Fodor's 91 Hawaii

Fodor's Travel Publications, Inc.
New York and London

ISBN 0–679–01912–X

Grateful acknowledgement is made to the following for permission to reprint previously published material: Alfred A. Knopf, Inc. and Garrett Hongo: "Village: Kahuku-*mura*" from *The River of Heaven* by Garrett Hongo. Rights in the British Commonwealth administered by Garrett Hongo. Rights in all other territories administered by Alfred A. Knopf, Inc. Copyright © 1987 by Garrett Hongo. Reprinted by permission of Alfred A. Knopf, Inc. and Garrett Hongo.

Pleasant Hawaii: The Aloha State Magazine: "The Underwater World" by Barbara Brundage. Copyright © 1989 by Barbara Brundage.

Fodor's Hawaii

Editor: Jillian Magalaner
Editorial Contributors: Gary Diedrichs, Michael Flynn, Betty Fullard-Leo, Anita Guerrini, Linda Kephart, Carolyn Price, Marty Wentzel
Art Director: Fabrizio La Rocca
Cartographer: David Lindroth
Illustrator: Karl Tanner
Cover Photograph: Paul Chesley/Photographers/Aspen

Design: Vignelli Associates

Special Sales

Contents

Maps and Plans

Foreword

We wish to express our gratitude to the offices of the Hawaii Visitors Bureau in Oahu, the Big Island, Maui, and Kauai for their assistance in the preparation of this guidebook.

While every care has been taken to assure the accuracy of the information in this guide, the passage of time will always bring change, and consequently, the publisher cannot accept responsibility for errors that may occur.

All prices and opening times quoted here are based on information supplied to us at press time. Hours and admission fees may change, however, and the prudent traveler will avoid inconvenience by calling ahead.

Fodor's wants to hear about your travel experiences, both pleasant and unpleasant. When a hotel or restaurant fails to live up to its billing, let us know and we will investigate the complaint and revise our entries where the facts warrant it.

Send your letters to the editors of Fodor's Travel Publications, 201 E. 50th Street, New York, NY 10022.

Highlights'91 and Fodor's Choice

Highlights '91

Oahu

What's New in Waikiki
Waikiki properties continue to follow each other's clean-up act. Outrigger Hotels Hawaii has polished up its chain with a $125 million renovation, including a $5 million refurbishment of the **Outrigger East Hotel.** The **Hyatt Regency Waikiki**'s $35 million renovation, scheduled for completion in 1990, includes improvements to restaurants, the unveiling of a dazzling $1.2-million ballroom, and the exterior painting of its two towers. On the outskirts of Waikiki, the swanky **Kahala Hilton** has embarked on a $5.5 million upgrade of its lagoon and beachfront rooms, sprucing them up while retaining the old Kahala charm.

There's not much room for new hotels in Waikiki, but the **Hawaii Prince Hotel** found the last available spot and is scheduled for a mid-1990 grand opening. The only other new construction planned for Waikiki is its **convention center** at the site of the International Market Place on Kalakaua Avenue. The state-sanctioned center is in the design stages, while a privately developed convention facility is on the drawing boards for a vacant lot on the fringe of Waikiki.

Hotels aren't the only things in the renovation act. At press time, **Duty Free Shoppers,** Hawaii's largest retailer, planned to open its improved facility in mid-1990, after pouring $70 million into tripling the size of its old operation.

Westward Ho
Since there's no room left in Waikiki, developers have cast an eye to the western reaches of Oahu. That's the site of **Ko Olina Resort,** a $2 billion project embracing a 400-slip marina, an 18-acre shopping center, an 18-hole golf course, four man-made lagoons, two condominiums, and eight hotels. Late 1989 saw the opening of the golf course, followed by the visitor information center in early 1990, and hotels and condos by the fall of 1992.

Looking North
Oahu's north shore soon will be the home of the **Kawela Bay Hotel,** part of the 808-acre Kuilima Resort. Ground was broken for the 20-acre site in early 1990 and work should be finished by late 1991. Next door at the **Turtle Bay Hilton,** a $20 million clean-up includes a new golf course, electronic lock systems for the rooms, and a new Japanese restaurant, scheduled for completion by press time.

New to Hawaii's Skies
Hawaii welcomed a new carrier called **Discovery Airways** in 1990. Flying 97-seat aircrafts, Discovery offers continuous service between Oahu, Maui, Kauai, and the Big Island. Over at the **Aloha Airlines** interisland terminal, two new

boarding gates were added in 1989, with large lobbies, a new snack bar area, and open garden café.

Pineapple Growth The **Dole Pineapple Pavilion** in Wahiawa has always been a big hit with Oahu sightseers since it opened in 1951. Now it's even bigger, thanks to a new visitor pavilion, a pineapple variety garden, a 10,000-square-foot marketplace, a gift shop, a restaurant, and parking for 216 cars. The buildings reflect long, low, plantation-style architecture.

A Taste of Restaurant Row The newest forum for eating and drinking has become downtown Honolulu's trendiest gathering place. It's called **Restaurant Row,** and it encompasses more than 50 restaurants and stores on 9 acres. Recent openings include **Trattoria Manzo,** where you can mix and match a variety of pastas and sauces, and **Touch The East,** a Japanese restaurant and karaoke lounge. They're settling in next to such popular hangouts as Tom Selleck's **Black Orchid** and a family-style eatery called **Marie Callender's.** The complex is a 10-minute walk from the Honolulu business district and a 10-minute cab ride from Waikiki.

The Big Island of Hawaii

Bigger Resorts The Big Island is off and running on the first lap of a race to build bigger, more plush, and more imaginative resorts than any other Hawaiian island to attract upscale tourists. Most of the development is targeted for West Hawaii—specifically the arid, lava-covered Kohala Coast. This area already has five upper-end destination resorts, including wonder developer Chris Hemmeter's latest fantasyland, the Disneyesque **Hyatt Regency Waikoloa,** which opened its doors to eager fun-seekers in 1988. Landowners and developers have aspirations of building hotels and condominiums on virtually every sandy pocket along the coast, but only the Ritz Carlton at Mauna Lani, planned as another posh resort for the well-heeled, moves ahead toward completion, set for this fall. The elegant 542-room hotel boasts such major conference facilities as a 14,000-square-foot ballroom.

One side effect of the glut of "upscale" resorts is the increasing popularity of bed-and-breakfast accommodations. A fledgling network has information on many of the B&Bs, but often finding out about "the cabin out back that so-and-so has for rent" depends on luck, listening to returning visitors, and reading tiny classified ads in travel magazines (*see* Lodging section, Chapter 4).

Hotel Update The modest Kona Hukilau Hotel is now part of the **Kona Seaside Hotel.** The renovated lodging with 155 rooms has a central location in Kailua-Kona, within walking distance of the Lanihau Shopping Center; the latter is in the midst of a $40 million expansion with **Liberty House** department store as an anchor tenant this year.

A few miles down the road at Keauhou, the **Kona Lagoon** is closed for conversion from a 454-room hotel into a 250-suite hotel. It is due to reopen early in 1991 as part of the **Keauhou Beach Resort.**

To the northwest, along the "gold coast," the lovely, laid-back **Kona Village** has completed construction of a second swimming pool and 19 new thatch-roof *hales* (houses), but has chosen not to add telephones or televisions to the new rooms. The resort's fine dining room, the Hale Samoa longhouse, has been spruced up but retains its languorous Polynesian atmosphere.

The **Royal Waikoloan** plans to spend $25 million on an expansion program through 1991. Changes include a swimming pool addition, poolside restaurant, lavascapes and gardens with medicinal Hawaiian plants, and the new Royal Canoe Club. A third golf course is under construction and at least two more are on the drawing boards. At **Mauna Lani Bay Hotel,** a $10 million expansion effort has added five luxury bungalow suites (each with a private swimming pool), a casual California-style restaurant, and an expanded fitness facility.

Dining Out   In Kailua-Kona, **Waterfront Row,** which opened on the ocean side of Alii Drive at the beginning of 1989, is a treasure trove of restaurants and shops. The **Chart House** broils a reliable and reasonably priced steak, and **Phillip Paolo** has added his Italian cooking to the Row.

Inland in *paniolo* (cowboy) country, **Waimea** town is rounding up some of the island's finest chefs, as well as a number of the most talented artists around, if you judge by the number of new restaurants and galleries. Two favorites are **Merriman's,** a restaurant opened at Opelu Plaza by Peter Merriman, the creative chef from the Gallery at the Mauna Lani Resort; and the **Bree Garden,** the brainstorm of Berndt Bree, a former chef at the Mauna Kea Beach Resort.

Newest to the Waimea scene is **Hale Kea,** an estate built in 1897, restored to its historic grandeur, and reopened in late 1989. The building has a series of small dining rooms where guests can sample local ingredients prepared in gourmet recipes. Hale Kea also boasts 11 acres for horseback riding, crafts demonstrations, and shopping in nine small cottages.

Volcano Update   Kilauea Volcano has been acting up again, as it did in 1977, 1986, and 1987. At press time, more than 100 homes in the Puna coastal village of Kalapana had been destroyed. The lava flow has not hindered the tourism flow; in fact, many tourists make the trip to Kalapana specifically to wonder at the lava formations.

Maui

Hotel News   The **Four Seasons Hotel and Resort** had its grand opening in March of 1990. The 347-room property touts itself as the creme-de-la-creme, and the owners spent just less than $400,000 on each room. Accommodations include large, marbled bathrooms, video cassette recorders, teak lanai furniture, and built-in refrigerated bars.

In the fall of 1990, construction should be finished on Maui's second Hyatt property, a $400-million, 800-room hotel called the **Grand Hyatt Wailea Resort and Spa.** Also in Wailea, the **Grand Champions Beach Resort** is slated to offer an additional 426 rooms in 1990, while progress continues on another all-suite resort on 20 acres in Wailea.

Airport Renovations The Kahului Airport is the focus of $41 million in improvements. Work started several years ago, with projects done in phases. In 1988, additions included an 82,000-square-foot lobby; a two-story, 78,000-square-foot central building; and a 45,000-square-foot concourse and holding area. Phase II will begin by 1991 with the conversion of the present terminal into a baggage claim area.

Traffic Patterns If you wonder whether or not to rent a car, consider that Maui has more rental cars per mile of road than anywhere else in the nation. Because of the high visitor counts in the last several years, major rental car companies have opened their doors on Maui to cash in on the increased business. Moreover, Maui has seen a rapid rise in exotic car rental companies.

More cars mean more traffic. A few years ago, West Maui tourists found car congestion especially bad during the hours when hotel/resort employees were going to work in the morning and coming home at night. Finally, the county approved a $2 million improvement to the Honoapiilani Highway, which circles the West Maui mountains from Wailuku to Kapalua. Although traffic can still get congested between Olowalu and Kaanapali, the highway's new third lane eases the situation considerably. A fourth lane is expected sometime in 1990.

For Art's Sake The long-awaited **Maui Community Arts and Cultural Center** (MCACC) finally broke ground in early 1989, providing a venue for local acting groups as well as major touring companies. The plan for this center began more than 20 years ago and was finally put into motion by corporate backers and a grant from the state. Now MCACC is scheduled to open by the end of 1990 in Kahului with two theaters—one that will seat 1,150 and an experimental theater with 200 retractable seats. There will also be a 3,500-square-foot gallery space and a gift shop. Both the Maui Community Theatre and Maui Youth Theater are expected to move into their own satellite wings.

Molokai

Hotel News The **Pau Hana Inn** in Kaunakakai, built in 1942, recently celebrated the completion of a $250,000 renovation. The project included the rebuilding of the 39-unit hotel's frame cottages, plus total refurbishing of interiors with new furniture, carpeting, drapes, spreads, bath fixtures, and ceiling fans. The three-and-a-half-acre complex has been relandscaped with tropical trees and flowering plants, and the swimming pool has been resurfaced.

To the west, the owners of the 4,500-acre **Kaluakoi Resort** plan two more golf courses and another hotel, but they are approaching development slowly. Their decision on when to build is linked to the timing of the adjacent 22-acre **Kaiaka Rock Hotel** site, which has been tied up in a civil suit between developers and landowners.

Safari Additions At the end of 1989, the **Molokai Ranch Wildlife Park** near Kaluakoi created a penned-in area where guests can now stand as they safely feed the giraffes. Also new to the park are a group of exotic zebras.

Travel Update At the end of 1989, Air Molokai folded up shop and stopped serving the Friendly Isle. The good news, however, is that **Panorama Air** has begun service between Oahu and Molokai to help fill the void.

Sweet Dreams Rudolph Wilhelm Meyer settled in the highlands of Molokai in 1851 and ran a sugarcane plantation and mill at Kalae from 1878 to 1889. A $1.5 million project to restore the historic mill on the one-acre site was completed in 1989. Plans call for the future creation of a museum that will share information with visitors and serve as a showcase of valuable Meyer family artifacts.

Lanai

Additional Lodging Since 98% of Lanai is owned by **Castle & Cooke,** just about every news item is generated by that company. For instance, after its new hotel is finished at Manele Bay, C & C will look ahead to adding 400 rooms to the property. Then they will begin work on a small condominium and 275 home lots in the same area.

Lanai Greenery Look around the town of **Lanai City,** and you'll notice just about every home has lots of greenery—fruit trees, vegetable gardens, and the like. C & C has been encouraging island residents to keep their yards attractive to the tourists and has been giving residents free yard plants. There is a landscaped town center in the works, plus an assortment of new buildings that will add to the number of Lanai's shops while maintaining the town's rustic atmosphere.

Teeing Off The building of the new **Lodge at Koele** has signaled the improvement of the island's nine-hole **Cavendish Golf Course,** which previously had no starter, no pro, and no carts. Time was when folks would simply bring their own carts, or else walk around from tee to tee. Now a clubhouse is being built, and word has it that the fee will go up now that the Lodge at Koele is open.

Kauai

Hotel Update A number of Kauai hotels are keeping their customers satisfied by renovating and upgrading their properties. The **Sheraton Mirage Princeville Hotel** has undergone an extensive refurbishment at an undisclosed price tag. At press time, the re-opening date was early 1991.

The **Hanalei Bay Resort** recently enjoyed a multimillion-dollar refurbishment to recapture a turn-of-the-century Hawaiian feeling. Accommodations reflect the motif of rooms in an old plantation guest house, and the work of local artists hangs throughout the resort. A newly constructed stream flows from the porte cochère, through the lobby, and into a cascading waterfall that drops into a new swimming pool.

With a target opening date of November 1, 1990, the $160 million, 605-room **Hyatt Regency Kauai** will be the chain's first hotel on the island. The architecture will be traditional Hawaiian-style with four-story structures and hip roofs. Plans call for the same elaborate attractions as have been included in other Hyatt properties. There will be three restaurants, two swimming pools, a snorkeling lagoon, various pools and waterways, two ballrooms, 12,000 square feet of shopping, and Hawaiian art from the early 1900s. Look for it on the south shore, in Poipu. Room rates will start at about $175 a night.

Prolific developer Chris Hemmeter has poured an estimated $600 million into the **Kauai Lagoons Resort,** his most expensive project to date. The first two phases of the Kalapaki Beach property are the $275 million **Westin Kauai Hotel** and the newly completed Lagoons retail complex, featuring 53 luxury boutiques such as Louis Vuitton. The third phase, headed for a mid-1991 opening, is a $325 million, 750-room hotel with two golf courses, a spa, eight tennis courts, and five restaurants.

Garden Isle Gifts Set on Kauai's lush northeast shore, the Kilauea area has done very well with its guava crops. In fact, each year Kilauea Agronomics harvests more than 10 million pounds of the heavenly fruit. Now the company is putting the finishing touches on its visitor center, which displays its guava products. The two-building complex is called **Mauna La'i Plantation,** and it features a guava museum, snack bar, and display area for guava products like juice, jelly, chutney, cakes, and pies. A trellis-covered pedestrian walkway connects the two buildings, which look rural and rustic with Hawaiian-style double-pitched roofs.

Fodor's Choice

No two people will agree on what makes a perfect vacation in the Aloha State, but it's fun and helpful to know what others think. We hope you'll have a chance to experience some of Fodor's Choices yourself while visiting Hawaii. For detailed information about each entry, refer to the appropriate chapters in this guidebook.

Beaches

Oahu Hanauma Bay in the morning (it gets too crowded in the afternoon)

Kailua Beach

Waikiki in front of the Royal Hawaiian Hotel

Waimea Bay in summer (the best time to swim there)

The Big Island Anaehoomalu Beach, especially for windsurfing

Hapuna Beach

Kaunaoa Beach at Mauna Kea Beach Resort

Spencer Beach, especially for children

Punaluu Black Sand Beach to watch the turtles

Maui Wailea Beach in the morning as the sun comes over Haleakala

Hookipa Beach to watch world-class windsurfing

Kapalua Beach for sheer class

Hana Beach for that Old Hawaii experience

Molokai Halawa Beach Park

Kawakiu Beach

Kepuhi Beach

Papohaku Beach

Lanai Hulopoe Beach

Shipwreck Beach

Kauai Hanakapiai Beach

Lumahai Beach

Polihale Beach State Park

Tunnels Beach

Best Buys

Oahu Aloha shirts—Andrade for quality; F.W. Woolworth for price

Fine jewelry—Maui Divers

Hawaiian arts and crafts—Little Hawaiian Craft Shop

Most fun—Shirokiya

Variety—Ala Moana Shopping Center

The Big Island Ethnic finds—Woodblock prints by Dietrich Varez at Volcano Art Center; woven lauhala baskets, hats, and mats at Kimura's Lauhala Store in Holualoa

Gifts—Wooden bowls by Jack Straka, boxes or cutting boards

Hawaiian arts and crafts—Alapaki's at the Keauhou Shopping Center

Most fun—Ira Ono's Trashface earrings at Volcano Art Center

Orchid corsages and cut anthuriums from Volcano Store

Maui Fine art in Lahaina

Hawaiian quilts

Made on Maui crafts and food

Tedeschi wine at the vineyards in Kula

Molokai Aloha shirts and muumuus—Molokai Gift Shop

Jewelry—Imports Gift Shop, Molokai Mountain Jewelers

Hawaiian arts and crafts—Molokai Island Creations

Most fun—Big Wind Kite Factory

Lanai Lanai T-shirts at Richard's Shopping Center

Kauai Art—Kahn Galleries; The Poster Shop

Ethnic finds—Half Moon Japanese Antiques; Indo-Pacific Trading Company

Hawaiian arts and crafts—Kapaia Stitchery; The Station

Jewelry—Kauai Gold; Jim Saylor Jewelers; Remember Kauai

Variety—Coconut Plantation Market Place; Koloa Town

Drives

Oahu From Hawaii Kai to Waimanalo

Likelike Highway on the windward side

Pali Highway on the leeward side

The Big Island From Hilo to Waipio Valley along the Hamakua coast

From Kona to Waimea to stop-and-shop in cooler weather

Maui The road to Hana

From Lahaina to Maalaea during whale season

Coming down Haleakala

Molokai Shoreline route east to Halawa Valley Overlook

Lanai Lanaihale in a jeep

Kauai North Shore—The oceanside drive from Hanalei to Ke'e Beach Park

Waimea Canyon Road from Waimea to the Kalalau Lookout

For Kids

Oahu Children's Touch and Feel Museum

Honolulu Zoo, especially the petting zoo

Sea Life Park

Waikiki Aquarium

The Big Island Thomas Jaggar Museum, Volcanoes National Park

Swimming with dolphins at the Hyatt Regency Waikoloa

Hiking through the Thurston Lava Tube or into Kilauea Iki Crater

Watching monkeys and tigers at Panaewa Zoo

Maui Haleakala Crater

Lahaina Sugar Cane Train

Maui Tropical Plantation

Whale watching

Molokai Molokai Ranch Wildlife Safari

Kauai Kamokila

Smith's Tropical Paradise

Snorkeling excursion along the south shore

Hotels

Oahu Kahala Hilton (*Very Expensive*)

Royal Hawaiian Hotel (*Very Expensive*)

Hyatt Regency Waikiki (*Expensive*)

Manoa Valley Inn (*Moderate*)

Royal Grove Hotel (*Inexpensive*)

The Big Island	Hyatt Regency Waikoloa (*Very Expensive*)
	Kona Village Resort (*Very Expensive*)
	Mauna Kea Beach Resort (*Very Expensive*)
	Mauna Lani Bay Hotel (*Very Expensive*)
	Aston Shores at Waikoloa (*Expensive–Very Expensive*)
Maui	The Four Seasons (*Very Expensive*)
	Hotel Hana-Maui (*Very Expensive*)
	Kapalua Bay Hotel (*Very Expensive*)
	Coconut Inn (*Moderate*)
	Plantation Inn (*Moderate*)
Molokai	Paniolo Hale (*Expensive*)
	Hotel Molokai (*Moderate*)
	Pau Hana Inn (*Inexpensive*)
Lanai	Hotel Lanai (*Inexpensive*)
Kauai	Sheraton Kauai (*Very Expensive*)
	Sheraton Mirage Princeville Hotel (*Very Expensive*)
	Aston Kauai Resort (*Expensive*)
	Hanalei Bay Resort (*Moderate*)
	Kokee Lodge (*Inexpensive*)

Kamaaina (Islanders') Favorites

Oahu	Manapua from any lunch wagon at Sandy Beach
	Morning snorkel at Hanauma Bay
	Poi luncheon at the Willows
	Shave ice with vanilla ice cream and azuki beans at Matsumoto's in Haleiwa
	Sunset jog around Diamond Head
The Big Island	Edelweiss in Waimea for dinner
	Kona Inn for cocktails or dinner at sunset
	Liliuokalani Park in Hilo on a Sunday afternoon
	Ohelo berry picking at Volcano
	Suisan Fish Auction in Hilo
Maui	Browsing through Hasegawa's Store
	Cream puffs at Komoda's
	People-watching at Longhi's
	Sunrise from Haleakala
	Wine-tasting at Tedeschi

Molokai   Family swimming at Pohakuloa Beach

Hiking the Halawa Valley Trail

Watching the Molokai-to-Oahu Canoe Race

Lanai   Cocktails on the porch of Hotel Lanai

Hamburgers from Dahang's Bakery

Snorkeling in Hulopoe Bay

Kauai   Bodysurfing at Brennecke's Beach, Poipu

Eggs Benedict at the Eggberts in Lihue

Sunday lunch at the Green Garden Restaurant, Hanapepe

Sunset picnic at Hanalei Beach Park

Local Dining

Oahu   Haupia at Ono Hawaiian Foods

Macadamia nut cream pie at the Willows

Mahimahi in any preparation, at Bali by the Sea

Portuguese sausage omelette at Eggs 'n Things

The Big Island   Breakfast or lunch at Ocean View Inn, Kailua-Kona

Loco-moco (eggs, rice, and hamburger dish that originated at Cafe 100 in Hilo)

Luau at Haile Church, Hilo

Teshima's at Honalo

Maui   Plate lunch from Hazel's

Fresh fish

Maui onion rings at the Maui Onion

Maui potato chips

Molokai   Beef adobo from Oviedo's

Lilikoi sundaes at Jojo's Cafe

Mahimahi at the Mid-Nite Inn

Molokai bread from Kanemitsu Bakery

Lanai   Filipino-style doughnuts from Dahang's Bakery

Kauai   Kalua pig and lomilomi salmon at Tahiti Nui

Lilikoi chiffon pie at the Green Garden Restaurant

Sashimi and poke at Club Jetty

Shave ice from carry-out trucks at Haena Beach Park

Nightlife

Oahu Aikane Catamaran Sunset Dinner Cruise

Brothers Cazimero Show, Royal Hawaiian Hotel

Danny Kaleikini Show, Kahala Hilton

Royal Hawaiian Luau

Rumours, Ramada Renaissance Ala Moana Hotel

The Big Island Reflections in Hilo for dancing

Spats at the Hyatt Regency Waikoloa

Vanda Lounge at the Royal Waikoloan for mellow music and dancing

Maui Blackie's Boatyard

Inu Inu Lounge at the Maui Inter-Continental

Old Lahaina Luau

Molokai Weekend dancing at Hotel Molokai and Pau Hana Inn

Kauai Club Jetty

Na Kaholokula, Sheraton Coconut Beach Hotel

Park Place

Tahiti Nui Luau

Restaurants

Oahu La Mer, Halekulani Hotel (*Very Expensive*)

Maile, Kahala Hilton Hotel (*Expensive*)

Orchids, Halekulani Hotel (*Moderate*)

Roy's (*Moderate*)

Eggs 'n Things (*Inexpensive*)

The Big Island Batik Room at the Mauna Kea Beach Hotel (*Expensive*)

Le Soleil at Mauna Lani Bay Resort (*Expensive*)

Edelweiss (*Moderate*)

La Bourgogne (*Moderate*)

Roussel's (*Moderate*)

Hartwell's Restaurant at Hale Kea (*Inexpensive–Moderate*)

Maui Raffles at the Stouffer Wailea (*Very Expensive*)

Plantation Veranda (*Expensive*)

Mama's Fish House (*Moderate*)

Haliimaile General Store (*Inexpensive–Moderate*)

Polli's on the Beach (*Inexpensive*)

Molokai Ohia Lodge (*Moderate*)

Hop Inn (*Inexpensive*)

Mid-Nite Inn (*Inexpensive*)

Lanai Dahang's (*Inexpensive*)

Hotel Lanai (*Inexpensive*)

Kauai Nobles, Sheraton Mirage Princeville Hotel (*Very Expensive*)

Tamarind (*Expensive*)

Casa di Amici (*Moderate*)

Gaylord's (*Moderate*)

The Eggberts (*Inexpensive*)

Romantic Hideaways

Oahu Breakfast at Michel's at the Colony Surf

Dinner at Nick's Fishmarket

Picnic lunch at the top of Diamond Head

Picnic dinner at the Waikiki Shell

Room in the old section of the Royal Hawaiian Hotel

The Big Island Kilauea Lodge at Volcano (light a fire in the bedroom fireplace)

Kona Village Resort in a thatched hale beside the sea

The Beach Club for dinner at Kona by the Sea (so private it's hard to find)

Waipio Wayside Bed and Breakfast

Maui Candlelight dinner at La Bretagne

Kula Lodge chalets with fireplaces

Royal Lahaina cottages with private pools

Waianapanapa cabins

Molokai Condo with a hot tub on the lanai at Paniolo Hale

Moaula Falls, at the back of Halawa Valley

Papohaku Beach

Lanai Lanaihale

Shipwreck Beach

Kauai Cottage at Kokee State Park

Horse-drawn carriage ride at Kilohana

Picnic at Lumahai Beach

Sunset cruise on the *Na Pali Queen*

Sunsets

Oahu Diamond Head Lighthouse

Sunset Beach, North Shore

The Big Island From the end of Kona Pier or from the lounges at Kona Inn or the Kona Hilton

From deckside on Captain Bean's Booze Cruise

From Keauhou lookout

In the Kohala mountains

Maui From Kimo's in Lahaina

From Kapalua's Bay Club

From the beach at Kaanapali

From the beach at Wailea

Molokai Kepuhi Beach

Ohia Room, Kaluakoi Resort

Lanai Hulopoe Beach

Kauai Kekaha Beach, west shore

Polihale Beach State Park

Views

Oahu Makapuu Point

Nuuanu Pali Lookout

Top of the Ilikai Waikiki Hotel

Upper ocean-view rooms at the Hilton Hawaiian Village and the Halekulani

The Big Island Upper ocean-view rooms of Mauna Kea Beach and Mauna Lani resorts

Horizon and flanks of Mauna Kea from the observatories

Kealakekua Bay from upcountry Kona

Waipio Valley and Pololu Valley from the overlooks at road's end

Maui All of Maui from Haleakala

Islands of Molokai, Lanai, Kahoolawe, and Molokini

Underwater at Wailea

Waterfalls along the Hana Highway

Molokai Halawa Valley Overlook

Kalaupapa Overlook

Lanai Lanaihale

Molokai from Shipwreck Beach

Kauai Hanalei Valley Overlook

Kalalau Lookout

Na Pali coast from a boat

Niihau by helicopter tour

Waimea Canyon

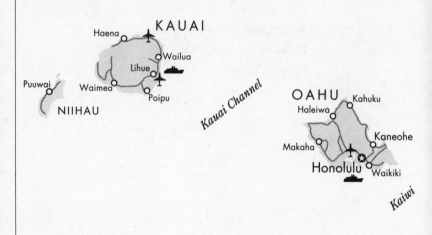

KAUAI

Haena

Wailua

Lihue

Puuwai

Waimea

Poipu

NIIHAU

Kauai Channel

OAHU

Kahuku

Haleiwa

Kaneohe

Makaha

Honolulu

Waikiki

Kaiwi

P A C I F I C   O C E A N

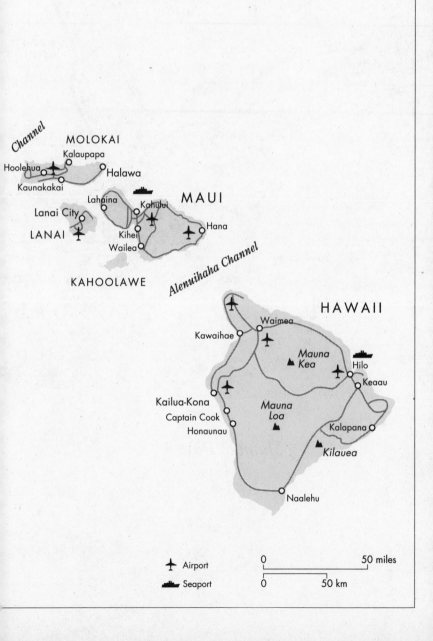

N

Channel

MOLOKAI

Kalaupapa

Hoolehua ✈

Halawa

Kaunakakai

Lanai City

LANAI ✈

Lahaina

Kahului 🚢

MAUI

Kihei ✈

Hana

Wailea

KAHOOLAWE

Alenuihaha Channel

HAWAII

Waimea ✈

Kawaihae ✈

▲ Mauna Kea

Hilo 🚢

Keaau

Kailua-Kona ✈

Captain Cook

Honaunau

▲ Mauna Loa

Kalapana

▲ Kilauea

Naalehu

✈ Airport

🚢 Seaport

0   50 miles

0   50 km

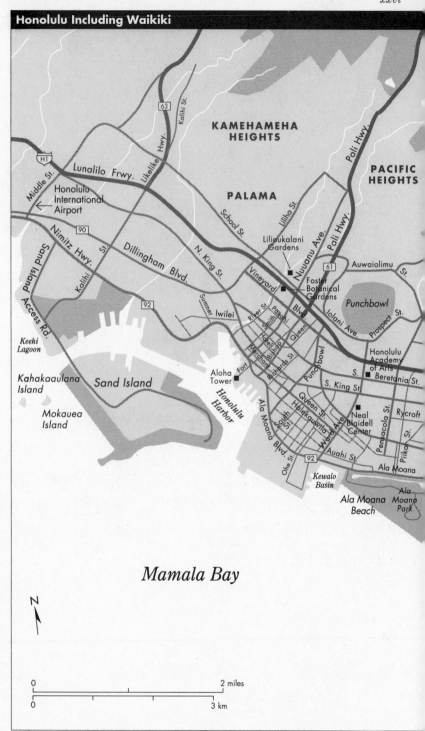

Honolulu Including Waikiki

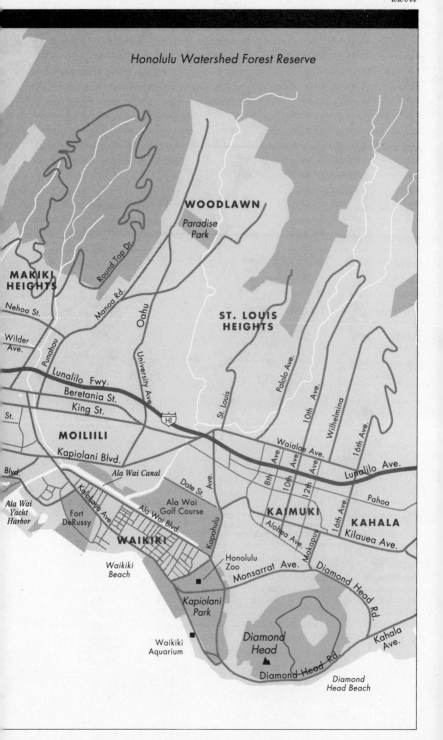

Honolulu Watershed Forest Reserve

WOODLAWN

Paradise Park

MAKIKI HEIGHTS

Round Top Dr.

Nehoa St.

Manoa Rd.

Oahu

ST. LOUIS HEIGHTS

Wilder Ave.

Punahou

University Ave.

St. Louis

Palolo Ave.

10th Ave.

Wilhelmina

16th Ave.

St.

Lunalilo Fwy.

Beretania St.

King St.

H1

MOILIILI

Kapiolani Blvd.

Ala Wai Canal

Date St.

Ave.

Waialae Ave.

Lunalilo Ave.

Blvd.

8th

10th

12th

Pahoa

Ala Wai Yacht Harbor

Kalakaua Ave.

Ala Wai Blvd.

Fort DeRussy

Ala Wai Golf Course

Kapahulu

KAIMUKI

Alohea Ave.

Makapuu

16th Ave.

KAHALA

Kilauea Ave.

WAIKIKI

Honolulu Zoo

Monsarrat Ave.

Diamond Head Rd.

Waikiki Beach

Kapiolani Park

Diamond Head

Kahala Ave.

Waikiki Aquarium

Diamond Head Rd.

Diamond Head Beach

World Time Zones

Numbers below vertical bands relate each zone to Greenwich Mean Time (0 hrs.).
Local times frequently differ from these general indications,
as indicated by light-face numbers on map.

Algiers, **29**
Anchorage, **3**
Athens, **41**
Auckland, **1**
Baghdad, **46**
Bangkok, **50**
Beijing, **54**

Berlin, **34**
Bogotá, **19**
Budapest, **37**
Buenos Aires, **24**
Caracas, **22**
Chicago, **9**
Copenhagen, **33**
Dallas, **10**

Delhi, **48**
Denver, **8**
Djakarta, **53**
Dublin, **26**
Edmonton, **7**
Hong Kong, **56**
Honolulu, **2**

Istanbul, **40**
Jerusalem, **42**
Johannesburg, **44**
Lima, **20**
Lisbon, **28**
London (Greenwich), **27**
Los Angeles, **6**
Madrid, **38**
Manila, **57**

xxix

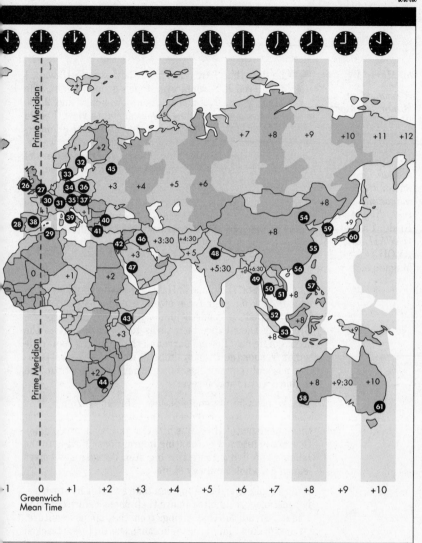

Mecca, **47**
Mexico City, **12**
Miami, **18**
Montreal, **15**
Moscow, **45**
Nairobi, **43**
New Orleans, **11**
New York City, **16**

Ottawa, **14**
Paris, **30**
Perth, **58**
Reykjavík, **25**
Rio de Janeiro, **23**
Rome, **39**
Saigon, **51**

San Francisco, **5**
Santiago, **21**
Seoul, **59**
Shanghai, **55**
Singapore, **52**
Stockholm, **32**
Sydney, **61**
Tokyo, **60**

Toronto, **13**
Vancouver, **4**
Vienna, **35**
Warsaw, **36**
Washington, DC, **17**
Yangon, **49**
Zürich, **31**

Introduction

by Marty Wentzel

A resident of Honolulu, Marty Wentzel is a freelance writer whose articles have appeared in several local and national magazines, including Modern Bride, Pleasant HAWAII, *and* ALOHA Magazine.

The first time I traveled from California to Hawaii, I wondered if I would ever touch ground again. The flight seemed endless. Then, 5½ hours and 2,390 miles later, a landscape new to me came into view. I could see the green spires of the Koolau Mountains, the glimmering high rises of Waikiki, the aqua intensity of the water, the fleets of white sails dotting the sea, and the network of crisscrossing freeways, pineapple plantations, and sugarcane fields.

A trip to Hawaii from anywhere else in the world makes you aware of its remoteness. It waits in the middle of the Pacific Ocean like a crossroads as well as a cloister; although it is influenced by all its neighbors, it remains very much its own destination. As a state, it often seems as exotic as a foreign land.

Visitors get off the plane in Hawaii with a sort of dizzy, uncertain look on their faces after spending as many as 18 hours cooped up inside a jumbo jet and sterile airports. Gradually their expression turns to astonishment as the scents of myriad flowers surround them and the cool trade winds freshen their weary limbs. Within a few hours, paradise has smitten their hearts, and they become determined to find a way to stay forever.

That's how a lot of people discover Hawaii. Like me, they visit it on vacation and decide they want to live there. Yet the experience of Hawaii is broader and far more complex than those first few enchanting impressions. Moving to the Islands and living there is a big step because it involves learning a whole new way of life.

Even simple Island customs can take a visitor by surprise. For instance, residents remove their shoes before entering a home, a tradition that springs from the Japanese culture. (It also makes a lot of sense, because less dirt gets tracked in that way.)

People operate on Hawaiian time, which means that if you're late for a party, an appointment, a meeting, a dinner party, or any other social function, you don't worry about it. Sure, there is rush-hour traffic, and there are schedules for movies and airplanes. But on Hawaiian time, people take a more laid-back approach to everything, which may be why the residents live much longer than those in other states.

Living in Hawaii teaches you to respect nature. You stay out of the water when the huge winter waves come up on the north shores of the islands. You avoid hiking in the valleys during rainy days because flash floods have been known to race down out of the mountains and wash people away. You tape your windows before a hurricane (the last one, Hurricane Iwa in 1982, hit Kauai with such intensity that it wiped out much of the island, especially the western portions). And when the sun starts to make its descent to the horizon, you stop what you're doing to enjoy the sunset, a guaranteed spectacle almost every day of the year.

Islands of Discovery

Today Hawaii offers much of the same mystique that it presented to the earliest Polynesian explorers, who navigated their huge voyaging canoes throughout the South Pacific until they stumbled upon paradise. The Hawaiian Islands amazed them back in the 4th century AD; that magnificent landscape has been preserved and, if anything, it has improved over the centuries.

Fortunately, Hawaii's six major islands are readily and rapidly accessible to each other. A flight from the northernmost island (Kauai) to the southernmost (the Big Island, Hawaii) takes no more than an hour. Each island has its own personality and warrants your attention, time, and exploration.

For instance, the Garden Island, Kauai, is so green and lush that it has served as a backdrop for Hollywood movies. On the other hand, much of Lanai is a dry and windswept panorama of red soil and rocky coastlines. Oahu is cosmopolitan, with its world-famous tourist mecca, Waikiki, while Molokai consists mostly of family-run businesses and natural attractions.

There are incredible heights on Maui, such as its 10,023-foot-high dormant volcano, Haleakala, as well as on the Big Island, with its 13,796-foot-high Mauna Kea and 13,677-foot-high Mauna Loa (the world's largest shield volcano). On the other hand, Kauai boasts amazing depths, such as Waimea Canyon, a 3,657-foot-deep chasm, while Molokai has the 4-mile-long and ½-mile wide Halawa Valley.

Traveling from one island to the next, you will most likely find yourself doing things you never dreamed of back on the mainland. Imagine this: On the least populated island, Lanai, you're riding a mountain bike through pineapple fields, whose sweet fragrance is truly intoxicating. You pedal through groves of ironwood trees along bumpy dirt roads, then climb steadily until you come to the clearing at the Garden of the Gods, a breathtaking assemblage of rocks and boulders that are scattered across a barren landscape overlooking the sea. You catch your breath and think, surely some greater being reached its arm to create this work of natural art on such a wild island.

Picture yourself on Kauai, the oldest island, hiking the Kalalau Trail on the Na Pali coast. You meander through ancient landscapes and along 1,000-foot-high cliffs, whose great walls of sheer rock rise above untamed surf. The trail winds up and down the edges of those cliffs, past exceptionally beautiful Pacific vistas, through groves of guava and *lilikoi* (passion fruit) trees, until you reach your destination: Kalalau Valley. You stand under a fresh, bracing waterfall off the beach; then you relax in a sea cave and gaze upon little birds with long legs skittering along the mile-long expanse of isolated sand.

Perhaps you would prefer to see the Big Island in the most dramatic way: on a "flightseeing" trip. A helicopter tour whisks you to places that are otherwise inaccessible. It hovers above volcanoes steaming with oozing orange lava, then zips along the coast, where you can see the new lava as it flows into the water, sending steam clouds into the air as it creates new land. Your whirlybird allows you to explore long, lush valleys with shimmering waterfalls hundreds of feet high and flies you over macadamia nut groves, orchid plantations, and anthurium farms.

Next, close your eyes and you'll find yourself on Molokai, the Friendly Isle, where you are climbing aboard a mule and riding down the cliff-side, switchback trail to Kalaupana. You meet a sensitive, gentle tour guide named Richard Marks who paints images with his words of a people banished from the rest of Hawaii in the late 1800s because of their disfiguring plight, Hansen's disease (leprosy). You chat with a few of the 90 or so residents who are proud to live in this tiny town on the remote peninsula, with its historic church and simple homes, all of which comprise a National Historic Landmark.

Or imagine yourself on Maui, the Valley Isle. At 3:30 AM you stumble out of bed and join the dozens of sun worshipers who are driving up Haleakala in time to see the sunrise. The clouds part before you as the sun makes its grand entrance and fills the crater with colors of every hue and shadows of every size. Then you walk down into the crater, so big, they say, that all of Manhattan could fit into it. You wander through lunar landscapes along lava and sand, and you get the once-over from a flock of nene (Hawaiian geese), the state bird, which is now endangered. Then you discover enormous purple berries growing by the cabin at Paliku, an Edenesque setting at the far end of the crater.

If you visit Oahu, you just might find yourself following a road that runs right through a tunnel in the wall of Diamond Head. Once inside that famous crater, you see a trail that leads you on a half-hour walk up its inner cliffs. Near the top, you lumber up 99 steps and hold onto a railing while wandering through the dark bunkers where U.S. soldiers once kept a watch for enemy forces. Climbing up the lookout at the 760-foot-high summit, you can see what appears to be the entire southern coast of the island. To the east, a crater called Koko Head rises over Hanauma Bay, while to the west stretch the Waianae Mountains. When you turn around you can gaze upon the interior, with its green-gilded Koolau Mountains, and be-

low you is the majestic shoreline of Waikiki, with its shiny
high rises, Ala Wai Canal, and Kapiolani Park.

Natural Beauty

Hawaii is America's most exotic and unusual state, with its
132 islands and atolls stretching across some 1,600 miles of
ocean. It is blessed with a uniform climate of predictably
warm temperatures and cool trade winds; except for the occasional squalls of January and February, the rains pass
quickly.

It's hard to believe that such a gentle place sprang from
such a violent beginning, as islands were forced up from the
ocean by mighty volcanic explosions. For centuries, the fiery heights steamed and sizzled, after which they were
worked on by the elements; crashing surf, mighty sea
winds, and powerful rivers carved and chiseled the great
mountains and lush valleys that are visible today.

Each year, more than 6 million visitors come to Hawaii to
see the results of nature's handiwork. While most of them
used to head straight for Waikiki, more and more people are
bypassing Oahu altogether and making the Neighbor Islands (as the rest of Hawaii is called) their final destination.
What they find on any island is a combination of the wild
and the tame, the simple and the slick.

Sun worshippers can't go wrong in Hawaii. On Oahu alone
there are more than 50 miles of beaches. Among the
beaches on Molokai is Papohaku, which measures a whopping 3 miles long, and Lumahai Beach on Kauai is so
splendid that it was featured in the movie *South Pacific*.
The Big Island's sands are a photographer's delight, including the black-sand beaches that are formed when hot lava
touches cold seawater. Even more unusual is the Big Island's green-sand beach, which was created long ago when
a cinder cone of the mineral olivine collapsed into a bay.

Throughout Hawaii, nature lovers find countless delights
to satisfy the senses. On an easy hike in the Tantalus hills
above Waikiki, you pass by tropical plants with leaves 10
times the size of ordinary house plants. Birds with bright
yellow wings and unusual names, such as o'o'a'a, flit in the
highlands of Kaunai and come into view if you're in the right
place at the right time. Perhaps most miraculous of all, as
you walk along the bleak, steamng floor of Kilauea Iki Crater on the Big Island, you can see new life growing up from
the cracks of the lava, such as ferns, grasses, and ohia trees
with scarlet lehua blossoms.

This rich natural environment now needs special protection. The people of Hawaii are aware of their fragile
surroundings, and they have joined forces in order to take
care of it. In the forefront of this movement is the Nature
Conservancy of Hawaii, a dedicated group of volunteers

who manage lands on most every island. They oversee such projects as Kamakou Preserve on Molokai, where they protect endangered birds, such as the *olomao* (Molokai thrush), *kakawahi* (Molokai creeper), and *pueo* (Hawaiian owl), as well as Pepeopae, Hawaii's most ancient bog. They are also fighting to preserve Molokai's Moomomi Dunes, one of the few remaining coastal dune areas in Hawaii. On Maui, the Conservancy's Waikamoi Preserve protects two types of birds that are found only in the rain forests of Haleakala: the Maui creeper and the crested honeycreeper.

As Hawaii's people give to the earth, so it has given to them. Millions of acres of this generous land have produced pineapple and sugarcane, the Islands' two most famous exports. If anything, Hawaii is growing increasingly prolific as its farmers become more diversified, first with macadamia nut farms and coffee plantations, then with orchid and anthurium groves along with such fruits and vegetables as guava, mango, bananas, corn, and sweet onions. Farmers on Kauai are growing baby vegetables for use in Hawaii's upscale restaurants, which have come to rely more and more on local products. On the Big Island, Excelsior Dairy is making its own butter from local herds and creating a fresher, more flavorful product. And Maui is becoming well-known for its upcountry farms, which cultivate such fresh herbs as fennel, basil, and thyme.

Painters, sculptors, weavers, photographers, and other types of artists have responded to their beautiful island environment in innovative ways. With a flash of fingers and a flick of the wrist, crafts people can handily turn lauhala leaves into a basket, or plumeria blossoms into a fresh, fragrant lei. An entourage of backwoods artists can be found at the volcano's edge on the Big Island, including photographer Boone Morrison and wood-print carver Deitrich Varez. On Maui, world-famous poet W.S. Merwin lives and writes about the inspiration he receives from his delicate island home. Robert Lyn Nelson creates colorful paintings of the humpback whales that each winter make their pilgrimage to the channels between the islands. On Oahu, photographer Joe Carini dedicates himself to documenting the hula; his line of note cards pays tribute to the hula *halau* (schools) that preserve the island heritage through traditional dance. These and many other islanders share their vision of Hawaii in a heartfelt outpouring of creativity, as if they were nature's own spokespeople.

Hawaii's magnificent environment also encourages sports, the number-one pastime in the islands. A veritable ragatta of vessels takes to the sea each day, from snorkeling-cruise boats to ocean liners. People hit the tennis courts, the golf courses, the running routes, the bridle paths, and the bike trails. Most of the major hotels offer some sort of fitness program, be it aerobics classes, nature walks, weightlifting rooms, or guided hikes to nearby outdoor attractions.

The superstars of sports love Hawaii's climate as well. Robbie Nash, one of the world's best windsurfers, wows folks with his 360-degree flips in the waves of Hookipa on Maui. Outstanding ocean paddlers, such as Marshall Rosa, brave the waves of the Pacific for the grueling Molokai-to-Oahu kayak race, a 38-mile contest that is similar to the annual Molokai-to-Oahu outrigger canoe race.

Hawaii is also famous for its endurance tests. Two such events that have thrust Hawaii into the international sports spotlight are the Ironman Triathlon (combination swim-bike-run) on the Big Island and the 15-year-old, 26.2-mile road race called the Honolulu Marathon on Oahu. Why do people do these crazy things? Simply put, there's something about Hawaii that makes people want to push themselves to do their very best.

The Past in the Present

The natural beauty of the Islands has allowed for a variety of accommodations from the countrified to the chic. You might find yourself on Kauai, staying at a bed-and-breakfast spot and hearing stories about the Garden Island from a sprightly resident in her 70s. Or you might wind up on the Big Island in a posh South Kohala hotel decorated with fish ponds, waterfalls, tropical gardens, gondolas, and a multimillion-dollar collection of international art. The cosmopolitan side of Hawaii has become more visible, with the backcountry options less easy to track down. The east side of Maui has become a seaside parade of luxury resorts, and developer Chris Hemmeter has recently opened a pair of fantasyland hotels on Kauai and the Big Island. Even little Lanai is seeing big changes as two very classy new hotels opened their doors in 1990.

However, the old will never completely disappear in Hawaii because traditions are paramount. To this day, the locals have a custom of blessing all things that are new by paying tribute to the past, with a dance, a chant, a lei, or even just a few words spoken by a minister. They respect the legend of their ancestors and honor the gods as they see fit. Dancers return reverently to the huge hula pavilion on the north shore of Kauai, a site that is dedicated to the goddess of the dance, Laka. Hikers leave rocks wrapped in ti leaves to thank the gods for their smooth passage. On the Big Island, those who visit the steaming Halemaumau pit toss in flowers and other gifts to the volcano goddess, Pele, to appease her unpredictable wrath.

Many island traditions can be learned and enjoyed by guests. In fact, as soon as you step off the plane you encounter your first island custom, as a fresh plumeria lei is draped around your neck. Centuries ago, garlands of leaves, nuts, or flowers were offered to the gods, and today the practice continues as they are given to family and friends on special occasions. It is said that the idea of bestowing a kiss along with a lei dates back to World War II, when during a show a female entertainer smooched a soldier after draping him with a flower lei. Then she justified it by saying, "It's tradition in Hawaii." It has been ever since.

The past endures thanks to several concerned organizations that have been fighting to save the visible remnants of days gone by. For instance, a nonprofit group called the Historic Hawaii Foundation works to preserve the unique decades-old structures of the state despite the enormous new high rises that are springing up around them.

The results are within plain view. Just look around downtown Honolulu and you can see such historic masterpieces as Iolani Palace, which dates back to 1882. King Kalakaua commissioned this colonial-style building for his short but dynamic reign. The only royal palace built on American soil, it is slowly but carefully being put back together inside and out, complete with the restored furnishings from its original days. Down the street from the palace is the Mission Houses Museum, whose restored buildings hark back to the 1820s, when they were the homes of the first missionaries on Oahu.

They now sit near one of the busiest intersections in downtown Honolulu and serve as quiet yet effective representations of the past.

The old also blends with the new in the form of the Hawaii Theatre, another Honolulu landmark, which dates from 1922 and is now being restored as 1,700-seat center of performing arts. The project will take several years during which time the theater can be used for fund-raisers, fashion shows, private parties, and meetings.

The Neighbor Islands offer further examples of architectural restoration. In Kona you can see the charming Mokuaikaua Church, constructed in 1837 of coral and lava rock; on Kauai, one of the most popular visitor attractions is Kilohana Estate, a gracious sugar plantation dating back to 1835. In Hana on Maui stands Wananalua Church, built in 1838 out of native lava rock, timbers from the surrounding mountains, and coral from the sea. Molokai features the historic 19th-century churches built by the caring priest Father Damien. On Lanai, during construction of the new Lodge at Koele, the developers actually took the time to relocate the historic Kalokahi O Ka Malamalama Church and the former homes of two old cowboys in order to preserve them.

Perhaps even more crucial to the restoration and preservation of Hawaiiana is the upkeep of its *heiaus*, or ancient sacred sites. On the Big Island, you can visit Mookini Heiau, the birthplace of King Kamehameha the Great and now a National Historic Landmark. On Molokai awaits Iliilopae, the largest outdoor shrine in the islands, which is as big as a football field. In Pupukea on Oahu is Pu'u o Mahuka, a "hill of escape" where Hawaiians still leave offerings to the gods, while on Lanai is another time-honored gathering place called Halulu Heiau, near the summer home of that great king.

Cultural Potpourri

At the heart of Hawaii are the people who live there every day and who turn life into a rewarding experience for both visitors and residents. From its earliest days the Islands have beckoned to races from around the world, beginning way back when Polynesian kings and queens ruled its lands. Along the way, Russia and France both tried to claim Hawaii for their own, as did Great Britain. Many people came from the Orient to work on the island's sugar and pineapple plantations. From Japan, China, the Philippines, Korea, Vietnam, Samoa, Thailand, and Portugal they have come, bringing with them their beliefs, their thoughts, and their traditions and turning Hawaii into what many people call a melting pot of cultures.

You can witness Hawaii's multicultural diversity in the way people dress. Go on a shopping spree and you'll encounter everything from designer Pierre Cardin blouses and classically casual Reyn's island fashions to shocking pink muumuus and Oriental-style slippers, the ubiquitous island footwear. There are kimonos from Japan, saris from India, and other exotic imports from China, the Philippines, and Korea. Most popular of all is the aloha shirt, which has become synonymous with Hawaii around the world and which has been worn with pride by such celebrities as Arthur Godfrey, Robin Williams, and Tom Selleck.

You can taste the local color in Hawaii's foods, a wonderful stew of cuisines from around the globe. On any given night you can dine on Japanese sashimi, Thai curry, Hawaiian lomilomi salmon, or Chinese roast duck, not to mention French, German, Korean, American, Mexican, Indian, Italian, and Greek dishes.

There are, of course, tastes that are uniquely tropical, especially when it comes to fruit. Hawaii's trademark bananas, papayas, and pineapple grow throughout the year, while the prized mangos, watermelons, and lychees appear only in the summer. Island seafood is equally splashy, with gourmet Pacific delicacies as exotic as their names: *mahimahi* (dolphin fish), *opakapaka* (blue snapper), *ulua* (crevelle), and *ahi* (tuna), to name a few.

Hawaii is making headway in the international dining scene, thanks to a recent influx of talented chefs from around the world. These culinary masters are coming to Hawaii primarily to cater to the ever-growing visitor population, and the results of their craft can be savored in the finer hotels throughout the state.

In Hawaii, meals are presented in environments as diverse as the menus. As you sip the finest champagne, you can enjoy an oceanside, candlelit dinner of fresh *opakapaka* fish that has been lavished with a sauce of three caviars. Or you can have just as much fun at a beachside carryout, munching on a lunch of teriyaki beef over rice served on paper plates with plastic utensils, then topping off your meal with a "shave ice" (snow cone) flavored with coconut, mango, and *lilikoi* (passion fruit) syrups.

Hawaii's ethnic mix is also in evidence on the cultural calendar, which is a wonderful hodgepodge of events, such as Japanese *bon* dances, Filipino festivals, Samoan shindigs, Chinese New Year celebrations, Scottish Highland flings, Greek galas, and the yearly Aloha Week festival. Vying for attention are the annual performances by the San Francisco ballet, a trio of productions presented by the Hawaii Opera Theater, chamber-music concerts, Broadway-style plays featuring top mainland stars, and community theater starring Hawaii's best local talent.

Standing out among the international din is that which is uniquely Hawaiian, as best exemplified by the dance and music of the Islands. Highly cherished are the hula and chants, which find their roots in ancient island history and have been handed down for centuries. Today they are praticed almost religiously; in fact, children can learn hula in school. Each year enthusiastic audiences applaud performances at such events as the Merrie Monarch Hula Festival on the Big Island, the Prince Lot Hula Festival on Oahu, and the Keiki Hula Festival, in which Hawaii's children carry on the tradition of Hawaiian poetry in motion.

Along with the swaying hips and stamping feet of the hula, the strumming sound of the ukulele has become innately associated with Hawaii. The ukulele (the name means "jumping flea") was brought from Portugal by sugarplantation workers. Today most every musical group that plays old-time Hawaiian songs has a ukulele in the band. Some of Hawaii's most cherished songsters play it, too, such as old-timer Andy Cummings, who wrote the hit song "Waikiki" and who strums and sings beloved standards each week in a Honolulu restaurant called Buzz's.

While many of Hawaii's performers faithfully strive to re-create the songs and dances of the past, a renaissance of the Hawaiian culture has spurred on a new generation of composers. Leading the wave of entertainers who make new music in the old tradition are the Brothers Cazimero, who perform at the Royal Hawaiian Hotel on Oahu, and Peter Moon, who plays at various clubs around the Islands. Their sounds are upbeat and easy to relate to for audiences unfamiliar with Hawaiian musical history.

The Aloha Spirit

Since the earliest days, island hospitality has played a key role in Hawaiian lifestyle. In fact, in ancient times members of the community who were not friendly to incoming guests were shunned by the rest of society. Since then it has been a revered island custom that when people come to call, they are not treated like tourists but instead are embraced like cherished guests or long-lost friends. In this very special way, Hawaii becomes everyone's home, and each visitor is a new and welcome member of the family.

Hawaii has a precious asset in its people. They go out of their way to help each other. On the freeway during rush hour, drivers often smile and wave you into their lane of traffic when you signal. At your hotel, a bellman carries your bag as if it's an honor, and your waitress seems genuinely excited that you're about to taste your first mai tai. Goodwill is not just a job to those in the visitor industry; it's their nature.

That sort of spirit just naturally rubs off on the people who visit Hawaii. Perhaps you first feel it as you smell the floral perfume in the air, that fragrance of the tropics. Dissected, it's a blend of plumeria, ginger, mock-orange blossoms, freshly clipped hedges, newly mown lawns, and the salt air from the Pacific surf. Together it presents an alluring essence that turns the most level-headed traveler into a giddy aficionado of Hawaii. The name for the way it makes you feel? Why, aloha spirit, of course!

Hawaii is full of living embodiments of this spirit. Take Tom Araki. He's an elderly taro farmer who lives in Waipo Valley, a remote spot on the Big Island that is accessible only by a four-wheel-drive vehicle. Tom runs a five-room "hotel" that has no official name, although he jokingly refers to it as the Waipio Hilton. It could very well be the most rustic accommodaton in all of Hawaii: It has no electricity, no front desk, no cable TV, no hot water. Guests bring their own food to cook on the Coleman stoves in his basement kitchen, and during the day they go on hikes, read a book, or venture down to the beach. Despite its limitations, this humble, out-of-the-way spot draws guests by the dozens. The main attraction is Tom himself; his good humor is contagious. In his unpretentious way he shares his island home with those who come to call, regaling them with stories of old Waipio Valley and sipping a glass of wine with them on the front porch.

Another fun example of Hawaiian hospitality awaits at the end of the Hana Highway on Maui. There you'll find the Hasegawa General Store, a surprisingly well-stocked emporium that has become famous in the tourist industry (there has even been a song written about it). No one knows how Harry Hasegawa can keep the place organized, because it's chock-full of everything from fishing poles and baby bottles to pickled cabbage and Maui T-shirts. Everyone loves to stop at Hasegawa's, to buy a cold soda, perhaps, but mainly to say hello to Harry, the "unofficial mayor" of Hana.

On Oahu, one of the most memorable embodiments of the aloha spirit is Irmgard Farden Aluli, who has written more than 300 songs in her 80 years of life. She is the leader of a singing group called Puamana, which includes her two daughters and a niece. They perform twice a month during luncheons at the Willows, a well-established restaurant where folks gather to eat, drink and listen to Hawaiian music. It's not strictly the food that packs the place, nor is it just the tropical ambience. No, folks flock to the Willows to meet "Auntie Irmgard," who, with the wink of an eye, a hike of her skirt, and the strumming of a guitar, sings the story of Hawaii in her own inimitable fashion.

Or perhaps you'd like to meet Beatrice Krauss, who, in her 80s, defies her age by leading tours around Honolulu's old Chinatown district. She takes visitors through her favorite Chinatown groceries, past the old tailor shops, the open-air emporiums, the ethnic markets, and the fish auction. Under the sponsorship of Lyon Arboretum, this gray-haired dynamo is a charming resource, and her excursions are full of fascinated tourists who adore her stories about growing up in Hawaii.

People like Tom, Harry, Irmgard, and Beatrice aren't in it for the money. They do what they do because they love their island home, and they want to share it with visitors. Like countless others in Hawaii, they're proud of their heritage, and they've found a way to express that happiness to others.

That undeniable aloha spirit permeates each island with such strength that it is impossible to ignore. It keeps people in Hawaii much longer than they originally plan to stay. It's also the best reason to pay a visit to the 50th state. Enjoy your trip, and remember that you are invited to stay as long as you like.

1 Essential Information

Before You Go

Visitor Information

A trip is a considerable investment in both time and money, and a travel agent who has been to Hawaii can help you cut through a lot of the details. He or she will also know most of the airline packages and special tours. Most travel agents work on a commission from the airlines, hotels, and attractions. You pay no more—and often less—than if you made your arrangements on your own.

The source of all information on Hawaii is the **Hawaii Visitors Bureau** (HVB). The bureau's main office is located right in Waikiki at Waikiki Business Plaza (2270 Kalakaua Ave., Suite 801, Honolulu, 96815, tel. 808/923–1811).

HVB is a communications network, attuned to the needs of the visitor and consumer oriented. The bureau publishes three free booklets. The *Calendar of Events* lists all the special holidays and annual festivals for the current year. The bureau also publishes an *Accommodation Guide*, which lists the various HVB-member lodging choices in Hawaii, in every price range. The guide tells you how close an accommodation is to the beach, and whether it has a pool and such amenities as refrigerators and televisions. If you specify that you are looking for budget accommodations, HVB will supply a list of helpful suggestions. The third is a *Restaurant Guide*, listing the 560 HVB-member restaurants in the state with a one-line description and a price category. There are no rating systems in the guides, just the bare facts.

The bureau also maintains regional offices.

New York: 441 Lexington Ave., Suite 1003, NY 10017, tel. 212/986–9203.
Los Angeles: 3440 Wilshire Blvd., Suite 502, CA 90010, tel. 213/385–5301.
Chicago: 180 N. Michigan Ave., Suite 1031, IL 60601, tel. 312/236–0632.
San Francisco: 50 California St., Suite 450, CA 94111, tel. 415/392–8173.
Great Britain: 2 Cinnamon Row, Plantation Wharf, York Place, London SW11 3TW, tel. 071/924–3999.
Japan: Hibiya Kokusai Building, 11th floor, 2-3-Uchisaiwaicho, 2-chome. Chiyoda-ku, Tokyo 100, tel. 81/3-597–7951.
Hong Kong: W. Tower, Suite 3702A, Bond Centre, Queensway, tel. 852/5-260387.

HVB Meetings and Conventions office:

Washington, DC: 1511 K St., NW, Suite 519, DC 20005, tel. 202/393–6752.

Tour Groups

Package tours to Hawaii usually include airfare, accommodations, transfers, some sightseeing, and plenty of free time for the beach. Choosing a tour comes down to how inclusive you want it to be: Do you want to know all your meals are paid for before you leave, or would you rather hunt out a local eatery?

Would you prefer to arrange a private sail, or is a group outing on a catamaran fine with you?

When considering a tour, be sure to find out (1) exactly what expenses are included—particularly tips, taxes, side trips, additional meals, and entertainment; (2) ratings of all hotels on the itinerary and the facilities they offer; (3) cancellation policies for both you and the tour operator; (4) the number of travelers in your group; and (5) if you are traveling alone, the cost of the single supplement. Note whether the tour operator reserves the right to change hotels, routes, or even prices after you've booked, and check out the operator's policy regarding cancellations, complaints, and trip-interruption insurance. Most tour operators request that bookings be made through a travel agent—in most cases there is no additional charge for doing so.

General-Interest Tours **Maupintour** (Box 807, Lawrence, KS 66044, tel. 913/843–1211 or 800/255–4266) combines Oahu with Maui, Kauai, and the Big Island of Hawaii in various itineraries. A 13-day trip to all of the four larger islands includes helicopter "flightseeing." **American Express Vacations** (Box 5014, Atlanta, GA 30302, tel. 800/241–1700) and **Pleasant Hawaiian Holidays** (2404 Townsgate Rd., Westlake Village, CA 91361, tel. 818/991–3390 or 800/2–HAWAII) are veritable supermarkets of tours, offering both escorted and independent packages. Other major operators include **Cartan Tours** (2809 Butterfield Rd., Oak Brook, IL 60521, tel. 708/571–1400 or 800/422–7826), **Island Holidays Tours** (2255 Kuhio Ave., Box 8519, Honolulu, HI 96830–0519, tel. 808/945–6000), **Talmage Tours** (1223 Walnut St., Philadelphia, PA 19107, tel. 215/923–7100), and **Trieloff Tours** (23521 Paseo de Valencia, Laguna Hills, CA 92653, tel. 714/855–2126 or 800/248–6877).

Special-Interest Tours
Adventure **Sobek Expeditions** (Box 1089, Angels Camp, CA 95222, tel. 800/777–7939) offers tours in Hawaii by bicycle or sea kayak as well as an off-the-beaten-track camping trip.

Camping The several tours offered by the **Sierra Club** (730 Polk St., San Francisco, CA 94109, tel. 415/776–2211) combine elements of the adventure packages (*see* above) and the conservationist program (*see* below). The Sierra Club spreads its conservation message by taking people on-site to see for themselves why an area should be preserved.

Conservation **Oceanic Society Expeditions** (Fort Mason Center, Bldg. E, San Francisco, CA 94123, tel. 415/441–1106) is a nonprofit environmental group with a variety of research and preservation projects open to public participation. Its Hawaii expedition includes whale-watching, sailing, and snorkeling as well as gathering valuable research on humpback whales as part of an ongoing project.

Golf **"Golf in Hawaii"** from **Trieloff Tours** (*see* General-Interest Tours, above) features five courses on three islands, along with first-class hotels.

Natural History **Questers Worldwide Nature Tours** (257 Park Ave. S, New York, NY 10010, tel. 212/673–3120) hikes into undeveloped areas throughout the islands to study native plant and animal life, volcanoes, and other exceptional settings.

British Tour Operators **Albany Travel** (Manchester) Ltd. (Central Buildings, 2H Deansgate, Manchester M3 3NW, tel. 061/833–0202) offers seven nights at Waikiki Beach from £738–£1,215 per person or 14 nights £843–£1,796. It also has self-catering vacations.

Hawaiian Holiday Tours, Inc. (308 Regent Street, London W1R 5AL, tel. 07/580–9998/9) is the only Hawaiian company directly available to the European market, and all its prices are quoted in dollars. A three-night stay in Waikiki ranges $128–$566 per person in a twin room. Seven nights in a condominium costs from $638 for two people. It also offers escorted tours to Waikiki, Maui, and Kauai, with prices starting from $1,045. Round-trip airfares from London to Honolulu are *not* included.

Kuoni Travel (Kuoni House, Dorking, Surrey RH5 4AZ, tel. 030/674–0500) offers six nights on Waikiki Beach from £694, and 13 nights combining New York and Waikiki from £849. It also offers "Hawaiian Magic" tours, visiting Waikiki and Maui, from £1,048 for 13 nights.

Jetsave (Sussex House, London Rd., East Grinstead, West Sussex RH19 1LD, tel. 0342/328231) offers seven nights at Waikiki Beach £705–£865 per person or 14 nights £795 to £959.

Package Deals for Independent Travelers

American Express Vacations and **Pleasant Hawaiian Holidays** (*see* General-Interest Tours, above) both offer catalogues full of air/hotel packages. **Liberty Travel/GoGo Tours** (68 offices across the country; if you can't find one near you, call GoGo's headquarters at 201/934–3500) has packages ranging from 2 to 16 days with options for sightseeing and discount car rental. **Classic Hawaii** (1 N. 1st St., San Jose, CA 95113, tel. 408/287–9101 or 800/221–3949) features the Islands' more upscale hotels and resorts. Also check with **American Fly AAway Vacations** (tel. 800/443–7300), **Continental Grand Destinations** (tel. 713/821–2100 or 800/356–4080), **Delta Airlines** (tel. 800/221–6666), and **United Vacations** (tel. 800/328–6877).

Passports, Visas, and Customs

Travel Documents Persons who are not citizens of the United States require a passport and a visa. Canadians only need to prove their place of birth, with a passport, birth certificate, or similar document. British travelers will need a valid, 10-year passport (cost £15) and a U.S. Visitor's Visa, which you can get either through your travel agent or by post from the **United States Embassy, Visa and Immigration Dept.** (5 Upper Grosvenor St., London W1A 2JB, tel. 071/499–3443 recorded message, or 499–7010). The embassy no longer accepts visa applications made by personal callers.

No vaccinations are required.

Restrictions on Import and Export If you are 21 or over, you may take in 200 cigarettes or 50 cigars or 2 kilograms of tobacco; one liter of alcohol; and duty-free gifts to a value of $100. Avoid illegal drugs like the plague.

Plants and plant products are subject to control by the Department of Agriculture, both on entering and leaving Hawaii. Pineapples and coconuts pass freely; avacados, bananas, lychees, and papayas must be treated. All other fruits are banned for export to the U.S. mainland. Flowers pass except for gardenia, rose, jade vine, and mauna loa. Seeds, except in leis and jewelry, are banned. Also banned are insects, snails, coffee, cotton, cacti, sugarcane, all berries, and soil.

Customs for British Travelers Returning to the UK, you may take home, if you are 17 and over: (1) 200 cigarettes or 100 cigarillos or 50 cigars or 250 grams of tobacco; (2) two liters of table wine and (a) one liter of alcohol over 22% by volume (most spirits) or (b) two liters of alcohol under 22% by volume (fortified or sparkling wine), (3) 60 milliliters of perfume and 1/4 liter of toilet water; and (4) other goods up to a value of £32.

Pets Leave dogs and other pets at home. A strict 120-day quarantine is imposed to keep out rabies, which is nonexistent in Hawaii. For full details, write to the **Animal Quarantine Station, Department of Agriculture,** State of Hawaii, 99-770 Moanalua Rd., Aiea, HI 96701.

When to Go

Hawaii's long days of sunshine, fairly mild year-round temperatures, and activities throughout each season allow for 12 months of pleasurable island travel. In resort areas near sea level, the average afternoon temperature during the coldest winter months of December and January is 80°F; during the hottest months of August and September the temperature can sometimes reach as high as 90°F. Cold weather (30°F) can occur in Hawaii during the winter, but only near the summit of the Big Island's Mauna Kea crater, where snow skiers occasionally have enough accumulation for a run or two.

Slight differences exist when it comes to monthly rainfall, high- and low-season travel rates, and the number of fellow travelers you'll find upon arrival. Winter is the season when most travelers prefer to head for the Islands. During mid-December through mid-April, visitors from the Mainland and other areas covered with snow find Hawaii's sun-splashed beaches and balmy trade winds particularly appealing. Not surprisingly, this high season also means that fewer travel bargains are available; room rates average 10%–15% higher during this season than the rest of the year.

The only weather change most areas experience during the December–February span is a few more days of rainfall, though the sun is rarely hidden behind the clouds for a solid 24-hour period. Visitors should remember that regardless of the season, the northern shores of each island usually receive more rain than those on the south. And Kauai and the Big Island's northern sections get more annual rainfall than the rest of Hawaii.

Rain- or sun-splashed, the Aloha State offers more than the weather to think about during the winter months. December ranks as the best time to see the magnificent crashing surf on Oahu's North Shore, where surfers gather from around the world to participate in competitions. This month also boasts such activities as Bodhi Day, the traditional Buddhist Day of Enlightenment; the annual Honolulu Marathon; and collegiate football's Aloha Bowl Game.

January and February also have their share of seasonal events. The Narcissus Festival, which begins in early January and runs through March, marks the Chinese New Year with an extended celebration, and the six-week Japanese Cherry Blossom Festival of traditional cultural activities kicks off at the same time. Kickoffs of a different kind take place when the Hula Bowl and NFL Pro Bowl games come to Honolulu. And for golf fans there's the annual Hawaiian Open International Golf Tournament.

Spring, marked by families on outings and college students taking a break from classes, is busy in Hawaii. In March, a fun-filled St. Patrick's Day parade cavorts through Waikiki; April brings the Merrie Monarch Festival, the Olympics of hula dancing held in Hilo.

Summer months mean warmer, humid weather, though the trade winds generally keep temperatures in the low to mid-80s most of the season. At this time of year, activity lessens only slightly and on the visitor front, the Islands still have much to offer to those who do choose to come then. Travelers can attend a range of events from June's King Kamehameha Celebration to the Hawaii State Farm Fair in July. In August there's Japanese Bon Dance and floating lantern festivals.

Fall also has its share of fun. September offers the annual Rough Water Swim in the waters off Waikiki; and October brings a popular canoe race from Molokai to Oahu, as well as ghoulish gaiety throughout Waikiki and Lahaina, Maui, on Halloween. When it comes to November and early December, the biggest event on the local calendar is the Hawaii International Film Festival, which draws award-winning filmmakers and their audiences from Asia, the Pacific, and the United States.

Climate The following are average maximum and minimum temperatures for certain areas of the Hawaiian Islands:

Waikiki, Oahu

Jan.	81F	27C	**May**	83F	28C	**Sept.**	88F	31C
	63	17		70	21		70	21
Feb.	81F	27C	**June**	85F	29C	**Oct.**	86F	30C
	63	17		70	21		70	21
Mar.	83F	28C	**July**	86F	30C	**Nov.**	85F	29C
	68	20		72	22		70	21
April	83F	28C	**Aug.**	88F	31C	**Dec.**	83F	28C
	67	19		72	22		65	18

Hilo, the Big Island

Jan.	79F	26C	**May**	81F	27C	**Sept.**	83F	28C
	63	17		65	18		67	19
Feb.	79F	26C	**June**	83F	28C	**Oct.**	83F	28C
	63	17		67	19		67	19
Mar.	79F	26C	**July**	83F	28C	**Nov.**	81F	27C
	63	17		67	19		67	19
April	79F	26C	**Aug.**	83F	28C	**Dec.**	79F	26C
	65	18		68	20		65	18

Lahaina, Maui

Jan.	85F	29C	**May**	86F	30C	**Sept.**	88F	31C
	61	16		63	17		70	21
Feb.	83F	28C	**June**	88F	31C	**Oct.**	88F	31C
	59	15		65	18		68	20
Mar.	85F	29C	**July**	88F	31C	**Nov.**	86F	30C
	63	17		65	18		67	19
April	85F	29C	**Aug.**	88F	31C	**Dec.**	83F	28C
	63	17		68	20		65	18

Molokai Airport, Molokai

Month	°F	°C	Month	°F	°C	Month	°F	°C
Jan.	79F	26C	May	81F	27C	Sept.	85F	29C
	63	17		67	18		70	21
Feb.	77F	25C	June	83F	28C	Oct.	85F	29C
	63	17		68	20		68	20
Mar.	79F	26C	July	85F	29C	Nov.	81F	27C
	63	17		70	21		67	19
April	79F	26C	Aug.	85F	29C	Dec.	79F	26C
	65	18		70	21		65	18

Lanai City, Lanai

Month	°F	°C	Month	°F	°C	Month	°F	°C
Jan.	76F	24C	May	79F	26C	Sept.	81F	27C
	58	14		63	17		63	17
Feb.	76F	24C	June	79F	26C	Oct.	81F	27C
	59	15		63	17		63	17
Mar.	76F	24C	July	81F	27C	Nov.	79F	26C
	58	14		65	18		63	17
April	77F	25C	Aug.	83F	28C	Dec.	76F	24C
	61	16		65	18		61	16

Lihue, Kauai

Month	°F	°C	Month	°F	°C	Month	°F	°C
Jan.	79F	26C	May	81F	27C	Sept.	85F	29C
	61	16		67	19		70	21
Feb.	79F	26C	June	83F	28C	Oct.	83F	28C
	61	16		70	21		68	20
Mar.	79F	26C	July	83F	28C	Nov.	81F	27C
	63	17		70	21		67	19
April	79F	26C	Aug.	83F	28C	Dec.	79F	26C
	65	18		70	21		65	18

Updated hourly weather information in 750 cities around the world—450 of them in the United States—is only a phone call away. Dialing WeatherTrak at 900/370–8725 will connect you to computer, with which you can communicate by touch tone—at a cost of 75 cents for the first minute and 50 cents a minute thereafter. A taped message will tell you to dial the three- digit access code to any of the 750 cities. The code is either the area code (in the United States) or the first three letters of the foreign city. For a list of all access codes, send a stamped, self-addressed envelope to Cities, Box 7000, Dallas, TX 75209. For further information, phone 800/ 247-3282.

Festivals and Seasonal Events

Hawaii has a busy calendar of holidays and special events; listed below are some of the most important or unusual ones. For further information contact the **Hawaii Visitors Bureau** (*see* Visitor Information, above).

Jan.: Hawaii Formula 40 World Cup (Oahu). Twelve 40-foot catamarans and trimarans participate in a challenging race that starts and ends at the Ala Wai Yacht Harbor, Honolulu.
Jan.: Kodak Hula Bowl (Oahu). This annual college all-star football game is played at Aloha Stadium, Honolulu.
Jan.: NFL Pro Bowl (Oahu). This annual pro football all-star game is played at Aloha Stadium.
Jan.: International Boogie Body Board Championships (Oahu). Thirty-six of the world's best bodyboarders participate in a one-day competition; the exact date depends on the best wave action.
Late Jan.: Kilauea Volcano Wilderness Marathon and Rim Runs

(the Big Island). More than 1,000 athletes from Hawaii, the mainland, and Japan run 26.2 miles across Kau desert, 10 miles around the Kilauea Caldera rim, and 5.5 miles into Kilauea Iki Crater and out again. The event takes place in Hawaii Volcanoes National Park.

Jan.–Feb.: Narcissus Festival (Oahu). Welcoming the Chinese New Year are a queen pageant, coronation ball, cooking demonstrations, and a noisy evening of fireworks in Chinatown.

Feb.: Hawaiian Open Golf Tournament (Oahu). Top golf pros tee off for $500,000 or more in prizes at the exclusive Waialae Country Club.

Feb.: Punahou Carnival (Oahu). Hawaii's most prestigious school stages an annual fund-raiser with rides, arts and crafts, local food, and a great flea market.

Feb.: Captain Cook Festival (Kauai). Honoring the British explorer who came to the island in 1778, Kauai offers a re-enactment of the captain's landing, canoe races, and a three-day fair at Waimea.

Feb.: Sandcastle Building Contest (Oahu). The students of the University of Hawaii School of Architecture take on Hawaii's professional architects in a friendly competition; the result is some amazing and unusual sand sculpture.

Feb.–March: Cherry Blossom Festival (all islands). This popular celebration of all things Japanese includes a run, cultural displays, cooking demonstrations, music, and the inevitable queen pageant and coronation ball.

Mar.: Buffalo's Annual Big Board Surfing Classic (Oahu). The event features surfing as it used to be, on old-fashioned 12- to 16-foot boards, plus food and entertainment.

Mar.: Opening Day of Polo Season (Oahu). Games are held every Sunday through August at 2 PM at the Hawaii Polo Club, Mokuleia.

Mar. 26: Prince Kuhio Day (all islands). The local holiday honors Prince Kuhio, who might have been a king if Hawaii had not been granted statehood. Instead the man became a respected congressman.

Mar. or Apr.: Merrie Monarch Festival (the Big Island). A full week of ancient and modern hula competition begins with a parade the Saturday morning following Easter Sunday. Tickets must be purchased months in advance; the competition is held at the Edith Kamakaole Auditorium in Hilo.

Mar.: Art Maui (Maui). This prestigious annual event highlights the best of a wide variety of media.

Apr.: Buddha Day (all islands). Flower pageants are staged at temples throughout the islands to celebrate the birth of Buddha.

Apr.: Carole Kai International Bed Race and Parade (Oahu). Big names in town turn out for this wild event centered in Waikiki. The race and parade are part of a charity fund-raiser.

May 1: Lei Day (all islands). The annual flower-filled celebration includes music, hula, food—and lots of leis on exhibit and for sale, some of them exquisite floral masterpieces.

May–June: 50th State Fair (Oahu). Produce exhibits, food booths, entertainment, and amusement rides mark this Hawaiian-style bit of Americana held at Aloha Stadium.

June: Festival of the Pacific (Oahu). This week-long affair of sports, music, songs, and dances highlighting regional ethnic culture has become very popular.

June: Pro Surf Championships (Oahu). Board, body, and skim surfing highlight this summer surfing event held on and around Sandy Beach.

June: King Kamehameha Day (all islands). Kamehameha united all the islands to become Hawaii's first king (and making Hawaii the only state to have a royal background). In addition to parades and fairs, twin statues of the king—in Honolulu, Oahu, and Hawi on the Big Island—are draped in giant leis.

June–July: Hawaii State Farm Fair (Oahu). Farm products, agricultural exhibits, arts and crafts, a petting zoo, contests, and a country market are featured at one of Hawaii's best farm fairs.

July: Makawao Statewide Rodeo (Maui). This old-time upcountry rodeo, held at the Oskie Rice Arena, includes the annual Makawao Rodeo Parade.

July 4: Independence Day (all islands). The national holiday is celebrated with a tropical touch, including fairs, parades, and, of course, fireworks. Special events are the 44th Walter J. MacFarlane Regatta and Surf Race, an outrigger canoe regatta featuring 30 events held on and off Waikiki Beach.

July: Prince Lot Hula Festival (Oahu). A whole day of hula unfolds beneath the towering trees of Oahu's Moanalua Gardens.

July: International Festival of the Pacific (the Big Island). The event features music, dance, and food from Japan, China, Korea, Portugal, Tahiti, New Zealand, and the Philippines.

End of July–Aug. Bon Odori Season (all islands). Buddhist temples invite everyone to festivals that honor ancestors and feature Japanese dancing.

Aug.: Hawaii International Billfish Tournament (the Big Island). Billed as the world's leading international marlin fishing tournament, the event, held in Kailua-Kona, includes a parade with amusing entries.

Aug.: Queen Liliuokalani Keiki Hula Competition (Oahu). The crowds turn out to see the children's hula competition, which is held over three days. Tickets are usually available at the end of June and sell out soon after.

Aug. 18: Admission Day (all islands). The state holiday recognizes Hawaii's statehood.

Sept.: Waikiki Rough Water Swim (Oahu). Swimmers of all ages and skill levels can compete in this 2-mile outing.

Sept.–Oct.: Aloha Week Festivals (all islands). This traditional celebration, started in 1946, preserves Hawaiian native culture. Crafts, music, dance, pageantry, street parties, and canoe races are all part of the festival.

Sept., Oct.: Bankoh Molokai Hoe. Two annual canoe races from Molokai to Oahu finish in Waikiki. The women's race is in Sept.; the men's is in Oct.

Oct.: Bud Light Ironman Triathlon World Championships (the Big Island). This popular annual sporting event is limited to 1,250 competitors who swim, run, and bicycle.

Nov.: Pearl Harbor Aloha Festival (Oahu). This event is the largest military festival of its kind in Hawaii. Major concerts, from rock to country and traditional Hawaiian, are common during the fair.

Nov.: King Kalakaua Kupuna and Keiki Hula Festival (the Big Island). Another big, popular hula contest, this one features both a children's competition and one for *kupuna*–adults 55 years and older.

Nov.: Kona Coffee Festival (the Big Island). A week-long celebration follows the coffee harvest. The Miss Kona Coffee contest, and a coffee cupping (tasting) contest are capped by a parade and family day at Hale Halawai Recreation Pavilion with ethnic foods and entertainment.

Nov.: Mission Houses Museum Annual Christmas Fair (Oahu). Artists and craftspeople sell their creations in an open market.

Nov.–Dec.: Hawaii International Film Festival (Oahu). The visual feast showcases films from the United States, Asia, and the Pacific.

Dec.: Triple Crown of Surfing (Oahu). The world's top pro surfers gather for the big winter waves and some tough competition.

Dec.: Honolulu Marathon (Oahu). Watch or run in one of the country's most popular marathons.

Dec.: Bodhi Day (all islands). The traditional Buddhist Day of Enlightenment is celebrated at temples throughout the islands. Visitors are welcome to the services.

Dec.: Eagle Aloha Bowl (Oahu). Two top college football squads meet in this annual contest held at Aloha Stadium.

Dec. 25: Christmas (all islands). The hotels outdo each other in extravagant exhibits and events like Santa arriving by outrigger canoe.

What to Pack

You can pack lightly because Hawaii is casual. Bare feet, bathing suits, and comfortable, informal clothing are the norm.

The Man's Suitcase In the Hawaiian Islands, there's a saying that when a man wears a suit during the day, he's either going for a loan or he's a lawyer trying a case. Only a few upscale restaurants require a jacket for dinner, and none requires a tie. Hawaii regulars wear their jackets on the plane—just in case—and many don't put them on again until the return flight. The aloha shirt is accepted dress in Hawaii for business and most social occasions. A visitor can easily buy one after arriving in Hawaii.

Shorts are acceptable daytime attire, along with a T-shirt or polo shirt. If you want to be marked as a tourist, wear your shorts with dark shoes and white socks. Local-style casual footwear consists of tennis or running shoes, sandals, or rubber slippers. You'll also see a lot of bare feet, but state law requires that footwear be worn in all food establishments.

Pack your toiletries, underwear, and a pair or two of easy-care slacks to wear with those aloha shirts, and you're all set.

Female Fashion During the winter months, be sure to bring a sweater or wrap for the evening because the trade winds cool things off as soon as the sun goes down. If you have an elaborate coiffure, a scarf will help keep it from getting windblown.

Sundresses, shorts, and tops are fine for daytime. During the summer months, synthetic slacks and shirts, although easy to care for, can get uncomfortably warm. If you have a long slip, bring it for the muumuu you say you won't buy, but probably will. As for shoes, sandals and tennis or running shoes are fine for daytime, and sandals are perfect for the evening. If you wear boots, you'll wish you hadn't.

If you don't own a pareu, buy one in Hawaii. It's simply a length (about 1½ yards long) of light cotton in a tropical motif that can be worn as a beachwrap, a skirt, or a dozen other wrap-up fashions. A pareu is useful wherever you go, regardless of climate. It makes a good bathrobe, so you don't have to pack one. You can even tie it up as a handbag or sit on it at the beach.

For Everyone Don't forget your bathing suit. Sooner or later, the crystal-clear water tempts even the most sedentary landlubber. Of course, bathing suits are easy to find in Hawaii. Shops are crammed with the latest styles. If you wear a bathing cap, bring one; you can waste hours searching for one.

Probably the most important thing to tuck in your suitcase is sunscreen. This is the tropics, and the ultraviolet rays are much more powerful than those to which you are accustomed. Doctors advise putting on sunscreen when you get up in the morning. Women can wear it as a moisturizer under makeup. The upper chest area of a woman is hypopigmented and should be protected. Don't forget to reapply sunscreen periodically during the day, since perspiration can wash it away. Consider using sunscreens with a sun protection factor (SPF) of 15 or higher. There are many tanning oils on the market in Hawaii, including coconut and kukui oils, but doctors warn that they merely sauté your skin. Too many Hawaiian vacations have been spoiled by sunburn.

Visitors who wear glasses are wise to pack an extra pair. Eyeglasses are easy to lose, and you can waste days of your precious Hawaiian holiday replacing them.

If you're planning to visit a volcano area, bring along a lightweight jacket, especially in the winter months.

It's a good idea to tuck in a few jumbo zip-lock plastic bags when you travel—they're ideal for wet swimsuits or food souvenirs that might leak. All hotels in Hawaii provide beach towels. Some hotels provide hair dryers and some don't. Unless you know for sure, bring your own.

Luggage Passengers on U.S. airlines are limited to two carry-on bags.
Carry-on Luggage For a bag you wish to store under the seat, the maximum dimensions are 9″ × 14″ × 22″. For bags that can be hung in a closet or on a luggage rack, the maximum dimensions are 4″ × 23″ × 45″. For bags you wish to store in an overhead bin, the maximum dimensions are 10″ × 14″ × 36″. Any item that exceeds the specified dimensions may be rejected as a carryon and taken as checked baggage. Keep in mind that an airline can adapt the rules to circumstances, so on an especially crowded flight don't be surprised if you are only allowed one carry-on bag.

In addition to the two carryons, you may bring aboard a handbag (pocketbook or purse); an overcoat or wrap; an umbrella; a camera; a reasonable amount of reading material; an infant bag; and crutches, cane, braces, or other prosthetic device. An infant/child safety seat can also be brought aboard if parents have purchased a ticket for the child or if there is space in the cabin.

Foreign airlines have slightly different policies. They generally allow only one piece of carry-on luggage in tourist class, in addition to handbags and bags filled with duty-free goods. Passengers in first and business class are also allowed to carry on one garment bag. It is best to call your airline to find out its current policy.

Checked Luggage U.S. airlines allow passengers to check in two suitcases whose total dimensions (length + width + height) do not exceed 62 inches and whose weight does not exceed 70 pounds.

Rules governing foreign airlines can vary, so check with your travel agent or the airline itself before you go. All airlines allow passengers to check in two bags. In general, expect the weight restriction on the two bags to be not more than 70 pounds each, and the size restrictions on the bags to be 62 inches total dimensions.

Cash Machines

Virtually all U.S. banks belong to a network of ATMs (Automatic Teller Machines), which gobble up bank cards and spit out cash 24 hours a day in cities throughout the country. There are eight major networks in the United States, the largest of which are Cirrus, owned by MasterCard, and Plus, affiliated with Visa. Some banks belong to more than one network. These cards are not automatically issued; you have to ask for them. If your bank doesn't belong to at least one network, you should consider moving your account, for ATMs are becoming as essential as check cashing. Cards issued by Visa, MasterCard, and American Express may also be used in the ATMs, but the fees are usually higher than the fees on bank cards (and there is a daily interest charge on the "loan," even if monthly bills are paid on time). Each network has a toll-free number you can call to locate machines in a given city. The Cirrus number is 800/4-CIRRUS; the Plus number is 800/THE-PLUS. Check with your bank for fees and for the amount of cash you can withdraw on any given day; also ask for a list of banks in Hawaii that will honor your bank cash card.

Insurance

Travelers may seek insurance coverage in three areas: health and accident, loss of luggage, and trip cancellation. Your first step is to review your existing health and homeowner policies; some health insurance plans cover health expenses incurred while traveling, some major medical plans cover emergency transportation, and some homeowner policies cover the theft of luggage.

Health and Accident Several companies offer coverage designed to supplement existing health insurance for travelers:

Carefree Travel Insurance (Box 310, 120 Mineola Blvd., Mineola, NY 11501, tel. 516/294-0220 or 800/645-2424) provides coverage for medical evacuation. It also offers 24-hour medical phone advice.

Health Care Abroad, International Underwriters Group (243 Church St. West, Vienna, VA 22180, tel. 703/281-9500 or 800/237-6615) offers comprehensive medical coverage, including emergency evacuation, for trips of 10-90 days.

International SOS Insurance (Box 11568, Philadelphia, PA 19116, tel. 215/244-1500 or 800/523-8930) does not offer medical insurance but provides medical evacuation services to its clients, who are often international corporations.

Travel Guard International, underwritten by Cygna (1100 Centerpoint Dr., Stevens Point, WI 54481, tel. 715/345–0505 or 800/782–5151) offers medical insurance, with coverage for emergency evacuation when Travel Guard's representatives in the United States say it is necessary.

For British Travelers We recommend that to cover health and motoring mishaps, you insure yourself with **Europ Assistance** (252 High St., Croydon, Surrey CRO INF, tel. 01/680–1234).

Lost Luggage The loss of luggage is usually covered as part of a comprehensive travel insurance package that includes personal accident, trip cancellation, and sometimes default and bankruptcy insurance. Several companies offer comprehensive policies:

Access America Inc., a subsidiary of Blue Cross-Blue Shield (Box 807, New York, NY 10163, tel. 800/851-2800).
Near, Inc, (1900 North MacArthur Blvd., Suite 210, Oklahoma City, OK 73127, tel. 800/654-6700).
Travel Guard International (*see* Health and Accident Insurance above).

For British Travelers It is also wise to take out insurance to cover the loss of luggage (although check that such loss isn't already covered in any existing homeowner's policies you may have). Trip-cancellation insurance is another wise buy. **The Association of British Insurers** (Aldermary House, Queen St., London EC4N 1TT, tel. 01/248–4477) will give comprehensive advice on all aspects of vacation insurance.

Trip Cancellation Flight insurance is often included in the price of a ticket when paid for with American Express, Visa, and other major credit and charge cards. It is usually included in combination travel insurance packages available from most tour operators, travel agents, and insurance agents.

Traveling with Film

If your camera is new, shoot and develop a few rolls of film before leaving home. Pack some lens tissue and an extra battery for your built-in light meter. Invest about $10 in a skylight filter and screw it onto the front of your lens. It will protect the lens and also reduce haze.

Film doesn't like hot weather. If you're driving in summer, don't store film in the glove compartment or on the shelf under the rear window. Put it behind the front seat on the floor, on the side opposite from the exhaust pipe.

On a plane trip, never pack unprocessed film in check-in luggage; if your bags get X-rayed, you can say good-bye to your pictures. Always carry undeveloped film with you through security, and ask to have it inspected by hand. (It helps to isolate your film in a plastic bag, ready for quick inspection.) Inspectors at American airports are required by law to honor requests for hand inspection; abroad, you'll have to depend on the kindness of strangers.

The old airport scanning machines—still in use in some countries—use heavy doses of radiation that can turn a family portrait into an early morning fog. The newer models—used in all U.S. airports—are safe for anything from five to 500 scans, depending on the speed of your film. The effects are cumulative; you can put the same roll of film through several scans without worry. After five scans, though, you're asking for trouble.

If your film gets fogged and you want an explanation, send it to the National Association of Photographic Manufacturers (550 Mamaroneck Ave., Harrison, NY 10528). They will try to determine what went wrong. The service is free.

Traveling with Children

Publications   *Family Travel Times* is an 8- to 12-page newsletter published 10 times a year by TWYCH (Travel with Your Children, 80 8th Ave., New York, NY 10011, tel. 212/206-0688). Subscription includes access to back issues and twice-weekly opportunities to call in for specific information. Send $1 for a sample issue.

Great Vacations with Your Kids, by Dorothy Jordan (founder of TWYCH) and Marjorie Cohen, offers complete advice on planning a trip with children (toddlers to teens) and details everything from city vacations to adventure vacations to child-care resources ($12.95, E.P. Dutton, 2 Park Ave., New York, NY 10016, tel. 212/725-1818).

Kids and Teens in Flight is a Department of Transportation brochure with information on young people traveling alone. To order free copies, call 202/366-2220.

Getting There   On domestic flights, children under two not occupying a seat travel free. Various discounts apply to children two to 12 years of age. Regulations about infant travel on airplanes are in the process of changing. Until they do, however, if you want to be sure your infant is secured in his/her own safety seat, you must buy a separate ticket and bring your own infant car seat. (Check with the airline in advance; certain seats aren't allowed. Or write for the booklet *Child/Infant Safety Seats Acceptable for Use in Aircraft,* from the Federal Aviation Administration, APA–200, 800 Independence Ave. SW, Washington, DC 20591, tel. 202/267-3479.) Some airlines allow babies to travel in their own safety seats at no charge if there's a spare seat available on the plane, otherwise safety seats will be stored and the child will have to be held by a parent. If you opt to hold your baby on your lap, do so with the infant outside the seatbelt so he or she won't be crushed in case of a sudden stop.

Also inquire about special children's meals or snacks. See the February 1990 and 1992 issues of *Family Travel Times* for "TWYCH's Airline Guide," which contains a rundown of the children's services offered by 46 airlines.

Hints for Disabled Travelers

In Hawaii   The Society for the Advancement of Travel for the Handicapped has named Hawaii the most accessible vacation spot for the disabled; the number of ramped visitor areas and specially equipped lodgings in the state attests to its desire to make everyone feel welcome. Several agencies and companies make helping the disabled their number one priority. **The Commission on Persons with Disabilities** (5 Waterfront Plaza, 500 Ala Moana Blvd., Suite 210, Honolulu 96813, tel. 808/548-7606) publishes a *Travelers Guide for Persons with Disabilities,* available at a nominal fee, which features the addresses and telephone numbers of support services for handicapped visitors on all islands. The guide also lists accessibility ratings of the island's hotels, beaches, shopping centers, entertainment, and major visitor attractions.

Information concerning accessibility on the Neighbor Islands can be obtained by writing or calling the **Commission on Persons with Disabilities:** on the Big Island (1190 Waianuenue Ave., Box 1641, Hilo 96820, tel. 808/935–7257); on Kauai (3060 Eiwa St., Room 207, Lihue 96766, tel. 808/245–4308); and on Maui (54 High St., Wailuku 96793, tel. 808/244–4441). Call the Commission for more detailed information about special displays, services, or assistance for the handicapped.

Several transportation options are available to disabled Hawaii travelers. They may receive curb-to-curb service from **Handi-Vans** (867 Ahua St., Honolulu 96819, tel. 808/833–2222) as long as riders give the company 24 hours' notice. You must meet the Handi-Vans administrator once in person, however, to prove your disability. All rides cost $1. A private company, **Handi-Cabs of the Pacific** (Box 22428, Honolulu 96822, tel. 808/524–3866), offers van service on Oahu for an $8 curb-side pickup charge plus $1.95 per mile. Twenty-four hours' notice is required.

Those who prefer to do their own driving may rent hand-controlled cars from **Avis** (tel. 800/831–8000), which are available on a request basis, so allow at least 24 hours notice to reserve one. **Hertz** (tel. 800/654–3131) also rents left- or right-hand controlled cars at no additional charge on all the major islands. A two-day notice is required, and an additional $25 deposit is required from customers renting on a cash basis. Handicapped-parking passes for Oahu may be obtained at the **Department of Transportation Services** (650 S. King St., Honolulu 96813, tel. 808/523–4021). Open Mon.–Fri. 8–4. If you already have a windshield card from your own state, that's all you need. However, the administrator says they like to meet disabled travelers and help if they can, so stop in the office anytime. Information concerning handicapped-parking on the Neighbor Islands may be found in the Commission on the Handicapped brochures (*see* above).

Travelers may rent wheelchairs, walkers, oxygen, lifts, and overbed tables from companies such as **a'a Medical Supplies** (711 S. Queen St., Honolulu 96813, tel. 808/537–5933) and **Abbey Medical** (500 Ala Kawa St., Honolulu 96817, tel. 808/845–5000). The companies should be contacted in advance.

Additional Information **Greyhound/Trailways** (tel. 800/531–5332) will carry a disabled person and companion for the price of a single fare. **Amtrak** (tel. 800/USA–RAIL) requests 72 hours' notice to provide Redcap service, special seats, or wheelchair assistance at stations equipped to provide this service. All handicapped elderly passengers are entitled to an additional 25% discount on regular, discounted coach fares. There are exceptions to these discounts on certain prescribed days with various routes. For a free copy of *Amtraks Travel Planner,* which includes its services for elderly and handicapped travelers, write to Amtrak (National Railroad Corporation, 60 Massachusetts Ave. NE, Washington, DC 20002).

The Information Center for Individuals with Disabilities (Fort Point Place, 1st floor, 27 Wormwood St., Boston, MA 02210, tel. 617/727–5540) offers useful problem-solving assistance, including lists of travel agents who specialize in tours for the disabled.

Moss Rehabilitation Hospital Travel Information Service (12th St. and Tabor Rd., Philadelphia, PA 19141, tel. 215/329–5715) provides information on tourist sights, transportation, and accommodations in destinations around the world for a small fee.

Mobility International (Box 3551, Eugene, OR 97403, tel. 503/343–1284) is a membership organization with a $20 annual fee offering information on accommodations, organized study, and travel around the world for disabled persons of all ages.

The National Park Service provides a **Golden Access Passport** free of charge to those who are blind or who have a permanent disability; the passport covers the entry fee for the holder and anyone accompanying the holder in the same private, noncommercial vehicle and a 50% discount on camping, boat launching, and parking. All charges are covered except lodging. Apply for the passport in person at any national recreation facility that charges an entrance fee; proof of disability is required. For additional information, write to the National Park Service (U.S. Dept. of Interior, 18th and C Sts. NW, Washington, DC 20240).

The Society for the Advancement of Travel for the Handicapped (26 Court St., Penthouse, Brooklyn, NY 11242, tel. 718/858–5483, fax 718/596–6310) offers access information. Annual membership costs $45, $25 for students and travelers over 65. Send $2 and a stamped, self-addressed envelope.

Travel Industry and Disabled Exchange (TIDE, 5435 Donna Ave., Tarzanna, CA 91356, tel. 818/368–5648) is an industry-based organization with a $15 per person annual membership fee. Members receive a quarterly newsletter and information on travel agencies and tours.

Publications *Access America: An Atlas and Guide to the National Parks for Visitors with Disabilities* (published by Northern Cartographic, Box 133, Burlington, VT 05402, tel. 802/860–2886) contains detailed information about access for the 37 largest and most visited national parks in the United States. It costs $40 plus $5 shipping.

Access to the World: A Travel Guide for the Handicapped, by Louise Weiss, is available from Henry Holt & Co. (tel. 800/247–3912, the order number is 0805 001417) for $12.95 plus $2 shipping and handling.

Hints for Older Travelers

The American Association of Retired Persons (AARP, 1990 K St. NW, Washington, DC 20049, tel. 202/872–4700) has two programs for independent travelers: (1) The Purchase Privilege Program, which offers discounts on hotels, airfare, car rentals, and sightseeing; and (2) the AARP Motoring Plan, which furnishes emergency aid (road service) and trip-routing information for an annual fee of $33.95 per couple. AARP members must be at least 50 years old. Annual dues are $5 per person or per couple. Group tours are arranged by **Olson-Travelworld** (100 N.Sepulveda Blvd., El Segundo, CA 90245, tel. 213/615–0711 or 800/421–2255). As of 1991, tours will be arranged by **American Express Vacations** (*see* Tour Groups, above).

To use an AARP or other identification card, ask for a reduced hotel rate at the time you make your reservation, not when you check out. At restaurants, show your card to the maître d' before you're seated, since discounts may be limited to certain set menus, days, or hours. Your AARP card will identify you as a retired person but will not ensure a discount in all restaurants. When renting a car, remember that economy cars, priced at promotional rates, may cost less than cars that are available with your ID card.

Elderhostel (80 Boylston Street, Suite 400, Boston, MA 02116, tel. 617/426–7788) is an educational travel program for people age 60 or over (only one member of a traveling couple needs to qualify). Participants live in dormitory-style housing on some 1,400 campuses in the United States and around the world. Mornings are devoted to lectures and seminars, afternoons to sightseeing and field trips. The fee for a trip includes room, board, tuition (in the U.S. and Canada) and round-trip transportation (overseas). Special scholarships are available for those who qualify financially in the United States and Canada.

The Golden Age Passport is a free lifetime pass to all parks, monuments, and recreation areas run by the federal government. Permanent U.S. residents over age 62 may pick them up in person at any of the national parks that charge admission. Proof of age is necessary. The passport covers the entrance fee for the holder and anyone accompanying the holder in the same private (non-commercial) vehicle. It also provides a 50% discount on camping, boat launching, and parking (lodging is not included). For additional information, contact National Park Service (U.S. Dept. of Interior, 18th and C Sts. NW, Washington, DC 20240).

Greyhound/Trailways (tel. 800/531–5332) offers special fares for senior citizens; the rates are subject to date and destination restrictions. **Amtrak** (tel. 800/USA–RAIL) requests 72 hours' notice to provide Redcap service, special seats, or wheelchair assistance at stations equipped to provide this service. (*See* Hints for Disabled Travelers, above, for more information.)

Mature Outlook (6001 N. Clark St., Chicago, IL 60660, tel. 800/336–6330), a subsidiary of Sears, is a travel club for people over 50 years of age, offering Holiday Inn discounts and a bimonthly newsletter. Annual membership is $9.95 per couple.

National Council of Senior Citizens (925 15th St. NW, Washington, DC 20005, tel. 202/347–8800) is a nonprofit advocacy group with some 5,000 local clubs across the country. Annual membership is $12 per person or per couple. Members receive a monthly newspaper with travel information and an ID for reduced-rate hotels and car rentals.

September Days Club (tel. 800/241–5050) is run by the moderately priced Days Inns of America. The $12 annual membership fee for individuals or couples over 50 entitles them to reduced car-rental rates and reductions of 15%–50% at 95% of the chain's more than 350 motels.

Publications *The Discount Guide for Travelers over 55,* by Caroline and Walter Weintz, lists helpful addresses, package tours, reduced-rate car rentals, etc., in the United States and abroad. To order, send $7.95, plus $1.50 shipping and handling, to NAL/Cash Sales (Bergenfield Order Dept., 120 Woodbine St., Bergenfield, NJ 07621, tel. 800/526-0275). Include ISBN 0-525-48358-6.

The International Health Guide for Senior Citizen Travelers, by Dr. W. Robert Lange, MD, is available for $4.95, and *The Senior Citizens Guide to Budget Travel in the United States and Canada,* by Paige Palmer, is available for $3.95, plus $1 for shipping from Pilot Books (103 Cooper St., Babylon, NY 11702, tel. 516/422-2225).

Further Reading

Hawaii, by James A. Michener, ranks as one of the best novels from which to gain an overall historical perspective of the Islands. *Hawaii: An Uncommon History,* by Edward Joesting, gives a behind-the-scenes look at the factual side of some of the same events in the Michener novel. *A Voyage to the Pacific Ocean,* by Captain James Cook, ranks as one of the first guidebooks to the Islands and still contains many valid insights; *Shoal of Time,* by Gavan Daws, chronicles Hawaiian history from Cook's time to the 1960s. Information concerning the gods and goddesses once thought to inhabit the region can be found in *Hawaiian Mythology,* by Martha Warren Beckwith. *Chanting the Universe,* by John Charlot, examines Hawaiian culture through its poetry and chants. Another level of early Island spiritual life is recorded in the missionary memoirs titled *A Residency of Twenty-one Years in the Sandwich Islands,* by Hiram Bingham.

More recent history comes to life in the pages of *Travels in Hawaii,* by Robert Louis Stevenson, while *Stevenson in Hawaii,* by Sister Mary Martha McGaw, makes an interesting story of the traveling storyteller himself. *History Makers of Hawaii,* by A. Grove Day, provides a biographical dictionary of the key people who shaped the territory from past to present. A more recent view (1984) of the state comes from the text and photographs of *A Day in the Life of Hawaii,* by Rick Smolen and David Cohen.

Those interested in the physical attractions of the Islands may want to read *A Guide to Tropical and Semitropical Flora,* by Loraine Kuck and Richard Tongg. The *Handbook of Hawaiian Fishes,* by W.A. Gosline and Vernon Brock, is a must for snorkelers; *Hawaii's Birds* by the Hawaii Audubon Society is perfect for birdwatchers.

The athletic-minded might consider *Hawaiian Hiking Trails,* by Craig Chisholm, just the guide for day hikers and backpackers. *Surfing: The Ultimate Pleasure,* by Leonard Lueras, covers everything about the sport from its early history to the music and films of its later subculture.

ALOHA Magazine, (Box 3260, Honolulu 96801), a colorful magazine devoted to the 50th State, contains scenic photo essays and articles about history, arts, culture, sports, food, and fashion, as well as visitor attractions and a calendar of events. *ALOHA Magazine* is published bimonthly; subscription rates are $14.95 per year. *Aloha Travelers' Newsletter,* with travel tips and savings specifically aimed for Hawaii visitors, is a sister publication also offered bimonthly for $14.95 a year.

Pleasant HAWAII (270 Lewers St., Penthouse, Honolulu, HI 96815), a colorful magazine devoted to the 50th State, contains excellent photography and feature articles about a broad range of topics, including history, sports, the arts, local customs, food, fashion, lifestyle, and the natural beauty of the Islands. Each issue features personal portraits of local residents and helpful travel tips. *Pleasant HAWAII* is published quarterly; subscription rates are $9 per year.

Arriving and Departing

By Plane

Booking your Hawaii flight will be easy because a number of major airlines regularly service the destination. If, however, you are traveling from anywhere other than a West Coast city, you should know the distinction among the types of flights available. The quickest way to get from your home to a Hawaiian beach is to catch a nonstop flight from one of the country's major gateway cities. On direct flights you stay on the same aircraft, but make one or more stops; connecting flights involve one or more plane changes at one or more stops. If you can tolerate the plane-hopping, connecting flights are often the least expensive way to go.

Airports Hawaii's major airport is **Honolulu International** (tel. 808/836–6411), about a five-hour flight from West Coast cities and a 20-minute drive from Waikiki. The facility currently is undergoing major renovation that makes it more cumbersome to navigate now, but this should ease congestion when work is finished in 1993. The Honolulu Airport is packed with shops perfect for last-minute buying: places where you can get a lei, a pineapple, T-shirts, and even Gucci bags. If you're flying from Honolulu to another island, you'll need to locate one of the two separate interisland terminals (one for Aloha Airlines and one for Hawaiian Airlines) to the left of the main terminal as you exit. For 50¢, a Wiki Wiki Shuttle will take you to and from the interisland terminals; however, it's an easy five-minute walk between the international and the interisland terminals.

As for the Neighbor Islands, some airports there are also getting major facelifts. Maui's **Kahului Airport** (tel. 808/877–0078) is an efficient facility in Maui's central town of Kahului, but like its sister in Honolulu, it will spend the next several years undergoing renovation. Maui's other airport, the **Kapalua-West Maui Airport** (call either Aloha IslandAir or Hawaiian Airlines, *see* Interisland Flights, below) opened in 1987 and capably handles the traffic it gets. For visitors to West Maui, landing at the Kapalua facility is the easiest way to arrive, and will save about an hour's drive from the Kahului airport. The tiny town of **Hana** in east Maui also has an airstrip (tel. 808/248–8208), but it is only serviced by one commuter airline and one charter airline.

On Kauai, visitors have a choice between the recently expanded **Lihue Airport** (tel. 808/246–1400), on the east side of the island, and **Princeville Airport** (tel. 808/826–3040) near the north shore. The main facility in Lihue has finished a major portion of its renovation, making it a dramatically new and clean airport, while the airstrip in Princeville is partly maintained by private funds, and is the best way to reach hotels on Kauai's northern shore.

Those flying to the Big Island can land at one of three fields. Kona's **Ke-ahole Airport** (tel. 808/329–2484) on the west side best serves Kailua-Kona, Keauhou, and the Kohala Coast. While this airport is slated for major expansion, it still is new enough to provide a pleasurable airport experience for passengers who land there. **Hilo International Airport** (tel. 808/935–0809), formerly General Lyman Field, also is a large, new airport but is more appropriate for those going to the east side. Those destined for the north end of the island might want to consider **Waimea-Kohala Airport** (tel. 808/885–4520), which is served daily by commuter airline Aloha IslandAir.

Nearby **Lanai** (tel. 808/565–6757) and **Molokai** (tel. 808/567–6140) airports are centrally located on those islands. Both are small, rural airports that can handle only a limited number of flights and planes per day.

Flights from Mainland U.S. Flying into Honolulu International Airport are **Air America** (tel. 800/247–2475), or in CA 800/654–8880, **America West** (800/247–5692), **American** (tel. 800/433–7300), **Continental** (tel. 800/525–0280), **Delta** (tel. 800/221–1212), **Hawaiian** (tel. 800/367–5320), **Northwest** (tel. 800/225–2525), **Pan Am** (tel. 800/221–1111), **TWA** (tel. 800/221–2000), and **United** (tel. varies from city to city). Many of those flights originate in Los Angeles and San Francisco, but it's also possible to fly from Dallas, Chicago, St. Louis, New York, Seattle, Minneapolis, San Diego, and other gateways. United Airlines—which boasts some 50% of the airline traffic to Hawaii—flies directly into the Big Island's Ke-ahole Airport, Maui's Kahului Airport, and Kauai's Lihue Airport. Air America, American, and Delta fly into Kahului.

International Flights Foreign air carriers are prohibited by law from serving Hawaii from American cities. Should your travel plans bring you from other parts of the world, however, **Canadian Airlines** (tel. 808/922–0533), **Qantas** (tel. 800/227–4500), **Air New Zealand** (tel. 800/521–4059), **China Air Lines** (tel. 800/421–1289, or in CA 800/227–5118), and **Japan Air Lines** (tel. 808/525–3663), among others, fly to Honolulu.

American, Continental, Delta, and **TWA** are among the airlines that fly from Britain to Honolulu. An APEX ticket costs about £559 for a midweek flight, plus taxes. Check the back pages of *Time Out* and the Sunday papers for good offers. **Trailfinders** (42–48 Earl's Court Rd., Kensington, London W8 6EJ, tel. 071/937–5400) can arrange flights from £535.

Interisland Flights While some national airlines make it possible to fly directly into Kauai, Maui, and the Big Island, the majority of travelers to Hawaii still fly to Honolulu and connect with interisland shuttle flights. Aircraft vary in size from Boeing 737 jets to twin-prop Cessna 402s. One advantage of the smaller planes is the option of flying into some of the more remote airfields around the state.

Interisland, **Aloha Airlines** (tel. 800/367–5250) and **Hawaiian Airlines** (tel. 800/367–5320) serve the following airports: Honolulu International (Oahu), Ke-ahole and Hilo International Airport (the Big Island), Kahului (Maui), and Lihue (Kauai). In addition, Hawaiian serves the Kapalua–West Maui, Molokai, and Lanai airports.

In 1990, **Discovery Airways** (tel. 800/733–2525 or 808/946–1500) began service between Honolulu International; Kahului, Maui; Ke-Ahole, the Big Island; and Lihue, Kauai. **Aloha IslandAir** (tel. 800/323–3345) serves the following airports: Honolulu International, Kamuela (the Big Island), Kahului, Kapulua–West Maui, Kapalua, and Hana (Maui), Molokai, and Lanai.

Lei Greeting When you walk off a long flight from the mainland, perhaps a bit groggy and stiff from at least 4½ hours in the air, nothing quite compares with Hawaiian lei greeting. The casual ceremony ranks as one of the fastest ways to make the transition from the worries of home to the joys of your vacation. Unfortunately, the state of Hawaii cannot bedeck each of its 6 million-plus annual visitors. Still, it's possible to arrange for a lei ceremony for yourself or your companions before you arrive. At least 10 companies make lei greetings all or at least part of their businesses. Try contacting **Greeters of Hawaii** (Box 29638, Honolulu 96820, tel. 800/367–2669), the oldest greeting company in the islands, or one of the more recent arrivals, such as **Aloha Lei Greeters** (Box 29133, Honolulu 96820, tel. 800/367–5255) or **Kamaaina Leis, Flowers & Greeters** (2222 Kalakaua Ave., Honolulu 96815, tel. 800/367–5183). All can arrange greetings on any major island. Prices for the flowered necklaces range from about $6 to $19; 24 hours' notice is suggested.

By Ship

When Pan Am's amphibious *Hawaii Clipper* touched down on Pearl Harbor's waters in 1936 it marked the beginning of the end of regular passenger ship travel to the Islands. From that point on, the predominant means of transporting visitors would be by air, not by sea. Today, however, cruising to Hawaii still holds a special appeal for those with the time and money to afford sailing, and with a bit of work, you can arrange passage aboard the luxury liners that call on Honolulu when traveling the Seven Seas.

No regularly scheduled American ships steam between the mainland and Hawaii. Although foreign-owned vessels often ply the Pacific, the Jones Act of 1896 prohibits them from carrying passengers between two U.S. ports unless the ships first stop at an intervening foreign port or carry the passengers to a foreign destination. What that means to those wishing for the relaxing ways of ship travel is that they'll have to book with one of the major lines passing through Honolulu. For details, check with such lines as **Cunard/N.A.C. Line** (tel. 212/880–7500, **Holland American Line** (tel. 206/281–3535), and **Royal Viking** (tel. 800/426–0821).

Cruises within the islands are available on the 800-passenger twin ships the SS *Constitution* and the SS *Independence*, under the direction of **American Hawaii Cruises** (550 Kearny St., San Francisco, CA 94108, tel. 800/765–7000). Both companies offer seven-day cruises that originate in Honolulu and visit the Big Island, Maui, and Kauai. American Hawaii also sells three- and four-day packages with fewer stops.

Staying in Hawaii

Getting Around by Car

Driving   Your mainland driver's license is valid in Hawaii for up to 90 days. If you plan to stay longer, you can apply for a Hawaii driver's license at the Honolulu Police Department, Main Station (1455 S. Beretania St., tel. 808/973–2700).

Be sure to buckle up. Hawaii has a strictly enforced seatbelt law for front-seat passengers. Children under age 3 must be in a car seat, available for a fee from your car-rental agency. Other standard traffic laws apply to driving in the Aloha State. Highway speeds are 55 mph; in-town traffic moves from 25 to 40 mph. A word of warning: Jaywalking is very common in Hawaii. Be particularly watchful, especially in highly congested areas such as Waikiki, for pedestrians.

It's difficult to get lost in most of Hawaii. Roads and streets, although they may challenge the visitor's tongue (Kalanianaole Highway, for example), are at least well-marked. Keep an eye open for the Hawaii Visitor Bureau's red-caped warrior signs that mark major visitor attractions and scenic spots along your route. Free visitor publications that contain quality maps can be found on all islands. Pick up several and choose the route that best suits your needs and destination.

Asking for directions will almost always produce a helpful explanation from the locals, but you should be prepared for an island term or two. Instead of compass directions, Hawaii residents refer to places as being either *mauka* (toward the mountains) or *makai* (toward the ocean) from one another. Other directions depend on your location: in Honolulu, for example, people say to "go Diamond Head," which means toward the famous landmark, or to "go ewa," meaning the opposite direction. A shop on the mauka–Diamond Head corner of a street is on the mountain side of the street on the corner closest to Diamond Head. It all makes perfect sense once you get the lay of the land.

Technically, the Big Island of Hawaii is the only island you can completely circle by car, but each island offers plenty of sightseeing from its miles of roadways. Oahu can be circled except for the roadless west-shore area around Kaena Point. Elsewhere, major highways follow the shoreline and traverse the island at two points. Rush-hour traffic (6:30–8:30 AM and 3:30–6 PM) can be frustrating around Honolulu and the outlying areas. Parking along many streets is curtailed during those times, and towing is strictly practiced. Read the curbside parking signs before leaving your vehicle, even at a meter.

Kauai has a well-maintained highway running south from Lihue to Barking Sands Beach; a spur at Waimea takes you along Waimea Canyon to Kokee State Park. A northern route also winds its way from Lihue to end at Haena, the beginning of the rugged and roadless Na Pali Coast. Maui also has its share of impenetrable areas, although four-wheel-drive vehicles rarely run into problems on the island. Saddle roads run between the east and west land masses composing Maui. Although Molokai and Lanai have fewer roadways, car rental is still worthwhile and will allow plenty of interesting sightseeing. Opt for a four-wheel-drive vehicle if dirt road exploration holds any appeal.

Car Rentals Finding rental cars during your Hawaii visit is about as difficult as finding palm trees in paradise. They're everywhere. Not only do bustling Oahu and Maui have more than their fair share of U-drive outlets, even the tiny island of Lanai, with only 32 miles of paved roadway, has three rental agencies. You can find yourself driving anything from a $13-a-day econobox to a $1,100-a-day Ferrari.

Before leaving home, find out if your hotel and air package includes a car—many packages do, and the deals offered by tour wholesalers are often less than the prices you'll find when you arrive in Hawaii. Airlines such as Hawaiian Airlines and Aloha Airlines often provide car tie-ins with a lower than normal rate. On fly/drive deals, ask whether the car rental company will honor a reservation rate if it must upgrade you to a larger vehicle upon arrival.

Reserving your vehicle before you arrive is always a good idea if you plan to rent from a national chain, especially if you will be in Hawaii during the winter and other busy travel times.

Before calling or arriving in person at the rental desk, do a bit of homework to save yourself some money. Check with your personal or business insurance agent to see if your coverage already includes rental cars. Signing up for the collision damage waiver (CDW) offered by the rental agency quickly inflates that "what-a-deal" rate before you ever leave the parking lot. Some credit card companies also offer rental-car coverage.

When booking over the phone, be certain to ask whether you're responsible for additional mileage and for returning the car with a full fuel tank, even if you don't use all the gas. In addition, be sure to get a confirmation number for your car reservation, and check to see if the rental company offers unlimited mileage and a flat rate per day, which are definite advantages. Last but not least, check beforehand on the credit cards honored by the company.

Avis (tel. 800/331–1212), **Budget** (tel. 800/527–0707), **Dollar** (tel. 800/367–7006), and **Tropical** (tel. 800/367–5140) rent on Oahu, the Big Island, Kauai, Maui, and Molokai. **Alamo** (tel. 800/327–9633), **Hertz** (tel. 800/654–8200), and **National** (tel. 800/CAR–RENT), offer cars on each of the major islands except Molokai. Thrifty (tel. 800/367-2277) offers cars on Oahu, Maui, and Kauai. **Aloha Funway Rentals** (tel. 808/942–9696), on Oahu, and the statewide **United Car Rental System** (tel. 808/923–0052) offer some of the lowest rates. If you decide to drive on Lanai, call **Lanai City Service** (tel. 808/565–7227), **Dollar** (tel. 800/367–7006), or **Oshiro U-Drive** (tel. 808/565–6952).

Shopping

Next to relaxing on the beach and eating, shopping is probably the most popular activity among Hawaii tourists. That may be less of a reflection on the visitors themselves than on the variety of products available in the Islands. Where else in the world, for example, could you find a strip of shops, all in one place, that sells rare black coral jewelry, *University of Waikiki* T-shirts, and intricately etched scrimshaw pieces?

Retail outlets abound in the Aloha State. You'll find someone selling something whether you're in the large city of Honolulu on Oahu or the town of Hanalei on Kauai. One-stop shopping malls are prevalent, although not in the same numbers as those in many mainland destinations. On Oahu, Ala Moana Center is one of the largest shopping spots; it's within easy walking distance of Waikiki. The Royal Hawaiian Shopping Center is centrally located in Waikiki itself. Farther away, you'll find Ward Warehouse, the Kahala Mall, and Pearlridge Center.

The Neighbor Islands offer more in the way of smaller strips of shops. Still, it's possible to find larger stores grouped in areas such as Kauai's Kukui Grove Center in Lihue, Maui's Kahului Shopping Center, and the Big Island's Prince Kuhio Mall in Hilo. Exclusive shops can often be found in the lobbies of the luxury hotels on all islands.

See the individual island chapters for more specific shopping information.

The following is a rundown of some of the most sought-after items in Hawaii:

Aloha Wear Aloha shirts and muumuus are standard businesswear on Friday of every work week, so you're sure to find plenty of shops selling high-quality prints. In fact, it's nearly impossible to walk through any shopping area without coming upon at least one store selling the clothing. Liberty House, Sears, and JC Penney department stores offer a wide selection of the latest styles. A number of new designers sell their originals from small shops in Waikiki, Lahaina, and other major destinations. Great deals on slightly worn older styles can be picked up in second-hand stores throughout the state.

Coral Jewelry "Going to great depths for the customer" is no exaggeration when it comes to coral jewelry. Island divers bring up the raw materials for the black, pink, and gold coral trinkets from the bottom of the sea. Honolulu's Maui Divers of Hawaii (*see* Shopping in Chapter 3) offers tours of its design center, as well as a large showroom of rings and necklaces. Shops throughout the Islands carry this jewelry.

Kona Coffee The country's only commercial coffee plantations are found on the western slopes of the Big Island, which is also the best place in the state to buy the rich roasted Kona coffee beans. If you want the strongest java, go for pure Kona coffee; Kona blends are often sold, with little distinction made for the buyer.

Macadamia Nuts Also grown on the Big Island, macadamia nuts are among the richest and most delicious foodstuffs in Hawaii. You'll find them everywhere and in every way—from chocolate-covered to chopped for cookie filling. Almost all supermarkets and convenience stores statewide sell the mac nuts in small tins and larger cans.

Pineapples Nothing, visitors claim, evokes the real Hawaii like the taste of a locally grown pineapple. Taking the fruit of the Islands home with you is simple: You may either purchase the fruit in a shop or grocery store, or buy it preboxed, for a slightly higher price, from the vendors at Honolulu International Airport. Pineapple does not ripen further once it's picked, so any fruits with good firmness and color should be good.

T-shirts Hawaii must surely be the T-shirt capital of the Pacific, providing plenty of inexpensive souvenirs and gifts for Island visitors. Everything from "Hang Loose" to "Don't Worry—Be Happy" can be found in local shops. Sidewalk artists in Waikiki and smaller Neighbor Island towns will airbrush a custom T-shirt design for a higher price. The least expensive shirts can be found in convenience stores and F. W. Woolworth, which often sell them two- and three-for-the-price-of-one.

Wood Products Attractive trays, bowls, furniture, and other products are among the wonderful creations wrought from island woods. Shops in towns around the state have a wide selection and can put you in touch with woodworkers who specialize in custom pieces. Rich koa (the wood favored for outrigger canoes), mango, milo, and monkeypod are the favorites of local craftsmen. Because the great koa forests are dwindling, visitors might consider buying only antique koa products.

Beaches

Ask people why they vacation in Hawaii and most of them will tell you they go there for the beaches. The 50th State boasts some of the most beautiful stretches of sand and surf in the world, and with the short travel distances, they are never far away. All beaches are open to the public.

Oahu's **Waikiki Beach** is nearly synonymous with Hawaii. Stretching from the Hilton Hawaiian Village to the foot of Diamond Head, the strip still ranks as the premier place to soak up the sun. Waikiki Beach, as most people know it, is actually a collection of smaller areas such as Fort De Russy, Gray's, and Queen's Surf beaches. By whatever name, though, it's tough to beat Waikiki in terms of convenience to the hotels, restaurants, and shopping.

Oahu offers an array of other sandy seashores. The North Shore's **Sunset Beach** is famous in the surfing world; **Kailua Beach Park** has hosted windsurfing athletes for international competition; and **Makapuu Beach,** near Sea Life Park, has some of the best body surfing to be found in the state.

Neighbor Island beaches hold equal attraction. The Big Island lures beach bums and beauties with its unique and diverse collections of sand. There visitors can wiggle their toes in everything from the sparkling white sands of **Hapuna Beach** to the green and black sand beaches near the southeastern town of **Kalapana.** The Big Island also has the newest beaches in the state—black sand stretches that form daily as hot lava from the active Kilauea volcano flows into the sea.

The nearby luxury hotels of Maui's **Kaanapali Beach** make it a fine place to get a tan while watching for movie stars and other celebrities. **Hookipa Beach Park,** near the town of Paia, has become known as the Mecca of windsurfing, and is as likely to be full of European and Japanese sailors as Hawaiians.

Molokai has several uncrowded beaches, but perhaps the most sensational on the island is the three-mile-long **Papohaku Beach,** the largest white sand beach in the state. Not far away, the south shore of Lanai offers **Hulopoe Beach**, with its excellent snorkeling opportunities.

Kauai's south shore has **Poipu Beach Park,** popular with bodysurfers and sunbathers. On the opposite side of the island is **Lumahai,** a small beach rimmed in black lava and vegetation that proved the perfect setting for the movie *South Pacific*.

Families and singles alike use all of Hawaii's beaches together, and seldom will anyone feel out of place at any area. What can be found in the way of facilities, however, will vary greatly from place to place. Most areas have fresh running water, bath and changing rooms, and outside showers. Picnic tables are less common. Hawaii's beaches are clean compared to other coastal areas, and visitors are asked to do their part in keeping them that way.

As with any sort of water-related activity, swimming and wading from Hawaii's beaches should be approached with caution until you are familiar with the local conditions. Forceful waves and undertows can surprise even experienced swimmers. Swimming is always at your own risk, and prudence should be the rule. Those guidelines extend to other ocean activities as well. More popular areas offer equipment rentals for windsurfing, snorkeling, sailing, and parasailing, but participants should be well aware of the dangers present in venturing upon unknown waters.

See the individual island chapters for detailed information on beaches.

Sports and Outdoor Activities

Bicycling Hawaii's near-perfect climate makes for ideal cycling conditions. Match that with the well-maintained coast-hugging roadways, and you come up with an exciting place for a cycling vacation. All of Hawaii is accessible to cyclists, but the Big Island, with its extra mileage, offers the best bet when it comes to long-distance tours.

Diving Crystal-clear waters, interesting marine life, and a variety of sunken wrecks add up to a diver's paradise for Hawaii. Nearly 50 dive operators offer introductory lessons to beginners and advance certification courses to experienced scuba enthusiasts. You may bring your own gear or rent from the many shops around the Islands.

Fishing Hawaii residents know how to take advantage of the waters surrounding their state, and they'll pass on their fishing secrets to anyone with an interest in hooks, lines, and sinkers. The biggest lure to visiting fishing enthusiasts is the deep-sea fishing for marlin, especially off the shores of the Big Island. Each morning an entire fleet of sportfishing boats leaves Kona in search of the elusive gamefish. If the marlin aren't biting, reels are often whining with catches of local *ahi* (tuna) or *opakapaka* (blue snapper).

Golf The large number of luxury hotels and resorts in the 50th state provide an instant tip about the prevalence of golf courses. One cruise ship company even goes so far as to offer its passengers a round of golf at a course on a different island each day of the sail. Whether you want to tee-off on the latest course designed by Arnold Palmer or play 18 holes overlooking wave-crashing coastline, Hawaii has the course for you. Some of Hawaii's top spots for golfing include the courses at the Sheraton Makaha Resort and the Turtle Bay Hilton on Oahu; the courses at the

Mauna Kea Beach Resort and the Mauna Lani Resort on the Big Island; the Royal Kaanapali Golf Course and the Kapalua Golf Club on Maui; and the Princeville Makai Course on Kauai.

Hiking The ancient Hawaiians blazed a wide variety of trails across their island domains, and many of these paths can still be hiked today. The state offers trails through rain forests, along palm-lined beaches, and around volcanic landscapes, such as Diamond Head on Oahu, Hawaii Volcanoes National Park on the Big Island, and Haleakala National Park on Maui.

Horseback Riding Riders may saddle up on all the major islands for guided horseback trips through a range of terrain. Some recommended rides explore Maui's Haleakala Crater or Kauai's south shore, while on Molokai you can reach Kalaupapa, the site of a 19th-century leper colony, by mule.

Hunting Deer, wild boar, big-horn sheep, mountain goat, turkey, and a variety of game birds can be hunted in Hawaii. The Big Island and Lanai are the two prime hunting grounds, where a number of guide services offer day trips. Rifles, shotguns, and archery equipment may be rented on-site.

Snow Skiing Believe it or not, you can ski in Hawaii—atop the Big Island's Mauna Kea volcano. Because of the fickleness of the snowfall, guide companies melt away faster than a snowball in Hana. As soon as one operator fades from the scene, however, another seems to come along for a shot at running what has to be one of the world's most unique ski areas. December through February is your best bet for skiing Hawaiian-style.

Surfing Hawaii names such as the Bonzai Pipeline and Sunset Beach are to surfers what the Super Bowl and the Astrodome are to football players. Little surprise then that surf enthusiasts from around the world come to Hawaii to ride the waves. Waikiki Beach is probably the best spot for first-time surfers to pick up the basics; Oahu's North Shore makes for excellent viewing of the veterans, especially during the December–January period of high surf.

Tennis The court sport is popular at many Island hotels and condominiums. Forget your racquet? No problem, the accompanying pro shops and retail centers will be happy to rent the latest ball-swatter to you and will even offer a brush-up lesson if you need it.

Waterskiing Skimming across the water's surface in Hawaii usually translates into surfing, but waterskiing also has its fans in the state. Oahu and Maui offer ocean skiing; companies on Kauai offer ski trips up and down the Wailua River near Lihue.

Windsurfing Hawaii's steady winds and surf conditions have helped to make it one of the premier windsurfing spots around the globe. Today, the world's fastest growing sport can be seen and experienced throughout the state, with Oahu and Maui attracting the best athletes. Beginning, intermediate, and advanced equipment can be rented from a variety of shops, and lessons abound.

National and State Parks

Like many states, Hawaii has sought to protect some of its natural beauty by designating portions of its property national and state parkland. The Islands have seven national parks, national historic parks, and national memorials. There are also 76 state parks and historic sights throughout the chain.

Federal park information may be obtained from the **National Park Service** (300 Ala Moana Blvd., Suite 6305, Box 50165, Honolulu, 96813, tel. 808/541–2693); details of state parks and historic areas come from the **District Office of the Hawaii Department of Land and Natural Resources,** Division of State Parks (1151 Punchbowl St., Room 310, Honolulu 96813, tel. 808/548–7455).

Hawaii's two national parks are the Big Island's **Hawaii Volcanoes National Park,** with 207,643 acres, and Maui's 27,350-acre **Haleakala National Park.** Both offer excellent views and opportunities to learn about volcanoes and their role in the formation of the Islands. As of January 1989, Kilauea volcano in Hawaii Volcanoes National Park was continuing on its seventh year of uninterrupted eruption. Helicopter tours over the active volcano represent the best way to see the action. Several of the roads into the area have been closed because they were overrun with flowing lava. Haleakala, which means "house of the sun," draws a large number of tours and individuals who make the two-hour drive to the summit to see the sun rise each morning. Any time of day, however, will find plenty of sights on, in, and around the dormant volcano.

The Big Island encompasses three other national areas: **Kaloko-Honokohau National Historical Park,** a royal fish pond area; **Puuhonua o Honaunau National Historical Park,** better known as the City of Refuge; and **Puukohola Heiau National Historic Site,** an ancient worship place. Molokai's **Kalaupapa National Historical Park,** site of Father Damien's leper colony, and the **U.S.S.** *Arizona* **Memorial** at Pearl Harbor round out the national selection.

State parks range in size from the 2.5-acre state wayside at Oahu's **Nuuanu Pali Lookout** to the 6,175-acre **Na Pali Coast State Park** on Kauai. Falling somewhere in between are other popular state areas including Maui's haunting **Iao Valley State Monument,** Kauai's **Kokee State Park** and the **Wailua River State Park,** and the Big Island's **Hapuna Beach State Recreation Area**—often said to hold the prettiest beach on that island.

Dining

Honolulu ranks in the top five cities nationally in the propensity of its residents to dine out, and restaurateurs there and throughout the Islands have been quick to take the hint and fulfill the need for good food. The result is a high number of restaurants, cafés, and other eateries, which makes it easy to find food service but difficult to decide among all the options.

Hawaii's melting-pot population also accounts for its great variety of epicurean delights. In addition to American and Continental cuisines, you can choose from Hawaiian, Thai, Korean, Japanese, Chinese, Philippine, Vietnamese, and other kinds of cooking as well. Such diversity need not cause indigestion; it just means you'll have that much more to sample from the international buffet Hawaii offers.

Hawaiian food, obviously, has a loyal following among visitors to the state. Many rate their trip to a luau among the highlights of their stay. Delicacies you're likely to find at one of these out-door feasts include the traditional *kalua* pig, often roasted underground in an *imu* (oven); *poi*, the starchy, bland paste made from the taro root; and *laulau*—fish, meat, and other ingredients wrapped and steamed in ti leaves. Luaus are presented at many hotels and visitor attractions around the state, or you can ask most any local for directions to a favorite Hawaiian-style feast.

With the heavy influx of Japanese into Hawaii, you'll find ample opportunity to sample foodstuffs from the land of the rising sun. Sushi (sliced raw fish and seafood served on balls of vinegared rice) and sashimi (raw fish without the rice) make the biggest hits. Other favorites include miso soup and tempuras, a variety of fish and vegetables deep fried with a light batter coating. Thai cuisine also has its fans in Hawaii. First-timers will be amazed at the interesting sauces and flavors—as well as such dish names as Evil Jungle Prince—that the cooks can concoct from a few simple ingredients.

Rest assured you'll also find plenty in the way of Continental offerings. Nearly every European country is represented in Island dining circles, from Austria to Spain, Italy to Switzerland. Almost all luxury hotels have at least one gourmet dining spot for Continental cuisine, and a healthy number of independent operations can be found as well.

A word of caution concerning the origins of the seafood served in Hawaii: Although the state's surrounded by water, don't be surprised to find that many of the *fruits de mer* come to the Islands the same way you did—by airplane. Several varieties of local tuna, dolphin (not porpoise), and snapper can be found under names such as *ahi*, *mahimahi*, and *opakapaka* respectively; and lobster, the clawless species known as spiny lobster, is also taken from the local reefs. Trout, oysters, and other ocean-dwellers, however, have most likely been caught somewhere else.

Lodging

Hotels Hawaii hosts most of the nationwide and worldwide hotel operators within its chain of islands. Hilton, Sheraton, Westin, Hyatt, Four Seasons, Marriott, Ritz-Carlton, Embassy Suites, and others operate or have plans to open resorts within the state. A number of large, locally based operators such as Aston Hotels and Resorts and Outrigger Hotels Hawaii round out the accommodations scene, and a number of independents also have loyal followings. The result is an extensive range of rooms, from rock-bottom economy units to suites fit for, and occasionally used by, kings.

Condominiums Hawaii is known for developing the resort condominium concept in the early 1970s, and the destination continues to maintain its status as a leader in the field. Condominiums, from simple studios to multiroom spreads, are now available on all islands. Besides large living areas and full kitchens, many condos have recently begun offering front-desk and daily maid services just like their hotel counterparts. Nearly 100 companies in Hawaii and around the United States rent out condominium space in the Islands. Your travel agent will be the most helpful in finding the condo you desire.

Bed-and-Breakfasts B&Bs have made heavy in-roads into the Hawaiian market in the last several years. It's now possible to find the combination room-and-meal lodgings throughout the state. Operations range from beachside rooms on Maui to comfortable accommodations bordering the Big Island's Hawaii Volcanoes National Park. Most operators advertise their own lodgings, but three centralized booking services, **Bed and Breakfast Hawaii** (Box 449, Kapaa 96746, tel. 800/657–7832) **Bed and Breakfast Pacific Hawaii** (19 Kai Nani Pl., Kailua 96734, tel. 808/262–8270), and **Bed and Breakfast Honolulu** (statewide) (3242 Kaohinani Dr., Honolulu 96817, tel. 800/288–4666), list a variety of properties.

House Rentals For stays ranging from overnight to a month or more, you might want to consider a house rental in Hawaii. Homes are often complete with everything down to crystal in the cabinets and silver in the drawers. Accommodations of this sort provide not only the utmost in privacy and freedom; they'll also give you a feel for what its like to actually live in the Islands. More than 15 companies act as rental agents for Hawaii houses; some, such as **Villas of Hawaii** (4218 Waialae Ave., Suite 203, Honolulu 96816, tel. 800/522–3030) offer accommodations on Oahu, Maui, the Big Island, and Kauai, while others such as **Hawaiian Properties Ltd.** (1784 Ala Moana Blvd., Honolulu 96815, tel. 808/955–3341) offer listings only on Oahu.

Camping and RV Facilities Camping offers an inexpensive alternative to higher-priced accommodations and allows the opportunity to appreciate Hawaii's great outdoors. A variety of national, state, and county parks are available, some with bathroom and cooking facilities, others a bit more primitive. For federal park information, contact the **National Park Service** (300 Ala Moana Blvd., Suite 6305, Box 50165, Honolulu 96813, tel. 808/541–2693); state information can be obtained from the **District Office of the Hawaii Department of Land and Natural Resources,** Division of State Parks (1151 Punchbowl St., Room 310, Honolulu 96813, tel. 808/548–7455); and details on county camping are available from the individual counties. The **City and County of Honolulu** (tel. 808/523–4525) can provide addresses and telephone numbers for the neighboring counties. You can pack up your own sleeping bag and bring it along, or you can rent camping equipment from several companies in the Islands. The following are a few outfits that rent equipment: (Oahu) **Omar the Tent Man** (650A Kakoi St., Honolulu 96819, tel. 808/836–8785); (the Big Island) **Pacific Rent-All** (1080 Kilauea Ave., Hilo 96720, tel. 808/935–2974); (Kauai) **Jungle Bob's** (Box 1245, Hanalei 96714, tel. 808/826–6664).

Credit Cards

The following credit card abbreviations are used in this guide: AE, American Express; CB, Carte Blanche; D, Discover; DC, Diners Club; MC, MasterCard; V, Visa.

2 Portraits of Hawaii

Hawaii at a Glance: A Chronology

c. AD 500   First human beings set foot on Hawaiian shores: Polynesians travel 2,000 miles in 60- to 80-foot canoes to the islands they name *Havaiki* after their legendary homeland.

c. 1750   Birth of King Kamehameha

1778   January: *HMS Resolution* and *Discovery*, captained by James Cook, land on Kauai; first Western encounter with Hawaii, which was not on any known Western map. Cook names the islands the Sandwich Islands after his patron, the Earl of Sandwich
November: Cook returns to Hawaii for the winter, anchors at Kealakekua Bay, on the Big Island

1779   February: Cook is killed in a battle with indigenous people

1786   Fur traders spend the winter in Hawaii (this becomes a common practice); Kamehameha consolidates his rule over the Big Island and attempts to extend his power over the other islands

1790   First Westerners settle on islands

1791   Kamehameha builds Puukohola Heiau temple; dedicates it by killing a rival chief

1794   Kamehameha uses Western arms to complete his conquest of the islands

1810   Chief of Kauai acknowledges Kamehameha's rule, uniting the islands under one chief

1819   Death of Kamehameha; first whaling ships land at Lahaina on Maui

1820   First missionaries arrive from Boston

1835   First commercial sugar plantation on Kauai, financed by Americans

1840   The Wilkes Expedition, sponsored by the U.S. Coast and Geodetic Survey, pinpoints Pearl Harbor as a potential naval base

1852   Depopulation owing to Western diseases creates labor shortage; Chinese laborers brought in to work cane fields; they are followed by Portuguese, Japanese, Koreans, and Filipinos

1863   Queen Emma, half-Caucasian widow of King Kamehameha IV, attempts to succeed her husband to the throne but the Hawaiian legislature elects Chief David Kalakaua king.

1875   Treaty with United States establishes virtual protectorate, gives sugar planters trade protection

1882   King David Kalakaua builds Iolani Palace on the site of the previous royal palace, after a visit to the United States

1887   Treaty with United States renewed; grants United States exclusive use of Pearl Harbor

1891–1893   Reign of Queen Liliuokalani. She is removed from throne by American business interests led by Sanford B. Dole (son of a missionary), and imprisoned in Iolani Palace

1898   Hawaii annexed by United States.

1900   Pineapples become a profitable crop

1901   First major tourist hotel, the Moana (now called the Sheraton Moana Surfrider), built on Waikiki Beach

1907   Fort Shafter Army Base built; first U.S. military post

1908   Construction of base begins at Pearl Harbor

1919   Pearl Harbor dedicated

1927   Matson Navigation Company builds Royal Hawaiian Hotel as destination for its cruise ships

1941   Pearl Harbor bombed by Japanese, causing United States to enter World War II

1942   James Jones, with thousands of others, trains at Schofield Barracks on Oahu; unlike the others, he later writes about it in *From Here to Eternity*

1959   Hawaii granted statehood; later in the year the first Boeing 707 jets make the flight from San Francisco in five hours; tourism greatly increases, becoming Hawaii's major industry

1968   Oahu hosts the first professional surfing competition for a money prize

1969   Astronauts Neil Armstrong, Edwin E. Aldrin, Jr., and Mike Collins return to Oahu after their lunar landing

1977   Tourists outnumber residents by four to one

Volcano Country

by Gary
Diedrichs

A former editor
for Los Angeles
magazine, Gary
Diedrichs is now
President of The
Publications
Company, based
in Michigan. He
has written
previously on
Jamaica and
Maui for Fodor's.

Dawn at the crater on horseback. It's cold at 10,023 feet above the warm Pacific—maybe 45°. The horses' breath condenses into a smoky cloud, and the riders cling against their saddles. Eerily quiet except for the creak of straining leather and the crunch of volcanic cinders under hooves, those sounds magnify absurdly in the vast and empty space that yawns below. . . .

This is Haleakala, which literally means "house of the sun." It's the crown of east Maui and the largest dormant volcano crater in the world. Every year thousands of Maui visitors shake themselves awake at three in the morning to board vans that take them from their comfortable hotels, up the world's most steeply ascending auto route to the crater in Haleakala National Park. Sunrise is the show of shows here, from the palest pink to the most fiery red spreading across the lip of the crater. Mark Twain called it "the sublimest spectacle" he had ever witnessed.

But sunrise is only the beginning of the spectacle that this volcano offers. The park encompasses 28,665 acres, and the crater itself is 21 miles in circumference and 19 square miles in area. At its deepest, it measures 3,000 feet from the summit. The two towers of Manhattan's World Trade Center could be stood end to end and not reach the top.

More than anything, entering Haleakala is like descending to the moon. Trails for hiking and horseback riding crisscross the crater for some 32 miles. The way is strewn with volcanic rubble, crater cones, frozen lava flows, vents, and lava tubes. The colors that surround the descent are muted yet dramatic—black, yellow, russet, orange, lavender, browns, and grays, even a pinkish-blue. It seems as if nothing could live here, but in fact this is an ecosystem that sustains, among other, more humble life forms, the sure-footed mountain goat, the rare nene goose (no webbing between its toes, to better negotiate the rugged terrain), and the strange and delicate silversword. The silversword, a spiny, metallic-leafed plant, once proliferated on Haleakala's slopes. Today it survives in small numbers at Haleakala and at high elevations on the Big Island of Hawaii. The plants live up to 20 years, bloom only once, scatter their seeds, and die.

The crater's starkness is overwhelming. Even shadows cast in the thin mountain air are flinty and spare. It's easy to understand why, in the early days of this nation's space program, moon-bound astronauts trained in this desolate place.

It is also not difficult to see this place as a bubbling, sulfurous cauldron, a direct connection not to the heavens but to the core of the Earth and to the origins of this island. Haleakala's last—and probably final—eruption occured in 1790, a few years after a Frenchman named La Perouse became the first European to set foot on Maui. That fiery outburst was only one of many in Hawaii over the millennia, just as Maui and its now-cold crater are just one facet of the volcanic variety of the Aloha State.

Large and small, awake or sleeping, volcanoes embody Hawaii's history and its heritage; behind their beauty is the story of the flames that created this ethereal island chain. This tale began some 25 million years ago, yet it is still unfinished.

The islands in the Hawaiian archipelago are really only the very crests of immense mountains rising from the bottom of the sea. Formed by molten rock known as magma, the islands were slowly pushed up from the Earth's volatile, uneasy mantle, forced through cracks in the thin crust that is the ocean floor.

The first ancient eruptions cooled and formed pools on the Pacific bottom. Then, as more and more magma spilled from the vents over millions of years, the pools became ridges and grew into crests; the latter built upon themselves over the eons, until finally, miles high, they at last towered above the surface of the sea.

As the islands cooled in the Pacific waters, the stark lava slopes slowly bloomed, over centuries, with colorful flora— exotic, jewel-like species endemic only to these islands, with their generous washings of tropical rain and abundant sunshine. Gradually, as seeds, spores, or eggs of living creatures were carried by the winds and currents to this isolated area, more than 2,000 miles from the closest continental land mass, the bare and rocky atolls became a paradise of greenery, with the occasional new eruption expanding their domain.

This type of volcano, with its slowly formed, gently sloping sides, is known as a shield volcano, and each of the Hawaiian isles is comprised of them. As long as the underwater vents spew the lifeblood lava out from the Earth's core and into the heart of the mountain, a shield volcano will continue to grow.

The Hawaiian Islands rest upon an area called the Pacific Plate, and this vast shelf of land is making its way slowly to the northwest, creeping perhaps two to three inches every year. The result is that contact between the submarine vents and the volcanoes' conduits for magma is gradually disrupted and closed off. Slowly, the mountains stop growing, one by one. Surface eruptions slow down and finally halt completely, and these volcanoes ultimately become extinct.

That, at least, is one explanation. Another—centuries older and still revered in Hawaiian art and song—centers upon Pele, the beautiful and tempestuous daughter of Haumea, the Earth Mother, and Wakea, the Sky Father. Pele is the Hawaiian goddess of fire, the maker of mountains, melter of rocks, eater of forests, and burner of land—both creator and destroyer. Legend has it that Pele came to the Islands long ago to flee from her cruel older sister, Na Maka o Kahai, goddess of the sea. Pele ran first to the small island of Niihau, making a crater home there with her digging stick. But Na Maka found her and destroyed her hideaway, so Pele again had to flee. On Kauai she delved deeper, but Na Maka chased her from that home as well. Pele ran on— from Oahu to Molokai, Lanai to Kahoolawe, Molokini to Maui—but always and ever Na Maka pursued her.

Pele came at last to Halemaumau, the vast firepit crater of Kilauea, and there, on the Big Island, she dug deepest of all. There she is said to remain, all-powerful, quick to rage, and often unpredictable; the mountain is her impenetrable fortress and domain—a safe refuge, at least for a time, from Na Maka o Kahai.

Interestingly, the chronology of the old tales of Pele's flight from isle to isle match closely with modern volcanologists' reckonings on the ages of the various craters. Today, the Big Island's Kilauea and Mauna Loa retain the closest links with the Earth's superheated core and are active and volatile, though three other volcanoes that shaped the island are not. The remainder of the Hawaiian volcanoes have been carried beyond their magma supply by the movement of the Pacific Plate. Those farthest to the northwest in the island chain are completely extinct. Those at the southeasterly end of the island chain—Haleakala, Mauna Kea, and Hualalai—are dormant and slipping away, so that the implacable process of volcanic death has begun.

Eventually, experts say, in another age or so, the same cooling and slow demise will overtake all of the burning rocks that are the Hawaiian Islands. Eventually, the sea will claim their bodies and, to Pele's rage, Na Maka o Kahai will win in the end. Or will she? Offshore the Big Island of Hawaii, a new island is forming. It's still a half mile below the water's surface. Several thousand years more will be required for it to break into the sunlight. But it already has a name: Loihi.

At this time, it's hard to imagine the demise of that burgeoning Grand Canyon of fire that is Pele's current home on the Big Island. Kilauea is today very much the living center of volcanic activity in the Hawaiian islands.

By far the largest of the archipelago, the Big Island of Hawaii, measured at the summit of Mauna Kea, is some 13,796 feet above sea level, with the tip of Mauna Loa nearly as lofty at 13,667 feet. Taken as a whole, from their bases on the ocean floor, these shield volcanoes are the largest mountain masses on the planet. Geologists believe it required more than 3 million years of steady volcanic activity to bring these peaks up above the waters of the Pacific.

Mauna Loa's little sister, Kilauea, at about 4,077 feet, is the most active volcano in the world. Between the two of them, they have covered nearly 200,000 acres of land with their red-hot lava flows over the past 200 years or so. In the process, they have ravished trees, fields, meadows, villages, and more than a few unlucky human witnesses. For generations, Kilauea, in a continually eruptive state, has pushed molten lava up from the earth's magma at 1,800° and more. But as active as she and Mauna Loa are, their eruptions are comparatively safe and gentle, producing continuous small and especially liquid lava flows rather than dangerous bursts of fire and ash. The exceptions were two violently explosive displays during recorded history—one in 1790, the other in 1924. During these eruptions, Pele came closest to destroying the Big Island's largest city, Hilo, although she gave residents another scare as recently as 1985.

It is around these major volcanoes that the island's Hawaii Volcanoes National Park is located. A sprawling natural preserve, the park attracts geology experts, volcanologists, and ordinary wide-eyed visitors from all over the world. They come for the park's unparalleled opportunity to view, up close and in person, the visual wonders of Pele's kingdom of fire and fantasy. They come to study and to improve methods for predicting the times and sites of eruptions. They have done so for a century or more. It has not been unusual for tourists to send back postcards with edges deliberately scorched by Kilauea's heat, or for the more adventurous to wander into the firepit when the volcano was quiet, with an egg and frying pan in hand, to cook breakfast in nature's most sizzling cauldron.

Thomas Augustus Jaggar, the preeminent volcanologist and student of Kilauea, built his home on stilts wedged into cracks in the volcanic rock of the crater rim. Harvard-trained and universally respected, he was the driving force behind the establishment of the Hawaiian Volcano Observatory at Kilauea. When he couldn't raise research funds from donations, public and private, he raised pigs to keep the scientific work going. After his death, his wife surreptitiously scattered Jaggar's ashes over the great fiery abyss.

The park is located on the Big Island's southeastern flank, about 30 minutes out of Hilo on the aptly named Volcano Highway. Wear sturdy walking shoes and carry a warm sweater. It can be a long hike across the lava flats to see Pele in action, and at 4,000 feet above sea level temperatures can be brisk, however hot the volcanic activity. So much can be seen at close range along the road that circles the crater that Kilauea has also been dubbed the "drive-in volcano."

At the park's Visitor Center sits a large display case. It contains dozens of lava-rock "souvenirs"—removed from Pele's grasp and then precipitantly returned, accompanied by letters of apology. They are sent back by visitors who say they regret having broken the *kapu* (taboo) against removing even the smallest grain of native volcanic rock from Hawaii. A typical letter might say: "I never thought Pele would miss just one little rock, but she did, and now I've wrecked two cars . . . I lost my job, my health is poor, and I know it's because I took this stone." Some of the letters are humorous, but more are poignant, full of remorse and requests for Pele's forgiveness. They are replaced, at frequent intervals, by a whole new batch.

It is surprisingly safe at the crater's lip. Unlike Japan's Mount Fuji or Washington State's Mount St. Helen, Hawaii's shield volcanoes spew their lava downhill, along the sides of the mountain. Still, the clouds of sulphur gas and fumes produced during volcanic eruptions are noxious and heady and can make breathing unpleasant, if not difficult. It has been pointed out that the chemistry of volcanoes—sulfur, hydrogen, oxygen, carbon dioxide—closely resembles the chemistry of the egg.

It's an 11-mile drive around the Kilauea crater, via the Crater Rim Road, and the trip takes about an hour. But it's better to walk a bit. There are at least eight major trails in the park, ranging from short 15-minute strolls to the 3-day, 18.3-mile (one-way) Mauna Loa Trail, which is, as you might expect, only for the seasoned hiker. A comfortable walk is Sulfur Banks, with its many vast, steaming vents creating halos of clouds around the rim of Kilauea. The route passes through a seemingly enchanted forest of sandalwood, flowers, and ferns.

Just ahead is the main attraction: the center of Pele's power, Halemaumau. This yawning pit of flame and burning rock measures some 3,000 feet wide and is a breathtaking sight. When Pele is in full fury, visitors come here in droves, on foot and by helicopter, to see her crimson expulsions coloring the dark earth and smoky sky.

Recently, however, Kilauea's most violent activity has occurred along vents in the mountain's sides instead of at its summit crater. Known as rift zones, they are lateral conduits that often open in shield volcanoes. Kilauea has two rift zones, one extending from the summit crater toward the southwest, through Kau. The other extends east-northeast through Puna, past Cape Kumakahi and into the sea. In the last two decades, repeated eruptions in the east rift zone have blocked off 12 miles of coastal road—some under more than 300 feet of rock—and have covered a total of 10,000 acres with lava. Where the flows entered the ocean, roughly 200 acres have been added to the Big Island.

Farther along the Crater Rim Road (about 4 miles from the Visitor Center) is the Thurston Lava Tube, an example of a strangely beautiful volcanic phenomenon common on the islands. Lava tubes are formed when lava flows rapidly downhill; the sides and top of this river of molten rock cool, while the fluid center flows on. Most of these formations are short and shallow, but some measure 30 to 50 feet high and hundreds of yards long. Dark, cave-like places, lava tubes were often used to store remains of the ancient Hawaiian royalty—the *alii*. All around the site of the Thurston Lava Tube is the justly famed Fern Jungle, a beautiful prehistoric fern forest.

Throughout the park, new lava formations are continually in the process of being created. Starkly beautiful, these volcanic deposits demonstrate the different types of lava produced by Hawaii's volcanoes: *'a'a*, the dark, rough lava that solidifies as cinders of rock; and the more common *pahoehoe*, the smooth, satiny lava that forms the vast plains of black rock in ropy swirls known as lava flats, which in some areas go on for miles. Other terms that help identify what may be seen in the park include *caldera*, which are the open, bowl-like lips of a volcano summit; *ejecta*, the cinders and ash that float through the air around an eruption; and *olivine*, the semiprecious chrysolite (greenish in color) found in volcanic ash.

But it isn't all fire and flash, cinders, and devastation in Volcano Country. Hawaii Volcanoes National Park is also a repository for some of the most beautiful of the state's black-sand beaches; humid forest glens full of lacy butterflies and colorful birds like the dainty flycatcher called the *'elepaio;* and exquisite grottoes sparked with bright wild orchid sprays and crashing waterfalls. Even as the lava cools, still bearing a golden, glassy skin, lush, green native ferns—the *amaumau* and *kupukupu* and *okupukupu*—spring up in the midst of Pele's fallout, as if defying her destructiveness or simply confirming the fact that after fire, she brings life.

Some 12 centuries ago, in fact, Pele brought mankind himself to her verdant islands: The fiery explosions that lit Kilauea and Mauna Loa like twin beacons in the night probably led to Pele's side the first stout-hearted explorers to Hawaii from the Marquesas Islands, some 2,400 miles away across the trackless, treacherous ocean.

Once summoned, they worshiped her from a discreet distance. Great numbers of religious *heiau* (temples) dot the landscapes near the many older and extinct craters scattered throughout Hawaii, demonstrating the great reverence the native islanders have always held for Pele and her creations. But the ruins of only two heiau are to be found near the very active crater at Halemaumau. There, at the center of the capricious Pele's power, native Hawaiians caution one even today to "step lightly, for you are on holy ground."

For all the teeming tourism and bustle that is modern Hawaii, no man today steps on the ground that Pele may one day claim for her own. In future ages, when mighty Kilauea is no more, this area will still be Volcano Country. Beneath the blue Pacific waters, fiery magma flows, and new mountains form and grow. Just below the surface, Loihi waits.

The Underwater World

by Barbara
Brundage

Scuba diver
Barbara
Brundage is
executive director
of Dive Hawaii, a
marketing
association of
Hawaii dive
shops.

People who've peered beneath the ocean's surface around the world say the Hawaiian Islands boast some of the most spectacular underwater scenery anywhere. Much of the credit goes to the rare and unusual volcanic structures rising from Hawaii's ocean floor. As the islands emerged many millions of years ago, molten lava spilled into the sea, cooling instantly to form huge cavernous rooms, mammoth archways, tall pinnacles needling skyward, and networks of tunnels called lava tubes. Over time, tiny polyps colonized to form the colorful corals carpeting the volcanic plains, while individual coral trees flourished along the rifts and ledges.

These corals began the food chain for many other marine organisms. Today more than 600 species of tropical fish thrive in Hawaiian waters. Nearly a third of these fish can be found *only* in Hawaii, and each species exhibits its own distinctive behavior. Brilliant yellow lemon butterfly fish traverse the reefs in massive schools while others, such as the delicate moorish idol, spend their lives in pairs. For newcomers, pronouncing the Hawaiian names of these fish can become a sport in itself. Consider the state fish, for instance—the *humuhumunukunukuapua'a*, translated as "fish that sounds like a pig" and otherwise known as the trigger fish.

The rugged volcanic terrain also provides protective hideaways for many varieties of shellfish. Shy lobsters thrive within the dark confines of cavern walls, their probing antennae shifting back and forth like TV rabbit ears. Colorful nudibranches, flatworms, and tube worms provide other curious finds within the cracks and crevices.

Because of all this diversity Hawaii is now rated the fourth most popular scuba diving destination worldwide. Some 60,000 certified divers visit the Islands each year, and another 55,000 experience their first half-day introductory scuba dive in the Aloha State. Snorkeling is also extremely popular; more than 125,000 people arrange snorkeling charters annually. More than 60 dive operations have emerged in response to the increasing demands of visiting divers seeking Hawaii's spectacular underwater adventures. Since scuba diving is a fairly safe and easy sport, it's become a popular family activity, too.

A number of marine preserves scattered throughout the Islands provide safe homes for the diverse marine life. No fishing or taking of shells is allowed in these areas. Fish have become extremely tame and will follow divers and

"The Underwater World" first appeared in Pleasant
HAWAII *magazine.*

snorkelers for handouts of bread or frozen peas. Divemasters have even befriended a number of moray eels, most of whom enjoy a pat on the head and an offering of squid.

Other marine life have become accustomed to visiting divers. Several areas are common ground for green sea turtles who spend much of their time sleeping under ledges but will wake to the passing sound of bubbles. Some of these turtles have become so accustomed to divers, they will approach and position themselves just above them as if to feel the tickle of the exhaust bubbles. Because of Hawaii's quickly plummeting dropoffs into deep water, game fish such as tuna, jacks, mackerel and *mahimahi* (dolphin) swim into view with regularity.

Due to the remoteness of the Islands from other land masses, Hawaii is an oasis in the sea for larger pelagic (ocean-going) marine life. Spinner dolphins often trail-blaze ahead of the boat bow en route to the dive sites. On occasion, the dive boat will stop so divers can snorkel with the pod. Several species of sharks inhabit Hawaiian waters. Divemasters can point out where white tip sharks, for example, rest under ledges and in lava tubes. Whale sharks exceeding 50 feet that are seldom seen have come into shallower depths to bask on the sun-warmed surface. Manta rays and spotted eagle rays are often seen sailing gracefully through the sun-shafted waters.

Hawaiian waters are well known for the humpback whales which make their seasonal trek from Alaska to the Islands between November and May. These are most often spotted from dive boats. Many times divers will hear the haunting songs underwater. Lesser known cetaceans include the many toothed whales that make Hawaii their year-round home; pilot whales, false killer whales, melon-head whales, and even giant sperm whales have been sighted offshore where depths plummet to 2,000 feet.

A number of fascinating wrecks also make for great diving. These include a 165-foot minesweeper and two barges that were scuttled several years ago to form artificial reefs off the coast of East Honolulu. Other wrecks of airplanes and WWII tanks are watery monuments in memory of Hawaii's war days. The state government is currently working with the dive industry to create additional artificial reefs throughout the Islands. A government-sanctioned mooring buoy program has recently been approved whereby divers will place permanent buoys at popular sites in an effort to conserve coral reefs.

Hundreds of sites have become dive tour favorites, while much of the waters throughout the Islands remain virgin and still ripe for exploration. Many of the popular sites are located on the south and west shores—the lee sides—protected from the trade winds. Dive sites along the north and east shorelines become accessible during the summer months when the large winter surf subsides. Throughout the Islands, water visibility often exceeds 100 feet and water temperature remains a comfortable 75 to 80 degrees year-round.

A comprehensive 24-page guide to dive spots also lists dive shops. To obtain the guide, send $2 to University of Hawaii (Seagrant Extension, MSB, 1000 Pope Rd., Honolulu, HI 96822).

Real Dives

The Hawaiian Islands feature more than 200 established diving sites of immense variety—for boat dives or shore dives, and for certified divers or wet-behind-the-ears beginners. Following are some of the most spectacular and, in many cases, most popular spots.

Oahu

Site	Location and Depth (in feet)	Description
Hanauma Bay	East Honolulu 10–70	A state underwater park; one of Hawaii's most popular diving sites. Shallow inner reef, gradually sloping outer reef. Tame, colorful tropical fish include butterflyfish, goatfish, parrotfish, surgeonfish; sea turtles, too.
	Mahi Waianae 50–90	A 165-foot minesweeper sunk in 1982 to serve as an artificial reef. Fully intact, can be penetrated. Goatfish, tame lemon butterflyfish, blue-striped snapper, and a six-foot moray eel.
Maunalua Bay	East Honolulu 30–80	Sites include Turtle Canyon, with lava flow ridges and sandy canyons teeming with green sea turtles of all sizes; *Kahala Barge*, a penetrable, 200-foot sunken vessel with functioning pilot house; Big Eel Reef with many varieties of moray eels; and Fantasy Reef, a series of lava ledges and archways with larger marine life including barracuda and eels.
Shark's Cove	North Shore 15–45	For experienced divers. Large, roomy caverns where sunlight from above creates stained-glass effect. Most popular cavern dive on Oahu. Easy access from shore. Summer months only.
Three Tables	North Shore 15–60	Named for trio of flat rocks breaking the surface near beach. Large rock formations, caverns, and ledges. Easy access from shore. Summer months only.

The Big Island of Hawaii

Site	Location and Depth	Description
Aquarium	Kealakekua Bay 15–110	A state underwater park popular for introductory boat dives. Great variety of tropical fish including rudderfish, taape, yellow tang, bird wrasses, and trumpetfish—all tame for hand feeding.
Pine Trees	North Kona 10–50	Overall area includes Carpenter's House, Golden Arches, and Pyramid Pinnacles—two underwater lava towers with tubes, arches, and large schools of pyramid butterflyfish and flase moorish idols.
Plane Wreck Point	Keahole Point 115	For experts only. Twin Beechcraft airplane lying broken in half on ripples of white sand. Penetrable wreck features damselfish, fantail filefish, and menpachi hovering in the shadows.
Red Hill	Near Kainaliu 25–70	Six different dive sites encompassing large caverns and lava tubes. Includes Boat Wreck Reef, Long Lava Tube, and Fantasy Reef. Encrusting sponges, octopus, shells, sleeping reef sharks, and abundant tropical fish.

Maui

Site	Location and Depth	Description
Honolua Bay	West Maui 20–50	Marine preserve with many varieties of coral and tame tropical fish, including large ulua, kahala, barracuda, and manta rays. Popular for introductory and night dives; generally summer months only.
Molokini Crater	Alalakeiki Channel 10–80	Crescent-shape islet formed by top of a volcanic crater; marine preserve popular for introductory dives. Many tame eels and hand feeding of all fish, including lemon butterflyfish, large ulua, and surgeonfish.

Molokai

Site	Location and Depth	Description
Mokuhooniki Rock	East End 30–100	Formerly a military bombing target: WWII artifacts common. Many pinnacles and drop-offs, home to barracuda, gray reef sharks, and large ulua. Black coral also found here.

Lanai

Site	Location and Depth	Description
Cathedrals	South Shore 10–70	Several pinnacles rise from 60 feet to just below the surface, with spacious caverns creating a cathedral effect. Beautiful chambers house friendly spotted moray eels, lobster, and ghost shrimp.
Sergeant Major Reef	South Shore 15–50	Three parallel lava ridges, a cave, and an archway, with rippled sand valleys between ridges. Several large schools of Sergeant Major fish. Other nearby sites include Lobster Rock, Menpachi Cave, Grand Canyon, Sharkfin Rock, and Monolith, the home of Stretch, a five-foot moray eel.

Kauai

Site	Location and Depth	Description
Cannon's Reef	North Shore 30–60	Reef drops quickly from shoreline forming a long ledge permeated with lava tubes. Plate coral found here. Turtles commonly sighted. White tip shark sleeping in caverns or cruising the ledge. Summer months only.
General Store	Kukuiula 65–80	Site of 19th-century shipwreck with five large anchors and chain. Horseshoe-shape ledge with two caverns teeming with many tropical fish. Large schools of lemon butterflyfish follow divers. Green moray eels and black coral under ledges.
Sheraton Caverns	Poipu 35–60	Three immense lava tubes parallel one another to form Kauai's most popular cavern dive. Turtles swimming in caverns, lobster nursery in one cavern, occasional white tip shark present.

Source: Dive Hawaii

Village: Kahuku-*mura*

by Garrett Hongo

Born in Volcano, Hawaii, Garrett Hongo is the author of two poetry collections, Yellow Light and The River of Heaven.

I'm back near the plantation lands of cane and mule trails
and narrow-gauge track rusting in the rainbow distance
against the green cliffs and bridal veils of the *pali*.

I know the mill is just beyond my sight,
around the sand point, past old caneland
cleared now for prawn farms and melon patches,
and that the village is beyond them, Quonset huts
and barracks in clusters arranged without pattern.

I remember someone—Iiyama-*san*—kept a carp pond,
and someone else made bean curd, fresh,
every day, and my chore was to fetch it,
in a bucket or a shallow pail or a lunchbox,
and I'd rush through the dusty, unpaved streets
winding past the rows of tiny shotguns,
thrilled with my job, anxious to get to
the low, barnlike building all in shadow
and cool as a cave in the middle of the day.

I'd knock or call—*Tadaima!*—as I was taught,
in Japanese for this Japanese man (other words
for the Portuguese or Chinese or Hawaiian),
and he'd slide the grey door back, *shōji*-like,
on its runner, opening up, and I'd see,
under dim lab-lights, long sinks like flumes
in three rows all brimming with a still water
lustrous and faintly green in the weak light.

There was an odor too, stark as dawnlight,
of fermentation I'd guess now, the cool paste
curdling in the damp, cold dark, silting
clear water milky under the coarse wire screens,
the air gaseous and fragrant and sharp.

It must have been a dime or a nickel—
I remember its shine and the coin's neat fit
in my hand—and he'd take it, drop it in
a slotted coffee can, then reach a slick palm,
small spade of flesh, into the supple water,
draw the raw, white cube, delicate and new,
drenched in its own strange juice, and place it,
without words or ceremony, into the blank pail
I held before me like a page to be written on.

How did I know it would all recede into nothing,
derelict shacks unpainted and overgrown
with morning glories, by canefields fringed
with *ekoa* and castor beans, swinging
their dark, brittle censers over the road?
How did I know my own joy's beginning
would be relic in my own lifetime?

I turn up the dirt road that took me in,
the green cane all around me, flush by the roadside,
a parted sea of masts and small sails scissoring the air,
whispering their sullen history on a tuneless wind.

3 Oahu

by Marty Wentzel The person who dreamed up Oahu's nickname, "The Gathering Place," was prophetic. Hawaii's most populated island is an eclectic blend of people, places, customs, and cuisines. Its geography ranges from peaks and plains to rain forests and beaches. A day that dawns clear and cool can end with the most fiery of sunsets. The only common denominators are the reliably warm weather and clear skies that enhance a beautiful natural environment.

Third largest of the Hawaiian Islands, Oahu was formed by two volcanoes that erupted 4 million to 6 million years ago and eventually created a peaceable kingdom of 608 square miles. More than 80% of Hawaii's 1 million residents live on Oahu, yet somehow there is enough room for wide-open spaces and sufficient time to take a deep breath and relax.

More and more Hawaiians are stepping forward to say that Oahu is their favorite island, and many claim that it has the most spectacular scenery of all Hawaii. Part of its dramatic appearance can be attributed to its majestic highlands: the western Waianae Mountains, which rise 4,000 feet above sea level, and the verdant Koolaus, which cross the island's midsection at elevations of more than 3,000 feet. After eons of erosion by wind and weather, these ranges now have sculptured, jagged peaks, deep valleys, sheer green cliffs, and dynamic vistas. If you drive just half an hour from Waikiki to the panoramic views from the Pali Lookout, you'll agree that this is one awesome island.

Below the mountains, Oahu is a gathering place of beach parks, with more than 50 draped around its edges like a beautiful lei. The sands of Waikiki are filled with sun bunnies, honeymooners, couples celebrating anniversaries, Marines on holiday, and every other type of tourist imaginable. The beaches to the west and north are surprisingly unspoiled and uncrowded, and their clientele sports a clearly local look.

Inside that sandy circumference are the vast pineapple and sugar plantations that have helped put Oahu on the map. Smaller family farms grow such gifts of nature as bananas, papayas, watermelons, lychees, mangoes, corn, and gardens full of exotic flowers. There are also modern-day "farmers" who are running successful experiments in aquaculture, as well as wind farms, which harness the power of air currents through enormous windmills on the slopes of Kahuku.

When fierce volcanoes formed Oahu's mountains, they also deposited shelves of rock beneath the sea, creating the two great harbors, Honolulu and Pearl, that together have determined Oahu's destiny as a Pacific capital. It was the December 7, 1941, Japanese attack on Pearl Harbor that launched the United States into World War II and brought thousands of servicemen to lodgings on Oahu. Today the military is still a major force on Oahu, occupying a quarter of the island's land and accounting for an eighth of the local population.

At the southeastern tip of this diverse island is a rectangular subdivision that, on a map, looks small and obscure. Don't let its size fool you. This is Waikiki, the international resort city to which more than 4 million tourists flock each year.

Even though it was thick with duck ponds and swampland until the building of the Ala Wai Canal in 1928, Waikiki has always been considered "holiday central" for kings and commoners alike. King Kalakaua kept a boat house there, and the lovely Princess Kaiulani had a home there. It was here that Robert Louis Stevenson penned poetry under an old banyan tree, Amelia Earhart took time out from her adventures, and the Prince of Wales (later Edward VII), danced under the stars.

From the oldest standing hotel, the 1901 Moana (now a part of the Sheraton Moana Surfrider), to the newest high rises that punch holes in the sky, the resorts of Waikiki continue to be a destination vacationers dream about. No wonder, since the area has more than 30,000 rooms of varying prices, sizes, and styles and nearly 250 restaurants, some of which are considered Oahu's finest. It has the green open spaces of Kapiolani Park, and it is presided over by the most familiar of Hawaiian natural landmarks, Diamond Head Crater. Waikiki has also seen a $10.5-million face-lift of its main thoroughfare, Kalakaua Avenue, which is now an inviting, intriguing strip for people-watching and window-shopping.

From subdued hues of dawn to brilliant orange-pink sunsets, Waikiki's days are long, and the sun bathes this little area more consistently than anywhere else on Oahu. Its 2½-mile-long stretch of sand is, to many, the world's greatest beach, and the gentle, aquamarine waters beside it are great for surfing, snorkeling, and swimming. By night Waikiki sizzles with excitement. Megastars from around the world share the stage with reliable local talent, from the venerable Don Ho and his Las Vegas–style revue to live rock 'n' roll bands that jam until the doors close at 4 AM.

Like most resort cities, Waikiki also has its downside. With 173 hotels and condos crammed into about 1½ square miles, it can be very crowded. The traffic can be horrendous, and the one-way streets are confusing. If you start to feel hemmed in, you can always escape to quieter parts of the island.

Waikiki is a subdivision of Honolulu, where the past and present mingle charmingly. Honolulu is America's only city with a royal palace, from which Hawaii's kings and queens ruled in the 1800s. Today that palace stands in the center of downtown, right down the street from the island's oldest homes, the Mission Houses, dating back to the 1820s. All around is a bustling, modern-day business center where executives make major international decisions in aloha shirts rather than suits and ties.

The flip side of Honolulu is the north shore, affectionately dubbed "the country" by residents who seek refuge from city life. The North Shore is dotted with such country towns as Haleiwa, Kahuku, Laie, and Kaaawa, tiny burgs where arts-and-crafts shops stand next to trendy fashion boutiques. Along the roads are fruit stands, mom 'n' pop stores, cattle ranches, and pretty parks where flying a kite or flicking a Frisbee is the order of the day.

Deeply rooted traditions of Hawaiian hospitality remain strong in Oahu, despite all the modern trappings. Yes, there are the inevitable plans for the island's future, including talk of a much-needed mass-transit system to ease the desperately choked freeway traffic. Designs are in the works for upgrading Honolulu's waterfront, creating dozens of new golf courses around the island, and expanding residential and resort developments toward the west end.

Yet on Oahu, there are things you can always count on. There will always be rainbows in beautiful Manoa Valley. The winter waves will always return to the Banzai Pipeline. Scarlet lehua blossoms will forever burst into bloom on the ridges high above the city. And best of all, the spirit of aloha will always spread like a blanket of love from one shore to the other.

Essential Information

Arriving and Departing by Plane

Airport **Honolulu International Airport** (tel. 808/836–6413) is the only commercial airport on Oahu, and it is one of the busiest in the nation. Flying time from Los Angeles is about 5 hours, and from New York, about 10 hours, plus layovers.

The airport has been completely renovated and now consists of the main terminal (for domestic and international flights), a pair of smaller terminals for the three major interisland carriers (Aloha, Hawaiian, and Discovery), and a tiny commuter terminal for small craft. When you fly out of Honolulu International Airport, plan to check in 90 minutes before departure for a domestic flight and one hour before departure for a flight to one of the Neighbor Islands.

Last year, various members of Oahu's transportation industry banded together in a cooperative effort to streamline the greeting of arriving passengers. As you enter the terminal, you now hear recorded Hawaiian music. People who are meeting individuals or collecting tour participants are asked to stand in roped-off areas away from the arrival gate in order to allow a smooth flow of passengers off the plane. In addition, a Wikiwiki Bus transports passengers arriving at gates that are far from the baggage-claim area.

If you have extra time at the airport, visit the new **Pacific Aerospace Museum** (tel. 808/531–7747) on the upper level of the central concourse of the main terminal. It was scheduled to open during 1991.

Flights from the U.S. carriers serving Oahu include **United** (tel. 808/547–2211),
Mainland U.S. **Northwest** (tel. 808/955–2255), **American** (tel. 808/526–0044), **Continental** (tel. 800/231–0856), **Delta** (tel. 800/221–1212), **TWA** (tel. 800/221–2000), **Hawaiian** (tel. 808/537–5100), and **Pan American** (tel. 800/221–1111). Most flights to Hawaii originate in Los Angeles or San Francisco, which, of course, means they are nonstop. There are also nonstop flights from Dallas/Fort Worth, Chicago, Seattle, and San Diego. There are direct flights (there are one or more stops along the route, but you don't have to change planes) from Anchorage, New York, and other cities in the East, Southwest, and Midwest. Connecting flights are available from almost every American city.

Flights from By law, foreign carriers serving Oahu may not originate in
Foreign Countries other American cities. Airlines that bring passengers to Honolulu from foreign destinations include **Qantas** (tel. 800/227–4500), **Canadian Airlines International** (tel. 808/922–0533), **Air Canada** (tel. 800/422–6232), **Japan Airlines** (tel. 808/521–1441), **Philippine Air Lines** (tel. 800/435–9725), **Air New Zealand** (tel. 800/521–4059), **China Air Lines** (tel. 808/536–6951), **Korean Air**

Lines (tel. 808/932–7302), **Singapore Air Lines** (tel. 808/524–6063), and **Air Tungaru** (tel. 808/735–3994).

Charter Flights Charter flights, though less expensive than regularly scheduled commercial flights, are also less reliable, with chronically late departures and occasional cancellations. In addition, they tend to depart less frequently (usually once a week). If the savings are worth the potential irritation, charter flights serving Honolulu International Airport include **Associated Aviation Activities** (tel. 808/836–3106) and **Trans Air** (tel. 808/833–5557). Consult your travel agent for further information.

Lei Greetings Many visitors are disappointed to find that everyone who arrives at Honolulu International Airport is not automatically given a lei. But with the visitor count at more than 6 million, universal lei greetings would bankrupt the state.

If you have booked through a tour company and are being met at the airport, you will probably be given a lei by the person who meets you. If you have friends meeting you, most definitely they will have a lei for you. If you are traveling independently, you can arrange for a lei greeting from **Greeters of Hawaii** (Box 29638, Honolulu 96820, tel. 800/367–2669) or **Hawaii 800** (Box 89696, Honolulu 96830–0810, tel. 800/367–5270). They require 24 hours notice. The cost runs from $9.95 to $33.95 per person. The standard $9.95 lei usually contains plumeria or an orchid-carnation mixture. It's a great way to surprise your traveling companion.

Between the Airport and Waikiki Since the majority of hotels on Oahu are located in Waikiki, chances are that's where you will be heading. There are several ways to get to Waikiki, which is only 20 minutes from the airport during off-peak times but twice that during rush hour. Before you use one of the following methods, check with your hotel to see if it has a free airport shuttle. For instance, the two main hotels outside Honolulu (the Sheraton Makaha Resort and Country Club and the Turtle Bay Hilton) offer that service.

By Bus **Gray Line** (tel. 808/834–1033) and **Airport Express** (tel. 808/949–5249) offer airport shuttle service to and from specific hotels and condos in Waikiki at a cost of $5. Oahu's **municipal bus** (tel. 808/531–1611) costs only 60¢, but you are allowed only one bag, which must fit on your lap. Buses 19 and 20 pick up passengers by the upper level exits every 10–15 minutes.

By Taxi Taxis are easy to catch at the airport exit. At $2.80 for the first mile plus $1.40 for each additional mile, the fare to Waikiki will run approximately $15 plus a tip. Drivers are also allowed to charge 25¢ per suitcase. For your trip back to the airport at the end of your visit, call **Charley's** (tel. 808/531–1333) or **SIDA of Hawaii, Inc.** (tel. 808/836–0011).

By Limousine When you want to be transported with a touch of class, Oahu has a fleet of limousine companies at your service. They charge anywhere from $30 to $50 for a run from the airport to Waikiki. Most have a two-hour minimum, so you might want to ask the driver to take a scenic route to your hotel. Try **Silver Cloud Limousine Service** (tel. 808/524–7999) or **Roberts Limousines** (tel. 808/973–2308).

By Car Many car-rental firms have locations near the airport, with free shuttle service from the baggage area to their offices. Call them from one of the courtesy phones when you arrive. (*See* Getting Around, below, for further car-rental information.)

The main highway into Waikiki from the airport is Lunalilo Freeway (H-1). Take the Punahou exit and turn right on Punahou Street, then make the first right (onto Beretania Street) and the first left (onto Kalakaua Avenue), which leads you straight into Waikiki. For a more coastal but congested route, you can take Nimitz Highway to Ala Moana Boulevard, which eventually spills into Kalakaua Avenue. Either way, beware of the traffic, especially during rush hour. It can be fierce.

Arriving and Departing by Ship

Boat Day used to be the biggest day of the week. Jet travel has almost obscured that custom, and it's too bad, because arriving in Honolulu by ship is a great experience. If you have the time, it is one sure way to unwind. As you approach the docks you have tremendous views of historic Aloha Tower, sparkling downtown Honolulu, and the majestic Koolau Mountains rising above it all. Many cruises are planned a year or more in advance and fill up fast.

Because of customs regulations, if you sail on a foreign ship from any U.S. port, you must return with that ship to that port. If you arrive in Hawaii from a foreign port, you may disembark in Honolulu. Most cruise-ship companies today offer a fare that includes round-trip air travel to the point of embarkation.

Cunard/N.A.C. Line (tel. 212/880–7500), **Holland American Line** (tel. 206/281–3535), and **Royal Viking** (tel. 800/426–0821) have cruise ships passing through Honolulu once or twice a year. Contact your local travel agent for further information.

Getting Around

Oahu is a diverse isle, and its transportation options are as plentiful as its attractions. If you plan to spend most of your time frolicking on the sands of Waikiki Beach, you can walk to the shops, hotels, and restaurants nearby. If your sightseeing will be limited to Honolulu, buses or taxicabs will do the trick. If you enjoy sightseeing in groups, there are many tour companies that provide islandwide van transportation. If you're an independent type with an urge to visit the north shore, the windward side, and other Oahu highlights on your own, you should rent a car.

By Car The rules of the road on Oahu are the same as on the mainland. Traffic can be very heavy during rush hour (6:30–8:30 AM and 3:30–5:30 PM), so allow plenty of time to get places. It's easy to drive around Oahu, because roads, streets, and major attractions are well marked.

Be sure to buckle up. Hawaii has a seat-belt law for front-seat passengers. Children under age three must be in a car seat, available from your car-rental agency.

Lock your car and take your valuables when you park to avoid theft, which occurs with unfortunate frequency in the city. Also, feed the meters to avoid having a tow truck ruin your vacation, because parking rules are strictly enforced.

Car Rentals You're advised to reserve a car before you arrive, particularly during the peak seasons of summer, the Christmas holidays, and February. Often, the companies near Honolulu Airport charge a bit more per day for their cars ($35–$45) than those in Waikiki ($30–$40), with lower rates at local budget companies.

Companies with airport and downtown offices include **Avis** (tel. 800/831–8000), **Hertz** (tel. 800/654–3131), **Budget** (tel. 800/527–0700), **Thrifty** (tel. 800/367–2277), **National** (tel. 800/328–4567), **Sears** (tel. 800/527–0770), **Dollar** (tel. 800/421–6868), and **American International** (tel. 800/527–0202).

Local budget and used rental-car companies include **Tropical** (tel. 808/836–1041), which also serves the other islands; **Roberts Hawaii** (tel. 808/947–3939); **Five-O** (tel. 808/836–1028), which offers special deals for members of the armed forces; **VIP** (tel. 808/946–1671); **Island World** (tel. 808/839–2222); and **Honolulu Rent-a-Car** (tel. 808/941–9099).

By Bus If you're staying in Waikiki, there's no reason to rent a car. You can walk to where you are going or hop on Honolulu's municipal transportation system, called **The Bus** (tel. 808/531–1611). The Bus will take you all around the island or just down Kalakaua Avenue for 60¢ a ride, and you are entitled to one free transfer per fare if you ask for it when boarding. Boarding is at the front of the bus, and exact change is required. The student fare (grades 1–12) is 25¢, and children under six ride free. A free bus pass for senior citizens (age 65 or over and able to prove it) may be obtained by applying in person at 725 Kapiolani Boulevard between 8 AM and 4 PM, but it takes two to three weeks to be processed. Monthly bus passes are available at $15 for adults, $7.50 for students. In Waikiki, get them at Pioneer Federal Savings Bank, Waikiki Business Plaza, 2270 Kalakaua Avenue, tel. 808/971–6520.

No official bus-route maps are available, but you can find privately published booklets at most drugstores and other convenience outlets. The important route numbers for Waikiki are 2, 4, 5, 8, 19, and 20. If you venture far afield, you can always get back on one of those.

There are also a number of brightly painted private buses, many free, that will take you from Waikiki to such commercial attractions as dinner cruises, garment factories, and the like.

By Waikiki Trolley An open **trolley** cruises Waikiki and the Ala Moana area and makes 27 stops along a 90-minute route. The trolley ride is a good way to get oriented. The conductor narrates, pointing out sights as well as shopping, dining, and entertainment opportunities along the way. *In Waikiki, the trolley originates at the corner of Royal Hawaiian Ave. and Kalakaua Ave., tel. 808/ 599–2561. Cost: $7 for an all-day pass (from the conductor), $4 children under 12. Daily, every hour on the hour 8–3.*

By Taxi You can usually get a cab right at the doorstep of your hotel, and most restaurants will call one for you. Rates are $2.80 for the first mile and $1.40 for each additional mile. Drivers are generally courteous, and the cars are in good condition and often air-conditioned. The two biggest taxicab companies are **Charley's**, a fleet of company-owned cabs (tel. 808/531–1333); and **SIDA of Hawaii, Inc.**, an association of individually owned cabs (tel. 808/836–0011).

By Limousine If you want to see the island in style, you can rent a Ferrari 328 GTS convertible for $399 a day plus $50 insurance from **Silver Cloud Limousine Service** (tel. 808/524–7999). It also provides other luxury cars and private yachts and planes. **Roberts Limousines** (tel. 808/973–2308) rents Cadillacs for $55 an hour.

By Moped/ Bicycle **Aloha Funway** (tel. 808/942–9696) has mopeds for $14.95 per 24-hour period. Ten-speed mountain bikes start at $12.95.

Important Addresses and Numbers

Tourist Information On Oahu, you can get plenty of information from the main office of the **Hawaii Visitors Bureau,** which is located right on the main street of Waikiki at 2270 Kalakaua Avenue, 8th floor, Honolulu 96815, tel. 808/923–1811. It's open weekdays 8–4:30.

Several informative tourist publications are available for free along the main streets of Waikiki, at the airport, in hotels and restaurants, and at other spots frequented by visitors. These include *Spotlight Oahu, This Week on Oahu,* and *Guide to Oahu,* which are all full of money-saving coupons and weekly calendars of events.

Emergencies For police, ambulance, fire department, or suicide center, dial 911.

Doctors **Doctors on Call.** This 24-hour service provides excellent care without an appointment; the doctors will even make "house" calls to your hotel room. Three clinics are located in Waikiki, *Hyatt Regency Hotel, 4th floor, tel. 808/926–4777; Reef Towers Hotel, Room 242, tel. 808/926–0664; Hawaiian Regent Hotel, 2nd floor, tel. 808/923–3666.*

Honolulu County Medical Society (1360 S. Beretania St., 2nd floor, Honolulu, tel. 808/536–6988) offers information on doctors when you're looking for reliable referrals.

Straub Walk-in Health Center. A doctor, a laboratory/radiology technician, and nurses are on duty. No appointment is necessary. Services include diagnosis and treatment of illness and injury, laboratory testing and X-rays on site, and referral, when necessary, to Honolulu's Straub Hospital. More than 150 kinds of medical insurance are accepted, including Medicare, Medicaid, and most kinds of travel insurance. Sunburn care is a specialty. *Royal Hawaiian Shopping Center, 2233 Kalakaua Ave., Bldg. B, Suite 304, Waikiki, tel. 808/971–6000. Clinic open weekdays 8:30–5:30. At other times, call the duty doctor at 808/926–4777.*

Waikiki Acupuncture Clinic. The ancient, highly respected art of acupuncture is available to you here, by appointment only. *305 Royal Hawaiian Ave., Suite 208, Waikiki, tel. 808/923–6939.*

Waikiki Health Center. Doctors are on hand to take care of general medical problems as well as physical exams, pediatrics, pregnancy testing, and VD screening and treatment. This is a nonprofit Aloha United Way agency. *277 Ohua Ave., tel. 808/922–4787. Open Mon.–Thurs. 9–7:30, Fri.–Sat. 9–3:30.*

Hospitals **Straub Clinic,** 888 S. King St., Honolulu, tel. 808/522–4000; **Queen's Medical Center,** 1301 Punchbowl St., Honolulu, tel. 808/547–4311; **Kapiolani Medical Center for Women and Children,** 1319 Punahou St., Honolulu, tel. 808/947–8633.

Dentists **Waikiki Royal Hawaiian Dental Group.** This group offers the full range of dental services for visitors and accepts all insurance plans. You need to call ahead for an appointment. *Waikiki Medical Bldg., 305 Royal Hawaiian Ave., Suite 209, tel. 808/ 926–5732. Open Mon. 8:30–noon, Tues, Thurs., and Fri. 8:30–5, Wed. 1–8.*

Late-Night Pharmacies The two pharmacies that are the most reliable and accessible to tourists are both in Waikiki. **Outrigger Pharmacy** (Outrigger Hotel, 2335 Kalakaua Ave., tel. 808/923–2529) and **Kuhio Pharmacy** (Outrigger West Hotel, 2330 Kuhio Ave., tel. 808/923–4466) both advertise as sunburn specialists.

Others **Coast Guard Rescue** (tel. 808/536–4336).
Foreign Money Exchange (tel. 808/521–0787).
Hawaii Council of Churches (tel. 808/263–9788).
Passport Information (tel. 808/541–1919).
Surf Report (tel. 808/836–1952).
Time of Day (tel. 808/983–3211).
Weather (tel. 808/836–0121).

Opening and Closing Times

Most Oahu banks are open Monday through Thursday 8:45–3 or 4:30, Fridays 8:45–6. Most financial institutions are closed on weekends and holidays.

Major museums are open daily 9 or 10–4:30 or 5. The Honolulu Academy of Arts is closed Sunday morning and all day Monday. Most museums are closed on Christmas.

Major shopping malls are generally open daily 10–9, although some shops may close at 4 or 5. Ala Moana Center is open weekdays 9:30–9, Saturday 9:30–5:30, Sunday 10–5.

Guided Tours

Types of Tours **Circle Island Tour.** There are several variations on this theme, so you should read the Circle Island Driving Tour (*see* Tour 5 in Exploring, below) to decide what's important to you and then decide which tour comes the closest to matching your desires. A standard all-day tour includes Diamond Head Crater, Hanauma Bay, Byodo-In Temple, famous surfing beaches, either Waimea Falls Park or the Polynesian Cultural Center, the Mormon Temple, and pineapple and sugarcane fields. Some of these all-day tours include lunch. Cost: $35–$40, depending on whether lunch is included and whether you go by bus or minibus, the latter being slightly more expensive.

Little Circle Tour. These tours cover the territory discussed in the East Oahu Ring Tour (*see* Tour 4 in Exploring, below). Most of these tours are the same, no matter which company you sign up with, and include Nuuanu Valley, the Pali Lookout, Makapuu Beach, Sea Life Park, Koko Head, Hanauma Bay, and the Halona Blowhole. Cost: about $26.

Scenic Honolulu City Tour. This tour encompasses Diamond Head Crater, the University of Hawaii, Punchbowl National Cemetery, Kawaiahao Church, sites in historic downtown and Chinatown, Iolani Palace and the state capitol building, Washington Place, and the King Kamehameha statue. Cost: about $17.

Pearl Harbor and Punchbowl. This half-day tour includes Pearl Harbor, the *Arizona* Memorial, historic Honolulu, and Punchbowl National Cemetery. Cost: about $20.

Polynesian Cultural Center (*see* Tour 5 in Exploring, below, for details). The only advantage of the guided tour is that you won't have to drive yourself back to Waikiki after dark if you take in the evening show. Cost: about $56, including admission to the center.

Tour Companies Many ground companies handle the excursions mentioned above. Some herd you onto an air-conditioned bus, and others use smaller vans. Vans are recommended, because less time is spent picking up passengers, and you get to know your fellow sightseers and your tour guide. Whether you go by bus or by van, you'll probably be touring in top-of-the-line equipment. The competition among these companies is fierce, and everyone has to keep up. If you're booking through your hotel travel desk, ask whether you'll be on a bus or a van and exactly what "get-off-the-bus" stops and "window sights" the tour includes.

Most of the tour guides have been in the business for years. Many have taken special Hawaiiana classes to learn the history and lore of the Islands. They expect a tip ($1 per person at least), but they're just as cordial without one. In almost all cases, you will be picked up at your hotel.

These are some of the most reliable and popular of the many tour companies.

Akamai Tours (Waikiki Business Plaza, 2270 Kalakaua Ave., Suite 1702, Honolulu, tel. 800/922–6485). Akamai sponsors a one-day circle-island snorkel and picnic tour.

American Express (1778 Ala Moana Blvd., Honolulu, tel. 808/924–6555). American Express books through several tour companies and can help you choose which tour best suits your needs.

Diamond Head Tours (2222 Kalakaua Ave., Honolulu, tel. 808/ 922–0544). Guides must complete the Bishop Museum's Hawaiiana classes.

E Noa Tours (1133 Waimanu St., Honolulu, tel. 808/599–2561). This company uses vans exclusively and likes to get you into the outdoors. On one of its Circle Island Tours, you get to swim at Hanauma Bay.

Polynesian Adventure Tours (2200 Kuhio Ave., Honolulu, tel. 808/922–0888). Some of the tours are action-oriented.

Roberts Hawaii (440 Hobron La., Honolulu, tel. 808/947–3939). This outfit has a variety of vehicles, from 15-passenger vans to 29-passenger motor coaches with kitchen and bar.

Trans Hawaiian Services (3111 Castle St., Honolulu, tel. 808/ 735–6467 or 800/654–2282). Multilingual services are available.

Walking Tours **Chinatown Walking Tour.** Meet at the Chinese Chamber of Commerce for a fascinating morning-long peek into herbal shops, an acupuncturist's office, and specialty stores. The tour is sponsored by the Chinese Chamber of Commerce. *42 King St., tel. 808/533–3181. Reservations required. Cost: $4; add $5 for lunch in a Chinese restaurant. Tues. only.*

Historic Downtown Walking Tour. Volunteers from the Mission Houses Museum (553 S. King St.) take you on a two-hour walk through Honolulu, where the historic sites rub shoulders with the modern business towers. If it's Friday, end the tour by picking up a fast-food lunch and enjoying the noontime concert on the Iolani Palace lawn. *Tel. 808/531–0481. Reservations required. Cost: $7 adults, $2 children. Mon.–Thurs.*

Aunty Malia's Historic Waikiki Walking Tour. Aunty Malia B. Solomon is a Pacific anthropologist who has long been headquartered in the Hyatt Regency Waikiki. Now she's leading 2-mile guided excursions past the landmarks, hideaways, and little-known spots of Waikiki. Highlights include the Wizard Stones of Kapaemahu and the waters where the Olympic swimming champ Duke Kahanamoku once trained. *Departs from Hyatt Regency Waikiki, 2424 Kalakaua Ave., tel. 808/923–1234, ext. 6410. Free. Mon.–Wed., 9–4.*

Great Outdoors Tours
Action Hawaii Adventures. This company manages to compress into a single day adventures the tourist rarely experiences in a week. You'll go on guided hikes through rain forests and valleys, swim beneath waterfalls, and snorkel at "insider" spots. *Box 75548, Honolulu 96836, tel. 808/944–6754. Cost: $69 adults, $59 students under 16.*

Windward Expeditions. The guides provide local history and lore as they take you by inflatable boat along the leeward coast of Oahu, past offshore islands and the private estates of stars. The water can get rough, so you should ask about surf conditions before you book. This tour departs from Hawaii Kai and takes you to a point off Diamond Head where you can snorkel and swim off the boat. Along the way you stop at a sea cave to do some exploring in calm waters. A local-style "plate lunch" and sodas are part of the package, and there's a cooler on board if you want to bring your own beer or wine. *789 Kailua Rd. Kailua 96734, tel. 808/263–3899. Cost: $35 for a 2-1/2 hr trip.*

Helicopter Tours
Hawaii Pacific Helicopters. People always think of helicopter rides as expensive, and they can be. But if you've never been up in a whirlybird, you might want to try this company's 10-minute view of Waikiki for $45. The 30-minute flight for $99 to the Pali Lookout is beautiful, or you can circle the island for one hour for $187. Best of all, these helicopters take off from the Ala Wai Helipad by the Hilton Hawaiian Village Rainbow Tower, so you don't have to bother with the confusion of airport traffic. *228 Lagoon Dr., Honolulu 96819, tel. 808/836–1566.*

Exploring

Oahu is a mixed bag, with enough sightseeing attractions and adventures to fill an entire vacation. Most of the time it's just too warm and sunny to spend all day exploring in the car or on a walking tour. So plan ahead, see only what you are interested in, and relax the rest of the time.

The area around Honolulu, including Waikiki, is called the leeward side. It is a hodgepodge of residential, tourist, and business developments, plus shopping centers, schools, and parks, all wedged between a series of ridges and valleys on one side and the ocean on the other.

Two tunnels cut through the Koolau Mountains to allow easy access from the big city to the windward side. Here, the coast and its bays offer spectacular views of mountain ridges that are folded like an Oriental fan. There are fewer tourist operations here and more residential communities, pasturelands, and beaches.

The eastern end of Oahu begins with suburbs, then trails off to stretches of golden sands and stately cliffs just waiting to be photographed. Meanwhile, on the north shore, the beach takes precedence throughout the year. In the summer the waters are as calm as a lake, while in winter the waves are wildly unpredictable.

To the west of Oahu, the land becomes drier and much less populated, until at last you reach the Waianae coast and a series of one-street towns that look as if they're straight out of the 1950s. Tourists rarely visit this untamed area of the island, except to play golf at the Sheraton Makaha Resort and Country Club. However, resort development is well underway in the West Beach area, so in years to come, who knows? This could be as popular as Waikiki.

Be careful when you're exploring Oahu's beaches in the winter months, for few are manned by lifeguards. If you see a sign warning of dangerous surf or currents, pay attention. Don't walk right next to the shore break or out on rocky promontories for a better view. A sudden set of huge waves could sweep you out to sea.

Oahu's mountains and valleys are lush and appealing, but they also come with a set of warnings. If you hike, don't go alone. You don't know the territory, and some valleys are subject to flash floods after heavy rains. Should you encounter trouble—and you might—there won't be any help around. Never leave valuables in your car, even in remote areas. Criminals can spot a rented car a mile away, and they count on the fact that in most cases the visitor will be long gone before they're caught or the case comes to trial.

In this exploring guide, the island is divided into two walking tours (Waikiki and Historic Downtown Honolulu), a trip to the Bishop Museum, and two driving tours (the East Oahu Ring and Circle Island Tour). For a one-day overview, combine the East Oahu Ring with the Circle Island trip, carefully budgeting your time. It's easy if you get a road map. Your car-rental agency will provide you with an adequate one.

Those who want to make these trips with a guide should see Guided Tours in the Essential Information section. The Circle Island and East Oahu Ring are the most popular offerings and cover most of the highlights.

You can also circle the island by bus, taking No. 57 or No. 58 from the Ala Moana Shopping Center to tour the East Oahu Ring and No. 52 or No. 55 to tour the North Shore. Call 808/531–1611 for information on transfer points.

Whether you're driving, taking a tour, or riding the bus, this section will give you an idea of what you want to see. Ready? If you're driving, KCCN 1400 on your AM radio dial plays Hawaiian music exclusively, to set the right mood.

Directions on Oahu are often given as *mauka*—toward the mountains (north), and *makai*—toward the ocean (south). In Honolulu and Waikiki, you may also hear people referring to "Diamond Head"—toward that landmark (east); and *ewa*—away from Diamond Head (west). You'll find these terms used throughout this section.

Highlights for First-time Visitors

Arizona **Memorial,** Tour 5

Bishop Museum, Tour 3

Diamond Head Crater, Tour 4

Honolulu Zoo, Tour 1

Iolani Palace, Tour 2

Pali Lookout, Tour 4

Polynesian Cultural Center, Tour 5

Sea Life Park, Tour 4

Waikiki Aquarium, Tour 1

Waimea Falls Park, Tour 5

Tour 1: A Walking Tour of Waikiki

Numbers in the margin correspond with points of interest on the Waikiki map.

Whether you're staying in Waikiki or bunking on the North Shore, you'll certainly want to take a stroll through this Pacific playground, a meeting place for young and old, the past and the present. This tour is flexible and can last from an hour to a day. Some of the sights are a bit off the beaten track—not in distance but in what's been hyped.

❶ Begin this tour at the **Royal Hawaiian Hotel** (2259 Kalakaua Ave., tel. 808/923–7311). This gracious pink palace was built in 1927 and continues to exude the charm of days gone by. The lovely lobby has impressive high ceilings, and one end opens up to the ocean lawn and the beach beyond. A stroll through the old gardens, with their tall, swaying coconut palms, branching banyans, vivid flowers, and cooing doves, will take you back to an era when Waikiki was a sleepy, tropical paradise with just a pair of resort hotels.

Time Out **Breakfast at the Surf Room** (Royal Hawaiian Hotel, 2259 Kalakaua Ave., tel. 808/923–7311). Since you're at the Royal, you might want to linger over some early morning treats in alfresco elegance. Set right at the edge of the sand, the Surf Room is a great place from which to watch the comings and goings on Waikiki Beach, including the outrigger canoers, surfers, swimmers, and sunbathers. The restaurant has a nice à la carte menu as well as an enormous breakfast buffet.

From the old, enter the new. On the other side of the hotel's ❷ gardens is the **Royal Hawaiian Shopping Center.** There are so many interesting shops tucked away here, it's a wonder how some of them survive, especially those on the upper floors (*see*

Waikiki

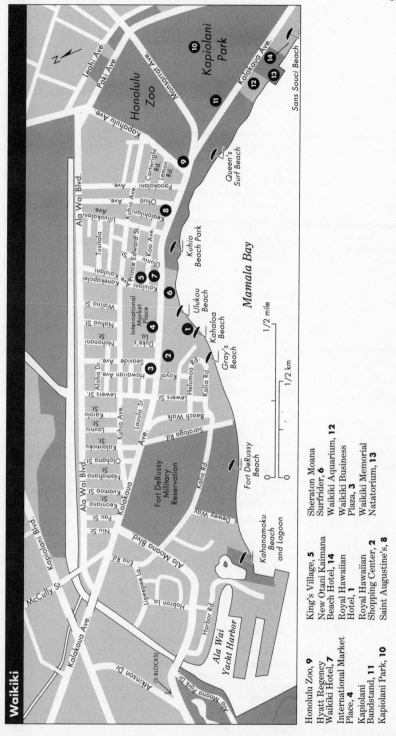

Honolulu Zoo, **9**
Hyatt Regency
Waikiki Hotel, **7**
International Market
Place, **4**
Kapiolani
Bandstand, **11**
Kapiolani Park, **10**

King's Village, **5**
New Otani Kaimana
Beach Hotel, **14**
Royal Hawaiian
Hotel, **1**
Royal Hawaiian
Shopping Center, **2**
Saint Augustine's, **8**

Sheraton Moana
Surfrider, **6**
Waikiki Aquarium, **12**
Waikiki Business
Plaza, **3**
Waikiki Memorial
Natatorium, **13**

Shopping, below). *2201 Kalakaua Ave., tel. 808/922–0588. Open Mon.–Sat. 9 AM–10 PM, Sun. 9–9.*

Across the street from the Royal Hawaiian Shopping Center is the **Waikiki Business Plaza** (2270 Kalakaua Ave.), recognizable by its fish-mosaic mural and little fountain. The **Hawaii Visitors Bureau** (tel. 808/923–1811) is on the eighth floor. Pick up free booklets on hotels, buses, and restaurants, as well as a calendar of events.

On the same block, also on the makai (ocean) side of Kalakaua Avenue, is the **International Market Place** (2330 Kalakaua Ave.), with its spreading banyan and Swiss Family Robinson–style tree house. Just follow the yellow line on the pavement to keep from getting lost in the tangle of wood-carvers, basket weavers, and other artisans from various Pacific islands who create and sell their handicrafts here. Most of the souvenir items, both tacky and 24-karat, are displayed in little Asian-style pushcarts. There's a vendor selling fresh orange juice, and several sit-down eateries, including Trader Vic's, are here. *2330 Kalakaua Ave., tel. 808/923–9871. Open daily 9 AM–11 PM.*

For a shopping mall with a different character altogether, from Kalakaua Avenue, turn mauka (toward the mountains) on Kaiulani Avenue to **King's Village.** Billing itself as a stroll through old Honolulu, it depicts a section of Waikiki as it might have looked at the turn of the century. It's ultra-cute, with cobblestone streets and salespeople in period garb. There's a Burger King here, as well as a restaurant serving authentic Japanese food and a hearty British-style pub. A Changing of the Guard ceremony is enacted every evening at 6:15, with "soldiers" in Hawaiian monarchy–era uniforms. *131 Kaiulani Ave., tel. 808/944–6855. Open daily 9 AM–11 PM.*

Cross the street and take yet another step back in time at the **Sheraton Moana Surfrider** (2365 Kalakaua Ave., tel. 808/922–3111). Formerly the 1901 Moana Hotel, the newly renovated "First Lady of Waikiki" has been dressed up to look like the original. A broad veranda stretches along the ocean side of the building, where you can sit and sip tea as you contemplate the banyan tree that has served as the focal point of the hotel for years and years. A stroll through the resplendent lobbies, past chic boutiques and nostalgic antiques, is worth the time.

Next to the Sheraton Moana Surfrider on the makai side of Kalakaua Avenue, you'll find the **Wizard Stones of Waikiki,** which, according to legend, were placed there in tribute to four prophets who came to Hawaii from Tahiti around the 15th century. Before disappearing, the prophets are said to have transferred their healing powers to the stones. The stones are located near the beach showers, and more often than not, they are irreverently draped in wet towels.

Time Out If you need to rest your feet, cross Kalakaua Avenue and stop off at **Harry's Cafe and Bar** (tel. 808/922–9292) which is in the atrium area on the ground floor of the **Hyatt Regency Waikiki Hotel** (2424 Kalakaua Ave.). Harry's is a fun place to people-watch, and the inexpensive menu includes tasty sandwiches, homemade croissants, and other deli treats.

While you're in the Hyatt, stop by **Hyatt's Hawaii** on the second floor. It's a small museum of artifacts, quilts, and crafts run by

Auntie Malia Solomon, the hotel's resident Hawaiian authority. Auntie Malia loves to help visitors become acquainted with Hawaiian handiwork and always has a charming story to tell.

From the Hyatt, walk two blocks toward Diamond Head and you'll find the only church in Waikiki with its own building, the **8** Roman Catholic **Saint Augustine's** (130 Ohua Ave., tel. 808/ 923-7024).

Next walk two more blocks toward Diamond Head and cross **9** Kapahulu Avenue; you'll be facing the entrance to the **Honolulu Zoo,** which merits a walking tour of its very own. When it opened in 1914, the zoo had a monkey, a Malayan honey bear, two lion cubs, and some imported birds; two years later, it added an African elephant named Daisy. Now the zoo houses about 1,000 animals, including such indigenous birds as the *pueo* (short-eared owl) and *elepaio* (flycatcher). An improved petting zoo with 100 creatures has recently been added, and a $5 million savanna with 200 animals of east Africa is on the drawing board. In the summertime, the zoo hosts "The Wildest Show in Town" each Wednesday night, with free admission and live music, singing, and dancing. Check the newspaper for what's playing and join the local families for a night out at the zoo. *151 Kapahulu Ave., tel. 808/971-7171. Admission: $3 adults and children 13-17. Open daily 8:30-4. Petting zoo hours: Tues.-Sun. 9-2. Closed Christmas and New Year's Day.*

10 The zoo is part of **Kapiolani Park,** founded in the late 1800s by King Kalakaua for his people. The people use it, that's for sure. On any given day there are Frisbee players, kite flyers, soccer games, softball leagues, joggers, you name it. *Admission free. Open all day.*

11 One of the park's major entertainment areas is the **Kapiolani Bandstand.** There's usually a free show by the Royal Hawaiian Band on Sunday afternoons at 2. Some excellent hula dances are performed here by local groups that don't frequent the hotels, and every year a ukulele festival fills its stage. Check the newspaper for particulars.

If you walk toward Diamond Head on the ocean side of **12** Kalakaua Avenue for about ½ mile, you'll reach the **Waikiki Aquarium,** another great place for families. The third-oldest aquarium in the United States continues to play host to schools of tropical wonders, including the *humuhumunukunukuapua'a* (Hawaii's state fish), monk seals, sharks, and more than 300 other Hawaiian and South Pacific marine species. Check out the giant clam and the chambered nautilus. Sometimes the aquarium offers reef walks in the nearby waters, and during the summer months there is weekly live entertainment by popular island performers. Call for the current schedule. *2777 Kalakaua Ave., tel. 808/923-9741. Admission: $2.50 adults and children 16-17. Open daily 9-5.*

13 Adjacent to the aquarium is the **Waikiki Memorial Natatorium,** a 1927 open-air structure that contains a large outdoor swimming pool built to commemorate lives lost in World War I. The pool is no longer open for swimming, and the structure itself is tattered and torn. However, a dedicated group called the Friends of the Natatorium has saved it from the wrecker's ball, and plans are in the works to renovate this proud monument to Hawaii's past.

Time Out Next to the natatorium is the beautiful **New Otani Kaimana**
⑭ **Beach Hotel** (2863 Kalakaua Ave.), home of the **Hau Tree Lanai**
(tel. 808/923–1555). Jutting out from the hotel onto the sand,
this is the perfect spot to watch the cruise boats on the water as
the giant orange orb of the sun slips silently into the sea. What
better way to wind up a Waikiki walking tour than with sunset
drinks at a shoreside cocktail lounge and restaurant?

See also Beaches, below, for information about Waikiki sunning
and swimming areas.

Tour 2: Historic Downtown Honolulu

*Numbers in the margin correspond with points of interest on
the Downtown Honolulu map.*

Honolulu's past and present play a delightful counterpoint
throughout the downtown sector. Modern skyscrapers stand
directly across the street from a series of piers where huge
ocean liners come to call, as they have for decades. To reach this
area from Waikiki by car, take Ala Moana Boulevard to Alakea
Street. Turn right, and drive mauka (toward the mountains)
three blocks to Hotel Street. Turn right, and right again on
Richards Street, where there is a municipal parking lot. You
can also try the metered parking in the Aloha Tower parking
lot, across Ala Moana Boulevard from Alakea Street.

If you travel by public transportation, take the No. 2 bus from
Waikiki. Get off at Alapai Street and walk makai (toward the
ocean) to King Street. Most of the historic sites are clustered
within easy walking distance.

❶ Begin this tour at the **Hawaii Maritime Center,** which is across
Ala Moana Boulevard from Alakea Street in downtown Honolulu. Opened in late 1988, it features such attractions as the *Falls
of Clyde*, a century-old, four-masted, square-rigged ship now
used as a museum. Pier 7 was the international steamship pier
in turn-of-the-century Honolulu. Aloha Tower, built in 1926
and once the tallest building in Hawaii, provides a panoramic
view of the city and coastline. The Kalakaua Boat House includes exhibits covering Hawaii's whaling days, the history of
Honolulu Harbor, and canoes, plus the Pacific Ocean Theater
and open-air restaurants. *The Hokule'a* is a double-hulled canoe used on the Polynesian Voyaging Society's "Voyage of
Rediscovery" to the South Pacific. *Pier 7, Ala Moana Blvd.,
Honolulu, tel. 808/536–6373. Admission: $6. Open daily 9–5.*

The **Children's Touch and Feel Museum** is also part of the
Hawaii Maritime Center. At this 1,000-square-foot aquatic
attraction, kids can play captain of a mock submarine complete
with periscope, engine, steering and diving controls, and
crew's quarters. A lifeboat and the deck of a 19th-century sailing vessel with steering wheel, capstan, and cargo winch, are
also here to explore. A cassette tour narrated by William Con-
rad guides you through the museum. *Pier 7, Ala Moana Blvd.,
Honolulu, tel. 808/536–6373. Admission: $6 adults, $3 ages 6–
17. Open 9–5.*

❷ Cross Ala Moana Boulevard, walk a block ewa (away from Diamond Head) and turn mauka (toward the mountains) on **Fort
Street Mall,** a pedestrian walkway that passes buildings historic and new. Sit on a bench for a few minutes and watch the

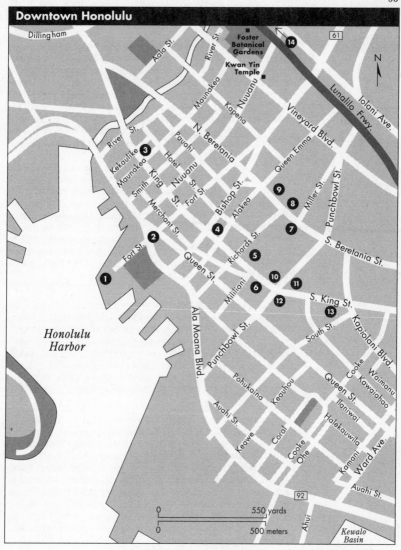

Downtown Honolulu

Aliiolani Hale (Kamehameha I statue), **6**

Bishop Museum, **14**

Chinatown, **3**

Fort Street Mall, **2**

Hawaii Maritime Center, **1**

Hawaii State Capitol, **7**

Hawaii State Library, **10**

Honolulu Hale, **11**

Iolani Palace, **5**

Kawaiahao Church, **12**

Mission Houses Museum, **13**

Saint Andrew's Cathedral, **9**

Tamarind Park, **4**

Washington Place, **8**

fascinating parade of everyone from businesspeople to street preachers.

③ Turn left on King Street, and in a few blocks you'll reach **Chinatown,** the old section of downtown Honolulu, which is crammed with interesting shops. Slightly on the tawdry side, it has lately been getting a piecemeal face-lift as little art galleries open up in renovated structures. There are lei stands, herb shops, acupuncture studios, noodle factories, Chinese and Thai restaurants, and the colorful Oahu Market, an open-air emporium with hanging pig heads, display cases of fresh fish, row after row of exotic fruits and vegetables, and plenty of smiling vendors of all ethnic backgrounds.

Time Out   There are plenty of fun Chinese restaurants in Chinatown, but **Wo Fat** (115 N. Hotel St., 1 block north of King St., tel. 808/537–6260) is a great lunchtime stop on your walking tour. Reputed to be Hawaii's oldest restaurant, this Hotel Street landmark has been doing business since 1882, with no indication of slowing down. Authentic Cantonese food is the fare in this three-story establishment with tile floors, and the meals are a great bargain. Be sure to order some of Wo Fat's special fried noodles with beef in oyster sauce.

④ Walk back toward Diamond Head along King Street until it intersects with Bishop Street. On the mauka (mountain) side is lovely **Tamarind Park,** where folks gather at lunchtime to hear live music, from jazz and Hawaiian to the U.S. Marine band. Check the newspaper to find out the schedule. Friday is the most likely day to catch an act. Do as the locals do: Pick up lunch at one of the many carryouts bordering the park, pull up a bench or some lawn, and enjoy. *Admission free. Open all day.*

⑤ Continue along King Street until you reach **Iolani Palace,** on the mauka side. This graceful Victorian structure was built by King David Kalakaua on the site of an earlier palace. Beautifully restored, it is America's only royal palace and contains the thrones of King Kalakaua and his successor (and sister) Queen Liliuokalani. Also on the palace grounds is the **Kalakaua Coronation Bandstand,** where the Royal Hawaiian Band performs at noon most Fridays. Stop at the **Iolani Barracks,** built to house the Royal Guard and now a gift shop. *King St. at Richards St., tel. 808/522–0832. Reservations required. Admission: $4 adults, $1 children 5–12; children under 5 are not permitted. Open only for guided tours, Wed.–Sat. 9–2:15.*

⑥ Across King Street from the palace is **Aliiolani Hale,** the old judiciary building that once served as the parliament hall during the monarchy era. In front of it is the gilded **statue of Kamehameha I,** the Big Island chieftain who united all the warring Hawaiian Islands into one kingdom. He stands with one arm outstretched in welcome. The original of this statue is on the Big Island, in Kapaau, near the birthplace of the king. Each year on June 11, his birthday, the statue is draped in leis.

⑦ Walk one block mauka up Richards Street to see the **Hawaii State Capitol** (S. Beretania St. between Punchbowl St. and Richards St., tel. 808/548–5420). Built in 1969, this architectural gem is richly symbolic: The columns look like palm trees, the legislative chambers are shaped like volcanic cinder cones, and the central court is open to the sky, representing Hawaii's open society. The capitol is surrounded by reflecting pools, just as the Islands are embraced by water. Between the capitol and the palace is a statue of Queen Liliuokalani, Hawaii's last reigning monarch. In front is a statue of Father Damien, the Belgian priest who gave his life caring for the victims of Hansen's disease, or leprosy, on the island of Molokai.

8 Almost across the street from the state capitol is **Washington Place** (320 S. Beretania St.). This graceful 1846 mansion is currently the home of Hawaii's governor. Queen Liliuokalani lived here until her death in 1917. You can only peer through the wrought-iron gates, since the residence is not open to the public.

9 Next to Washington Place is **Saint Andrew's Cathedral** (S. Beretania St. at Queen Emma St.), Episcopal headquarters in Hawaii. Queen Emma, widow of Kamehameha IV, supervised the construction of the church and was baptized in the sanctuary. The building was designed in England, and parts of it were shipped from there.

Time Out Walk back to King Street and continue 1 block farther, to Merchant Street. Turn right and you'll discover a charming open-air restaurant ideal for lunch, a snack, or a cool drink. True to its name, the **Croissanterie** (222 Merchant St., tel. 808/533–3443) features fresh-baked breads, muffins, and croissants, great for sandwiches or on their own. Order a beer or a cup of Hawaii's own Lion Coffee, get a salad with your sandwich, and enjoy the relaxed atmosphere of this homey indoor-outdoor spot.

10 Return to King Street, stay on the mauka side, and proceed in a Diamond Head direction. Past the palace is the **Hawaii State Library,** whose "Asia and the Pacific" room has a fascinating collection of books old and new about Hawaii's history. The library was under renovation at press time, but should reopen by 1991. *478 King St., tel. 808/548–4775. Open Tues. and Thurs. 9–8; Mon., Wed., Fri., and Sat. 9–5.*

11 Next on the mauka side is **Honolulu Hale,** or City Hall (530 S. King St. at Punchbowl St.), a Mediterranean/Renaissance-style building constructed in 1929. You can walk into the cool, open-ceiling lobby, which sometimes displays works by local artists.

12 Across the street, on the corner of King and Punchbowl, is **Kawaiahao Church,** Hawaii's most famous religious structure. Fancifully called Hawaii's Westminster Abbey, the coral-block church witnessed the coronations, weddings, and funerals of generations of Hawaiian royalty. The graves of missionaries and of King Lunalilo are in the yard. The upper gallery has an exhibit of paintings of the royal families. *957 Punchbowl St. at King St., tel. 808/522–1333. Services in English and Hawaiian each Sun. morning at 10:30. Free tours Mon.–Fri. 9–12 and Sun. after the service. Call ahead to schedule one.*

13 On the Diamond Head side of the church is the **Mission Houses Museum,** a historic complex where the first American missionaries in Hawaii lived. Arriving in 1820, the stalwart band gained royal favor and influenced every aspect of island life. Their descendants have become leaders in government and business. The white frame house was prefabricated in New En-

gland and shipped around the Horn. *553 S. King St., tel. 808/
531–0481. Admission: $3.50 adults, $1 children 6–15. Museum
can be seen only on a guided tour, which is held once an hour,
with the last tour at 3. Open Tues.–Sat. 9–4, Sun. noon–4.
Closed New Year's Day, Easter, Thanksgiving, and Christmas.*

Tour 3: A Side Trip to the Bishop Museum and Planetarium

Anyone who is interested in any facet of Hawaiian or Pacific
culture should make the time to take this special tour. The
building alone, with its huge Victorian turrets and immense
stone walls, is a sight worth seeing.

⑭ Founded in 1889 by Charles R. Bishop as a memorial to his
wife, Princess Bernice Pauahi, the **Bishop Museum** began as a
repository for the royal possessions of this last direct descendant of King Kamehameha the Great. It has since achieved
world fame as a center of Polynesian archaeology, ethnology,
and history.

There are lustrous feather capes, scary god images, the skeleton of a giant sperm whale, an authentic, well-preserved grass
house, and changing displays of old photographs and ethnic
crafts. The planetarium next door spotlights "Polynesian
Skies," a narrated show that helps you unravel the mysteries of
the tropical skies. Arts and crafts demonstrations take place
regularly. *1525 Bernice St., tel. 808/848–4129. Admission:
$4.95 adults, $2.50 children 6–17, including the planetarium.
Open Mon.–Sat. 9–5 and the first Sun. of each month, which is
"Family Sunday." Closed Christmas. By car, take Lunalilo
Fwy. to Houghtailing exit. Make an immediate right on
Houghtailing St., then a left onto Bernice St. By public transportation, take Bus No. 2 ("School Street") from Waikiki. Get
off at the Kamehameha Shopping Center, walk makai (toward
the ocean) 1 block to Bernice St., then go left.*

Tour 4: A Driving Tour of the East Oahu Ring

*Numbers in the margin correspond with points of interest on
the Oahu map.*

From Waikiki, there are two routes to Lunalilo Freeway (H-1).
On the Diamond Head end, go mauka (toward the mountains)
on Kapahulu Avenue and follow the signs to the freeway. On
the ewa (away from Diamond Head) end, take Ala Wai Boulevard and turn mauka at Kalakaua Avenue, staying on it until it
ends at Beretania Street, which is one-way going left. Turn
right off Beretania at Piikoi Street, and the signs will direct
you onto the freeway heading west.

Take the freeway exit marked **Pali Highway,** one of two roads
that cut through the Koolau Mountains.

❶ On the right is the **Queen Emma Summer Palace.** The colonial-
style white mansion, which once served as the summer retreat
of King Kamehameha IV and his wife, Queen Emma, is now a
museum maintained by the Daughters of Hawaii. It contains
many excellent examples of koa furniture of the period, including the beautiful cradle of Prince Albert, heir to the throne,
who died at age four. *2913 Pali Hwy., tel. 808/595–3167. Ad-*

mission: $4. Guided tours daily 9–4. Closed Thanksgiving, Christmas, New Year's Eve, Easter, and July 4.

As you drive toward the summit of the highway, the road is lined with sweet ginger during the summer and red poinsettias during the winter. If it has been raining, waterfalls will be tumbling down the sheer, chiseled cliffs of the Koolaus, creating a veritable wonderland in green.

② Watch for the turn to the **Pali Lookout** (Nuuanu Pali). There is a small parking lot and a lookout wall from which you can see all the way up and down the windward coast—a view that Mark Twain called the most beautiful in the world. It was in this region that King Kamehameha I drove defending forces over the edges of the 1,000-foot-high cliffs, thus winning the decisive battle for control of Oahu.

As you descend the highway on the other side of the mountain, continue straight along what becomes Kailua Road. If you are interested in Hawaiian history, look for the YMCA at the big Castle Hospital junction of Kalanianaole Highway and Kailua **③** Road. Behind it is **Ulu Po Heiau.** Though it may look like a pile of rocks to the uninitiated, Ulu Po Heiau is a sacred platform for the worship of the gods that dates back to ancient times.

④ If you're ready for a detour to **Kailua Beach,** which many people consider the best on the island, continue straight on Kailua Beach Road, no matter how many times the road changes its name, until it forms a "T" with Kalaheo Avenue.

Make a right on Kalaheo and continue until you come to the corner of Kailua Road. On one side is the **Kalapawai Market.** Generations of children have gotten their beach snacks here, and you might like to as well, since there's no concession stand at Kailua Beach. Across the street is the **Kailua Beach Center,** where you can rent windsurfing equipment and arrange for lessons at either **Naish Hawaii** (tel. 808/262–6068) or **Kailua Sailboards** (tel. 808/262–2555; *see* Sports, below, for further information). **Wild Bill's Sandwich Saloon** (tel. 808/261–5518) will fix you up with a great lunch to take to the beach.

Past the market, the road crosses a little bridge. On your left is Kailua Beach Park, where there are showers and picnic areas, plus a small parking lot (*see* Beaches, below).

Retracing your route back to Castle Junction, turn left at the intersection onto Kalanianaole Highway. Soon you will come to **⑤** the town of **Waimanalo,** traditionally a depressed area. Down the side roads, heading mauka, are little farms that grow a variety of fruits and flowers. Toward the back of the valley, flanked by cliffs, are small ranches with grazing horses. In a small shopping plaza on the makai (ocean) side of the road, there's a **Dave's Ice Cream** (41–1537 Kalanianaole Hwy., tel. 808/259–8576), which has some of the best ice cream in the Islands, including such exotic, tropical flavors as lychee and mango.

If you see any trucks selling corn on the cob and you're staying at a place where you can cook it, be sure to get some. It may be the sweetest you'll ever eat, and the price is the lowest on Oahu.

⑥ Bellows Beach (off Kalanianaole Hwy. in Bellows Air Force Station) is open to the public on weekends and holidays. The entrance is on the makai (ocean) side of the highway. The beach is

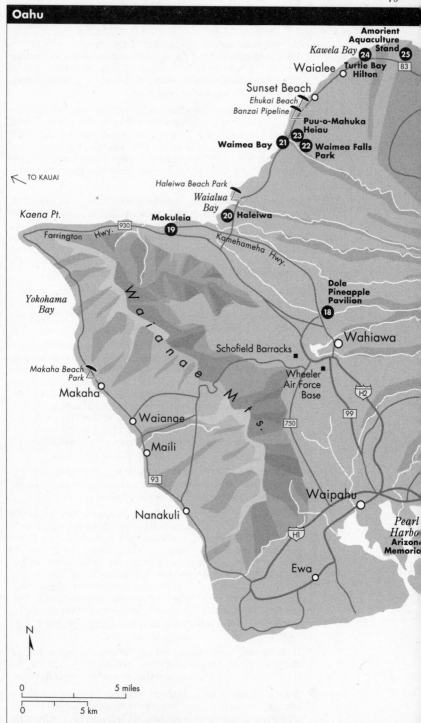

Oahu

Amorient Aquaculture Stand **25**

Kawela Bay **24**

83

Waialee · **Turtle Bay Hilton**

Sunset Beach

Ehukai Beach

Banzai Pipeline · **Puu-o-Mahuka Heiau**

Waimea Bay **21** **23** **22** **Waimea Falls Park**

Haleiwa Beach Park

Waialua Bay **20** **Haleiwa**

Mokuleia **19**

← TO KAUAI

Kaena Pt.

Farrington Hwy. 930

Kamehameha Hwy.

Dole Pineapple Pavilion **18**

Yokohama Bay

W a i a n a e

Schofield Barracks ◾ ○ **Wahiawa**

Wheeler Air Force Base ◾

Makaha Beach Park

Makaha

M t s.

750

H2

99

Waianae

Maili

93

Waipahu ○

Pearl Harbor

Arizona Memorial

Nanakuli

H1

Ewa ○

N

0   5 miles

0   5 km

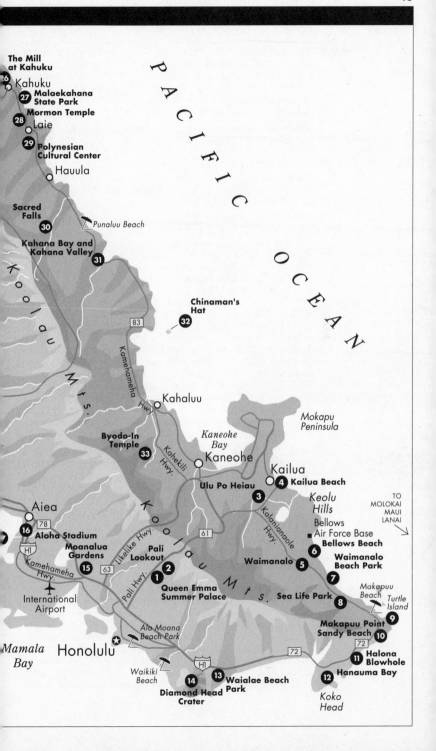

PACIFIC OCEAN

The Mill at Kahuku
26
Kahuku
27 Malaekahana State Park
Mormon Temple
28 Laie
29 Polynesian Cultural Center
Hauula

Sacred Falls
30
↟ Punaluu Beach

Kahana Bay and Kahana Valley
31

Chinaman's Hat
32

Koolau Mts.

Kamehameha Hwy.
83

Kahaluu

Byodo-In Temple
33

Kahekili Hwy.

Kaneohe Bay
Kaneohe

Mokapu Peninsula

Ulu Po Heiau
3

Kailua
4 Kailua Beach

Keolu Hills

TO MOLOKAI MAUI LANAI

Aiea
16 78
Aloha Stadium
Moanalua Gardens
15 63

H1
Kamehameha Hwy.
7

Pali Hwy.
Likelike Hwy.
Pali Lookout

1 2
Queen Emma Summer Palace

61

Koolau Mts.

Kalanianaole Hwy.

Bellows Air Force Base
Bellows Beach

Waimanalo **5**
6 Waimanalo Beach Park
7

Sea Life Park **8**

Makapuu Beach
↟ Turtle Island
9

International Airport

Mamala Bay
Honolulu ★

Ala Moana Beach Park

Waikiki Beach

14 **13** Waialae Beach Park
Diamond Head Crater

H1

72

Makapuu Point Sandy Beach
10
72
11 Halona Blowhole

12 Hanauma Bay

Koko Head

uncrowded and great for swimming and bodysurfing. There's plenty of shade as well as picnic areas (*see* Beaches, below).

Time Out Just past the entrance to Bellows Beach, on the makai side of the highway, is **Bueno Nalo** (41–865 Kalanianaole Hwy., tel. 808/259–7186), a funky Mexican eatery with fantastic south-of-the-border specialties at low prices. The space is small and unpretentious, but the food is terrific. It's BYOB; stop next door at Jimmy's Market if you'd like a cold one.

For dessert (if you're still hungry), go next door to **Ken's,** a no-frills bakery with delicious cinnamon rolls (tel. 808/259–9084).

7 A block farther and you reach **Waimanalo Beach Park,** on the makai side of the road. The beach is safe for swimming, although the park area often draws young toughs. Pass it by (*see* Beaches, below).

8 Another mile down the highway takes you to **Sea Life Park,** a marine attraction definitely worth a stop. Its finned menagerie includes the world's only "wholphin," the offspring of a romance between a whale and a dolphin. Children will especially enjoy watching dolphins leap and spin, penguins frolic, and a killer whale perform impressive tricks at the shows in the outdoor amphitheater. There's also an 11,000-gallon exhibit called "The Rocky Shores" recreating the surf-swept marine ecology of Hawaii's shoreline. The Pacific Whaling Museum teaches you about the fascinating history of whaling in Hawaii. Snacks and sodas are available, and there's a sit-down restaurant called The Galley. Even if you've seen trained cetaceans at other marine parks, the distinctively Hawaiian flavor makes this place special. The setting alone, right across from the ocean and Rabbit Island, is worth the price of admission. *Makapuu Point, Waimanalo, tel. 808/259–7933. Admission: $9.95 adults, $7.75 juniors 7–12, $3.75 children 4–6. Open Sat.–Thurs. 9:30–5, Fri. 9:30–10 PM. Live local music in the Galley Restaurant, Fri. 8:30 PM. Cost: $4.*

From the cliffs above Sea Life Park, colorful hang gliders often soar in the breezes. It takes a lot of daring to leap from these imposing heights, and there have been several fatalities here. Nestled in the cliff face above the water is the Makapuu Lighthouse (not open to the public).

Across the highway from Sea Life Park is **Makapuu Beach,** a beautiful cove that is great for seasoned bodysurfers but treacherous for the weak swimmer (*see* Beaches, below). Parking is hard to find, too, so just keep driving. The road winds up a hill, at the top of which is a pull-off on the makai side of the
9 road. This is **Makapuu Point,** a fabulous photo opportunity, with breathtaking views of the mountains and bay, ocean and islands, including the large Rabbit Island and the smaller Turtle Island. The peninsula jutting out in the distance is Mokapu, site of a U.S. Marine base. The spired mountain peak is Mount Olomana. In front of you on the long pier is part of the Makai Undersea Test Range, a research facility that is closed to the public. The facility recently launched a manned submersible to study Loihi, the active undersea volcano that is forming another Hawaiian island. Loihi should surface in about a thousand years.

Continue along the highway past the **Hawaii Kai Championship Golf Course** (tel. 808/395–2538), on the mauka side of the road (*see* Sports, below). Across the highway is the area known as **Queen's Beach**. In recent years, developers and conservationists have fought over the shoreline here. During the 1988 elections the people of Oahu voted to make it conservation land.

⑩ Next you'll see a long stretch of inviting sand called **Sandy Beach**. Tempting as this beach looks, it is not advisable to swim here. Notice that the only people in the water are local and young. They know the powerful and tricky waves well. Even so, the fierce shore break lands many of them in the hospital every year with back and neck injuries. The steady onshore winds make Sandy Beach a popular place to fly kites (*see* Beaches, below).

Time Out   Across Kalanianaole Highway from Sandy Beach is a fleet of **carryout trucks** offering fast-food specialties ideal for a break from the car. They're lined up along the shoulder, with colorful banners and enormous signs boasting their menus. On any given day they'll be selling shave ice (snow cones), plate lunches, cold sodas, and such dim sum goodies as *manapua* (dough wrapped around diced pork) and pork hash. Indulge yourself. You still have some traveling to do.

After Sandy Beach, the road takes you along the **Koko Head shoreline**—untamed and open to the ocean. This is a favorite stretch of coastline for visitors and residents alike, because the road twists and turns next to steep cliffs. Offshore, the islands of Molokai and Lanai call like distant sirens, and every once in a while, Maui is visible in blue silhouette. Pull into at least one scenic turnoff.

⑪ One stop features the famous **Halona Blowhole,** a lava tube that sucks in the ocean and then spits it out in lofty plumes. The blowhole may or may not perform, depending on the currents. If you do get out here, lock up, because the spot is frequented by thieves.

Soon on the makai side of the road you will see a sign for **⑫** **Hanauma Bay.** If you make only one stop during your drive, this one should be it. Even from the overlook, the horseshoe-shaped bay is a beauty, and you can easily see the reefs through the clear aqua waters. You can also see the crowds of people snorkeling and sunbathing, but it's still worth a visit (*see* Beaches and Sports, below).

From here back to Waikiki the highway passes several residential communities. First there is the sprawling **Hawaii Kai** development. Ancient Hawaiian fish ponds once flourished in this valley, but now the waterways are lined with suburban homes with two cars in the garage and a boat out back. The next communities are **Niu Valley** and **Aina Haina,** each of which has a small shopping center with a food store if you need a drink or a snack. Best to keep driving, however, because during rush hour, Kalanianaole Highway becomes choked with commuter traffic.

Right before you turn off from Kalanianaole Highway you'll notice a long stretch of green on the makai side. This is the private **Waialae Country Club** (4997 Kahala Ave., tel. 808/734–

2151), scene of the annually televised Hawaiian Open golf tournament (*see* Sports, below). Take the Kahala exit, right before the highway becomes the freeway. Turn left at the stoplight onto Kilauea Avenue. Here you'll see **Kahala Mall** (4211 Waialae Ave.), an upscale shopping complex with yuppie eateries, high-fashion stores, and five movie theaters.

Take a left on Hunakai Street and follow it to Kahala Avenue. If you want to hit one more beach, turn left and drive several blocks to **Waialae Beach Park,** where there is a shower house, beach pavilion, and nice sand for strolling. People enjoy windsurfing here. Just down the road is the fancy Kahala Hilton Hotel, where movie stars and royalty stay when they're in town.

Kahala Avenue takes you back toward Waikiki through **Kahala,** Oahu's wealthiest neighborhood. Here the oceanfront homes have lately been selling for more than $15 million, mostly to Japanese investors. At intervals along this tree-lined street are narrow lanes that provide public access to the beach.

As you reach a small, triangular park on the right, you have the option of continuing straight on what becomes Diamond Head Road or turning right on Monsarrat Avenue. A right turn will take you up to the top of a hill, where there is a sign pointing left to **Diamond Head Crater.** The famous extinct volcano got its common name from sailors who thought they had found precious gems on the slope; the diamonds proved to be volcanic refuse. If you're feeling energetic, drive through the tunnel to the inside of the crater and take the half-hour (one-way) hike to the lookout at the top. From 760 feet, you'll get a tremendous view of where you've been and where you're going. *Monsarrat Ave. near 18th Ave., tel. 808/548–7455. Admission free. Open daily 6–6.*

If you continue straight along Diamond Head Road from the triangular park, you will crest a hill next to Diamond Head Crater. Pull off at one of the two scenic turnouts on the makai side of the road for a pretty view of the multicolored sails of the windsurfers below. A bit farther on the makai side is the picturesque **Diamond Head Lighthouse,** one of the oldest in the Pacific.

Drive along the road to Kapiolani Park, and stay on the right side of the park until you hit Kapahulu Avenue. Take a left, and you're back in Waikiki.

Tour 5: Circle Island Driving Tour

Numbers in the margin correspond with points of interest on the Oahu map.

Follow the directions to the H-1 Freeway heading west that appear at the beginning of the East Oahu Ring Tour. The freeway will diverge into Moanalua Freeway (Route 78). Stay on this past **Moanalua Gardens,** a lovely park with huge, spreading monkeypod trees. A hula festival is held on the ancient hula mound during the third weekend in July. Hikes are offered into historic Moanalua Valley; call for specific times. *1401 Mahiole, Honolulu, tel. 808/833–1944. Admission free. Open weekdays 8–4.*

16 On your left you'll pass **Aloha Stadium.** This 50,000-seat park has movable stands, and the seating configuration changes at the touch of a switch to conform to the type of event, be it a football or baseball game or a rock concert. There's no reason to stop here unless there's a game you plan to attend.

Across the street from the stadium is **Castle Park.** If you're used to big mainland amusement parks, this small one won't appeal to you. But it does have a great "grand prix," bumper boats, putt-putt golf, and a video arcade—perfect for children. *4561 Salt Lake Blvd., tel. 808/488–7771. Admission free to the park, then you pay for each attraction. Open daily 10–10.*

As you approach the stadium on the freeway, bear right at the sign to Aiea, then merge left onto Kamehameha Highway (Route 90) going south to Pearl Harbor. Turn right at the
17 Halawa Gate for a tour of the ***Arizona* Memorial,** a must-see stop. The gleaming white memorial shields the hulk of the USS *Arizona*, which sank with 1,102 men aboard when the Japanese attacked Pearl Harbor. The tour includes a 20-minute documentary and a shuttle-boat ride to the memorial. Afterward, you may also tour the USS *Bowfin*, a World War II submarine moored near the Visitor Center. You will be issued a "wand" for a self-guided tour that takes you through the vessel, including the torpedo room and engine room. *USS* Arizona *Memorial and Visitor Center, U.S. Naval Reservation, Pearl Harbor, tel. 808/422–0561. Admission free. Open daily 8–3. Tues. is the most crowded, with afternoon waits sometimes as long as 2 hours. Late in the week and early in the day are your best bets. For safety reasons, no children under 45 in. tall are permitted aboard the shuttle or the memorial. Also prohibited are people in bathing suits or with bare feet.*

After Pearl Harbor, retrace your steps and take either Kamehameha Highway or the H-2 Freeway to Wahiawa, home of the U.S. Army base at **Schofield Barracks.** This old plantation town has a distinctly military flavor.

Time Out | **Kemoo Farms** (1718 Wilikina Dr., Wahiawa, tel. 808/621–8481), a pleasant restaurant for lunch, is situated right on the main road in Wahiawa. Although there is no longer live music, this family-style, no-frills eatery on the shores of Lake Wilson still has a genuine feeling of aloha. It's closed Saturday.

If you're really into plants, stop by the **Wahiawa Botanical Gardens.** *1396 California Ave., Wahiawa, tel. 808/621–7321. Admission free. Open daily 9–4.*

For a modest glimpse of ancient Hawaiiana, take Kamehameha Highway, now Route 80, just over the bridge and turn onto the dirt road on the left. It's a short ride to the **Hawaiian Birth Stones,** once a sacred site for royal births.

Back on the main road, there is a scrubby-looking patch ambitiously called the **Del Monte Pineapple Variety Garden.** Unpromising as it looks, it's actually quite interesting, with varieties of the ubiquitous fruit ranging from thumb-size pink ones to big golden ones.

18 Turn left on Kamehameha Highway and you'll see the **Dole Pineapple Pavilion,** a big hit with Oahu sightseers since 1951. It has become even bigger with a new visitor pavilion, pineapple variety garden, 10,000-square-foot plantation gift shop, and restaurant. All of this, along with tram tours of an agricultural field, is a vast improvement over the old Dole Visitor Center. *64-1550 Kamehameha Hwy., tel. 808/621-8408. Admission free. Open daily 9-5:30.*

From here, the road north cuts through acres of pineapple fields, followed by more acres of sugarcane. Once you hit the traffic circle, you have some choices to make. If you go around the circle and continue to **Mokuleia,** you'll come to the **polo fields** (*see* Sports, below). Beyond that is the **Dillingham Airfield,** where you can watch the gliders or book a sailplane ride and try it yourself. *Glider Rides, Dillingham Airfield, Mokuleia, tel. 808/677-3404. Cost: $40 for one passenger, $60 for two. Open daily 10:30-5:30. No reservations, with 20-min flights every 20 minutes.*

Another option at the circle is to follow the signs to **Haleiwa,** a sleepy old plantation town that has come of age. In the 1920s it was a fashionable retreat at the end of a railroad line that no longer exists. During the '60s, the hippies gathered here. Now, Haleiwa is a fun mix of old and new. Old general stores peacefully coexist with contemporary boutiques and art galleries. Among the highlights are a pair of great fashion stores, **O'ogenesis** (66-249 Kamehameha Hwy., tel. 808/637-4580) and **RIX** (66-145 Kamehameha Hwy., tel. 808/637-9260). At a wonderful Haleiwa restaurant named **Jameson's by the Sea** (62-540 Kamehameha Hwy., tel. 808/637-4336), you can sit on the porch, sip a drink, and watch the boats go by.

Time Out For a real slice of Haleiwa color, stop at **Matsumoto's** (66-087 Kamehameha Hwy., tel. 808/637-4827). Many sources claim that this place serves the best shave ice—a tropical snow cone, only better. They shave the ice right before your eyes and offer every flavor imaginable, including banana, mango, papaya, coconut, or combinations thereof. If you want to do it right, get it with vanilla ice cream and sweet azuki beans.

Leaving Haleiwa and continuing along Kamehameha Highway, you'll pass the famous north shore beaches, where the winter surf comes in size large. The first of these is **Waimea Bay,** a popular family picnic spot with a big, broad beach and fine facilities.

Across the street, on the mauka (mountain) side of the road, is **Waimea Falls Park.** An ancient Hawaiian community once thrived in Waimea Valley and today you can see remnants of that early civilization, as well as more than 2,500 species of flora from around the world. The garden trails are well marked, and the plants are labeled. An interesting assortment of animals roams the grounds, including the Hawaiian nene (goose), and there's a spectacular cliff-diving show at the 45-foot-high falls. Hawaiian games and dances are presented, there's a restaurant and picnic areas, and two evenings a month during the full moon, the park is open for free "moonwalks." *59-864 Kamehameha Hwy., Haleiwa, tel. 808/638-8511. Admission: $9.95 adults, $6 juniors 7-12. $2 children 4-6. Open daily 10-5:30.*

If you're interested in seeing a fine example of an ancient Hawaiian heiau (sacred stone platform for the worship of the gods), turn mauka (toward the mountains) at the Foodland store and take the Pupukea Road up the steep climb, not quite a mile, to the dirt road leading to the **Puu-o-Mahuka Heiau.** Once a site of human sacrifice, it is now on the National Register of Historic Places. The views are spectacular.

Continue along the coastal road past more famous surfing beaches, including **Ehukai** and **Sunset** (*see* Beaches, below). If it's wintertime, keep clear of those waves, which sometimes rise as high as 30 feet. Leave the sea to those daring (some say crazy) surfers who ride the towering waves with amazing grace.

㉔ The only hotel of any consequence in these parts is your next landmark: the **Turtle Bay Hilton** (57-091 Kamehameha Hwy., tel. 808/293–8811). If it's Sunday between 9 AM and 2 PM, you might want to stop for its incredibly extensive champagne brunch, served in a pretty oceanside dining room ($21 for adults, $11 for children under 12).

Time Out   Down the road from Turtle Bay is the **Amorient Aquaculture** ㉕ **Stand,** a fascinating example of what has become an extremely successful venture for Oahu. Amorient (Kamehameha Hwy., Kahuku) is one of several companies that grow prawns, shrimp, and other fish and sea creatures in controlled environments. The results are as tasty as their natural counterparts. Stop by this stand on the makai side of the road and take a cup of carry-out shrimp cocktail to one of the picnic benches. The stand also sells fresh prawns, shrimp, and fish that you can take back to your condominium and cook for dinner.

Across the road, there is often a small lean-to set up with **Kahuku watermelons** for sale. By all means, buy one. They're the juiciest, sweetest melons you'll find in the Islands.

The old Kahuku Sugar Mill on Kamehameha Highway, which shut down in 1971 and then enjoyed a brief stint as a tourist at-
㉖ traction, has reopened as **The Mill at Kahuku** (56-565 Kamehameha Hwy., tel. 808/293–2414), with a restaurant and businesses. Visitors may take a free self-guided tour from 10 to 6 of parts of the turn-of-the-century mill, with its steam engines and enormous gears. There's also a gift shop and a craft area. The Country Kitchen Restaurant is open for breakfast, lunch, and dinner and serves a variety of American dishes.

As you approach the town of Laie, on the makai (ocean) side is a long stretch of pine trees. Look for the entrance to
㉗ **Malaekahana State Park,** a lovely place to take a break from driving. You can park in the big lot and wander the shady grounds or stroll on the long beach. At low tide you can even wade to Goat Island. *Admission free. Open Oct.–Mar. 7–6:45; Apr.–Sept. 7–7:45.*

㉘ Coming up on the makai side is a road that leads to the **Mormon Temple** (55-415 Iosepa St., tel. 808/293–9167), a white structure made of pulverized volcanic rock and coral. It is a house of worship, not a visitor attraction. The Mormons also run Brigham Young University's Hawaii campus, in Laie.

㉙ The Mormons also operate the sprawling **Polynesian Cultural Center,** next on the makai side of the road. A visit to the center isn't cheap, but it's worth it to see the 40 acres of lagoons and seven re-created South Pacific villages representing Hawaii, Tahiti, Samoa, Fiji, the Marquesas, New Zealand, and Tonga. Shows and demonstrations enliven the area, and there's a spectacular evening dinner show. If you're short on time, you can try to sandwich this attraction into a driving tour, though you'll miss much of what makes it so popular. If you're staying in Honolulu, it's better to see the center as part of a van tour, so you won't have to drive home after the evening show. *55-370 Kamehameha Hwy., Laie, tel. 808/293–3333 or 808/923–1861. Cost: Standard Package (general admission to all villages and daytime shows plus American dinner) $37 adults, $15 children 5–11. Luau Package (general admission, afternoon shows, and the luau) $42 adults, $20 children 5–11. Ambassador Passport (this VIP ticket includes standard shows and attractions, plus a kukui-nut-lei greeting, an escorted tour, a special dinner, prime show seating, and more) $65 adults, $40 children 5–11. Open Mon.–Sat. 12:30–12:30.*

About 4 miles down the highway on the mauka (toward the mountains) side of the road, look for the Hawaii Visitors Bureau sign for **Sacred Falls.** This wild state park, with a strenuous 2-mile hike to an 80-foot-high waterfall, is Hawaiian country as you dreamed it would be. A swim in the pool beneath the falls is a welcome refresher after the hike. Be sure to hike with someone else, and don't attempt the trail if there has been rain; the valley is subject to flash flooding, and the trail can be slippery. *Admission free. Open Oct.–Mar., daily 7–6:45; Apr.–Sept., daily 7–7:45.*

A bit farther down the road you'll pass **Kahana Bay** and **Kahana Valley,** where ancient Hawaiians once lived. Don't bother stopping here; the water is too shallow for decent swimming, and the valley is not safe for hiking during hunting season.

The next thing to look for, although it's not spectacular, is the **Crouching Lion** mountain formation on the ridge line behind an inn of the same name. If someone tells you it has a deeply significant Hawaiian legend attached to it, don't believe them. The lion was an idea thought up by modern-day promoters. As you continue driving along the shoreline, you'll notice a picturesque little island called, for obvious reasons, **Chinaman's Hat.**

At the town of Waiahole is a little market with an unlikely name, Hygienic Store. Here you can branch off the Kahekili Highway (Route 83) and head for the Valley of the Temples and its lovely **Byodo-In Temple.** This replica of a 900-year-old temple in Kyoto, Japan, dramatically set against the sheer green cliffs of the Koolau Mountains, is surrounded by Japanese gardens and a two-acre lake stocked with prize carp. A two-ton statue of Buddha presides over all. *47-200 Kahekili Hwy., Kaneohe, tel. 808/239–8811. Admission: $2 adults, $1 children under 12. Open daily 8–4:30.*

Continue on Kahekili Highway to the Likelike Highway, where you turn mauka and head back toward Honolulu through the Wilson Tunnel. The highway leads to the Lunalilo Freeway going east. Exit at Pali Highway and go south through downtown Honolulu to Nimitz Highway, then turn left on Ala Moana Boulevard, which leads to Kalakaua Avenue in Waikiki.

Oahu for Free

Hawaii can be expensive, but a visitor on any budget can still enjoy the Islands. Here are a few of the gratis events of special interest to Oahu's guests.

***Arizona* Memorial.** *See* Tour 5, above.

Hilo Hattie's Fashion Factory Tour. The Hawaiian Islands' multimillion-dollar garment industry specializes in such tropical togs as muumuus, aloha shirts, and floral-design sportswear. You can find out how it's all made on this fun, 15-minute factory tour. Multicolored buses will provide transportation from your Waikiki hotel if you call ahead of time. *700 Nimitz Hwy., Honolulu, tel. 808/537–2926. Open daily 8:30–5.*

Honolulu Academy of Arts. Hawaii's premier art gallery houses a stunning collection of works from Hawaii, Asia, and the Pacific, with pieces dating from the 9th century to the present. The galleries are situated around six garden courtyards, and there is a Garden Cafe offering pleasant luncheons. *900 S. Beretania St., Honolulu, tel. 808/538–1006. Open Tues.–Sat. 10–4:30 and Sun. 1–5. Take the No. 2 bus from Waikiki.*

Kapiolani Park Rose Garden (Paki St. and Monsarrat Ave., Waikiki). Inaugurated in 1927 and used as a victory garden during World War II, this cozy outdoor park was officially dedicated to roses in 1971. If you come from an area where roses thrive, you've probably seen better. But the price is right, and there are picnic tables where you can relax. Open daily 24 hrs.

Polynesian Cultural Center Mini Show. The enthusiastic young entertainers from Hawaii's number-one paid visitor attraction stage a miniproduction. Of course they're hoping you'll rush right into their Waikiki ticket office and sign up for the complete package, but there's no pressure. *Royal Hawaiian Shopping Center, 2201 Kalakaua Ave., Bldg. C, 1st floor, tel. 808/922-0588. Tues., Thurs., Sat. 9:30 AM.*

Evening at City Hall. A free concert is offered on the fourth Thursday of each month in the courtyard of City Hall. *King and Punchbowl Sts., tel. 808/527-5666. Concerts start at 7 PM.*

National Memorial Cemetery of the Pacific. Better known as Punchbowl Crater, this is the final resting place for thousands of men and women who served in World War I, World War II, the Korean War, and the Vietnam War. The top of the crater affords an excellent view of Honolulu. Several guided tours stop at Punchbowl as part of their itineraries. *2177 Puowaina Dr., Honolulu, tel. 808/541-1430. Open daily 8-5:30.*

Royal Hawaiian Band. Spiffy musicians in aloha uniforms perform marches from the days of Hawaii's monarchy as well as popular tunes. These twice-weekly open-air concerts, featuring both singers and dancers, have become a tradition since the band's beginnings in the mid-1800s. *Coronation Bandstand, Iolani Palace grounds, tel. 808/922-5331. Fri. at noon. Also, Kapiolani Park Bandstand, Sun. at 2 PM.*

Royal Hawaiian Shopping Center (2201 Kalakaua Ave., tel. 808/ 922–0588). Every day of the week, this open-air Waikiki shopping mall is filled with gratis events, including hula lessons, ukulele lessons, Hawaiian language instruction, lei-making demonstrations, pineapple carving, and assorted arts and crafts classes. The free Polynesian Cultural Center minishow is staged there on Tuesday, Thursday, and Saturday mornings at 9:30 and 11:30.

U.S. Army Museum. What was once a pre–World War II bunker with 22-foot-thick concrete walls is now the home of a museum devoted to the nation's armed forces. Items from the American

Revolution, Spanish-American War, Boxer Rebellion, Philippine Insurrection, World Wars I and II, and the Korean and Vietnam wars are on display. *Randolph Bldg., Fort DeRussy, Kalia Rd., Waikiki, tel. 808/438–2821. Open Tues.–Sun. 10–4:30.*

What to Do and See with Children

Most Hawaiian attractions that charge admission offer reduced rates for children. "Children" is usually defined as under 13, although the categories are sometimes broken down into juniors (ages 7–12) and children (ages 4–6).

Castle Park. *See* Tour 5, above.

Children's Touch and Feel Museum. *See* Tour 2, above.

Honolulu Zoo. *See* Tour 1, above.

Kite Fantasy (2863 Kalakaua Ave., Waikiki, tel. 808/922–5483). Kids of all ages get a free kite-flying lesson (with no purchase required) when they visit this delightful sky-toy store, right across the street from Oahu's best kite-flying venue, Kapiolani Park.

Sea Life Park. *See* Tour 4, above.

Waikiki Aquarium. *See* Tour 1, above.

Waikiki Offshore Glass-bottom Cruise. This leisurely cruise along Waikiki's shoreline is perfect for families who want to explore the wonders of the Pacific deep. Large picture windows afford glimpses of exotic coral formations and tropical fish. *Departs from Kewalo Basin, tel. 808/947–9971. Cost: $9.95 adults, $5.50 children under 12. Daily 10, 11, 1:30, and 2:30.*

Off the Beaten Track

Dole Cannery Square. Oahu boasts the biggest pineapple in the world, weighing in at 28.5 tons and standing 199.3 feet tall, with 46 leaves sticking out of its crown. This mega-pineapple is actually a 100,000-gallon water tower built in 1928 by Hawaii Pineapple Company, the predecessor to Dole. More important, it marks the location of the cannery, at whose new visitor center you can learn all about the 103-year-old business history of Hawaii's fruit export. The center has a 27-projector film, exhibits, specialty shops, a food court, and a fascinating factory tour lasting 35 minutes. Complimentary Dole products are served at the end of the tour. *650 Iwilei Rd., Honolulu, tel. 808/531–8855. Free "Pineapple Transit" buses leave from Waikiki hotels on a regular schedule; ask at your hotel front desk for times. Entrance to the square is free; admission to tour and film, $5 adults and children 13–17. There are continuous cannery tours daily every 15 min, 9–4.*

Maui Divers' Jewelry Design Center. The folks who run this attraction like to say they'll take you "40 fathoms in five languages." Intrigued? Then stop by this center to discover how Hawaii's official state gemstone—coral—is mined. The 30-year-old company presents the story of coral in state-of-the-art video theaters. Then you move on to the manufacturing exhibit area, where goldsmiths and artisans make new jewelry designs, cut and polish coral, and set it with diamonds before your very eyes. In the last room the finished products are on display and for sale. *1520 Liona St., Honolulu, tel. 808/946-7979. Tours weekdays 10–3. Closed Sun. By car from Waikiki, take the Ala Wai Canal to Kalakaua Ave. and turn right. Turn left on Beretania, left on Keeaumoku, and left on Liona. By public transportation, take the No. 2 bus from Waikiki, get off at the corner of Beretania and Keeaumoku, and walk 3 blocks makai (toward the ocean) to Liona.*

Senator Fong's Plantation and Gardens. Though Fong hasn't been a senator for more than a dozen years, this enterprising 82-year-old ex-legislator hosts an agricultural attraction showcasing the splendors of Hawaii's rich soil and climate. Flowering vines, ethnic gardens, edible bushes, and tropical fruit trees cover 725 acres of windward Oahu. Guests get a 40-minute guided tour of the plantation and gardens in an open-air minibus. The visitor center includes a snack bar, rest rooms, and a gift shop. *47-285 Pulama Rd., Kahaluu, tel. 808/239-6775. Admission: $6.50 adults, $3 children 5–12. Open daily 9–4. 35 min from Honolulu on the way to the Polynesian Cultural Center, 2 mi past Byodo-In Temple.*

Urasenke Foundation Teahouse. In this oasis of tranquillity amid the commerce of Waikiki, ladies in kimonos perform an intricate tea ceremony in which every gesture has significance. The Urasenke Foundation is a centuries-old institution based in Kyoto, Japan, that hosts ritualized tea ceremonies based on the Zen philosophy of enlightenment through meditative living. The Waikiki teahouse, donated by the Kyoto foundation, was the first to be built outside Japan and gives you a good, basic introduction to Japanese culture. Wear something comfortable for sitting on the floor. *245 Saratoga Rd., tel. 808/923-3059. Cost: $1. Wed. and Fri. 10–noon.*

Shopping

Locals used to complain about the lack of shopping options in the Islands. Some even went so far as to hop on a plane and fly to the mainland to find the latest fashions or that perfect gift. Happily, those days are past, and Hawaii (particularly Oahu) has assumed its place as an international crossroads of the shopping scene.

As the capital of the 50th state, Honolulu is the number-one shopping town in the Islands. It features sprawling shopping malls, spiffy boutiques, hotel stores, family-run businesses, and a variety of other enterprises selling brand-new merchandise as well as priceless antiques and one-of-a-kind souvenirs and gifts. What makes shopping on Oahu so interesting is the unusual cultural diversity of its products and the many items unique to Hawaii.

As you drive around the island, you'll find souvenir stands and what appear to be discount stores for island products. Watch out, because you could end up buying something tacky and expensive. Start with the reliable stores listed below; they're bound to have what you're looking for, and a little extra.

Major shopping malls are generally open daily from 10 to 9, although some shops may close at 4 or 5.

Shopping Centers

Oahu's many fine shopping malls assemble a little of everything at a wide range of prices. Be sure to wander to the upper levels, where the rents are cheaper and the shops are usually smaller and more original.

In Waikiki The Royal Hawaiian Shopping Center (2201 Kalakaua Ave., tel. 808/922–0588), fronting the Royal Hawaiian and Sheraton Waikiki hotels, is three blocks long and contains 120 stores on three levels. There are such Paris shops as **Chanel** (tel. 808/923–0255) and **Louis Vuitton** (tel. 808/926–0621), as well as local arts and crafts from the **Little Hawaiian Craft Shop** (tel. 808/926–2662), which features Bishop Museum reproductions, Niihau shell leis (those super-expensive leis from the island of Niihau), feather hat bands, and South Pacific art. **Bijoux Jewelers** (tel. 808/926–1088) has a fun collection of baubles, bangles, and beads for your perusal. The **Friendship Store** (tel. 808/926–1255), one of the few Chinese government stores outside mainland China, showcases Chinese arts and crafts, from baskets to fine rugs. The **Accessory Tree** (tel. 808/922–6595) carries an assortment of belts, bags, and jewelry, some crafted from shells, others hand-painted, plus a limited selection of clothing.

The **Waikiki Shopping Plaza** (2270 Kalakaua Ave., tel. 808/923–1191) is across the street; its landmark is a 75-foot-high water-sculpture gizmo, which looks great when it's working. Two clothing shops worth checking out are **Chocolates for Breakfast** (tel. 808/923–4426), with its trendy, fairly expensive items from the high-fashion scene; and its sister store, **Villa Roma** (tel. 808/923–4447), equally trendy but younger and less pricey. There's a **Waldenbooks** (*see* Gift Ideas, below) and "Voyage," a show featuring Polynesian song and dance, at 6:45 and 8:30 PM, on the fourth floor.

The **Waikiki Trade Center** (at the corner of Kuhio and Seaside Aves., tel. 808/922–7444) is slightly out of the action and features shops only on the first floor. Included are such prizes as **It's Only a Paper Moon** (tel. 808/924–8521), with greeting cards that go beyond the usual Hallmark variety. **Bebe's Boutique** (tel. 808/926–7888), which leans to the leather look, is for the slim and affluent. **C. June Shoes** (tel. 808/926–1574) offers European designer shoes, clothing, handbags, belts, and accessories, featuring Carlo Fiori of Italy.

Waikiki also boasts three theme-park-style shopping centers. Right in the heart of the area is the **International Market Place** (2330 Kalakaua Ave., tel. 808/923–9871), a tangle of souvenir stalls under a giant banyan tree. It spills into adjacent **Kuhio Mall** (2301 Kuhio Ave., tel. 808/922–2724), which has more of the same beads, beach towels, and shirts. **King's Village** (131 Kaiulani Ave., tel. 808/944–6855) looks like a Hollywood stage set of monarchy-era Honolulu, complete with a changing-of-the-guard ceremony every evening at 6:15.

Around Honolulu **Ala Moana Shopping Center** (1450 Ala Moana Blvd., tel. 808/946–2811) is a gigantic open-air mall just five minutes from Waikiki on the No. 8 bus. The 50-acre center is on the corner of Atkinson and Ala Moana boulevards. All the main Hawaiian department stores are here, including **Sears** (tel. 808/947–0211) and **J. C. Penney** (tel. 808/946–8068). **Liberty House** (tel. 808/941–2345) is highly recommended for its selection of stylish

Hawaiian wear, and high fashion is available at **Chocolates for Breakfast** (tel. 808/947–3434). For stunning Hawaiian prints, try the **Art Board** (tel. 808/946–4863), and buy your local footwear at the **Slipper House** (tel 808/949–0155).

Also at Ala Moana is **Shirokiya** (tel. 808/941–9111), an authentic Japanese department store where someone is usually demonstrating the latest state-of-the-art kitchen gadget in at least two languages, one of them Japanese. The upper-level food section is like a three-ring circus of free samples, hawkers, and strange Japanese specialties, both fresh and tinned. The toy department whirls and clinks with windup wonders.

Ala Moana also features a huge assortment of local-style souvenir shops, such as **Hawaiian Island Creations** (tel. 808/941–4491) and **Irene's Hawaiian Gifts** (tel. 808/946–6818). Its **Makai Market** is a food bazaar, with central seating and 20 kitchens serving everything from pizza to health food, poi, ribs, sushi, and Thai food. Stores open their doors daily between 7 and 9:30 AM. The shopping center closes weekdays at 9 PM; Saturday it closes at 5:30, and Sunday at 5, with longer hours during the Christmas holidays.

Heading west, toward downtown Honolulu, you'll run into **Ward Centre** (1200 Ala Moana Blvd., tel. 808/531–6411) and **Ward Warehouse** (1050 Ala Moana Blvd., tel. 808/531–1611). Both are eclectic mixes of boutiques and restaurants. Two of their best-loved shops are **Thongs 'N Things** (tel. 808/524–8229), notable for its huge collection of casual footwear, and **Neon Leon** (tel. 808/545–7666), which features racks and racks of outrageous notecards.

Farther west awaits **Waterfront Plaza** (500 Ala Moana Blvd. between South and Punchbowl Sts., tel. 808/538–1441), a new conglomeration of fun retailers and eateries. Be sure to stop by **Nothing You Need** (tel. 808/533–0029), an ultra-high-tech shop of electronic toys, gadgets, and gizmos.

Kahala Mall (4211 Waialae Ave., tel. 808/732–7736) is located 10 minutes by car from Waikiki in the chic residential neighborhood of Kahala, near the slopes of Diamond Head. This single-story mall features such upscale clothing stores as **Liberty House** (tel. 808/941–2345; *see* listing in Ala Moana Shopping Center, above) and **Carol & Mary** (tel. 808/926–1264), which offers high-level fashions for those evenings out. **Reyn's** (tel. 808/737–8313) is the acknowledged place to go for men's resort wear; its aloha shirts have muted colors and button-down collars, suitable for most social occasions. Along with a fun assortment of gift shops, Kahala Mall also features eight movie theaters (tel. 808/735–9744) for post-shopping entertainment.

Around the Island A scattering of shopping centers serves the various residential communities of Oahu. Heading ewa (west) out of Honolulu you'll reach **Pearlridge Center** (1005 Moanalua Rd., Aiea, tel. 808/488–0981), featuring most of the same major stores as Honolulu's shopping centers. On the other side of the island, **Windward Mall** (46–056 Kamehameha Hwy., Kaneohe, tel. 808/235–1143) provides the Kaneohe and Kailua areas with the major department stores, assorted gift shops, and carryout-food stands. As you drive farther away from the city and toward the north shore, the shopping centers give way to small plaza with strings of independently run markets and boutiques.

Gift Ideas

Aloha Shirts and Muumuus For stylish local Hawaiian wear, look in **Liberty House** (*see* Shopping Centers, above); **Carol & Mary** (*see* Shopping Centers, above); and **Andrade** (several locations, including Ala Moana Shopping Center, tel. 808/926–1380). If you want something bright, bold, and cheap, there are a number of "garment-factory-to-you" outlets and street stalls in Waikiki. For a collector's item, check out **Bailey's Antique Clothing Shop** (2051 Kalakaua Ave., Waikiki, tel. 808/949–8172), which carries a huge selection of vintage aloha shirts from $3 to $500.

Books Several Island authors and photographers have produced successful word and picture books reflecting the mood and magic of the Islands. These books make special keepsakes. Two stores worth browsing in are **Honolulu Book Shops** (Ala Moana Shopping Center, tel. 808/941–2274, and Pearlridge Center, tel. 808/487–1548) and **Waldenbooks** (Kahala Mall, tel. 808/737–9550, and Waikiki Shopping Plaza, tel. 808/922–4154); they carry several Hawaiian titles.

Clothing Fashion is Hawaii's third-largest business, behind tourism and agriculture. Getting into costume is part of the fun of any Hawaiian vacation, and almost every visitor buys at least one Hawaiian garment. Local fashion specialties are muumuus (the lovely flowing, loose-fitting garment worn by Hawaiian women) and aloha shirts (sport shirts in tropical prints worn both in the office and at parties).

Hawaii is also one of the leaders in the manufacture of resort wear. Many shops carry seasonal clothing, woolens, and leathers, catering to the needs of visitors who might not have the leisure to shop at home. There's even a fur salon, **Jindo** (1500 Kapiolani Blvd., tel. 808/942–5601, and 2424 Kalakaua Ave., Rm. 216, tel. 808/926–5601).

Fruits and Nuts Pineapples, papayas, and coconuts are always a big hit with friends and family back home. However, be sure all fresh-fruit products have been inspected by the Department of Agriculture. **Fresh from Hawaii** (Woolworth Waikiki, 2424 Kalakaua Ave., Honolulu 96815, tel. 808/831–0444) and **Tropical Fruit Distributors** (429 Waiakamilo Rd., Honolulu 96817, tel. 808/847–3234) carry only inspected fruit, ready for shipment, and will deliver right to your hotel or to airport baggage check-in counters.

Jams are also a yummy way to carry home the taste of Hawaii, and such flavors as *poha* (tangy gooseberry), passion fruit, and guava are all available. **ABC Stores** (24 locations in Waikiki, tel. 808/538–6743) and **Woolworth** (2225 Kalakaua Ave., Waikiki, tel. 808/923–2331) put together beautiful gift boxes of jams, macadamia nuts, exotic teas, pancake syrups, and cookies.

Hawaiian Arts and Crafts One of the nicest gifts is something handcrafted of native **Hawaiian wood.** Koa and milo, two species of trees that grow only in Hawaii, have a beautiful color and grain. The great koa forests are dwindling because of such demand, however. Buying only antique Koa items will help preserve those forests. Or choose other local crafts: framed arrangements of delicate *limu* (seaweed), feather leis, polished kukui-nut leis, wooden bowls, and hula implements.

Some of the best selections of Hawaiian handiworks can be found at any of the regularly scheduled **crafts fairs** around the island. Consult the local newspaper for times and places. The best are held in Kapiolani Park in Waikiki and at the Bishop Museum, Mission Houses Museum, Thomas Square, and Ala Moana Park in Honolulu.

Haleiwa, on the North Shore, features several fun art stores along its main strip. The **Fettig Gallery** (66–030 Kamehameha Hwy., tel. 808/637–4933) is a longtime landmark, showcasing the works of local painters, potters, and sculptors. For silk-screen wall graphics in custom-made frames, try **Haleiwa Arts** (66-220 Kamehameha Hwy., tel. 808/637–4618).

Another artistic gift is a photograph or print depicting the beauties of the Islands. Two Ward Warehouse (1050 Ala Moana Blvd.) establishments, the **Frame Shack** (tel. 808/523–8866) and the **Art Board** (tel. 808/521–6203), offer a variety of options.

High Fashion Again, **Liberty House** is recommended, and **Carol & Mary** has been known for high quality and designer labels since 1937. **Altillo** (2139 Kuhio Ave., Waikiki, tel. 808/926–1680) carries a line of European menswear, with shirts ranging from $20 to more than $200. **Chocolates for Breakfast** (*see* Shopping Centers, above) offers wonderful women's clothing for those who don't care about the price tag. For the latest in shoes and bags, try **C. June Shoes** (*see* Shopping Centers, above), featuring an elegant array of unusual and expensive styles.

International Gifts Japanese goodies await you at **Iida** (Ala Moana Center, tel. 808/946–0888) and **Shirokiya** (Ala Moana Center, tel. 808/941–9111). **India Imports** features spangled shirts and smocks (Ala Moana Center, tel. 808/949–5777), and **The Friendship Store** (*see* Shopping Centers, above) features rare items produced in the People's Republic of China.

Jewelry You can buy gold chains by the inch and jade and coral trinkets by the dozen on street corners in Waikiki. **Bernard Hurtig's** (Kahala Hilton Hotel, Honolulu, tel. 808/732–0721) has a fine jewelry department, specializing in 18K gold and antique jade. Hurtig's boutique jewelry is a collection of fabulous fakes, many of them reproductions of famous pieces, priced from $35. **Maui Divers' Jewelry Design Center** (1520 Liona St., Honolulu, tel. 808/946–7979) features beautiful coral of black, pink, brown, white, and green in settings both simple and elaborate. Necklaces, rings, charms, earrings, and brooches are $25–$25,000. **Tiffany and Co.** (2365 Kalakua Ave., tel. 808/922–2722) is a showcase shop at the Sheraton Moana Surfrider. The store features lovely window displays, and some items are surprisingly inexpensive.

Resort Wear After you've surveyed **Liberty House**, try **Chapman's** (Ala Moana Center, tel. 808/941–4330, plus several hotel locations in Waikiki), a fine specialty shop for men's clothing. **McInerny** (Royal Hawaiian Shopping Center, tel. 808/926–1351) has a couple of theme shops and a clearance shop. **Andrade** (*see* Gift Ideas, above) has a compact but good inventory of both men's and women's resort fashions. Its hotel shops offer a particularly rewarding selection.

The hip young crowd frequents **O'ogenesis Originals** (66–249 Kamehameha Hwy., tel. 808/637–4580) and **Rix** (66–145 Kamehameha Hwy., tel. 808/637–9260), a pair of Haleiwa stores selling hand-painted fashions by North Shore talents.

Women who like clothing that is conservative and well designed rave about **Alfred Shaheen** (tel. 808/947–2433), with outlets at King's Village, Royal Hawaiian Shopping Center, Hyatt Regency Hotel, Sheraton-Waikiki Hotel, Outrigger Waikiki Hotel, and Ilikai Waikiki Hotel.

Beaches

Beaches are synonymous with Hawaii, and Oahu's selection delivers on that promise. Each has its own distinctive character, which means there's a beach for everyone. Singles looking for action generally head for the beaches in Waikiki, while families prefer the sheltered waters of Ala Moana Beach Park or Hanauma Bay. Bodysurfers find challenges at Makapuu and Sandy Beach, and windsurfers like the steady trade winds off Kailua Beach. Most of the 50-plus beach parks scattered around the island have excellent facilities, including indoor and outdoor showers, toilets and changing houses, lifeguards, picnic tables, and in some cases, snack bars and shady areas nearby for retreat from the noonday sun. Parking can sometimes be a problem, since beachgoing is the number-one sport on Oahu.

Thankfully, pollution is rarely a problem off Oahu's shores. The occasional flotilla of Portuguese men o'war come floating in when "Kona Winds" blow from the south, but otherwise the waters are remarkably clear and clean.

You should keep in mind some words of caution when approaching any Hawaiian beach. Before you stretch out beneath a swaying palm, check it for coconuts. The trade winds can bring them tumbling down on you with enough force to cause serious injury. And don't forget the sunscreen. The sun-protection factor in some new preparations goes as high as 52! It's a good idea to reapply sunscreen after swimming. Oahu is only 21 degrees north of the equator, and the ultraviolet rays are extremely potent.

Take notice of the signs posted on Oahu's beaches. If they warn of dangerous surf conditions or currents, pay attention. During the winter, the north shore beaches are pounded by huge surf that nobody (repeat, *nobody*) should enter. In fact, it's dangerous even to stand anywhere near the shore break during those months. However, the big winter waves—and the experienced surfers who dare to ride them—are a wonder to behold from a safe distance.

It's sad to say, but true: Beaches are a prime spot for theft. Try not to bring any valuables with you, and be sure to lock your car to avoid an unhappy vacation incident. Also, no alcoholic beverages are allowed on the beaches, which is why you may notice some people drinking out of brown paper bags.

On a happier note: All of Oahu's beaches are free, so you can plop down with aplomb in front of the most elegant hotel. The beaches do not have phone numbers, but if you want additional information about any of them, call the **Hawaii Department of Land and Natural Resources** (tel. 808/548–7837) and the **City and County Parks and Recreation Department** (tel. 808/527–6316). Listed below are the beaches a visitor would most enjoy, though there are certainly more options to choose from.

The word *makai*, used in directions given below, means "toward the ocean."

Waikiki Beaches

The 2½-mile stretch of sand called Waikiki Beach is actually a chain of beaches extending from the Hilton Hawaiian Village on one end to the base of Diamond Head on the other. The sands of Waikiki are harder, coarser, and more crowded than some of the less-frequented beaches out of town. On the other hand, food stands, beach amenities, and equipment rentals are much more accessible in Waikiki. The following beaches are listed in geographical order from west to east.

Kahanamoku Beach and Lagoon. The swimming is good here, the surf is gentle, and the snorkeling is not bad. You may find the water in the lagoon a touch too torpid, but it's perfect for small children, and you can lazily paddle around in a little boat. The area is named for Hawaii's famous Olympic swimming champion, Duke Kahanamoku. There's a snack concession, a surfboard and beach-equipment rental shop, showers, catamaran cruises, and a volleyball court. *Fronting the Hilton Hawaiian Village.*

Fort DeRussy Beach. This is the widest part of Waikiki Beach, and it trails off to a coral ocean bottom. There are volleyball courts, food stands, picnic tables, dressing rooms and showers, and snack concessions. The beach is frequented by military personnel but is open to everyone. *Fronting Fort DeRussy and the Hale Koa Hotel.*

Gray's Beach. A little lodging house called Gray's-by-the-Sea once stood on this site, and it left its name behind. The Hawaiians used to consider this a place for spiritual healing and baptism and called it *Kawehewehe* (the removal). High tides often cover the narrow beach here. Beyond the reef are two good surfing spots, called Paradise and Number Threes. You'll also find food concessions, surfboard and beach-equipment rental shops, and canoe and catamaran rides. *Fronting the Halekulani Hotel.*

Kahaloa and Ulukou Beaches. Probably the best swimming, and certainly the most activity, is at this little stretch of Waikiki Beach. There are snack bars, catamaran rides, and outrigger-canoe rides, and you can sign up for a surfing lesson. The Royal Hawaiian Hotel cordons off a small section of sand for its guests, bringing to mind a rich kid's sandbox. The heart of beach activities is the Waikiki Beach Center. Facilities include public rest rooms, changing rooms, showers, and a snack stand. The police station is located here. *Fronting the Royal Hawaiian Hotel and Sheraton Moana Surfrider.*

Kuhio Beach Park. A seawall jutting into the ocean acts as a breakwater to keep shoreside waters calm. The area is deceptive, though, and children should be watched closely, because there are unpredictably deep holes in spots. (There have been several drownings here.) Beyond the wall, surfers and bodysurfers ride the waves. The wall is a great place for sunset watching, but be careful of your footing. *Extending from the Waikiki Beach Center to the wall.*

Queen's Surf. Beyond the seawall, toward Diamond Head, is what is known as the other end of Waikiki, where beaches beginning with Queen's Surf Beach laze along the makai (south) side of Kapiolani Park. The sand is softer than by the hotels, and the beach slopes gently to the water. A mixture of families and gays gathers here, and it seems as if someone always has a bongo drum. There's a lawn, good shade trees, picnic tables, and a changing house with showers. This is a nice place for a sunset picnic. *Across from the entrance to the Honolulu Zoo.*

Sans Souci. This small rectangle of sand, a favorite with singles, is nicknamed Dig-Me Beach due to its outlandish display of skimpy bathing suits. The waters it borders are shallow and safe for children, and the spot draws many ocean kayakers and outrigger canoers. The beach also features a pair of outdoor showers (no changing house) and a grassy area that is popular with picnickers and volleyball buffs. The beach wall is a good vantage point for sunset watching. There's no food concession, but adjacent to one end of the beach is the Hau Tree Lanai, a wonderful open-air eatery that is part of the hotel. *Makai side of Kapiolani Park, between the New Otani Kaimana Beach Hotel and the Waikiki War Memorial Natatorium.*

Beaches Around Oahu

Here is an alphabetical listing of some of the finer beaches scattered around Oahu's shores.

Ala Moana Beach Park. Waikiki aside, this is the most popular beach for tourists. Residents love Ala Moana as well, because it features a protective reef, which keeps the waters calm. The sand is hard and packed, and bodies are everywhere, tanning, listening to radios, practicing acrobatics, eating picnics, and watching the surf action outside the reef. To the Waikiki side is a peninsula called Magic Island, with picnic tables, shady trees, and paved sidewalks ideal for jogging. Ala Moana also features playing fields, changing houses, indoor and outdoor showers, lifeguards, concession stands (owned by Burger King), and tennis courts. This is a beach for everyone; don't expect to find easy parking on the weekends. *Honolulu, makai side of Ala Moana Shopping Center and Ala Moana Blvd. For public transportation from Waikiki, take the No. 8 bus, get off at the shopping center, and walk across Ala Moana Blvd.*

Bellows Field Beach. Locals come here for the fine swimming on the weekends, when the Air Force opens the beach to civilians. The waves are great for bodysurfing, and the sand is soft for sunbathing. There are showers, abundant parking, and plenty of places for picnicking underneath shady ironwood trees. There are no food concessions here, but right outside the entrance gate is a McDonald's and some other carryouts. *Entrance is on Kalanianaole Hwy., near Waimanalo town center. It is marked with signs on the makai side of the road. Open to the public on weekends and holidays.*

Ehukai Beach Park. Ehukai is part of a series of beaches running for many miles along the north shore. There's a grassy area above the beach and a steep dune dropping down to it. The long, wide, and generally uncrowded beach has a changing house with showers and an outdoor shower and water fountain. Bring along a cooler with sodas, as there is virtually no shade here, and the nearest store is a mile away. The winter waves are fierce, and the lifeguards are constantly warning people to be careful. Right offshore is the famous Banzai Pipeline, site of international surfing competitions. *North shore, 1 mi north of the Foodland store at Pupukea. Turn makai off Kamehameha Hwy. onto the dirt road that parallels the highway. The small Ehukai parking lot is about 2 blocks away.*

Haleiwa Beach Park. The winter waves are impressive here, but in the summertime the ocean is like a lake, ideal for family swimming. The beach itself is big and pleasant and often full of locals. Broad lawns between the highway and the beach are busy with volleyball action, Frisbee games, and groups of barbecuers. There is a changing house with showers. No food concession, but Haleiwa has everything you need for provisions. *North shore, makai side of Kamehameha Hwy., north of Haleiwa town center and just past the boat harbor.*

Hanauma Bay. Crowds flock to this horseshoe-shaped, palm-lined, sunken crater rimmed with a long, narrow crescent of packed sand. The main attraction here is the snorkeling, and the coral reefs are clearly visible through the turquoise waters. Beyond the reef is a popular site for scuba-diving classes. The bay is best early in the morning (7 AM), before the crowds arrive. There is a busy food concession on the beach, plus changing houses and indoor and outdoor showers. You can't rent equipment here, so do that before you leave town, or sign up with a Hanauma Bay snorkeling tour (*see* Sports, below). *Makai of Kalanianaole Hwy., at the top of the hill just east of Hawaii Kai. A big sign points to the parking lot. A jitney runs down the steep slope to the beach for 50¢, one-way. The Hanauma Bay Shuttle Service (tel. 808/737–6188) runs to and from Waikiki and costs $1.50 each way.*

Kahana Bay Beach Park. Parents often bring their children to wade in safety at this pretty beach cove with very shallow, protected waters. A grove of tall ironwood and pandanus trees keeps the area cool, shady, and ideal for a picnic. There are changing houses, showers, and picnic tables. An ancient Hawaiian fish pond, which was in use until the 1920s, is visible nearby. Across the highway is Kahana Valley, burgeoning with banana, breadfruit, and mango trees. *On the windward side of the island, makai of Kamehameha Hwy., just north of Kualoa Park.*

Kualoa Regional Park. Grassy expanses border a long, narrow stretch of beach with spectacular views of Kaneohe Bay and the Koolau Mountains. The highlight of the landscape/seascape is an islet called Mokoli'i (more commonly known as Chinaman's Hat), which rises like a little oceanic beret 206 feet above the water. At low tide you can wade out to the island on the reef. This is without doubt one of the island's most beautiful picnic, camping, and beach areas. The one drawback is that it's usually windy. Bring a cooler; no refreshments are sold here. There are places to shower, change, and picnic in the shade of palm trees. *On the windward side, makai of Kamehameha Hwy., just north of Waiahole.*

Kailua Beach Park. Steady breezes attract windsurfers by the dozens to this long, palm-fringed beach with gently sloping sands. You can rent equipment in Kailua and try it yourself (*see* Sports, below). Young athletes and members of the military enjoy this beach, as do local families, so it gets pretty crowded on the weekend. There are showers, changing houses, and picnic areas, but no concession stands. Buy your provisions at the Kalapawai Market nearby. *On the windward side, makai of Kailua town. Turn right on Kailua Rd. at the market, cross a bridge, then turn left into the beach parking lot.*

Makaha Beach Park. Tourists generally don't visit the 20-mile stretch of the Waianae coast because it has just one hotel, the Sheraton Makaha. It features a string of beaches where the swimming is generally decent in the summer, and the scene is much more local than in Honolulu. At Makaha Beach families string up tarps for the day, unload hibachis, set up lawn chairs, get out the fishing gear, and strum ukuleles while they "talk story," or chat. This quarter-mile-long beach has a changing house and showers and is the site of a yearly big-board surf meet (*see* Sports, below). *On the Waianae coast, 1½ hours west of Honolulu on the H-1 Fwy. and Farrington Hwy. On the makai side of the highway.*

Makapuu Beach. This tiny crescent cove at the base of high sea cliffs is a gem of a sunbathing spot. From the beach you can see Rabbit Island, a picturesque cay so named because some say it looks like a swimming rabbit. If you look up you might see a hang glider who has just launched from the cliffs above. Swimming at Makapuu should be reserved for strong strokers and bodysurfers, because the swells can be big and powerful here. Makapuu is a popular beach with the locals. Because the lot is small, parking can be tricky, and you may have to park on the narrow shoulder and walk down to the beach. There is a changing house with indoor and outdoor showers. *Makai of Kalanianaole Hwy., across from Sea Life Park, 2 mi south of Waimanalo.*

Malaekahana Beach Park. Families love to camp here, because there are groves of ironwood trees that provide lots of shade and breezes during the heat of the day. The beach itself is fairly narrow but long enough for a 20-minute stroll, one-way. The waves are never too big to swim in, and sometimes they're just right for the beginning bodysurfer. At low tide, you can wade out to tiny Goat Island, just offshore, and the water never gets much more than waist high. If you decide to wade, be sure to wear sneakers so you don't stub your toe on a rock. There are several changing houses and indoor and outdoor showers, plus picnic tables. *On the windward side. Entrance gates are makai of Kamehameha Hwy., ½ mi north of Laie. They're easy to miss, because you can't see the beach from the road.*

Sandy Beach. There's generally a rescue truck parked on the road by Sandy's, which means that people are swimming where they shouldn't and hurting themselves. The shore break is mean here, but that doesn't stop young men and women from jumping in. It should, however, stop *you* unless you are a strong swimmer. Sandy's is a popular spot for the high school and college crowd. Due to the strong, steady, onshore winds, it is a kite-flyer's paradise. There's a changing house with indoor and outdoor showers here, and food trucks across the highway. *Makai of Kalanianaole Hwy., 2 mi east of Hanauma Bay.*

Sunset Beach. This is another link in the chain of north shore beaches, which extends for miles. Sunset has a tiny parking lot, so it's easy to miss. It is popular for its gentle summer waves and crashing winter surf. The beach is broad, and the sand is soft. It's a fun place to look for puka shells, the ones with the holes in the middle. Across the street there are usually carry-out trucks selling shave ice, plate lunches, and sodas. No facilities except a portable outhouse. *On the north shore, 1 mi north of Ehukai Beach Park, on the makai side of Kamehame-ha Hwy.*

Waimanalo Beach Park. The lawn at Waimanalo plays host to hundreds of local people who set up minicamps for the day, complete with hibachis, radios, lawn chairs, coolers, and shade tarps. Sometimes these folks are not very friendly to tourists. However, the beach itself is more welcoming, and from here you can walk a mile along the shore for fantastic windward and mountain views. Boogie boarders and bodysurfers enjoy the predictably gentle waves of this beach. The grassy, shady grounds have picnic tables and shower houses. *On the wind-ward side. Look for the signs makai of Kalanianaole Hwy., just south of Waimanalo town.*

Waimea Bay. Made popular in that old Beach Boys song, "Surfin' U.S.A.," Waimea Bay is a slice of hang-ten heaven. Winter is when you should stand well away from the shore break and leave the 25-foot-high waves to the hotdogs. Try walking near the water and the lifeguards will shoo you away through their bullhorns. Summer is the time to swim and snor-kel in the calm waters. The beach is a broad crescent of soft sand, backed by a grassy, shady area with picnic tables, a changing house, and showers. Parking is almost impossible in the lot on weekends, so folks just park along the road and walk down. *On the north shore. Across the street from Waimea Falls Park, 3 mi north of Haleiwa, on the makai side of Kamehame-ha Hwy.*

Yokohama Bay. This Waianae-coast beach at the very end of the road feels remote and untouched, which may explain its lack of crowds. Locals come here to fish and swim in waters that are calm enough for children during the summer. Bring provisions, because the nearest town is a 15-minute drive away. The beach is narrow, and rocky in places. There's a changing house and showers, plus a small parking lot, but most folks just pull over and park on the side of the bumpy road. *On the Waianae coast, at the northern end of Farrington Hwy., about 7 mi north of Makaha.*

Sports

Participant Sports

Biking The good news is that the coastal roads are flat and well paved. On the downside, they're also awash in vehicular traffic. Frank-ly, biking is no fun in either Waikiki or Honolulu, but things are a bit better outside the city. Be sure to take along a nylon jacket for the frequent showers on the windward side and remember that Hawaii is Paradise After the Fall: Lock your bike, or be prepared to hike.

Mountain bikes are available for rent at **Aloha Funway Rentals** (1778 and 1984 Kalakaua Ave., Waikiki, tel. 808/942–9696 and 947–4579). Day rate: $12.95 for a 10-speed. You can buy a bike or, if you brought your own, you can get it repaired at **Eki Cyclery Shop** (1603 Dillingham Blvd., Honolulu, tel. 808/847– 2005). If you want to find some biking buddies, write ahead to the **Hawaii Bicycling League** (Box 4403, Honolulu 96813, tel. 808/988–7175). This organization can tell you about upcoming races, which are frequent on all the Islands.

Fitness Centers **Clark Hatch Physical Fitness Center** has complete weight-training facilities, an indoor pool, a racquetball court, aerobics classes, treadmills, and indoor running apparatus. *745 Fort St., Honolulu, tel. 808/536–7205. Daily, weekly, and monthly guest rates work out to approximately $7 a day. Open weekdays 6 AM—8 PM, Sat. 7:30 AM–5:30 PM.*

World Gym is Waikiki's most accessible fitness center. In fact, 80% of its business comes from tourists. Full free-weight facilities, Nautilus machines, Universal gyms, and a pro shop are open to men and women. *1701 Ala Wai Blvd., Honolulu, tel. 808/942–8171. $9 a day, $35 a week, $50 for 2 weeks. Open daily 24 hrs.*

Among the hotels that have established fitness centers are the following:

Halekulani Hotel (2199 Kalia Rd., Waikiki, tel. 808/923–2311) has aerobics classes three times a week. Universal weight machines, a treadmill, two exercise bikes, and a massage room are available, for guests only.

Hilton Hawaiian Village (2005 Kalia Rd., Waikiki, tel. 808/949–4321) has an extensive fitness center open to those staying in the hotel's Alii Tower, including a Nautilus weight room and a Jacuzzi.

Kahala Hilton (5000 Kahala Ave., Kahala, tel. 808/734–2211) has an excellent, sophisticated fitness center available for its guests. The hotel is affiliated with Maunalua Bay Club, which has tennis courts, a swimming pool, aerobics classes, Nautilus machines, rowing machines, and treadmills. The Kahala offers a shuttle to the club, which is only 5 minutes away from the hotel.

Golf Oahu is honeycombed with golf holes. It has more golf courses than any other Hawaiian Island—more than two dozen—most of them open to the public. One of the most popular facilities is the **Ala Wai Golf Course** (404 Kapahulu Ave., tel. 808/296–4653) on Waikiki's mauka (north) end, across the Ala Wai Canal. It's par 70 on approximately 6,424 yards and has a pro shop and a restaurant. Greens fees: $18 weekdays; $20 weekends and holidays; carts $11. The waiting list is long, so if you plan to play, call the minute you land.

You'll stand a better chance of getting to play at the 6,350-yard **Hawaii Kai Championship Course** or the neighboring 2,386-yard **Hawaii Kai Executive Course** (8902 Kalanianaole Hwy., Honolulu, tel. 808/395–2358 for either). Fees are $50 with a cart for the former and $17.50 with a cart for the latter. Another good buy is the **Olomana Golf Links** on the windward side (41-1801 Kalanianaole Hwy., Waimanolo, tel. 808/259–7926). Fees, including carts, are $39 weekdays, $49 weekends and holidays. The **Sheraton Makaha Resort and Country Club** has an exceptional course in a beautiful valley setting (84-626 Makaha Valley Rd., Waianae, tel. 808/695–9544). Rates, including cart: $45 for guests, $95 for nonguests. The 18-hole golf course at the **Turtle Bay Hilton** (57–091 Kamehameha Hwy., Kahuku, tel. 808/293–8811) costs $65 for hotel guests, $80 weekdays, $90 weekends for nonguests, with cart.

Horseback Riding   **Kualoa Ranch** (49–560 Kamehameha Hwy., Kaaawa, tel. 808/ 237–8515; in Honolulu, tel. 808/538–7636), on the windward side, across from Kualoa Beach Park, features trail rides in Kaaawa, one of the most beautiful valleys in all Hawaii. (Cost: $15 per hour.) It also has an activities club. For $90 a day, you can go horseback riding, fly in a helicopter, ride a dune buggy, go snorkeling, try the shooting range, and have lunch (weekdays only). **Sheraton Makaha Lio Stables** (Box 896, Waianae, tel. 808/695–9511 ext. 7646) offers escorted rides into Makaha Valley; a one-hour guided trail ride costs $18.50 per person, and sunset rides are available. **Turtle Bay Hilton** (57–091 Kamehameha Hwy., Kahuku, tel. 808/293–8811) has 75 acres of hotel property (including a private beach) for exploring on horseback, at $20 per guest, $22 per nonguest, per 45 minutes.

Jogging   In Honolulu, the most popular places are the two parks, **Kapiolani** and **Ala Moana,** at either end of Waikiki. In both cases, the loop around the park is just under 2 miles. You can also run a 4.6-mile ring around **Diamond Head Crater,** past scenic views, luxurious homes, and herds of other joggers. If you jog along the 1.5-mile **Ala Wai Canal,** you'll probably glimpse outrigger-canoe teams practicing on the canal. If you're looking for jogging companions, show up for the free **Honolulu Marathon Clinic** that starts at the Kapiolani Park Bandstand (Mar.–Nov., Sun. 7:30 AM).

Once you leave Honolulu, it gets trickier to find places to jog that are scenic as well as safe. Best to stick to the well-traveled routes, or ask the experienced folks at the **Running Room** (559 Kapahulu Ave., Honolulu, tel. 808/737–2422) for advice.

Tennis   In the Waikiki area there are 4 free public courts at **Kapiolani Tennis Courts** (2748 Kalakaua Ave., tel. 808/923–7927); 9 at the **Diamond Head Tennis Center** (3098 Paki Ave., tel. 808/923–7927); and 10 at **Ala Moana Park** (tel. 808/521–7664). Several Waikiki hotels have tennis facilities open to nonguests, but guests have first priority. The **Ilikai Waikiki Hotel** (1777 Ala Moana Blvd., tel. 808/949–3811) has seven courts, one lighted for night play, plus a pro shop, daily tennis clinics, instruction, a ball machine, and a video. The hotel also offers special tennis packages that include room and court fees. There's one court at the **Hawaiian Regent Hotel** (2552 Kalakaua Ave., tel. 808/922–6611), with lessons and clinics by Peter Burwash International. The two courts at the **Pacific Beach Hotel** (2490 Kalakaua Ave., tel. 808/922–1233) also offer instruction.

Water Sports   The seemingly endless ocean options can be arranged through any hotel travel desk or beach concession or at the **Waikiki Beach Center,** next to the Sheraton Moana Surfrider.

Deep-Sea Fishing   For fun on the high seas, try **Coreene-C Sport Fishing Charters** (tel. 808/536–7472), **Island Charters** (tel. 808/536–1555), or **Tradewind Charters** (tel. 808/533–0220). Another reliable outfit is **ELO–1 Sport Fishing** (tel. 808/947–5208). All are berthed in Honolulu's Kewalo Basin. Plan to spend $85–$110 per person to share a boat for a full day (7 AM–3:30 PM). Half-day rates are

$50–$65. Boat charters run $425–$595 for a full day and $325–$495 for a half day. All fishing gear is included, but lunch is not. The captain usually expects to keep the fish. Tipping is customary, and $20 to the captain is not excessive, especially if you keep the fish you caught.

Sailing Lessons may be arranged through **Tradewind Charters** (350 Ward Ave., Honolulu 96814, tel. 808/533–0220). Instruction follows American Sailing Association standards. Cost: $35 per hour for the first student, $15 for each additional student, up to four. Transportation from Waikiki is available. Tradewinds specializes in intimate three-hour sunset sails for a maximum of six people at $59 per person, including hors d'oeuvres, champagne, and other beverages. The same price will buy you a half-day snorkel or scuba sail.

Silver Cloud Limousine Service (Box 15773, Honolulu 96830, tel. 808/524–7999) arranges private yacht charters, complete with limousine pickup at your hotel. A four-hour sail for one to six passengers is $450, and a seven-hour sail is $550.

Scuba Diving Contact **Destination Hawaii** (1777 Ala Moana Blvd., Honolulu
and Snorkeling 96815, tel. 808/946–0061). This nonprofit association of dive operations has a 24-page guidebook of dive sites on all the islands. It's yours for $3. **Dan's Dive Shop** (660 Ala Moana Blvd., tel. 808/536–6181) offers an introductory boat dive for $55 (no experience necessary) and a two-tank boat dive for $65, as well as a certification program. **The City and County of Honolulu Department of Parks and Recreation** (650 S. King St., Honolulu 96813, tel. 808/483–7853) offers free snorkeling lessons for children.

The most famous snorkeling spot in Hawaii is Hanauma Bay (*see* Beaches, above). **Seahorse Snorkeling** (6650 Hawaii Kai Dr., Suite 109, Honolulu 96825, tel. 808/395–8947) has a half-day Hanauma Bay excursion for $5.99, including transportation and equipment. **Steve's Diving Adventures** (1860 Ala Moana Blvd., Honolulu 96815, tel. 808/947–8900) offers the same for $7.

Ocean Kayaking This relatively new sport to the islands is catching on fast. You sit on top of a one-person board and paddle on both sides—great fun for catching waves or just exploring the coastline. Bob Twogood, a name that is synonymous with Oahu kayaking, runs a shop called **Twogood Kayaks Hawaii** (46-020 Alaloa St., Suite B-6, Kaneohe, tel. 808/262–5656), which makes and sells the fiberglass craft and runs free demonstrations on Kailua Beach at least every two weeks. Twogood rents kayaks for $20 a half day, $25 a day, and $40 a weekend.

Surfing If you'd like to look into free surfing lessons, call the **Honolulu Department of Parks and Recreation** (tel. 808/527–6343) to see if it has a clinic scheduled.

Windsurfing This sport was born in Hawaii, and Oahu's Kailua Beach is its cradle. World champion Robby Naish and his family build and sell boards, rent equipment, run "windsurfari" tours, and offer instruction. They also have the only commercial accommodations on Kailua Beach: **Naish Hawaii** (160 Kailua Rd., Kailua 96734, tel. 800/262–6068).

Spectator Sports

Basketball Each April, four teams of the nation's best players shoot and dribble during the **Aloha Basketball Classic** at the Neal Blaisdell Center (777 Ward Ave., Honolulu, tel. 808/948-7523).

Football The **Pro Bowl,** featuring the NFL elite, is played here a week after the Super Bowl. In December collegiate football hits the stadium during the **Aloha Bowl.** The **Hula Bowl,** held each January at Aloha Stadium in Honolulu (tel. 808/486-9300), is a sports classic bringing together All-American college stars and presenting a field full of hula girls at halftime. For local action, the **University of Hawaii Rainbows** take to the field at Aloha Stadium in season, with a big local following. There are often express buses from Kapiolani Park (tel. 808/531-1611 for details).

Golf The giants of the greens return to Hawaii every February to compete in the **Hawaiian Open Golf Tournament,** a PGA tour regular with a $500,000 purse. It is held at the exclusive Waialae Country Club (4997 Kahala Ave., tel. 808/734-2151) near Waikiki, and it's always mobbed.

Polo Mokuleia on the North Shore is a picturesque oceanside setting for weekly polo matches. Local teams compete against international players during the season, which runs from March to August. *Dillingham Field, tel. 808/637-POLO. Admission: $5 adults and children 12-17. Food concession available, or pack a tailgate picnic. Game: 2 PM.*

Rugby Every other year in October, the **Pan Am World International Rugby Tournament** takes place at Kapiolani Park.

Running **The Honolulu Marathon** is a thrilling event to watch as well as to participate in. Join the throngs who cheer at the finish line at Kapiolani Park as internationally famous and local runners tackle the 26.2-mile challenge. It's held on a Sunday in December and is sponsored by the Honolulu Marathon Association (tel. 808/734-7200).

Surfing For two weekends each March, **Buffalo's Annual Big-Board Surfing Classic** fills Makaha Beach with Hawaiian entertainment, food booths, and the best in big-board surfing (tel. 808/696-3878 or consult the newspaper). In the winter you can head out to the north shore and watch the best surfers in the world hang ten during the **Triple Crown Hawaiian Pro Surfing Championships.** This two-day event, scheduled according to the wave conditions, is generally held at the Banzai Pipeline and Sunset Beach during November and December. Watch the newspapers for details.

Volleyball This is an extremely popular sport in the Islands, and no wonder. The **University of Hawaii Rainbow Wahines** (women's team) has blasted to a number-one league ranking in years past. Crowded, noisy, crazy, and very exciting home games are played during the September-December season in Klum Gym (1337 Lower Campus Rd., Honolulu, tel. 808/948-6376). Admission: $4.

Windsurfing Watch the pros as they jump and spin on the waves during July's **Pan Am Hawaiian Windsurfing World Cup** off Kailua Beach. There are also windsurfing competitions off Diamond

Head point; consult the sports section of the daily newspaper for details on these events.

Dining

The strength of Hawaii's tourist industry has allowed Oahu's hotels to attract and pay for some of the best culinary talent in the world. Consequently, Honolulu is one of the few cities where the best dining in town is in the hotels, and Waikiki is the area where you will pay the highest dinner prices.

A wide variety of restaurants serve excellent ethnic food, especially Chinese and Japanese. So pervasive is the Eastern influence that even the McDonald's menu is posted in both English and *kanji*, the universal script of the Orient. In addition to its regular fare, McDonald's serves saimin, a Japanese noodle soup that ranks as the local favorite snack.

Honolulu is most, but not all, of the Oahu dining picture. As you head away from town there are a handful of culinary gems sparkling among many lesser restaurants not worth a second look. So diverse are the island's restaurants that on successive nights you may eat with silver and fine linen napkins, from monkeypod dishes, with chopsticks, or with your fingers. There may be candlelight, moonlight, or neon light. You can choose from some of the most delectable fish, including *opakapaka* (blue snapper) and mahimahi (white dolphin fish, not to be confused with Flipper). Or you may want to tackle a bowl of brown paste called poi, the traditional starch that Hawaiians lap up with love.

For snacks and fast food around the island, look for the *manapua* wagons, the food trucks usually parked at the beaches; and *okazu-ya* stores, the local version of delis, which dispense tempura, sushi, and plate lunch, Hawaii's unofficial state dish. A standard plate lunch has macaroni salad, "two scoops rice," and an entrée that might be curry stew, kalua (roasted) pig and cabbage, or sweet-and-sour spareribs.

New dining spots keep opening their doors at Restaurant Row (500 Ala Moana Blvd., tel. 808/538–1441) in downtown Honolulu. For a mere 50¢, there's a trolley service between Waikiki and Restaurant Row Thursday–Sunday 5:30–9:15 PM. A free shuttle service is also available between Honolulu's business district and Restaurant Row on weekdays 11:20 AM–1 PM.

Few restaurants require men to wear jackets. An aloha shirt and pants for men and a simple dress or pants for women are acceptable in all but the fanciest establishments.

Restaurants are open daily, unless otherwise noted.

Highly recommended restaurants in each area are indicated by a star ★.

Category	Cost*
Very Expensive	over $60
Expensive	$40–$60

Moderate	$20–$40
Inexpensive	under $20

per person excluding drinks, service, and sales tax (4%)

Waikiki

American ★

Orchids. You can't beat the setting, right beside the sea, with Diamond Head looming in the distance and fresh orchids everywhere. The restaurant is terraced, so every table inside and out has a view. The popovers are huge, and the salads are light and unusual. The most popular meal of the week here is the special Sunday brunch, featuring table after table of all-you-can-eat buffet delights; one spread features an impressive variety of Island sashimi. Chafing dishes give you a range of options, from eggs Benedict to chicken curry. Desserts, such as plum cake, are all made in the Halekulani's own kitchen. *Halekulani Hotel, 2199 Kalia Rd., tel. 808/923–2311. Reservations advised. Dress: casual. AE, CB, DC, MC, V. Moderate.*

Eggs 'N Things. This breakfast-only eatery with unusual hours is popular in part for its waitresses. They have names like Mitch and Yoshi, and their breezy, chatty style makes you feel right at home. Late-night revelers often stop here after a night on the town. Omelets are as huge as your plate and come with a variety of fillings; chili and cheese is a favorite. Blackened Cajun-style fish is great with scrambled eggs, and the macadamia nut waffle topped with whipped cream is rich enough to be called dessert. The best bargain is the $1.99 Early Riser Special, two eggs and three pancakes, served 5–9 AM, 1–2 PM, and 1–2 AM. *1911 Kalakaua Ave., tel. 808/949–0820. No reservations. Dress: casual. No credit cards. Open 11 PM–2 PM. Inexpensive.*

Harry's Cafe and Bar. Located right in the thick of the action at the Hyatt Regency Waikiki, this sidewalk cafe in an atrium with a waterfall is a great place to take in the passing parade of people. The reasonably priced menu includes no entrées but does boast some tasty sandwiches, homemade croissants, and other deli treats. The California salad features marinated shrimp, avocado, and tons of fresh vegetables. Another winner is the salmon with bagel chips and cream cheese. *Hyatt Regency Waikiki Hotel, 2424 Kalakaua Ave., tel. 808/922–9292. Dress: casual. AE, CB, DC, MC, V. Inexpensive.*

Hau Tree Lanai. Renovations have made this restaurant right beside the sand at Kaimana Beach more charming than ever. It is often overlooked and shouldn't be. At breakfast, lunch, or dinner, you can dine under graceful hau trees and hear the whisper of the waves. Breakfast offerings include a huge helping of eggs Benedict, a fluffy Belgian waffle with your choice of toppings (strawberries, bananas, or macadamia nuts), and a tasty fresh salmon omelet. This is the only restaurant we know of that features an authentic Japanese-style breakfast with a raw egg, fish, rice, miso soup, and other delicacies. *New Otani Kaimana Beach Hotel, 2863 Kalakaua Ave., tel. 808/923–1555. Reservations required at dinner. Dress: casual. AE, CB, DC, MC, V. Inexpensive.*

Wailana Coffee House. If you like coffee shops, this is a reliable one. Nothing fancy—just booths and tables, waitresses who look like someone's favorite auntie, and all the coffee you can drink. Pancakes, waffles, omelets, and everything else that

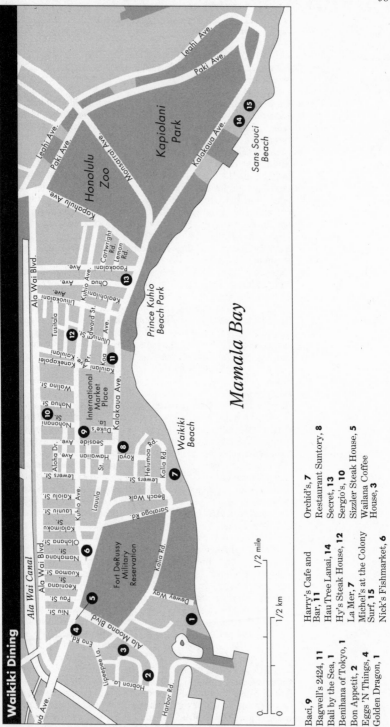

Waikiki Dining

Ala Wai Canal

Ala Wai Blvd.

Mamala Bay

Honolulu Zoo

Kapiolani Park

Sans Souci Beach

Prince Kuhio Beach Park

Waikiki Beach

Fort DeRussy Military Reservation

International Market Place

Duke's Ltd.

1/2 mile

1/2 km

Baci, **9**
Bagwell's 2424, **11**
Bali by the Sea, **1**
Benihana of Tokyo, **1**
Bon Appetit, **2**
Eggs 'N Things, **4**
Golden Dragon, **1**

Harry's Cafe and
Bar, **11**
Hau Tree Lanai, **14**
Hy's Steak House, **12**
La Mer, **7**
Michel's at the Colony
Surf, **15**
Nick's Fishmarket, **6**

Orchid's, **7**
Restaurant Suntory, **8**
Secret, **13**
Sergio's, **10**
Sizzler Steak House, **5**
Wailana Coffee
House, **3**

goes with breakfast are among the specialties of this budget diner. *1860 Ala Moana Blvd., tel. 808/955–1764. Dress: casual. AE, DC, MC, V. Inexpensive.*

Chinese　**Golden Dragon.** Local Chinese people consider this the best.
★　Chef Dai Hoi Chang has been here for 30 years and has developed quite a tasty bill of fare, including Szechuan, Cantonese, and unconventional nouvelle Chinese cuisine. Set right by the water, the restaurant has a stunning red-and-black decor, with big lazy Susans in the middle of each table for easy sharing of food. Among the best items are stir-fried lobster with *haupia* (coconut), and Szechuan beef. The Peking duck and beggar's chicken (whole chicken baked in a clay pot) must be ordered 24 hours in advance. *Hilton Hawaiian Village, 2005 Kalia Rd., tel. 808/949–4321. Reservations required. Dress: casual. AE, CB, DC, MC, V. Moderate.*

Continental　**Bagwells 2424.** A waterfall cascading over etched glass sets the
★　tone for this restaurant, which is decorated in mauve with crystal chandeliers and an antique Chinese screen. Chef On-Jin Kim has introduced an innovative East-meets-West concept to the nouvelle Hawaiian fare, reflected in his opakapaka Chinatown, blue snapper steamed with soy sauce, ginger, and Hawaiian peppers, coated in sesame oil. There's also an appetizer of opakapaka in phyllo pastry on mango purée and an entrée of broiled *ulua* (a local fish) on *lilikoi* beurre blanc (passion-fruit butter) with pink and green peppercorns. The double-chocolate pâté with warm orange zabaglione is a chocoholic's Waterloo. The adjacent wine bar lists 400 selections, many of which are available by the glass. *Hyatt Regency Waikiki Hotel, 2424 Kalakaua Ave., tel. 808/922–9292. Reservations required. Jacket suggested but not required. AE, CB, DC, MC, V. Expensive.*

★　**Bali by the Sea.** Like the island it's named for, this restaurant is breeze-swept and pretty, with an oceanside setting offering glorious views of Waikiki Beach. But don't be fooled by the name. This is not an Asian ethnic eatery but an internationally acclaimed restaurant featuring such entrées as roast duck with papaya puree and macadamia nut liqueur. Another favorite is the poached mahimahi and opakapaka, a pair of island fish served with two sauces. Pastry chef Gale O'Malley is the only American pastry chef to have been decorated by the French government. His magnificent tarts, cakes, and sweets are displayed on the rolling pastry cart. *Hilton Hawaiian Village, 2005 Kalia Rd., tel. 808/949–4321. Reservations advised. Dress: casual. AE, CB, DC, MC, V. Expensive.*

★　**Michel's at the Colony Surf.** With mirrors, candlelight, piano music, crystal, and chandeliers, this is easily the most romantic restaurant in town. One wall opens up to panoramas of the sea, lovely by day or night. The service is superb, and the waiters' mastery of tableside cooking is a wonder to behold. For starters, try the lobster bisque, flamed with cognac and laced with lobster chunks and homemade croutons. Pepper steak flamed with Jack Daniels whiskey is another winner. Breakfast, an insider's secret, features crepes suzette sautéed with fruit. *Colony Surf Hotel, 2895 Kalakaua Ave., tel. 808/923–6552. Reservations required. Dress: casual at breakfast, jacket required at dinner. AE, CB, DC, MC, V. Expensive.*

Secret. Formerly called The Third Floor, this restaurant feels like Europe—maybe Spain—with extravagant food displays and big rattan chairs to hide in. For what the staff calls a

"Promising Start," you can sample the 20 or so dishes in the appetizer bar, including everything from artichoke hearts to melon balls. For an entrée, try the casserolette, an exquisite dish made with lobster, scallops, shrimp, and opakapaka in fennel sauce. Tournedos Windsor combines filet mignon with Canadian bacon, chanterelles, Swiss cheese, and a demiglace sauce. A wonderful German fellow named Siggy is your host, and he makes each guest feel welcome, like the oldest of friends. Finish things off with the surprise complimentary dessert of . . . well, let's not spoil the surprise. *Hawaiian Regent Hotel, 2552 Kalakaua Ave., tel. 808/922–6611. Reservations required. Dress: casual. AE, CB, DC, MC, V. Expensive.*

French **La Mer.** In the exotic, elegant atmosphere of a Mandalay man-
★ sion, you'll be served a unique blend of French and nouvelle Hawaiian cuisine that most connoisseurs consider the finest dining experience in Hawaii. Portions are delicate and beautifully presented. A favorite appetizer is new-potato salad with sour cream and caviar, and a standout among the entrées is breast of duck with fresh pears and spiced apples in a light ginger sauce. Each evening there are two complete dinner menus, which run $65–$90, soup through dessert. Highly recommended is the cheese and port course, offered in lieu of dessert. *Halekulani Hotel, 2199 Kalia Rd., tel. 808/923–2311. Reservations required. Jacket required. AE, CB, DC, MC, V. Very Expensive.*

Bon Appetit. Country French cuisine is presented in a cozy atmosphere reminiscent of a European bistro. Elegantly decorated in pink and black with French-style paintings on the wall, this restaurant is the brainchild of owner-chef Guy Banal, who has created a fascinating menu. Appetizers include a Scandinavian plate of Norwegian salmon and trout marinated in champagne with Gravlak sauce (cream, mustard, horseradish, lemon juice, and dill). Tempting entrées include broiled fresh fillet of fish with ginger-lobster butter, and broiled lamb with sweet pimientos, fresh basil, mint, and garlic. The fixed-price dinner goes for $21.95. *Discovery Bay, 1778 Ala Moana Blvd., tel. 808/942–3837. Reservations required. Dress: casual. AE, CB, DC, MC, V. Closed Sun. Moderate.*

Italian **Baci.** This is one of Waikiki's great finds. Tucked away in the Waikiki Trade Center, it's a place you might miss unless you know about it. The spacious interior is decorated with a nice blend of modern and traditional, with chrome finishings and cloth napkins. The service is attentive, and the emphasis is on nouvelle Italian cuisine. The star appetizer is charcoaled shrimp with lime, mint, and feta cheese. You have a long list of pastas from which to choose, headlined by the ever-popular lobster ravioli. *Waikiki Trade Center, 2255 Kuhio Ave., tel. 808/924–2533. Reservations advised. Dress: casual. AE, CB, DC, MC, V. Moderate.*

Sergio's. Sergio Battistetti's popular dining room offers a tantalizing taste of Italy smack-dab in the heart of Waikiki. The atmosphere is sophisticated and romantic, with dark-brown booths providing plenty of intimacy. The appetizer menu offers nearly two dozen hot and cold options, including shiitake mushrooms in butter and garlic or spicy calamari (squid) marinara. Among the 16 pasta dishes is the *bugili puttanesca*, whose wide noodles swim in a tomato sauce spiced by anchovies and capers. Other fine entrées include saltimbocco, osso bucco, veal marsala, and Dover sole, pan-fried or broiled. The wine list is extensive and impressive. *445 Nohonani St., tel. 808/926–3388. Reservations advised. Dress: casual. AE, DC, MC, V. Moderate.*

Japanese   **Benihana of Tokyo.** These restaurants are as famous for their theatrical knife work at the *teppan* (iron grill) tables as they are for their food. You are seated at a long table with other diners and together you watch as steak, chicken, seafood, and a variety of vegetables are sliced, diced, tossed, and sautéed before your eyes. There's not much variety to the menu, but it's still a lot of fun. Finish off the meal with some green-tea ice cream, a Benihana tradition. *Hilton Hawaiian Village, 2005 Kalia Rd., tel. 808/955–5955. Reservations required. Dress: casual. AE, CB, DC, MC, V. Moderate.*

Restaurant Suntory. This unique restaurant offers Japanese dining at its most elegant. You can choose to eat in four areas: a sushi bar, a *teppanyaki* room (with food prepared on an iron grill), a *shabu shabu room* (thinly-sliced beef boiled in broth), or a private dining room. The waiters and waitresses are stiff and the atmosphere formal, but the food is very good. Beef sashimi and assorted shellfish top the shabu shabu entrées. A complete *teishoku* dinner served teppanyaki-style includes miso soup, vegetable and fish tempura, rice, and dessert. The sushi chef is a wizard to watch as he creates inventive morsels of delicate raw seafood and rice. *Royal Hawaiian Shopping Center, 2233 Kalakaua Ave., tel. 808/922–5511. Reservations advised. Dress: casual. AE, CB, DC, MC, V. Moderate.*

Seafood   **Nick's Fishmarket.** Television and film star Tom Selleck spent
★   so much time here that he went into partnership with the owners and opened another Honolulu restaurant, the Black Orchid. His favorite dish at Nick's is the bouillabaisse, but there are many other wonderful offerings to recommend in this dark, candlelit dining room with black booths and elegant table settings. Nick's special salad with spinach cream dressing is special indeed. Unique to Nick's is the Monterey abalone, served with a Ricci sauce containing morsels of tender fish. For dessert, bananas flambé, beautifully prepared tableside, is as dramatic for the eye as for the palate. *Waikiki Gateway Hotel, 2070 Kalakaua Ave., tel. 808/955–6333. Reservations required. Dress: casual. AE, CB, DC, MC, V. Expensive.*

Steak   **Hy's Steak House.** Things always seem to go well at Hy's, from
★   the steak tartare and oysters Rockefeller right through to the flaming desserts, such as cherries jubilee. The atmosphere is snug and librarylike, and you can watch the chef perform behind glass. Tuxedoed waiters, catering to your every need, make helpful suggestions about the menu. Hy's is famous for its broiled lobster tail, *kiawe*-broiled rack of lamb ("kiawe" is a mesquite-type wood), and glazed New York peppercorn steak. The Caesar salad is excellent, as are the potatoes O'Brien. *Waikiki Park Heights Hotel, 2440 Kuhio Ave., tel. 808/922–5555. Reservations required. Dress: casual. AE, CB, DC, MC, V. Moderate.*

Sizzler Steak House. This neon-and-chrome, low-budget steak and seafood eatery is designed for people who are stopping in for a quick meal. There's generally an all-you-can-eat special, with soup, salad, and hot bread. You walk through a cafeteria-style line to place your order for such items as fried shrimp, steak, and lobster. Breakfast here is pretty good, and the pancakes are substantial. The salad bar is a popular stop. *1945*

Kalakaua Ave., tel. 808/955-4069. No reservations. Dress: casual. No credit cards. Inexpensive.

Honolulu

American   **Hala Terrace.** This restaurant has an open-air setting and a healthy lunch menu that stars unusual salads and vegetarian dishes. There is also a full low-calorie menu, with calories listed, along with more substantial offerings, such as a corned beef sandwich on rye with sauerkraut or the excellent home-made lobster ravioli. The Sunset Supper Menu is an excellent buy and includes tropical chicken coated with coconut. The Hala Terrace is the site of the long-running Danny Kaleikini Show, a delightful Polynesian revue that is performed Monday through Saturday. *Kahala Hilton Hotel, 5000 Kahala Ave., tel. 808/734-2211. Reservations required. Dress: casual. AE, CB, DC, MC, V. Moderate.*

Sunset Grill. The smell of wood smoke greets you as you enter the Sunset Grill, which specializes in *kiawe*-broiled foods ("kiawe" is a mesquite-type wood). The place is supposed to feel unfinished, with the marble bar top and white tablecloths contrasting nicely with the concrete floors. The salad niçoise, big enough for a whole dinner, includes red-top lettuce, beans, tomato, egg, potatoes, and olives, as well as marinated grilled *ahi* (tuna). The trout and scallops, cooked in a wood oven, are both very good. *Restaurant Row, 500 Ala Moana Blvd., tel. 808/521-4409. Reservations advised. Dress: casual. AE, MC, V. Moderate.*

★ **The Willows.** Thatched dining pavilions set amid carp ponds full of prize fish make this a cherished landmark on Oahu's dining scene. The jungle elegance of the setting makes the perfect backdrop for chef-consultant Kusuma Cooray's golden touch. She has added an international flavor to the tropical entrées, curries, and "mile-high" pies. The sautéed opakapaka with spinach sauce is excellent, as are the lamb medallions in brandy and honey. Hawaiian curry salad is another good choice. For a glimpse of real down-home Hawaii, reserve a space at the Thursdays-only Kamaaina Luncheon. You'll discover lots of local food, music, and spontaneous hula. *901 Hausten St., tel. 808/946-4808. Reservations required. Dress: casual. AE, CB, DC, MC, V. Moderate.*

Columbia Inn. "At the top of the boulevard" sits this well-established, recently renovated coffee shop with a tradition of offering three square meals, low prices, and plenty of camaraderie. Solo diners sit at the long counter, while others take up the booths. The walls are covered with sports memorabilia and photos of personalities who have stopped by over the years. For breakfast, the banana pancakes are good. At lunch, go for the Reuben sandwich. Dinner specials include such American standards as roast chicken and such local fare as saimin and broiled teriyaki pork chops. *645 Kapiolani Blvd., tel. 808/531-3747. No reservations. Dress: casual. AE, DC, MC, V. Inexpensive.*

Hard Rock Cafe. One of the latest links in this international chain of formula restaurants, the Honolulu Hard Rock is filled with musical memorabilia. You can see guitars signed and donated by rock stars, a black outfit once worn by John Lennon, gold and platinum records by the likes of Tina Turner and Michael Jackson, and one of Tom Selleck's aloha shirts. Over the bar hangs a shiny aqua '57 Cadillac woodie. The Hard Rock has mystique but is more famous for its T-shirts than for its food.

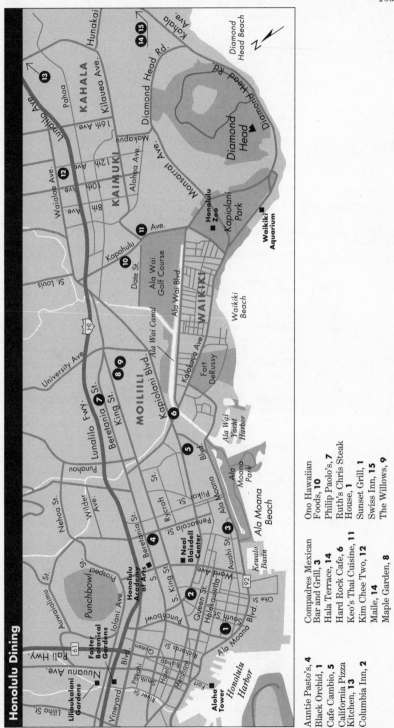

Honolulu Dining

Auntie Pasto's, **4**
Black Orchid, **1**
Cafe Cambio, **5**
California Pizza Kitchen, **13**
Columbia Inn, **2**

Compadres Mexican Bar and Grill, **3**
Hala Terrace, **14**
Hard Rock Cafe, **6**
Keo's Thai Cuisine, **11**
Kim Chee Two, **12**
Maile, **14**
Maple Garden, **8**

Ono Hawaiian Foods, **10**
Philip Paolo's, **7**
Ruth's Chris Steak House, **1**
Sunset Grill, **1**
Swiss Inn, **15**
The Willows, **9**

The menu includes some decent half-pound burgers, ahi steak sandwich, baby back ribs, french fries, and all-American hot apple pie à la mode. Watch out: The oldies can get pretty loud. *1837 Kapiolani Blvd., tel. 808/955-7383. Lunch reservations only. Dress: casual. AE, MC, V. Inexpensive.*

Chinese **Maple Garden.** The fine reputation of Maple Garden is founded on spicy Szechuan cuisine but certainly not on decor. There are some booths, some tables, an oriental screen or two, and lights that are a little too bright at times. It's comfortable, however, and that's all that matters, because the food is delicious. A consistent favorite is the eggplant in a tantalizing hot garlic sauce. Smoky Szechuan duck comes with succulent little dumplings, and the hot-and-sour soup may just be the best in town. *909 Isenberg St., tel. 808/941-6641. Reservations advised. Dress: casual. AE, DC, MC, V. Inexpensive.*

Continental **Black Orchid.** This exceptionally formal restaurant became an immediate success when it opened in 1988, due in part to the fact that Tom Selleck is one of its owners. Now it has established itself as a fine dining experience in its own right. Dark wood and the art-deco decor make this a glittering place for lunch or dinner. Black-and-blue ahi (tuna), cooked with Cajun spices, seared on the outside and left raw inside, is reputed to be Selleck's favorite dish, and deservedly so; it is excellent. Also try the red-hot prawns, which are marinated in 15 spices and then sautéed. The best dessert: chocolate mousse with a hazelnut sauce. *Restaurant Row, 500 Ala Moana Blvd., tel. 808/521-3111. Reservations required. Jacket preferred. AE, CB, DC, MC, V. Expensive.*

★ **Maile.** The signature restaurant in this "hotel of the stars" is glamorous and glimmering. Situated on the lower level, the Maile has no view but instead casts an indoor spell with magic all its own. Trickling waterfalls, tropical flowers and greenery, and soft live music create a lovely background to the exceptional dishes, which include both continental favorites and Island cuisine. Steaks and meats are the pride of the restaurant. Roast duckling Waialae has long been its most famous entrée, prized for its sauce of lychees, bananas, and mandarin orange slices. The gingerbread soufflé laced with cinnamon ice and fresh strawberry compote is a must-try dessert. *Kahala Hilton, 5000 Kahala Ave., tel. 808/734-2211. Reservations required. Jacket advised. AE, CB, DC, MC, V. Expensive.*

Hawaiian **Ono Hawaiian Foods.** Locals frequent this no-frills hangout for a regular hit of their favorite foods. You can tell it's good, because there's usually a line outside after about 5 PM. Housed in a plain storefront site and furnished simply with tables and booths, this small (it seats about 40) restaurant is a good place to do some taste testing of such Island innovations as *poi* (taro paste), *lomilomi* salmon (massaged until tender and served with minced onions and tomatoes), *laulau* (steamed bundle of ti leaves containing pork, butterfish, and taro tops), *kalua* (roasted) pig, and *haupia* (dessert made from coconut). The beef curry is superb, and the house specialty is chicken long rice soup. Appropriately enough, the Hawaiian word *ono* means delicious. *726 Kapahulu Ave., tel. 808/737-2275. No reservations. Dress: casual. No credit cards. Inexpensive.*

Italian **Cafe Cambio.** Those in the know love Cafe Cambio for its toned-down trendiness. The unusual decor of this cafe includes imported marble, a mural in pastel shades along one wall, and another wall where you're invited to write your own personal review of the place. Chef-owner Sergio Mitrotti creates every dish himself, cooking what he calls contemporary Northern Italian cuisine. Try the fettuccine al cafe, made with a hint of fresh-ground espresso coffee in a light-cream Parmesan sauce. Experimental and exciting daily specials include shrimp in lemon and wine sauce over linguine. Try the Italian beer. *1680 Kapiolani Blvd., tel. 808/942-0740. No reservations. Dress: casual. MC, V. Moderate.*

Phillip Paolo's. The talented Phillip Paolo creates Italian cuisine with a flair all his own. The restaurant is set in an old colonial-style house, with rooms of different sizes, wooden floors, and high ceilings. The outdoor garden is a charming place for casual dinners under the trees. The lobster parmigiana is a classic dish, and the steak capri is served with fresh crab legs and shrimp, all covered with béarnaise sauce. There are always specials here. For dessert, try vanilla cheesecake with a sauce of mangoes from Paolo's own tree. *2312 S. Beretania St., tel. 808/946-1163. Reservations advised. Dress: casual. AE, MC, V. Moderate.*

Auntie Pasto's. Here's a cute, casual Italian eatery with high ceilings, brick walls, and planters that divide the room into smaller sections. The kitchen is open to the dining room, making things pretty noisy when the pots and pans start banging. The quality of the food makes up for it, however. Huge menus hang on the wall for all to see. Start with an order of basil bread, a wonderful variation on the garlic bread theme. The antipasto salad is big enough to be a main dish, as is the pasta salad. Eggplant Parmesan has a red sauce so tasty that you'll want to scoop it up with extra bread. Mud pie makes for a sinfully good dessert. *1099 S. Beretania St., tel. 808/523-8855. No reservations. Dress: casual. MC, V. Inexpensive.*

Korean **Kim Chee Two.** Here's an unassuming little carryout and sit-down restaurant featuring Korean food. The prices are low and the portions are big. You get little side dishes of spicy *kimchee* (pickled vegetables) with your meal. This is a fun place to try such specialties as *bi bim kook soo* (noodles with meat and vegetables), meat *jun* (barbecued beef coated with egg and highly seasoned), *chop chae* (fried vegetables and noodles), and fried *man doo* (plump meat-filled dumplings). *3569 Waialae Ave., tel. 808/737-0006. No reservations. Dress: casual. No credit cards. BYOB. Inexpensive.*

Mexican **Compadres Mexican Bar and Grill.** The after-work crowd gath-
★ ers here for frosty pitchers of potent margaritas and yummy *pupus* (hors d'oeuvres). An outdoor terrace with patio-style furnishings is best for cocktails and chips. Inside, the wooden floors, colorful photographs, and lively paintings create a festive setting for imaginative Mexican specialties. Fajitas, chile rellenos, baby back ribs, and grilled shrimp are just a few of the many offerings. Most popular menu item: the chimichanga (a burrito filled with chicken or beef, deep-fried, and served with beans, rice, and salad). The six-layer dip is a good starter, with beef, cheese, beans, guacamole, sour cream, and chips. *The Ward Centre, 1200 Ala Moana Blvd., tel. 808/523-1307. No reservations. Dress: casual. AE, MC, V. Inexpensive.*

Pizza **California Pizza Kitchen.** This dining and watering hole for young fast-trackers is worth the probable wait to get a table. A glass atrium with tiled and mirrored walls and one side open to the shopping mall creates a sidewalk-cafe effect. The pizza features toppings you'd never expect, such as Thai chicken, Peking duck, and Caribbean shrimp. The pastas, made fresh daily on the premises, include angel hair, fettuccine, rigatone, fusilli, and linguine. Look for a new (and bigger) CPK on Ala Moana Boulevard in Waikiki. It's scheduled to open sometime in 1990. *Kahala Mall, 4211 Waialae Ave., tel. 808/737-9446. No reservations. Dress: casual. AE, MC, V. Inexpensive.*

Steak **Ruth's Chris Steak House.** At last, a steak joint that doesn't look like one, with its pastel-hued and sophisticated decor. Salads are generous, and steak cuts are hefty. The char-broiled fish serves as an excellent alternative to the meat dishes. *Restaurant Row, 500 Ala Moana Ave., tel. 808/599-3860. Reservations recommended. Dress: casual. AE, MC, V. Moderate.*

Swiss **Swiss Inn.** Waitresses in dirndls and color photos of Alpine vil-
★ lages create a Swiss setting for the concoctions of Swiss-born chef Martin Wyss. Appetizers include *bundnerfleisch* (thinly sliced air-dried beef) and *croûte emmental* (creamed mushrooms on toast with ham and Swiss cheese). Dinners come complete with soup, salad, vegetables, and coffee or tea. Veal medallions florentine, served on a bed of spinach and covered with sliced bacon and Swiss cheese, is an outstanding entree. With her sparkling aloha spirit, Martin's wife, Jeanie, does an excellent job of keeping things running smoothly. *Niu Valley Shopping Center, 5730 Kalanianaole Hwy., tel. 808/377-5447. Reservations advised. Dress: casual. AE, CB, DC, MC, V. Moderate.*

Thai **Keo's Thai Cuisine.** Hollywood celebrities have discovered this
★ twinkling nook with tables set amid lighted trees, big paper umbrellas, and sprays of orchids everywhere. In fact, Keo has a whole wall devoted to photos of himself with a variety of stars. The food is exceptional. Favorites include Evil Jungle Prince (shrimp, vegetables, or chicken in a sauce flavored with fresh basil, coconut milk, and red chile) and *chiang mai* salad (chicken salad seasoned with lemongrass, red chile, mint, and fish sauce). Ask for the mild or medium; they'll still be hot, but not as hot as they could be. The crispy Thai noodles have a wonderful, barely-there sauce. The food comes in serving dishes Chinese-style, so you can share. For dessert, the apple-bananas in coconut milk are wonderful, as is the Thai tea with a twist of lemon. *625 Kapahulu Ave., tel. 808/737-8240. Reservations required. Dress: casual. AE, CB, DC, MC, V. Moderate.*

Around the Island

Haleiwa **Steamer's.** Whether you're seated at a comfortable booth or a
Seafood table, you'll have the finest meal available on the north shore amid this restaurant's mirrored walls and ceiling fans. The emphasis is on seafood, including a chowder with fresh fish chunks. Daily seafood specials are prepared nicely, including a delicious caper sauce that enhances mahimahi as well as red snapper. The meat entrées are not as successful. Carrot cake is a sweet ending to a pleasant meal. *Haleiwa Shopping Plaza, 66-165 Kamehameha Hwy., tel. 808/637-5071. Reservations advised. Dress: casual. AE, MC, V. Moderate.*
Pacific Broiler. This relative newcomer has made a splash with its waterside location and innovative food. Owner Kono Wong

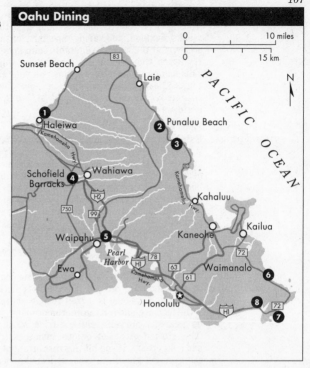

Oahu Dining

uses his expertise to bring upscale California-style fare to the islands. The decor is casual, friendly, and smart, with big picture windows facing the canal and an open kitchen where chefs prepare meals on the hardwood broiler. All broiler entrées start with garlic cheese toast. Appetizers are headlined by unique quesadillas filled with creamy brie cheese, seedless grapes, sour cream, and piquant mango salsa. Try the salad with buffalo mozzarella, beefsteak tomatoes, and Maui onions. Entrées include marinated breast of chicken topped with hollandaise. *Koko Marina Shopping Ctr., tel. 808/395–4181. Reservations advised. Dress: casual. AE, DC, MC, V. Moderate.*

Hawaii Kai
Mixed Menu
★

Roy's. Roy Yamaguchi, the widely acclaimed chef of 385 North fame in Los Angeles, has brought his talents to Oahu. His Island venture is a two-story restaurant with Pacific colors and casual furnishings. Two walls of windows offer views of Maunalua Bay and Diamond Head in the distance, and a glassed-in kitchen affords equally fascinating views of what's cooking. Roy's cuisine combines the best of Island flavors with French, Italian, Japanese, Thai, and Chinese accents. His lemon-thyme fettuccine with chicken and corn is a crowd-pleaser, as are the rack of veal with ginger and lime, and grilled lamb with balsamic vinegar. *Hawaii Kai Corporate Plaza, 6600 Kalanianaole Hwy., tel. 808/396–7697. Reservations advised. Dress: casual. AE, CB, DC, MC, V. Moderate.*

Kaaawa
American

Crouching Lion Inn. This historic residence on the windward side has been a landmark restaurant since 1957. The oceanside setting is dramatic and you have the choice of indoor or outdoor seating. The food is decent enough, with homestyle soups, steaks, seafood, and salads. Specialty of the house is Slavonic steak, and the turkey-vegetable soup is delicious. Also worth trying is the vegetarian combination topped with cheese. This makes a good stop for lunch on your circle-island driving tour. *51-666 Kamehameha Hwy., tel. 808/237-8511. Reservations required. Dress: casual. AE, CB, DC, MC, V. Moderate.*

Pearl City
American/Japanese

Pearl City Tavern. Be forewarned: This is a real local hangout. Established in 1944, it boasts the world-famous Monkey Bar, with *live* monkeys who frolic behind glass panels, plus a bonsai garden upstairs and Japanese decorations everywhere. Japanese and American dinners are the fare, including very good beef sukiyaki, ahi (tuna) sashimi, *tonkatsu* (pork cutlet served over rice), and fish *misoyaki* (fish cooked in soybean paste). Live Maine lobsters are also well prepared. Service is a little slow, giving you plenty of time to soak in your surroundings over a few beers. *905 Kamehameha Hwy., tel. 808/455-1045. No reservations. Dress: casual. AE, DC, MC, V. Inexpensive.*

Punaluu
Tex/Mex
★

Texas Paniolo Cafe. Saddle up for some countrified fun at this rustic windward retreat. The decor is distinctly south-of-the-border, and the beer is served up in frosty mason jars. Tex-Mex is the food of choice on the enormous menu, which includes jumbo jalapeño burgers, chicken-fried steak, and border-town tacos stuffed with beef, onions, tomatoes, lettuce, black olives, and sour cream. If you hit this restaurant at the right time, you can even get genuine Texas rattlesnake meat. There's live entertainment in the evenings, and free dance lessons to boot. *53-146 Kamehameha Hwy., tel. 808/237-8521. No reservations. Dress: casual. AE, MC, V. Inexpensive.*

Wahiawa
American

Kemoo Farms. Housed in a 1915 building overlooking Lake Wilson, this restaurant has a rural, farmhouse feeling to it. Its large interior, seating up to 100 people, is divided into smaller areas where you can have a drink, buy a souvenir, or dine at cloth-covered tables. Dinners are a bargain, and include soup and salad. Rainbow trout is the standout dish here, and roast duck filled with macadamia-nut stuffing is unique to Kemoo Farms. Skip dessert and proceed directly to the Hawaiian *keoki* coffee liqueur, a tasty finale. *1718 Wilikina Dr., tel. 808/621-8481. Reservations advised. Dress: casual. AE, CB, DC, MC, V. Closed Sat. lunch, Mon. dinner. Moderate.*

Waimanalo
Mexican
★

Bueno Nalo. Don't blink or you'll drive right by this hole-in-the-wall, which serves authentic Mexican food. The decor is a riot of colors, with velvet Day-Glo paintings, piñatas, and year-round Christmas tinsel, and sometimes the lack of air-conditioning makes the rooms uncomfortably warm. The food, however, is reliably good, and it's worth standing in the line that sometimes forms outside in the evening. Topopo salad is a heap of greens, tomatoes, onions, tuna, olives, cheese, and beans on top of a tortilla. Combination plates with tacos, enchiladas, and tamales are all bargains. The chile rellenos are expertly seasoned. *41-865 Kalanianaole Hwy., tel. 808/259-7186. No reservations. Dress: casual. No credit cards. BYOB. Inexpensive.*

Lodging

Oahu boasts a huge variety of accommodations, so it takes some planning ahead to find your perfect vacation home-away-from-home.

When considering the options, first decide if you want to get away from the everyday hustle and bustle. If your answer is yes, then you should look at the accommodations listed in the "Around the Island" category. If you prefer proximity to the action, go for a hotel or condominium in Honolulu or near Waikiki, where the majority of the island's lodgings are located.

Tiny as it is, Waikiki offers you everything from tidy, simple accommodations (bed, bath, room service, and telephone) away from the beach to elegant oceanside suites furnished with all your heart's desires. There are bed-and-breakfast establishments and condominiums with fully equipped kitchens. If you want a hotel right on the beach in Waikiki, just ask for it. However, Waikiki is small enough that you don't have to pay a premium for a hotel *near* the beach. You can rent a little room three blocks from the ocean and still spend your days on the sand rubbing elbows with the rich and famous.

Some people look at a hotel as simply a place to sleep at night. Others prefer a bit of ambience. The hotels that are recommended in each price category offer a good range of options. A place doesn't have to be expensive to be clean, friendly, and attractive. For a complete list of every hotel and condominium unit on the island, write to the Hawaii Visitors Bureau for the free *Accommodation Guide*. It details amenities and gives each hotel's proximity to the beach.

One asset Oahu's hotels do have in common is the service—in other words, the people with whom you come in contact every day. Their hospitality is part of the aloha spirit, a spirit you can find at the simplest of boarding houses as well as at the top-of-the-line properties. Hawaii's hotel personnel often receive their training at the college level, and tourism is their profession; they have pride in what they do.

Except for the peak months of January, February, and August, you'll have no trouble getting a room if you call ahead of time. When making your reservations, either on your own or through a travel agent, ask about packages and extras. Some hotels have special tennis, golf, or honeymoon deals. Others have periodic room-and-car packages. Oahu hotel prices usually follow a European plan, meaning no meals included.

Highly recommended hotels in each price category are indicated by a star ★.

Category	Cost*
Very Expensive	over $120
Expensive	$90–120
Moderate	$60–90
Inexpensive	under $60

All prices are for a standard double room, excluding 9¼% tax and service charges.

Waikiki

Very Expensive **Colony Surf Hotel.** This small hotel with impeccable and per-
★ sonal service is like a condominium; each unit is equipped with
a full kitchen and an attractive living area. The same is true of
the hotel's annex, the **Colony Surf East,** though units are smaller there. Wealthy patrons like to keep this one a secret;
they appreciate the fine points, such as a staff that will hold
your aloha shirts and beach paraphernalia until your next
visit. The hotel is way up on the Diamond Head (east) end of
Waikiki, beyond the mainstream. Its restaurant, Michel's,
is French, fashionable, open to the sea, and considered the
most romantic dining room in town. *2895 Kalakaua Ave., Honolulu 96815, tel. 808/923–5751 or 800/252–7873. On the beach.
Of 171 units, 50 are available for booking. There are an additional 50 units in the Colony Surf East. Facilities: 2 restaurants, 2 cocktail lounges in the 2 buildings. AE, CB, DC,
MC, V.*

Halekulani Hotel. Today's sleek, modern, and luxurious Halekulani was built around the garden lanai and historic 1931
building of the gracious old Halekulani Hotel. Throughout its
colorful history, it has attracted visitors looking for an elegant
oceanside retreat. The marble-and-wood rooms have accents of
white, beige, blue, and gray. All have lanais, sitting areas, refrigerators, bathrobes, and dozens of little touches that are
sure to pamper. The in-room check-in service means no waiting
in the lobby. The hotel has two of the finest restaurants in Honolulu and an oceanside pool with a giant orchid mosaic. Try to
get a room with an ocean view, looking toward Diamond Head.
*2199 Kalia Rd., Honolulu 96815, tel. 808/923–2311 or 800/367–
2343. On the beach. 456 rooms with bath. Facilities: pool,
shops, meeting rooms, 3 restaurants, 3 lounges. AE, CB, DC,
MC, V.*

★ **Hilton Hawaiian Village.** Hilton spent $100 million to remake
this complex into a brand-new, lavishly landscaped resort, the
largest in the state. There are four towers, 19 restaurants,
three swimming pools, cascading waterfalls, colorful fish and
birds, and even a botanical garden of labeled flora. Rooms are
decorated in attractive colors of raspberry or aqua, with rattan
and bamboo furnishings. The top floor and lower floors of the
Rainbow Tower tend to be noisy, but the pricey suites of the
Ocean Tower offer all the amenities. A variety of views are offered; ask for an ocean view. The hotel has a private dock for its
catamaran and a fine stretch of oceanfront. *2005 Kalia Rd.,
Honolulu 96815, tel. 808/949–4321 or 800/HILTONS. On the
beach, 2,524 rooms with bath. Facilities: 2-tier superpool
(10,000 sq. ft.), 2 additional pools, 19 restaurants, 11 lounges.
AE, CB, DC, MC, V.*

★ **Royal Hawaiian Hotel.** This "Pink Palace of the Pacific" was
built in 1927, an age of gracious and leisurely travel when people sailed on Matson luxury liners and spent months at the
Royal. As befits that grand era, the hotel has high ceilings, period furniture, and flowered wallpaper. People who have been
coming here for 30 years insist on a favorite chair or bureau, but
the hotel appeals to newlyweds as well as old-timers. Dreams
are made of breakfast at the beachside Surf Room, the pink telephones in each room, the corridors of pink carpeting, and the
great crystal chandeliers tinkling in the wind. The modern
wing is more expensive, but for charm, the original building

Waikiki Lodging

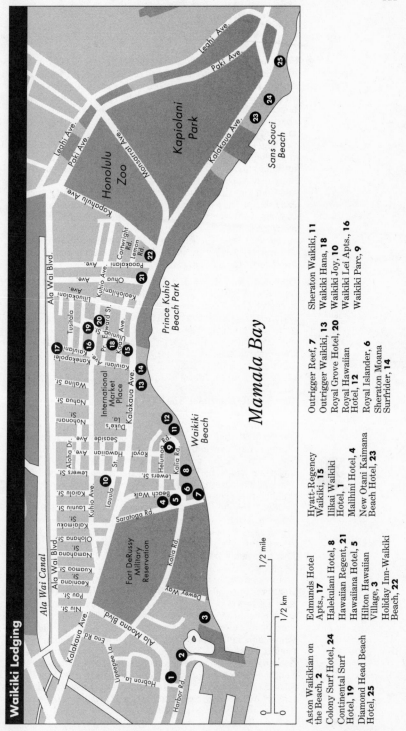

Ala Wai Canal

Ala Wai Blvd.

Mamala Bay

Kapiolani Park

Honolulu Zoo

Sans Souci Beach

Prince Kuhio Beach Park

Waikiki Beach

Fort DeRussy Military Reservation

International Market Place

1/2 mile
1/2 km

Aston Waikikian on the Beach, **2**
Colony Surf Hotel, **24**
Continental Surf Hotel, **19**
Diamond Head Beach Hotel, **25**

Edmunds Hotel Apts., **17**
Halekulani Hotel, **8**
Hawaiian Regent, **21**
Hawaiiana Hotel, **5**
Hilton Hawaiian Village, **3**
Holiday Inn-Waikiki Beach, **22**

Hyatt-Regency Waikiki, **15**
Ilikai Waikiki Hotel, **1**
Malihini Hotel, **4**
New Otani Kaimana Beach Hotel, **23**

Outrigger Reef, **7**
Outrigger Waikiki, **13**
Royal Grove Hotel, **20**
Royal Hawaiian Hotel, **12**
Royal Islander, **6**
Sheraton Moana Surfrider, **14**

Sheraton Waikiki, **11**
Waikiki Hana, **18**
Waikiki Joy, **10**
Waikiki Lei Apts., **16**
Waikiki Parc, **9**

can't be beat. *2259 Kalakaua Ave., Honolulu 96815, tel. 808/ 923–7311 or 800/325–3535. On the beach. 550 rooms with bath. Facilities: pool, meeting rooms, 2 restaurants, 2 lounges. AE, CB, DC, MC, V.*

★ **Sheraton Moana Surfrider.** The Moana Hotel, the "First Lady of Waikiki," was built in 1901 and restored to her original grandeur in 1989. Sheraton has taken great pains and spent millions on this landmark structure, which has been merged with the newer Surfrider next door. Accommodations retain their cozy charm, and, as in the old days, the furnishings on each floor are made of a different kind of wood: mahogany, oak, maple, cherry, and rare Hawaiian koa. Each room has a colonial-reproduction armoire and such modern amenities as a minibar, in-room movies, Hawaiian soaps and toiletries, a hair dryer, daily newspaper delivery, and 24-hour room service. The Banyan Court is still the focal point for beachside activity, and you can relax on the gracious veranda, sip tea, and tune yourself in to turn-of-the-century living. *2365 Kalakaua Ave., Honolulu 96815, tel. 808/922–3111 or 800/325–3535. On the beach. 803 rooms with bath. Facilities: pool, recreation deck, shops, meeting rooms, 3 restaurants, 3 lounges, poolside snack stand, beach bar. AE, CB, DC, MC, V.*

Expensive **Diamond Head Beach Hotel.** Right on the ocean, but at the quiet end of Waikiki, this is a smaller hotel that appeals to those in search of peaceful accommodations that are still close to the action of Waikiki. Irwin Stroll & Associates, a popular Los Angeles design firm, has decorated many of the rooms with mirrors, glass, and fine fabrics. Some rooms have kitchenettes. Continental breakfast is served to all guests. *2947 Kalakaua Ave., Honolulu 96815, tel. 808/922–1928 or 800/367–6046. Of 61 units, 53 are available for booking. AE, CB, DC, MC, V.*

Hawaiian Regent Hotel. The huge lobbies and courtyards, open to the breezes, are sunlit and contemporary in feel. With two towers and two lobbies, the layout is a bit confusing, but if you can get past that, this is an outstanding hotel. It has several dining choices, including the award-winning Secret (formerly The Third Floor) and two Japanese restaurants, Regent Marushin and Kobe Fogetsudo. A complimentary breakfast is served each morning, and your bed will be turned down and an orchid left for you each evening. *2552 Kalakaua Ave., Honolulu 96815, tel. 808/922–6611 or 800/367–5370. Across the street from the beach. 1,346 rooms with bath. Facilities: shops, meeting rooms, 2 pools, 1 tennis court, 2 lounges, 1 disco, 6 restaurants. AE, CB, DC, MC, V.*

★ **Hyatt Regency Waikiki.** The focal point of this twin-towered beauty is the 10-story atrium lobby with its two-story waterfall and mammoth metal sculpture. Shops, concerts, and Harry's Bar make this one of the liveliest lobbies anywhere, though you may get lost in it. Each guest room has an oriental art print to complement the warm earth tones, wall-to-wall carpeting, private lanai, color TV, air-conditioning, and combination desk/ game table and chairs. Spats is the hotel's fun Italian restaurant and disco, and Trappers presents hot live jazz. Since the hotel has two towers, there are two Regency Clubs and eight penthouses. *2424 Kalakaua Ave., Honolulu 96815, tel. 808/ 923–1234 or 800/233–1234. Across the street from the beach and a short walk from Kapiolani Park. 1,234 rooms with bath. Fa-*

cilities: 7 restaurants; 6 lounges, including a disco and a jazz club; a pool; 70 shops. AE, CB, DC, MC, V.

Ilikai Waikiki Hotel. It's not on the beach, but this is the acknowledged tennis center of Waikiki. It's also the closest hotel to the Ala Moana Shopping Center and the popular Ala Moana Beach Park. There are three towers and a huge esplanade, which is always busy, and crowds usually gather for the hula-dancing demonstrations and local musicians. You can get a good look at the Ala Wai Yacht Harbor from here, and Annabelle's lounge atop the hotel affords the best view of Waikiki. *1777 Ala Moana Blvd., Honolulu 96815, tel. 808/949–3811 or 800/367–8434. 800 rooms with bath. Facilities: 2 pools, 7 tennis courts, meeting rooms, shops, 5 restaurants, 2 lounges. AE, CB, DC, MC, V.*

Outrigger Waikiki Hotel. The star beachfront Outrigger property, located right on Kalakaua Avenue, is in the heart of the shopping and dining action, with some of the nicest sands in Waikiki spread out on the other side. Rooms are decorated with a Polynesian motif, and each has a lanai. Some have kitchenettes, for a higher price. For more than twenty years, the main show room has been the home of the sizzling Society of Seven and the group's Las Vegas–style production. *2335 Kalakaua Ave., Honolulu 96815, tel. 808/923–0711 or 800/367–5170. 529 rooms with bath. Facilities: pool, shops, 6 restaurants, 6 lounges. AE, CB, DC, MC, V.*

Sheraton Waikiki. Towering over its neighbors, this hotel has a lobby done in tones of periwinkle and peach, which look much too sedate in a building of such extravagant proportions. Fortunately, the gigantic capiz-shell chandeliers that clatter in the trade winds have survived the renovations. The rooms are spacious, many with a grand view of Diamond Head. The hotel is located just steps away from the multilevel Royal Hawaiian Shopping Center and next to the Royal Hawaiian Hotel. Be sure to take the glass elevator up to the Hanohano Room, an elegant dining room with breathtaking panoramas of the sea and Waikiki. *2255 Kalakaua Ave., Honolulu 96815, tel. 808/922–4422 or 800/325–3535. On the beach. 1,900 rooms with bath. Facilities: 2 pools, shops, meeting rooms, 5 restaurants, 3 lounges. AE, CB, DC, MC, V.*

Waikiki Joy. With rooms ranging in price from Moderate to Very Expensive, this 1988 addition to the Waikiki lodging scene has something for everybody. Some rooms have refrigerators, others have full kitchens, and still others have complete wet bars. There are five types of rooms; one tower has all suites, and another has standard hotel rooms. Bed sizes range from double to king and queen, and you can also ask for ocean or partial ocean views. The common denominators: Each room has a lanai, a Jacuzzi, a deluxe stereo system with Bose speakers, and a control panel by the bed. *320 Lewers St., Honolulu 96815, tel. 808/923–2300 or 800/367–8047. 101 rooms with bath. Facilities: pool, sauna, restaurant, lounge. AE, CB, DC, MC, V.*

★ **Waikiki Parc.** Billing itself as offering "affordable luxury," this hotel lives up to that promise in all essentials except the main entrance, which is down a narrow side street, and the location, which is not on the beach. The lobby is light and airy, with mirrors and pastel tones. Guest rooms are done in cool blues and whites, with lots of rattan, plush carpeting, conversation areas, tinted glass lanai doors, and shutters. Some rooms are in the Very Expensive category, but others start as low as $90. Each room features a lanai, a refrigerator, central air-conditioning, an electronic in-room safe, and a high-security electronic-card entry system. The hotel has a fine Japanese restaurant called Kacho and the lovely Parc Cafe. *2233 Helumoa Rd., Honolulu 96815, tel. 808/921–7272 or 800/422–0450. 298 rooms with bath. Facilities: pool, recreation deck, 2 restaurants, 2 shops. AE, CB, DC, MC, V.*

Moderate **Aston Waikikian on the Beach.** It's one of the few low-rise ho-
★ tels left, although it does have a newer, air-conditioned Tiki Tower. This hotel is a little gem, perhaps unpolished in spots, but the romance of old Hawaii is definitely here in the South Seas architecture, high-pitched roofs, and junglelike gardens. Rooms are decorated in old Polynesian style, very different from more modern accommodations, and windows and doors open onto a garden path. The hotel is not technically on the beach, but it fronts the Duke Kahanamoku Lagoon, which has a sandy shore. The Tahitian Lanai restaurant has a faithful local following. *1811 Ala Moana Blvd., Honolulu 96815, tel. 808/949–5331 or 800/922–7866; in Canada, 800/423–8733. 135 rooms with bath. Facilities: pool, shops, restaurant, cocktail lounge. AE, CB, DC, MC, V.*

Hawaiiana Hotel. One of the cherished old-timers of Waikiki, this hotel has definitely improved with age. The aloha spirit permeates the place. When you arrive you are offered fresh pineapple, and when you leave you get a flower lei. Two- and three-story sections are arranged around a gorgeous tropical garden, and the sands of Fort DeRussy Beach are a short walk away. Open your door, and the gardens and pools are right there. The decor is simple and basic, and rooms come with electronic safes, air-conditioning, phones, and kitchens. Many have lanais as well. Complimentary newspapers, juice, and coffee are offered each morning on the patio. *260 Beach Walk, Honolulu 96815, tel. 808/923–3811 or 800/367–5122. ½ block from the beach. 95 rooms with bath. Facilities: pool, free washers and dryers. AE, MC, V.*

Holiday Inn–Waikiki Beach. The location—almost next to Kapiolani Park, the zoo, and other attractions—is excellent, and the seawall in front of the hotel offers the best sunset views. The mauka (north) tower has been completely refurbished and offers mainly ocean views. The rooms have nice rattan furniture, right down to the headboards. Each room is equipped with a color TV, private lanai, and air-conditioning. The Captain's Table serves meals in surroundings modeled after old-time luxury liners. *2570 Kalakaua Ave., Honolulu 96815, tel. 808/922–2511 or 800/465–4329. Across the street from the beach. 716 rooms with bath. Facilities: pool, 2 restaurants, 3 lounges, shops. AE, CB, DC, MC, V.*

New Otani Kaimana Beach Hotel. Extensive renovations have taken this establishment a long way. The ambience is cheerful and charming and the lobby has happily maintained its unpretentious feel. Polished to a shine, it is open to the trade winds and furnished with big, comfortable chairs and good magazines. Best of all, the hotel is right on the beach at the quiet end of Waikiki, practically at the foot of Diamond Head. Hotel manager Steve Boyle has received national recognition for his efforts to preserve the beauty of Diamond Head, and he often leads hikes to the summit. The staff is also friendly and helpful. Rooms are smallish but very nicely appointed, with soothing pastels, off-white furnishings, and color TV. Get a room with an ocean view, if possible. *2863 Kalakaua Ave., Honolulu*

96815, tel. 808/923–1555 or 800/421–8795 in the United States and Canada; in California, 800/252–0197. 138 rooms with bath. Facilities: 3 restaurants (1 Japanese), 1 lounge, shops, meeting rooms. AE, CB, DC, MC, V.

Outrigger Reef Hotel. The big recommendations here are the location right on the beach and the price—which is right. The extensive renovations have definitely improved the appearance of the lobby and rooms. Charming fashion and souvenir boutiques have replaced the random lobby vendors, and the rooms are now done in soft mauves and pinks; many have lanais, and all have air-conditioning and color TVs. Ask for an ocean view; the other views are decidedly less delightful. The seventh floor is for nonsmokers. *2169 Kalia Rd., Honolulu 96815, tel. 808/923–3111 or 800/367–5170. 883 rooms with bath. Facilities: pool, 4 restaurants, 4 lounges, nightclub, shops, meeting rooms. AE, CB, DC, MC, V.*

Waikiki Hana. Behind the Hyatt Regency sits this little-known secret, a moderately priced hotel in a superb location. Although the building is not new, it has been renovated, and the lobby is charmingly furnished with wicker furniture. The rooms are attractively decorated, with pink walls, blue quilted bedspreads, and light wood. Each room has a color TV, a telephone, and air-conditioning. Some have kitchenettes. All that, and it's just a block to the beach (the hotel has no pool). Go during the off-season, and the prices are $10 lower. *2424 Koa Ave., Honolulu 96815, tel. 808/926–8841 or 800/367–5004. 73 rooms with bath. AE, CB, DC, MC, V.*

Inexpensive **Continental Surf Hotel.** One of the great budget hotels of Waikiki, this appealing high rise is located along the Kuhio Avenue strip, two blocks from the ocean and convenient to tons of shopping and dining options. The lobby is large and breezy, and the comfortable rooms are decorated in standard Polynesian hues of browns and golds. Each room has a color TV, a telephone, and individually controlled air-conditioning. However, there are real views and no lanais. Some rooms have a well-equipped kitchenette. *2426 Kuhio Ave., Honolulu 96815, tel. 808/922–2755 or 800/245–7873. 2 blocks from the beach. 140 rooms with bath. Facilities: guests may use the facilities of its sister hotel, the Miramar, 1½ blocks away. AE, CB, DC, MC, V.*

Edmunds Hotel Apartments. Located on the Ala Wai Canal, four blocks from the ocean, this has been a budget gem for more than 20 years. Long lanais wrap around the building so that each room has its own view of the pretty canal and glorious Manoa Valley beyond—views that look especially lovely at night, when lights are twinkling up the mountain ridges. The rooms are small, nondescript studios, but they have all the basics: kitchenette, toaster, ironing board, and TV set. If you can put up with the occasional sounds of traffic on the boulevard, this is a real bargain. *2411 Ala Wai Blvd., Honolulu 96815, tel. 808/923–8381. 4 blocks from the beach. 12 rooms with bath. No credit cards.*

Malihini Hotel. There's no pool, it's not on the beach, none of the units has a television or air-conditioning, and the rooms are spartan. Still, the atmosphere of this low-rise complex is cool and pleasant, and the gardens are well maintained. All rooms are either studios or one-bedrooms, and all have kitchenettes, daily maid service, and fans. The low prices and good location make this a popular place, so be sure to book well in advance.

217 Saratoga Rd., Honolulu 96815, tel. 808/923-9644. 28 rooms with bath. Facilities: 1 shop. No credit cards.

Royal Grove Hotel. You won't go wrong with this flamingo-pink hotel, reminiscent of Miami. With just six floors, it is one of Waikiki's smaller hotels. The lobby is comfortable; the rooms, though agreeably furnished, have no real theme and no views. They do, however, all have kitchens and air-conditioning, plus color TVs and telephones. The pool area is bright with tropical flowers (the hotel is not on the beach). Most people enjoy the family atmosphere. *15 Uluniu Ave., Honolulu 96815, tel. 808/923-7691. 87 rooms with bath. Facilities: pool. AE, CB, DC, MC, V.*

Royal Islander. The location—only two minutes from a very nice section of Waikiki Beach—is the key to this inexpensive link in the Outrigger hotel chain. The rooms have tapa-print bedspreads and ceramic lamps with matching patterns, and there are Island-inspired pictures on the walls. Each room also has a private lanai, color TV, and air-conditioning. Choose from studios, one-bedroom apartments, or suites. The staff is helpful in arranging activities, such as golf and scuba packages and sightseeing tours. *2164 Kalia Rd., Honolulu 96815, tel. 808/922-1961 or 800/367-5170. 101 rooms with bath. Facilities: no pool, but guests are allowed to use the pools at other Outrigger Hotels. AE, CB, DC, MC, V.*

Waikiki Lei Apartments. A favorite with repeat guests looking for affordable lodging in the heart of the action, this four-story pink establishment is one-of-a-kind. There's no elevator; guests use the outside staircase. Everything is well maintained, and the studio units have a kitchen and refrigerator. You need to ask ahead if you want a room with a TV and air-conditioning, and there is no maid service. The decor is dark wood and light-colored spreads, with tile floors. The longer you stay, the lower the daily price. *241 Kaiulani Ave., Honolulu 96815, tel. 808/923-6656 or 808/734-8588. 2 blocks from the beach. 19 units with bath. Facilities: pool, coin-operated washers and dryers. No credit cards.*

Honolulu

Very Expensive ★ **Kahala Hilton.** Minutes away from Waikiki, on the quiet side of Diamond Head, this elegant and understated hotel is situated in the wealthy neighborhood of Kahala. Here's where kings, Hollywood stars, and presidents stay. The Kahala Hilton's impressive lobby features chandeliers, tropical flower displays, and a musician playing a grand piano. The very large rooms, decorated in earth and natural tones, have his and her dressing rooms and parquet floors. The hotel also has a porpoise pond and four distinguished restaurants, including Maile, with Continental cuisine, and the Hala Terrace supper club, featuring local star Danny Kaleikini. The staff prides itself on its service. The hotel is affiliated with the Maunalua Bay Club, a fitness center just a short shuttle away. *5000 Kahala Ave., Honolulu 96816, tel. 808/734-2211 or 800/367-2525. On the beach. 309 rooms and suites with bath, plus 60 cottage-style units in the Lagoon Terrace. Facilities: pool, tennis court, shops, meeting rooms, 4 restaurants, 2 lounges. AE, CB, DC, MC, V.*

Expensive **Ramada Renaissance Ala Moana Hotel.** This 20-year-old landmark boasts an excellent location, right next to the popular Ala Moana Shopping Center (they're connected by a pedestrian ramp) and one block from Ala Moana Beach Park. A $30 million renovation has transformed the 36-floor hotel into a gorgeous showcase, and the rooms have been refurbished to include color TVs, air-conditioning, AM/FM radios, electronic-card door locks, and private safes. Each has a lanai for a view of the ocean, the Koolau Mountains, or Diamond Head. Preferred floors with special suites feature complete bar service, a spa, and free newspaper and breakfast delivery each morning. The Mahina Lounge, a sleek lobby bar with a white grand piano, hosts live entertainment. *410 Atkinson Dr., Honolulu 96814, tel. 808/955–4811 or 800/367–6025. 1,200 rooms with bath. Facilities: 5 restaurants, 2 lounges, nightclub, shops, pool, pool bar. AE, CB, DC, MC, V.*

Moderate **Manoa Valley Inn.** Here's an intimate surprise tucked away in Manoa Valley, just 2 miles from Waikiki. Built in 1919, this stately hotel features a complimentary Continental-breakfast buffet on a shady lanai, and fresh tropical fruit and cheese in the afternoon. Rooms are furnished in country-inn style, with antique four-poster beds, marble-topped dressers, patterned wallpaper, and fresh flowers. *2001 Vancouver Dr., Honolulu 96822, 808/947–6019 or 800/634–5115. 7 guest rooms, 4 with private bath; 1 cottage with bath. Facilities: TV and VCR in the reading room. MC, V.*

Pagoda Hotel. Minutes away from the four-level, 50-acre Ala Moana Shopping Center and from Ala Moana Beach Park, the Pagoda has a convenient location, and there's also a free shuttle bus between the hotel and its sister property, the Pacific Beach in Waikiki. That, along with the moderate rates, makes this a good choice if you're simply looking for a place to sleep and to catch a couple of meals. Studio rooms include a full-size refrigerator, a stove, and cooking utensils. No real views are offered here, since the hotel is situated in the middle of a lot of high rises. However, the rooms are all air-conditioned, and each has a color TV. The hotel features Koi, one of Honolulu's most interesting restaurants, notable for its Japanese gardens and waterways filled with colorful carp. *1525 Rycroft St., Honolulu 96814, tel. 808/941–6611 or 800/367–6060. 341 rooms with bath. Facilities: pool, shops, 2 restaurants. AE, CB, DC, MC, V.*

Around the Island

Very Expensive **Turtle Bay Hilton.** The only place to stay for miles and miles along the island's north shore. Though it's not swanky, this oceanside retreat has everything it takes for a relaxing stay away from town. The rooms, in three separate wings, have private lanais and are furnished with basic wicker, brass, pastels, and light woods, with pastel prints on the walls. A lot of people like the hotel for its golf course and horseback-riding facilities. Others drive out just to enjoy its mammoth Sunday champagne brunch, where you dine next to huge windows with a view of the crashing surf. The sunsets are wonderful, so try to get a room with a view of the water. The cottages adjacent to the hotel are pricier but offer more privacy. *Box 187, Kahuku 96731, tel. 808/293–8811 or 800/HILTONS. On the beach. 487 rooms, suites, and cottages with bath. Facilities: pool, golf, tennis, horses, shops, restaurants. AE, CB, DC, MC, V.*

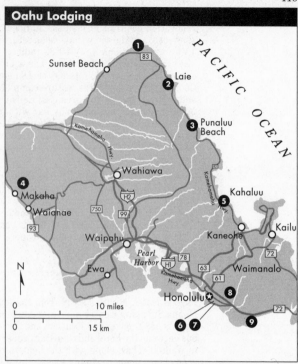

Oahu Lodging

Expensive
★

Sheraton Makaha Resort and Country Club. It takes an hour-plus by car to get from Waikiki to this country resort set in glorious Makaha Valley, and the trip is worth it. Clusters of low-rise cottages and open-air pavilions keep this place simple and sweet. The Polynesian architecture and steep A-framed roofs look a little dated, but the interiors are done in a lovely combination of natural colors and woods. Each room has a private lanai with chairs and a table, plus a refrigerator, air-conditioning, a telephone, and a color TV. Most of the guests here play golf on one of the two highly acclaimed Makaha courses. Makaha Beach, popular with the locals, is about a mile away. Be sure to sign up for the horseback ride to the valley's restored ancient heiau (sacred Hawaiian site). *Box 896, Makaha 96792, tel. 808/695–9511 or 800/334–8484. 200 rooms with bath. Facilities: golf, tennis, horses, pool, shops, lounge, 2 restaurants. AE, CB, DC, MC, V.*

Inexpensive

Laniloa Lodge. Situated on the main road right next to the Polynesian Cultural Center, this plain, two-story establishment is the only hotel in Laie. That means you can break your round-the-island driving tour in two and spend the night here in basic comfort. The rooms are all studios, with color TVs and air-conditioning. The motif is Polynesian. Five separate wings form a circle around the swimming pool, and all the lanais face inward. *55109 Laniloa St., Laie 96762, tel. 808/293–9282 or 800/367–8047 ext. 359. 46 rooms with bath. Facilities: pool. AE, CB, DC, MC, V.*

Pat's at Punaluu. Families find everything they need at this unpretentious condominium hotel located between the windward side and the North Shore, an ideal base for seeing the attractions of Oahu's "other side." The mood is decidedly country here. The hotel is set on a reef-protected, palm-fringed beach whose waters are nice for swimming, snorkeling, windsurfing, and fishing. Golf and tennis are also nearby. Fully furnished rental apartments include studio and cottage units with kitchens and dishwashers; many have washer/dryers. Rooms are done in greens and browns, with rattan furniture, and each unit has a lanai. *Box 359, Hauula 96717, tel. 808/293–8111 or 293–9322. On the beach. 136 rooms with bath. Facilities: pool, restaurant, saunas, gym, stores, recreational areas. MC, V.*

Schrader's Windward Marine Resort. Here is another rural resort with fewer luxuries than you would find in Waikiki but with perhaps a little more personalized attention from the staff. Some of the one-, two-, and three-bedroom apartments have kitchens and refrigerators. Each unit has a color TV, air-conditioning, a couch and coffee table; beds are turned down for the guests at night. The fancier rooms include full cooking facilities and remote-control TV. Some rooms open onto Kaneohe Bay, so close that people have been known to fish right off their lanais. Other rooms face the Koolau Mountains. Set on a peninsula, this is a popular spot for water activities. Jet skiing, snorkeling, windsurfing, and other excursions are offered to guests at special rates. *47-039 Lihikai Dr., Kaneohe 96744, tel. 808/239–5711 or 800/367–8047 ext. 239; in Canada, 800/423–8733 ext. 239. On the beach. 55 rooms with bath. Facilities: water sports, pool, spa. AE, CB, DC, MC, V.*

Bed-and-Breakfasts

Bed and Breakfast Hawaii. This reliable booker offers homestays around Oahu, as well as on the other Islands. *Box 449, Kapaa 96746, tel. 808/822–7771 or 800/657–7832.*

Bed and Breakfast Honolulu. This company has an especially good selection of rooms in Honolulu, including a place to stay in one of the few remaining private homes in Waikiki. *3242 Kaohinani Dr., Honolulu 96817, tel. 808/595–7533 or 800/288–4666.*

Pacific Hawaii Bed and Breakfast. These folks will help you book a B & B unit in the moderate range. *19 Kai Nani Pl., Kailua 96743, tel. 808/262–6026 or 254–5030.*

The Arts

The arts thrive right alongside the tourist industry in Oahu's balmy climate. The island has a symphony orchestra, an opera company, chamber-music groups, and theater troupes. The major ballet companies also come gliding through from time to time. Check the local newspapers, the morning *Honolulu Advertiser* and the afternoon *Honolulu Star-Bulletin*, for the latest happenings.

Dance

Every autumn, the Honolulu Symphony (tel. 808/537–6191) imports the **San Francisco Ballet.** A local company, **Ballet Hawaii** (tel. 808/988–7578), is active during the holiday season with its annual production of **The Nutcracker,** which is usually held at the Mamiya Theater (3142 Waialae Ave., Chaminade University, Honolulu).

Film

Art films. Art, international, classic, and silent films are screened at the little theater at the Honolulu Academy of Arts. *900 S. Beretania St., Honolulu 96814, tel. 808/538–1006. Tickets: $3. Dinner in the garden courtyard (tel. 808/531–8865) is served Thurs. at 6:30 PM.*

The Hawaii International Film Festival (1777 East-West Rd., Honolulu 96822, tel. 808/944–7666) may not be Cannes, but it is unique and exciting. The week-long festival, held from the end of November to early December, is based on the theme "When Strangers Meet." Top films from the United States, Asia, and the Pacific are aired day and night at several theaters on Oahu. Many local people plan their vacations around this time and spend days viewing free films and attending lectures, workshops, and social events with visiting film experts.

The Varsity Theater (1106 University Ave., tel. 808/946–4144) is a two-theater art house that brings internationally acclaimed motion pictures to Honolulu.

Waikiki generally gets the first-run films at its trio of theaters dubbed, appropriately, the **Waikiki 1, Waikiki 2,** and **Waikiki 3** (tel. 808/923–2394). Check newspapers for what's playing.

Music

Chamber Music Hawaii (tel. 808/261–4290) gives 25 concerts a year at the Honolulu Lutheran Church (1730 Punahou St.), Honolulu Academy of Arts (900 S. Beretania St.), and other locations around the island.

The Hawaii Opera Theater's season spans February and March, beginning with Verdi's *Aida,* Feb. 1, 3, and 5; Mozart's *The Marriage of Figaro,* February 15, 17, and 19; and Bernstein's *Candide,* March 1, 3, and 5. *Neal Blaisdell Concert Hall, Ward Ave. and King St., tel. 808/521–6537. Tickets: $15–$40 at the box office. To charge on credit cards, tel. 808/ 521–2911. MC, V.*

The Honolulu Symphony's season runs September to April, Tuesday evenings and Sunday afternoons at Blaisdell Concert Hall (Ward Ave. at King St.). The Symphony on the Light Side series is on Friday evenings during the same season. Well-known Island musicians often play with the symphony, and occasionally international performers are headlined. During the summer, the popular Starlight Series is held outdoors at the Waikiki Shell in Kapiolani Park. Write or call for a complete schedule. *1441 Kapiolani Blvd., Suite 1515, Honolulu 96814, tel. 808/942–2200. Tickets: $10–$30.*

During the school year, the faculty of the **University of Hawaii Music Department** (tel. 808/948–7756) gives concerts at Orvis Auditorium on the Manoa campus.

Rock concerts are usually performed at the cavernous Neal Blaisdell Center Arena (tel. 808/521–2911). Internationally famous stars also pack them in at Aloha Stadium (tel. 808/486–9300).

Theater

Because the Islands are so expensive to get to and stay on, major touring companies seldom come to Hawaii. As a result, Oahu has developed several excellent local theater troupes, which present first-rate entertainment all year long.

American Theater Company Hawaii, the newest ensemble on the scene, is Hawaii's only full-fledged professional acting company. It features Broadway actors and local professionals and mounts productions in various locations around town. *720 Iwilei Rd., Suite 290, Honolulu 96817, tel. 808/599–5122. Prices vary.*

The **Honolulu Community Theater** is in residence five minutes away from Waikiki, right next to Diamond Head. Its repertoire includes a little of everything: musicals, dramas, experimental, contemporary, and classics. *520 Makapuu Ave., Honolulu 96816, tel. 808/734–0274. Tickets: $11.75–$15.75.*

The **Honolulu Theater for Youth** stages delightful productions for children around the Islands from July to May. Write or call for a schedule. *2846 Ualena St., Honolulu 96819, tel. 808/839–9885. Tickets: $6 adults, $4 youth.*

The **John F. Kennedy Theater** at the University of Hawaii's Manoa campus is the setting for eclectic dramatic offerings—everything from musical theater to Kabuki, Noh, and Chinese opera. *1770 East-West Rd., Honolulu 96822, tel. 808/948–7655. Prices vary.*

Kumu Kahua, now in its 20th season, is the only troupe presenting shows and plays written on and about the Islands. It offers up five productions a year in Tenney Theatre, on the grounds of St. Andrew's Cathedral. *224 St. Emma Sq., Honolulu 96813, tel. 808/737–4161. Tickets: $6 adults, $5 students and seniors.*

The **Manoa Valley Theater** offers wonderful nonprofessional productions in an intimate theater in Manoa Valley. Its season is September to June. Write or call for a schedule. *2833 E. Manoa Rd., Honolulu 96822, tel. 808/988–6131. Tickets $12–$14.*

The **Starving Artists Theater Company** is the theater-in-residence at Mid-Pacific Institute. Its creative productions draw on both student and community talent. *2445 Kaala St., Honolulu 96822, tel. 808/942–1942. Tickets: $5–$7.*

The **Windward Theater Guild** is now in its 34th year of offering live family entertainment on the windward side of Oahu. Since it has no theater of its own, check the newspapers for location. *Box 624, Kailua 96734, tel. 808/261–4885. Tickets: $8–$10.*

Nightlife

Nightlife on Oahu can be as simple as a barefoot stroll in the sand or as elaborate as a dinner show with all the glittering choreography of a Las Vegas production. You can view the vibrant hues of a Honolulu sunset during a cocktail cruise, or hear the mystifying melodies of ancient chants at a luau on a remote west-shore beach.

Waikiki is where nearly all of Oahu's night action takes place, and what action there is! Kalakaua and Kuhio avenues come to life when the sun goes down and the lights go on. It's fun just to watch the parade of people. Some strollers walk purposefully, knowing they have dinner reservations. Others wander along the strip reading every sign, every posted menu, looking for something to strike their fancy, whether it's the right atmosphere, the right price, or the catchiest tune.

Outside Honolulu, the offerings are slimmer but equally diverse. You can dance the two-step at a waterfront cafe one night and the next night boogie to live bands in a tiny second-story windward bar. The north shore is more conducive to settling back to the music of a slack-key guitar and lilting falsetto voice, while the ranch country of Waimanalo lends itself to country tunes and fiddle playing.

Wafting through the night air of Oahu is the sound of music of every kind—from classical to contemporary. Music has been the language of Hawaii from the beginning, and Oahu has the best selection of any Island. Along with the music of the ancients, there's a new music in the soul of Hawaii. Traditional Hawaiian music has absorbed or fused with rock and disco to create a distinctively Hawaiian contemporary sound. Strong currents of jazz, country, and reggae also run through the local music pool.

Meanwhile, hula dancers wear sequined skirts in Waikiki and authentic ti-leaf skirts at Paradise Cove; they are accompanied by everything from *ipu* drums to electric guitars, mercifully not on the same stage in most cases. The latest high-tech, ultrastereo video discos may also be found on Oahu, but then, so are acoustic ukulele trios.

Bars/Cabarets/Clubs

The drinking age is 21 on Oahu and throughout Hawaii, although many bars admit younger people without serving them alcohol. By law, all establishments that serve alcoholic beverages must close at 2 AM. The only exceptions are those with a cabaret license, which may have a 4 AM curfew. These may be billed as discotheques, but they are required to have live music. Most of the places listed below have a cover charge of $2 to $5.

Waikiki **Annabelle's** (Ilikai Waikiki Hotel, 1777 Ala Moana, tel. 808/949-3811). This spot, which offers disco dancing atop the hotel with the Honolulu city lights spread out below, attracts a casual crowd—what might be classified as the "beer bunch." Happy hour nightly 5–9, open until 2 on weekdays, 4 on weekends.

Bavarian Beer Garden (Royal Hawaiian Shopping Ctr., 3rd floor, 2201 Kalakaua Ave., tel. 808/922-6535). You can polka to your heart's content in this old-world atmosphere and quaff some of the world's best brews. Oktoberfest specials are a big deal each fall. Nightly 5–midnight.

Bobby McGee's Conglomeration (2885 Kalakaua Ave., tel. 808/922-1282). The club has disco dancing for adults in the 21–30 age group. Nightly 7–2.

Cilly's (1909 Ala Wai Blvd., basement, tel. 808/942-2952). This is another place where the fast-moving younger-adult crowd goes for disco dancing. Evening drink specials come as cheap as 25¢. Nightly 9–4.

Cupid's Lobby Bar (Prince Kuhio Hotel, 2500 Kuhio Ave., tel. 808/922–0811). Singer and pianist Pat Sylva tickles the ivories Mondays through Thursdays, while on Friday he's joined by friends to form the Pat Sylva Hawaiian Trio. Weekends feature guitar player Scott Moulton. Daily 11–11 with live music 6–10.

Esprit (Sheraton Waikiki Hotel, 2255 Kalakaua Ave., tel. 808/922–4422). Bernadette and the Sunshine Company play Tuesday through Saturday, and the Love Notes fill the Sunday and Monday slot. Tourists flock here to dance, and so do local men looking for tourist women. Nightly 9–1.

Genesis Nightclub (2888 Waialae Ave., tel. 808/734–3772). After the dinner show there's dancing to live music amid stainless-steel decor. Nightly 11–3:30.

Hawaii Prince Hotel's Captain's Room (100 Holomoana St., tel. 808/956–1111). Hot sounds of the island's most exciting jazz performers fill this new nightspot. Nightly 10–2.

Jazz Cellar (205 Lewers St., tel. 808/923–9952). Live rock every night and 25¢ drinks on Monday make this a popular spot with the young-adult set. Music nightly 9–4. Late-night happy hour 2–4 AM.

Maile Lounge (Kahala Hilton Hotel, 5000 Kahala Ave., tel. 808/734–2211). A band called Kit Samson's Sound Advice has kept folks swinging on the small dance floor for more than 15 years, playing everything from contemporary hits to '40s favorites. Mon.–Sat. 8:15–12:45.

Monarch Room (Royal Hawaiian Hotel, 2255 Kalakaua Ave., tel. 808/923–7311). Tea dancing is a tradition at this historic hotel. Dancers spill out onto the grassy area near the ocean to dance to music by the Del Courtney Orchestra with vocalist Jimmy Borges. Sunday 4–8:30.

Moose McGillycuddy's Pub and Cafe (310 Lewers St., tel. 808/923–0751). A variety of bands play for the beach-and-beer gang in a casual setting. Nightly 9–1:30.

Nick's Fishmarket (Waikiki Gateway Hotel, 2070 Kalakaua Ave., tel. 808/955–6333). This is probably the most comfortable of the Waikiki dance lounges, with an elegant crowd, inspiring music, and an intimate, dark atmosphere. There's some singles action here. Nightly 9–1:30.

Nicholas Nickolas (Ramada Renaissance Ala Moana Hotel, 410 Atkinson Dr., tel. 808/955–4466). The view is splendid, the music is good, and the crowd dresses well, but the place is a bit on the stuffy side. Dancing Sunday–Thursday nights 9:30–2:15, Friday and Saturday 10–3:15.

Paradise Lounge (Hilton Hawaiian Village, 2005 Kalia Rd., tel. 808/949–4321). It's expensive, which is reflected in the crowds appearance. A piano player sets the tone for the dancing, nightly 5:30–11. One of Honolulu's top jazz crooners, Jimmy Borges, headlines with the Betty Loo Taylor Trio Friday and Saturday 8–midnight.

Pink Cadillac (478 Ena Rd., tel. 808/942–5282). The hard rock music draws a rowdy crowd. You can dance by yourself or with your partner. Nightly 9–2.

Point After (Hawaiian Regent Hotel, 2552 Kalakaua Ave., tel. 808/922–6611). This club, with video dancing for young adults, is a cut above most. Nightly 7–4.

Rumours (Ramada Renaissance Ala Moana Hotel, 410 Atkinson St., tel. 808/955–4811). The after-work crowd loves this spot, which offers video and disco dancing with all the lights and action. Sun.–Thurs. nights 5–3, Fri. and Sat. nights 5–4.

On Big Chill nights, the club plays oldies from the '60s and '70s and serves free pupus, or hors d'oeuvres (call for schedule).

Scruples (Waikiki Market Place, 2310 Kuhio Ave., tel. 808/923–9530). The club features disco dancing to Top 40 tunes, with a young adult, mostly local crowd. Nightly 8–4.

Shore Bird Beach Broiler (Outrigger Reef Hotel, 2169 Kalia Rd., tel. 808/922–2887). This beachfront disco that spills right out to the sand features a large dance floor and 10-foot video screen. Karaoke singalongs are held nightly, 9–2.

Trappers (Hyatt Regency Waikiki, 2424 Kalakaua Ave., tel. 808/923–1234). This is an elegant night spot featuring such popular musicians as the New Orleans Jazz Band and jazz flautist Herbie Mann. Stars stop by to jam when they're in town. Nightly 5–2.

Wave Waikiki (1877 Kalakaua Ave., tel. 808/941–0424). Dance to live rock 'n' roll until 1:30, recorded music after that. It can be a rough scene, but the bands are tops. Nightly 9–4.

Honolulu **Anna Banana's** (2440 S. Beretania St., tel. 808/946–5190). At this two-story, smoky dive, the live music is fresh, loud, and sometimes experimental. Local favorites the Pagan Babies perform ultra-creative reggae music regularly, but the likes of blues singer Taj Mahal have been known to slip in for a set or two. Open nightly 11:30–2. Live music Wednesday–Sunday, 9–2.

Black Orchid (Restaurant Row, 500 Ala Moana Blvd., tel. 808/521–3111). A very upscale atmosphere pervades this restaurant and club, which is partially owned by Tom Selleck. Azure McCall sings hot jazz weeknights 5:30–9 and Sundays 8:30–1:30. Live dance bands play Tuesday–Saturday nights 10–3:30.

Buzz's Original Steak House (2535 Coyne St., tel. 808/944–9781). The lounge area of this comfortable restaurant is the forum for mellow folk/jazz singers on Friday and Saturday nights 8–11:30. For a real treat, catch old-time song-writer Andy Cummings as he strolls around strumming his ukulele and telling stories about the old days, Sunday nights 6–9.

Jubilee Nightclub (1007 Dillingham Blvd., tel. 808/845–1568). If you can see through the smoke and hear over the noise, this local hangout is a great spot to experience live, authentic Hawaiian music. It's not a fancy place, so don't dress up. Nightly 8–4.

Studebakers (Restaurant Row, 500 Ala Moana Blvd., tel. 808/526–9888). Exhausting "nonstop bop" revives the early rock 'n' roll era with an all-American '50s and '60s look. Free pupus weekdays 4–8. Open Monday–Saturday 11 AM–2 AM, Sunday noon–2 AM. Minimum age: 23.

Around the Island **Pecos River Cafe** (99-016 Kamehameha Hwy., tel. 808/487–
Aiea 7980). Billing itself as Hawaii's premier country and western nightclub, this easygoing establishment features two live bands. Keyed Up Country plays Sunday–Tuesday nights, and Straight Shot takes over Wednesday–Saturday nights, 9–1:20.

Kahuku **Bayview Lounge** (Turtle Bay Hilton, tel. 808/293–8811). A truly beautiful place to watch the sun set over the north shore water. Regulars the Ohana Trio play contemporary Hawaiian tunes Thursday nights 6–9.

Kailua **Fast Eddie's** (52 Oneawa St., tel. 808/261–8561). If you want to boogie, visit this hot spot for live local and national bands playing everything from rock to Top 40 songs. Nightly 8–4. Attention, ladies: The Fast Eddie's Male Revue is a longstanding tradition not to be missed. Friday and Saturday nights 8:30–10:30.

Makaha **Lobby Lounge** (Sheraton Makaha Resort and Country Club, tel. 808/695–9511). If you're staying at this tranquil resort, stop in the Lobby Lounge for Karaoke Night, when you can try your hand at performing, Friday–Saturday 8:30–12:30.

Makapuu **The Galley** (Sea Life Park, Makapuu Point, tel. 808/259–7933). Some of the top names in Island entertainment play at this relaxed restaurant in the popular marine park. Friday nights 8:30–10, with park admission.

Cocktail and Dinner Shows

Some Oahu entertainers have been around for years, and others have just arrived on the scene. Either way, the dinner-show food is usually acceptable, but certainly not the main event. If you want to dine on your own and then take in a show, sign up for a cocktail show. Dinner shows are all in the $35–$45 range, with the cocktail shows running $17–$25. The prices usually include one cocktail, tax, and gratuity. In all cases, reservations are required.

Al Harrington (Polynesian Palace, Reef Towers Hotel, 247 Lewers St., tel. 808/923–9861). Dubbed "the South Pacific Man," Harrington is a tall, handsome singer with a rich voice and a cast of 16 musicians and dancers to back him up. Sunday to Friday, first dinner seating at 5, cocktail seating at 5:45 for show at 6. Second dinner seating at 8, second cocktail seating at 8:45 for show at 9.

Brothers Cazimero (Monarch Room, Royal Hawaiian Hotel, 2259 Kalakaua Ave., tel. 808/923–7311). Robert and Roland Cazimero put on a class act, complete with their own hula dancers and a splendid blend of traditional and contemporary Hawaiian tunes. The Monarch Room is a lovely oceanside setting. Dinner show Tuesday to Saturday at 8:30, cocktail show Friday and Saturday at 10:30.

Charo (Tropics Surf Club, Hilton Hawaiian Village, 2005 Kalia Rd., tel. 808/949–4321 or 942–7873). Charo has appeared on Johnny Carson, David Letterman, and Merv Griffin's shows and has guest starred on countless television programs. This "coochie-coochie" girl's latest venture is a live act in Waikiki's newest showroom, located beachside. Latin rhythms, flamenco dancing, songs of the islands, and international music add up to a fiery evening with an explosive performer. Dinner seating at 6:30; cocktail seating at 7:30 for the show at 8.

Comedy Club (Ilikai Hotel, 1777 Ala Moana Blvd., tel. 808/922–5998). Some of the most outrageous national and local comics take to the stage of this relatively new and increasingly popular establishment. Show times are Tuesday to Thursday nights at 9; Friday at 8 and 10; Saturday at 7, 9, and 11; and Sunday at 9. There's dancing after the show, too.

Danny Kaleikini (Kahala Hilton Hotel, 5000 Kahala Ave., tel. 808/734–2211). This mellow fellow has been serenading guests for more than 20 years with songs, stories, and an occasional tune on the nose flute. Kaleikini's a gentleman, and a very gifted one. He performs an interesting mix of songs from Hawaii and Japan, where he's also a major star. Book early, because there's rarely an empty table. Dinner and cocktail show Monday to Saturday at 9.

Don Ho (The Dome, Hilton Hawaiian Village, 2005 Kalia Rd., tel. 808/949–4321). Waikiki's old pro still packs them in with his glitzy Las Vegas–style Polynesian revue. His memorable show features a huge cast of attractive performers from around the South Pacific, led by the "King of Hawaiian Entertainment" himself. Dinner seating Sunday to Friday at 6:30, cocktail seating at 8 for an 8:30 show.

Flashback (Hula Hut Theater Restaurant, 286 Beach Walk, tel. 808/923–8411). This is one of Waikiki's biggest draws. The movie-star look-alikes really pour on the nostalgia. The Elvis imitator—Jonathan Von Brana—looks pretty close to the real thing. The faux Diana Ross, Supremes, and Tina Turner are also tops. Monday–Saturday dinner seating begins at 8, cocktail seating at 8:30 on a first-come, first-served basis for the show at 9.

Frank DeLima (Peacock Room, Queen Kapiolani Hotel, 150 Kapahulu Ave., tel 808/922–1941). Local funny man Frank DeLima presides over this comedy forum. He places a heavy accent on the ethnic humor of the Islands, and does some pretty outrageous impressions. By the end of the evening he's poked fun at everyone in the audience—and folks eat it up. Wednesday–Sunday nights, 9:30 and 11.

Polynesian Cultural Center (55-370 Kamehameha Hwy., Laie, tel. 808/293–3333). Easily one of the best shows in the Islands. The actors are students from Brigham Young University's Hawaii campus. The production has soaring moments and an "erupting volcano." Dinner served from 4:30 on for the 7:30 show. During peak seasons (Christmas to March and June to August) there are two shows, at 6 and 7:45.

Sheraton's Spectacular Polynesian Revue (Ainahau Showroom, Sheraton Princess Kaiulani Hotel, 120 Kaiulani Ave., tel. 808/971–5300). From drumbeats of the ancient Hawaiians to Fijian war dances and Samoan slap dances, this show takes audiences on a musical tour of Polynesia. The highlight is a daring Samoan fire knife dancer. Two dinner and cocktail shows nightly.

Society of Seven (Outrigger Waikiki Hotel, 2335 Kalakaua Ave., tel. 808/922–6408). This lively, popular septet has great staying power and, after 20 years, continues to put on one of the best shows in Waikiki. They sing, dance, do impersonations, play instruments, and above all, entertain with their contemporary sound. Monday–Saturday nights, 8:30 and 10:30. No 10:30 show on Wednesday.

Dinner Cruises

The fleet of boats gets bigger every year. Most set sail daily from Fisherman's Wharf at Kewalo Basin, just beyond Ala Moana Beach Park, and head along the coast toward Diamond Head. There's usually dinner, dancing, drinks, and a sensational sunset. You'll find it hard to go indoors to dance, because the sea and sky are just too spectacular. Dinner cruises cost approximately $40, except as noted.

Aikane Catamarans (677 Ala Moana Blvd., Honolulu 96813, tel. 808/522–1533). The table seating for dinner is a plus. This is one of the veteran outfits, with catamarans based on an ancient Hawaiian design. Also offered: a package that takes you to the Outrigger Waikiki Hotel after the cruise to spend the rest of the evening with the Society of Seven entertainers. On Fridays there's a rock 'n' roll cruise, 8–10.

Alii Kai Catamarans (Pier 8, street level, Honolulu 96813, tel. 808/522–7822). Patterned after an ancient Polynesian vessel, the huge *Alii Kai* catamaran casts off from historic Aloha Tower with 1,000 passengers. The deluxe dinner cruise features two open bars, a huge dinner, and an authentic Polynesian show full of colorful hulas and upbeat music. The food is good, the after-dinner show loud and fun, and everyone dances to the Alii Kai musicians on the way back to shore.

Hawaiian Cruises' Sunset Dinner Sail (343 Hobron Ln., Honolulu 96815, tel. 808/947–9971). A full Polynesian revue breaks out on the high seas on board this 110-foot vessel, which holds 550 passengers. There's an open bar followed by a sit-down dinner.

Hilton Hawaiian Village Cruise (2005 Kalia Rd., Honolulu 96815, tel. 808/949–4321). With fewer than 150 passengers, this is a more intimate cruise than the others. The boat has distinctive rainbow sails. A two-hour champagne breakfast cruise is offered, as well as the twilight dinner sail.

Tradewind Charters (350 Ward Ave., Honolulu 96814, tel. 808/533–0220). This is a real sailing experience, a little more expensive and a lot more intimate than the other cruises mentioned. The sunset sail carries no more than six people. Cost: $60. Champagne and hors d'oeuvres are extra.

Windjammer Cruises (2222 Kalakaua Ave., 6th Floor, Honolulu 96814, tel. 808/922–1200). The pride of the fleet is the 1,500-passenger *Rella Mae*, done up like a clipper ship. It was once a Hudson River excursion boat in New York. Cocktails, dinner, a Polynesian revue, and dancing to a live band are all part of the package. Then you're whisked off for more fun at "Flashback," the Hula Hut show which takes you back to the legendary performers of the '50s and '60s.

Luaus

Just about everyone who comes to Hawaii goes to at least one luau. Traditionally, the luau would last for days, with feasting, sporting events, hula, and song. But at today's scaled-down and, for the most part, inauthentic version, you're as likely to find macaroni salad on the buffet as *poi* (taro paste) and big heaps of fried chicken beside the platter of *kalua* (roasted) pig. Traditional dishes that visitors actually enjoy include *laulau* (steamed bundles of ti leaves containing pork, butterfish, and taro tops), *lomilomi* salmon (massaged until tender and served with minced onions and tomatoes), and *haupia* (dessert made from coconut). As for the notorious poi, the clean, bland taste goes nicely with something salty, like bacon or kalua pig.

If you want authenticity, look in the newspaper to see if a church or civic club is holding a luau fund-raiser. You'll not only be welcome, you'll experience some down-home Hawaiiana. One luau that can be recommended as the real thing is **Hanohano Family Luau** (tel. 808/949–5559). During a day spent in Punaluu on Oahu's north shore, you help a family prepare a luau; go fishing; and participate in sports and games. Transportation is included in the cost: $38.95 adults, $29.95 children 12–16, $19.95 children 5–11.

Here are some other good luaus that emphasize fun without giving much thought to tradition. They generally cost $30–$50 adults, $25 children. Reservations are required.

Germaine's Luau (tel. 808/941–3338). You and a herd of about a thousand other people are bused to a remote beach near the industrial area. The bus ride is actually a lot of fun, while the beach and the sunset are pleasant. The service is brisk in order to feed everyone on time, and the food is so-so, but the show is warm and friendly. The bus collects passengers from 13 different Waikiki hotels; luaus start daily at 6.

Luau on the Beach (tel. 808/395–0677). Here's a nice switch—a luau right on Waikiki Beach. It takes place in front of the Outrigger Waikiki Hotel and begins with refreshing drinks at sunset. Dinner is all-you-can-eat, followed by an entertaining Polynesian show hosted by Doug Mossman of "Hawaii Five-O" fame. Tuesdays, Fridays, and Sundays at 7.

Paradise Cove Luau (tel. 808/973–5828). Another mass-produced event for a thousand or so. Once again, a bus takes you from one of six Waikiki hotel pickup points to a remote beach beside a picturesque cove on the western side of the island. There are palms and a glorious sunset, and the pageantry is fun, even informative. The food—well, you didn't come for the food, did you? Luaus begin daily at 5:30 (doors open at 5).

Royal Luau (Royal Hawaiian Hotel, 2259 Kalakaua Ave., tel. 808/923–7311). This is a notch above the rest of the commercial luaus on Oahu, perhaps because it takes place at the wonderful pink palace. With the setting sun, Diamond Head, the Pacific Ocean, and the enjoyable entertainment, who cares if the luau isn't totally authentic? Mon. at 6.

4 The Big Island of Hawaii

*by Betty
Fullard-Leo*

*A Hawaii resident
since 1962, Betty
Fullard-Leo writes
and edits for*
ALOHA, The
Magazine of
Hawaii and the
Pacific, *and for the*
Aloha Travelers'
Newsletter.

Nearly twice as large as all the other Hawaiian Islands combined, this youngest island of the chain is still growing, with lava adding black-sand beaches and more than 70 acres of land in the last decade on its southeast side. As a matter of fact, the Big Island has the world's most active volcano: the east rift zone below Halemaumau on Kilauea has been spewing lava intermittently since January 3, 1983.

The Big Island is accustomed to setting records. It is hyped as having the tallest mountain in the world (if you measure from Mauna Kea's origins some 32,000 feet beneath the ocean's surface to its lofty 13,796-foot peak). The island's southern tip extends farther south than any other state in the United States. To the southeast, far beneath the surface of the ocean, Loihi, a sea mount bubbling lava, is slowly building another Hawaiian Island, due to emerge in a few million years. On a higher plane, the Big Island has the world's most powerful telescope (at Keck Observatory), which searches the universe from the summit of Mauna Loa, the clearest place on earth for peering into the heavens.

The most diverse of all the islands, it offers skiing (but only for experts) in the winter and year-round sunshine on its southern and western shores, where the average temperature range is 69–84 degrees in July and 53–75 degrees in January. Yet there is so much rain near Hilo, its major city, that its only zoo is situated right in the middle of a rain forest.

Two of the Big Island's golf courses, the Mauna Kea Beach Resort course and the Francis I'i Brown Course at Mauna Lani Resort, are repeatedly chosen by golfing magazines as the best, the most spectacular, and the favorite of businesspeople and others. If locals were the bragging type, they could give Texans a run for their money—particularly since the Parker Ranch is touted as the largest privately owned ranch in the United States (though the folks at the King Ranch in Texas might justifiably say that's open to debate).

Yet visitors have been known to lack appreciation for, or to miss completely, the spiritual, sensual, untamed feel of this vast island. One Oahuan returned home after three days in Kailua-Kona to report, "I got bored. I couldn't find the beach, the shopping wasn't any different from Waikiki, and I walked the length of the town the first day!"

The first secret to enjoying the Big Island to the max is: Rent a car! The second secret is: Stay more than three days, or return again and again until you've seen all the facets of this fascinating place.

With 266 miles of coastline made up of white-coral, black-lava, and a dusting of green-olivine beaches, and with its cliffs of lava and emerald gorges slashing into jutting mountains, the Big Island is so large and so varied that it is easiest to split it up when planning a visit, in the same way former mayor Dante Carpenter divided it to discuss the exciting changes taking place. "Kona," he said, "is where the jobs are. Hilo and the Puna District are where the people are." Unfortunately, it's a bumpy 60 miles along Saddle Road, which runs between the Big Island's two largest volcanos, Mauna Kea and Mauna Loa, to travel from Hilo to the fancy resorts along the Kona–Kohala coast. This latter area, however, is where you'll find growth.

Luckily, there is plenty of room to grow on the Big Island. Land along the Kona–Kohala coast is generally dry, uninhabited stretches of lava. When a developer snakes a road to the ocean across a barren flow and supplies the water that creates a green oasis, many of us think it's an improvement.

In earlier times, Hawaii's kings and queens lived and played along this coastline. King Kamehameha I was born close to its northern shore, near the 500-year-old Mookini *Heiau* (a sacred stone platform for the worship of the gods). All along the water's edge are reminders of earlier inhabitants. At Kawaihae, two heiaus, Puukohola and Mailekini, mark the site of the final victory in Kamehameha's battle to unite the Hawaiian Islands in 1810. At Puako, an easy 15-minute walk from the road, are abundant examples of petroglyphs, the carvings etched by early Hawaiians into lava flows that depict everyday events in their lives.

In 1812 King Kamehameha I chose to build his principal residence, Kamakahonu, in Kailua-Kona. From this site, now on the grounds of the Hotel King Kamehameha, he ruled Hawaii in his later years, in a large enclosure bordered on one side by the Ahuena Heiau. Today the hotel offers free tours of these historic structures.

What perhaps stirs the most controversy when a new resort goes up is the potential destruction of significant archaeological finds. Most developers are aware of the reverence the Hawaiian people feel for their *aina* (land), and they attempt to preserve and restore the bits and pieces of Hawaiian history that come to light when a bulldozer rakes the land. Such modern resorts as the Royal Waikoloan and Kona Village conduct tours of the petroglyph fields on their grounds. The Royal Waikoloan at Anaehoomalu Bay and the Mauna Lani Resort have restored the fish ponds that once supplied the tables of Hawaiian royalty and have placed tasteful signs so that a stroll around the beachfront ponds is an interesting and informative experience.

This awareness of the past intrudes on the consciousness no matter where you go on the Big Island. In the calm tranquility of the Kohala Mountains to the north, where *paniolos* (cowboys) ride the range, or in the windswept isolation of South Point, which is thought to have been populated as early as AD 750, you wonder about the early Hawaiians who crossed this land on foot. Did they bring their gods and goddesses from their ancient homeland in the Tahitian islands? Or was the goddess Pele conceived as an explanation for some violent volcanic eruption?

Five volcanos formed the Big Island perhaps a half-million years ago: Kohala, Hualalai, Mauna Kea (white mountain), Mauna Loa (long mountain), and Kilauea, which is currently active. Early Hawaiians believed that Pele lived in whichever crater was erupting. Even today, eerie stories are repeated as fact; they tell of a woman hitchhiker who dresses in red and wanders the volcano area, accompanied by a small white dog. "My neighbor gave her a ride, but when he looked in the mirror she was gone!" is how one oft-repeated tale goes. As far as volcanic eruptions, those Pele has caused in recent years have been relatively nondestructive, flowing from rift zones through ohia forests on Kilauea's gentle slopes. Lava has

The Big Island of Hawaii (Boxes Refer to Detail Maps)

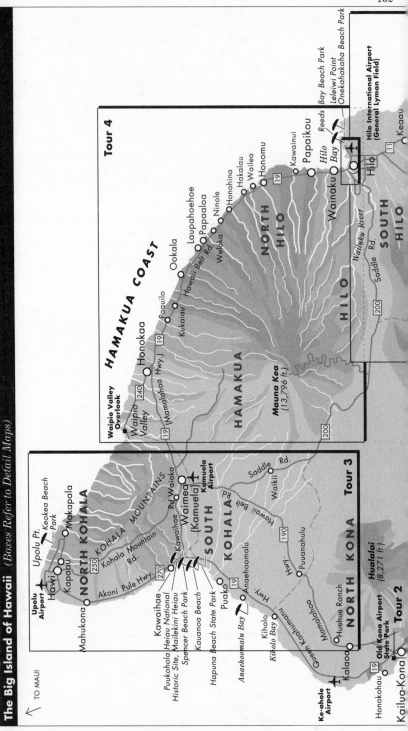

↖ TO MAUI

Tour 4

HAMAKUA COAST

Bay Beach Park
Leleiwi Point
Onekahakaha Beach Park

Hilo International Airport
(General Lyman Field)

Kawainui
Papaikou
Reeds
Hilo
Bay
Wainaku
Hilo
Keaau

Honomu
Wailea
Hakalau
Honohina
Weloka
Ninole
Papaaloa
Laupahoehoe
Ookala

Kukaiau
Paauilo

Honokaa

19

Hawaii Belt Rd.

19 (Mamalahoa Hwy.)

240

Waipio Valley Overlook
Waipio Valley

19

NORTH HILO

SOUTH HILO

HILO

Wailuku River

Saddle Rd.

200

11

HAMAKUA

Mauna Kea
(13,796 ft.)

200

NORTH KOHALA

Upolu Pt.
Keokea Beach Park

Upolu Airport

Hawii
Kapaau
Makapala

Mahukona

250

Kohala Mountain Rd.

KOHALA MOUNTAINS

Akoni Pule Hwy.

270

Kawaihae
Puukohola Heiau National
Historic Site, Mailekini Heiau
Spencer Beach Park
Kauanoa Beach
Hapuna Beach State Park
Puako

19

Anaehoomalu

Anaehoomalu Bay

Kiholo
Kiholo Bay

SOUTH KOHALA

Kawaihae Rd.

Rd. Waiaka
Waimea
(Kamuela)

Kamuela Airport

Saddle Rd.

Waikii

190

Hawaii Belt Rd.

Puuanahulu

Tour 3

NORTH KONA

Hualalai
(8,271 ft.)

Ocean Kohumann

Mamalahoa

Hwy

Huehue Ranch

Kalaoa

Honokohau
Old Kona Airport
State Park

Ke-ahole Airport

19

Tour 2

Kailua-Kona

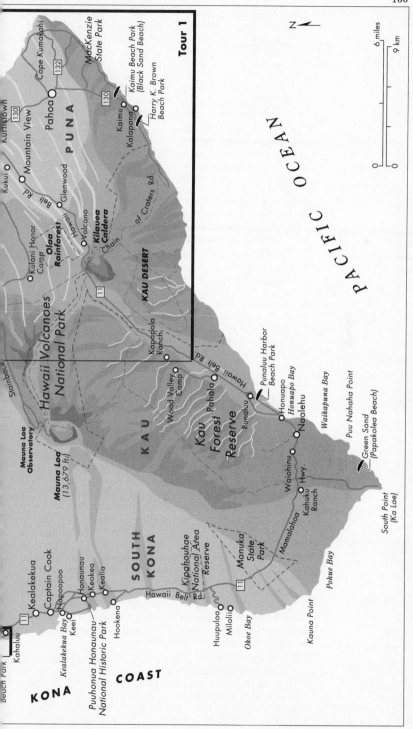

Tour 1

N

6 miles
9 km

PACIFIC OCEAN

Cape Kumakahi

MacKenzie State Park

132

Kaimu Beach Park (Black Sand Beach)

130

Pahoa

Kurtistown

PUNA

Kaimu

Harry K. Brown Beach Park

130

Mountain View

Kalapana

Kukui

Glenwood

Bell Rd.

Olaa Rainforest

Hawaii Belt Rd.

Volcano

Kilauea Caldera

Kulani Honor Camp

Chain of Craters Rd.

KAU DESERT

11

Hawaii Volcanoes National Park

Kapapala Ranch

Mauna Loa Observatory

Hawaii Belt Rd.

Mauna Loa (13,679 ft.)

Wood Valley Camp

Punaluu Harbor Beach Park

KAU

Pahala

Punaluu

Honuapo Bay

Punaluu

Honuapo

Kau Forest Reserve

Naalehu

Waikapuna Bay

Puu Nahaha Point

Staircase

Waiohinu

Green Sand (Papakolea Beach)

Kealakekua

Mamalahoa

Kahuku Hwy. Ranch

Captain Cook

SOUTH KONA

South Point (Ka Lae)

Napoopoo

Honaunau

Keokea

11

Keei

Kealakekua Bay

Kealia

Puuhonua Honaunau National Historic Park

Kipahoehoe National Area Reserve

Manuka State Park

Mamalahoa

Hookena

11

Hawaii Belt Rd.

Pohue Bay

Kahaluu

Beach Park

KONA COAST

Huupuloa

Miloli'i

Okoe Bay

Kauna Point

flowed through Kalapana and the remote Royal Gardens subdivision repeatedly since 1983, however, destroying 139 housing units and blocking Chain of Craters Road; but no lives have been lost. You can drive to the end of the road, but because of the unstable ground, sightseers without a guide are discouraged from hiking to where the molten lava flows into the ocean. Helicopters carry passengers to view the 2.5-mile lava lake called Kupaianaha, an 800-foot cinder cone, and the clouds of steam that rise as hot lava hits the ocean waters.

The drive along the Hamakua Coast to Hilo, the island's county seat and the fourth-largest city in the state, brings attention to modern developments on the island. Fields of sugarcane still wave in the breeze, but these are rapidly being replaced by orchards of macadamia nut trees. With such major companies as C. Brewer turning to macadamias, the nuts have become big business on the Big Island, supplying 90% of the state's yield. Kona coffee, anthuriums and orchids, and *pakalolo* (marijuana —said to be the state's biggest income-producing [though illegal] crop—are adding a new chapter to the agricultural history of the state.

Hilo is a town of modern and rustic buildings, stretching from the banks of the Wailuku River to Hilo Bay, where a few major hotels rim stately Banyan Drive. Nearby, the 31-acre Liliuokalani Garden, a Japanese-style park with arched bridges and waterways, was established as a safety zone after a devastating tidal wave swept away businesses and homes on May 22, 1960, killing 60 people. Residents don't worry much about a tidal wave recurring, but they haven't built anything except hotels, the park, and a golf course in that area, either.

Though it is the center of business, shipping, and government for the island, Hilo is primarily a residential town. Indications of the weather and the character of the residents are provided by the perfectly kept yards with tree ferns and the lush tropical foliage surrounding older wooden houses with rusty red and green corrugated roofs. Bring your umbrella—the rainfall averages 139 inches per year—but do plan to spend a day absorbing the charm of Hilo. It's a friendly community, populated primarily by descendants of the contract laborers— Japanese, Chinese, and Portuguese—brought in to work the sugarcane fields in the 1800s.

You'll have fun experiencing the culture of this town. Try to interpret the bidding at the Suisan fish auction at the end of Banyan Drive any morning at about 7:30 or 8. The combination of dialects, called *pidgin*, might seem like a foreign language, but the fish get sold in good time. At the Malamalama and Haili churches, the choirs still sing Hawaiian hymns, while the annual luau at Haili is a feast of authentic ethnic foods. In the last couple of years, Hilo has been sprucing up. Old buildings are being restored, and Keawe Street is a shopper's mecca, with galleries, boutiques, candy, crafts, and other specialty shops featuring a potpourri of merchandise.

The island of Hawaii—with all the diversity and activity it offers—is just beginning to attract hordes of visitors. In the past, hotel occupancy has often dropped to only 50%. Perhaps there's confusion over its name. Sometimes it's called the Orchid Isle or the Volcano Isle (both apt descriptions, by the way), but residents always say "the Big Island," since the en-

tire chain—Kauai, Oahu, Molokai, Lanai, Maui, Hawaii, Kahoolawe, Niihau—is called Hawaii as well. Perhaps it's the silly
rumor that good beaches are scarce, or the fact that the
nightlife is a little low-key. The fact remains that the Big Island
excites the senses and inspires the adventurer. Here you can
hike into a crater; catch marlin weighing hundreds of pounds;
discover another universe from the top of Mauna Kea; and out-
stare a shark from the safety of a submarine's viewing port.
The Big Island is a place for big dreams to become reality.

Essential Information

Arriving and Departing by Plane

Airports
The Big Island has two main airports. Visitors whose accommodations are on the west side of the island, at Keauhou,
Kailua-Kona, or the Kohala coast, normally fly into Kona's **Ke-
ahole Airport** (tel. 808/329–2484; visitor information tel. 808/
329–3423), 6.8 miles from Kailua. Those staying on the eastern
side, in Hilo or near the town of Volcano, fly into **Hilo International Airport** (tel. 808/935–0809; visitor information tel. 808/
935–1018), just 2 miles from Hilo's Banyan Drive hotels. In addition, one Oahu-based airline, Aloha IslandAir, has a schedule
of regular flights into **Waimea-Kohala Airport,** called Kamuela
Airport by residents (tel. 808/885–4520). Located midway between Hilo and Kailua-Kona, Kamuela Airport is used
primarily by residents of Waimea-Kamuela to commute between islands. Another airstrip, at Upolu Point, services small
private planes only.

Flights from the Mainland U.S.
Hawaiian (tel. 800/367–5320) and **United Airlines** (tel. 800/241–
6522) are the only two carriers that fly daily from the mainland
to the Big Island. United flies to both Ke-ahole and Hilo International Airport airports (with about an hour layover in
Honolulu) from Los Angeles, San Francisco, and Chicago. Hawaiian Airlines flies from San Francisco and Seattle to Ke-
ahole. Both flights make Honolulu and Maui stops. Flying time
from the West Coast is about 4½ hours.

Flights from Honolulu
Between the Neighbor Islands, both **Aloha Airlines** (tel. 800/
367–5250) and **Hawaiian Airlines** offer jet flights, which take
about 34 minutes from Honolulu to Hilo International Airport
and 45 minutes from Honolulu to Ke-ahole. In addition, Hawaiian operates a Dash prop, which adds a few minutes to the flight
times. **Discovery Airways** began service to Ke-ahole Airport in
1990. Fares are approximately $50, though both Aloha and Ha-
waiian discount their first (6 AM) and last (8 or 9 PM, depending
on the airline) flights of each day from $35 to $40. Complaints
about any airline often have to do with being on time. In general,
the earlier in the day you fly interisland, the better assurance you
have of departing and arriving on time.

Aloha Airlines owns **Aloha IslandAir** (tel. 808/833–3219), the
former Princeville Airlines, which flies from Honolulu to
Kamuela Airport three times daily and returns two times daily.

The standard round-trip fare between two islands on the major
carriers is about $100, though a book of six one-way tickets can
be purchased, providing about a $10 savings per ticket.

Between the Airport and Hotels The distance from Ke-ahole Airport to Kailua, the resort area on the western side of the Big Island, is 6.8 miles, or a 10-minute drive, while the Keauhou resort area stretches another 6 miles to the south beyond Kailua. Visitors staying at the upscale resorts along the Kona–Kohala coast north of Ke-ahole Airport should allow 30–45 minutes driving time to reach their hotels.

On the eastern side of the island, Hilo International Airport is situated just 2 miles, or a five-minute drive, from Hilo's Banyan Drive hotels. If you've chosen Volcano Lodge or a bed-and-breakfast accommodation near the little mountain town of Volcano, plan on a half-hour drive from Hilo International Airport.

The adventuresome souls who have booked out-of-the-way accommodations near Waimea might want to fly into Kamuela Airport, but be sure to arrange your rental car in advance (*see* Getting Around, below), as few auto-rental companies service that airport.

Unfortunately, no buses operate from the airports.

By Shuttle There is no regularly scheduled shuttle service from either main airport, although a private service is offered by four major Kohala-coast resorts to the north of Ke-ahole Airport. Mauna Kea, Mauna Lani, the Hyatt Regency Waikoloa, and the Royal Waikoloan offer lei greetings and transportation to their hotels for about half the cost of a taxi. The rates vary depending on the distance each resort is from the airport. Arriving guests must simply check in at the Kohala Coast Resort Association counters at the Aloha and Hawaiian Airlines arrival areas.

Guests staying in Kailua or at the Keauhou resort area to the south of the airport should check with their individual hotels upon booking to see if shuttle service is available.

By Taxi Taxis are generally on hand for plane arrivals at both major airports. Some local services are: **ABC** (tel. 808/935–0755); **Ace** (tel. 808/935–8303); **Aloha** (tel. 808/935–1600); and **City** (tel. 808/935–1690). Taxis from Hilo International Airport to Hilo charge about $7 for the 2-mile ride to the Banyan Drive hotels.

A number of taxis service Ke-ahole Airport. The following also offer guided tours: **Kona Airport Taxi Company** (tel. 808/329–7779), **Paradise Taxi** (tel. 808/329–1234), and **Marina Taxi** (tel. 808/329–2481). From Ke-ahole Airport to the Hotel King Kamehameha, taxi fares are about $15; to the Kona Surf in Keauhou, the cost is about $27. Taxis to South Kohala from Ke-ahole are even more expensive: approximately $32 to the Royal Waikoloan and $45 to the Mauna Kea Beach Hotel.

By Limousine For real luxury, limousine service with a chauffeur who will act as your personal guide is between $55–$60 an hour, with a two-hour minimum. **Luana's** in Kona (tel. 808/326–5466) provides all the extras—TV, bar, and narrated tours, plus Japanese-speaking guides. **Roberts'** offers service in both Kailua-Kona (tel. 808/329–1688) and Hilo (tel. 808/935–2858).

By Car The best way to see the Big Island is by car, if you want to explore beaches and trails and don't mind driving across wide open stretches of lava that can sometimes become a bit monotonous. Especially in the summer, when temperatures can hit 90 degrees, you'll want to travel in air-conditioned comfort.

Though there are perhaps two dozen companies to choose from (*see* Getting Around, below, for specific car-rental information), cars can be scarce during peak seasons—from mid-December through mid-March—and sometimes on weekends during August. If you haven't reserved a car far in advance for the October Bud Light Ironman Triathlon or for the Merrie Monarch Festival the first week in April, chances are you'll end up walking. Major rental agencies at both Ke-ahole Airport and Hilo International Airport have service desks across the street from the baggage-claim areas. Others furnish free shuttle service to their car yards.

From Ke-ahole Airport, the main road is Highway 19, or Queen Kaahumanu Highway. Turn right, or south, as you leave the airport to reach Kailua-Kona. To the left, or north, along this highway are the major resorts of Kona Village, Royal Waikoloan, Hyatt Regency Waikoloa, Aston Shores at Waikoloa (an elegant condo-resort), Mauna Lani Resort, and Mauna Kea Resort. Highway 19 turns inland to Waimea, then emerges along the northeastern Hamakua coast, eventually terminating in Hilo (96 miles from Kailua-Kona via this northern route), on the east side of the island. South from Hilo, Highway 11 bypasses Hilo International Airport, angling inland as the Hawaii Belt Road through the volcano area and continuing around the south and southwest coasts of the island as Mamaloha Highway to Kailua-Kona (126 miles from Hilo via this southern route). From Kailua-Kona, Mamaloha Highway is the older, more curvy, up-country route to Waimea, while Queen Kaahumanu is a straight, well-paved highway that follows a coastal route to Kawaihae and then turns inland to Waimea.

Arriving and Departing by Ship

From Honolulu **American Hawaii Cruises** also runs seven-day excursions departing Honolulu Harbor every Saturday on two ships, the SS *Constitution* and the SS *Independence*. You have the option of choosing a four-day cruise and disembarking on the island of Hawaii, where special rates can be arranged at the Kona Surf, Aston Shores at Waikoloa, or Aston Royal Sea Cliff resorts. Pre- and postcruise hotel packages are offered at a variety of rates. *American Hawaii Cruises, 530 Kearny St., San Francisco, CA 94108, tel. 800/765–7000 for information or a free brochure about cruises or cruise-and-land packages.*

Getting Around

By Car An automobile is necessary to see the sights of the Big Island in any reasonable amount of time. Even if you're solely interested in relaxing at your self-contained megaresort, you may still want a car, simply to travel to Kailua-Kona or Waimea so you can try cuisine other than hotel fare.

If you pick up an auto at either airport and drop it off at the other, be aware that it could cost you as much as $30 extra. If you decide to return a car to the original pickup point, allow 2¼ hours to drive the 96-mile Hamakua-coast route. To get the best rate on a rental car—and surprisingly, Hawaii's rates are often better than mainland rates—book it in conjunction with a round-trip interisland Hawaiian or Aloha Airline flight, or ask your travel agent to check out room and car packages for you.

The national car-rental firms represented on the Big Island are: **Alamo** (tel. 800/327–9633), **Avis** (tel. 800/831–8000), **Budget** (tel. 800/527–7000), **Dollar** (tel. 800/421–6868), **Hertz** (tel. 800/654–3131), **National** (tel. 800/227–7368), and **Tropical** (tel. 800/352–3923). The Hawaii-based companies are **Harper's** (tel. 808/969–1478), **VIP Car Rentals** (tel. 808/329–7328), **Phillip's** (tel. 808/935–1936), **Roberts Hawaii** (tel. 808/935–2858), **Sunshine** (tel. 800/367–1977 or 808/329–2926), and **World** (tel. 808/329–1006). Harper's is the only agency with a rental contract that allows its four-wheel-drive vehicles to be taken on Saddle Road (a rough, winding shortcut from Hilo to Waimea), although a number of other agencies have four-wheel-drives in their fleets.

By Bus/Shuttle A locally sponsored **Hele-On Bus** (*hele* translates roughly as "go") operates Monday–Saturday between Hilo and Kailua-Kona. The bus goes from Kailua-Kona to Hilo and back again, at $6 each way. For luggage and backpacks that do not fit under the seat, an additional $1 is charged per piece. Hele-On (tel. 808/935–8241) departs from Mokuaikaua Church, on Alii Drive in Kailua-Kona at 6:43 AM arriving in Hilo at 9:45 AM. It leaves from the Mooheau Bus Terminal, between Kamehameha Avenue and Bayfront Highway in Hilo at 1:30 PM to arrive in Kailua-Kona at 4:30 PM. In Hilo, a Hele-On operates amid Banyan Drive, downtown, and the shopping malls for 75¢ (exact fare required).

Within Keauhou, a free shuttle (tel. 808/322–3500 or 808/322–3000) runs from hotels and condos to Keauhou Shopping Village and the Kona Country Club golf course.

By Taxi Several companies advertise guided tours by taxi, but it is an expensive way to travel, with a trip around the island totaling about $300. Meters automatically register $2 on pickup, and most click off another $1.60 with each passing mile. If you've got the urge to splurge, in Hilo call **Ace Taxi** (tel. 808/935–8303) or **Hilo Harry's** (tel. 808/935–7091). In Kona, try **Kona Airport Taxi Company** (tel. 808/329–7779), **Paradise Taxi** (tel. 808/329–1234), or **Marina Taxi** (tel. 808/329–2481).

By Moped Mopeds and scooters can be rented in Hilo from **Ciao! Activities Center** (tel. 808/969–1717) and in Kailua-Kona from **Rent Scootah** (tel. 808/329–3250) and **Hawaii Speed Sports** (tel. 808/326–1419). Some words of warning: Big Island roads often have narrow shoulders, and the drafts from oversize tour buses swooping by can double the excitement of a simple Sunday ride. Helmets are advised but not mandatory in Hawaii.

By Plane Big Island Air (tel. 800/367–8047, ext. 207 or 808/329–4868) offers charter flights to any island in a six-passenger Citation jet at a basic hourly rate of $950. "Wait time" (for example, if you fly to Kamuela for lunch and the plane sits on the ground for several hours while you dine) is charged at a lesser rate, unless you've totaled up more than four hours of flight time.

Important Addresses and Numbers

Tourist Information The minute you step off the plane at any Hawaii airport, grab a handful of the free brochures that describe attractions, restaurants, scheduled events, and tours and often contain free discount coupons. At the Big Island's airports, brochures are dispensed at the **Hawaii Visitors Bureau** (HVB) booths, and you can ask the booth attendent anything you need to know. In addition, if you rent a car, be sure to get a "Drive Guide," as these handy little booklets have all the maps you'll probably need to navigate the island. *HVB office in Hilo: Hilo Plaza, 180 Kinoole St., Suite 104, tel. 808/961–5767; in Kailua-Kona: 75-5719 W. Alii Dr., Kailua-Kona 96740, tel. 808/329–7787. Open weekdays 8–noon and 1–4.*

Before you go, you can write HVB for its accommodation and restaurant guides. Another helpful source of information is the **Kohala Coast Resort Association** (Box 5000, Kohala Coast 96743-5000, tel. 808/885–4915), a group of resorts and luxury hotels cooperating to promote the Kohala coast as a resort destination. For visitors staying in Keauhou, the **Keauhou Visitors Association** (78-6831 Alii Dr., Suite 234, Kailua-Kona 96740, tel. 808/322–3866) is a source of information. For questions about east Hawaii, write **Destination Hilo,** Box 1391, Hilo 96721.

Emergencies **Police, fire,** or **ambulance,** dial 808/935–3311 (East Hawaii–Hilo); 808/329–3311 (West Hawaii–Kona).

Kailua-Kona **Police** (tel. 808/323–2645).
Hospital. Kona Hospital (Hwy. 11, Box 69, Kealakekua 96750, tel. 808/322–9311).
Dentist. Ask the hospital to call a dentist who will take emergency patients.
Pharmacy. Long's Drug Store (Lanihau Center, 75-5595 Palani Rd., tel. 808/329–1632; open Mon.–Sat. 8:30–9, Sun. 8:30–5).

Hilo **Police** (tel. 808/935–3311).
Hospital. Hilo Hospital (1190 Waianuenue Ave., tel. 808/969–4111).
Dentist. Ask the hospital to call a dentist who will take emergency patients.
Pharmacy. Long's Drug Store (555 Kilauea Ave., tel. 808/935–9075; open Mon.–Thurs. and Sat. 8:30–6, Fri. 8:30–7, Sun. 8:30–5).

For All Areas **Ambulance or fire** (tel. 808/961–6022).
Poison Control Center (tel. 800/362–3585).
Help Line (Crisis Center, tel. 808/329–9111).
Volcano watchers (tel. 808/967–7977 for 24-hr recorded information).

Parks and Recreation **County:** Tel. 808/961–8311. Open weekdays 7:45–4:30. **State:** Tel. 808/961–7200. Open weekdays 8–4:15.

Weather Tel. 808/961–5582.

Opening and Closing Times

Banks are open Monday through Thursday 8:30–3:30 and Friday 9–6.

In general, major stores and shopping centers on the Big Island open at 9 or 9:30 and close by 4:30 or 5. Hilo's Prince Kuhio Shopping Center (111 E. Puainako, tel. 808/959–3555) stays open until 9 PM on Thursday and Friday. In Kona, most of the stores at the Kona Coast Shopping Center (Palani Rd., no tel.) are open until 7 PM, though the KTA Super Stores outlet (a supermarket) is open from 7 AM to 11 PM. Many small grocery stores also maintain longer hours, as do the shops along Kona's main Alii Drive that are geared to tourism.

Guided Tours

Orientation Tours At least four established companies offer circle-island orientation tours at fares just under $40. Tours are 9–11 hours long
from pickup to drop-off at your hotel or the airport. The circle-
island tours generally include Waimea, the Hamakua coast,
Hilo, and Volcanoes National Park. All the companies use air-
conditioned vehicles, but only **Akamai** (tel. 800/922–6485 or
808/329–7324) limits tours to a maximum of 12 people in a van.
Akamai also has shorter North Kohala scenic tours and Kona
scenic tours, and it furnishes transportation and makes arrangements so you can join a Waipio Valley tour. Other
companies drive motor coaches or minibuses, depending on the
number of bookings. **Gray Line Hawaii** (tel. 800/367–2420 or
808/833–8000) has a circle-island tour originating in Kailua-
Kona, a Hilo/Volcano/Kalapana tour, a Hilo/Volcano/Kona tour,
and a Kona historical tour. **Roberts Hawaii** (444 Hobron Lane,
Honolulu 96815, tel. 808/947–3939) offers a Hilo/Volcano/Kona
tour for under $30; a Hilo/Volcano/Hilo tour, which takes eight
hours; and a shorter Kona historical tour. **Hawaii Resorts
Transportation** (Box 183, Honokaa 96727, tel. 808/885–7484) offers adventures to Waipio, Mauna Kea, and Kohala; a look at
historical Kona; and a $36 circle-island tour. Hawaii Resorts
also has an unforgettable limousine/helicopter trip for $275 per
person, with complimentary champagne served along the way.

Aerial Tours Hovering over a waterfall that drops a couple of thousand feet
into multiple pools is absolutely breathtaking—never mind the
noise. You can fly above the lava lake on Mauna Loa, then follow
the flow to the ocean, where huge clouds of steam billow into
the air. (Currently the flow is mostly underground, through a
lava tube, but that can change, so ask exactly what you'll see
when you book your flight.) Some passengers have a tendency
to feel woozy in a helicopter, so if you're prone to car, sea, or air
sickness, you might want to take a shorter flight, or try the new
wristbands we've seen in pharmacies that work on pressure
points and are said not to induce such side effects as drowsi-
ness.

Volcano Heli-Tours (Box 626, Volcano 96785, tel. 808/967–7578)
is the only helicopter that departs from the Volcano area (right
near the golf course), and since flying time over the lava lake
and to the ocean is minimized, the 45-minute flights are somewhat cheaper at $99.84. You must make reservations in
advance, however, as the flights are well booked. Countless
other tour companies are available: **Mauna Kea Helicopters**
(tel. 808/885–6400) pilot Scott Shupe has plenty of experience,
while **Io Aviation** (tel. 808/935–3031) takes off from Hilo International Airport with helicopter tours. From Kamuela
Airport, **Lacy Helicopters** (tel. 808/885–4657) flies over Waipio
Valley. From the Waikoloa Helipad, **Papillon Helicopters** (tel.
800/367–7095 or 808/329–0551) is reputable. Ask at your hotel
desk for additional operators. Flight tours range vastly in
price. **Hawaii Pacific Aviation** (tel. 808/961–5591) advertises a
60-minute volcano tour from Hilo International Airport for
$65. Papillon Helicopters also describes a longer flight from
Kona-coast hotels over Kilauea and Volcanoes National Park
for $245.

Big Island Air (tel. 800/367–8047, ext. 207 or 808/329–4868)
flies two-hour circle-island tours with a minimum of four pas-

sengers on its six-passenger Citation jet for $150 per person. Flights depart from Ke-ahole Airport at 7:45 AM and 11 AM seven days a week. In addition, a five-hour excursion to Molokai takes in Kahoolawe, Lanai, and Maui's Hana coastline, including two hours on the ground at Kalaupapa Peninsula, Molokai, for $195 per person. Weight is critical on these smaller planes, so be prepared to divulge your true body weight.

Special-Interest Tours
Garden Tours

So far, tour agencies have not specialized in offering garden tours, perhaps because most nurseries welcome visitors free of charge in order to sell and ship their orchids and anthuriums on the spot. Most of the nurseries that sell tropical flowers are on the Hilo side near Puna or on the way to Volcano. Close to the center of Hilo, **Nani Maui Gardens'** 20 acres have 100 varieties of tropical fruit trees and 2,000 varieties of ginger, orchids, and anthuriums. The Nitahara family established the gardens in 1970. *421 Makalika St., Hilo, tel. 808/959-3541. Admission: $5 adults, $2 children age 13-18. Open daily 8-5.*

Hawaii Tropical Botanical Garden (Onomea Bay, Hilo, tel. 808/964-5233) charges a tax-deductible admission but is an extensive botanical garden, with plants imported from around the world (*see* Tour 4 in Exploring, below). *Open daily 8:30-4:30.*

On Volcano Highway 11 you will see signs indicating anthurium gardens, as well as a Hawaiian-warrior sign 22 miles from Hilo pointing the way to **Akatsuka Orchid Gardens** (tel. 808/967-7660; open daily 8:30-5 PM). Also off Highway 11, **Rainbow Tropicals** grows 62 acres of anthuriums (ranging from the green-white obake to the deep red beefsteak), orchids, and other tropical blooms that you can purchase and have shipped home. Little water-filled balloons around their stems keep them fresh. *Box 4038, W. Mamaki St., Hilo, tel. 808/959-4565. Visitor Center open daily 10-4:30.*

In West Hawaii, **Wakefield Garden** is an easy stop and a self-guided walk, appropriate if you want to stretch your legs and have a cool drink at the casual restaurant, but not particularly impressive as far as plants. *Hwy. 160 at Honaunau, tel. 808/328-9930. Open daily 8-sunset. Lunch daily 11-3.*

Off Mamalahoa Highway 180 at the intersection of Kuakini Highway 11 south of Kailua, watch for the new **Fuku Bonsai Center,** a visitor center with nine different bonsai gardens not yet open at press time. Educational exhibits of these miniature plants will show the differences in the cultivation and training of Japanese, Chinese, and Hawaiian bonsai. This will be the largest bonsai center and the only one of its kind outside Japan.

Mauna Kea

The clearest place in the world for viewing the heavens is reputedly the summit of 13,796-foot Mauna Kea. The trick is getting there. It takes a four-wheel-drive vehicle to reach the top, and you must traverse Saddle Road on the way. Driving on Saddle Road is restricted by most car-rental companies, because it twists and turns and has no gas stations or emergency phones from Waimea to Hilo. Only **Harper's Car Rental** (1690 Kamehameha Ave., Hilo 96720, tel. 808/969-1478) allows use of its $60-a-day Isuzu Trooper IIs and Broncos on Saddle Road.

If you decide to strike out on your own, follow the access road off Highway 20 between Hilo and West Hawaii to reach Onizuka Center for International Astronomy, about 30 miles from Hilo. Every Saturday and Sunday four-wheel-drive vehicles caravan for free tours to the Mauna Kea observatories, which sprout like mushrooms from the otherworldly landscape. Departure is from Onizuka Visitor Center at 2 PM Saturday and Sunday and at 6:30 Saturday evenings. Information and reservations can be obtained by calling **Mauna Kea Support Services** (tel. 808/935–3371). Freezing temperatures are common at the summit, even when the heat is high at the seashore, so you must take along warm parkas.

Three companies take all the worry out of a trip to the top. You may book a day or evening van tour with knowledgeable Pat Wright of **Paradise Safaris** (Box AD, Kailua 96745, tel. 808/322–2366). He supplies lunch for the day excursion as well as hotel pickup and warm parkas. **Waipio Valley Shuttle** tours (Box 5128, Kukuihaele 96727, tel. 808/775–7121) conduct Mauna Kea summit tours that leave from Parker Ranch Shopping Center in Kamuela with a minimum of four passengers. **Hawaii Resorts Transportation Company** (Box 183, Honokaa 96727, tel. 808/885–7484) furnishes transportation by jeep and a box lunch. Prices among the various companies are $50–$85.

Parker Ranch **Parker Ranch** (*see* Tour 3 in Exploring, below) has expanded its visitor facilities to attract not only art lovers but also would-be cowboys. Van tours originate at the Parker Ranch Visitor Center at the Parker Ranch Shopping Center in Waimea. A video orientation to the ranch (founded in 1847), its history, and its operations is presented at a small museum. A three-hour tour to the ranch includes lunch and a chance to watch the paniolos at work. Shorter tours are available daily (except Sunday), 9 AM–3:30 PM. Ranch exhibits and artisan demonstrations are featured at Puukalani Stables. Mana, the original, koa-wood residence of ranch founder John Palmer Parker, is open, as is Puuopelu, the century-old residence of Richard Smart, the ranch's current owner and a sixth-generation Parker. Smart is an avid collector of art: Venetian glass, antique Chinese vases, bronze sculptures, and oils by a variety of artists, including Maurice Utrillo, Lloyd Sexton, and Pierre Auguste Renoir, are all on view at Puuopelu. *Box 458, Kamuela-Waimea 96743, tel. 808/885–7655. Cost of tour: $15–$38 adults, $7.50–$19 children 4–11.*

Walking Tour You can take a self-guided walking tour of downtown Hilo with the help of a "Discover Downtown Hilo" map from the **Lyman House Memorial Museum.** Points of interest are indicated at Kalakaua Park and at 15 historic buildings (*see* Tour 4 in Exploring, below). *276 Haili St., tel. 808/935–5021. Map $1.25. Open Mon.–Sat. 9–5.*

Exploring

If you have only three or four days on the Big Island and you want to reserve some time for relaxing as well as sightseeing, you should look over a map before or upon your arrival and choose the highlights you want most to see. For three- or four-day stays, you might choose to book a hotel along the west coast, in Kailua-Kona or Keauhou, or at one of the resorts on the Kohala coast in order to be near the best restaurants, beaches, and suntanning weather.

If, on the other hand, your schedule allows a week or 10 days on the island, you might want to spend a night or two in the county

seat of Hilo, a night at the Volcano House, and another in
Waimea before finishing up your vacation at a resort on the sunny side of the island. It's best to follow this east-coast-to-west-
coast order for accommodations so you won't go home with
memories of Hilo's often gray skies.

To orient yourself, divide the island into sightseeing sections
roughly corresponding to its six official districts: Hilo on the
eastern side; Hamakua, the northeast seacoast; Kohala, the
northern mountainous region, and the northwestern coastline;
Kona, the western seaside village of Kailua-Kona, and the upcountry coffee region; Ka'u and the vast stretches of lava and
desert to the south; and Puna, which is east of Volcano.

Reserve Hilo and the rugged Hamakua Coast to Waipio Valley
for one or two days of exploring. Another day (more for hikers
and outdoor types) could be spent investigating Hawaii Volcanoes National Park, which is slightly east of the center of the
island; you could follow Chain of Craters Road to the point
where lava blocks it, then retrace your route and continue
through the Puna District, with its ebony lava flows and black-
sand beaches, to where the road is again blocked by recent
flows. On a third or fourth day you might journey all the way
around to the southern tip, through the Ka'u district, to a new
base at one of the tourist centers on the west coast—the Kona
district. The seaside village of Kailua (generally referred to as
Kailua-Kona to distinguish it from the Kailuas on Oahu and
Maui) is a mecca for shoppers but should also be explored for its
historical significance (*see* Tour 2, below). From here, day trips
can easily be made to cowboy country in Waimea, and you can
return via a circle route through the Kohala Mountains to
Upolu Point at the northern tip, past Kawaihae, and back.

Make reservations with a tour agency for another day or evening to go stargazing from the top of Mauna Kea, where 10
observatories crop up like mushrooms in the barren cinder and
lava landscape. Access to Mauna Kea is via Saddle Road, the
most direct route between Hilo and the Kohala coast; however,
nearly all car-rental contracts prohibit driving on this remote,
winding, and sometimes rough track. Finally, you'll want a day
to get off the beaten track in up-country Kona, simply to enjoy
the riot of tropical flora: the bougainvillea, poinsettias, breadfruit, impatiens, and shiny-leaved coffee trees delight the eye.
You might make Holualoa (*see* The Arts, below) the destination
for this day, as this little town houses the Kona Arts Center and
a number of fine art galleries for browsing.

If you are short of time, give Hilo a once-over-lightly look, then
see Volcanoes National Park on your first day, traveling the
Hamakua-coast route and making your new base in Kailua-
Kona that night. This unfortunately eliminates the 126-mile
drive around the southern end of the island, which gives a wonderful sense of space, history, and isolation with its miles of
macadamia nut orchards, lava flows, and ranch lands; however,
this area needs correspondingly bigger stretches of time to explore adequately.

For this guide, the island is divided into a car trip from Hilo to
the volcano area; a walking tour of Kailua-Kona; a trip around
the northwest section, including Waimea and the Kohala Mountains; and a tour of the Hamakua coast. Later in this chapter,
we've included a section on beaches you won't just want to drive

past. Generally, in addition to this book, you will find the Drive Guides furnished by car-rental agencies helpful; they are marked with major sightseeing stops. If you want detailed street maps, **Basically Books** (169 Keawe St., Hilo 96720, tel. 808/961–0144) is a complete map shop. Maps are also available at the **Middle Earth Bookshoppe** (75-5719 Alii Dr., Kailua-Kona, tel. 808/329–2123). Each of the following tours can be divided into two separate sightseeing trips, but they can also be accomplished in one day, if you have plenty of stamina and limited time.

Highlights for First-time Visitors

Akaka Falls State Park, Tour 4
Chain of Craters Road, Tour 1
Devastation Trail, Tour 1
Halemaumau Fire Pit in Kilauea Crater, Tour 1
Hawaii Volcanoes National Park, Tour 1
Hulihee Palace, Tour 2
Lava Tree State Park, Tour 1
Lyman Museum and House, Tour 4
Mokuaikaua Church, Tour 2
Parker Ranch Visitor Center and Museum, Tour 3
Puukohola Visitor Center and Heiaus, Tour 3
Suisan Fish Market, Tour 4
Thurston Lava Tube, Tour 1
Waipio Valley, Tour 4

Tour 1: From Hilo to Hawaii Volcanoes National Park and Puna

Numbers in the margin correspond with points of interest on the Tour 1: Hawaii Volcanoes National Park and Puna map.

The most popular attraction on the Big Island, Hawaii Volcanoes National Park, is home to most of the Kilauea volcano. If you're in the area and lucky enough to be visiting when lava is flowing from Kilauea, you'll want to make the park your top-priority destination. Kilauea's recent series of eruptions began in 1983.

Even if you don't witness a fiery display, you'll have plenty to see in the park, which also includes the summit caldera and gently sloping northeast flank of the 13,680-foot Mauna Loa volcano. You'll also be impressed with the lush greenery of the tree ferns and other tropical plants, the lava tubes, cinder cones, odd mineral formations, and trails beside steam vents, and the vast barren craters of Chain of Craters Road. Don't forget to take a sweater (or a jacket in winter), as temperatures can get nippy at the park's 3,700-foot elevation.

Start from Hilo's Banyan Drive and continue out on Highway 11—or Kanoelehua Avenue—which takes you directly to Hawaii Volcanoes National Park, 30 miles to the southeast. You can cover the distance from Hilo to the park in a quick 45-minute drive along the smooth divided highway. You might also choose to start early in the day, take your time, and perhaps visit sights along the way.

On Highway 11, keep your eyes peeled for the Hawaiian-warrior markers, the distinctive red-and-white signs, installed by the Hawaii Visitors Bureau, that designate visitor attrac-

❶ tions. To the right of the road you'll see the sign for the **Pan-aewa Rain Forest Zoo.** Children love the monkeys and tigers here. The trails tend to get muddy because of the rain-forest location, so you and your children shouldn't wear good shoes if you plan to come here. Turn right at Hawaiian Warrior sign. Zoo is just off Stainback Hwy. *Administrative office: 25 Aupuni St., Hilo, tel. 808/959-7224. Admission free. Open daily 9–4. Closed Christmas and New Year's Day.*

❷ About 5 miles south of Hilo on Highway 11 on the left is the marker for the **Mauna Loa Macadamia Nut Orchard.** The entry road meanders 3 miles through macadamia trees. The processing plant here has large viewing windows, and a videotape describes the harvesting and preparation of the nuts. Kids can run off their energy on the nature trail; there's also a place to buy snacks or enjoy your own picnic lunch. *Macadamia Rd. on Hwy. 11 south of Hilo, tel. 808/966-8612. Admission free. Open daily 9–5.*

❸ Continue on Highway 11 and turn left at the sign marking the entrance to **Hawaii Volcanoes National Park** (Box 52, Volcano 96718, tel. 808/967-7311). The 344-square-mile park, which was established in 1916, has an admission fee of $5 per car between 8:30 and 4:30 (it's free outside those hours); an annual permit costs $15. Those on bicycles or on foot are charged $2, while a Golden Age pass for those 62 and older is free. Once you're inside the park, all visitor attractions are free. The park is open 24 hours every day, and the gate is manned from 8:30 to 4:30.

❹ **Kilauea Visitor Center** (open 7:45–5) is just beyond the entry booth to the right. Displays and a movie focus on past eruptions; if you can't see the real thing, don't miss the movie shown hourly from 9 to 4. The center posts the latest information on volcanic activity, and hikers can obtain trail information.

❺ From the Visitor Center, walk over to the **Volcano Art Center** (tel. 808/967-7511), which was built as a Volcano House, or lodge, in 1877. The first Volcano House was actually a thatch-roofed hut built in 1846. The art center features the work of Big Island photographers, artists, and craftspeople. Items in a wide range of prices are available, including koa rice paddles, koa cutting boards, and framed batik-on-silk paintings by Phan Nguyen Barker. Be sure to take a look at the block prints by Dietrich Varez depicting Hawaiian legends and the unusual hand-painted T-shirts.

❻ Across the street from the art center is today's **Volcano House** (tel. 808/967-7321), a charming old lodge dating from 1941 with a huge stone fireplace, 37 rooms for rent, the Ka Ohelo Dining Room, and a snack bar. The restaurants attract tour groups at lunchtime, but dinner at the Ka Ohelo Dining Room can be a romantic experience (*see* Dining, below).

❼ Walk right through the snack bar to the edge of **Kilauea Caldera** and peer into the steaming fire pit, called **Halemaumau Crater,** at its center. The volcano currently is erupting not from here but from a rift zone on the flanks of Kilauea. Visitors can fly over that area (*see* Guided Tours in Essential Information, above). From the lodge you can hike around or into the crater; then return to your car for the 11.1-mile drive around the crater's circumference.

Tour 1: Hawaii Volcanoes National Park and Puna

Saddle Rd.

200

Saddle Rd.

S O U T H

H I L O

Powerline Rd.

Olaa Flume Rd.

Tree Planting Rd.

Stainback Rd.

Stainback Hwy.

Kulani Honor
Camp

Ola'a
Rainforest

Glenwood

11

**Volcano
Art
Center**
5

Volcano Golf and
Country Club

Kilauea
Visitor
Center
4

Hawaii Belt Rd.

**Sulfur
Banks**
8

Kipuka Puaulu

19

17

20 **Volcano Store**

Mauna Loa
Rd.

18

Tree Molds

9 **6** **3** **Hawaii Volcanoes**
National Park

Steam Vents

Thomas A. Jaggar Museum **10** **7** **Volcano House**

Kilauea Caldera

13 **Thurston Lava Tube**

12

11

Devastation Trail

Halemaumau
Overlook

11

Chain of Craters
14 **Road**

Hawaii Volcanoes
National Park

Hilina Pali Rd.

Chain of Craters Rd.

KAU DESERT

Puuloa
Petroglyphs

PACIFIC OCEAN

HILO

Kanoelehua Ave.

Puainako St.

28 Prince Kuhio Plaza

29 Hirose Nursery

11

Panaewa
ain Forest
Zoo 1

2 Mauna Loa
Macadamia Nut Orchard

Macadamia Rd.

Keaau

Kaloli Point

Kurtistown

Kaloli Rd.

Kukui

ani Rd.

130

Mountain View

Kahakai Blvd.

Cape Kumukahi
Lighthouse

24

Kapoho 23

Lava Tree
State Park 22

Pahoa

132

P U N A

Pahoa Pohoiki Rd.

25

Isaac Hale
Beach Park

21

26 MacKenzie
State Park

137

130

Kaimu

27 Kaimu Black Sand Beach

Kalapana

130 16

Waha'ula Heiau

N

0   5 miles

0   5 km

Scenic stops along the way include the yellow, acrid-smelling
⑧ **sulfur banks** (sure to elicit loud complaints from children—
⑨ unless they like the smell of rotten eggs), **steam vents,** and the
⑩ park's new **Thomas A. Jaggar Museum,** on the edge of Kilauea
Caldera. At this hands-on museum, seismographs that measure the earth's movement will also record a child's footfall. You
can also see fascinating filmstrips of current and previous eruptions. Park rangers lead educational walks from the museum.
Museum tel. 808/967-7643. Admission free. Open 8:30-5.

From the museum, rangers escort groups on three scenic
walks, or you can follow the walks on your own: a 10-minute
⑪ walk to the **Halemaumau Overlook,** with another view of the
⑫ crater; a 30-minute stroll along **Devastation Trail;** and a 20-min-
⑬ ute jaunt through a fern forest and into the **Thurston Lava
Tube.**

On Devastation Trail, a boardwalk leads you through an eerie,
barren landscape that may make you feel you're on another
planet; this area was created after a 1959 eruption, when fiery
lava from the smaller, adjacent Kilauea Iki Crater (*iki* means
little) burned the surrounding ohia forest.

The walk to the Thurston Lava Tube takes you to a natural tunnel about 10 feet high that formed when the cooling top and
sides of a lava flow hardened and the lava inside drained away.
You can walk 450 feet into the tube. Lorrin A. Thurston, for
whom the tube is named, was a descendant of New England
Protestant missionaries and a Honolulu newspaper publisher
who helped establish the park.

Next, if you still have the time and the stamina, drive from the
⑭ center of the park to **Chain of Craters Road** (you'll understand
how it got its name when you see all the huge depressions),
which descends 3,700 feet in 24 miles to the Kalapana coastal
district of the park. No food or gasoline is available until you
return, so be sure to top off both the tank and your appetite before you go; the round-trip can take two or three hours,
depending on how often and how long you stop to gawk. The
road offers a breathtaking ocean view, while the historic lava
flows are awesome to behold.

⑮ A sign on the left marks a trail across the lava to the **Puuloa
petroglyphs,** about a 15-minute walk inland. Etchings of people, boats, and animals made by early Hawaiians are spread
over a vast area of black lava. The round depressions are *piko*
holes, where umbilical cords of newborns were burned. Along
the Kohala Coast, other easily accessible petroglyph sites may
be found, so don't be disappointed if you don't have time for
these.

Approximately 28 miles from the Kilauea Visitor Center on the
makai (ocean) side of Chain of Craters Road is the site where
⑯ **Waha'ula Visitor Center** was demolished by lava in June 1989.
At press time, Hawaii's oldest sacrificial temple ruin was also
in danger of being covered with lava. Constructed in the 13th
century, the huge stone platform, enclosed by a thick stone
wall, once contained house sites and a *luakine* (sacrificial)
heiau, where human sacrifices were made to appease the gods.
Check at Kilauea Visitor Center to see if guided walks to some
of the world's youngest lava flows and newest black-sand
beaches are still being offered in the area. Lava has overflowed

the road just beyond the center repeatedly since 1984; the road is now closed.

When hiking in the Waha'ula area, do not go beyond established barriers, as coastal regions do collapse and the ground can be unstable. Not too long ago, there used to be another site worth visiting just off a narrow dirt road just beyond the park boundaries in the Puna district. **Queen's Bath,** or Punalu'u, once ostensibly reserved for Hawaiian *alii* (royalty), was a freshwater pool about 10 feet deep that was a favorite swimming hole for neighborhood kids. The pool was buried in lava in 1988— another recent reminder that the Big Island is still a brash, rumbling, changing land.

Return via Chain of Craters Road to exit the park; turn right onto Highway 11 if you are ready to go back to Hilo, and left if you are game for some more sightseeing. Then, if you need a bite to eat, make the first right turn, which leads to **Volcano Golf and Country Club** (Box 46, Volcano 96718, tel. 808/967– 7331).

Time Out   **Volcano Country Club Restaurant** (tel. 808/967–8550), at the golf course, has big plate-glass windows that afford a view of mist-shrouded greens, rare golden-blossomed lehua trees, and an occasional nene goose, Hawaii's state bird. Coffee and a devil-on-horseback (corned beef) sandwich can be a soul-saver on a cool, wet Volcano day.

Return to Highway 11, continue in a southwesterly direction to the next right, and turn onto Mauna Loa Road. Then stop at the sign on the right that says **"Tree Molds."** These molds were created when molten lava hardened around a tree and burned it away in the process. Farther on is a little park with picnic tables, and at the end of the road you can take a self-guided mile-long walk around **Kipuka Puaulu.** A *kipuka* is a green, forested island surrounded by a sea of lava. Here you'll discover a koa tree and other endemic plants and (if you've got sharp eyes) native birds, such as the *apapane* or the *elepaio*. (You can pick up a written guide with numbers that correspond to sites along the kipuka's trail at Volcano National Park's Kilauea Visitor Center.)

Return toward Hilo by driving back on Highway 11 through **Volcano.** The old volcano highway runs parallel to Highway 11, and it's fun to take a side trip to the **Volcano Store** (turn left about a mile from the park entrance to Volcano Village at the sign; tel. 808/967–7210). The shop has excellent bargains in cut flowers; when in stock, charming little orchid corsages are only a couple of dollars.

Continuing back to Hilo on Highway 11, notice the yellow and white ginger (the aromatic flower prized for leis) and tiny purple wild orchids that grow in profusion along the sides of the road. Nobody minds if you stop to pick a blossom or two, or you might prefer to stop at any of the anthurium nurseries along the road to see how the bright red, pink, white, and varicolored "little boy" flowers (notice the stamen at the flower's center) grow. You'll see round wooden water tanks beside weathered houses until you draw nearer to Mountain View and Kurtistown, where the city supplies water.

㉑ Take a side trip to **Puna** (or, if you prefer, save this excursion for another day). Turn right onto Highway 130 at Keaau; 11 miles out, pause at Pahoa, a little town with wooden boardwalks and rickety buildings reminiscent of the wild West. The restaurants outnumber the art galleries in the quaint old buildings that are fun to wander through. After Pahoa, angle left

㉒ onto Highway 132 and continue to **Lava Tree State Park**. Tree molds formed here in 1790 when a lava flow swept through the ohia forest. These molds rise like blackened smokestacks 6 or more feet into the cool, damp air. *Admission free. Open 24 hours.*

Keeping to the left, continue on Highway 132 toward the coast

㉓ to **Kapoho**—if you can find it, ? today it is simply a place where two roads cross. In 1960 the entire town was covered with lava. Luckily, everyone was safely evacuated. Near the coast, after 2

㉔ miles on an unpaved road, you'll come across **Cape Kumukahi Lighthouse,** directly in the path of lava that stopped 6 feet away, splitting into two fingers to encircle the lighthouse and tumble into the sea, as if the quixotic goddess Pele had suddenly changed her mind about its destruction. Returning to the Kapoho crossroads, turn left to follow Highway 137 along the

㉕ ㉖ coast, stopping at either **Isaac Hale Beach Park** or **MacKenzie State Park** to take time out for picnicking or to use the facilities.

The Puna area has many black-sand beaches. Southwest of the

㉗ parks on Highway 137 lies **Kaimu Black Sand Beach**. The black sand is formed when hot *'a'a* (chunky, cinder-type lava) hits the cold ocean water, bursting into tiny black granules that are broken down even further by wave action. Bear in mind that tricky currents make swimming at Kaimu dangerous (*see* Beaches, below). At press time, the beach was on its way to becoming the most recent victim of Kilauea Volcano's latest eruption. Since 1977 more than 170 homes have been destroyed or moved as a result of the longest lava eruption in recorded history.

In 1990 the **Star of the Sea Painted Church** (Hwy. 137, Kalapana, tel. 808/965–8202), built in 1931, had to be moved when lava inundated Kalapana. The little white steepled structure contains religious frescoes painted in vivid blue, red, yellow, and green on the walls and ceiling. Lava flows came close to destroying the church in 1977 and again in 1986 and 1987, when lava closed Chain of Craters Road (Highway 130), which joins Highway 137 less than a mile inland. At press time there was no news about where the church will be resituated.

The return to Hilo via Pahoa and Keaau on Highway 130 to Highway 11 will take about 45 minutes. As you enter town you might want to pick up souvenirs or snacks at Hilo's most mod-

㉘ ern shopping center, **Prince Kuhio Plaza** (11 E. Puainako at Hwy. 11, tel. 808/959–3555), where such fine stores as **Liberty House** also carry muumuus and resort wear. If you would like to

㉙ avoid packing souvenirs, visit **Hirose Nursery** (2212 Kanoelehua Ave., tel. 808/959–4561), near Prince Kuhio Plaza. You can order flowers to be sent to your friends on the Mainland; the owners will even present you with a complimentary blossom to tuck behind your ear when you go out to dinner.

Tour 2: Kailua-Kona

*Numbers in the margin correspond with points of interest on
the Tour 2: Kailua-Kona map.*

The touristy seaside village of Kailua-Kona rests at the base of
the 8,271-foot Mt. Hualalai. With the Hotel King Kamehameha
at the northern end of Alii Drive, the village has restaurants
and shops laid out along a mile strip of oceanfront that culmi-
nate in the new Waterfront Row complex at the southern end.
You can walk the whole length of "downtown" Kailua-Kona and
back again in 45 minutes, or else spend an entire day here, taking time to browse in the shops, do the historical tours, and
simply breathe in the atmosphere. Just beyond the new Waterfront Row shopping and dining complex, the Kona Hilton and
Tennis Resort marks the beginning of the 6 miles of hotels and
condos along Alii Drive that ends at the Kona Surf Resort in
Keauhou.

For visitors who are driving, the easiest place to park (and
parking fees are not out of line) is at the Hotel King Kamehameha, but free parking is available if you enter Kailua via Palani
Road, or Highway 190. Turn left onto Kuakini Highway; in half
a block turn right and then immediately left into the parking
lot. Walk makai (toward the ocean) on Likana Lane half a block
to Alii Drive.

Time Out   The caramel–macadamia nut Danish is finger-licking good at
Suzanne's Bake Shop (75-5702 Alii Dr., tel. 808/329-3365).
There are five outdoor tables to the left of the lane if you want
sustenance before you begin your walking tour. The gingerbread hula boys and girls are especially scrumptious.

Cross Alii Drive to the **seawall,** where fishermen cast their
lines. If the *lau hala* weavers are set up on their mats, stop to
"talk story" (chat) and they will explain the technique of weaving hats and mats; perhaps they'll weave a bird for you.
Pranksters delight in telling visitors that hala trees, which produce the long flat leaves for weaving lau hala items, are actually
pineapple trees, because the fruit of the tree is similarly
shaped.

❶ Angle to the left, keeping the ocean on your right until you
come to the wrought-iron gate that fronts **Hulihee Palace** and
museum. The two-story palace was built in 1838 by the island's
governor, John Adams Kuakini, and served as King David
Kalakaua's summer palace in the 1880s. Tour guides at the restored palace talk about the artifacts and the royal lifestyle and
furnish a good basis for appreciating the history of the Big Island. Oversize doors and koa-wood furniture in the elegant
home graphically illustrate how huge some of the Hawaiian
people were. *75-5718 Alii Dr., tel. 808/329-1877. Admission:
$4 adults, $1 children 12–18, 50¢ children under 13. Open daily
9–4. Closed Christmas and New Year's Day.*

❷ Return along the seawall, where fishermen daily cast their
lines, past **Kailua Pier.** You may want to return here to watch
the fishing fleet come in at dusk, especially during marlin tournament season in August and September. Regular daily
catches of the big game fish are now generally weighed in at
Honokohau Harbor, north of Kailua-Kona.

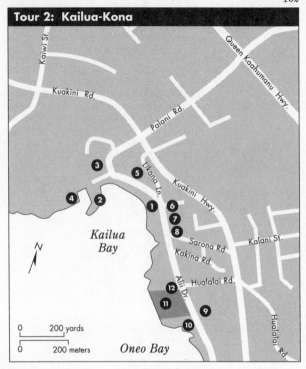

Tour 2: Kailua-Kona

Kaiwi St.

Queen Kaahumanu Hwy.

Kuakini Rd.

Palani Rd.

Likana Ln.

Kuakini Hwy.

Kailua Bay

N

Sarona Rd.

Kalani St.

Kakina Rd.

Alii Dr.

Hualalai Rd.

Hualalai Rd.

0 — 200 yards
0 — 200 meters

Oneo Bay

❸ Beyond the pier, enter the **Hotel King Kamehameha** for a stroll through the high-ceilinged, extensive lobby, reminiscent of a covered shopping mall. Some of the nicest shops in town, including **Liberty House** department store, **Jafar** clothing boutique, **Lalana's** (for hand-painted silks and cottons), **Mynah Bird Fabrics**, the **Shellery**, and **Trader's Hawaiian Gifts** are side by side with museum-quality displays of Hawaiian artifacts and trophies and mounted marlin from past Hawaiian International Billfish Tournaments. You'll see the 1986 winner of the Hawaiian Billfish Tournament, which weighed in at 1,062 pounds.

Exit the hotel on the makai (ocean) side past the swimming pool and **Moby Dick's Restaurant** and continue on the pathway past Kamakahonu Beach and the lagoon. This is where King Kame-
❹ hameha I lived between 1813 and 1819. **Ahuena Heiau** has been restored with thatched houses, so be sure you have your camera ready. Built by early Hawaiians, heiaus often had grass huts on top. Many heiaus can be found in the Islands; only a few have been restored. *75-5660 Palani Rd., tel. 808/329–2911. The hotel offers free historic tours of its grounds and the heiau Sat.–Thurs. at 1:30 and Fri. at 3, beginning at the mural across from the registration desk. Free ethnobotanical tours identifying and discussing the uses of endemic plants are offered Tues., Thurs., and Sun. at 10 and 11.*

Retrace your steps through the hotel, crossing Palani Street to Kona Square, the first of many shopping villages and lanes that lead off Alii Drive.

Time Out The **Shave Ice Company** is right on the corner of Alii Drive and Palani Street. Can't make up your mind on one flavor? Try a rainbow shave ice (a multiflavored Hawaiian snow cone) to quench your thirst. You can have it with *azuki* beans (similar to pinto beans) or a little ice cream tucked inside, or you can get a plain Dreyers ice-cream cone here.

If you continue on the *mauka* (mountain) side of the street, ⑤ you'll find **Kona Arts and Crafts** (75-5699 Alii Dr., tel. 808/329–5590) at the Kailua Bay Inn Shopping Plaza. Everything in this shop is locally produced—petroglyph earrings, iridescent volcano-glass necklaces, pictures made of banana bark, and blown-glass dolphins on coral bases that have been painted black to resemble lava. (A coral substitute is used for lava because it is widely believed that anyone taking lava from Hawaii risks incurring the wrath of the volcano goddess Pele.)

Farther along Alii Drive, past Ocean View Inn and across the ⑥ street from Hulihee Palace, is **Mokuaikaua Church,** (tel. 808/329–0655), or the Church of the Chimes, which sound on the hour. The present church was built in 1836, though the original Mokuaikaua Church was founded in 1820 by Hawaii's first missionaries and was the earliest Christian church in the Islands. When the Congregationalists arrived on the brig *Thaddeus*, the old Hawaiian religion with all its *kapus* (taboos) had just been banned by the new king, Liholiho, at the insistence of his mother, Keopuolani, and Queen Kaahumanu. Many of the kapus governed the behavior of women; for instance, they could not eat certain foods, such as bananas, nor could they eat with men. The Islands were ripe for a new religion, and Queen Kaahumanu helped to pave the way for the Protestants.

Mokuaikaua Church is built of black stone from an abandoned heiau, which has been mortared with white coral and topped by an impressive steeple. Inside are pews, balconies, and at the back a panel of gleaming koa wood, behind which is a model of the *Thaddeus* and a reproduction of a page written by Lucy Thurston (a missionary wife), detailing her early impressions.

At this point, you might opt to return to your car to drive along the waterfront, or you can continue browsing through the shopping plazas that extend off Alii Drive. At the **Kona Shopping Arcade,** behind the Crazy Shirts store and the pink awnings of ⑦ the second-floor Rusty Harpoon Restaurant, is the **Hawaii Visitors Bureau** (75-5719 Alii Dr., tel. 808/329–7787). Ask the staff anything—until *pau hana* (closing) time at 4:30. Maps of the Big Island and Kailua-Kona are sold at the **Middle Earth Bookshoppe** (75-5719 Alii Dr., tel. 808/329–2123), around the corner in the same arcade.

At the next shopping arcade, **Kona Bazaar,** rest rooms are located upstairs, and next door, clear at the back, is the movie ⑧ theater. **World Square Theater** (75-5719 Alii Dr., tel. 808/329–4070) shows recent movies at 6 and 8:15 PM. Kona Shopping Arcade and the Kona Bazaar are collectively known as the **Kona Marketplace.**

Time Out Entertainment gets a bit more local a few steps up the street at **Uncle Billy's Kona Bay Hotel** (75-5739 Alii Dr., tel. 808/329–1393). Sip a cool drink at the open-air Kimo's Steak and Seafood

Restaurant by the pool beside Alii Drive and enjoy one, or both, of two free hula shows presented Monday through Saturday nights at 6:30 and 7:30.

9 Next you'll find a grotto shrine constructed of coral that holds a statue of the Virgin Mary at the pink **St. Michael's Church** (Alii Dr., tel. 808/329–0655), half a block up the street. To the left of the church, a small thatched structure at the entrance to a poorly maintained graveyard marks the site of the first Catholic Church built in Kona in 1840.

10 At this point, it's time to stroll across the street to the new **Waterfront Row** (75-5770 Alii Dr.), which has more shops and restaurants, and begin the return walk. Alii Drive continues for 6 more miles along the oceanfront, past Disappearing Sands Beach, the tiny blue-and-white St. Peter's Catholic Church, the ruins of a heiau, and Kahaluu Beach Park. Elegant condos with beautifully landscaped grounds, the Kona Country Club (golf course), and the Keauhou Shopping Center are all part of the scenery before the road ends at the **Kona Surf Resort.**

11 For the footsore, the benches under the trees at the ocean's edge in front of the **Hale Halawai** recreational pavilion furnish a welcome respite, or you can continue your return through the **12** **Kona Inn Shopping Village** (75-5744 Alii Dr.). The boardwalk, with still more shops and restaurants, takes you all the way back along the waterfront to your point of origin. You might decide the Kona Inn Shopping Village deserves a return visit just for the shopping. **Exotic Skins** has reasonable eelskin wallets and purses, **Big Island Hat Company** has great tropical toppers, **Lady L.** offers raw silk resort wear, and hand-painted T-shirts in pretty pastels are everywhere. Shop at more than one place to find the best buys on these shirts and ask about seconds; sometimes an almost unnoticeable flaw or misplaced brushstroke can bring down the price.

Children (if they've tagged along this far) deserve a break at **Fernandez Fun Factory** (tel. 808/329–1992). In addition to the standard electronic diversions, it's got Skeeball and Whacknole, a couple of games that take some physical effort. This will give mom and dad the chance to walk through **Fisherman's Landing Restaurant** (tel. 808/326–2555) just to enjoy the tropical foliage at the entrance and the lagoons inside. A saltwater pool lies between the restaurant and the ocean.

Time Out Pause next door at the **Kona Inn Restaurant** (75-5744 Alii Dr., tel. 808/329–4455), where cocktails at sunset are a local tradition. Some visitors bring lawn chairs and stretch out with a good book in the afternoon beneath the coconut trees on the lawn between the restaurant and the ocean.

Near the exit of the arcade, **Old Time Portraits** (tel. 808/326–5447) will be happy to create a look as old as you might be feeling after this long stroll. Then cross the street and return to your car via Likana Lane.

Tour 3: The Kohala District

Numbers in the margin correspond with points of interest on the Tour 3: The Kohala District map.

If you're staying in Kona, you can begin this tour early in the morning by driving north on Queen Kaahumanu Highway 19. You'll pass both brightly colored bougainvillea along the roadside and white coral rocks carefully arranged by local youths to spell out names and messages on the black lava. Speed on by the glamorous luxury resorts along the Kona–Kohala coast; you can save those to inspect on another day. This is big country we're covering, and you can't see it all in a single swoop. Most of the lava flows that stretch from the mountains to the sea, which are interrupted only by the green oases of irrigated golf courses, resulted from the last eruptions of **Mt. Hualalai** in 1800–1801. You should be able to see the looming mountain to your right clearly in the morning light, though often mist descends later in the day. If you start late, you may not have time to take in every attraction on the Kohala Loop.

When you get to the split in the road 33 miles from Kailua-Kona, go left on Highway 270 toward Kawaihae and stop at **Puukohola Visitor Center.** The guide at this National Historic Site will tell you the history of the two large heiaus (stone temples), and a third which is submerged just off shore, that King Kamehameha I had his men rebuild from 1790 to 1791. A prophet had told him to rebuild **Puukohola Heiau** (originally constructed about 1550) and dedicate it to the war god Kukailimoku by sacrificing his principal Big Island rival, Keoua Kuahuula, on the temple so that Kamehameha could fulfill his goal of conquering the Hawaiian Islands. The sacrifice was made, and the prophecy was finally fulfilled in 1810. It is a short, downhill walk over arid landscape from the visitor center to Puukohola Heiau and then across the road to the smaller **Mailekini Heiau** for a snapshot that will include both of the stone structures. *Box 44340, Kawaihae 96743, tel. 808/882-7218. Admission free. Open 7:30–4.*

You can also get a photo of the two heiaus by driving a bit farther down the road and turning into **Samuel M. Spencer Beach Park** (tel. 808/882-7094; *see* Beaches, below).

Retrace your route and continue up Highway 19 through Parker Ranch land toward Waimea-Kamuela. You can actually call this town by either part of the name. The community is generally called **Waimea,** but in the past it was affectionately named Kamuela, the Hawaiian word for Samuel, after Samuel Parker, the son of the founder, and mail to the town should be addressed to Kamuela.

Right where the road splits and Kohala Mountain Road (Highway 250) makes a sharp left, you'll find **Kamuela Museum.** Parker descendants Albert and Harriet Solomon have amassed a fascinating array of Hawaiian and other artifacts from around the world. The Solomons don't worry that the things on display are too eclectic; instead, they think people will be attracted to whatever interests them, whether it's a satiny-smooth koa table that once graced Iolani Palace or a stuffed black bear from British Columbia. Most of the items are neatly labeled, and there's an impressive number of antique poi pounders, calabashes, and bone fishhooks. *At the junction of Hwys. 19 and 250, Box 507, Kamuela 96743, tel. 808/885-4724. Admission: $2.50 adults, $1 children under 12. Open daily 8–5.*

Continue inland on Highway 19 (Kawaihae Road) to pause again at the new shopping complex called **Hale Kea,** to the left

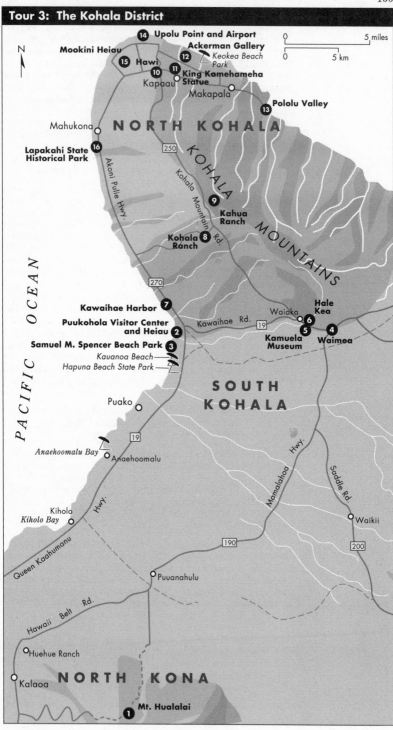

Tour 3: The Kohala District

N

14 Upolu Point and Airport
Mookini Heiau
12 Ackerman Gallery
Keokea Beach Park
15 Hawi
10 **11** King Kamehameha
Kapaau Statue
Makapala
13 Pololu Valley

NORTH KOHALA

Mahukona

Lapakahi State **16**
Historical Park

Akoni Pule Hwy.

250

Kohala Mountain Rd.

9
Kahua
Ranch

Kohala **8**
Ranch

270

Kawaihae Harbor **7**

Kawaihae Rd. Waiaka Hale
Kea

Puukohola Visitor Center 19 **6**
and Heiau **2** **5** **4**
Samuel M. Spencer Beach Park **3** Kamuela Waimea
Kauanoa Beach Museum
Hapuna Beach State Park

**SOUTH
KOHALA**

PACIFIC OCEAN

Puako

19

Mamalahoa Hwy.

Saddle Rd.

Anaehoomalu Bay
Anaehoomalu

Kiholo
Kiholo Bay

Queen Kaahumanu Hwy.

Puuanahulu

190

Waikii

200

Hawaii Belt Rd.

Huehue Ranch

Kalaoa **NORTH KONA**

1 Mt. Hualalai

0 — 5 miles
0 — 5 km

KOHALA MOUNTAINS

of the main road. This area was the ranch of Laurance Rockefeller (the same mogul who built the Mauna Kea Resort). During 1989 the ranch house and outbuildings were remodeled, and now they house wonderful little shops, art galleries, and Hartwell's Restaurant. Take a look at the finely crafted milo- and koa-wood sculptures, furniture, bowls, and boxes, hand-made paper, and other collectibles in **Maya Gallery** and the hand-dyed silk and batik clothing at **Noa Noa,** designed by C. Marie.

You'll also want to take some time to poke around and shop at **Parker Square** (those red buildings with white trim to the right of Kawaihae Rd. as you enter town, tel. 808/885-7178), and at **Opelo Plaza** (Hwy. 19, Waimea). If you're lucky enough to be in Waimea on a Saturday before 11:30 AM, drop by the tiny swap meet (flea market) called **Mother's Den** across from the public school to pick up cookies, cut flowers, or any number of second-hand finds that residents offer for sale (*see* Shopping, below).

Waimea has attracted a surprising number of fine restaurants run by chefs who have defected from the luxury resorts on the coast. You'll want to make a point of coming back here to dine at **Bree Garden, Merriman's, Hartwell's,** or the established stand-by, **Edelweiss** (*see* Dining, below).

Time Out   For now, however, a quick lunch at the **Bread Depot** (808/885-6354) in Opelo Plaza should suffice, or ask for a picnic lunch to go. The Depot bakes all the breads for its fabulous sandwiches; you can also get soup and a daily special, often pasta or curry.

The traditional visitor attraction in Waimea is the **Parker Ranch Visitor Center and Museum,** which was opened in 1975 by Richard Smart, a ranch owner and an heir of John Palmer Parker. The latter founded Parker Ranch in 1847, when King Kamehameha I gave the newcomer two acres of land. The museum delves into the history of ranching by the Parkers with life-size replicas and a slide show detailing the growth of the ranch.

A few years ago Smart opened **Mana,** the original koa-wood residence of the ranch founder, as well as the century-old Smart family home, **Puuopelu,** so the public could view an extensive private art collection. More recently tours have been added, which include demonstrations at Puukalani Stables (*see* Guided Tours in Essential Information, above). *At Parker Ranch Shopping Center, junction of Hwys. 19 and 190, Box 458, Kamuela 96743, tel. 808/885-7655. Admission to museum: $4 adults, $2 children 4–11. Open Mon.–Sat. 9–4:30. Admission to Historic Homes: $5 adults, $2.50 children 4–11. Open Mon.–Sat. 9:30–4:30. Cost of tours: $15–$38 adults, $7.50–$19 children 4–11.*

If you leave Parker Ranch Visitor Center and drive northeast on Highway 19, you'll pass the **Keck Control Center** on the left (it is the headquarters for the Keck Observatory, containing the world's largest mirrored telescope, at the top of Mauna Kea). Then drive by the first church on the left, but stop to peek into the cream-colored church called **Imiola Congregational** (Box 669, Kamuela 96743, tel. 808/885-4987). The entrance of the church, which was built in 1832, is behind the pulpit (be careful not to walk in while a service is in progress).

Note the all-koa interior and the very unusual wooden calabashes hanging from the ceiling.

Return through town and turn right on **Kohala Mountain Road** (Highway 250) for a scenic ride through the Kohala Mountains to Hawi. An overlook affords a view of the entire coastline; see **❼** if you can pick out the protective breakwater at **Kawaihae Harbor** directly below. This harbor is second in size only to Hilo Harbor on the east coast. Farther on, through the ironwood trees that act as windbreaks along the road, you'll see whiteboard fences that extend across the emerald pastures. These fences divide into 3-, 5-, and 10-acre lots an exclusive country-home subdivision called **Kohala Ranch.** Here the impressive **❽** new Arena Polo and Equestrian Center sets the stage for frequent exhibition polo matches, which visitors are welcome to attend. You can arrange at your hotel desk for guided horse-back rides through this country with **Ironwood Outfitters** (tel. 808/885–4941). The air is crisp and clear, until the mist sets in and all you can see are the outlines of horses or cattle appearing and disappearing on the pastures.

❾ Across the road you may see the windmilled farm of **Kahua Ranch,** a 23,000-acre operation with progressive cowboys who round up the cattle astride horses or motorcycles and spend part of their days tending sheep and long-stemmed carnations. Owner Monte Richards realized that the best way to remain economically viable was to diversify his ranching efforts. Sunset in the Kohala Mountains turns the hills into a muted watercolor in shades of mauve, wheat, and cerulean blue.

The road drops gradually from 3,564 feet, and after about 20 miles it rejoins Highway 270 at the dilapidated old sugar village **❿** of **Hawi.** Turn right to Kapaau, where on the right of Highway **⓫** 270 you'll see the original **King Kamehameha Statue** (which is just like the one in front of the Judiciary Building on King Street in Honolulu). This statue was cast in Florence in 1880 but was lost at sea when the German ship that was transporting it sank near the Falkland Islands. A replica was ordered and shipped to Honolulu, and two years later an American sea captain found the original in a Port Stanley (Falkland Islands) junkyard and brought it to the Big Island. The legislature voted to erect it near Kamehameha's birthplace.

Across the street, painter Gary Ackerman and his wife, Yesan, have a fine collection of local gifts and artifacts for sale in their **⓬** **Ackerman Gallery** (Box 961, Kapaau 96755, tel. 808/889–5971).

Time Out | If riding and history have made you hungry, **Tropical Dreams** (tel. 808/889–5386), a little restaurant next to the Ackerman Gallery on the main street in Kapaau, dishes out freshly made ice cream.

⓭ The road ends at an overlook at **Pololu Valley.** A hiking trail for the very hearty leads into the valley and over several ridges beyond. The trail eventually reaches Waipio Valley. On the return via Highway 270, feel free to pass up **Kapaa Beach Park** and **Mahukona Beach Park;** you've earned the break, and these parks do not have particularly enticing swimming beaches.

⓮ But we do recommend you take the turnoff to **Upolu Point** and the **Upolu Airport** if you are truly intent on not missing anything historically important. At the airport a rough lane to the

⑮ left leads to the **Mookini Heiau.** Few people seem to seek out this isolated luakine (sacrificial) heiau, but it is so impressive in size it will give you "chicken skin" (the local equivalent of goosebumps), especially when you think that it was built about AD 480.

⑯ The final stop off is **Lapakahi State Historical Park,** if it's not too late in the afternoon, as this beach park closes at 4 PM. It's a healthy walk down an arid hillside to take the self-guided tour through the ruins of an ancient fishing village. Displays illustrate early Hawaiian fishing, salt gathering, legends, games, shelters, and crops. You might want to take only part of the trail—unless, of course, you've driven the Kohala Loop in the opposite direction and are ready for some fine snorkeling and a bit of feasting on a picnic lunch. *Box 100, Kapaau 96755, tel. 808/889-5566. Admission free. Open daily 8-4.*

Return to Kona via Highway 270 and perhaps have dinner or drinks at Harrington's or Café Pasta at Kawaihae Harbor.

Tour 4: Hilo and the Hamakua Coast to Waipio Valley

Hilo *Numbers in the margin correspond with points of interest on the Tour 4: Hilo Vicinity map.*

When the sun shines and the snow glistens on Mauna Kea 25 miles in the distance, Hilo is truly beautiful. In the rain, the town becomes an impressionist painting, with the brilliant greenery muted alongside the weather-worn brown, red, and blue buildings. In the last couple of years, these buildings have been the focus of a $1.4 million refurbishment, undertaken in hopes of revitalizing the downtown area by attracting more businesses and visitors. The whole town has only 1,200 hotel rooms, most of them strung along Banyan Drive, right on Hilo Bay. In comparison, a single hotel on the west coast, the Hyatt Regency Waikoloa, has 1,240 rooms.

Nonetheless, Hilo (with a population of 40,000) is the fourth-largest city in the state: it is home to a branch of the University of Hawaii. Often the rain blows away by noon, and a colorful arch will appear in the sky. Some people nickname Hilo "the City of Rainbows."

❶ From the **Naniloa Hotel** (93 Banyan Dr., tel. 808/969-3333), go southwest on Banyan Drive, keeping to the right with Hilo Bay to your right. Those banyan trees along the drive, by the way, were planted in the 1930s by visiting celebrities; you will find such names as Amelia Earhart and Franklin Delano Roosevelt on plaques on the trees.

Time Out For a pleasant breakfast, try **Queens Court** at the **Hilo Hawaiian Hotel** (71 Banyan Dr., tel. 808/935-9361). Both the window seats and the raised booths that are set back from the windows have a good view of Hilo Bay. Prices here are not exorbitant for a hotel restaurant.

❷ Next, you might want to meander across the footbridge to **Coconut Island** to watch children play in the tidal pools while fishermen try their luck. The wide green expanse on either side of Banyan Drive housed Hilo businesses until a *tsunami*, or tidal wave, in 1960 swept them away and took the lives of 60

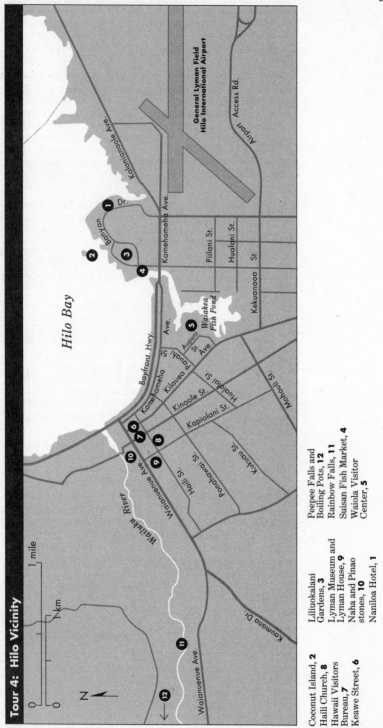

Tour 4: Hilo Vicinity

Hilo Bay

General Lyman Field
Hilo International Airport

Waiakea Fish Pond

Coconut Island, **2**
Haili Church, **8**
Hawaii Visitors Bureau, **7**
Keawe Street, **6**

Liliuokalani Gardens, **3**
Lyman Museum and Lyman House, **9**
Naha and Pinao stones, **10**
Naniloa Hotel, **1**

Peepee Falls and Boiling Pots, **12**
Rainbow Falls, **11**
Suisan Fish Market, **4**
Waiola Visitor Center, **5**

❸ people in the process. Today, **Liliuokalani Gardens,** with its fish-stocked streams and oriental bridges, pagodas, and ceremonial teahouse, is a favorite Sunday destination for residents.

Banyan Drive turns left onto Lihiwai Street. This is where the most action in town takes place Monday through Saturday, starting at about 7:30 or 8 AM. A fishing fleet arrives sometime in the wee hours with its catch to be auctioned to retailers at the **❹** **Suisan Fish Market.** Take your camera (and a flash) to get pictures of the bright red aweoweo, aku, ahi, marlin, and other fish as buyers and sellers do their thing, generally in unintelligible pidgin English.

Leaving Lihiwai Street, turn right onto Kamehameha Avenue, unless construction forces you to partially retrace your route. Ignore the connecting Bayfront Highway, which is the fast way to bypass town to drive to the Hamakua coast. In 3 blocks, turn left on Pauahi Street and left again after 1 block onto Piopio Street. Park and walk across Liliuokalani Park beside **❺** Waiola Pond to the **Waiola Visitor Center,** where a photographic exhibit shows the aftermath of the 1960 tidal wave. *Box 936, Piopio St., tel. 808/961-7360. Open Mon., Tues., Thurs., Fri. 8–4:30, Wed. noon–8:30, Sat. 9–3.* Back in the car, drive until you reach Kilauea Avenue.

Next, drive up Pauahi Street and continue on Kilauea Avenue until it angles to the right to become Keawe Street and is crossed by Haili Street. For inveterate shoppers, it is time to park the car and take out the credit cards. The charming shops **❻** on **Keawe Street** are your goal. While away time at **Basically Books,** or browse in the **Most Irresistible Shop in Town** (containing an eclectic array of items, including English china cups, ceramic fireplaces, and handbags), the **Futon Connection, Cunningham Gallery, Louise Dumaine Antiques, Da Ceramic Shop,** and the **Potter's Gallery.**

Time Out We guarantee that a few minutes at the **Chocolate Bar** (98 Keawe St., tel. 808/961-5088), topped off with a few sips of fresh-brewed Kona coffee at **Bear's Coffee Shop** (110 Keawe St., tel. 808/935-0708), will revive the tired shopper.

If you walk from Keawe Street *mauka* (toward the mountains) **❼** on Haili Street, you'll find the Hilo branch of the **Hawaii Visitors Bureau** (180 Kinoole St., tel. 808/329-7787), marked by a red and white Hawaiian Warrior sign. Where Ululani Street **❽** crosses Haili Street is the historic **Haili Church,** built by Protestant missionaries in 1859. On Sunday the choir sings Hawaiian hymns, and services are conducted in both Hawaiian and English.

❾ Farther up the block on the right are two attractions, **Lyman Museum and Lyman House,** of particular interest to history buffs. The house was built in 1839 by missionaries who came from Boston to run a school for boys. The adjacent museum was dedicated in 1973 to house the museum's unique acquisitions— wooden cuspidors carved by Hawaiians, the world's only display of Hawaiian land shells (snails), and historical dress representing Hawaii's various ethnic groups.

The Lyman Museum operates a refurbished **sampan bus,** a brown-and-yellow 1948 Plymouth that old-time Hiloans remember with fond nostalgia, as these open-sided autos were once used for public transportation. Call the museum for information about narrated, hour-long city tours ($6.50 per person) conducted in the sampan bus in conjunction with a visit to the museum. A walking-tour map of old Hilo Town, explaining the significance of historic sites and buildings, is available in the museum's gift shop for $1.25. *276 Haili St., tel. 808/935–5021. Admission (includes guided tours): $3.50 adults, $2.50 ages 13–18, $1.50 ages 6–12. Open Mon.–Sat. 9–5.*

Retrace your steps half a block to go along Kapiolani Street and around the corner to 300 Waianuenue Avenue. In front of the public library you'll find two large oblong stones, the legendary **Naha and Pinao stones.** The Pinao stone is reportedly an entrance pillar of an ancient temple that stood on this site. Legend decreed that the person who could move the 5,000-pound Naha stone would become king of all the islands. Kamehameha I, who united the Hawaiian Islands, is said to have moved the Naha stone when he was still in his teens.

Return to your car to follow Waianuenue Avenue a mile west of town. (When the road forks, remain on Waianuenue Avenue to the right. The left fork, Kaumana Drive, becomes Saddle Road, which bisects the island between Mauna Loa and Mauna Kea mountains and continues on to Waimea and the Kohala coast. Also, be advised that Waianuenue Avenue from 7:15 to 8 AM is a one-way street entering Hilo). You'll see the Hawaiian-warrior marker for **Rainbow Falls,** which thunders into Wailuku River Gorge. If the sun peeks out in the morning hours, a rainbow forms above the mist.

Continue another 2 miles or so up the road, keeping to the right; you may think you've gotten lost, but eventually you'll see a green sign for **Peepee Falls.** The falls drop in four streams of water into a series of circular pools, and the resultant turbulent action of the water has earned the name **Boiling Pots.**

Hamakua Coast   *Numbers on the map correspond with points of interest on the Tour 4: Hamakua Coast map.*

Return along Waianuenue Avenue through Hilo and turn left onto Bayfront Highway if you're still interested in sightseeing along the Hamakua coast, or if you prefer, save the farther reaches of this drive for another day. You'll be traveling north on Highway 19. It is 95 miles to Kona via this shorter of the two coastal routes and approximately 50 miles to Waipio Valley, the turnaround point of this excursion.

Seven miles out of town, turn right onto a **4-mile scenic drive.** Lush vegetation, flowers, bridges over rushing, tumbling streams, and stunning coastline views appear around each curve. On the left you'll see an old church, now a partially burned ruin, and a small office, the headquarters of **Hawaii Tropical Botanical Garden.** Tickets are available at the office, where you also catch a van to visit the 17-acre nature preserve just down the hill on Onomea Bay. Pathways lead through more than 1,000 species of plants and flowers, including palms, bromeliads, ginger, heliconia, and ornamentals. You'll see waterfalls and, in the lily lake, the fish called koi, prized by many Japanese collectors. Allow yourself enough time to explore the grounds at a leisurely pace. *Box 415, Hilo, tel. 808/964–5233. Admission (tax deductible, as the nature preserve is a nonprofit organization): $10 adults, $9.50 seniors. Open daily 8:30–4:30.*

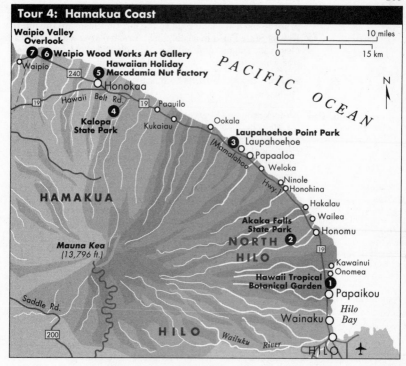

Tour 4: Hamakua Coast

Waipio Valley Overlook ⑦ ⑥ Waipio Wood Works Art Gallery
Hawaiian Holiday
⑤ Macadamia Nut Factory

Waipio · 240 · Honokaa

19 · Hawaii Belt Rd. · 19 · Paauilo

④ Kalopa State Park · Kukaiau · Ookala

③ Laupahoehoe Point Park
Laupahoehoe
(Mamalahoa) · Papaaloa
Weloka
Ninole
Honohina
Hakalau
Wailea
Akaka Falls State Park ② · Honomu

HAMAKUA

Mauna Kea (13,796 ft.)

NORTH HILO · 19
Kawainui
Onomea
Hawaii Tropical Botanical Garden ① · Papaikou

Saddle Rd.

· 200 · HILO · Wailuku · River · Wainaku · Hilo Bay

HILO

PACIFIC OCEAN

0 ——— 10 miles
0 ——— 15 km

N

When the scenic drive rejoins Highway 19, turn left at Honomu
② to travel 5 miles inland to **Akaka Falls State Park.** On the way to
the park you pass through the old plantation town of **Honomu,**
home of a little gift shop and gallery, but mostly you'll see fields
of sugarcane on both sides of the car and perhaps a loaded cane
truck or two.

There are two falls at the park, **Akaka** and **Kahuna;** you have to
be willing to walk perhaps 20 minutes total to see them. If you
follow the easier downhill trail to your right, you'll pass the 100-
foot Kahuna Falls first. Akaka Falls drops more than 420 feet,
tumbling far below into a pool drained by Kolekole Stream amid
a profusion of fragrant white, yellow, and red torch ginger. *Admission free. Open all day.*

Sit back and enjoy the ride through sleepy little towns with
music in their names: Honohina, Ninole, Papaaloa. If you
remember to say every letter and pronounce *i* as "ee" and *e* as in
"hey," you'll come pretty close to the correct pronunciation.
Drive off Highway 19 on the ocean side when you see the sign
③ for **Laupahoehoe Point Park.** It's not a place for swimming, but
it is a stunning point of land dotted with ironwood trees that
overlooks the pounding surf and the jagged black rocks of the
northeast coastline. Still vivid in the minds of longtime Hilo
residents is the April 1, 1946, tragedy when 20 schoolchildren
and four teachers were swept to sea by a tidal wave. In 1988 the
state constructed **Laupahoehoe Harbor,** and today the area features bathrooms, showers, picnic tables (open and covered),
and stone barbecue pits. *Admission free. Open all day.*

Highway 19 will lead you to the old plantation town of **Paauilo;** past the town is a side road to the left that leads up the hill to ❹ **Kalopa State Park,** in a cool, lush, forested area with picnic tables, rest rooms, and cabins. *Tel. 808/775–7114. Admission free. Open all day.*

Waving sugarcane turns to macadamia orchards as you near Honokaa.

Time Out A quick stop on Highway 19 at **Tex Drive Inn** (191 Hualani St., tel. 808/775–0598) will give you a chance to taste the snack it is famous for: a *malassada*, a puffy, doughy Portuguese doughnut (sans hole), deep-fried and rolled in sugar and best eaten while it's hot. For lunch with a little local flavor, turn right down the hill onto Highway 240 to Honokaa, stopping at the dilapidated old **Hotel Honokaa Club** (Manane St., Honokaa, tel. 808/775–0678 or 808/775–0533). This may well be the only place in town with a salad bar, and the prices are certainly right. It's been owned by the same family for umpteen years, and the present proprietor confides that he even serves lobster for dinner if patrons call in advance to request it.

The town of **Honokaa** marks the place where the first macadamia nut trees were planted in Hawaii in 1881 by an Australian named William Purvis. Today Honokaa is hailed as the macadamia capital of the world, mostly by the public-relations ❺ department of **Hawaiian Holiday Macadamia Nut Factory** (tel. 808/775–7743), which may be reached by following Highway 240 through Honokaa and turning right at the Hawaiian Holiday sign. *Open for tours and nut purchases daily 9–6.*

If you continue through Honokaa on Highway 240 for about 8 miles, to the end of the road, you'll reach Waipio. A sign on the way out will take you to the right on a loop with no street name ❻ off the main road; here you'll find the **Waipio Wood Works Art Gallery** (Box 5091, Kukuihaele, tel. 808/775–0958). Finely crafted wooden bowls, *ipus* (gourds), art by local artists, jewelry, and stitchery items are for sale. Make arrangements here ❼ or at the **Waipio Valley Overlook** for a tour (*see* Off the Beaten Track, below) to the floor of the valley, bounded by 2,000-foot cliffs. Nicknamed "the Valley of the Kings," Waipio was once a favorite retreat of Hawaiian royalty. Waterfalls drop 1,200 feet from the Kohala Mountains. A few residents still operate taro farms in the pastoral valley, and horses roam among the flowers and fruit, lotus ponds, and freshwater rivers.

If you have stopped to explore the sleepy plantation towns that look like relics from the past, with wooden boardwalks and dogs dozing in backyards, night is undoubtedly falling. Don't worry, the return to Hilo via Highway 19 will take only about an hour, or you can continue on the same road to Waimea (20 minutes) and then to the Kohala-coast resorts (another 40 minutes).

The Big Island for Free

Hawaii compares very favorably cost-wise with any popular resort destination in the world. However, in the interest of economy, we are including a listing of fabulous freebies, just in case you've reached your credit limit but not your departure day.

Hikiau Heiau. Unless you take a snorkeling cruise or go hiking, this is the closest you can get to where Britain's Captain Cook landed in 1778. He was warmly welcomed the first time he arrived, as it was the *makahiki* season, a festival time when war was suspended, taxes in the form of food and goods were paid to the king and distributed to the chiefs, and games of strength and swiftness were the order of the day. Whether the Hawaiians thought Cook was the returning festival god, Lonokamakahiki, is considered doubtful today. At any rate he was greeted with abundant gift-giving, and he gladly accepted the chance to restock his ships, going so far as to take the wooden railing from the heiau (temple) dedicated to Lono to use for firewood.

When he was forced to return a short month later to repair the foremast of the *Resolution*, the makahiki season was over. One Hawaiian stole a longboat from the accompanying British ship, the *Discovery*. Fighting broke out when Cook and his men tried to hold a chief hostage to exchange for the boat, and Cook was killed. His bones were stripped of their flesh to be kept for their *mana* (spiritual power) and taken to another heiau near the bay. When Cook's sailing master, Captain William Bligh of HMS *Bounty* fame, asked for the return of Cook's body, he was given only the skull, hands, arms, and legs.

If you look across Kealakekua Bay from Hikiau Heiau you can see the 27-foot obelisk erected by the British Commonwealth as a memorial in 1874. Today the heiau is a large barren black stone platform. Grass houses once stood on the site. A small beach is beyond the heiau. *Drive south on Hwy. 11 to Captain Cook. Turn right on Napoopoo Rd. for a scenic drive to Kealakekua Bay and Hikiau Heiau.*

Hilo Hattie Fashion Centers actually furnish transportation from hotels in Hilo or Kona, as well as a lei and complimentary refreshments. You can tour the garment factory and see resort wear being made, and of course, ample shopping time is allowed. *75-5597A Palani Rd., Kailua-Kona, tel. 808/329–7200; 933 Kanoelehua St., Hilo, tel. 808/961–3077.*

Hilo Tropical Gardens. Time your visit for a Saturday at 10 AM, when a free hula show is presented. Photographers will revel in the opportunity to snap exotic orchids and colorful tropical flowers in a natural setting in this 2-acre garden. A number of other orchid and anthurium gardens near Hilo and on the way to the volcano are also open to visitors (*see* Guided Tours in Essential Information, above). *1477 Kalanianaole Ave., tel. 808/935–4957. Open daily 8:30–5.*

Kailua Candy Company. Here's a place on the Big Island where you are welcome to indulge in a free dessert. Take the tour, or bypass it and go straight to the salesroom if you're trying to make a departing plane. In 1977 Jack and Ginny Smoot started producing chocolates using fresh ingredients and no preservatives. They conduct personalized tours of their tiny plant (even if you're a family of only three or four). *A Hawaii Visitor Bureau sign marks the entrance, in the industrial area of Kailua-Kona. 74-5552 C Kaiwi St., tel. 808/329–2522, or 800/622–2462. Open weekdays 9–5. Sat. 9–noon. Tours are weekdays 9–3.*

Macadamia Nut Factories. The best factory visitor center is at the **Mauna Loa Macadamia Nut Factory**, 5 miles south of Hilo off Route 11 (*see* Tour 1 in Exploring, above). Two other factories that welcome the public behind the scenes are the **Hawaiian Holiday Macadamia Nut Factory** in Honokaa (*see* Tour 4 in Exploring, above) and **Mrs. Field's Macadamia Nut Factory** (Halekii St. off Hwy. 11, Kealakekua, tel. 808/322–9515). A guide at the latter factory leads the way every half hour 9–3. Products are always for sale at the above locations, but often you can buy the same boxes of chocolate-covered macadamia nuts on sale at Long's or Pay'n Save Drug stores for less. One other place that deserves mention is the old **Kona Coast Nut and Candy Factory** (tel. 808/328–8141) on Middle Keei Road, between Highway 11 and Honaunau. The methods and machinery here are old-fashioned, but you can crack a nut yourself at one display, and the little shop sells off-grade, unsalted nuts that are great to use in your own home-baked cookies.

Mauna Kea Royal Kona Coffee Mill and Museum. Sip freshly brewed coffee while you wander through the photo gallery that illustrates 150 years of coffee growing in Hawaii. The Big Island, with orchards at about the 1,200-foot elevation, is the only place in the United States that grows coffee commercially. School vacations in Kona used to be timed to coincide with the harvesting of the ripe beans so the children of family-owned plantations could help with the picking. *Above Kealakekua Bay, 3.3 mi. off Hwy. 11 near Captain Cook, tel. 808/328–2511. Open daily 8–4:30.*

Polo. Spectators can enjoy this "sport of kings" on weekend-afternoon picnic outings at two locations on the Big Island. At press time, admission was free, but call first to make sure that games are scheduled and policies have not changed. *Waikii Ranch, 7 mi from Waimea on Saddle Rd., tel. 808/885–6668; Kohala Ranch, Kohala Mountain Rd., Rte. 250, tel. 808/329–9551.*

Puako petroglyphs. Watch for the Puako turnoff from Queen Kaahumanu Highway 19 between the Mauna Lani and Mauna Kea Beach Resorts. Near the end of Puako Beach Road, 3 miles from the turn, is a white sign with petroglyph figures. On foot, follow the white arrows painted sporadically on the ground for 15 minutes, and when you're just about ready to give up on the hot, dusty walk, the trail opens out to a lava bed covered with carved figures. Hawaiian warriors, fish, and geckos are spread out in three groupings.

Punaluu Village Museum displays old photos of C. Brewer's history in raising cane—for sugar, that is. As the industry became less and less profitable, with a lack of trade restrictions allowing the importation of sugar from other countries, C. Brewer began replanting fields in vast orchards of macadamia nuts in this area. A video about the volcano's activity and a mural painted by Big Island artist Herb Kane are also at the museum. *Hwy. 11, Punaluu, tel. 808/928–8528. Open daily 10:30–3.*

Television Tour. When you think you've seen it all, turn on **Channel 6** (tel. 808/322–3672) for a television tour of the Big Island from 6 AM to 6 PM and from 9:30 PM to 6 AM. Use it to plan your day or to view volcanic eruptions, scenic waterfalls, and remote destinations you might have missed on this trip.

What to See and Do with Children

In the last few years, the major resorts have become aware that children do travel with parents, particularly during the summer months and the Christmas season—so special activities are planned with the younger set in mind during those times. Sometimes an additional charge is assessed, with the amount based on how long the *keikis* (children) will be in the program and whether meals will be included. Supervised activities cover a broad spectrum, from lei making to fishing with a bamboo pole to sailing to dabbling with the crawly things in tide pools. **Mauna Lani Bay Hotel** offers Camp Mauna Lani; **Kona Village, Mauna Kea Beach Resort,** and the **Royal Waikoloan** also sponsor children's programs.

Fishing. Youngsters seem to like to try their luck casting at the seawall right in Kailua-Kona. A bamboo pole and hook are easy to come by in the village, and plenty of locals are willing to give pointers.

Hiking at Hawaii Volcanoes National Park. Kids will run off excess energy on **Devastation Trail** or through the **Thurston Lava Tube.** If you are in the park for a full day or more, a hike into **Kilauea Iki Crater** is exhilarating and can be accomplished in less than half a day. Hiking information and maps are available at the Kilauea Visitor Center (*see* Tour 1 in Exploring, above).

Hyatt Regency Waikoloa. This hotel has free train and boat rides; small children will probably find the monorail a nifty experience. Swimming with the dolphins is done through a special lottery—winners pay $65 for the privilege. Unfortunately, to use the water slides in the pools, you are required to have a bracelet that is only distributed on request to guests. *1 Waikoloa Beach Resort, Kohala Coast, tel. 808/885–1234 or 800/228–9000.*

Nautilus Submarine. A boat shuttles passengers from Kailua Pier to the 65-foot *Atlantis IV* submarine, which is so clean and new it feels more like an amusement-park ride than the real thing. A large glass dome in the bow and 13 viewing ports on the sides allow up to 48 passengers clear views of the watery world outside. A scuba diver feeds fish along a coral reef, keeping the viewing ports filled with the colorful finned creatures of the deep. Night dives to view nocturnal fish are also available. *Sign up at the Hotel King Kamehameha, 75-5660 Palani Rd., Kailua-Kona, tel. 808/329–6626. Cost: $67 adults, $33.50 children.*

Panaewa Zoo. *See* Tour 1, above.

Puuhonua o Honaunau. This 180-acre national historic park is perfect for a painless dose of education. In early times, kapu (taboo) breakers, criminals, and prisoners of war who escaped and reached this "city of refuge" were allowed to live and to escape punishment upon purification by the priests who lived within the walls. On the site, Hale-o-Keawe Heiau, built in 1650, has been restored, and the wooden images of Hawaiian gods have been replaced along its outer boundaries. Proceed at your own pace with a map for self-guided tours. Demonstrations of Hawaiian skills, games, poi pounding, canoe making, and more are frequently scheduled. Tidal pools and a picnic area with showers and bathrooms lie just beyond Puuhonua o Honaunau. *Follow Hwy. 11 south of Kailua-Kona to Keokea, turn right and follow Hwy. 160 3.6 mi to Puuhonua o Honaunau. Box 129, Honaunau 96726, tel. 808/328–2326. Admission: $1 adults, free under 17. Seniors in a car enable all passengers to get in free. Open daily 7:30–5:30.*

Thomas A. Jaggar Museum, Volcanoes National Park. *See* Tour 1, above.

Whale Watching. The season for watching these gentle giants is roughly from December through April, when the humpbacks migrate from the north to Hawaiian waters. Pacific Whale Foundation runs 2½-hour cruises from Kailua Pier daily. All profits go to benefit research and conservation of whales. Other pluses: The guides are knowledgeable, hydrophones allow you to hear the whales, and if the whales don't surface, you receive a "Just a Fluke" coupon for another trip. Take your own binoculars to save a rental fee. *Pacific Whale Foundation, 101 N. Kihei Rd., Kihei, Maui 96753, tel. 800/WHALE–1–1 or 808/329–3522. Cost: $25 adults, $15 children 3–12.*

Off the Beaten Track

South Point The southernmost point of land in the United States, South Point (Ka Lae) is easily accessible by car, but unless you have ample time for exploring all aspects of the Big Island, it is one destination you might choose to pass up. If you do take the 3½-hour, 126-mile Highway 11 route from Hilo to Kona, Ka Lae is slightly farther than midway. The turn to South Point is just beyond Naalehu, the southernmost U.S. town; you go 12 miles down a narrow road to treeless, windswept Ka Lae, where you'll find the small Kalalea Heiau and abandoned structures once used to lower cattle and produce to ships anchored below the cliffs. Old canoe-mooring holes were carved through the rocks, possibly by settlers from Tahiti as early as AD 750.

If you're determined to get even farther into the outback and lucky enough to be driving a four-wheel-drive vehicle, follow 3 miles along the shoreline to Mahana, or Green Sand Beach. The beach is at the base of a low sea cliff. There are no facilities, and the rip current is dangerous. The beach has a distinct green tint from the glassy olivine formed by the minerals that combine when hot 'a'a (chunky) lava hits the sea.

If you continue on Highway 11 to Kailua-Kona, **Manuka State Park** (tel. 808/961–7200) is a cool picnic stop on the long route. The botanical park is between Hookena and Naalehu and has signs naming the plants and trees. The picnic tables and covered pavilion are always open.

Waipio Valley At 6 miles deep, **Waipio Valley** in the north of the Big Island at the end of Highway 240 is the largest valley on the island. In 1823, the first white visitors found 1,500 inhabitants living in this Eden-like environment, amid wild fruit trees, banana patches, taro fields, and fish ponds. Dubbed the Valley of the Kings because it was once a vacation spot for Hawaiian royalty, the area today is home to only a handful of families. Here, in 1780, Kamehameha I was singled out as a future ruler by reigning chiefs. In 1791, he fought Kahekili in his first naval battle at the mouth of the valley. Now as then, waterfalls frame the landscape; one of them drops from a 2,000-foot cliff to the valley floor.

The no-name hotel (no electricity or private baths, either)—although sometimes it's called the Waipio Hotel—is the only hotel for overnighters, and arrangements must be made in advance. Hikers or outdoor types need to pack their own food and bring mosquito repellent and mosquito punks. You can walk into the valley or arrange to be dropped off by one of the four-wheel-drive tours that run daily. *Write to Tom Araki, 25 Malana Pl., Hilo 96720, tel. 808/775–0368. 5 rooms. Facilities: kerosene lamp, community kitchen and bath. No credit cards.*

Hawaii Resorts Transportation Company (Box 183, Honokaa 96727, tel. 808/885–7484) hosts a trip into Waipio Valley and includes a stop at Hawaiian Holiday Macadamia Nut Factory in Honokaa. (Cost: $26 adults from Kohala Coast hotels.) In addition, the company offers "Waipio on Horseback," a 2½-hour ride for a maximum of 6 riders. (Cost: $65 plus tax per person.) Reservations are needed 24 hours in advance, and children under 12 are allowed only if they are good riders and are accompanied by an adult.

Waipio Valley Shuttle leaves Waipio Woodworks Art Gallery daily on 1½-hour tours. *Box 5128, Kukuihaele 96727, tel. 808/ 775–7121. Cost: $20 adults, $10 children under 12.*

Waipio Valley Wagon Tours departs from the Last Chance Store in Kukuihaele for two-hour excursions. *Box 1340, Honokaa 96727, tel. 808/775–9518. Cost: $25 adults, $12.50 children under 13.*

Shopping

Residents like to complain that there isn't much to shop for on the Big Island. However, unless you're searching for career clothes or sweaters or a formal ball gown, you'll find plenty to deplete your pocketbook. Kailua-Kona has a range of souvenirs from farflung corners of the globe, such as Hong Kong, the Philippines, Taiwan, India, and Tahiti. Destination resorts along the Kohala coast offer quality goods. The **Mauna Lani Hotel,** for example, has **Collections,** an exclusive apparel shop that is a subsidiary of Liberty House. The **Mauna Kea Beach Resort** has a gift and jewelry shop that offers museum-quality objets d'art and unusual jewelry from around the world.

Everybody in the family can find at least one thing to take home from the **Kona Country Fair.** You'll find local produce, flowers, island crafts, and gifts of crystals, eelskin wallets and purses, sea urchin jewelry, T-shirts, and towels, all dispensed with a dash of aloha spirit, not to mention reasonable prices. *Look for the tree house and new visitor center on Hwy. 11 in Honaunau, tel. 808/328–8088. Open daily 8–4.*

In general, major stores and shopping centers on the Big Island open at 9 or 9:30 and close by 4:30 or 5. Hilo's Prince Kuhio Shopping Plaza (*see* below) stays open until 9 on Thursday and Friday. In Kona, most of the stores at the Kona Coast Shopping Center (*see* below) are open until 7, though the KTA Super Stores outlet (a supermarket) is open from 7 AM to 11 PM. Many small grocery stores also maintain longer hours, as do the shops along Kona's main Alii Drive, which are geared toward tourists.

Shopping Malls

In Hilo the most comprehensive mall, similar to mainland malls, is **Prince Kuhio Shopping Plaza** (111 E. Puainako, at Hwy. 11, tel. 808/959–3555). Here you'll find **Liberty House** and **Sears** for fashion, **House of Adler** and the **Diamond Company** for jewelry, **Safeway** for food, and **Long's Drugs** and **Woolworth** for just about everything else, plus a smattering of specialty shops: **The Puka, Once Upon a Time,** and a one-hour photo store if you want to send home a really current picture.

The older **Hilo Shopping Center** (70 Kekuanaoa St. at Kilauea Ave., tel. 808/935–6499) has more than 40 air-conditioned shops and restaurants and plenty of free parking, and the centrally located **Kaiko'o Mall** (777 Kilauea Ave., tel. 808/935–3233) has 27 shops, including **J C Penney, Singer's,** and **Kinney Shoe Store.**

On the western side of the island, **Keauhou Shopping Village** (78-6831 Alii Dr., tel. 808/322–3000) offers an attractive steak and seafood restaurant, **Drysdale's Two** (tel. 808/322–0070), and upscale boutiques: **Plus Ten** for large sizes, **Small World** for children, **Showcase Gallery** for works by Hawaiian artists and imaginative feather jewelry, **Collector's Cottage** for the unusual gift, and a post office so you can drop a card and make the folks back home envious.

Right in Kailua-Kona, there are so many shopping malls along Alii Drive that they tend to blend into one another. Virtually all of them offer merchandise to appeal to visitors. On the ocean side of Alii Drive, extending an entire block, is **Kona Inn Shopping Village** (75-5744 Alii Dr., no phone), while the major mall across the street is **Kona Marketplace** (tel. 808/329–3539). A block off Alii Drive, **Lanihau Center** (75-5595 Palani Rd., tel. 808/329–9333) houses **Long's Drug Store** and 21 other stores, or you might want to stop across the street at **Kona Coast Shopping Center** (no phone) to pick up groceries or a bottle of wine at **KTA Super Stores.**

In Waimea, the **Parker Ranch Shopping Center** (at the junction of Hwys. 19 and 190, tel. 808/885–7178) houses 35 shops and the Parker Ranch Visitor Center. **Parker Square** (Kawaihae Rd., tel. 808/885–7178) and **Opelo Plaza** (Hwy. 19, Waimea) have galleries and specialty boutiques. The new **Waimea Center,** with the area's first McDonald's, was completed in 1990.

Hawaiian Arts and Crafts

For souvenirs that truly characterize the Big Island, visitors should take home either foods or crafts and artwork by local artisans. Local artists seem to draw inspiration from the almost spiritual beauty of their island. You'll find gifts and galleries in the most out-of-the-way spaces, as well as in Kailua-Kona and at Keauhou Shopping Village. Finely crafted wooden bowls and boxes and beautiful drawings and paintings are not inexpensive, but they can enhance your home for years to come, and they are authentically Big Island. Following are galleries we've oohed and ahhed our way through:

At **Kona Arts and Crafts** (75-5699-0 Alii Dr., tel. 808/329–5590), absolutely everything is handcrafted in Hawaii. It's right on Kailua-Kona's main waterfront street, next to McGurk's blue awning. You'll find koa- and milo-wood carvings, crystal sculptures, scrimshaw, coral and sea urchin jewelry, and prints of ocean scenes by James H. O'Neil.

At the opposite end of Alii Drive, at Waterfront Row, as well as 6 miles down the road at **Keauhou Shopping Village** (78-6831 Alii Dr., tel. 808/322–3000), check out **Alapaki's Hawaiian Things.** Here you'll find fine commemorative Hawaiian plates, wooden *konane* game boards (a Hawaiian board game reminiscent of checkers played with white and black stones), and necklaces of rare Niihau shells. The shells are found only around Niihau, a privately owned island near Kauai, and the necklaces are intricately strung by Hawaiian women from that island; unfortunately, it's a dying art.

Those who are handy with a needle might want to stop by **Stitch Witches** (Lunapule and Walua Rd., tel. 808/329–3898), which carries Hawaiian designs for needlepoint, counted cross-stitch, and quilted pillow kits. The shop is not far from Keauhou Shopping Village.

In Hilo, you can go through the workshop of **Hawaiian Handcraft** (760 Kilauea Ave., tel. 808/935–5587), where master bowl-turner Dan Deluz creates works of art from 50 types of exotic woods grown on the Big Island; his wares are sold in the adjoining shop.

The **Potter's Gallery** (95 Wainuenue Ave., tel. 808/935–4069), just off Keawe Street, shows *raku* (dark Japanese earthenware), baskets, porcelain, furniture, and jewelry by local artists. Be sure to amble down Keawe Street (it's only a few blocks long) at the same time. Shops like the **Futon Connection** (104 Keawe St., tel. 808/935–8066), with attractive bedroom furnishings, **Louise Dumaine Antiques** (140 Keawe St., tel. 808/935–9604), **Cunningham Gallery** (116 Keawe St., tel. 808/935–7223), and the **Most Irresistible Shop in Hilo** (110 Keawe St., tel. 808/935–9644) are hard to pass up.

Within Volcanoes National Park, the **Volcano Art Center** (tel. 808/967–7511) remains a favorite with everyone. The Dietrich Varez block prints that depict Hawaiian legends are recommended. Unframed, these come in two sizes, for about $10 and $15. Here, too, are tie-dyed *pareus* (the colorful strips of material that can be tied in a variety of ways to become all-purpose wearing apparel), handpainted 100% cotton T-shirts ($15), and funky Trashface jewelry, which is made of exactly what the name implies (one person's trash is another's treasure). Koa cutting boards range in price from $12 to $47, koa rice paddles are $5, and wonderfully thin wooden bowls by Ron Kent are $250 and up.

One other locale deserves special mention for its fine art galleries, and that's Waimea (*see* Tour 3 in Exploring, above). This is such an artsy community that even the old fire station has been turned into an arts center. Don't pass up the new **Hale Kea** (tel. 808/885–6094) restaurant and boutique complex, and search out **Maya Gallery** there. At **Parker Square** (the red buildings on Kawaihae Rd., tel. 808/885–7178), in the **Gallery of Great Things,** you'll drool over the bowls by Jack Straka ($300–$700), but there are attractive mirrors and wooden earrings for much less. Artist Kathy Long does charcoal sketches of Hawaiian dancers that are so detailed they capture more than a photo could, and the oils by her mother, Mary Koski, are superb. A new branch of **Kamaaina Woods** (tel. 808/885–5521) has opened at **Opelo Plaza** on Highway 19 in Waimea; so stop by if you didn't have time to drop by the main branch of this factory and gift shop on Lehua Street in Honokaa (tel. 808/775–7722).

Resort Wear

Hotel shops generally offer the most attractive and original resort wear. In Kailua-Kona, **Andrade's Sale Studio** (tel. 808/329–2323) marks down its quality resort clothing from other outlets and sells it at its Hotel King Kamehameha store. **Kona Inn Shopping Village** (75-5744 Alii Dr.), that long boardwalk on the ocean side of Alii Drive, is stuffed with intriguing shops. Here, two places that have creatively hand-painted clothing are **Noa Noa** (also across from Hulihee Palace on Alii Dr., tel. 808/329–8187) and **Cottage Crafted in Hawaii** (no phone), which has 100% cotton hand-painted and silk-screened Aloha Fashions.

Up-country in the one-street town of Kainaliu, **Paradise Found** (Mamalahoa Hwy. #11, tel. 808/322–2111) has hand-painted raw silk and cropped pants. Or, if you'd rather take home some of Hawaii's splashy material to make your own, also on Kainaliu's main street is **Kimura's Fabrics** (Mamalahoa Hwy. #11, 808/322–3771).

Across the island in Hilo, **Sig Zane** (140 Kilauea Ave., tel. 808/935–7077), a popular designer of dance costumes for the Merrie Monarch Festival, sells his designer fabrics and aloha shirts.

Hilo Hatties (*see* The Big Island for Free, above) is such an old standby, it has to be mentioned (though most people who live in Hawaii would prefer to buy their muumuus from **Liberty House** at the Prince Kuhio Shopping Plaza in Hilo, the Hotel King Kamehameha in Kona, or the Keauhou Beach Hotel in Keauhou). The styles are bright, cool, and loose-fitting, and if matching his-and-her aloha wear is your thing, Hilo Hattie's is the place to go (Hilo, tel. 808/961–3077; Kailua, tel. 808/329–7200 for free transportation).

Menswear

Virtually every golf course has a logo shop; even the casual **Volcano Golf Course** (tel. 808/967–7331) has a monogrammed line of golf shirts, shorts, and visors. But men shouldn't forgo shopping just because the prices look high on this logo leisure wear. More reasonable prices (advertised as "the best clothing prices on the Big Island") are to be found at the **Aloha Gift Factory** (tel. 808/324–1112) in the little town of Kealakekua, 9 miles from Kona on Highway 11. The Gift Factory is an official distributor of Ironman Triathlon T-shirts, towels, and aloha wear with the telltale logo. In Kona, you'll find **Kona Gift Shop** (75-5703 Alii Dr., tel. 808/329–3259) distributing Ironman products, as well as pocketknives with scrimshaw decorating the handle.

For those men who need a little top-level protection from the tropic sun, the old-time, family-run **Kimura Lauhala Shop** (Holualoa Rd., Hwy. 182, tel. 808/324–0053) in the up-country town of Holualoa has authentic made-in-Hawaii lauhala hats.

While he's admiring his new look, others will have time to browse here among the baskets, purses, table mats, hot pads, etc. You can also order wonderful Christmas wreaths custom-made of natural Hawaiian materials.

Beaches

Don't believe it if anyone tells you the Big Island lacks beaches. It actually has 80 or more, and in 1989 a new black sand beach, Kamoamoa, actually formed when molten lava shattered as it hit cold ocean waters. Located 1½ miles west of the now lava-covered Waha'ula Visitor Center, Kamoamoa is the largest of the black sand beaches, more than half a mile long and 25 yards wide. Though currents are dangerous and suntanning on the coarse sand is not particularly comfortable, nearby Kamoamoa Campground is one of the nicest on the island. Some beaches are just a little hard to get to—several are hidden behind elaborate hotels or down unmarked roads—and others have dangerous undertow and should be used for suntanning and fishing rather than swimming. In Kailua-Kona and even in Keauhou, it's true, there are not broad expanses of coral sand. The most beautiful, swimmable white-sand beaches stretch along the Kohala coastline. The surf tends to get rough during the winter months; to be safe, swim only when you see or otherwise know that local people swim in the area. The tropical sun can be deceptive. Even on a cloudy day, it's wise to take along a sunscreen with a SPF (protection rating) of 15 or more and re-apply it often, as saltwater and perspiration reduce its effectiveness. Public transportation to beaches does not exist. Few public beaches have lifeguards or manned beach centers.

Anaehoomalu Beach, at the Royal Waikoloan Resort. This expansive beach on the west coast is perfect for swimming, windsurfing, snorkeling, sailing, and scuba-diving. Equipment rental and instructors can be arranged at the north end. Be sure to wander around the ancient fish ponds and petroglyph fields that the hotel has preserved. *Take Waikoloa Beach Rd. to the Royal Waikoloan Resort. Follow the signs to the park and beach right-of-way to the south.*

Green Sand (or Papakolea) Beach. You have to have a four-wheel-drive vehicle to get to this beach, whose greenish tint is caused by an accumulation of the olivine that forms in volcanic eruptions. You can get to South Point (where you'll find ruins of a heiau and the winches once used to load cattle and produce onto boats from the cliffs) in a regular car, but it's another 2½ rough miles northeast to where the beach lies at the base of Pu'u o Mahana, a cinder cone formed during an early eruption of Mauna Loa. Swimming can be hazardous when the surf is up in this windy, remote area. There are no facilities and no shade trees.

Hapuna State Recreation Area. The beach is a half-mile crescent of glistening sand guarded by rocky points at either end. The surf can be hazardous in winter, but in summer months the gradual slope of a beach that stretches as wide as 200 feet into a perfectly blue ocean makes it ideal for swimming, snorkeling, and scuba diving. Children enjoy the shallow cove with tidal pools at the north end, while at the southern end, adventuresome swimmers like to jump from the sea cliffs into the ocean. Signs restrict the use of surfboards and similar beach equipment. State cabins and public facilities are available nearby. There are no lifeguards to rescue swimmers from rough seas in winter, so keep out of the water at that time. *Between the Mauna Kea Beach and Mauna Lani resorts off Hwy. 19, tel. 808/882–7995.*

Harry K. Brown Beach Park. Local people frequent Kalapana Black Sand Beach across the road from the park. The park facilities, fishing, sunning, and surfing are good, though the waves can be unsafe in winter. An offshore surfing spot called Drainpipes is known for its big waves. A safe, shallow area for children is located at the southwest end. The park includes a part of old Kalapana Village, remains of a heiau, and some historically significant stones—a rough grinding stone, a bell stone, and a fish god. Facilities include pavilions, camping sites, rest rooms, showers, drinking water, and tables. *On Hwy. 137, near Kalapana in the Puna district, tel. 808/965–9355.*

Honokohau and Alula. These two beaches are down the road to Honokohau Harbor. Alula is just a slip of white sand a short walk over the lava to the left of the harbor entrance. Honokohau Beach is north of the harbor (turn right at Gentry Marina and go past the boat-loading dock). Follow the trail to the right through the bush until you come upon the ¾-mile beach and the rocky ruins of the ancient fish ponds. The center portion of the beach is comparatively rock-free, though a shelf of lava along the water's edge lines most of the shore. The Aimakapa fish pond is directly inland. At the north end of the beach a trail leads mauka (toward the mountains) across the lava to a freshwater pool. The only public facilities are at the boat harbor. *Off Queen Kaahumanu Hwy. 19, 1 mi north of Kailua-Kona.*

Hookena Beach Park. You'll feel like an adventurer when you come upon Hookena, at the northern corner of Kauhako Bay, after the 2-mile drive off the main road, about 23 miles south of Kailua-Kona. When Mark Twain visited, 2,500 people populated the busy seaport village. You can still find gas lampposts dating back to the 1900s. Good swimming, bodysurfing, fishing, and hiking can be accomplished here, but there's no drinking water at this gray coral-and-lava-sand beach. Rest rooms, showers, and picnic tables are available at the park.

Kahaluu Beach Park. The swimming and snorkeling are fine here, and facilities include a pavilion, rest rooms, showers, a lifeguard tower, and parking. We suspect the reason it is the most popular beach in Kailua-Kona is that there are few others so close to town. The sand is speckled with lava fragments, and on weekends, there are just too many people. A strong rip current during high surf pulls swimmers away from the beach. *Beside Alii Dr. between Kailua-Kona and Keauhou.*

Kaimu Black Sand Beach Park. At press time, this once picture-postcard black-sand beach was in danger of being completely engulfed by lava. Before the damaging flow, the beach was lovely to look at but not so safe for swimming; there are no facilities. *Borders Hwy. 137 beyond Kaimu in the Puna district.*

Kauanoa Beach at Mauna Kea Beach Resort. It's a toss-up whether this or neighboring Hapuna is the most beautiful beach on the island. Kauanoa is long and white, and it slopes very gradually. The high surf that pounds the shore during the winter can give swimmers neck injuries. Hotel guests generally congregate near the hotel's beach facilities. Near the public-access end, there's plenty of shady and sunny beach if you prefer to stay away from the action. The amenities are hotel-owned. *Access is through the gate to Mauna Kea Beach Resort off Queen Kaahumanu Hwy. 19, which furnishes 30 public parking stalls.*

Keokea Beach Park. Driving back from the end of Highway 270 at the Pololu overlook to the north, you'll see a curvy road angle off to the right. Follow it for a mile, pass the cemetery with the weathered old stones, and you'll come upon the green lawns and large picnic pavilion of Keokea Beach Park. The black-bouldered beach is suited for fishing and snorkeling in the calm summer months, but heavy surf in the winter makes this a hazardous swimming beach. A shallow, protected cove on the northeastern side of the bay is great for keikis (children) to float around on boogie boards and inner tubes. Some of the picnic tables are under cover, others are in the open; rest rooms, showers, drinking water, electricity, and a camping site make this a popular weekend destination for local folks.

Kiholo Bay. Don't try to find the unmarked road branching off to the west on the makai (ocean) side from Queen Kaahumanu Highway 19 unless you have a four-wheel-drive. The road seems to disappear into nowhere across the lava, but it actually leads to homes built along the oceanfront and to Kiholo Bay. The huge, spring-fed Luahinewai Pond anchors the south end of the bay, while the three black-pebble beaches are fine for swimming in calm weather. At the northern end, Wainanalii Pond (a five-acre lagoon) is a feeding site for green sea turtles. Kamehameha I had a well-stocked fish pond here that was destroyed by lava in 1859. Secluded areas of the 2-mile bay are sometimes sought out by nude sunbathers. You'll find good swimming, fishing, and hiking here, but no facilities.

Leleiwi Beach Park and Richardson Ocean Center. Near Hilo, this tiny beach just beyond the seawall allows entry to the water for good snorkeling, swimming, bodysurfing, board surfing, and net fishing. Richardson Ocean Center is a recreation and interpretive center with free marine displays for public viewing. Showers, rest rooms, paved walkways, and lifeguard service are available. *2349 Kalanianaole Ave., tel. 808/935-3830.*

MacKenzie State Recreation Area. This spacious 13-acre park, shaded by ironwoods, is good for picnicking and camping. You can't swim here, but there are rest rooms, fresh water, and plenty of free parking. *In the Puna district between Hwy. 137 and the sea cliff.*

Mahukona Beach Park. Located next to the abandoned Port of Mahukona in the Kohala district, where sugar was once shipped by rail to be loaded on boats, Mahukona Beach has old docks and buildings that are a photographer's treat. Divers and snorkelers can view both marine life and remnants of shipping machinery in the clear water. Heavy surf makes water activities off-limits in the winter, however. Boats can be launched with the chain hoist and winch on the old dock. It's a pleasant picnicking spot, with rest rooms, showers, and a camping area, but there is no sandy beach.

Napo'opo'o Beach Park at Kealakekua Bay. The best way to see this black-sand beach and marine preserve is to take a snorkel, scuba, or glass-bottom boat tour from Keauhou Bay. A 27-foot white obelisk indicates where Captain James Cook was killed in 1779. This six-acre beach park has a picnic pavilion, tables, showers, rest rooms, and a basketball court.

Old Kona Airport Recreation Area. The unused runway is still visible above this beach at Kailua Park, which has showers, bathroom facilities, and palm trees strung out along the shore. The beach has a sheltered, sandy inlet with tide pools for children, but for adults it's better for snorkeling and scuba than it is for swimming. An offshore surfing break known as Old Airport is popular with Kona surfers. *Follow Hwy. 11 north to where it ends just outside of Kailua; tel. 808/329–6727.*

Onekahakaha Beach Park. A white-sand beach protected by a point of land makes this a favorite for Hilo families with small children. Lifeguards are on duty throughout the year. The park has picnic pavilions, rest rooms, and showers. *Follow Kalanianaole Ave. east along the water about 3 mi south of Hilo.*

Puako Beach. Turn off Queen Kaahumanu Highway 19 to Puako. At the end of the road, pull off to the right under the keawe trees. The water is clear and the snorkeling good by the tide pools, or you can follow the shoreline south to a better sunning area. Before you take your swim, you might want to walk to the petroglyphs off Puako Road. During the drive in, watch for the white sign with black stick figures on the inland side that marks the trailhead. The walk to see the rock carvings left by early Hawaiians takes 15 minutes each way (*see* The Big Island for Free, above).

Punaluu Beach Park. Turtles swim in the bay (you can watch them surface and submerge), nest, and lay their eggs in the black sand of this beautiful beach. Fish ponds are just inland, and you can find the ruins of a heiau and a flat sacrificial stone at the northern end of the beach near the boat ramp. Sugar was shipped by rail to this former port town, and in 1941 Army troops were stationed here. The tsunami (tidal wave) of 1946 destroyed the Army buildings. The offshore currents here can be dangerous, though you'll see a few local surfers riding the waves. There are rest rooms across the road and also at the **Punaluu Black Sand Restaurant** (tel. 808/928–8528), located inland from the ponds. Here a visitor center houses artifacts from the area, and you'll see a memorial to Henry Opukahaia. In 1809, when he was 17, Opukahaia swam out to a fur-trading ship in the harbor and asked to sail as a cabin boy. When he reached New England, he entered the Foreign Mission School in Cornwallis, Connecticut, but he died of typhoid fever in 1818. His dream of bringing Christianity to the Islands inspired the American Board of Missionaries in 1820 to send the first Protestant missionaries to Hawaii. *26.7 mi beyond Volcanoes National Park on Hwy. 11.*

Reeds Bay Beach Park. Rest rooms, showers, drinking water, and the proximity to downtown Hilo are the enticements that this cove has to offer. The waters are calm and safe. Most swimmers take a dip in the Ice Pond adjoining the head of Reed's Bay. Cold freshwater springs seep from the bottom of the pond and rise in the saltwater. *Banyan Dr. and Kalanianaole Ave., Hilo.*

Samuel M. Spencer Beach Park. This park is popular with local families because its gently sloping white-sand beach is reef-protected, making it safe for swimming year-round. There are cooking and camping facilities, showers, tennis courts, and a large covered pavilion with electrical outlets. Mynah birds and sparrows make their homes in large shade trees on the grounds. You can walk to see the Puukohola and Mailekini heiaus, midway between the park and Kawaihae Harbor, which is a mile to the north. *The entry road is off Hwy. 270, just up the hill from Kawaihae Harbor, tel. 808/882-7094.*

White Sands, Magic Sands, or Disappearing Sands Beach Park. Now you see it, now you don't. Overnight, winter waves wash away this small white-sand beach on Alii Drive just south of Kailua-Kona. In summer, you'll know you've found it when you see the body- and board-surfers. This isn't a great beach for swimming. Rest rooms, showers, a lifeguard tower, and a coconut grove create a favorite and convenient summer hangout. *Go south on Alii Dr. about 1 mi past the Kona Hilton in Kailua-Kona. The beach is just before the small seaside St. Peter's Catholic Church.*

Sports and Fitness

Participant Sports

The Big Island attracts active people. You'll see them running, bicycling, hiking, sailing, and even skiing. Any number of guides and services make it easy to be a joiner. In general, water-sports activities center on the Kailua-Kona area because of its calmer waters.

Biking Although pedalers should be fairly physically fit for extended bicycling tours, there seems to be no typical rider. Everyone from college students to retirees has completed tours of a week or longer, and how much you ride is up to you, as generally the support van that carries gear will also stop to pick up tired riders. Many Big Island roads have narrow shoulders and are traveled by large tour buses and sugarcane hauling trucks. No law requires the wearing of a helmet, but it is strongly recommended, and some operators do require them. Also, sheepskin seat covers and bicycle riding pants add greatly to personal comfort on long trips.

Backroads Bicycle Touring (Box 1626 M66, San Leandro, CA 94577, tel. 415/527-4005) has been pedaling the blacktop in Hawaii since 1985, offering 10-day, 220-mile circle-island trips. Hotel accommodations (sometimes in such out-of-the-way places as Naalehu and Captain Cook) and meals are included, but the bicycle and airfare are extra.

Island Bicycle Adventures, Inc. (569 Kapahulu Ave., Honolulu 96815, tel. 808/734-0700 or 800/233-2226), another locally based firm, offers bicycle tours on the Big Island, Maui, and Kauai, scheduled so that you can enjoy 12 days of bicycling on two islands by booking two consecutive tours. Each island tour price includes five nights' accommodations, meals, and such services as the support van, maps, and two tour guides. You pay your own airfare. Bicycle rental is additional, or you can bring your own. Optional routes make these tours suitable for bicyclists of any ability, while easy hikes off the beaten path offer occasional breaks from constant pedaling. Each island tour is $785 per person based on double occupancy.

On the Loose Bicycle Vacations (1030 Merced St., Berkeley, CA 94707, tel. 415/527–4005 or 800/346–6712) offers a 10-day circle–Big Island trip and a 7-day Big Island/3-day Maui combination.

Vermont Bicycle Touring (Box 711, Bristol, VT 05443, tel. 802/453–4811) hit Hawaii's highways in 1988, though the company has been pedaling for 17 years in Vermont.

For those hearty souls who want to strike out on their own, bicycles can be rented in Kailua at **B&L Bike and Sports** (74-5576 B Pawai Pl., Kailua-Kona, tel. 808/329–3309) or at **Dave's Triathlon Shop** (74-5588 M Pawai Pl., Kailua-Kona, tel. 808/329–4522).

Fitness Centers The gyms on the Hilo side look like places where Rambo might work out. There are no fitness centers exclusively for women, but those who are exercise addicts might try **Spencer Health and Fitness Center** (96 Keawe St., tel. 808/969–1511). In Kona, the **Club** (75-5722 Hanama St., Kona Center, tel. 808/326–2582) advertises high-tech fitness with child-care facilities as well. Three major hotels, the Mauna Lani, the Mauna Kea, and the Hyatt Regency Waikoloa on the Kohala coast, have spa facilities.

Of these, the **Hyatt Regency Waikoloa** (1 Waikoloa Beach Resort, Kohala Coast 96734, tel. 808/885–1234) has the finest facilities, with the 17,500-square-foot Anara health spa. You can tone up in weight rooms and the aerobics room; relax in saunas, steam baths, Jacuzzis, or the club room; and have a facial, an herbal wrap, a loofah treatment, or a massage. Currently, one free spa visit is included with each reservation.

Mauna Lani Bay Hotel (Box 4000, Kohala Coast 96743, tel. 808/855–6622) has a spa (with weight and aerobics rooms and a Jacuzzi) that is completely adequate but on a much smaller scale than the Hyatt's.

The use of the fitness center at the **Mauna Kea Beach Hotel** (1 Mauna Kea Dr., Kohala Coast 96743, tel. 808/882–7222) is complimentary to hotel guests and features 10 Nautilus machines and two Lifecycles, the latest in computerized stationary bicycles. Fitness instructors offer daily counseling sessions. The resort also has a scenic 2-mile jogging trail.

Golf If there is one thing the Big Island is known for, it's the beautiful golf courses that appear like green oases in the black, arid landscape of lava. Costs are very reasonable at the municipal golf courses. On the east side of the island, the **Hilo Municipal Golf Course** (340 Haihai St., Hilo 96720, tel. 808/959–7711) assesses greens fees of only $6 for nonresidents on weekdays, $8 on weekends. The public course most convenient to Hilo's major hotels is the nine-hole **Naniloa Country Club Golf Course** (120 Banyan Dr., Hilo 96720, tel. 808/935–3000). Farther afield, the 18-hole, par 72 course at **Volcano Golf and Country Club** (Box 46, Volcanoes National Park 96718, tel. 808/967–7331) is comfortably cool and countrified, though sometimes a bit soggy in winter. Rates are $30 per player.

About 30 miles south of Volcano Village is **Sea Mountain Golf Course** (at Punaluu, Box 85, Pahala 96777, tel. 808/928–6222), which stretches from the Pacific Coast up the slopes of Mauna Loa. Play is $41 at the 18-hole, par 72 course. **Hamakua Country Club** (Honokaa 96727, tel. 808/775–7244) is a nine-hole private course open to the public with greens fees of $10.

On the west coast, golf gets a bit more expensive at the **Kona Country Club** (78-7000 Alii Dr., Keauhou 96740, tel. 808/322–2595), but free shuttle service is available from Keauhou hotels and condos to this 27-hole course, which is par 36 for nine holes. Rates (anywhere from $50 to $100) are less expensive for Kona-area guests and also vary according to season. Don't confuse the two Robert Trent Jones, Jr.–designed Waikoloa courses— **Waikoloa Village Golf Course** is inland, in South Kohala (Waikoloa 96743, tel. 808/883–9621), while the **Waikoloa Beach Golf Course** (tel. 808/885–6060) is affiliated with the Royal Waikoloan Resort and the Hyatt Regency Waikoloa on the Kohala coast. A 72-par Tom Weiskoph/Jay Morrish–designed course, the **King's Course** (tel.808/885–1234), featuring four large lakes, opened adjacent to the Hyatt Regency Waikoloa in 1989.

Off Highway 19 are two gems that receive award after award from golf magazines: the **Mauna Kea Beach Resort's** par 72, 18-hole course (1 Mauna Kea Dr., Kohala Coast 94743, tel. 808/882–7222), designed by Robert Trent Jones, Sr.; and the **Francis I'i Brown Golf Course at the Mauna Lani Resort** (Box 4959, Kohala Coast 96743, tel. 808/885–6655). Mauna Kea charges $115 at its championship course. The men's tee at the sixth hole of the Mauna Lani's Francis I'i Brown course is famous among golfers because the ball must soar over a stretch of open ocean to complete play. Rates are $100, except from mid-December through March, when it costs $130 per player for 18 holes.

Hiking and Camping For the hearty and fit adventurer, hiking is a great way to explore the Big Island's natural beauty. In addition to hiking on Mauna Kea and into Kilauea Iki Crater (*see* Tour 1 in Exploring, above), a little-known trek to the top of 13,680-foot **Mauna Loa,** with overnight stops at two cabins, one at 10,000 feet and the other at the summit, can be arranged. *Write to the superintendent, Hawaii Volcanoes National Park, Volcano 96743. The cabins are free but must be reserved well in advance.*

Namakani Paio Cabins, at the 4,000-foot level 3 miles beyond the Volcano House, are managed by Hawaii Volcanoes National Park. Each cabin has a double bed, two bunk beds, and electric lights. *Write to Hawaii Volcanoes National Park, Box 53, Volcano 96718-0053, tel. 808/967–7321. A $15 refundable deposit allows guests to pick up bedding and keys (for the cabins and separate bath facilities) at Volcano House. Guests should bring extra blankets, because it gets cold. Rates: $24 single or double.*

For information on cabins at state parks, including Hapuna Beach Park and the three campgrounds at Kilauea, write to the **Department of Parks and Recreation** (25 Aupuni St., Hilo 96740, tel. 808/961–8311).

Two Oahu-based companies offer a variety of guided hikes on all islands: **Pacific Quest** (Box 205, Haleiwa 96712, tel. 808/638–8338 or 800/367–8047 ext. 523); and **Wilderness Hawaii** (Box 61692, Honolulu 96839, tel. 808/737–4697), which specializes in Big Island hikes in Volcanoes National Park.

Horseback Riding Some hotels, such as **Mauna Kea Beach Resort** (1 Mauna Kea Dr., Kohala Coast 96743, tel. 808/885–4288), maintain stables for their guests' use, while others offer transportation to commercial stables. Ask at your hotel Activities Desk. From the Kohala coast and Kailua-Kona, excellent guided rides are offered by:

Ironwood Outfitters at Kohala Ranch (take Hwy. 250 to the 13-mi marker; Box 832, Kamuela 96743, tel. 808/885–4941). This group offers a daily morning mountain ride on a 40,000-acre ranch in the Kohala Mountains. Groups are kept small, and the views are of the misty highlands trailing down to the blue Pacific.

Waikoloa Countryside Stables (Box 3466, Waikoloa Village 96743, tel. 808/883–9335) gives riding lessons.

Waiono Meadows Trail Rides (Box 628, Holualoa 96725, tel. 808/324–1544) offers one-, two-, or four-hour trail rides, 10 minutes from Kailua-Kona, with beautiful coastal views. The long rides include fishing in a mountain stream and breakfast or lunch.

Hunting Among its fantasy-vacation offerings, the Hyatt Regency Waikoloa offers guests the chance to hunt in paradise, but on the Big Island, hunting is not a fantasy. Anyone can make their own arrangements by contacting **Hawaii Hunting Tours** (Box 58, Paauilo 96766, tel. 808/776–1666) or **McCandless Ranch Gentleman's Hunt** (Kai Malino, tel. 808/328–2389). Game in Hawaii includes pheasant, turkeys, wild boar, and sheep. Hunting licenses are issued annually by the **State Department of Land and Natural Resources** (75 Aupuni St., Hilo, tel. 808/961–7291). Permits for birds and mammals are issued daily during the season, generally from the first weekend in November to the third weekend in January. The season is set by the Forestry and Wildlife Division and fluctuates according to game availability.

Skiing Skiing on Mauna Kea is for experienced adventure skiers only. Currently there are no equipment-rental facilities, nor does the ski area have a lodge or lifts. Christopher Langan of Mauna Kea Ski Corporation runs **Ski Guides Hawaii** (Box 1954, Kamuela 96743, tel. 808/889–6398, or in ski season, tel. 808/885–4188), which is licensed to furnish transportation, guide services, and ski equipment on Mauna Kea. Snow might fall from Thanksgiving through June, but the most likely months are February and March. For an eight-hour day trip for up to six people, Langen charges $100 to $150 per person, including refreshments and a mountaintop lunch. On an Alii Tour, for $250 he'll take you to places accessible by snowmobile where few have ever skied.

Tennis School and park courts are free and open to anyone who wishes to play, though students have first priority during school hours at high school courts. In Hilo, you will find courts at the **University of Hawaii–Hilo campus** (333 West Lanikaula Street); there are four free, lighted courts at **Lincoln Park** (Kinoole and Ponahawai streets). The eight courts (three lighted for night play) at **Hilo Tennis Stadium** (Piilani and Kalanikoa sts.) charge a small fee. **Waiakea Racket Club** (400 Hualani St., Hilo 96720, tel. 808/961–5499) is also open to the public for a reasonable fee.

Across the island, the Keauhou-Kona resorts have become renowned for their beautiful tennis courts. **Holua Stadium** is a headquarters for exhibition tennis. One of the few courts where not-so-heavy hitters can play free is at **Kailua Playground**—the wait may be long, however. Nonguests can play for a fee at the **Kona Surf Hotel's Racquet Club** and on the four courts at the **Kona Hilton Beach and Tennis Resort** (*see* Lodging, below). At the **Hotel King Kamehameha** (see Lodging, below) nonguests may purchase memberships to play. Farther afield, there are two free, lighted courts at **Waimea Park** (on Hwy. 19) in Waimea, while courts at the **Royal Waikoloan, Waikoloa Village,** and **Sea Mountain Resort** (see Lodging, below) are open at an hourly charge.

Resorts offering tennis for guests only include: **Mauna Kea Beach Resort** (with 13 courts in a beautiful 12-acre tennis park), **Mauna Lani Bay Resort, Hyatt Regency Waikoloa,** and **Kona Village Resort** (see Lodging, below). Closer to the town of Kailua-Kona, the following also have courts for guests only: **Kona Makai** (75-6026 Alii Dr., Kailua-Kona 96740, tel. 808/329–1511), **White Sands** (77–6469 Alii Dr., Kailua-Kona 96740, tel. 808/329–1264), **Kanaloa** (78-261 Manukai St., Kailua-Kona 96740, tel. 808/322–2272), and the **Keauhou-Kona Surf and Racquet Club** (78-6800 Alii Dr., Keauhou 96740, tel. 808/322–9131).

Water Sports
Deep-Sea Fishing
In Kona, excitement about game fishing hits a peak in July, August, and September, when a number of tournaments are held, but charter fishing goes on year-round. You don't have to be in a tournament to experience the thrill of landing a big Pacific blue marlin or a mahi, tuna, wahoo, or other game fish. More than 50 charter boats, averaging 36 to 42 feet, are available for hire, most of them out of Honokohau Harbor, just north of Kailua. Prices for a full day of fishing begin at about $300 and average $450, though there are a few luxury boats in the $500–$700 range. Half-day charters are also available in the $200 range and might be preferable if you've never experienced dawn-to-dusk fishing. Tackle and soft drinks are furnished. Most boats do not allow you to keep your catch, although it doesn't hurt to ask. Ask your hotel to pack a box lunch or purchase one at the Kona Marlin Center at Honokohau Harbor. If you want to bring stronger refreshments, most boats allow beer or liquor on board.

The biggest of the fishing tournaments is the **Hawaiian International Billfish Tournament** at the beginning of August, which attracts teams from around the world. During the HIBA, the Richard Boone Award is given by participating anglers. This award lists in order the boats on which tournament participants would most prefer to fish; the listing can serve as a helpful guide in choosing which boat to charter. In addition, be sure to describe your expectations when you book your charter so the booking agent can match you with a captain and a boat you will like.

Tournament catches are often weighed in at the pier adjacent to the Hotel King Kamehameha in Kailua-Kona, which, because of its central location, is a popular headquarters for tournament participants and viewers. Both old and young head for either the Kailua Pier or Honokohau Harbor's Fuel Dock between 4 and 5 PM to watch the weigh-in of the day's catch. *Make arrangements for deep-sea fishing at your hotel Activities Desk or call the Kona Activities Center (tel. 808/329–3171 or 800/ 367–5299) for information. At Honokohau Harbor, book charters or get information on tournaments from the Kona*

Marlin Center, 74-381 Kealakehe Pkwy., Kailua-Kona 96740, tel. 808/329-7529 or 800/648-7529.

Diving Two-tank dives should cost from $65 to $75, depending on whether they are in one or two locations and if they are dives from a boat or from the shore. Many dive outfits have underwater cameras for rent, in case you're lucky enough to glimpse humpback whales and their calves during the winter months or simply want to capture colorful reef fish on film. Instruction with PADI certification in three to five days is approximately $100 per day. The Kona coast has calm waters for diving, and dive operators there are helpful about suggesting dive sites. A 24-page guidebook giving the top 40 scuba and snorkeling sites on all islands and a listing of dive businesses is available for $2 from **University of Hawaii** (Seagrant Extension MSB, 1000 Pope Rd., Honolulu, HI 96822). Reputable scuba charters to consider in Kailua are: **Kona Kai Diving** (35-382 Aloha Kona Dr., Kailua-Kona 96740, tel. 808/329–6068), which offers classes in marine biology, Hawaiian history, and underwater photography; **Gold Coast Divers** (75-5744 Alii Dr., Kailua-Kona 96740, tel. 808/329– 1328), which, in its 12th year, offers classes, night and shore dives, and free snorkeling maps; and **Fair Wind Sailing and Diving Adventures** (78-7128 Kaleopapa Rd., Kailua-Kona 96740, tel.808/322–2788). First-time divers might want to try **Snuba** (tel. 808/326–5444), which alleviates the apprehension and discomfort of scuba novices by having divers breathe through an air hose connected to an overhead raft that carries the cumbersome air tanks.

Parasailing/ Windsurfing These are two of the newer water sports, and both are generally considered quite safe (though in 1988 one parasailer died in a freak accident because she did not strap in properly). Parasailers sit in a harness attached to a parachute that lifts off from the boat deck until they are sailing aloft. Call **Kona Water Sports** (75-56956 Alii Dr., Kailua-Kona 96745, tel. 808/329–1593) to make arrangements for parasailing.

One of the best windsurfing locations on the Big Island is at Anaehoomalu Bay, on the beach in front of the Royal Waikoloan Resort. You can take lessons or rent equipment right at the resort's beach services desk (Waikoloa Rd., Kohala Coast, tel. 808/885–6789). In remote Naalehu, **Kau Wind** (Naalehu 96772, tel. 808/929–9517) maintains a 24-hour wind line so you can check conditions before you make the long drive.

Sailing/Snorkeling Among the Big Island's wet and wild offerings is the **Captain Zodiac Raft Expedition** (Box 5612, Kailua 96740, tel. 808/329–3199) along the Kona coast. The four-hour trip begins at Honokohau Harbor, pokes into gaping lava-tube caves, and drifts through Kealakeua Bay where passengers can enjoy snorkeling and a light tropical lunch. Arrangements can be made for a six-hour land/sea trip which also includes a van ride to a macadamia nut factory, a Kona coffee plantation, and St. Benedict's Painted Church. St. Benedict's was originally painted at the turn of the century by its priest, who wanted it to look like a European cathedral; it was recently restored. Other excursions are shorter: January through April you might see the humpback whales, and private charters can be arranged. If you love water and crave adventure, sit at the front edge of the inflatable raft for an exciting, bouncy, wind-in-your-hair ride.

Wear a bathing suit (you'll get a chance for snorkeling) and take a towel, sunscreen, and camera. Captain Zodiac furnishes a plastic bag to keep your possessions high and dry.

For a more sedate daytime cruise, the **Captain Cook VII** (Hawaiian Cruises Ltd., 74-5543 Kaiwi Bay 11; Kailua-Kona 96740, tel. 808/329-6411) takes more than a look through its glass bottom at the fishy underworld. The boat departs from Kailua Pier and its destination is historic Kealakekua Bay, where Captain Cook met his death at the hands of Kamehameha's men in 1779. Today the bay is a snorkeler's paradise. The glass-bottom boat picks up passengers at 8:30 AM for a four-and-a-half-hour cruise; the cost is $35. Hawaiian Cruises' *Hawaiian Princess* is also available for charter groups.

Polynesian entertainers liven the decks of Captain Bean's 150-foot **Tamure** (Captain Bean's Kona Voyagers, 74-5626 Alapapa St., B-17, Kailua-Kona 96740, tel. 808/329-2955) as it departs Kailua Pier headed for Kealakekua Bay. A four-and-a-half-hour swim and snorkel sail departs at 8:30 AM, or you might opt for the one-hour sail leaving at 1:30 PM *(see* Dinner Cruise in Nightlife, below).

The family-owned and operated **Fair Wind Sail and Diving Adventures** sails for 4½ hours from Keauhou Bay at 8:30 AM to Kealakekua Bay. The 50-foot glass-bottom trimaran has a super water slide, inner tubes, and snorkel and scuba gear. *78-7128 Kaleopapa Rd., Kailua-Kona 96740, tel. 808/322-2788. Lunch and gear is included for $54 adults, $30 children 5-12. The 3½-hour afternoon sail departs at 1 PM.*

Many snorkel and scuba cruises are available. Shop for prices, ask the size of the boat, make sure you know what is included and how much the extras (i.e., underwater cameras) cost.

Spectator Sports

With the University of Hawaii-Hilo campus the only major college on the Big Island, such spectator sports as football and baseball exist only at the high school level. Volleyball is popular on the University of Hawaii-Hilo campus, and information about scheduled competition can be obtained by calling tel. 808/961-9520. On the other hand, the Bud Light Ironman Triathlon and polo attract record-breaking crowds.

Bud Light Ironman Triathlon. We call this a spectator sport because it is getting more and more difficult to get into the event. The Ironman is limited to 1,250 competitors, who do a 2.4-mile open-water swim, run a 26.2-mile marathon, and bicycle 112 miles, and most entrants must qualify by doing well in other international competitions, though a few slots are awarded by lottery. The annual competition begins with a swim from Kailua Pier at 7 AM on a Saturday at the beginning of October. Spectators cheer on their favorite contestants from vantage points along Alii Drive and the Queen Kaahumanu Highway. The course closes at midnight. *75-5737 Kuakini Hwy., Suite 208, Kailua-Kona 96740, tel. 808/329-0063.*

Kohala Ranch Arena Polo. Tournaments are staged every Sunday at 2 PM in September, October, and November. Initially, admission and parking were free to the public (with success, we suspect that may change). Spectators are encouraged to bring along a hibachi and food to grill. In addition, polo lessons are offered for $40 per hour at various times of the year by Dan Healy, an internationally known player and a member of the Kohala Ranch Polo Team. *Approximately 5 mi north of Kohala-coast resorts, accessible by the Kohala Mountain Rd. (Rte. 250), or Akoni Pule Hwy. (Rte. 270), tel. 808/329–9551.*

Waikiki Ranch Polo. The season runs six Sundays in November and December. *Just off Saddle Road, 7 mi. from Waimea, tel. 808/885–6668.*

Dining

Choosing a place to eat in the western part of the Big Island has become more difficult than in the past—not because of a lack of fine restaurants, but because there are many good, established restaurants and several more new and exciting places to try. The newest star on the Kailua-Kona horizon is the dining/shopping complex called Waterfront Row, which opened on Alii Drive at the beginning of 1989. Waterfront Row is built to reflect Kailua's seafaring past, with antiques and ship models displayed along the wooden decks. A 45-foot observation tower, accessible by glass elevator, is equipped with telescopes for whale watching. Within the complex, the old Spindrifter Restaurant has been remodeled and renamed the Jolly Roger, the two-story oceanfront Chart House has become the Row's outstanding showplace, and Phillip Paulo's dishes up fabulous pastas and other Italian specialties. On the lighter side, Hot Diggety Dog serves every kind of hot dog imaginable, and the Flying Fruit Fantasy whips up fresh fruit shakes that you can top off with one of their chocolate-dipped strawberries. Watch for additional restaurants to open at this oceanfront food arcade.

Little Waimea has also been enjoying a surge of new restaurants. With the Kohala-coast resorts booming, more and more visitors are willing to make the 40-minute drive inland for a change from hotel dining. Merriman's and Bree Garden are the ventures of two respected hotel chefs who have gone into business for themselves in Waimea. Hartwell's at Hale Kea offers a choice of settings (the Library, the Paniolo Room, the Sun Room, and the Pa'u Room) in which to enjoy its imaginative cuisine.

Hilo's dining scene, in contrast, has remained fairly stable. Hilo's restaurants are generally lower-priced family places where the food makes up for any lack in atmosphere. Fast-food restaurants can be found along Hilo's Kilauea Avenue, while near Kailua-Kona McDonald's golden arches are beside Kuakini Highway 11 and a Burger King is on Palani Road (Highway 190).

Highly recommended restaurants in each area are indicated by a star ★.

Category	Cost*
Very Expensive	over $60
Expensive	$40–$60

Moderate	$20–$40
Inexpensive	under $20

per person, without sales tax (4%), service, or drinks

Hilo

American
★

Harrington's. A popular and reliable steak and seafood restaurant with 27 tables right on Reed's Bay, Harrington's has a dining lanai that extends over the water. The fresh ono or mahimahi meunière, served with browned butter, lemon, and parsley, and the Slavic steak, thinly sliced and slathered with garlic butter, are two outstanding dishes. *135 Kalanianaole St., tel. 808/961–4966. Reservations advised. Dress: casual but neat. MC, V. Closed Christmas Day. Inexpensive–Moderate.*

Dick's Coffee House. The locals line up for breakfast on weekends at this old-fashioned coffee shop with its rows of low-backed booths—the price is right and everyone knows everyone else. Wall lamps and a big collection of football pennants set the mood for standard coffee shop fare. Try the "local boy favorite," fried rice topped with an egg and three crisp wonton on the side, or go for the chicken cutlet or chop steak Hawaiian, topped off with a hot fudge sundae. *Hilo Shopping Center, 70 Kekuanaoa St., tel. 808/935–2769. No reservations. Dress: casual. MC, V. No lunch or dinner Sun. Inexpensive.*

Don's Grill. This casual family-style restaurant with modest decor is located in a residential area, but it's worth seeking out for its reasonable prices. A complete dinner averages $5 or $6 and includes soup; salad; an entrée of teriyaki steak or chicken, barbecued back ribs, lasagna, or beef with rice; potatoes; beverage; and dessert. *485 Hinano St., tel. 808/935–9099. Reservations accepted for large parties. Dress: casual. MC, V. Inexpensive.*

Fiasco's. Booths with floor-to-ceiling dividers permit complete privacy in this cheerful restaurant that has something for everyone, from tasty fajitas and snacks to a garden-fresh fruit and salad bar. Porterhouse steak at $14 is Fiasco's most expensive item. Margarita specials and 23 varieties of domestic and imported beer liven the menu—not to mention the imbibers. *200 Kanoelehua Ave., tel. 808/935–7666. Weekend reservations advised. Dress: casual. MC, V. Closed Labor Day and Christmas Day. Inexpensive.*

Keaau Steak House. Locals award top honors to the steaks (midwestern beef) served at this plain, no-frills restaurant, formerly called the Olaa Steak House. Keaau's casual ice-cream-parlor booths will take you back to the '50s. Dinners come complete with salad from the salad bar, dessert, and beverage. Non–steak lovers can order chicken or pork chops. *Hilo Shopping Center, 70 Kekuanaoa St., tel. 808/961–3131. Dress: casual. MC, V. Closed New Year's Day. Inexpensive.*

Ken's Pancake House. For years, this 24-hour coffee shop has been a gathering place for Hilo residents for breakfast. Situated between the airport and the Banyan Drive hotels, Ken's serves good pancakes and omelets—they're cheap, too. Local favorites, such as hot and cold sandwiches, steaks, and fish, round out the lunch and dinner menu. *1730 Kamehameha Ave., tel. 808/935–8711. No reservations. Dress: casual. AE, CB, DC, MC, V. Open 24 hours. Inexpensive.*

Big Island Dining

Batik Room at Mauna Kea Beach Hotel, **9**

Beach Club at Aston Kona by the Sea, **34**

Bree Garden, **5**

Café Pasta, (a.k.a.) We're Talking Pizza, **2**

The Canoe House at the Mauna Lani Bay Hotel, **13**

Cascades at the Hyatt Regency Waikoloa, **19**

Cattleman's Steakhouse, **6**

Chart House at Waterfront Row, **29**

Dick's Coffee House, **41**

Donatoni's at the Hyatt Regency Waikoloa, **17**

Don's Grill, **42**

Edelweiss, **7**

Fiasco's, **44**

Fisherman's Landing, **27**

Gallery at Mauna Lani Resort, **12**

The Garden at Mauna Kea Beach Hotel, **10**

Hele Samoa at Kona Village Resort, **20**

Harrington's, **46**

Harrington's (Kawaihae), **1**

Hartwell's Restaurant at Hale Kea, **3**

Hale Mai at Kona Hilton Beach and Tennis Resort, **31**

Huggo's, **32**

Imari at the Hyatt Regency Waikoloa, **18**

Jameson's by the Sea, **35**

Jolly Roger, **30**

Ka Ohelo Room, **39**

Kana Zawa-Tei, **33**

Keaau Steak House, **41**

Ken's Pancake House, **45**

Knicker's at the Mauna Lani Resort, **14**

Kona Inn, **26**

Kona Provision Company at Hyatt Regency Waikoloa, **15**

Kona Ranch House, **23**

La Bourgogne, **36**

Le Soleil at Mauna Lani Bay Hotel, **11**

Makee Restaurant at the Kona Surf Resort, **37**

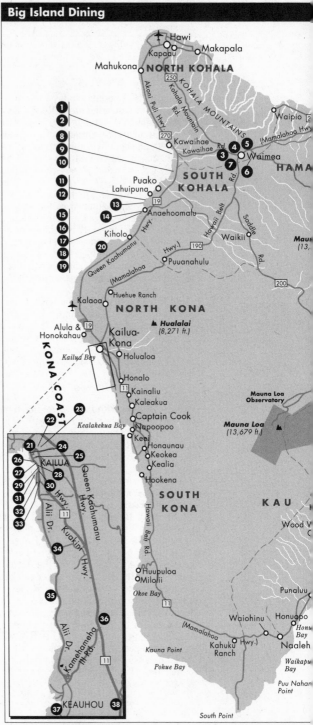

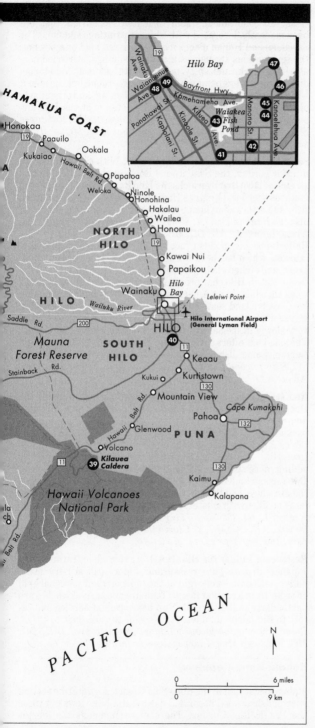

Merriman's, **4**

Moby Dick's at Hotel King Kamehameha, **21**

Ocean View Inn, **24**

Pavilion at Mauna Kea Beach Hotel, **8**

Phillip Paolo's at Waterfront Row, **28**

Quinn's, **22**

Reflections, **43**

Restaurant Fuji at the Hilo Hotel, **48**

Roussel's, **49**

Rusty Harpoon, **25**

Sandalwood Room at the Naniloa Hotel, **47**

Teshima's, **38**

Ting Hao, **40**

Water's Edge at Hyatt Regency Waikoloa, **16**

Chinese **Ting Hao.** The only Mandarin restaurant in town, Ting Hao is a clean, air-conditioned, family-oriented restaurant that has been modestly decorated with Chinese paintings and fans. The Szechuan and Hunan dishes may be ordered mild or spicy hot; the scrumptious specialties include dumplings, stir-fried noodles with pork, and spicy noodles with seafood. Vegetarian dishes, such as eggplant with garlic sauce, round out the menu, which is based on recipes from Taiwan, Peking, and other parts of China. Ting Hao is conveniently located near the Hilo airport. *Puainako Town Center (Kilauea Ave. and W. Kahaopea St.), tel. 808/959–6288. Dress: casual but neat. MC, V. Inexpensive.*

Continental **Sandalwood Room at the Naniloa Hotel.** With 40 tables and an interior garden, the Sandalwood Room opens on one side to a stretch of lawn that overlooks the Hilo Bay coastline. The menu features such local items as Hawaiian spiny-back lobster, fresh fish, and a Hawaiian luau plate served in a carved monkeypod dish. *93 Banyan Dr., tel. 808/969–3333. Reservations advised. Dress: informal. AE, DC, MC. Moderate.*

Reflections. Lily ponds grace the entry of this appealing restaurant, which has been decorated with touches of koa wood, brass, and etched glass. It is perhaps better known as one of the two places in Hilo that provide a band for dancing six nights a week than it is for its American and continental food. Nonetheless, fresh island seafood is presented in a number of creative ways, while the prime rib with Yorkshire pudding is cooked very slowly in special Alto Shamm ovens to a juicy tenderness. The salad bar offers a wide variety of items, including crab and shrimp. Some dishes are flambéed at tableside. *101 Aupuni St., Hilo Lagoon Center, tel. 808/935–8501. Dress: informal. AE, DC, MC, V. Inexpensive–Moderate.*

Creole **Roussel's.** This Cajun-Creole restaurant brings a bit of the
★ Deep South to Hawaii with arched doorways, a high-ceilinged dining room with 16 tables, gray and red decor, and cane-backed chairs. At the front of Roussel's, the cocktail lounge has tables facing the attractively restored Keawe Street in downtown Hilo. The chef has improved the quality of the menu by adding more specials and baking his own bread and desserts. Two recommended dishes are the shrimp creole, with a piquant tomato sauce, and the trout Alexander, which combines a boneless fish fillet with lobster, shrimp, mushrooms, and sherry. *60 Keawe St., tel. 808/935–5111. Reservations advised. Dress: informal. AE, DC, MC, V. Closed the fourth of July, Christmas Day, and New Year's Day. Moderate.*

Japanese **Restaurant Fuji at the Hilo Hotel.** At this plain, rather noisy Japanese *teppan-yaki* restaurant, diners can stir-fry marinated steak or chicken right at the table on their personal grill or order from a regular menu. Tempura and teriyaki dishes are particularly well-prepared. Fuji has excellent service and caters to Big Island families. *142 Kinoole St., tel. 808/961–3733. Reservations advised on holidays. Dress: casual. AE, DC, MC, V. Closed Mon. Inexpensive–moderate.*

Kohala-Kona-Keauhou

American **Makee Restaurant at the Kona Surf Resort.** An uplifting setting with polished wood decor and garden and bay views enhances the Pacific Rim Cuisine. The chef recommends the lobster wonton soup flavored with a dash of sesame and garnished with snow peas and onions, or the warm salad of Hawaiian seafood— ono, opakapaka, mahi mahi, crab, and prawns—served with lettuce and vegetables and a shallot and macadamia nut dressing. *78–128 Ehukai St., Keauhou, tel. 808/322–3411. Reservations advised. Dress: casual. AE, CB, DC, MC, V. Expensive.*

Pavilion at the Mauna Kea Beach Hotel. Whether you have a macadamia-waffle breakfast, or dinner from the menu, featuring lighter, California-style cuisine, the spectacular view of Kauna'oa Bay at this restaurant is mesmerizing. The spacious, airy interior, with arrangements of orchids and other tropical flowers, encourages diners to linger over coffee. Fresh island seafood served with lemon and caper cream, escalope of salmon with sun-dried tomato relish, and grilled veal chop pistoui with angel hair pasta are artfully presented with good health in mind. The Pavilion is in a resort hotel on Highway 19 on the Kohala coast, a half hour from Ke-ahole Airport. *1 Mauna Kea Dr., Kohala Coast, tel. 808/882–7222. Reservations advised. Dress: casual. AE, CB, MC, V. Expensive.*

Chart House at Waterfront Row. This spectacular two-story restaurant in the shopping and dining complex on Alii Drive overlooks the ocean. Koa-wood booths, a waterfall, and floral arrangements complement the fine artwork displayed in the restaurant. Dinners of thickly sliced prime rib, fresh local fish, and Alaskan king crab come with unlimited salad service and squaw (sourdough) bread. *75-5770 Alii Dr., Kailua-Kona, tel. 808/941–6669. No reservations. Dress: casual. AE, DC, MC, V. Moderate.*

Fisherman's Landing. Cobblestone paths lead to an elaborate display of fresh fish on ice at the entrance. Inside you'll find tropical foliage and saltwater ponds with reef fish and fountains. Five open-air dining rooms, divided by water and walkways, overlook the ocean in a relaxing, romantic setting that is more inspiring than the seafood and Oriental and Polynesian entrées served here. However, the steak and lobster, fresh fish, and shrimp Louis are *ono* (good). *75-5744 Alii Dr., Kailua-Kona, tel. 808/326–2555. Dress: informal. AE, CB, DC, MC, V. Moderate.*

Harrington's—Kawaihae. This place has the same reliable menu as Harrington's in Hilo. With a view overlooking the fishing fleet at Kawaihae Harbor, the dining spot offers a good and less expensive dinner alternative to visitors who are staying at the Kohala-coast resorts. *Wharf Rd. and Mahukona Hwy., Kawaihae Center, Kawaihae, tel. 808/882–7997. Reservations advised. Dress: casual but neat. MC, V. Closed Thanksgiving and Christmas Day. Moderate.*

Huggo's. The open windows look out over the rocks at the ocean's edge, so you can actually feed the fish, if you wish. Fresh local seafood (mahimahi, shrimp scampi) is the safest bet on the menu, though the prime rib is also recommended. *75-5828 Kahakai St., Kailua-Kona, tel. 808/329–1493. Reservations advised for parties of 6 or more. Dress: informal. AE, CB, D, DC, MC, V. Moderate.*

Jameson's by the Sea. Sit outside next to the ocean or just inside the picture windows for glorious sunset views over Magic Sands Beach. The co-owner and chef serves three or four island fish specials daily, plus a tasty baked shrimp stuffed with crab and garnished with hollandaise sauce. *77–6452 Alii Dr., Kailua-Kona, tel. 808/325–3195. Reservations advised. Dress: casual, DC, MC, V. Closed Christmas Day. Moderate.*

Knicker's at the Mauna Lani Resort. This open-air restaurant opened in 1989 overlooking the Francis I'i Brown Golf Course. Mahogany paneling, 26 teak tables in the restaurant and nine in the lounge, which is highlighted by a massive koa bar, create a comfortable clubhouse atmosphere. Dinner entrées include sautéed island snapper with artichokes and mushrooms in a brown butter sauce, and a bouillabaise of fish, lobster, shrimp, and shellfish enchanced with saffron and pernod. *Off Hwy. 19, 1/2 hour from Ke-ahole Airport, Box 4959, HCR 2, Kohala Coast, tel. 808/885–6699. Reservations advised. Dress: casual. AE, DC, MC, V. Moderate.*

Moby Dick's at the Hotel King Kamehameha. At this centrally located major hotel in the Kailua-Kona area, the tables, positioned near large windows, look out on a torch-lit lawn; beyond is the beach, with outrigger canoes and a thatched house built on a restored heiau (temple). Some of the tantalizing entrées served here are the mixed grill for two (with baby back ribs, Kona broil, and chicken breast) and a surf brochette of scallops and fresh fish. The Sunday champagne brunch is served from 9 to 1. *75-5660 Palani Rd., Kailua-Kona, tel. 808/329–2911. Reservations advised. Dress: informal. AE, DC, MC, V. Moderate.*

Kona Inn. This open-air restaurant, which faces a wide lawn with the ocean beyond, has been a longtime favorite for cocktails at sunset. The fresh fish and chicken entrées are consistently delectable. Burgers at lunch are reasonably priced, while the most expensive dinner item is a shellfish platter of scampi, scallops, and lobster. *75-5744 Alii Dr., Kailua-Kona, tel. 808/329–4455. Reservations advised. Dress: informal. AE, MC, V. Inexpensive–Moderate.*

Kona Provision Company at the Hyatt Regency Waikoloa. You'll have a spectacular view of the Kona-Kohala coastline as you sample the excellent salad bar, broiled and grilled steak, or seafood at this restaurant. Tables along the lanai open to sea breezes, while ceiling fans cool the rest of the dining room, which seats 189 people. Before or after dinner, sip cocktails on the lanai that overlooks the resort's impressive waterfall and swimming pool. The fresh fish include all the Hawaiian favorites: opakapaka (blue snapper), ono, onaga, mano, and more, and you can order it sautéed, grilled, poached, or blackened. *1 Waikoloa Beach Resort, Kohala Coast, tel. 808/885–1234. Reservations advised. Dress: informal. AE, DC, MC, V. Inexpensive–Moderate.*

Jolly Roger. This restaurant with a nautical theme and pink-and-gray decor sits right at the ocean's edge, though some of the 100 tables are set back from the water. We recommend the Jolly Roger for a leisurely breakfast rather than for dinner. Try the 4-ounce steak and a half order of eggs Benedict with a papaya wedge. *75-5776 Alii Dr., tel. 808/329–1344. No reservations. Dress: informal. AE, DC, MC, V. Inexpensive.*

Kona Ranch House. This reliable dining spot is known in the area for its reasonable prices and pleasant service. The Kona Ranch House has two sections; the Plantation Lanai is preferable, with its turn-of-the-century Hawaiian wicker furniture, tablecloths, and candles. The adjoining Paniolo Room serves food from the same kitchen, but the decor is simple café-style, with booths and no tablecloths. The fresh local fish and big barbecue platters warrant the short walk up the hill from the Hotel King Kamehameha. *75-5653 Olioli St., Kailua-Kona, tel.*

808/329–7061. Reservations advised for the Plantation Lanai. Dress: casual but neat. AE, MC, V. Inexpensive.

Ocean View Inn. If you're on a tight budget, this local hangout with an ocean view is a lifesaver for breakfast, lunch, and dinner. Chinese, American, and Hawaiian food are on the plate-lunch menu. Although there's no atmosphere, the servings are ample. *Alii Dr., Kailua-Kona, tel. 808/329–9998. Dress: casual. No credit cards. Closed Mon. Inexpensive.*

Quinn's. Don't be put off by the fact that you have to walk through the bar to reach the little garden restaurant in back. Located across Palani Street from the Hotel King Kamehameha, Quinn's is a convenient spot for good sandwiches, salads, and hamburgers. *75-5655A Palani Rd., tel. 808/329–3822. Dress: casual. MC, V. Inexpensive.*

Continental **Batik Room at the Mauna Kea Beach Hotel.** For a very special
★ night out, capture the spirit of Sri Lanka at the Batik Room, with its furnishings of tangerine and pink tapestries, Ceylonese batiks, brass service plates, and an *houdah* (used by the Asian upper class when riding on the back of an elephant). Chef Jean Marc Heim sprinkles the menu with Indian curries, as well as continental and regional dishes that satisfy the most discriminating palates. The enticing choices include veal medallions with ginger ravioli in a cilantro cream sauce, Thai-style opakapaka, and a classic chateaubriand. The extensive wine list includes French Bordeaux and burgundies and good California wines. The Batik Room is in a resort hotel overlooking Kauna'oa Bay on the Kohala coast (on Hwy. 19, a half hour north of Ke-ahole Airport). *1 Mauna Kea Dr., Kohala Coast, tel. 808/882–7222. Reservations advised. Jacket and tie required. AE, CB, MC, V. Expensive.*

★ **The Garden at Mauna Kea Beach Hotel.** This restaurant features beautiful Polynesian decor with table settings of Hawaiian koa and teak alongside French and Belgian crystal. Every item on the menu is grown or raised in Hawaii. Ohelo-berry-glazed wild boar, breast of pheasant, and Pacific lobster and prawns with melon and ginger sabayon are among the imaginative offerings guaranteed to please. The Garden is in a resort hotel overlooking Kauna'oa Bay on the Kohala coast (on Hwy. 19, a half hour north of Ke-ahole Airport). *1 Mauna Kea Dr., Kohala Coast, tel. 808/882–7222. Reservations advised. Jacket and tie required. AE, CB, MC, V. Expensive.*

Water's Edge at the Hyatt Regency Waikoloa. The multilevel dining room overlooks a lagoon and the ocean at this subdued restaurant that is the pride of the resort. The continental cuisine features such entrées as chateaubriand, lobster Newburg (topped with crabmeat, asparagus, and hollandaise sauce), veal Oscar, and Dover sole. Water's Edge seats 415, when the patrons are not dancing to the music of the 10-piece big-band orchestra. The morning after, perk up with a breakfast of apple-smoked salmon and bagels or fresh apple crepes. *1 Waikoloa Beach Resort, tel. 808/885–1234. Reservations advised. Dress: neat but casual. AE, DC, MC, V. Open for breakfast and dinner. Expensive.*

Beach Club. This hard-to-find establishment is hidden behind the basement-level parking garage of Aston's Kona by the Sea, but once you're seated, the menu will set your mouth watering with flavors of the Southwest. The food, however, may be a little hard to see, as the place is on the dark side. Ask to sit outside, with the ocean a stone's-throw away. Warm spicy shrimp is served with cool papaya relish, while a salad may have a hint of Hawaii in its Manoa lettuce and Waipio fern shoots with a creamy Molokai dressing. Sauté of shrimp with artichoke bottoms and sweet peppers in coconut sauce topped off with ohelo-berry mousse are other reasons why this restaurant's eclectic menu has gained a reputation for serving the most interesting food in town. In wines, if Chablis is a bit fruity for you, you'll be pleased to note that chardonnay is available by the glass as a house wine. *Aston Kona by the Sea, 75-6106 Alii Dr., Kailua-Kona, tel. 808/329–0290. Reservations advised. Dress: informal. AE, CB, DC, MC, V. Closed Sun., Mon. Moderate.*

★ **Gallery at Mauna Lani Resort.** Apart from the hotel at the tennis complex and surrounded by a golf course, the Gallery has a cozy, cheerful atmosphere that is enhanced by a friendly staff. A huge picture window on one side overlooks an exhibition tennis court. The restaurant has gained a reputation for unique cuisine with Pacific Rim touches. The chef is continuing a tradition of using fresh, island ingredients in new and creative ways, and you can make personal requests as well. The attractive menu includes tasty appetizers, such as grilled chicken with macadamia nut sauce and shrimp in phyllo, and such entrées as sautéed scallops with *lilikoi* (passion fruit) and cilantro sauce and fillet of steak *kiana* with shiitake mushrooms and cream sauce. *Off Hwy. 19, Kalahuipuaa, Kohala Coast, tel. 808/885–7777. Reservations advised. Dress: informal. AE, DC, MC, V. Moderate.*

Hele Mai at the Kona Hilton Beach and Tennis Resort. This open-air dining room overlooks Kailua Bay; at dusk, when the sun outlines the boats bobbing offshore, you'll have a lovely, peaceful view. Jumbo prawns and scallops in a black-bean sauce with fresh Chinese pea pods are especially succulent. Big eaters can go for the 22-oz. rib-eye-steak special. *Within walking distance of central Kailua-Kona; 75-5852 Alii Dr., Kailua, tel. 808/329–3111. Reservations required. Dress: casual but neat. AE, DC, MC, V. Closed Sun., Mon. Moderate.*

Rusty Harpoon. The pleasant peach decor, matched with natural oak and highlighted with the work of local artists, makes this second-floor restaurant, which overlooks Kailua-Kona's main street, the prettiest in the village center. An exceptional entrée is the oysters Rockefeller, served in an artichoke bottom with a creamy spinach mixture topped by three cheeses; for traditionalists, the prime rib is certified Black Angus beef, cooked in rock salt to seal in the flavor. *75-5719 N. Alii Dr., Kailua-Kona, tel. 808/329–8881. Reservations advised for parties of 8 or more. Dress: informal. AE, MC, V. Open for breakfast, lunch, and dinner. Inexpensive.*

French **Le Soleil at the Mauna Lani Bay Hotel.** This elegant restaurant
★ with 21 tables overlooks a tropical garden with waterfalls and fish ponds. The waiters wear tuxedos and pamper you as they serve such sumptuous delicacies as smoked lilikoi chicken, Maine lobster, and blackened ahi and onaga with four-pepper crust, but it's the desserts that will do you in. Even if you order a pastry or flambé dessert specialty, every diner receives the Pele flambé bonbons (dry ice is used in a beautiful presentation) and finger bowls; footstools and roses for the ladies add to the delight of dining here. *Off Hwy, 19, ½ hour from Ke-ahole Airport, Box 4000, Hwy. 19, Kohala Coast, tel. 808/885–6622. Jacket required. AE, CB, DC, V. Very Expensive.*

La Bourgogne. A genial husband-and-wife team owns this relaxing, country-style French restaurant with dark wood walls and blue velvet booths; it's just 4 miles out of town. Classic French cooking at its best keeps the 10 tables filled six nights a week. Chef Guy Chatelard is particularly proud of his sweetbreads of veal with Madeira sauce and his roast saddle of lamb with mustard sauce. *Kuakini Plaza S on Hwy. 11, 77-6400 Nalani St., Kailua-Kona, tel. 808/329-6711. Reservations advised (to be safe, call a couple of days in advance). Dress: informal. AE, CB, DC, MC, V. Closed Sun. Moderate.*

Italian **Donatoni's at the Hyatt Regency Waikoloa.** Lighter cuisine, shellfish, and the more subtle sauces of Italy, as well as specialty pizzas made to suit your personal tastes, are served in this romantic restaurant, complete with an accordion player during dinner. Reminiscent of an Italian villa, Donatoni's seats 337 in a building separate from the hotel's residence towers. Prices on the extensive Italian wine and champagne list range from $14 to $39. *1 Waikoloa Beach Resort, Kohala Coast, tel. 808/885-1234. Reservations advised. Dress: casual. AE, DC, MC, V. Moderate.*

Phillip Paolo's at Waterfront Row. Portions are generous at this Italian (with a French flair) restaurant. Dining is on two levels in a Mediterranean setting by the water. The Giuseppe fettucine is a wonderful blend of fresh snow crabmeat sautéed in fresh basil and oregano and garnished with bacon and olives. Or you might try the osso bucco (veal), or the opakapaka with crab, shrimp, mushrooms and capers served on oglio pasta. *75-5770 Alii Dr., Kailua-Kona 96740, tel. 808/329-4436. Reservations advised. Dress: Casual. AE, CB, MC, V. Inexpensive-moderate.*

Café Pasta (a.k.a.) We're Talking Pizza. Even people who don't like pizza like the pizza made here. The chef uses fresh island ingredients in his version of nouvelle cuisine. Hint: You can have pizza al pesto, with sun-dried tomatoes, eggplant, and fresh basil pesto, delivered right to your hotel room. Twenty tables seat 65 at this harborside restaurant with a contemporary art-deco decor. *Wharf Rd. and Mahukona Hwy., Kawaihae Center, 1st floor, Kawaihae, tel. 808/882-1071. Reservations advised for large groups. Dress: casual. Closed Thanksgiving and Christmas. D, MC, V. Inexpensive.*

Japanese **Imari at the Hyatt Regency Waikoloa.** The teriyakis and tempuras aimed to please mainland tastes are about the only way you can distinguish this Japanese restaurant, complete with waterfalls and a teahouse, from the most elegant of those in Japan. Beyond the display of Imari porcelain at the entrance, you'll find beef and chicken *shabu shabu* cooked at your table, complete teppan-yaki dinners prepared on a grill, and an outstanding sushi bar. Impeccable service by kimono-clad waitresses and modern, uncluttered Japanese decor (lacquer, bamboo, cloisonné vases, and Imari dinnerware in spotless, light surroundings) add to your dining pleasure. The restaurant seats 136. *1 Waikoloa Beach Resort, Kohala Coast, tel. 808/885-1234. Dress: informal. Reservations advised. AE, DC, MC, V. Moderate.*

Kana Zawa-Tei. Located across the street from the Kona Hilton and within walking distance of the central hotels, Kana Zawa-Tei has the only sushi bar (seats 11) in Kailua. Traditionally clad waitresses serve patrons in this authentic Japanese restaurant, which is decorated with black lacquered booths, 18 oak tables, and lanterns. The *bento* specials come in a lacquer serving dish and allow you to sample tempura, sashimi, eel, lobster, and other items. Kana Zawa-Tei serves 32 varieties of sushi. *75-5845 Alii Dr., Kailua-Kona, tel. 808/326-1881. Dress: informal. AE, DC, MC, V. Moderate.*

Teshima's. The local lawyers and doctors show up at Teshima's whenever they're in the mood for some Big Island Japanese-American cooking. Don't expect a soothing ambience; Teshima's is on the dark and questionably clean side, with scarred booths and clattering dishes. Service is so-so, but residents come for the sashimi, sukiyaki, and puffy shrimp tempura. You might also want to try a *teishoku* (tray) of assorted Japanese delicacies. The teriyaki steak is under $10. *15 min. from Kailua-Kona in Honalo, tel. 808/322–9140. Dress: casual. No credit cards. Open for breakfast, lunch, and dinner. Closed Christmas Day and New Year's Day. Inexpensive.*

Mixed Menu **Hale Samoa at Kona Village Resort.** Ferns, tapa screens, hurricane lamps, and mounted marlin and other fish, all bathed in the glow of sunset, set a magical mood at this Kona Village signature restaurant, with 18 tables. The escargots and artichokes, baked in Boursin cheese with garlic sauce, are heavenly, as are the Malaysian prawns stir-fried in black-bean sauce, both dreamed up by James Balanay, the Chinese-Filipino chef. The Hale Samoa serves Asian, French, and Hawaiian cuisines, while the prix fixe dinner includes appetizer, soup, salad, entrée, dessert, and coffee. The entry road to Kona Village is 7 miles out Highway 19 from Kailua; you'll see the thatched guard shack. *Box 1299, Kaupulehu, tel. 808/325–6787. Reservations required. Dress: informal. AE, DC, MC, V. No lunch. Closed Wed., Fri., and 1 week in Dec. when resort is closed. Expensive.*

The CanoeHouse at the Mauna Lani Bay Hotel. This open-air, beachfront restaurant, surrounded by fishponds, was a welcome addition to the Kohala Coast dining scene in the fall of 1989. An enormous koa canoe is the focal point of this restaurant serving Pacific Rim cuisine; entrées include wok-fried sesame shrimp on crispy noodles with lilikoi glaze and bamboo-steamed mahi mahi with ginger-scallion salsa and baby Chinese cabbage. *Off Hwy. 19, ½ hour from Ke-ahole Airport, Kohala Coast, tel. 808/885–6622. Reservations advised. Dress: casual. AE, CB, DC, MC, V. Moderate.*

Polynesian **Cascades at the Hyatt Regency Waikoloa.** This open-air restaurant, next to a cascading waterfall and a pond with swans floating by, seats 337. Cascades is open for breakfast and lunch (American-style omelets, etc.) and offers a Polynesian buffet at dinner, which includes items (such as curried veal, kalua pig, teriyaki beef, and seafood, to name a few) to suit every taste for $19.95. *1 Waikoloa Beach Resort, Kohala Coast, tel. 808/885–1234. Dress: casual but neat. AE, DC, MC, V. Inexpensive.*

Waimea-Kamuela, Honokaa

American **Hartwell's Restaurant at Hale Kea.** Built in 1897 and named for Parker Ranch manager who once lived here, this house is the centerpiece of the boutiques and shops at Kale Kea. Various rooms of the house—the Library, the Sun Room, the Pa'u Room, and the Paniolo Room, restored with period furnishings make Hartwell's seem like many restaurants in one. Chef Steve Hupp presents "Upcountry" cuisine, flavored with herbs grown on the property. Roast duckling with lilikoi sauce served with wild rice pancakes and a 14-oz. T-bone steak garnished with a sweet pepper and onion compote draw raves. A light dinner menu is available from 5 to 6:30. *Near entrance to Waimea on Kawaihae Rd. Box 982, Kamuela 96743, tel. 808/885–6094. Reservations advised. Dress: casual. AE, MC, V. Inexpensive–moderate.*

Cattleman's Steakhouse. This steakhouse is fronted by a popular cocktail lounge with a bar and polished redwood tables. The dining room with white-topped tables and pink linen napkins overlooks a grassy field and the Kohala foothills. A great salad bar, shrimp scampi, and a variety of steaks make this an all-American choice for lunch or dinner. *Adjacent to Waimea Center on Hwy. 190, Waimea, tel. 808/885–4077. Dress: casual. MC, V. No lunch Sat. and Sun. Inexpensive.*

Continental **Merriman's.** Pete Merriman opened his restaurant in December 1988, after winning rave reviews as the chef at the Mauna Lani's Gallery Restaurant. It's worth the 20-minute drive from the Kohala-coast hotels to cowboy country in Waimea to sample his imaginative Continental cuisine. Try opakapaka ravioli in orange dill sauce or the Parker Ranch beef Bourguignon. Merriman's, which is decorated in bright, playful colors, brings to mind the steamship days in Hawaii—a sort of Hawaiian art-deco decor features an exhibition kitchen that allows diners to watch the chef create. *Opelo Plaza II, corner of Rte. 19 and Opelo Rd., Kamuela, tel. 808/885–6822. Reservations advised. Dress: informal. AE, MC, V. Moderate.*

★ **Bree Garden.** This beautiful restaurant wraps around an East Indian banyan tree. Enter through the etched-glass doors; picture windows surround the banyan's fascinating root system. The split-level dining room has antiques and leather goods from Germany displayed on banquettes, with one side opening onto a cactus garden. Continental and weekly international menus, such as Vietnamese and French, are featured. Try the German beefsteak, fresh fish, or one of the pastas featured every night. The fettuccine Bernio—after Chef Bree's nickname—is similar to fettuccine Alfredo. *64-5188 Kinohou St., Kamuela, tel. 808/885–5888. Dress: informal. AE, MC, V. Open 4:30–10 daily. Inexpensive–Moderate.*

★ **Edelweiss.** Faithful local diners whisper that this popular place has slipped a bit, but we haven't noticed. This is a relaxed family-oriented restaurant with rustic redwood furnishings. The chef's rack of lamb is still excellent. The varied menu includes 14 daily specials (such as a sausage platter), many with a European flavor. Go early—5:30–6:30—to avoid a long wait for one of the 14 tables. *Hwy. 19 entering Waimea-Kamuela, tel. 808/885–6800. No reservations. Dress: informal. MC, V. Closed Mon., New Year's Day, and lunch on Christmas Day. Inexpensive.*

Volcano

American **Ka Ohelo Room.** The romance of the Ka Ohelo Room is not so much in its food but in the fact that it is right at the edge of Kilauea Crater in a mountain-lodge setting. It's lovely and romantic at night, with huge picture windows and traditional furnishings of natural wood. Recommended for dinner are the mahi Florentine or prime rib, topped off with pie made from Ohelo berries picked on the mountainside. *Volcano House, Volcanoes*

National Park, tel. 808/967-7321. Reservations advised. Dress: informal. AE, CB, DC, MC, V. Inexpensive.

Lodging

The types of accommodations vary tremendously on the Big Island: from hot and sunny resorts to condominiums on cool mountaintops and bed-and-breakfasts in damp, beautifully green little towns geared more toward fishing and farming than vacationing. That, in fact, is the beauty of a trip to this island: You can sample that elusive thing people like to call "the real Hawaii," yet complete your stay at a resort designed for fun and fantasy—or, if you're limited for time, opt only for the fantasy and never leave your "total destination resort." If you decide to spend an entire week or 10 days in more than one location on the Big Island, you'll need to plan the order of your moves. If, for example, you begin with fun and sun in Kailua-Kona or along the Kohala coast, you might be disappointed to end with a night or two in Hilo, particularly if it rains (and in Hilo that's a very likely prospect). Consequently, accommodations are listed by area in the order in which you might plan your stay. If you have only three nights on the Big Island, go directly to Keauhou, Kailua-Kona, or the Kohala coast and bask in the sun. Bed-and-breakfasts and small out-of-the-way hotels are listed in their own category, regardless of location.

Generally, you'll always be able to find a room on the Big Island; however, you might not get your first choice if you wait until the last minute to make reservations at the top resorts during the winter season, which runs from December 15 through April 15. Amazingly enough, you will not be able to find a room in Hilo during the first week in April, when the Merrie Monarch Festival *(see* The Arts, below) is in full swing. Hula *halau* (schools) from all Islands converge on Hilo to compete in the week-long contests staged to honor Hawaii's last monarch, King David Kalakaua. Across the island, Kailua-Kona bursts at the seams in mid-October, when athletes and their support teams fill the hotels, the ocean waters, and the highways during the Bud Light Ironman World Triathlon Championships. An even bigger problem than finding a room at these times is finding a rental car. Be sure to make reservations well in advance—six months to a year—if your stay coincides with the festival or the triathlon.

Room and car packages are often available in all price categories. A reputable travel agent should be able to furnish up-to-date information on these packages. The more expensive hotels offer special packages for tennis players, golfers, or honeymooners—but no one minds if you pretend to be a honeymooner to take advantage of the deal. Included in the package price are such things as lei greetings, perhaps a meal or two, free court time for tennis buffs, or carts and complimentary greens fees for golfers. We have indicated when hotels offer an American plan, meaning meals included. Otherwise, hotel rates are for a double room only.

Generally, all large hotels and condos have outdoor swimming pools—a particularly nice amenity to have if you're staying in Kailua-Kona, where the beaches are limited. Some of the older hotels do not have air-conditioning, but these will almost always be equipped with ceiling or room fans, which should be adequate except during the hot summer and early fall seasons. All rooms have a television set and telephone unless otherwise indicated.

Highly recommended hotels in each price category are indicated by a star ★.

Category	Cost*
Very Expensive	over $120
Expensive	$90–$120
Moderate	$60–$90
Inexpensive	under $60

All prices are for a standard double room, excluding 9¼% tax and service charges.

Hilo

★ **Hawaii Naniloa Hotel.** Be sure to ask for a renovated room with a harbor view when you book into this hotel. When all the rooms are redone in soft tones of beige and rose, this will again be the nicest place to stay in Hilo. Coffee makers in all rooms are a bonus. The 7- and 12-story towers are connected by a lobby area with shops, and on the lower level is the Sandalwood Dining Room; the Polynesian Room, a lounge that offers dancing Thursday through Sunday nights; and the Karaoke Bar for poolside cocktails. An executive golf course, the Naniloa Country Club, is just across Banyan Drive. *93 Banyan Dr., Hilo 96720, tel. 808/969–3333 or 800/367–5360. 386 air-conditioned rooms with bath. Facilities: pool, shops, cocktail lounges, restaurants, free parking. AE, CB, DC, MC, V. Moderate.*

★ **Hilo Hawaiian Hotel.** One of the most pleasant hotels on the shores of Hilo Bay, the Hilo Hawaiian has a lanai terrace and bayfront rooms with spectacular views of Mauna Kea, the bay, and Coconut Island. The rooms have rattan furniture; most have private lanais, and several are designed for guests in wheelchairs. Kitchenettes are available with one-bedroom suites. The Queen's Court Dining Room has reasonable prices for a hotel restaurant; it has a beautiful view of Hilo Bay and serves breakfast, lunch, and dinner buffets. The Menehune Lounge serves up cocktails and entertainment seven days a week. *71 Banyan Dr., Hilo 96720, tel. 808/935–9361 or 800/367–5004. 290 large, air-conditioned rooms with bath. Facilities: shops, pool, Monarchy meeting room, restaurant, cocktail lounge, free parking. AE, CB, DC, MC, V. Moderate.*

Waiakea Villas Hotel. Aku the macaw greets visitors and residents alike at the entry to the airy lobby. The hotel stands on 14 acres, surrounded by foliage, waterways, and carp ponds. Spacious rooms and one-bedroom suites are tropically decorated with rattan furniture and have bathtubs with showers. If not recently aired, the rather dark units can have a musty aroma, but they are clean. Waiakea Villas is located next to Waiakea Fish Pond and Wailoa State Park, near Hilo and shopping centers. *400 Hualani St., Hilo 96720, tel. 808/961–2841 or 800/367–7042. 141 of 292 condominium apartments in 3-story walk-up buildings available for daily rental. Facilities: golf, 2 tennis courts, pool, air-conditioning, John Michael's Restaurant*

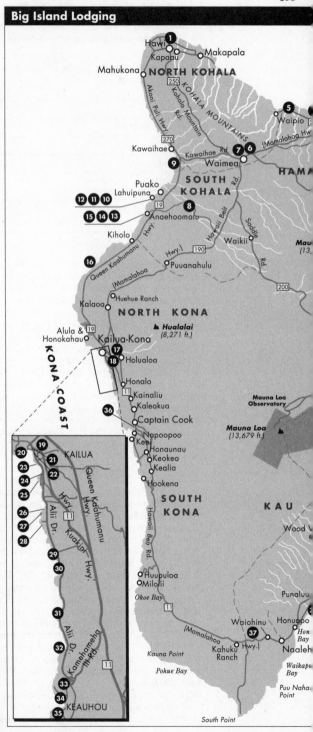

Big Island Lodging

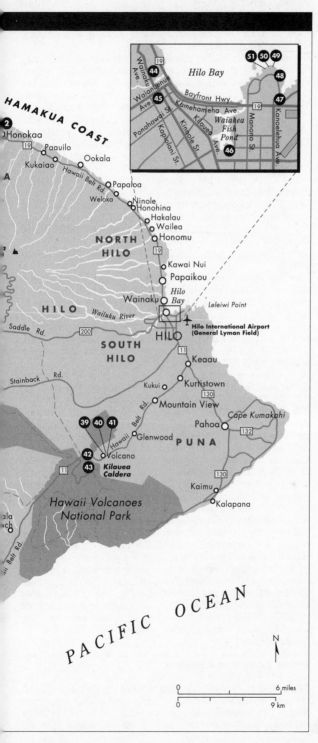

(American), Miyo's Restaurant (Japanese), Springwater Cafe, cocktail lounges, meeting room. 3-day minimum stay. AE, DC, MC, V. Inexpensive–Moderate.

Country Club Hotel. The rooms in this old bayfront, multistory building are large and clean, with indoor-outdoor style carpeting and showers with glass doors. Some rooms overlook the bay, while others face the Naniloa Country Club Golf Course. The exterior of the building has deteriorated in the Hilo humidity and needs to be painted; rust on doors and screens gives the place a worn look. Repair work is being done little by little. *121 Banyan Dr., Hilo 96720, tel. 808/935–7171. About 70 of 149 condominium units are available for daily rental. Facilities: restaurant, cocktail lounge, meeting room, pool; some rooms with TV. AE, MC, V. Inexpensive.*

Dolphin Bay Hotel. All rooms have kitchens in this clean, homey hotel in a lovely, green Hawaiian garden setting. The rooms do not have phones, but they do have desk fans to stir the air. The hotel is away from the beach in a residential area called Pueo. *333 Iliahi St., Hilo 96720, tel. 808/935–1466. 4 blocks from Hilo Bay. 18 units. Facilities: free parking. MC, V. Inexpensive.*

Hilo Bay Hotel, Uncle Billy's. Small to average-size rooms in this low-rise hotel on Hilo Bay are decorated with 1960s-style green shag carpeting and come equipped with showers (but no bathtubs). It's a popular stopover for Neighbor Islanders, who enjoy proprietor Uncle Billy Kimi's Hawaiian hospitality. A nightly hula show and entertainment during dinner are part of the fun. *87 Banyan Dr., Hilo 96720, tel. 808/935–0861 or 800/ 442–5841; in AK, 800/367–5102; in Canada, 800/423–8733. 150 air-conditioned rooms, most with kitchenettes. Facilities: shops, pool, Kimi's coffee shop, cocktail lounge, free parking. AE, CB, DC, MC, V. Inexpensive.*

Hilo Hotel. Favored by Japanese travelers and economy-minded visitors, this centrally located hotel has spotlessly clean studios and two-bedroom family suites that sleep up to six. The communal sitting room has a television, while the Fuji Japanese Restaurant is popular among residents. *142 Kinoole St., Hilo 96720, tel. 808/961–3733. 30 spartan rooms in downtown Hilo. Facilities: pool, cocktail lounge, restaurant, room and car packages, complimentary Continental breakfast. AE, DC, MC, V. Inexpensive.*

Hilo Seaside Hotel. Rooms in the two- and three-story walk-up buildings are pleasant and clean, though not plush. The nicest rooms have lanais and overlook the lagoon or are situated around the pool. Lots of foliage along the walkways and friendly local personnel create a very Hawaiian ambience. A peaceful place, except when planes take off and land, as the hotel is near the airport's flight path. *126 Banyan Dr., Hilo 96720, tel. 808/ 935–0821 or 800/367–7000. 145 rooms with bay and garden views. Facilities: ceiling fans, shops, pool, meeting rooms, restaurant, cocktail lounge, free parking. AE, DC, MC, V. Inexpensive.*

Kailua-Kona and Keauhou

Aston Kona by the Sea. Complete modern kitchens and tiled lanais can be found in every suite in this comfortable oceanfront condo. The spacious rooms are tastefully decorated in beige and ivory. An open-air lobby and a helpful reception desk add to the friendly atmosphere. There's no sandy beach, but the pool is situated next to the ocean. The casual Beach Club Restaurant has a local reputation for serving creative cuisine using island-grown ingredients. *75-6106 Alii Dr., Kailua-Kona 96740, tel. 808/329–0200 or 800/367–5124. 145 of 155 1- and 2-bedroom units are available for daily rental. Facilities: 2 pools, restaurant, air-conditioning. AE, CB, DC, MC, V. Very Expensive.*

★ **Kona Coast Resort.** The beautifully decorated rooms with contemporary soft rose and gray decor have modern wood-and-tile kitchens. This 12-acre, low-rise resort is across Alii Drive from the Keauhou Shopping Center. Units have every amenity you could ask for: Jennair ranges, microwaves, washers and dryers, hair dryers in the master bathrooms, and more. If you stay awhile, you'll get to know your neighbors at the complimentary weekly cocktail parties. Lanais have views of the ocean or golf course. *78-6842 Alii Dr., Kailua-Kona 96740, tel. 808/324–1721 or 800/367–8047, ext. 373. 68 1-, 2-, and 3-bedroom rental units. Facilities: pool and spa with waterfall, VCRs, room safes, barbecues, recreation pavilion. MC, V. Very Expensive.*

Aston Royal Sea Cliff. This is a Mediterranean-style condominium resort on seven coastal acres with pleasantly tree-shaded grounds. Plushly furnished one- and two-bedroom apartments, decorated in soft, tropical colors, have large lanais and kitchen/dining areas. *75-6040 Alii Dr., Kailua-Kona 96740, tel. 808/329–8021 or 800/922–7866. 150 rental units. Facilities: 2 pools, sauna, hot tub, tennis, free parking, air-conditioning, health spa, laundry. AE, CB, DC, MC, V. Expensive–Very Expensive.*

★ **Kanaloa at Kona.** The 13-acre grounds provide a lovely setting for this low-rise condominium bordering the Keauhou-Kona Country Club. Large one-, two-, and three-bedroom apartments have wall-to-wall carpeting, koa-wood cabinetwork, and tile and marble decor. The fully equipped kitchens have microwave ovens. Oceanfront suites are furnished with private Jacuzzis; the bathroom showers are big enough for two. The Terrace Restaurant has a romantically tropical atmosphere, in addition to serving reasonable and good American cuisine with local flavor. *78-261 Manukai St., Kailua-Kona 96740, tel. 808/322–2272. 166 rooms and villa apartments (condominiums) in 37 buildings. Facilities: 3 outdoor pools, hot tub, 2 tennis courts, ceiling fans, laundry, meeting area, free parking. AE, DC, MC, V. Expensive–Very Expensive.*

Kona Hilton Beach and Tennis Resort. Of the major hotels, the Kona Hilton is nearest to Kailua on the south side of town. It has a distinctive profile (built to resemble an early Hawaiian *holua* slide dropping toward the sea) that is easy to pick out from downtown. Rooms have coffee makers, safes, refrigerators, and standard rattan furniture. Corner rooms in the Beach Building are the best, because they have huge lanais that overlook the ocean. Full and modified American plans can be booked. A complimentary shuttle to Kona Country Club is available for golf foursomes. *Box 1179, Kailua-Kona 96745, tel. 808/329–3111 or 800/452–4411. 452 rooms in a main building, a beach building, and a village building. Facilities: Hele Mai dining room (continental), cocktail lounges, pool, shops, meeting and banquet rooms, 4 Laykold tennis courts, free parking. AE, DC, MC, V. Expensive–Very Expensive.*

Kona Surf Resort. Owned by a Japanese firm, Otaka, Inc., and catering to Japanese tour groups, this large, easy-to-get-confused-in hotel is the last property at the end of the road in Keauhou. Ask for a hotel map. The pink stuccoed rooms, with separate dressing areas and private lanais, are large almost to the point of feeling bare. A charming copper-roofed wedding chapel beside peaceful koi (carp) ponds caters mainly to Japanese couples, but it's available for all visitors who want to tie the knot during their vacation. Paths and open spaces allow strolls along the cliff edge with the waves crashing below. You can walk to Keauhou Bay, where arrangements can be made for sailing, snorkeling, and deep-sea fishing. Room and car packages are frequently offered. *78-128 Ehukai St., Kailua-Kona 96740, tel. 808/322–3411 or 800/367–8011. 535 rooms in 5 wings. Facilities: freshwater and saltwater pools, 3 tennis courts, golf course, restaurants, including the Makee Restaurant (steaks and seafood), cocktail lounges, shops, meeting rooms, air-conditioning, refrigerators, free parking. AE, CB, DC, MC, V. Expensive–Very Expensive.*

★ **Hotel King Kamehameha.** The most conveniently located of the major hotels, the King Kam is right next to Kailua Pier, where big game fish are weighed in during fishing tournaments. Though the rooms are not particularly special (the fifth- and sixth-floor oceanfront rooms are best), this hotel rates a star because it is the only centrally located Kailua-Kona hotel with a white-sand beach and a shopping mall in the lobby. Among the numerous shops is the only branch of Liberty House (a quality department store) in Kailua. The lobby also has educational Hawaiiana displays and fishing trophies; a mounted 1,062½-pound Pacific blue marlin, which set a record in the 1986 Hawaii International Billfish Tournament, hangs on one wall. Free historically oriented tours explore the grounds and the restored Ahuena Heiau, which King Kamehameha I ordered constructed in the early 1800s. *75-5660 Palani Rd., Kailua-Kona 96740, tel. 808/329–2911 or 800/227–4700. 460 rooms and suites. Facilities: pool, sauna, tennis courts, Moby Dick and Kona Veranda restaurants, cocktail lounges, shops, air-conditioning, free parking. AE, CB, DC, MC, V. Expensive.*

Keauhou Beach Hotel. New carpets, bedspreads (the headboards of a matching pastel-print fabric are trimmed with bleached cane wood), and roomy lanais insure comfort in this established oceanfront hotel next to Kahaluu Beach Park. Unfortunately, many lanais overlook a bare rooftop before opening to a spectacular vista of black lava and blue seas. Renovations to the public areas of the hotel are being completed, and the Kona Lagoons Hotel next door, which is closed for renovation, will eventually become part of the Keauhou Resort complex. *5 mi. from Kailua town, 78-6740 Alii Dr., Kailua-Kona 96740, tel. 800/367–6025 or 808/955–4811. 318 rooms, 6 suites. Facilities: 2 pools, sauna, exercise room, 6 tennis courts, 4 restaurants, lounge, shops, meeting room, air-conditioning, refrigerators. AE, CB, DC, MC, V. Moderate–Expensive.*

Kona Bali Kai. These older, family-style units midway between Kailua-Kona and Keauhou Country Club were decorated with new furnishings and carpeting in 1988. All units have kitchen/dining areas. The property is divided, so ask for a place on the ocean side rather than the mountain side of the road. *76-6246 Alii Dr., Kailua-Kona 96740, tel. 808/329–9381 or 800/367–6046. 91 condo units available for daily rental. Facilities: pools, sauna, restaurant, laundry, air-conditioning. AE, DC, MC, V. Moderate–Expensive.*

Hale Kona Kai. This small vacation condominium on the ocean's edge next door to the Kona Hilton requires a three-day minimum stay. Units are furnished differently, because they are privately owned; the corner units have the best views. Hale Kona Kai is within walking distance of Kailua-Kona restaurants and shopping. *75-5870 Kahakai Rd., Kailua-Kona 96740, tel. 808/329-2155. 39 1-bedroom rental units. Facilities: pool, full kitchens, air-conditioning, free parking. No credit cards. Moderate.*

Kona Bay Hotel, Uncle Billy's. These two- and four-story motel-type units are conveniently located in the center of town, across the street from the ocean. Owned and managed by the same local family that owns the Hilo Bay Hotel, these hotels have a friendly, fun-loving atmosphere. Open-air dining around the pool is a casual affair. Guests have access to a salt-water swimming pool at the ocean's edge, across the street in front of the Fisherman's Landing Restaurant. *75-5739 Alii Dr., Kailua-Kona 96740, tel. 808/329-1393 or 800/442-5841; in Alaska, 800/367-5120; in Canada, 800/423-8733. 125 rooms. Facilities: pool, restaurant, cocktail lounge, shops, air-conditioning, free parking. AE, CB, DC, MC, V. Moderate.*

Kona Islander Inn. Its close-to-the-village location and turn-of-the-century plantation-style architecture in a setting of palms and torch-lit paths make this pleasant but older apartment-style hotel a good value. Studios, some with built-in sofas, are located across the street from Kailua Bay. *Box 1239, Kailua-Kona 96745, tel. 808/329-3181 or 800/367-5124. 82 hotel units. Facilities: pool, air-conditioning, free parking. AE, CB, DC, MC, V. Moderate.*

Kona Magic Sands. A three-day minimum stay is required in this small beachside condominium, which has maid service on request. The studios do not have telephones, but they do have kitchenettes. Units vary, because they are individually owned, but all are oceanfront. Some have enclosed lanais to give more living space. The condo is located near Disappearing Sands Beach, which is a plus for swimmers and sunbathers when the sand is there in the summer months (it washes away in winter). *77-6452 Alii Dr., Kailua-Kona 96740, tel. 808/329-6488 or 800/ 367-5168, 800/423-8733, ext. 329 in Canada. 26 hotel units. Facilities: pool, Jameson's by the Sea seafood restaurant, cocktail lounge, free parking. AE, MC, V. Moderate.*

Kona Seaside Hotel. The old Hukilau Hotel and the adjoining Kona Seaside have been combined and renovated, with 155 rooms in four price categories (according to size and location). This hotel has the best central location in the area, across the street from Kailua Bay. Rooms nearest the main street are built around a pool with a grassy courtyard. The Garden Wing is set back, and the Tower Pool Wing opens onto Palani Road on the opposite side. The small rooms have tiny bathrooms and showers but are completely adequate for the budget traveler. *75-5646 Palani Rd., Kailua-Kona 96740, tel. 808/329-2455. Facilities: restaurant, cocktail lounge, 2 pools, meeting rooms, air-conditioning and/or ceiling fans, free parking. AE, MC, V. Inexpensive-Moderate.*

Kona Tiki Hotel. The best thing about this simple, older 3-story walk-up hotel about a mile south of Kailua-Kona is that all the units have lanais right next to the ocean. All the rental units have refrigerators, and others have kitchens for an extra $5. Decorated in outdated colors—brown, orange, etc.—the rooms are not luxurious, but the proximity to the ocean is a definite asset. Guests can sunbathe by the pool. A continental breakfast is provided. No in-room TV is available. *Box 1567, Kailua-Kona 96745, tel. 808/329–1425. 15 rental units. Facilities: pool, ceiling fans, free parking. No credit cards. Inexpensive.*

Kohala Coast and Waikoloa

★ **Hyatt Regency Waikoloa.** The guest rooms in this new fantasy resort are large, beautifully appointed, and decorated in soft beige and sand colors; the works of such well-known local artists as Yvonne Cheng grace the walls. Each room has its own small lanai, minibar, ample walk-in closet, couch, dining table, and chairs. Guests at this resort on 62 acres of rocky ocean shoreline can swim with dolphins (for a fee) in a protected area of a man-made four-acre lagoon, bordered on one side by a man-made sunning beach. No natural sand beach is available. A swimming pool nearly an acre in size has water slides and a grotto bar hidden behind an enormous waterfall; two other pools are connected by a river pool; and a third swimming pool is located in the Ocean Tower atrium. For vacationers who are not in a rush to make an early tee-time or the last interisland flight of the day, this resort is an adventure. Otherwise, one tends to grow weary of the advance planning and the waiting involved to get places via the Disneyesque trams and boats. It's no wonder a one-time fee of $10 is automatically added to your bill for luggage handling. The hotel is becoming known for its fine restaurants, including the Water's Edge, Donatoni's, Imari, and the Kona Provision Company. Spats Disco ($10 cover charge for nonguests unless you've patronized one of the restaurants) is one of the few places where the nightlife is actually lively along the Kohala coast. *1 Waikoloa Beach Resort, Kohala Coast 96734, tel. 808/885–1234 or 800/228–9000. 1,241 rooms in 3 6-story buildings. Facilities: 7 restaurants and adjoining bars, luau grounds, Spats Disco, 6 additional bars, 3 pools, 8 tennis courts, health spa, 2 racquetball courts. A Tom Weiskopf–Jay Morrish golf course and a Robert Trent Jones, Jr., course adjoin the resort. AE, DC, MC, V. Very Expensive.*

★ **Kona Village Resort.** Here is the ultimate retreat for privacy and peaceful surroundings. It's easy to feel you are part of an extended Polynesian *ohana* (family) with your own thatched roof *hale* (house) beside the sea. Houses are available in various island designs, such as Hawaiian, Tahitian, Tongan, Fijian, Samoan, and Marquesan. Access to the resort, with its crescent of sparkling beach, is down a narrow road leading off Queen Kaahumanu Highway, 15 miles north of Kailua. No phones, televisions, or radios are available in any of the *hales*, but you might have your own hammock right outside the door. The extra-large rooms are cooled by ceiling fans and decorated with bright tropical prints, many silk-screened or hand-painted by local artists. Families seem to return again and again; an added enticement is that the full American plan includes nearly everything: Meals, tennis, sailing, outrigger canoeing, snorkeling, volleyball, shuffleboard, and rides in the glass-bottom boat are at no additional charge. In keeping with the Polynesian mood, jackets and ties are not worn at dinner, even in the resort's finest restaurant, the Hale Samoa. *Box 1299, Kaupulehu-Kona 96745, tel. 808/325–5555 or 800/367–5290. 125 bungalows. Facilities: limited meeting and banquet space, "flightseeing" from the grounds, tennis, masseuse, scuba and* *sailing lessons, 2 pools, beach, 2 dining rooms, bars, general store, village goldsmith. AE, CB, DC, MC, V. Closed 1 week in Dec. Very Expensive.*

★ **Mauna Kea Beach Resort.** This discreetly low-key, world-class resort is located on what is possibly the most beautiful, gently sloping white-sand beach on the island; some guests are out and swimming by 7 AM. The peaceful hotel is not known for its nightlife, though dancing is offered in the Batik Room most evenings. The rooms, which can be completely darkened by closing off the spacious lanais with sliding louvered doors, have tropical furnishings, with touches of the Far East (such as Buddha-shaped lamp bases) appearing in accessories. The dressing rooms feature his-and-her closets, complimentary cotton *yukatas* (robes) to wear during your stay, and the biggest, softest towels I've ever seen in a hotel. Rooms do not have televisions, on the premise that guests will mingle if they watch television in a communal room. The hotel, which is known for its fine dining, particularly at the Batik Room and the Dining Pavilion, offers modified American-plan rates (two meals included). The Mauna Kea, developed by Laurance S. Rockefeller, opened its doors in 1965. *1 Mauna Kea Dr., Kohala Coast 96743–9706, tel. 808/882–7222 or 800/882–6060. 310 mountain- and ocean-view rooms and suites. Facilities: golf on the award-winning Robert Trent Jones, Sr., Mauna Kea Golf Course, 13 tennis courts, sailing, scuba diving, fitness center, exercise trail, shops, movies, sauna, 6 restaurants, luau garden. Sportfishing is available from nearby Kawaihae Harbor. Hunting and horseback riding are also within a short distance. AE, CB, MC, V. Very Expensive.*

★ **Mauna Lani Bay Hotel.** Almost all the spacious rooms in this exquisite modern hotel have views of the ocean. Soft chairs, a couch, a marble coffee table, and an oversize television are the comfortable furnishings in rooms decorated in soft beige and off-white hues with burgundy and blue accents. The rooms, with big, sunny lanais, are equipped with a dry bar and refrigerator, a clock radio, and a safe. The hotel is especially known for its spectacular Francis I'i Brown Golf Course and its famous sixth hole, where golfers tee off over a wide expanse of ocean. Jackets are required at the award-winning Le Soleil Restaurant (which is located by the waterfall on the first floor; its windows overlook the ocean and the golf course). *Box 4000, Kohala Coast 96743, tel. 808/885–6622 or 800/367–2323. 351 hotel rooms and suites. Facilities: golf, pool, 10 tennis courts, restaurants, bars, shops, air-conditioning. AE, CB, DC, MC, V. Very Expensive.*

Mauna Lani Point Condominiums. These elegant and roomy suites are set off by themselves near the sixth green of one of the world's most beautiful oceanside golf courses, a few steps away from the Mauna Lani Bay Hotel and its fine restaurants. This is the only condominium in Hawaii that offers full concierge services. Fans on the vaulted ceilings cool the rooms, which have a modern tropical decor in soft pink and eggshell colors. Kitchens, microwave ovens, and washer/dryers are in every unit, and daily maid service is standard. *2 Kaniku Dr., Kohala Coast 96743, tel. 808/885–5022 or 800/642–6284. 116 condominium units. Facilities: pool, Jacuzzi, sauna, golf and tennis, laundry, jogging trails, free parking. AE, CB, DC, MC, V. Very Expensive.*

Royal Waikoloan. The emphasis is on Hawaiiana in this recently remodeled hotel with its updated lobby and conference facilities. The lobby features demonstrations of Hawaiian quilting and other crafts. While the majority of rooms have an ocean view, all of them have private lanais, clock radios, and air-conditioning. The Royal Waikoloan has also opened 20 new plush cabanas with their own concierge. The resort is situated on 15.7 acres, bordered by royal fish ponds with a white-sand crescent beach and Anaehoomalu Bay just beyond. The bay is perfect for windsurfing and snorkeling. Luaus, *hukilaus* (communal fishing parties), and other special dining nights are regularly scheduled. *Box 5000, Waikoloa Rd., Kohala Coast 96743, tel. 808/885–6789 (resort) or 808/921–9700 or 800/537–9800 (reservations). 523 guest rooms in a multiwinged, 6-story hotel and 20 cabanas. Facilities: 2 18-hole golf courses, pool, shops, 6 tennis courts, conference facilities, free parking, petroglyph park and trails. AE, CB, DC, MC, V. Very Expensive.*

★ **Aston Shores at Waikoloa.** Wide curving driveways lead to individual white stucco and red-tile-roofed units set in a field of green. The spacious one-bedroom/one-bath and two-bedroom/two-bath condominiums have been decorated in muted shades, such as rose and light green. The plush carpets are even vacuumed in a shell pattern. Units all have kitchens and dining areas, as well as daily maid service. Oversize tubs and separate large glassed-in showers add to the luxury. Sliding glass doors in both the bedrooms and the living room open onto large lanais. The villas are landscaped with lagoons and waterfalls at the edge of the championship Waikoloa Golf Course. *Star Rte. 5200-A, Waikoloa 96743, tel. 808/885–5001 or 800/922–7866. 96 villas. Facilities: pool, hot tub, tennis, golf, equestrian center, air-conditioning and ceiling fans, free parking. AE, DC, MC, V. Expensive–Very Expensive.*

Ritz-Carlton, Mauna Lani. Set to open at the end of 1990 or early in 1991, this new Ritz-Carlton, located on secluded beachfront property, was planned to perpetuate the chain's high standards. The rooms are furnished warmly and traditionally with Drexel Heritage furniture. *50 Kaniku Dr., HC–02, Box 4320, Kohala Coast 96743, tel. 808/885–0099 or 800/241–3333. 542 rooms, 54 suites. Facilities: pool, 10 tennis courts, 2 golf courses, health club, sauna. AE, CB, DC, MC, V. Expensive.*

Waikoloa Villas at Waikoloa Resort. This is just about the only place to stay in the Waikoloa area (relatively near the Kohala-coast resorts) that is more moderately priced—and it's 6 miles inland. Individually owned condominium units are all decorated differently, but they each meet standards set by the rental agency. Two-night minimum stays are required, and maid service is on a weekly basis. The wide open spaces of cowboy country attract golfers and the horsey set. *Box 3066, Kamuela 96743, tel. 808/883–9144 or 800/657–7887. 55 1-bedroom rental units. Facilities: golf, tennis, horseback riding, pools, air-conditioning, free parking, restaurant at golf club. AE, DC, MC, V. Moderate.*

Out-of-the-Way Accommodations

It is practically imperative that you have a car if you choose to stay overnight at any of the places that follow. Generally, the hotels are small, family-run affairs that furnish a clean bed but little luxury. Many visitors are also beginning to "wake up and smell the coffee" when it comes to bed-and-breakfast lodgings, and on the Big Island a demand for less-expensive accommodations is being fulfilled by B&B hosts (usually outside the resort areas), who are opening their doors to guests.

A fledgling network under the directorship of Gordon Morse, himself a B&B host in the Volcano area, lists many of these widely spread private homes, cottages, and inns. For further information, write to: Gordon Morse, My Island Bed and Breakfast, Box 100, Volcano 96785, tel. 808/967–7216. Explain your expectations fully and ask plenty of questions before booking. For example, many B&Bs are located within a few miles of Volcanoes National Park, a haven for lovers of the great outdoors, though not the perfect location for beach and sun worshipers. Some require stays of two or three days.

Hamakua Coast **Hotel Honokaa Club.** A funky bargain place to stay in a pinch, but definitely not for luxury. This old, wood-frame hotel has been operated by the same family since 1908. The second-story rooms are more appealing for their views, if you don't mind the walk upstairs. The lunches are reasonably priced in the downstairs restaurant, which has a tiny salad bar. *Box 185, Honokaa 96727, tel. 808/775–0678. 12 hotel units. Facilities: desk fans, restaurant, bar. MC, V. Inexpensive.*

Waipio Wayside Bed and Breakfast. This former plantation manager's home, located near Honokaa on the way to Waipio Valley, has four sparkling clean rooms decorated with special touches that include light, airy curtains handpainted on silk by a local artist. One room is furnished with Chinese antiques, another (with private bath) has an early American theme, with blond wood paneling and a patchwork quilt. A pool and gazebo overlook fields of cane to the ocean. The B&B is about 15 minutes from Waimea (where at least four fine restaurants are located) and about 45 minutes from the Kohala Coast resorts. Breakfast is included. *Box 840, Honokaa 96727, tel. 808/775–0275 or 800/833–8849. 4 rooms, 1 with bath. Facilities: pool. No credit cards. Inexpensive.*

Up-country **Holualoa Inn.** Desmond and Karen Twigg-Smith rent a suite
Kona District and three rooms, each with private bath, in their cedar estate home. Situated in up-country Kona, amid coffee trees and bucolic fields above Kailua Bay, the artsy town of Holualoa is only 4 miles from Kailua-Kona. Each guest room is named for its decorating theme: Tahiti Suite, Bali Room, Oriental Room, and Polynesian Room. Constructed in 1978, the 5,000-square-foot inn features a rooftop gazebo. *Box 222, Holualoa 96725, tel. 808/324–1121. 3 rooms and 1 suite. Facilities: pool, hot tub, Ping-Pong and pool tables. MC, V. Moderate.*

Mango Cottage Bed and Breakfast. Tucked away in peaceful coffee country minutes above Kailua-Kona, the house has a wide veranda with a view of the ocean, and a large private pool in the front yard, which is lush with exotic plantings. Each of three rooms is highlighted with antiques. One suite has a big four-poster bed romantically draped in mosquito netting; adjoining it is a sitting room and a big bathroom with a deep furo tub, separate shower, and bidet. Another bedroom has an antique wicker bed, while the third bedroom has a separate entrance at the back of the house. Breakfast and wine and cheese service are included. *Box 5620, Kailua-Kona 96745, tel. 808/326–7220. 3 rooms with bath. Facilities: pool. No credit cards. Moderate.*

Manago Hotel. You'll get a great view high above the Kona coast in the newer wing of this older but clean family-run hostelry. The rooms are reminiscent of a mainland motel, except for one—a Japanese-style room with *tatami* (sleeping mats) instead of beds and a *furo* (deep bathtub), which the proprietor has kept in remembrance of his grandparents, who built the main hotel in 1917. If you seek something unusual, ask for this room; otherwise, request a room in the newer wing, as those in the main building share bathrooms. Large groups can arrange a Japanese dinner (leave your shoes at the door and sit on the floor) in a special dining room. *Box 145, Captain Cook 96704, tel. 808/323-2642. 42 rooms with bath in the newer wing. Facilities: restaurant, bar, free parking, shared TV. MC, V. Inexpensive.*

Volcano/ South Point

Sea Mountain at Punaluu. Avid golfers will enjoy the spacious Colony One condominiums, bordered on one side by the ocean and on the other by fairways. Units are not ultraplush but have a country feel, with comfortable wicker and rattan furnishings and complete kitchens. Owned by C. Brewer (the same company that planted all the macadamia orchards in the area), the property includes the Aspen Institute, a think-tank retreat. *Box 70, Pahala 96777, tel. 808/928-8301 or 800/367-8047, ext. 145. 27 rental units. Facilities: pool, nearby Broiler Restaurant and Punaluu Black Sands Restaurant, cocktail lounge, tennis courts, golf course, meeting rooms, free parking, weekly maid service. 2-day minimum stay. MC, V. Moderate-Expensive.*

Kilauea Lodge. A mile from the Volcanoes National Park entrance, this is possibly the most romantically appealing place to stay in the area. Remodeled and opened in April 1988, the lodge has four rooms and a cabin, each with a private bath and a fireplace; they are slickly decorated to reflect a theme. Kimura has oriental touches, while Noekolo, Paina, and Hapuu have a Hawaiian ambience. Seven new rooms which share a fireplace in a common sitting room were constructed in 1990. Set amid tree ferns and forests, the lodge offers cool mountain air and opportunities for brisk walks along the peaceful back roads of Volcano. A country-style restaurant, also with a fireplace, has earned a reputation for good food. A big breakfast is included in the price of the room. *Box 116, Volcano Village 96785, tel. 808/967-7366. 11 rooms and a cabin with bath. Facilities: restaurant, fireplaces, near Kilauea General Store, Volcano Golf Course. AE, MC, V. Moderate.*

Volcano House. The charm of the Volcano House is its location at the edge of Kilauea Caldera, so if you choose to stay, plan on paying a bit extra to book one of the rooms with a crater view. Furnished with green shag rugs and period koa furniture, the simple rooms are clean, with decent beds. Dinner at the Ka Ohelo Room can stir romance, as can a walk in the cool, crisp air, topped off with a nightcap sipped while nestling in commodious leather chairs by the ohia-wood fire in the lobby's stone fireplace. *Box 53, Hawaii Volcanoes National Park 96718-0053, tel. 808/967-7321. 38 rooms. Facilities: restaurant, bar, natural volcanic sauna, Volcano Golf Course. AE, CB, DC, MC, V. Moderate.*

Volcano Vacation. This luxury two-bedroom, one-bath cottage near the entrance to Volcanoes National Park is a cool, quiet escape for golfers who want to play at Volcano or Sea Mountain or for nature lovers who like to hike, pick ohelo berries, and bird watch. *Box 608, Kailua-Kona 96745, tel. 808/335-7708. Facili-*

ties: sauna, fireplace, kitchen, washer/dryer. No credit cards. Moderate.

My Island Bed and Breakfast. Gordon and JoAnn Morse opened their historic three-story, 100-year-old house to visitors four years ago. The house is the oldest in Volcano, built in 1886 by the Lyman missionary family (Hilo has the Lyman Museum). Three rooms are available in the house (one sleeps up to six), and you will definitely want a tour with the genial host. However, if you seek privacy and a brand-new, uncluttered haven, you might be happier in either the newly opened studio apartment with a kitchenette or in one of two new studios that are separate from the house. A full breakfast is included. *Box 100, Volcano 96785, tel. 808/967–7216. 6 rooms and studios. No credit cards. Inexpensive.*

Shirakawa Motel. In the remote Kau District, midway between Kona and Hilo near Naalehu, the southernmost town in the United States, this bare, basic, and clean motel has been run by the same family since 1921. Families can get connecting units with cooking facilities, though there are two drive-in restaurants and Elsie's Fountain Service in town. *Box 467, Naalehu 96772, tel. 808/929–7462. 13 double rooms, 4 with kitchenettes. Facilities: shower stalls. No credit cards. Inexpensive.*

Volcano Bed and Breakfast. Twelve years ago, Jim and Sandy Pedersen bought their 1930s-vintage house, about a mile from the park entrance, but they waited to complete extensive rebuilding and remodeling before opening their doors to guests in June 1988. The Pedersens live on the ground level of the three-story house, which has its main entrance on the second level, where there is a sun room, living room, dining room, fireplace, and one bedroom. A bathroom is shared with two other bedrooms on the third level. *Box 22, Volcano 96785, tel. 808/967–7779. 3 double rooms. Facilities: continental breakfast, bicycles, shared TV, VCR, piano. MC, V. Inexpensive.*

Waimea-Kamuela

Kamuela Inn B&B. You might choose to spend a night in Waimea-Kamuela just to stay at this nicely decorated country inn. Every room is attractively designed, but the penthouse suite, which sleeps six, is the pièce de résistance, with its own fireplace, sunset lanai, and full kitchen with microwave. Continental breakfast is served at the cheery breakfast lanai. The inn has a peaceful, lush, country setting, yet it's near shops, a theater, restaurants, and a museum. *Box 1994, Kamuela 96743, tel. 808/885–4243. 21 rooms. Facilities: private baths, pay phone in office, breakfast, free parking. AE, DC, MC, V. Moderate–Expensive.*

Parker Ranch Lodge. In cool up-country, the lodge has rustic rooms that look out onto green pastures. Each room has a kitchenette and a heater. The lodge is suitable for an overnight stay, but you wouldn't particularly want to spend a 10-day honeymoon here. *Box 458, Kamuela 96743, tel. 808/885–4100. 20 rooms. Facilities: meeting room, free parking. AE, MC, V. Moderate.*

The Arts

Artwork

Big Island residents rank second to none in artistic creativity, as becomes apparent by the number of galleries tucked in out-of-the-way places *(see* Shopping, above). Two hamlets are especially noted for their art communities. Just up-country of Kailua, the little town of Holualoa, on Highway 180, is a nest of artists, possibly because many years ago a California couple, Bob and Carol Rogers, moved to town and opened the **Kona Arts Center** in an old coffee mill. To this day they give classes, and their doors are open to curious drop-in visitors or aspiring students. Classes at the Kona Arts Center were what originally encouraged Hiroki Morinoue, who then studied in California and Japan and returned to Holualoa to open his own gallery, **Studio 7** (tel. 808/324–1335), a half block from the Kona Arts Center. You'll also want to investigate the **Little Gallery** (in an old church across the street from the Kona Arts Center), **Kim Starr's Gallery** (tel. 808/324–1769), and **Hale o Kula Goldsmith Gallery** (tel. 808/324–1688).

In Waimea, the **Waimea Arts Council** (Box 1818, Kamuela 96743, tel. 808/885–7671 or 808/969–2400) is dedicated to promoting the arts in Waimea, Hamakua, Kohala, and Waikoloa. The council sponsors free *kaha ki'is* (one-man shows) at the Art Center Gallery, located in the old fire station near the stoplight in Waimea (open Tues., Thurs., Sat. 10–2).

When it comes to art for viewing, three collections deserve mention. **Puuopelu,** the private home of Parker Ranch owner Richard Smart, is open for public viewing of his vast collection of paintings, Venetian glass, antique Chinese vases, and sculpture *(see* Guided Tours, above). For guests, the **Mauna Kea Beach Hotel** (tel. 808/882–7222) conducts free tours of its Pacific Rim collection on Sundays and Wednesdays at 10:30. The **Hyatt Regency Waikoloa** (tel. 808/885–1234) also offers free tours of its vast art collection for those who make reservations with the Aloha Services desk in the lobby.

Hula

For dance lovers, the biggest wingding of the year is the **Merrie Monarch Festival** (400 Hualani, Apt. 8-279, Hilo 96270, tel. 808/935–9168), staged in Hilo during the first week in April. Hula halau (schools) converge on the town to honor King David Kalakaua, Hawaii's last king, in a dance competition that names the best male, female, group, and so on. The Waiakea Villas Hotel *(see* Lodging, above) recently became the headquarters for the dancers; if you want to stay anywhere in Hilo, or even get tickets for the competition, it is best to make reservations as much as a year in advance.

Film

When you ask about cultural outings on the Big Island, you're just as likely to get directions to the nearest movie theater as anyplace else:

Kailua-Kona Hualalai Theaters 1, 2, and 3 (Hualalai Center, Kuakini Hwy. and Hualalai St., tel. 808/329–6641) and **World Square Theater** (Kona Marketplace, 75-5719 Alii Dr., tel. 808/329–4070).

Hilo Prince Kuhio Theaters 1 and 2 (Prince Kuhio Plaza, 111 E. Puainako Ave., tel. 808/959–4595) and **Waiakea Theaters 1, 2, and 3** (Waiakea Kai Shopping Plaza, 88 Kanoelehua Ave., tel. 808/935–9747).

Honokaa	**Honokaa People's Theater** (Hwy. 240, tel. 808/775–0629).
Pahoa	The **Akebono Theater** (on Hwy. 130, tel. 808/965–9943) shows occasional special-engagement movies, such as surfing films. Otherwise, the theater is used as a community center.

Theater

For legitimate theater, the little town of Waimea is your best bet. The **Kihulu Theater Foundation** (Kamuela, tel. 808/885–6017) produces plays and imports entertainment on a fairly regular basis. Nearer the resort areas, if you're dying to see a play, check with the **Aloha Community Players** (Aloha Theatre Café, Hwy. 11, Kainaliu, tel. 808/322–9924) for its next production.

Nightlife

Clubs and Cabarets

If you're the kind of person who doesn't come alive until after dark, you're going to be pretty lonely on the Big Island. In Hilo, the streets roll up at dusk. You can kick up your heels at only two places in town.

Reflections Restaurant (101 Aupuni St., tel. 808/935–8501) offers dancing to "oldies, goodies, and the Top 40" rendered by a small band, the Rainbow Connection, Wednesday through Saturday. At the Naniloa Hotel, the **Polynesian Room** (93 Banyan Dr., tel. 808/909–3333) has dance music on the weekends, which sometimes attracts a vocal local crowd.

Even on the visitor-oriented Kona–Kohala coast, there's not a lot doing after dark. Blame it on the plantation heritage (people did their cane-raising in the morning) or the fact that life is lived to the fullest during the daylight hours, but it has taken a newcomer to turn on the bright lights. The hottest place—actually half an hour out of town—is **Spats Disco,** at the Hyatt Regency Waikoloa (1 Waikoloa Rd., off Queen Kaahumanu Hwy., tel. 808/885–5737). If you aren't a guest or haven't eaten in a hotel restaurant, the $10 cover charge for this high-energy Toulouse-Lautrec–themed restaurant could break your party spirit. In Kailua, the **Eclipse Restaurant** (75-5711 Kuakini Hwy., tel. 808/329–4686) turns disco at 10 PM, except on Sundays, when a big-band sound is featured. Earlier in the evening, this is a pleasant place to dine, with continental cuisine and attentive service for about $15–$20 per person. At Kamehameha Square, behind the Hotel King Kamehameha on Kuakini Highway, the Poo Ping II Thai Restaurant transforms into the **Tech Disco** (755626 Kuakini Hwy., tel. 808/329–0010) every night at 10 PM. This casual disco has two DJs. Collared shirts and shoes are required Friday, Saturday, and Sunday nights when a $3 cover charge is assessed.

Dinner Cruise

Captain Bean's Kona Voyagers is the ever-popular standby in sunset dinner cruises. You can't miss it. As the sun sets in Kailua, look out over the water and you'll see a big, gaudy, orange-and-brown boat with distinctive orange sails. This cruise is corny, and you would get a better full-course dinner in a restaurant for less, but it's an experience. *74–5626 Alapapa St., B–17, Kailua-Kona 96740, tel. 808/329–2955. Cost: $42, adults only, for 5:15 sail with dinner, entertainment, and open bar.*

Luaus and Polynesian Revues

Four luaus are recommended in the Kohala coast and Waikoloa area:

The **Hyatt Regency Waikoloa** seats 750 outdoors at the Kamehameha Court for its "Legends of Polynesia" show, which features a buffet with samplings of Hawaiian food, as well as fish, beef, and chicken to appeal to all tastes, and two cocktails. *1 Waikoloa Beach Resort, Kohala Coast 96734, tel. 808/885–1234. Cost: $46 adults, $24 children 5–12. Mon., Wed., Fri. from 6 PM.*

Everybody knows **Kona Village Resort** has the best luau of the Big Island resorts, if you are judging by authenticity, atmosphere, and attitude—and they don't even use too much salt in the seasoning. Mainland taste buds might reject some items, such as *opihi* (a limpet considered a chewy delicacy in Hawaii that sells for about $24 a pound), but don't worry, there's plenty to appeal to everyone. A Polynesian show on a stage over a lagoon creates magic. *7 mi north of Ke-ahole Airport, off Queen Kaahumanu Hwy.; Box 1299, Kapulehu-Kona 96745, tel. 808/325–5555. Cost: $49 adults, $24.50 children 6–12. Fri. from 6:15 PM.*

Gourmet magazine called the **Mauna Kea Beach Resort's** Tuesday *pa'ina* (luau) "a Hawaiian feast elevated to haute cuisine." The luau food includes the regular kalua (roasted) pig, and the bar is open. *Half hour north of Ke-ahole Airport off Queen Kaahumanu Hwy., near Kawaihae; 1 Mauna Kea Dr., Kohala Coast 96743, tel. 808/882–7222. Cost: free for guests. $50 for nonguests, $29 children 3–8. Tues. 6 PM.*

The **Royal Waikoloan** does a nice job with its Sunday-night luau at the oceanside Volcano Grounds, where the "Back to Hawaii" theme showcases a local hula halau (dance school) presenting the entertainment and island artisans demonstrating and selling their products. *Box 5000, Waikoloa Rd., Kohala Coast 96743, tel. 808/885–6789. Cost: $40 adults, $26 children 4–12. Sun. 6–9 PM.*

In Kailua, two luaus fill the bill, with Polynesian entertainment, an *imu* ceremony (placing and removing the pig from the underground oven), pageantry, and an open bar:

Hotel King Kamehameha. *75-5660 Palani Rd., Kailua-Kona 96740, tel. 808/329–2911. Cost: $39.50 adults, $24 children under 13. Tues., Thurs., Sun. at 6 PM.*

The **Kona Hilton Beach and Tennis Resort** also lights luau torches three times a week. *Alii Dr., Box 1179, Kailua-Kona 96745, tel. 808/329–3111, ext. 4. Cost: $39 adults, $23 children under 13. Mon., Wed., Fri. at 6 PM.*

5 Maui

by Linda Kephart

A resident of Honolulu, Linda Kephart has edited Discover Hawaii, *a trade magazine, and has written articles for* Hawaii Business, Aloha, RSVP, Modern Bride, *and* Pleasant Hawaii.

Maui, say the locals, is *no ka oi*—the best, the most, the top of the heap. To those who know Maui well, there's good reason for the superlatives. The second-largest island in the Hawaiian chain, Maui has made an international name for itself with its tropical allure, heady nightlife, and miles of perfect-tan beaches. Maui magic weaves a spell over the 2 million people who visit its shores each year and leaves them wanting more. Often visitors decide to return for good.

In many ways, Maui comes by its admirable reputation honestly. The island's 729 square miles contain Haleakala, a 10,023-foot dormant volcano whose misty summit beckons the adventurous; several villages where Hawaiian is still spoken; more millionaires per capita than nearly anywhere else in the world; three major resort destinations that have set new standards for luxury; Lahaina, an old whaling port that still serves as the island's commercial crossroads; and more than 80,000 residents who work, play, and live on what they fondly call the Valley Isle.

Maui residents have quite a bit to do with their island's successful tourism story. Some 15 years ago, savvy marketers on Maui saw a way to increase their sleepy island's economy by positioning it as an island apart. Maui was tired of settling for its meager 50,000 or so visitors each year and decided it didn't want to be one of the gang anymore. So community leaders started advertising and promoting their Valley Isle separately from the rest of the state. They nicknamed West Maui "the Golf Coast," luring in heavyweight tournaments that, in turn, would bring more visitors. They went after the upscale visitor, renovating their finest hotels to accommodate a clientele that would pay more for the best. And they became the state's condominium expert, so that condos no longer meant second-best accommodations. Maui's visitor count swelled, putting it far ahead of that of the other Neighbor Islands.

That quick growth has led to its share of problems. During the busy seasons—from Christmas to Easter and then again during the summer—West Maui can be overly crowded. Although the County of Maui has seen success in its attempts to widen the two-lane road that connects Lahaina and Kaanapali, the stop-and-go traffic during rush hour reminds some visitors of what they face at home. It's not that residents aren't trying to do something about it—the Kapalua–West Maui Airport, with its free shuttle to and from Kaanapali, has alleviated some of the heavy island-circling traffic.

The heady explosion of visitors seeking out the Valley Isle has also created a large number of businesses looking to make a fast buck from the high-spending segment. Most of the time, the effect is harmless: Lahaina could easily be called the T-shirt capital of the Pacific (in close competition with Waikiki), and the island has perhaps too many art galleries and cruise-boat companies for its own good. As in other popular travel destinations, the opportunity to make money from tourists in Maui has produced its fair share of schlock.

But then consider Maui's natural resources. The island is made up of two volcanoes, one now extinct and the other dormant, that both erupted many years ago and joined into one island. The resulting depression between the two is what gives Maui its nickname, the Valley Isle. West Maui's 5,788-foot Puu Kukui was the first volcano to form, a distinction that gives the area's mountainous topography a more weathered look. Rainbows seem to grow wild over this terrain as gentle mists move quietly from one end of the long mountain chain to the other. Sugarcane seems to give the rocky region its life, with its green stalks moving in the trade winds born near the summit.

The Valley Isle's second volcano is the 10,023-foot Haleakala, a mountain so enormous that its lava filled in the gap between the two volcanoes. You can't miss Haleakala (House of the Sun), a spectacle that rises to the east, often hiding in the clouds that cover its peak. To the Hawaiians, Haleakala is holy, and it's easy to see why. It's a mammoth mountain, and if you hike its slopes or peer into one of its craters, you'll witness an impressive variety of nature. Desertlike terrain butted up against tropical forests. Dew-dripping ferns a few steps from the surface of the moon. Spiked, alien plants poking their heads out of the soil right near the most elegant and fragrant flowers.

In fact, the island's volcanic history gives Maui much of its beauty. Rich red soil lines the roads around the island— *becoming* the roads in some parts. That same earth has provided fertile sowing grounds for the sugarcane that has for years covered the island's hills. As the deep blue of ocean and sky mingle with the red and green of Maui's land, it looks as if an artist had been busy painting the scenery with his favorite colors. Indeed, visual artists love Maui. Maybe it's the natural inspiration; maybe it's the slower pace, so conducive to creativity.

Farmers also appreciate the Valley Isle. On the slopes of Haleakala, the volcanic miracle has wrought agricultural wonders, luring those with a penchant for peat moss to plant and watch the lush results. Sweetly scented flowers bloom large and healthy, destined later to adorn a happy brow or become a lovely lei. Grapes cultivated on Haleakala's slopes ripen evenly and deliciously, then are squeezed for wine and champagne. Horses graze languidly on rolling meadows of the best Upcountry grasses, while jacaranda trees dot the hillsides with spurts of luscious lavender. As the big brute of a volcano slides east and becomes the town of Hana, the rains that lavishly fall there turn the soil into a jungle. Ferns take over the forest, waterfalls cascade down the crags, and moss becomes the island's carpeting.

Distances are not great on Maui, and most points of interest are accessible by paved roads; yet sometimes the awesome terrain forces travelers to sit back and take their time, making a miniadventure out of a drive of a relatively short distance. The 55 miles from Kahului to Hana along the legendary serpentine Hana Highway—a trip rewarded by the sight of ancient taro patches, the fluttering of red petals from African tulip trees, and white water cascading for hundreds of feet past amazingly green ferns and mosses—can take two to three hours. The 38 miles from Kahului to the top of Haleakala—the most steeply ascending auto route in the world—require about two hours.

By all means, make the effort. Although a fantastic time can be had simply by bronzing on the silky-soft, white-sand beaches, the wonder of Maui is that much, much more awaits your discovery. Don't be surprised if quite a few of your fantasies are actually fulfilled. The Valley Isle hates to let anyone down.

Essential Information

Arriving and Departing by Plane

Airports   Maui's major airport, in Kahului, at the center of the island, is currently undergoing a $100-million, 10-year renovation, which began in 1982. Its new terminal won't open until later this year, so for now, the place continues to seem a bit cramped. While small, however, **Kahului Airport** (tel. 808/877–6431) is efficient and easy to navigate. Its major disadvantage is its distance from the major resort destinations in West Maui and Wailea. It will take you about an hour, with traffic in your favor, to get to a hotel in West Maui and about 20 to 30 minutes to go to Wailea. However, Kahului is the only airport on Maui that has direct service from the mainland.

If you're staying in West Maui, you might be better off flying into **Kapalua–West Maui Airport** (tel. 808/669–0228), an $8.5-million facility that opened in 1987. The only way to get to the Kapalua–West Maui Airport is on an interisland flight, however, since the short runway allows only small planes to land there. The little airport is set in the midst of a pineapple field with a terrific view of the ocean far below and provides one of the most pleasant ways to arrive on the Valley Isle. It was built by locally based carrier Hawaiian Air, which years ago had purchased small planes, giving it exclusive rights in West Maui. Before long, however, competitor Aloha Airlines figured out a way to fly into the Kapalua facility: It simply purchased commuter carrier Princeville Airways—which already flew the requisite-size prop planes—and renamed it Aloha IslandAir. Several major rental-car companies have desks right inside the terminal. Shuttles also run between the airport and the Kaanapali and Kapalua resorts.

The only other airport on Maui is **Hana Airport** (tel. 808/248–8208), which is really not much more than a landing strip. Only commuter Aloha IslandAir flies there, landing about once an hour. When there's no flight, the tiny terminal usually stands eerily empty, with no gate agents, ticket takers, or other people in sight. If you're staying at the Hotel Hana-Maui, your flight will be met; if you've reserved a rental car, the agent will usually know your arrival time and meet you. Otherwise you can call **Dollar Rent A Car** to pick you up (tel. 808/248–8237).

Flights from the Mainland United States   **United Airlines** (tel. 800/241–6522) flies directly to Kahului from Los Angeles, Chicago, Denver, Philadelphia, and San Francisco. **American Airlines** (tel. 800/433–7300) also flies into Kahului, with one stop in Honolulu, from Los Angeles, Chicago, Detroit, Houston, New York, and Dallas. **Delta** (tel. 800/221–1212) has through service to Maui daily from Salt Lake City, Atlanta, Dallas, and Los Angeles.

Maui is part of the world's most isolated chain of islands, so even if you fly directly to the Valley Isle, be prepared for a lengthy flight. From the West Coast, Maui is about 5 hours; from the Midwest, expect about an 8-hour flight; and coming from the East Coast will take about 10 hours. If you have to connect with an interisland flight in Honolulu, add at least another hour.

Maui is two hours behind Los Angeles, three hours behind Salt Lake City, four hours behind Chicago, and five hours behind New York. Hawaii doesn't turn back its clocks for daylight savings time, however, so add an extra hour to the time difference during the summer.

Flights from Honolulu
In addition, **Continental** (tel. 800/525-0280), **Hawaiian** (tel. 800/367-5320), **Northwest** (tel. 800/225-2525), **America West** (tel. 800/247-5692), **Pan Am** (tel. 800/221-1111), and **TWA** (tel. 800/221-2000) fly from the mainland to Honolulu, where Maui-bound passengers can connect with a 20- to 30-minute interisland flight. Interisland flights generally run about $50 one-way between Honolulu and Maui and are available many times each day from **Hawaiian Airlines** (tel. 800/367-5320), **Aloha Airlines** (tel. 800/367-5250), and **Discovery Airways** (tel. 808/946-1500). In fact, Maui is the most visited of the Neighbor Islands and therefore the easiest to connect to on an interisland flight. Commuter carrier **Aloha IslandAir** (tel. 800/323-3345) also makes the trip each day for about $55 one-way. Flying a commuter carrier can take a few minutes longer, since the planes are generally small prop planes. Flights on all carriers usually stop around 8 PM and begin again at about 6:30 the next morning.

Between the Airport and Your Destination
By Bus/Shuttle
If you're staying at the Kaanapali Beach Resort and fly into the Kapalua–West Maui Airport, you can take advantage of the resort's free shuttle and go back to the airport later to pick up your car. During daylight hours, the shuttle passes through the airport at regular intervals. Likewise, a **Grayline-Maui** bus (tel. 808/877-5507) operates between Kahului and Kaanapali every hour between 7 AM and 5 PM. If you book the Hotel Hana-Maui, the charge for pickup at Hana Airport is included in the rate.

By Taxi
You could also opt for a taxi. Maui has ever more than two dozen taxi companies, and they make frequent passes through the airport. If you don't see a cab, you can call **Yellow Cab** (tel. 808/877-7000) or **La Bella Taxi** (tel. 808/242-8011) for islandwide service from the airport, or **Kihei Taxi** (tel. 808/879-3000) if you're staying in the Kihei, Wailea, or Makena areas. Charges from Kahului Airport to Kaanapali run about $35; to Wailea, about $20; and to Lahaina, about $30.

By Car
Frankly, the best way to get from the airport to your destination is in your own rental car. You're going to need it for the rest of the trip; you might as well get it right away. Most major car-rental companies have conveniently located desks at each airport (*see* Getting Around, below).

Arriving and Departing by Ship

From Honolulu
Approaching the Valley Isle from the deck of a ship is a great orientation. Watching the land loom ever larger conjures up the same kinds of feelings the early Polynesians probably had on their first voyage—except they didn't get the kind of lavish treatment those on board a luxury cruise ship routinely receive. If this is an option that appeals to you, you can book passage through **American Hawaii Cruises** (550 Kearny St., San Francisco, CA 94108, tel. 800/765-7000), which offers seven-day interisland cruises departing from Honolulu on the SS *Constitution* and the SS *Independence*. Both have been renovated.

Getting Around

By Car
Driving

Maui has no major public transportation, unlike Oahu, where you can traverse the entire island and leave the driving to someone else for 60¢. Unless you want to stay in one place for your entire Maui vacation—or rely on a system of shuttles between hotels and selected shopping areas—you'll need a car.

Once you get your auto, the driving is fairly easy. The stretch between Kahului and Wailea is the best road on the island, a four-lane wonder that sees little traffic. In West Maui, constant improvements make the driving situation better all the time; what was once a rush-hour nightmare has become a fairly pleasant three-lane highway. If you're going to attempt the dirt roads between Kapalua and Wailuku or from Hana to Makena, you'll need a four-wheel-drive vehicle, but be forewarned: Rental-car companies prohibit travel off the pavement, so if you break down, you're on your own for repairs. The only other difficult road on Maui is the 56 miles from Kahului to Hana, which includes more twists and turns than a person can count. Take it slow and you should have no problems.

Rental Cars

During peak seasons—summer and Christmas through February—be sure to reserve your car well ahead of time. Although you'll generally pay a higher price in the peak seasons, you'll find Maui one of the cheapest U.S. destinations for renting an auto. Expect to pay about $20 a day for a compact car from one of the major companies. You can get an even more inexpensive deal from one of the locally owned budget companies. For these, you'll probably have to call for a shuttle from the airport since they often don't have rental desks there. On Maui, nearly all car rentals include unlimited mileage.

Budget (tel. 800/527–0707), **Dollar** (tel. 800/367–7006), and **Hertz** (tel. 800/654–8200) have desks at the Kapalua–West Maui Airport, while **Thrifty** (tel. 800/367–2277) and **Tropical** (tel. 800/367–5140) are nearby. All the above, plus **Avis** (tel. 800/331–1212), **National** (tel. 800/CAR–RENT), **Robert's** (tel. 808/947–3939), and **United** (tel. 800/657–7797), have desks at Maui's major airport, in Kahului. In addition, quite a few locally owned companies rent cars on Maui, including **Payless Car Rental** (tel. 800/345–5230), **Rent-A-Jeep** (tel. 808/877–6626), and **Trans-Maui** (tel. 800/367–5228). They are near the Kahului Airport and will pick you up only from there.

By Shuttle

If you're staying in the right hotel or condo, there are a few shuttles that can get you around the area. The **Kaanapali–Lahaina Shuttle** runs daily from the Royal Lahaina Hotel in Kaanapali to the Wharf Shopping Center in Lahaina every half hour between 8 AM and 10:25 PM with stops at all Kaanapali hotels. The cost is $1.50. The **Kaanapali Shuttle** runs within the resort between 7 AM and 11 PM and stops automatically at all hotels and at condos when requested. It also goes to and from Lahaina at 55-minute intervals. It's free. All Kaanapali hotels have copies of schedules, or you can call the Kaanapali Beach Operators Association (tel. 808/661–3271). The free **Aston Hotels Shuttle** in the Kaanapali area runs from 8 AM to 6 PM for guests who want to go to the Whalers Village Shopping Center and Lahaina. You can get schedules at Aston hotel desks. The **Wailea Shuttle** and the **Kapalua Shuttle** run within their respective resorts and are free; schedules are available throughout each resort.

By Taxi For short hops between hotels and restaurants, this can be a convenient way to go, but you'll have to call ahead. Even busy West Maui doesn't have curbside taxi service. **West Maui Taxi** (761 Kumukahi, Lahaina, tel. 808/667–2605) and **Yellow Cab of Maui** (Kahului Airport, tel. 808/877–7000) both service the entire island, but you'd be smart to consider using them just for the areas where they're located. **Alii Cab** (475 Kuai Pl., Lahaina, tel. 808/661–3688) specializes in West Maui, while **Kihei Taxi** (Kihei, tel. 808/879–3000) serves Central Maui.

By Limousine **Arthur's Limousine Service** (Box 11865, Lahaina 96761, tel. 800/345–4667) provides a chauffeured superstretch Lincoln complete with two TVs, three bars, and two sunroofs for $60 per hour. **Inlanda Inc.** (91 Alo Alo Pl., Lahaina 96761, tel. 808/669–7800) has Cadillacs and Lincolns from $48 an hour. Both companies are based in Lahaina but serve the entire island. There's a minimum time requirement—usually two hours—but the companies have put together personalized sightseeing tours just to make it easy for you.

By Moped/ Motorcycle **AA Go Go Bike Hawaii** (30-B Halawai Dr. #5, Lahaina, tel. 808/661–3063) rents mopeds from $20 a day. Mopeds from **A&B Moped Rental** (3481 Lower Honoapiilani Hwy., Lahaina, tel. 808/669–0027) go for about $25. You can get bicycles at AA Go Go for $10 to $20. Visitors in West Maui should find it especially convenient to rent a motorized two-wheeler, since both of these companies are based there. Be especially careful navigating the roads on Maui, since there are no designated bicycle or moped lanes.

Important Addresses and Numbers

Tourist Information **Maui Visitors Bureau** (380 Dairy Rd., Kahului 96733, in Kahului's industrial district, tel. 808/871–8691).
Maui Chamber of Commerce (26 Puunene Ave., Kahului 96732, also in the industrial district, tel. 808/871–7711).

Emergencies **Police, fire,** or **ambulance** (tel. 911).

Doctors **Doctors on Call** (Hyatt Regency Maui-Napili Tower #1, Kaanapali, tel. 808/667–7676) and **Maui Physicians** (3600 Lower Honoapiilani Rd., Lahaina, tel. 808/669–9600) are doctors serving West Maui. Another walk-in clinic at **Whalers Village** (2435 Kaanapali Pkwy., Suite H-7, Kaanapali, tel. 808/667–9721) also serves West Maui. Created by two doctors in 1980 to treat tourists, the clinic is open daily 8 AM–10 PM. **Kihei Clinic** and **Wailea Medical Services** (1993 S. Kihei Rd., Kihei, tel. 808/879–1440 or 808/879–7447) are based in the more central part of the Valley Isle. All of the above groups are geared toward working with visitors.

Hospitals **Hana Medical Center** (Hana Hwy., Hana, tel. 808/248–8294).

Kula Hospital (204 Kula Hwy., Kula, tel. 808/878–1221).

Maui Memorial Hospital (221 Mahalani, Wailuku, tel. 808/244–9056).

Pharmacies Maui has no 24-hour pharmacies but several where you can get prescriptions filled during daylight hours. The least expensive are the island's two **Longs Drug Stores** (Maui Mall, corner of

Kaahumanu and Puunene aves., Kahului, tel. 808/877–0068; Lahaina Cannery Shopping Center, Honoapiilani Hwy., tel. 808/667–4390; both open daily, 8:30 AM–9 PM). **Kihei Drug** is in the Kihei Town Center (1881 S. Kihei Rd., Kihei, tel. 808/879–1915; open weekdays 8:30–7, Saturday 8:30–5:30, Sunday 10–3).

Road Service On Maui, the one AAA garage that offers 24-hour islandwide service is **Sunset Towing** (Bldg. 30, Halawai Rd., Kaanapali, tel. 808/667–7048). It specializes in serving West Maui and Kahului but will travel anywhere on Maui with a tow truck.

Grocers Three major groceries are open 24 hours a day. **Safeway,** at the Lahaina Cannery Shopping Center (Honoapiilani Hwy., Lahaina, tel. 808/667–4392), serves West Maui, while **Foodland,** in the Kihei Town Center (1881 S. Kihei Rd., Kihei, tel. 808/879–9350), and Safeway (170 E. Kam Ave., tel. 808/877–3377) operate on the island's other side.

Weather **National Weather Service/Maui Forecast** (tel. 808/877–5111). **Haleakala Weather Forecast** (tel. 808/871–5054).

Others **Coast Guard Rescue Center** (tel. 808/244–5256). **Suicide and Crisis Center Help Line** (tel. 808/244–7407).

Opening and Closing Times

Banks on the island are generally open Monday–Thursday 8:30–3, Friday 8:30–6.

Shops are generally open seven days a week, 9–5. Shopping centers tend to stay open later (until 9 on certain days).

Guided Tours

If getting yourself oriented on an island doesn't come easily, try taking one of a variety of guided tours offered on Maui. This is a perfect opportunity to benefit from the services of an expert who can point out the sights you're most interested in and explain what it all means. Basically, you have your choice of getting oriented from the ground or from the air.

By Land **Circle Island Tour.** This is a big island to tour in one day, so several companies combine various sections of it—either Haleakala, Iao Needle, and Central Maui, or West Maui and its environs. Some stops include the historical sections of the county seat of Wailuku, while others focus on some of the best snorkeling spots. Call a selection of companies to find the tour that suits you. The cost is usually $25–$45 for adults, half that for children.
Haleakala Sunrise Tour. This tour starts before dawn so that visitors get a chance to actually make it to the top of the dormant volcano before the sun peeks over the horizon. Some companies throw in champagne to greet the sunrise. Cost of the six-hour tour: about $40.
Haleakala/Upcountry Tour. Usually a half-day excursion, this tour is offered in several versions by different companies. The trip often includes stops at a protea farm and at Tedeschi Vineyards and Winery, the only place in Hawaii where wine is made. Cost: about $40 adults, $20 children.
Hana Tour. This tour is almost always done in a van, as the winding road to Hana just doesn't provide a comfortable ride in bigger buses. Of late, Hana has so many of these one-day tours

that it seems as if there are more vans than cars on the road. Still, it's a more relaxing way to do the drive than behind the wheel of your own car. Guides decide where you stop for photos. Cost: about $60.

Tour Companies Ground-tour companies are usually statewide and have a whole fleet of vehicles. Some use air-conditioned buses, while others prefer smaller vans. Then you've got your minivans, your microbuses, and your minicoaches. The key is how many passengers each will hold. Be sure to ask how many stops you'll get on your tour, or you may be disappointed to find that all your sightseeing is done through a window.

Most of the tour guides have been in the business for years; some were born in the Islands and have taken special classes to learn more about their culture and lore. They expect a tip ($1 per person at least), but they're just as cordial without one.

There are many ground-tour companies. Here are some of the most reliable and popular ones, with their mailing addresses:

Akamai Tours (Box 395, Kahului 96732, tel. 800/922–6485) does a good job, and they're always recognizable by their bright yellow vans.
Gray Line Hawaii (273 Dairy Rd., Kahului 96732, tel. 800/367–2420 or 808/877–5507) uses air-conditioned motor coaches, limos, and vans.
No Ka Oi Scenic Tours (Box 1827, Kahului 96732, tel. 808/871–9008) specializes in a Hana tour.
Maui Fun Centers (777 S. Kihei Rd. #225, Kihei 96753, tel. 808/874–3773) offers van, bicycle, and hiking tours.
Polynesian Adventure Tours (536 Keolani Pl., Kahului 96732, tel. 808/877–4242 or 800/622–3011) has guides that keep up an amusing patter. The talk can get annoying, however, if you're more interested in the serious stuff.
Robert's Hawaii Tours (Box 247, Kahului 96732, tel. 808/871–6226) and **Trans Hawaiian Services** (3111 Castle St., Honolulu 96815, tel. 800/533–8765) are two of the largest companies in the state, but each manages to keep its tours personal.

By Air **Circle Island Tour.** Helicopter companies handle this in different ways. Some have fancy names, such as Ultimate Experience or Circle Island Deluxe. Some go for two hours or more. Cost: about $185–$200.
Hana/Haleakala Crater Tour. This takes about 90 minutes to travel inside the volcano, then down to the Hawaiian village of Hana. Some companies stop in secluded areas for refreshments, but local residents have had moderate success in getting this stopped. Cost: about $130.
West Maui Tour. Generally a 30-minute helicopter ride over Kaanapali and Lahaina. Frankly, this is not a very exciting helicopter tour. Cost: about $70–$95.

Tour Companies About eight helicopter companies regularly offer air tours over Maui. If you're at all nervous, ask about the company's safety record, although most are reliable. The best Maui operators include **Hawaii Helicopters** (Kahului Heliport, Hangar 106, Kahului 96732, tel. 808/877–3900 or 800/346–2403 from the mainland), **Maui Helicopters** (Box 1002, Kihei 96753, tel. 808/879–1601 or 800/367–8003 from the mainland), **Papillon Hawaiian Helicopters** (Box 1690, Lahaina 96761, tel. 808/669–4884 or 800/367–7095), and **South Sea Helicopters** (Kahului Airport,

Hangar 108, Kahului 96732, tel. 808/871–8844 or 800/247–5444).

Special-Interest Tours Once you have your bearings, you may want a tour that's a bit more specialized. For example, you may have a hankering for hunting but not know where to go. You might want to bike down a volcano or visit artists. Here are some tours to meet those needs:

Haleakala Downhills. It started back in 1983 with **Cruiser Bob's Original Haleakala Downhill** (505 Front St., Lahaina 96761, tel. 800/654–7717), which now has competition from **Maui Downhill Bicycle Safaris** (333 Dairy Rd., Suite 201E, Kahului 96732, tel. 800/535–2453) and **Maui Mountain Cruisers** (Box 1356, Makawao 96768, tel. 800/232–MAUI). All three companies will put you on a bicycle at the top of Haleakala and let you coast down. Safety precautions are top priority, so riders wear helmets and receive training in appropriate bicycle-bell ringing. Meals are provided. Cost: $85–$100.

Hiking Tours. Hike Maui (Box 330969, Kahului 96733, tel. 808/879–5270) is owned by naturalist Ken Schmitt, who guides some 50 different hikes himself. Prices range from $60 for a 4-mile, five-hour hike to $990 for a week-long trek with accommodations and all meals.

Horseback Tours. At least two companies on Maui now offer horseback riding that's far more appealing than the typical hour-long trudge over a boring trail with 50 other horses. Mauian Frank Levinson started **Adventures on Horseback** (Box 1771, Makawao 96768, tel. 808/242–7445) a few years back with five-hour outings into secluded parts of Maui. The tours traverse ocean cliffs on Maui's north shore, along the slopes of Haleakala, as they pass by streams, through rain forests, and near waterfalls. The $125-per-person price includes breakfast, lunch, and refreshments. **Charley's Trail Rides & Pack Trips** (c/o Kaupo Store, Kaupo 96713, tel. 808/248–8209) requires an even more stout physical nature, as the overnighters go from Kaupo—a *tiny* village nearly 20 miles past Hana—up the slopes of Haleakala to the crater. For parties of four to six, the per-person charge is $150, including meals and cabin or campsite equipment, or $125 without meals. Charges are higher for fewer people.

Hunting Adventures of Maui (645-B Kaupakalua Rd., Haiku 96708, tel. 808/572–8214). This is a guided excursion on more than 100,000 acres of private ranch land on Maui, a "fair chase" hunt for Spanish mountain goats and wild boar. Maui has a year-round hunting season, so this tour is always available. Cost: $400 for the first person, $150 for each additional hunter. Cost includes transportation, food, beverages, clothing, boots, packs, and meat storage and packing for shipping. Nonhunters can accompany the tour free.

Maui Art Tours (Box 1058, Makawao 96768, tel. 808/572–8374). Maui publisher Barbara Glassman produces a book every year that catalogues and pictures Maui artists and their work in exchange for an entry fee. That project has been successful, so Glassman now offers a tour that takes creative types into artists' homes for tea and conversation. Limo transportation and an elegant lunch are provided, as is the opportunity to buy art directly from the artists. This is a very enjoyable, refined tour that costs $150. Maui Art Tours will customize each tour, letting clients choose the type of art they want to see and even how many artists they want to visit.

Personal Guides **Guides of Maui** (333 Dairy Rd., Kahului 96732, tel. 800/228–6284). This is *the* best way to see Maui through the eyes of the locals. Started by Laurie Robello, who is part Hawaiian, the company now has more than a dozen guides. Your guide will come to your hotel, but then transportation is in your car, which he or she will drive. Guides of Maui tailors its tours to your particular interests—one elderly lady wanted to meet senior citizens who live on Maui, and that's exactly what she got to do. Others just want to sample life Hawaiian-style, so Guides of Maui takes them to the secret swimming holes, the hidden hot spots, and even home to meet the family. Guides of Maui charges $150 for two people all day; each additional person is $10.

Temptation Tours (RR1, Box 454, Kula 96790, tel. 808/877–8888). At the other end of the spectrum is this company, which leads you around luxuriously. Company president Dave Campbell has targeted members of the affluent older crowd who don't want to be herded into a crowded bus. He provides exclusive tours in his stretch-limo coach and specializes in full-day tours to Haleakala and Hana. Prices vary depending on the degree of customization; the average Hana tour, however, runs about $125, plus tax, per person.

Walking Tours The **Lahaina Restoration Foundation** (Baldwin Home, 696 Front St., Lahaina, tel. 808/661–3262) has published a walking-tour map for interested visitors. The map will guide you past the most historic sites of Lahaina, some renovated and some not. Highlights of the walk include the Jodo Mission, the Brig *Carthaginian II*, the Baldwin Home, and the old Court House. These are all sights you could find yourself, but the map is free, and it makes the walk easier.

Exploring

A visitor to Maui has plenty of things to see and do besides spending time on the beach. To help you organize your time, this guide divides the island into four tours—West Maui, Central Maui, Haleakala and Upcountry, and the Road to Hana (East Maui). Each tour lasts from a half day to a full day, depending on how long you spend at each stop. All tours require a car, but they include opportunities for walking.

Highlights for First-time Visitors

Alexander & Baldwin Sugar Museum, Tour 2
Baldwin Home, Tour 1
Brig *Carthaginian II*, Tour 1
Hale Hoikeike, Tour 2
Haleakala, Tour 3
Hana, Tour 4
Helani Gardens, Tour 4
Hookipa Beach, Tour 4
Iao Valley, Tour 4
Lahaina, Tour 1
Paia, Tour 4
Tedeschi Vineyards and Winery, Tour 3

Tour 1: West Maui

Numbers in the margin correspond with points of interest on the Maui map.

❶ Drive about as far north as you can on the Honoapiilani Highway (aka Highway 30), and make a left on Bay Drive at the Kapalua sign. We'll start this tour at the **Kapalua Bay Hotel** (1 Bay Dr., tel. 808/669–5656), set in a beautifully secluded location in upper West Maui. Surrounded by pineapple fields, this classy hotel was built in 1978 by Maui Land & Pineapple Company and now hosts celebrities who want to be left alone, as well as some of the world's richest folks. The Kapalua Villas are expansive condominiums on the resort property that start at $250 a night. Kapalua's shops and restaurants are some of Maui's finest, but expect to pay big bucks for whatever you purchase (*see* Shopping and Dining, below, for more details).

Back in the car, return from the hotel to Honoapiilani Highway and make a left. Drive north, and in less than a mile the road is less well-maintained. This used to be the route to Wailuku. It was never a good road, and a storm a few years back made it partly impassable. That means you may eventually have to turn back before reaching Wailuku. However, you'll discover some gorgeous photo opportunities along the road, and if you go far **❷** enough, you'll come to **Kahakuloa,** a tiny fishing village that seems lost in time. It is one of the oldest towns on Maui. Many remote villages that were similar to Kahakuloa used to be tucked away in the valleys of this area. This is the wild side of West Maui; true adventurers will find terrific snorkeling and swimming here, as well as some good hiking trails.

Kahakuloa is about as far as you can go on the "highway" that alternates between being called 30 and 340. From Kahakuloa, turn around and go back in the direction from which you came—south toward Kaanapali and Lahaina. Along the way to Kaanapali, you'll pass the beach towns of **Napili, Kahana,** and **Honokowai,** which are packed with condos and a few restaurants. Some of this area can be charming; if you wish to explore these towns, get off the upper Honoapiilani Highway and drive closer to the water.

Time Out If it's Monday or Thursday, check out the **Farmer's Market** in Kahana. County Council member Wayne Nishiki sets up his open-air fruit-and-veggie show in the parking lot at the ABC Store at 3511 Lower Honoapiilani Highway. The Farmer's Market specializes in quality produce at reasonable prices, and, of course, there's the flamboyant Nishiki himself. *Open Mon. 12:30–4:30, Thurs. 9–noon.*

❸ If you're staying at the **Kaanapali Beach Resort,** save exploring it for another day. Otherwise, you may want to see two hotels at Kaanapali, the **Hyatt Regency Maui** (200 Nohea Kai Dr., 808/661–1234) and the **Westin Maui** (2365 Kaanapali Pkwy., 808/667–2525). To reach these properties, from Kahakuloa take the third Kaanapali exit on Honoapiilani Highway (the one closest to Lahaina), then turn left on Kaanapali Parkway. Although the resort has six hotels and seven condos, the Hyatt and Westin hotels are of special interest because they were both built by Honolulu-based developer Christopher Hemmeter, whose resort projects have grown more and more opulent over the years. The Hyatt, for example, was built in 1980 at a cost of about $80 million. It has a waterfall in the swimming pool and eight more falls scattered around the property. The Westin, a $155-million makeover of the much older Maui Surf Hotel, also has waterfalls all over the place—15 at last count. Its extensive art collection, worth about $2 million, includes work from around the world, with emphasis on Asian and Pacific art.

Kaanapali Beach Resort also has some decent shopping at the **Whalers Village** (2435 Kaanapali Pkwy., tel. 808/661–4567), with such trendy mainland shops as ACA Joe, Benetton, and Esprit, as well as such Hawaiian boutiques as Blue Ginger Designs, Paradise Clothing, and Lahaina Printsellers.

❹ Back in the car, it's time to head for **Lahaina.** This little whaling town has a notorious past; there are stories of lusty whalers who met head-on with missionaries bent on saving souls. Both groups journeyed to Lahaina from New England in the early 1800s. To get oriented, take a drive down **Front Street**. At first, Lahaina might look touristy, but there's a lot that's genuine here as well. Lahaina has recently been concentrating on the renovation of its old buildings, which date from the time it was Hawaii's capital, in the 1800s. Much of the town has been designated a National Historic Landmark; further restrictions have been imposed on all new buildings, which must resemble structures built before 1920.

Numbers in the margin correspond with points of interest on the Lahaina map.

❺ One result of this reconstruction is **505 Front Street** at the southern end of Front Street, where you can park. Quaint New England–style architecture characterizes this mall, which houses small shops connected by a wooden sidewalk. It isn't as crowded as some other areas in Lahaina, probably because between here and the nearby Banyan Tree, the town turns into a sleepy residential neighborhood and some people give up before reaching the mall. A local hang-out called Sam's Pub, however, seems to lure its fair share of fun-lovers.

❻ The **Banyan Tree,** which is a short walk from 505 Front Street, was planted in 1873. It is the largest of its kind in the 50th state and provides a welcome retreat for the weary who come to sit under its awesome branches. When the sun sets each evening, mynah birds settle in for a screeching symphony (which can be **❼** an event in itself). Next to the tree is the **Court House,** which now houses two art galleries—one upstairs and one in what was an old prison in the basement. The Court House was originally built in 1859 and rebuilt in 1925. *649 Wharf St., tel. 808/661–0111. Admission free. Open daily 10–4.*

❽ About a half block northwest, you'll find what's left of a **Brick Palace** built by King Kamehameha I, as well as the four cannons he used to protect it. Actually, nothing much remains of the palace, so don't waste time looking for a building. All that's left is a space with several holes sectioned off in front of the Pioneer Inn, one of Hawaii's oldest hotels. Hawaii's first king lived only one year in the palace because his favorite wife, Kaahumanu, refused to stay there. After 70 years, it collapsed.

❾ The **Brig *Carthaginian II*** is anchored at the dock nearby and is open as a museum. It was made in Germany in the 1920s and is a replica of the type of ship that brought the missionaries around

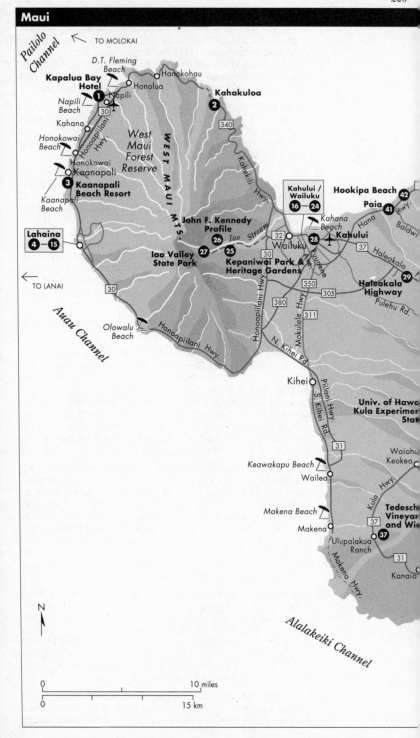

Maui

Pailolo Channel

← TO MOLOKAI

D.T. Fleming Beach

Hanokohau

Kapalua Bay Hotel ①

Honolua

Napili Beach Napili

Kahakuloa ②

Kahana

340

Honokowai Beach

West Maui Forest Reserve

Honokowai

Kaanapali

③ **Kaanapali Beach Resort**

Kaanapali Beach

WEST MAUI MTS.

Kahului / Wailuku 16 — 24

Hookipa Beach 42

Kahana Beach

Paia 41

Hwy.

Baldwi

John F. Kennedy Profile 26

Iao Stream

32

Kahului 28

Hana

37 Haleakala

Lahaina ④ — ⑮

Iao Valley State Park 27

25

Wailuku

Puunene

Haleakala Highway 29

← TO LANAI

Kepaniwai Park & Heritage Gardens

30

350

305

Pulehu Rd.

Anau Channel

Honoapiilani Hwy.

380

311

N. Kihei Rd.

Mokulele Hwy.

Olowalu Beach

30

Kihei

S. Kihei Rd.

Piilani Hwy.

Univ. of Hawa Kula Experimen Sta

Waiohu
Keokea

31

Keawakapu Beach

Wailea

Kula Hwy.

Makena Beach

Tedesch Vineyar and Win 37

Makena

37

Ulupalakua Ranch

31

Makena Hwy.

Kanaio

Alalakeiki Channel

N ↑

| 0 | | 10 miles |
| 0 | | 15 km |

PACIFIC OCEAN

Ulumalu

Rd.

43 **Twin Falls**

Huelo

Kailua

365

360

Puohokamoa
Stream

44 **45** **Kaumahina State**
Wayside Park

90

Kokomo

46 **Keanae Arboretum**

Makawao

Honomanu
Valley

47

48 Wailua

Pukulani

Keanae Overlook

49 **Wailua Lookout**

50

51 **Nahiku**

377

Waikane
Falls

Haleakala
Crater Rd.

Koolau
Forest
Reserve

360

Hana Hwy.

Waianapanapa
State Park

Park
Headquarters/
Visitor Center

Leleiwi
Overlook

Pinaau Stream

52

Helani Gardens **53**

Hotel Hana-Maui **55**

Hana

Hana Forest Reserve

38

7

378

30

31

54

36 **Kula Botanical**
Gardens

32

Halearnavu

Hasegawa's Store **56**

Kaihalulu
Beach

Kalahaku
Overlook

33

Trail

Haleakala
National Park

Hamoa

Mt. Haleakala

35

Puu Ulaula
Overlook

34

Haleakala Visitor
Center

Kaupo

Kahikinui
Forest Reserve

Trail

Muolea

57 **Oheo Gulch**

Kipahulu

31

58 **Charles Lindbergh's**
Grave

Piilani Hwy.

31

Kaupo

Alenuihaha Channel

TO HAWAII ↓

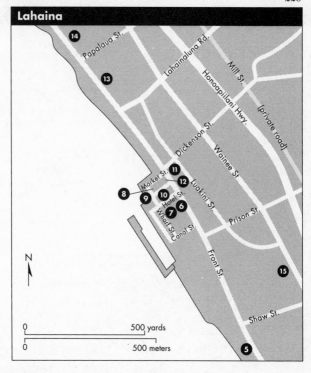

the Horn to Hawaii in the early 1800s. The Brig *Carthaginian II* is the only authentically restored square-rigged brig in the world. A small museum below deck features a film and exhibit about whaling. *At the harbor, tel. 808/661–3262. Admission: $2. Open daily 9–4:30.*

Time Out If you're in the mood for some local color, stroll into the **Pioneer Inn** (658 Wharf St., tel. 808/661–3636) for a refreshment. This hotel, built in 1920, has a few inexpensive rooms upstairs and a restaurant. The inn's ambience capitalizes on Lahaina's whaling era, during the 19th century. This is where the cruise-boat captains, fishermen, and brave tourists hang out during the afternoon. It can be fun or a little freaky, depending on how much everyone's had to drink and on your point of view.

If you walk from the *Carthaginian* to the corner of Front and Dickenson streets, you'll find the **Baldwin Home.** An early missionary to Lahaina, Ephraim Spaulding, built this plastered and whitewashed coral block home in 1834–35; in 1836 Dr. Dwight Baldwin—also a missionary—moved in with his family. The home is now run by the Lahaina Restoration Foundation and has been restored and furnished in a decor that reflects the period. You can view the living room with the family's grand piano, the dining room with the table appropriately set, the master bedroom with Dr. and Mrs. Baldwin's four-poster koa wood bed, and the boys' bedroom. Dr. Baldwin's dispensary is also on display, including his Hawaiian medical license. *696 Front St., tel. 808/661–3262. Admission: $2. Open daily 9–4:30.*

Next door is the **Master's Reading Room,** Maui's oldest building, constructed in 1833. In the early days, the ground floor was a mission's storeroom, while the reading room upstairs was for sailors. The **Lahaina Restoration Foundation** is housed in the building.

Continue north or south on **Front Street** for Lahaina's commercial side. Shops abound here; some are funky, a few are exquisite. Several little malls go back off the street, and some unique stores can be found there. Lahaina also boasts so many fine art galleries that it's occasionally referred to as SoHo West (*see* Shopping, below). At the Wharf Cinema Center (658 Front St.), you can see the **Spring House,** which was built by missionaries over a freshwater spring. The building is now home to a huge Fresnel lens once used in a local lighthouse that guided ships to Lahaina.

⓬

⓭ If you continue north on Front Street, you'll pass the **Wo Hing Society,** originally built as a temple in 1912. It now contains Chinese artifacts and a historic theater that features Thomas Edison's films of Hawaii, circa 1898. Upstairs is the only public Taoist altar on Maui. *858 Front St., tel. 808/661–3262. Admission to the temple: $1 adults, children free with their parents. Open Mon.–Sat. 9–4:30, Sun. noon–4:30.*

⓮ Head another block north and you'll find the **Seamen's Hospital,** which was built in the 1830s as a royal party house for King Kamehameha III. It was later turned over to the U.S. government, which used it as a hospital for whaling men. Now within the building, **Lahaina Printsellers** sells antique maps and charts. *1024 Front St., tel. 808/661–3262. Admission free. Open daily.*

Time Out There's nothing like watching the sun sink in the western sky while you sit near the ocean. In Lahaina, a couple of restaurants have situated their lanais right over the water. Try **Kimo's** (845 Front St., tel. 808/661–4811). Here, you can have simple food and a relaxing drink while you watch the parasailors, the cruise boats, and various water fanatics work in the last minutes of another great day.

⓯ If you're finished walking before dusk with a hankering for just one more stop, try the **Waiola Church** (535 Wainee St., tel. 808/661–4349) and the **Waiola Cemetery.** To reach the church and cemetery, walk south down Front Street, make a left onto Dickenson Street, then make a right onto Wainee Street and walk another few blocks. The cemetery is the older of the two sites, dating from the time when Kamehameha's sacred wife Queen Keopuolani died and was buried there in 1823. The church was erected next door in 1832 by Hawaiian chiefs and was originally named Ebenezer by the Queen's second husband, Governor Hoapili. It was later named Wainee, after the district in which it is located. After a few fires and some wind damage, the current structure was put up in 1953 and named Waiola Church.

Tour 2: Central Maui

*Numbers in the margin correspond with points of interest on
the Kahului-Wailuku map.*

This tour begins in **Kahului,** which looks nothing like the lush
tropical paradise most people envision when they think of Hawaii. This industrial and commercial town is home to many of
Maui's permanent residents, who find their jobs and the center
of commerce close by. Kahului was built in the early 1950s as
the answer to Alexander & Baldwin's problems. This large
company was tired of playing landlord to its many plantation
workers and sold land to a developer who promised to create affordable housing. The scheme worked, and Kahului became the
first planned city in Hawaii. Most tourists spend little time
here, merely passing through on their way to and from the airport. Kaahumanu Avenue (Highway 32) is Kahului's main
street and runs east and west.

16 Kahului does have Maui's largest shopping mall, the
Kaahumanu Center (275 Kaahumanu Ave., tel. 808/877–3369).
You might want to stop in at **Camellia Seed Shop** for what the
locals call "crack seed," a delicacy that's made from dried
fruits, nuts, and sugar. Other places to shop at Kaahumanu
Center include **Shirokiya,** a major department store brought to
Hawaii from Japan, and such American standards as Mrs.
Field's Cookies, Sears, Kay-Bee Toys, and Kinney Shoes.

17 Next take a detour to visit the **Alexander & Baldwin Sugar
Museum.** Get on Kaahumanu Avenue from the shopping center
and take a right onto Highway 350 (Puunene Ave.). Look for
the museum just off Highway 350 as you drive into the town
called Puunene (pronounced *Poo-nay-NAY*) in the direction of
Wailea. You'll be heading toward **Haleakala,** a 10,023-foot dormant volcano, which you should save most of a day to explore
(*see* Tour 3, below). Alexander & Baldwin, Maui's largest land-
owner, opened this museum in 1988 to detail the rise of
sugarcane in the Islands. Alexander & Baldwin was one of five
companies, better known as the Big Five, that spearheaded the
planting, harvesting, and marketing of the valuable agricultural product. Although Hawaiian sugar has been supplanted by
cheaper foreign versions—as well as by less costly sugar
beets—for many years, the crop was the mainstay of the Hawaiian economy.

The museum is located in a small, restored plantation-
manager's house next to the post office and the still-operating
sugar mill. At the refinery, black smoke billows up when cane is
burning; from the outside, the whole operation looks dirty and
industrial. Inside the museum, you'll find historic photos, artifacts, and documents that explain the introduction of
sugarcane to Hawaii and how plantation managers brought in
laborers from other countries, thereby changing the Islands'
ethnic mix. This fascinating exhibit is well worth your time.
*3957 Hansen Rd., Puunene, tel. 808/871–8058. Admission: $2
adults, $1 students 6–17. Open Mon.–Sat. 9:30–4:30.*

Time Out As you return to Kahului, head toward the Kaahumanu Center.
When you reach the corner of Puunene and Kaahumanu ave-
18 nues, you'll be at the **Kahului Shopping Center.** Here you'll find
Ah Fook's Super Market (tel. 808/877–3308), a geniune, local-

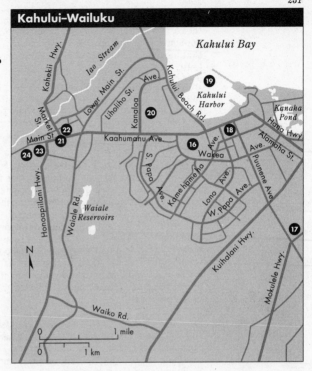

style grocery where you can also get prepared Japanese, Chinese, and Hawaiian food. There are no tables, but the shady mall offers a quiet stopping spot.

Return to Kaahumanu Avenue, head toward Wailuku, and take a right onto Kahului Beach Road. Here you can see any ships in **⑲** port at **Kahului Harbor.** This is Maui's chief port, since it's the island's only deep-draft harbor. Cruise ships call here, as do large freighters and tugboats. Surfers sometimes use this spot as a castoff to catch some good waves, but it's not a good swimming beach.

Continue on the beach road until you reach Kanaloa Avenue, **⑳** make a left and soon you'll find **Maui Zoological and Botanical Gardens.** This is a great spot for kids, since there's a small children's zoo that includes peacocks, African pygmy goats, spider monkeys, and lots more. The gardens of native Hawaiian plants actually take a much smaller role in this attraction than the name implies. *Kanaloa Ave. off Kaahumanu, tel. 808/243–7337. Admission free. Open daily 9–4.*

Press on to Wailuku by turning right from Kanaloa Avenue back onto Kaahumanu Avenue. (Kaahumanu eventually be-**㉑** comes Wailuku's Main Street.) You'll soon reach **Wailuku's Historical District,** mostly concentrated on High Street, as well as around Vineyard and Market streets. Much of the area is in the Register of Historic Places, and many of the old buildings are being preserved with their wooden facades intact. Overall, the little town is sleepy and belies its function as Maui's county seat. Wailuku is where you'll see the County Court House (on the corner of Main St. and Honoapiilani Hwy.), from which the popular Mayor Hannibal Tavares has for years run the county that includes the islands of Maui, Molokai, Lanai, and Kahoolawe.

In ancient times, Wailuku was a favored place for the inhabitants of Maui, who maintained two *heiaus* (temples) on the hills above. They used these heiaus primarily to watch for intruders, and villages grew up around the temples to support the cause. But the town really began to grow when the first missionaries arrived in the 1820s.

㉒ To get a closer look at this historical area, turn right at Market Street from Main Street, where you'll see the **Iao Theater** (68 North Market St., tel. 808/242–6969), one of Wailuku's most photographed landmarks. This charming movie house went up in Wailuku in 1927 and acted as a community gathering spot. A few years ago, several ambitious developers almost had the community convinced that the theater should be gutted and replaced with brand-new shops and offices. But then the Maui Community Theater started using it as its headquarters. The art deco–style building is now the focus of the Wailuku Main Street Program. Unless there's a play on, you can't usually get inside the theater.

Time Out Stop off at **Hazel's** (2080 Vineyard, tel. 808/244–7278). Owner Hazel Yasutomi serves no-nonsense food here—specialties like Spam and eggs, pork chops, and burgers. This is where the locals hang out to enjoy the relaxed environment. You'll see the Wailuku Grand Hotel nearby.

㉓ Next visit **Kaahumanu Church** (tel. 808/244–5189), which is on High Street around the corner from Main Street and across the way from the County Court House. It's said that Queen Kaahumanu attended services on this site in 1832 and requested that a permanent structure be erected. Builders first tried adobe, which dissolved in the rain, then stone. The present wooden structure, built in 1876, is classic New England style, with white exterior walls and striking green trim. You won't be able to see the interior, however, unless you attend Sunday services. The church features a Hawaiian service— completely in Hawaiian—each Sunday at 9 AM.

㉔ Return to Main Street and drive away from Kahului. After a few blocks, on your left, you'll see **Hale Hoikeike** (House of Display). This structure was the home of Edward and Caroline Bailey, two prominent missionaries who came to Wailuku to run the first Hawaiian girls' school on the island, the Wailuku Female Seminary; this school's function was mainly to train the girls in the "feminine arts."

Hale Hokeike's construction between 1833 and 1850 was supervised by Edward Bailey himself. The Maui Historical Society has opened a museum in the plastered stone house, with displays of a small artifacts collection from before and after the missionaries' arrival, and Mr. Bailey's paintings of Wailuku. Some rooms are decorated with missionary-period furniture. The Hawaiian Room has exhibits on the making of tapa cloth, as well as samples of pre–Captain Cook weaponry. Unfortunately, the girls' school is no longer standing. *2375A Main St., tel.*

808/244–3326. Suggested optional donation: $2 adults, 50¢ children. Open 10–4:30.

Numbers in the margin correspond with points of interest on the Maui map.

Back on Main Street, drive toward the mountains for this tour's last destination, Iao Needle. If you go straight, Main Street turns into Iao Valley Road. Before you're even out of town, the air cools and the hilly terrain gets more lush. Soon you'll come **25** to **Kepaniwai Park and Heritage Gardens.** This county park is now a memorial to Maui's melting pot, with ethnic displays dotting the landscape. There's an early Hawaiian shack, a New England saltbox, a Portuguese villa with gardens, and dwellings from other cultures, such as China, the Philippines, and Portugal. This is a lovely spot to take a break or bring a picnic lunch.

However, the peacefulness here belies the history of the area. During his quest for domination, King Kamehameha I brought his troops to the Valley Isle in 1790 and engaged in a particularly bloody battle near Kepaniwai Park. He succeeded in his plan to defeat Maui and thereby take over the entire group of islands, but the result was mass murder. Bodies blocked Iao Stream, so that the village downstream was given the name Wailuku, which means "bloody river."

As you drive toward the needle, you'll come to a landmark **26** called **John F. Kennedy Profile.** The Hawaiians, it seems, can see something in every rock formation throughout the Islands. But this one does uncannily resemble the profile of the late president.

27 Iao Valley Road ends at **Iao Valley State Park.** When Mark Twain saw this park, he dubbed it the Yosemite of the Pacific. Here you'll find the erosion-formed gray and moss-green rock called **Iao Needle,** a spire that rises 1,200 feet from the valley floor. You can take one of several easy hikes from the parking lot across Iao Stream and explore the jungle-like area. This park offers a beautiful set of walks, where you can stop and contemplate by the edge of a stream or look at some of the native plants and flowers. Mist occasionally rises if there's been a rain, making the spot even more magical. *Admission free. No set hours.*

Tour 3: Haleakala and Upcountry

Numbers in the margin correspond with points of interest on the Maui map.

The fertile western slopes leading up to majestic **Mt. Haleakala** are called Upcountry. This region is responsible for much of Hawaii's produce. Lettuce, tomatoes, and sweet Maui onions are some of the most popular crops grown here, but the area is also a big flower producer. As you drive along you'll notice plenty of natural vegetation, as clumps of cacti mingle with purple jacaranda, wild hibiscus, and towering eucalyptus trees. Carnations are the number one flower in the area, but the exotic-looking protea are rapidly gaining in popularity.

Upcountry is also fertile ranch land, with such spreads as the 30,000-acre Ulupalakua, long famous for raising cattle, and the 20,000-acre Haleakala Ranch, which throws its well-attended rodeo each July 4th. In addition, Tedeschi Vineyards and Winery dominates Hawaii's only wine-producing region, just a few acres of Ulupalakua land.

28 Start this tour of Haleakala in **Kahului.** Before setting out, call 808/871–5054 for Haleakala's weather conditions. Extreme gusty winds, heavy rain, and even snow in winter are not uncommon—even if it is paradise as usual down at beach level. Because of the high altitude, the mountaintop temperature is often as much as 30 degrees cooler than in sea-level Maui. If you didn't pack a warm jacket or can't borrow one, skip watching the sunrise until the next trip and settle for a morning or mid-day visit.

29 After you've checked out the weather conditions, drive on **Haleakala Highway,** or Highway 37, toward the big mountain of Haleakala (House of the Sun) in the center of the island. On this road, you'll travel from sea level to 10,023 feet in only 38 miles—a feat you won't be able to repeat on any other car route in the world. It's not a quick drive, however; it'll take you about two hours. We recommend that you start fairly early in the morning, since the clouds move over the top of the mountain as soon as 11 AM.

Try to make the drive up Haleakala without stopping, since you'll want the best views possible. Watch the signs, because Haleakala Highway will diverge in two directions. If you go straight, the road becomes Kula Highway, which is still Highway 37. If you veer to the left, the road becomes Highway 377. You want this latter road. After about six miles, make a left onto Haleakala Crater Road. The switchbacks begin here. With the ascent, you'll notice the weather getting a bit chilly. As you near the top, there's a **30** **Park Headquarters/Visitor Center,** where you can stop and orient yourself to the volcano's origins and eruption history. Mt. Haleakala is the centerpiece of the 27,284-acre Haleakala National Park, which was dedicated in 1961 to preserving the area. At the gift shop, you can get maps, as well as some nice posters and other memorabilia. *At the 7,000-foot elevation on Haleakala Crater Rd., tel. 808/572–9306. Cost: $3 car fee, $1 per person for hikers, seniors free. Visitor Center open daily 7:30–4.*

Several lookout areas are located within the park itself. The first you'll come to as you continue your ascent on Haleakala **31** Crater Road is **Leleiwi Overlook,** at about 8,800 feet elevation. There's parking here and the beginning of the Haleamauu Trail, which leads into the volcano crater. If you happen to be at this point in the late afternoon, it's possible you'll experience a unique phenomenon called the Brocken Specter. Named after a similar occurrence in East Germany's Harz Mountains, the "specter" allows you to see yourself reflected on the clouds and circled by a rainbow. Don't wait all day for this, because it is not an everyday thing.

32 Next is **Kalahaku Overlook,** a particularly interesting stop at about the 9,000-foot level. The famous silversword plant grows here amid the desertlike surroundings; in fact, the flowering plant grows in only one other place in the park, along the Halemauu Trail, within the crater. The silversword looks like a member of the yucca family and produces a stalk some 3 to 8 feet tall with several hundred yellow and purple flower heads.

At this lookout, the silversword is kept in an enclosure to protect it from nibbling wildlife.

㉝ Next you'll come to **Haleakala Visitor Center,** at about 9,800 feet. By now you're about 10 miles from park headquarters, but a ranger is on duty here as well. The center has exhibits inside and a trailhead that leads to White Hill, a small crater nearby. This is a short, easy walk that will give you an even better view of the volcano crater. Shortly after noon each day, the ranger gives an informative lecture on Haleakala geology. In the summer, a 90-minute walk with a ranger guide that goes partly down Sliding Sands trail starts daily at 9. *Center open sunrise–3.*

㉞ Continue on to reach the highest point on Maui, the **Puu Ulaula Overlook.** Here you'll find a glass-enclosed lookout that boasts a 360-degree view from the 10,023-foot summit. People gather here for the best sunrise view, as the building's open 24 hours a day. Sunrise generally begins between 5:45 and 7, depending on the time of year. On a clear day, you can see the islands of Molokai, Lanai, Kahoolawe, and the Big Island. On a *really* clear day, you can even spot Oahu glimmering in the distance.

On a small hill above, you'll see Science City, a research and communications center that looks like it's straight out of an espionage thriller. You can't visit the center, unfortunately, since the University of Hawaii and the Department of Defense don't allow visitors. The university maintains an observatory, while the Defense Department tracks satellites.

㉟ Now head back down the way you came and see the lower nooks and crannies of **Mt. Haleakala** . When you reach Highway 377 again, make a right.

Time Out Within about a quarter mile on Highway 377, you'll see **Kula Lodge** (Haleakala Hwy., tel. 808/878–2517). The Lodge is a popular post–Haleakala-sunrise spot; it offers a hearty breakfast of the best eggs Benedict you'll find this side of the Rockies. The views are spectacular, since the lodge has windows all around, allowing you to see all the way to the ocean. The flower fields outside are an added benefit.

㊱ Backtrack on Highway 377, then go past the 378 intersection about 2 more miles, where you'll come to **Kula Botanical Gardens** on your left. Specimens grow somewhat naturally here, and you'll see all kinds of flora that may be unfamiliar. There are koa trees, often made into finely turned bowls and handcrafted furniture, and kukui trees, which ancient Hawaiians used for lighting. In addition, the gardens have the requisite protea, varieties of ginger, and stands of bamboo orchid. *RR 2, Box 288, Upper Kula Rd., tel. 808/878–1715. $3 adults, 50¢ children 6–12. Open daily 9–4.*

㊲ Continue on Highway 377 away from Kahului and you'll soon join Highway 37 again. In about 8 miles, you'll come to **Tedeschi Vineyards and Winery,** where you can sample Hawaii's only homegrown wines: a pleasant Maui Blush, the Maui Brut-Blanc de Noirs Hawaiian Champagne, and Tedeschi's annual Maui Nouveau. You can also get a tour of the winery and purchase whatever wines you like. The most unusual wine, Maui Blanc, is made from pineapple concentrate; the winery owners started their operation by buying juice from their neighbor, Maui Land & Pineapple Company.

The winery's tasting room is unusual because it once served as the jail for James Makee's Rose Ranch, where the old-time farmer grew sugarcane back in the 1860s. A large plantation house perches on the slope above, dominating the scenery. Tedeschi is definitely worth a visit. *Ulupalakua Ranch, Haleakala Hwy., tel. 808/878–6058. Admission free. Open daily 9–5.*

Now return the way you came and head toward Kahului on Highway 37. When you get to the Highway 37/377 fork, bear to the left to stay on Highway 37. You're now on Kula Highway, which eventually turns back into Haleakala Highway (this isn't as confusing as it sounds). Within about 2 miles, you'll see a turnoff to the right called Copp Road. About ½ mile later, turn left onto Mauna Place. Here you can visit the **University of Hawaii's Kula Experimental Station.** The station planted the first protea here in the mid-'60s and since then has gained the reputation for being the foremost protea research and development facility.

Within the gates, you'll see as many as 300 varieties of the exotic bloom, most with names to match: Rickrack Banksia, Veldfire Sunburst, Pink Mink, Blushing Bride, and Safari Sunset, to name just a few. You can talk to the growers to find out more about the plants, which were brought to Maui from Australia in 1965 by Dr. Philip Parvin, a University of Hawaii horticulture professor. Then you can proceed to one of Upcountry Maui's many commercial outlets and buy your favorite blooms. *Mauna Place in Upcountry Maui, tel. 808/878–1213. Admission free. Open weekdays 7–3:30, but you must stop at the office and sign a sheet releasing the station from any liability. You'll then be given a map to help you find your way.*

Retrace your steps to Kula Highway and, again, head toward Kahului. In about 4 miles, you'll come to the town of **Pukalani,** essentially an Upcountry bedroom community for Kahului. If you're pressed for time, this is the point from which you can take Highway 37 back to Kahului.

Otherwise, take a right onto Highway 400, which you'll find right in Pukalani, and head toward the *paniolo* (Hawaiian cowboy) village of **Makawao.** This tiny town was settled long ago by Portuguese immigrants who were brought to Maui to work the sugar plantations. After their contracts ran out, many of them moved Upcountry, where their descendants now work the neighboring Haleakala and Ulupalakua ranches. Once a year on the Fourth of July, the paniolos come out in force for the Makawao rodeo.

Time Out One of Makawao's most famous landmarks is **Komoda Store & Bakery** (3674 Baldwin Ave., tel. 808/572–7261), where you can get a delicious cream puff. They sell hundreds each day, as well as offering all the other trappings of a general store.

Besides the annual rodeo, Makawao also provides an opportunity to browse through unusual shops. You can find casual attire at **Collections** (3677 Baldwin Ave., tel. 808/572–0781); original children's toys and books at **Maui Child Toys & Books** (3643 Baldwin Ave., tel. 808/572–2765); and trinkets, souvenirs, and collectibles at **Goodies** (3633 Baldwin Ave., tel. 808/572–0288) or **Coconut Classics** (3647 Baldwin Ave., tel. 808/572–7103). **Glassman Galleries** (3682 Makawao Ave., tel. 808/572–0395) is the newest enterprise of Barbara Glassman, who brought us Maui Art Tours (*see* Guided Tours, above).

From Makawao, it's a short drive down toward the ocean on Baldwin Avenue to the Hana Highway. Make a left on the Hana Highway to head back to Kahului.

Tour 4: The Road to Hana

Numbers in the margin correspond with points of interest on the Maui map.

Don't let anyone tell you the Hana Highway is impassable, frightening, or otherwise unadvisable. Because of all the hype, you're bound to be a little nervous approaching it for the first time. But once you try it, you'll wonder if maybe there's somebody out there making it sound tough just to keep out the hordes. Certainly the road is challenging, spanning some 55 miles of turns and bridges. But it's not a grueling, all-day drive. The road isn't a freeway, but it has been resurfaced to make it a pleasant drive.

41 Start your trip to Hana in the little town of **Paia** by having breakfast at one of the restaurants that line the main street. **Charley's** (142 Hana Hwy., tel. 808/579–9453) is recommended; you can get a good meal here and watch the locals go by. We suggest you also stop at **Picnics** (30 Baldwin Ave., tel. 808/579–8021) to buy a lunch for the road.

If you want to do some predrive shopping as well, Paia is a friendly little town. You can find clothing and keepsakes in shops run by retailers who'll stop and chat, ask where you're from, and, most likely, give you their card in case something doesn't fit or you'd like to return. Here you'll find artists, windsurfers, and some folks who've lived in these parts all their lives.

Paia was once a sugar-growing enclave, an operation complete with a mill and plantation camps. Shops opened by shrewd immigrants quickly sprouted to serve the workers, who probably found it easier to buy supplies near home. The town boomed during World War II when the Marines set up camp nearby. After the war, however, sugar grower Alexander & Baldwin closed its Paia operation, and the town's population began to dwindle. Many residents took off for the new city of Kahului, where they were able to purchase their own homes.

In the 1960s, Paia became a hippie town as dropouts headed for the sunny shores of Maui to open ethnic shops, bizarre galleries, and unusual eateries. By the late 1970s, windsurfers **42** discovered nearby **Hookipa Beach,** and soon Paia was the windsurfing capital of the world. You can see this in the youth of the town and in the budget inns that have cropped up to offer cheap accommodations to those who windsurf for a living. Paia is certainly a fun place.

As you begin your drive to Hana, remember that many people —mostly those who live in Hana—make this trip frequently. You'll recognize them because they're the ones who'll be zipping around every curve as if they had a death wish. They don't; they've just seen this so many times before that they don't care to linger. With stops, this drive should take you between two and three hours. Locals will do it in about 45 minutes. Pull over and let them pass.

About 10 miles from Paia, the famous road really begins to twist and turn (as it will for the next 40 miles or so). About 3 miles later, you'll come to the first of the Hana Highway's approximately 65 bridges. This is **Twin Falls,** so called because it boasts two waterfalls. You'll have to park and walk up the right side of the stream to find them. First you'll come to a pool, into which both waterfalls cascade gracefully. If you keep going for about ¼ mile, though, you'll come to another pool with a larger waterfall. There's good swimming here, especially during the wetter winter and spring seasons.

As you drive on, you'll pass the small villages of **Huelo,** with its two quaint churches, and **Kailua,** home to Alexander & Baldwin's irrigation employees. At about mile marker 11, you can stop at the bridge over **Puohokamoa Stream,** where there are more pools and waterfalls. If you walk up to the left of the first pool, you'll find a larger pool and waterfalls. Picnic tables are available at Puohokamoa Stream, so many people favor this as a stopping point.

If you'd rather stretch your legs *and* use a flush toilet, continue on another mile to the **Kaumahina State Wayside Park,** which has a picnic area and a lovely overlook to the Keanae Peninsula. Hardier souls can camp here with a permit. *Admission free. No set hours.*

A mile past the park, you'll see an enormous valley to your right. This is **Honomanu Valley,** carved by erosion during Haleakala's first dormant period. At the canyon's head, there are 3,000-foot cliffs and a 1,000-foot waterfall, but don't try to reach them. There's not much of a trail, and what does exist is practically impassable.

Another 4 miles brings you to the **Keanae Arboretum,** where you can admire many plants and trees that are now considered native to Hawaii. The meandering Piinaau Stream adds a graceful touch to the arboretum and provides a swimming pond besides. You can take a fairly rigorous hike from the arboretum, if you can find the trail at one side of the large taro patch. You have to be careful not to lose the trail once you're on it. A lovely forest waits at the end of the hike. *Admission free. No set hours.*

Near mile marker 17, you'll find the **Keanae Overlook.** From here, you'll notice the patchwork-quilt effect the taro farms create below. The ocean provides a dramatic backdrop, while in the other direction you have some awesome views of Haleakala through the foliage. This is a good spot for photos.

Coming up is the **halfway mark to Hana.** If you've had enough scenery, this is as good a time as any to turn around and head back to civilization. The scenery from here is essentially the same. Once you get to Hana, you can't expect a booming city. It's the road that's the draw. Diehards will want to stick with us.

Time Out At about mile marker 20, you can pull over at **Uncle Harry's,** (tel. 808/248–7019), a refreshment stand run by Harry Mitchell. Uncle Harry and his family also have souvenirs for sale, and they're planning a small museum next door, including a grass house to demonstrate how their ancestors lived. The Mitchells have some Hawaiian food available, including fruit, home-baked breads, and beverages.

49 Continue on from mile marker 20 for about ¾ mile to **Wailua Lookout.** From the parking lot, you can see Wailua Canyon, but you'll have to walk up steps to get a view of Wailua Village. The landmark in Wailua Village is a church made of coral, built in 1860. Once called St. Gabriel's Catholic Church, the current Our Lady of Fatima Shrine has an interesting legend surrounding it; as the story goes, a storm washed just enough coral up onto the shore to build the church, but then took any extra coral back to sea.

Another ½ mile, and you'll hit the best falls on the entire road to
50 Hana. **Waikane Falls** are not necessarily bigger or taller than the other falls, but they're dramatic just the same. That's partly because the water is not diverted for sugar irrigation; the taro farmers in Wailua need all the runoff. Here is another good spot for photos.

About 9 miles past the Wailua Lookout, or at about mile marker 25, you'll see a road that heads down toward the ocean and the
51 village of **Nahiku.** This was a popular spot in ancient times, providing a home to hundreds of natives. Now Nahiku's population numbers about 80, consisting mostly of native Hawaiians and some back-to-the-land types. Like so many other Hawaiian villages, Nahiku was once a plantation town. A rubber grower planted trees there in the early 1900s. The experiment didn't work out, so Nahiku was essentially abandoned.

52 As you continue on toward Hana, you'll pass **Waianapanapa State Park,** which has state-run cabins where you can stay with a permit for between $14 and $30 a night, depending on the number of people. (*see* Sports and Fitness, below). The park is right on the ocean, and it's a lovely spot to picnic, hike, or swim. An ancient burial site is located nearby, as well as a heiau, or temple. Waianapanapa also boasts one of Maui's few black-sand beaches and some caves for adventurous swimmers to explore. *Hana Hwy., tel. 808/248–8061. Admission free. No set hours.*

53 Closer to Hana, you'll come to **Helani Gardens,** a 60-acre enclave of plants collected and grown by Hana native Howard Cooper. Cooper is the crusty old guy you'll find wandering the place or hanging out in his treehouse. His wife, Nora, is editor of the *Maui News* in Kahului, but Howard just couldn't bear to leave his beloved Hana, so Nora commutes. Howard's philosophy of life crops up all over the garden in delightful, hand-painted signs. A tour of Helani Gardens is a self-guided one, but if Howard's around, he'll be glad to show you his favorite plants. *No street address; you can write to Helani Gardens, Box 215, Hana 96713, tel. 808/248–8274. Admission: $2 adults, $1 children 6–16. Open daily (weather permitting) 10–4.*

54 **Hana** is just minutes away from Helani Gardens. It's a blink-and-you'll-miss-it kind of place, with only a couple of roads and
55 clusters of houses. In Hana, a high spot is the **Hotel Hana-Maui** (Hana Hwy., tel. 808/248–8211), one of the best hotels in the state—if not the world (*see* Lodging, below). You can also
56 browse through **Hasegawa's Store** (Hana Hwy., tel. 808/248–8231), a general store packed with everything from A to Z. Im-

mortalized in song, the store is still run by Harry Hasegawa and his family. There's also a small museum in town, full of quaint Hawaiian memorabilia.

Time Out **Tutu's** (tel. 808/248–8224) is a snack shop down by the bay. Aside from the Hotel Hana-Maui and its two eating establishments, this is the only place for a meal in the entire town. Although nothing is fancy here (burgers are the typical fare), the prices are lower than those at the hotel restaurants. You'll also get a view of fishing boats bringing in their catch in the late afternoon.

As you wander around Hana, keep in mind that this is a company town. Although sugar was once the mainstay of Hana's economy, the last plantation shut down in the 1940s. In 1946, rancher Paul Fagan built the Hotel Hana-Maui and stocked the surrounding pastureland with cattle. Suddenly, it was the ranch and its hotel that were putting food on the most tables.

The Cross you'll see on the hill above the hotel was put there in memory of Fagan. After Fagan died in the mid-1960s, ranch-and-town ownership passed into the hands of 37 shareholders, most of whom didn't care about their property. Then Rosewood Corporation came along and purchased most of Hana's valuable land. Owned by Caroline Hunt, the company put megamillions into restoring the Hotel Hana-Maui and began teaching the *paniolos* (cowboys) all the latest techniques in grazing and breeding. Recently, however, Rosewood sold its Hana holdings to a Japanese company which handed over mangement to Sheraton. No news was available at press time about the resulting changes.

Because of the town's size, most of the townspeople are the hands-on suppliers of the services and amenities that make hotel guests happy. Moreover, many locals have worked at the hotel for years; a fascinating family tree that hangs near the lobby shows the relationships of all the employees. If you're at all adventurous, you'll no doubt be able to talk to several of the people who live and work in Hana. They're candid, friendly, and mostly native Hawaiian—or at least born and raised in Hana.

57 Once you've seen Hana, you might want to drive past the town for a dip in the pools at **Oheo Gulch.** Called the Piilani Highway once past Hana, the road that spans the 10 miles to the gulch is truly bad—rutted, rocky, and twisting. You're just sure you've passed the pools because the terrain is so awful, but don't give up. These refreshing pools are worth the drive. Oheo Gulch is often referred to as Seven Sacred Pools, but that is just a bit of promotional hype. There's nothing sacred here, unless you count sybaritic swimming as a religious pursuit, and the pools number far more than seven.

From the paved parking lot, you can walk a short way to the first of the pools. Rocks are available for sunbathing, and caves may be explored. In the spring and summer, it can get quite crowded here, and it doesn't even thin out when it rains.

58 A lot of people come this far just to see the **Grave of Charles Lindbergh,** the world-renowned aviator. Lindbergh chose to be buried here because he and his wife, Anne Morrow Lindbergh, spent a lot of time living in the area in a home they built. His grave is very difficult to spot, which is probably intentional. It's about a mile past Oheo Gulch on a road that goes toward the ocean. On this road you'll find Hoomau Congregational Church, next to which Lindbergh was buried in 1974. Remember, this is a churchyard, so be considerate and leave everything exactly as you found it.

Unless you've decided to drive completely around Maui and end up at Makena (which isn't advisable unless you have a four-wheel-drive vehicle), this is the place to turn around. You've seen just about all of Hana's high spots. The drive back isn't nearly as fun, so you might want to plan on spending a night in Hana (*see* Lodging, below).

Maui for Free

Hale Paahao/Old Lahaina Prison. Here you can see the original coral-block walls that were once the jail for rowdy sailors and whalers. This prison was built between 1852 and 1854 by the prisoners themselves; the small, brown building looks like a chapel. The rock for the coral prison came from the walls of an old fort, which Hale Paahao replaced. *Prison Rd. just off Wainee St., Lahaina, tel. 808/661–3262. Open daily 9–5.*

Hale Pai/Old Print Shop. Located on the grounds of Lahainaluna School in Lahaina, this print house was opened in 1837 and put out the first Hawaiian-language newspaper. Founded by the missionaries, it now houses the Lahaina Restoration Foundation's extensive archival collection and exhibits depicting Maui's early whaling and missionary days. *At the mountain end of Lahainaluna Rd., Lahaina, tel. 808/661–3262. Open Mon.–Fri. 10–4.*

Hui Noeau Visual Arts Center. This nonprofit cultural center is set in the Upcountry town of Makawao in the old Baldwin estate. There are regular exhibitions, as well as audiovisual presentations. *2841 Baldwin Ave., Makawao, tel. 808/572–6560. Open daily 10–4.*

Jodo Mission. The Lahaina Jodo Mission Cultural Park is one of the town's busiest tourist attractions, sitting on a parcel of land called Puunoa Point just off Front Street near Mala Wharf. The park's centerpiece is the largest Buddha outside Japan, placed there to commemorate the arrival of the first Japanese immigrants in 1868. The park includes the shrine, graveyards, a crematorium, and an extensive outdoor meeting area. *12 Ala Moana, Lahaina, tel. 808/661–4304. No set hours.*

Lahaina Whaling Museum. Crazy Shirts' owner, Rick Ralston, has opened this repository of more than 800 pieces of whaling memorabilia, including carved ivory, harpoons, and old photos. *865 Front St., tel. 808/661–4775. Open daily 9 AM–10 PM.*

Maui Zoological and Botanical Gardens (Kanaloa St. off Kaahumanu Ave., Kahului, tel. 808/243–7337). *See* Tour 2, above.

Muumuu Factory. Famous muumuu manufacturer **Hilo Hattie** advertises all over Maui. Owned by the same company that runs the Maui Tropical Plantation, Hilo Hattie stocks aloha wear made on the premises. The company will pick you up if you're staying in the Kaanapali or Lahaina area, or you can drive there yourself. Be forewarned that the clothing isn't much cheaper or better quality than what you'll find in the stores. *1000 Limihana Place, Lahaina, tel. 808/667–7911. Open daily 8:30–5.*

Pacific Brewery. Look for this operation on the grounds of the old Wailuku Sugar Mill. You can get 15-minute tours of this Maui Lager beer plant, which recently began shipping its product to the mainland. The tour acquaints you with brewing and bottling techniques and ends with a taste test. *Imi Kala St., Wailuku, tel. 808/244–0396. Open weekdays 10–4.*

Sandcastle Exhibition. Billy Lee is getting a reputation. The master sandcastle builder has set up his pails and shovels on the beach in front of 505 Front Street in Lahaina, and between 9 AM and sunset he sculpts whatever comes to mind—mermaids, castles, towers, lions, you name it.

Upcountry Protea Farm. On the slopes of Haleakala, Upcountry Protea Farm grows exotic blossoms and offers views of the gardens to all who stop by. You can also purchase protea here, or have them shipped home. *One mile off Hwy. 37, at the top of Upper Kimo Dr., tel. 808/878–2544. Open daily 8–4:30.*

Whalers Village Museum. On the shore at the Kaanapali Beach Resort, this museum's exhibits explore whaling history. The museum contains a 30-foot sperm whale skeleton, with information about whale biology, photos, and artifacts from 1825 to 1860. A video theater shows films, and an authentic whaling boat is displayed in the outdoor pavilion. Lectures and special tours are available. *2435 Kaanapali Pkwy., tel. 808/661–5992. Open daily 9:30 AM–10 PM.*

What to See and Do with Children

Lahaina–Kaanapali & Pacific Railroad. Affectionately called the Sugarcane Train, this choo-choo is Hawaii's only passenger train. It's an 1890s-vintage railway that once shuttled sugar but now moves sightseers between Kaanapali and Lahaina. This quaint little attraction is a big deal for Hawaii but probably not much of a thrill for those more accustomed to trains. The kids will like it. You can also get a package that combines a ride and lunch in Lahaina or a historic Lahaina tour. *1½ blocks north of the Lahainaluna Rd. stoplight on Honoapiilani Hwy., Lahaina, tel. 808/661–0080. Cost for round-trip ride: $9 adults, $4.50 children; one-way: $6 adults, $3 children. Open daily 9–4.*

Maui Tropical Plantation. This visitor attraction used to be a huge sugarcane field, but when Maui's once-paramount crop declined severely in importance, a group of visionaries decided to open an agricultural theme park. The 120-acre preserve now ranks as Hawaii's third most popular tourist attraction. Located on Highway 30 just outside Wailuku, the plantation offers a 30-minute tram ride through its fields with an informative narration of growing processes and plant types.

Kids will also probably enjoy a historical-characters exhibit, as well as fruit-testing, coconut-husking, and lei-making demonstrations and bird shows. There's a restaurant on the property, and a souvenir shop that sells fruits and vegetables. At night, the Maui Tropical Plantation features a country barbecue. *On Honoapiilani Hwy. right outside Wailuku toward Kaanapali,* *tel. 808/244-7643. Admission free to the park; cost of narrated tour, $8 adults, $3 children 6-12. Open daily 9-5.*

Whale watching. Appealing to both children and adults, whale watching is one of the most exciting activities in the United States. During the right time of year on Maui—between December and April—you can see whales breaching and blowing just offshore. The humpback whales' attraction to Maui is legendary. More than half the North Pacific's humpback population winters in Hawaii, as they've been doing for years. At one time, thousands of the huge mammals existed, but the world population has dwindled to about 1,500. In 1966, they were put on the endangered-species list, which restricts boats and airplanes from getting too close.

Experts believe the humpbacks keep returning to Hawaiian waters because of the warmth. Winter is calving time for the behemoths, and the whale babies, born with little blubber, probably couldn't survive in the frigid Alaskan waters. No one has ever seen a whale give birth, but the experts studying whales off Maui know that calving is their main winter activity, since the one- and two-ton babies suddenly appear while the whales are in residence.

Quite a few operations run whale-watching excursions off the coast of Maui. This allows you to get a closer view; it gives the whale a better vantage point, too. Sometimes, in fact, a curious whale can get so close that it makes the passengers downright nervous. **Pacific Whale Foundation** (Kealia Beach Plaza, Kihei 96753, tel. 808/879-8811) pioneered whale watching back in 1979 and now runs two boats.

Also offering whale watching in season are the following: **Ocean Activities Center** (1325 S. Kihei Rd., Suite 212, Kihei 96753, tel. 808/879-4485); **Leilani Cruises** (505 Front St., Suite 225, Lahaina 96761, tel. 808/661-8397); **Captain Zodiac Raft Expeditions** (Box 1776, Lahaina 96761, tel. 808/667-5351); **Seabern Yachts** (Box 1022, Lahaina 96767, tel. 808/661-8110; **Trilogy Excursions** (Box 1121, Lahaina 96767, tel. 808/661-4743); and **Alihilani Yacht Charters** (Box 1286, Lahaina 96767, tel. 808/871-1156). Ticket prices average about $30 adults, $15 children.

Off the Beaten Track

Kaupo Road. This stretch of road beyond Charles Lindbergh's grave is located near where the pavement stops 10 miles past Hana. Kaupo Road is rough, with more than a few miles of rocky, one-lane terrain not unlike that of the moon. Drop-offs plunge far down to the sea and washouts are common. It's a beautiful drive, however, and probably the closest to Old Hawaii you'll find. Along the way, the little Kaupo store, about 15 miles past Hana, sells a variety of essential items, such as groceries, fishing tackle, and hardware; it's also a good place to stop for a cold drink. You'll also pass the renovated Hui Aloha Church, a tiny, wood-framed structure surrounded by an old Hawaiian graveyard. You might want a four-wheel-drive vehicle for this road. You'll eventually wind up near Makena.

Maui Swap Meet. The Maui Swap Meet flea market is the biggest bargain on Maui, with crafts, gifts, souvenirs, fruits, flowers, jewelry, antiques, art, shells, and lots more. *At the*

Kahului Fairgrounds, Hwy. 35, just off Puunene Ave. Admission: 50¢. Open Sat. 8–1.

Yee's Orchard. If you're up for a little local shopping, look for Wilbert Yee's Orchard in Kihei. The Yee family has farmed the same 20-acre plot for more than half a century, raising mangoes, papayas, bananas, guavas, and tomatoes. *Near the Azeka Shopping Center (1280 S. Kihei Rd.) Open Wed. 10–4 and Sun. 9–5.*

Shopping

Maui is not the place to go if you're in a serious shopping mood, but you can have fun browsing through the little stores that line Front Street in Lahaina or the boutiques packed into the major resort hotels. In all fairness, Maui does have two major shopping malls, in Kahului and Lahaina.

No matter if you head for the mall or opt for the boutiques hidden around the Valley Isle, one thing you should have no problem finding is clothing made in Hawaii. The Hawaiian garment industry is now the state's third-largest economic sector, after tourism and agriculture.

Maui has an abundance of locally made arts and crafts in a range of prices. In fact, a group that calls itself Made on Maui exists solely to promote the products of its members—items that range from pottery and paintings to Hawaiian teas and macadamia caramel corn. Made on Maui has a booth at the Kaahumanu Shopping Center, or you can identify the group by its distinctive Haleakala logo. Maui also boasts plenty of food choices besides the usual pineapple or macadamia nuts. Maui onions, protea, and potato chips are only a few of the possibilities.

Business hours for individual shops on the island are usually 9–5, seven days a week. Shopping centers tend to stay open later (until 9 on certain days).

Shopping Centers

Kaahumanu Center is in the heart of Kahului. It takes up an entire block and boasts more than 60 shops and restaurants. The mall also has free parking. Its anchor stores are **Liberty House** (tel. 808/877–3361) and **Sears** (tel. 808/877–2221), as well as the popular Japanese retailer **Shirokiya** (tel. 808/877–5551). You'll also find such recognizable mainland stores as **Casual Corner, Kay-Bee Toys,** and **Radio Shack.** *Kaahumanu Center, 275 Kaahumanu Ave., Kahului, tel. 808/877–3369. Open Mon.– Wed. and Sat. 9–5:30, Thurs. and Fri. 9–9, Sun. 10–3.*

Lahaina Cannery Shopping Center, a newer mall, is set in a building reminiscent of an old pineapple cannery. Unlike many shopping centers in Hawaii, the Lahaina Cannery isn't open-air; it is air-conditioned. The center has some 50 shops, including **Arabesque Maui** (tel. 808/667–5337), with classy fashions for women; **Dolphin Galleries** (tel. 808/661–5000), featuring sculpture, paintings, and other Maui artwork; **Superwhale** (tel. 808/661–3424), with a good selection of children's tropical wear; and **Kite Fantasy** (tel. 808/661–4766), one of the best kite shops on Maui. *Lahaina Cannery Shopping Center, 1221*

Honoapiilani Hwy., Lahaina, tel. 808/661–5304. Open daily 9:30–9:30.

Art

Maui has more art per square mile than any other Hawaiian Island—maybe more than any other U.S. county. Artists love Maui, and they flock there to live and work. There are artists' guilds and co-ops, as well as galleries galore. The Provenance Gallery runs the **Art Information Desk of Maui** (122 Lahainaluna Rd., Lahaina, tel. 808/667–6224), which can answer questions about where to find the work of particular artists.

The **Old Jail Gallery,** located in the basement of the old Lahaina Court House (649 Wharf St., across the street from the Pioneer Inn and Lahaina Harbor), sells work by artists who belong to the Lahaina Arts Society (tel. 808/661–0111). The artists range from watercolorists to specialists in oil and sculpture. Down the street, the **Grycner Gallery** (758 Front St., Lahaina, tel. 808/667–9112) has exclusive rights in Hawaii to sell the work of famous American Indian artist R. C. Gorman, among other artwork. Gorman's languid Navajo women have often been compared to the native Hawaiian lasses painted by Island artist Pegge Hopper.

As for exclusivity, **Wyland Galleries** (697 Front St., Lahaina, tel. 808/661–7099) is the only Maui shop to sell the work of Wyland, the marine artist whose favorite technique is a simultaneous look at scenes from under and above the water. **Coast Gallery** in the Maui Inter-Continental Wailea (3700 Wailea Alanui, Wailea, tel. 808/879–2301) has an attractive selection of marine-related paintings and sculptures by such well-known artists as Richard Pettit, George Sumner, and Robert Lyn Nelson.

A popular Maui art enclave, **Village Gallery,** now has three locations—one in Lahaina (120 Dickenson St., tel. 808/661–4402), one at the Lahaina Cannery Shopping Center (tel. 808/661–3280), and one in the Embassy Suites (104 Kaanapali Shores Pl., tel. 808/667–5115)—featuring such local artists as Betty Hay Freeland, Wailehua Gray, and Margaret Bedell. **Lahaina Galleries** has three locations (728 Front St., Lahaina, tel. 808/667–2152; Whalers Village, Kaanapali Beach Resort, tel. 808/661–5571; Kapalua Resort, tel. 808/669–0202), making it the island's largest art gallery company. One of the most interesting galleries on Maui is the **Maui Crafts Guild** (43 Hana Hwy., Paia, tel. 808/579–9697), on the road to Hana. Set in a two-story wooden building alongside the highway, the Guild is crammed with work by local artists; the best pieces are the pottery and sculpture. Upstairs, antique kimonos and batik fabric are on display.

Clothing

Aloha Wear To find the kind of aloha wear, such as colorful shirts and muumuus, worn most by the people who live year-round on Maui, check out **Liberty House.** The store has six locations on the island, including shops in the Maui Marriott, Stouffer Wailea, and Maui Inter-Continental hotels and in Azeka Place Shopping Center (1280 S. Kihei Rd.) in Kihei, Whaler's Village (2435

Kaanapali Pkwy.) in the Kaanapali Beach Resort, and Kaahumanu Center in Kahului. The largest Liberty House store is the one at Kaahumanu Center (tel. 808/877–3361). Also in the Kaahumanu Center, **Sears** (tel. 808/877–2221) has a wide selection of authentic—as in subtly patterned—aloha shirts and muumuus at reasonable prices.

Resort Wear You can find lots of casual, easygoing clothes at Liberty House or any of the hotel shops. Whalers Village in the Kaanapali Beach Resort has several good resort-wear shops, including **Foreign Intrigue** (tel. 808/667–6671) and **Paradise Clothing** (tel. 808/661–4638).

Although stores for women's resort wear are easy to find on Maui, stores for men's resort wear are scarcer. Some recommended shops for men's clothing are: **Chapman's,** at the Hyatt Regency (tel. 808/661–4121) and at the Wailea Shopping Village (tel. 808/879–3644); **Kramer's Men's Wear,** at the Lahaina Cannery Shopping Center (tel. 808/661–5377) and Kaahumanu Center (tel. 808/871–8671); and **Reyn's,** in Kapalua (tel. 808/669–5260).

Food

Many visitors to Hawaii opt to take home some of the local produce: pineapples, papayas, guavas, coconut, or Maui onions. You can find jams and jellies—some of them Made on Maui products—in a wide variety of tropical flavors. Cook Kwee's Maui Cookies have gained quite a following, as have Maui Potato Chips. Both are available in most Valley Isle grocery stores. Maui has just started growing its own macadamia trees—but it takes seven years before nuts can be harvested! Still, macadamia nuts are a favorite gift back home.

Remember that fresh fruit must be inspected by the U.S. Department of Agriculture, so it's safer to buy a box that's already passed muster. **Paradise Fruit** (1913 Kihei Rd., Kihei, tel. 808/879–1723) sells ready-to-ship pineapples, Maui onions, and coconuts, while **Take Home Maui** (121 Dickenson St., Lahaina, tel. 808/661–8067) will deliver produce free to the airport or your hotel.

One highly recommended food item is **Chocolate Chips of Maui.** These delectables are the brainchild of entrepreneur Bonnie Friedman, who figured out a way to dip Maui potato chips in dark chocolate. They're delicious—bet you can't eat just one. Look for them in better gift shops or write to Ms. Friedman's company (Discriminating Taste, 221 Lalo, Kahului 96732, tel. 808/871–7127).

Maui is also the only place in Hawaii that commercially produces its own wine. You can find bottles of Maui Blanc (a pineapple wine), Maui Blush, and Maui Brut-Blanc de Noirs Hawaiian Champagne in grocery stores, but you might want to take a drive into Upcountry Maui and visit the **Tedeschi Winery** (tel. 808/878–6058). There, you can taste before you buy. Let's face it, the ambience is better there, too. To find the winery, take Highway 37 from Kahului toward Haleakala. Continue for about 25 miles, through Pukalani and past the Kula Sanatorium *(see* Tour 3 in Exploring, above).

Gifts

You may be looking for a unique gift—expensive and unlike anything already sitting on your recipient's dusty bookcase. On the grounds of the Kapalua Bay Hotel, look for two fine shops guaranteed to fit the bill: **By the Bay** (107 Bay Dr., Kapalua, tel. 808/669–5227), which specializes in shells, coral, and hand-crafted jewelry; and **Distant Drums** (125 Bay Dr., Kapalua, tel. 808/669–5522), a boutique that has put together a collection of primitive arts and crafts. **Maui on My Mind** (tel. 808/667–5597) at the Lahaina Cannery Shopping Center offers fine arts and crafts made right on Maui. **Maui's Best** (tel. 808/536–7629), with its two locations—Kaahumanu Center and Wailea Shopping Village—also has a wide selection of locally made gifts.

Hawaiian Arts and Crafts

Some visiting shoppers are determined to buy only what they can't get anywhere else. Some of the arts and crafts native to Hawaii can be just the thing. Woods like koa and milo grow only in certain parts of the world, and because of their increasing scarcity, prices are rising. In Hawaii, craftsmen turn the woods into bowls, trays, and jewelry boxes that will last for years. One of the best places to find Hawaiian crafts on Maui is in the Upcountry town of Haiku, at **John of Maui & Sons** (100 Haiku Rd., Haiku, tel. 808/575–2863). If you're driving east from Kahului, you'll need to turn right up Baldwin Avenue in Paia and drive for about 15 minutes. This little family operation turns out some of the most exciting wood products in the Islands.

Quilts may not sound Hawaiian, but the way they're done in the 50th state is very different from anywhere else in the world. Missionaries from New England were determined to teach the natives their homespun craft, but—naturally—the Hawaiians adapted quilting to their own style. **Lahaina General Store** (829 Front St., Lahaina, tel. 808/661–0944) and **Tutu's Palaka** (76 Hana Hwy., Paia, tel. 808/579–8682) have a few of these precious coverlets.

If you're looking for a unique experience while you're shopping for Hawaiian-made crafts, try the **Maui Rehabilitation Center** (95 Mahalani, Wailuku, tel. 808/244–5502). You won't find the world's most expert craftsmanship, but the prices are reasonable and you can meet some local folks who are just breaking into this segment of the visitor industry.

Jewelry

In Lahaina, a visit to **Claire the Ring Lady** (858-4 Front St., tel. 808/667–9288) can be a worthwhile jewelry-buying expedition. The somewhat eccentric craftswoman will make an original piece of jewelry for you while you wait. **Jack Ackerman's The Original Maui Divers** (640 Front St., tel. 808/661–0988) is a company that's been crafting gold and coral into jewelry for about 20 years. You can buy Hawaiian heirloom jewelry and tiny carved pendants from **Lahaina Scrimshaw** (tel. 808/661–3971) in the Lahaina Cannery Shopping Center or at two locations on Front Street. **Haimoff & Haimoff Creations in Gold** (tel. 808/669–5213), located at the Kapalua Resort, features the original work of award-winning jewelry designer Harry Haimoff.

Beaches

Maui has more than 100 miles of coastline. Not all of this is beach, of course, but Maui's striking white crescents do seem to be around every bend. All of Hawaii's beaches are free and open to the public—even those that grace the front yards of fancy hotels—so you can feel free to make yourself at home on any one of them.

While they don't appear often, be sure to pay attention to any signs on the beaches. Warnings of high surf or rough currents should be noted. Before you seek shade under a swaying palm tree, watch for careening coconuts. Though the trades seem gentle, the winds are strong enough to knock the fruit off the trees and onto your head. Also be sure to diligently apply that sunscreen. Maui is closer to the equator than the beaches to which you're probably accustomed, so although you may think you're safe, take it from those who've gotten a beet-red burn in 30 minutes or less—you're not. Drinking alcoholic beverages on beaches in Hawaii isn't allowed.

West Maui boasts quite a few beach choices. If you start at the northern end of West Maui and work your way down the coast in a southerly direction, you'll find the following beaches:

D. T. Fleming Beach is one of West Maui's most popular beaches. This charming, mile-long sandy cove is better for sunbathing than for swimming, because the current can be quite strong. There are rest-room facilities, including showers; picnic tables and grills; and paved parking. *Take Hwy. 30 about 1 mi north of the Kapalua Resort.*

The lovely **Napali Beach** is located right outside the **Napili Kai Beach Club,** a popular little condominium for honeymooners. This sparkling white crescent makes a secluded cove perfect for strolling. No facilities are available here unless you're staying at the condo, but you're only a few miles south of Kapalua. *5900 Honoapiilani Hwy. From the upper highway, take the cutoff road closest to the Kapalua Resort.*

Honokowai Beach is a bust if you're looking for that classic Hawaiian stretch of sand. Still, kids will enjoy the rocks here that have formed a pool. This beach does have showers and picnic tables. *Across from the Honokowai Superette at 3636 Lower Honoapiilani Rd.*

Fronting the big hotels at Kaanapali is one of Maui's best people-watching spots, **Kaanapali Beach.** This is not the beach if you're looking for peace and quiet, but if you want lots of action, lay out your towel here. Cruises, windsurfers, and parasails take off from this beach while the beautiful people take in the scenery. Although no facilities are available, the nearby hotels have rest rooms. You're also close to plenty of shops and concessions. *Take any one of the three Kaanapali exits from Honoapiilani Hwy. Park at any of the hotels.*

South of Lahaina at mile marker 14 is **Olowalu Beach,** a secluded snorkeling haven. There's no parking here—except right on the road—and no facilities, but it's one of Maui's best sandy spots. With mask and fins, you'll see yellow tangs, parrot fish, and sometimes the state fish, the humuhumunu-kunukuapuaa. You can call it a humu, if you like.

Farther south of Olowalu, you'll find **Wailea's five crescent beaches,** which stretch for nearly 2 miles with relatively little interruption by civilization. Two hotels call Wailea home, with three condominiums now under construction. So far, the buildings haven't infringed on the beaches in a noticeable way. With any luck, the population boom won't affect this area either. Swimming is good here—the crescents protect the shoreline from rough surf. Few people populate these beaches—mostly guests of the nearby lodgings—which makes Wailea a peaceful haven.

Just south of Wailea is **Makena,** with two good beaches. **Big Beach** is 3,000 feet long and 100 feet wide. The water off Big Beach is fine for swimming and snorkeling. If you walk over the cinder cone at Big Beach, you'll reach **Little Beach,** which is used for nude sunbathing. Officially, nude sunbathing is illegal in Hawaii, but several bathers who've pushed their arrests through the courts have found their cases dismissed. Understand, though, that you take your chances if you decide to partake of a favorite local pastime at Little Makena.

The beaches in Central Maui are far from noteworthy, but if you're staying in the area, try **Kanaha Beach** in Kahului. A long, golden strip of sand bordered by a wide grassy area, this is a popular spot for windsurfers, joggers, and picnicking Maui families. Kanaha Beach has toilets, showers, picnic tables, and grills. *In Kahului, take Dairy Rd. toward the airport. At Koeheke, make a left and head toward Kahului Bay.*

If you want to see some of the world's finest windsurfers, stop at **Hookipa Beach** on the Hana Highway. The sport has become an art—and a career, to some—and its popularity was largely developed right at Hookipa. Waves get as high as 15 feet. This is not a good swimming beach, nor the place to learn windsurfing yourself, but plenty of picnic tables and barbecue grills are available. *About 1 mi past Paia on Hwy. 36.*

In East Maui, **Kaihalulu Beach** was once a favorite spot for privacy-seeking nudists. Now, however, Hana's red-sand beach has gotten a little less secluded as more people have discovered it, but this is still a gorgeous cove, with good swimming and snorkeling. To get there, start at the Hana Community Center at the end of Hauoli Road and walk along the outside of Kauiki Hill. The hike won't be easy, but it's worth the effort. No facilities are available.

Sports and Fitness

Participant Sports

Biking Maui's roads are narrow, which can make bicycling a harrowing experience. Some visitors rent a bike just to ride around the resort where they're staying, but to go anywhere else requires getting on a two-lane highway. If it looks like something you'd like to try anyway, these companies rent bicycles: **AA Go Go Bike Hawaii** (30-B Halawai Dr. #5, Lahaina, tel. 808/661–3063) and **A & B Moped Rental** (3481 Lower Honoapiilani Hwy.,

Lahaina, tel. 808/669–0027). Both rent for between $10 and $20 an hour. If you're staying at the Kaanapali Resort, your best bet is **Let's Rent A Bike!** (2580 Kekaa Dr., Kaanapali, tel. 808/661–3037), with a location just off Highway 30 in the resort itself. Rates start at $5 an hour, with family discounts available.

Camping and Hiking Like the other Hawaiian islands, Maui is riddled with ancient paths. These were the roads the Polynesians used to cross from one side of their island home to another. Most of these paths today are too difficult to find. But if you happen to stumble upon something that looks like it might have been a trail, chances are good it was used by the ancients.

In fact, most trails on Maui are not well marked. Only three areas have clearly marked trailheads. Luckily, they're some of the best hikes on the island.

In Maui's center, **Haleakala Crater** in Haleakala National Park is an obvious hiking haven, boasting several trails. As you drive to the top of the 10,023-foot dormant volcano on the Haleakala Highway, you'll first come to **Hosmer Grove,** less than a mile after you enter the park. This is a lovely forested area, with an hour-long nature trail. You can pick up a map at the trailhead and camp without a permit in the campground. There are six campsites, pit toilets, drinking water, and cooking shelters. There's also **Halemauu Trail,** near the 8,000-foot elevation. The walk to the crater rim is a grassy stroll, then it's a switchback trail nearly 2 miles to the crater floor. Nearly 4 miles from the trailhead, you'll find **Holua Cabin,** which you can reserve—at least three months in advance—through the National Park Service (Box 369, Makawao 96768, tel. 808/572–9306). Nearby, you can pitch a tent, but you'll need a permit that's issued on a first-come, first-served basis at Haleakala National Park Headquarters/Visitors Center (Haleakala Crater Rd., 7,000-ft. elevation, tel. 808/572–9306. Open daily 7:30–4).

If you opt to drive all the way to the top of Haleakala, you'll find a trail called **Sliding Sands,** which starts at about the 10,000-foot elevation, descending 4 miles to the crater floor. The scenery is spectacular; it's colorful and somewhat like the moon. You can reach the above-mentioned Holua Cabin in about 7 miles if you veer off to the left and out of the crater on the Halemauu Trail. If you continue on the Sliding Sands Trail, however, you'll come to **Kapalaoa Cabin** within about 6 miles, and at about 10 miles you'll hit **Paliku Cabin,** both also available from the park service with at least three months' notice. All three cabins have bunks, firewood, water, and a stove and are limited to 12 people. They can be reached in less than a day's walk. Paliku Cabin has tent camping nearby with toilets and drinking water. Tent permits, again, are issued at park headquarters on the day you want to use them.

Maui's second hiking area, in East Maui, is called **Oheo Gulch.** The gulch is part of Haleakala National Park, but it's very different from the crater. That's because it's over on the Hana side of the park—which actually extends far beyond the mountain you see in the clouds. This is a lush, rainy, tropical area. You can reach Oheo Gulch by continuing on the Hana Highway about 10 miles past Hana. Oheo Gulch includes the Seven Pools, where the two major trails begin. The first trail is **Makahiku Falls,** a half-mile jaunt from the parking lot to an overlook. You can go around the barrier and get closer to the falls if you want. From here, you can continue on the second trail for another 1½ miles. You'll dead-end at **Waimoku Falls.** There's camping in this area, with no permit required, although you can only stay three nights. Toilets, grills, and tables are available here, but no water.

Another camping and hiking area is located on the southern slope of Haleakala. Called **Polipoli Forest,** this place will remind you of a Walt Disney movie. It was once heavily forested, until cattle and goats chewed away most of the natural vegetation. Starting in about 1930, the government began a program to reforest the area, and soon redwoods, cedar, pine, and cypress took hold. To reach the forest, drive on Highway 377 past Haleakala Road to Waipoli Road. Go up the hill until you reach the park. Next to the lot, you'll see a small campground and a cabin you can rent from the Division of State Parks (write far in advance for the cabin to: Box 1049, Wailuku 96793, tel. 808/244-4354; for the campground, you can wait until you arrive in Wailuku, then visit the State Parks office at 54 High St.). Once you're at Polipoli, there are three trails from which to choose.

Fitness Centers There are more fitness centers in hotels than anywhere else on Maui, and those will probably be the most convenient for you. At the Kaanapali Resort, the **Hyatt Regency** has a guests-only health spa with all the trimmings and daily aerobics classes; the **Maui Marriott** boasts a weight room and aerobics with a $3 charge for nonguests; and the **Westin Maui** has a health club with weights, aerobics, and massage. If you're a Westin guest, this is the best spa. At Wailea, both the Maui Inter-Continental and Stouffers offer aerobics daily.

Outside the resorts, the **Lahaina Nautilus Center** (180 Dickenson St., Suite 201, tel. 808/667-6100) has more than a dozen weight machines as well as aerobics classes and massage therapists. The **Kahana Gym** (4310 Lower Honoapiilani Hwy., Kahana, tel. 808/669-7622) specializes in free weights. There are other clubs as well, but they are simply not convenient unless you want to drive to Kahului or Wailuku—about an hour from West Maui and 45 minutes from Wailea.

Golf How do you keep your mind on the game in a place like Maui? It's very hard, because you can't ignore the view. The island's three major resorts all have golf courses, each of them stunning. They're all open to the public as well.

The **Royal Kaanapali Golf Course** (Kaanapali Beach Resort, Lahaina, tel. 808/661-3691) is one of Maui's most famous, due to television exposure. The layout consists of two 18-hole courses, which are each celebrities in their own right. The North Course was designed by Robert Trent Jones, Sr., while the South Course architect was Arthur Jack Snyder. Greens fees run about $90 for guests and nonguests.

The **Kapalua Golf Club** (300 Kapalua Dr., West Maui, tel. 808/669-8044) has two 18-holers—the Village Course and the Bay Course—both designed by Arnold Palmer. Kapalua is also well-known among television sports watchers. One of the Kapulua Bay Hotel owners is Mark Rolfing, who's made a name for himself as a producer of sporting events (he founded the Kapalua International) and as an announcer on ESPN. Rolfing, who's barely 40, started as a grease monkey in the cart barn. Greens fees at Kapalua are $75 for nonguests, $45 for guests. Carts go for $15 and clubs for $25.

The **Wailea Golf Club** (120 Kaukahi St., Wailea, tel. 808/879–2966) also has two courses—the Orange and the Blue—which were designed by Arthur Jack Snyder. In his design, the golf architect incorporated ancient lava-rock walls and heiaus (temples) for an even more unusual golfing experience. Between December and April, greens fees are $90 for nonguests and $45 for guests.

The island's newest resort, the Makena, has a golf course as well, the lovely **Makena Golf Course** (5415 Makena Alanui, Kihei, tel. 808/879–3344), designed by Robert Trent Jones, Jr. Of all the resort courses, this one is the most remote. At one point, golfers must cross a main road, but there are so few cars that this poses no problem. Greens fees are $90; guests pay $55. Twilight fees are $50; guests pay $40.

Maui has two municipal courses as well, where the fees are lower. Be forewarned, however, that the weather can be cooler and wetter, while the locations may not be as convenient. The **Waiehu Municipal Golf Course** (tel. 808/244–5433) is set on the northeast coast of Maui a few miles past Wailuku off Highway 340. Greens fees are $25; carts are $12. The **Pukalani Country Club** (360 Pukalani, tel. 808/572–1314) is in Upcountry Maui with views of much of the island. Fees are similar to those at Waiehu.

Tennis The state's finest tennis facilities are at the **Wailea Tennis Club** (131 Wailea Ike Pl., Kihei, tel. 808/879–1958), often called "Wimbledon West" because of its grass courts; there are also 11 Plexipave courts and a pro shop. You'll pay between $10 and $12 a day per person for the hard courts, and between $40 and $60 per court per hour for the grass numbers. At the Makena Resort, just south of Wailea, the **Makena Tennis Club** (5415 Makena Alanui, Kihei, tel. 808/879–8777) has six courts. Rates are $8 per person per hour for guests, $5 for nonguests. After an hour, if there's space available, there's no charge.

Over on West Maui, the **Royal Lahaina Tennis Ranch** (2780 Kekaa Dr., tel. 808/661–3611 ext. 2296) in the Kaanapali Beach Resort offers 11 courts and a pro shop. Guests pay $6 a day per person, while nonguests are charged $9. The **Hyatt Regency Maui** (200 Nohea Kai Dr., Kaanapali, tel. 808/661–1234 ext. 3174) has five courts, with rentals and instruction. Courts go for $12 an hour for singles, $15 for doubles. Farther north, **Kapalua Tennis Gardens** (100 Kapalua Dr., Kapalua, tel. 808/669–5677) serves the Kapalua Resort with 10 courts and a pro shop. You'll pay $9 a day if you're a guest, $10 if you're not.

There are other facilities around the island, usually one or two courts in smaller hotels or condos. Most of them, however, are open only to their guests. The best free courts are the five at the **Lahaina Civic Center** (1840 Honoapiilani Hwy., Lahaina, tel. 808/661–4685), near Wahikuli State Park; they're available on a first-come, first-served basis.

Water Sports If fishing is your sport, Maui is the place for it. You'll be able to
Deep-Sea Fishing throw in hook and bait for fish like *ahi* (yellowfin tuna), *aku* (a skipjack tuna), barracuda, bonefish, *kawakawa* (bonito), mahimahi, (a dolphin fish—*not* the mammal), Pacific blue marlin, *ono* (wahoo), and *ulua* (jack crevalle). On Maui, you can fish throughout the year, and you don't need a license.

Plenty of fishing boats run out of Lahaina and Maalaea harbors. If you charter a boat by yourself, expect to spend in the neighborhood of about $600 a day. But you can share the boat with others who are interested in fishing the same day for about $100. While there are at least 10 companies running boats on a regular basis, these are the most reliable: **Excel Charters** (Box 146, Makawao 96768, tel. 808/877–3333), **Finest Kind Inc.** (Box 10481, Lahaina 96767, tel. 808/661–0338), and **Luckey Strike Charters** (Box 1502, Lahaina 96761, tel. 808/661–4606). **Ocean Activities Center** (1325 S. Kihei Rd., Suite 212, Kihei 96753, tel. 808/879–4485 or 800/367–8047 ext. 448) can arrange fishing charters as well. You're responsible for finding your own transportation to the harbor.

Sailing Because of its proximity to the smaller islands of Molokai, Lanai, Kahoolawe, and Molokini, Maui can provide one of Hawaii's best sailing experiences. Most sailing operations like to combine their tours with a meal, some throw in snorkeling or whale watching, while others offer a sunset cruise. If you want to really sail—as opposed to cruising on a motorized catamaran or other vessel—try **Genesis Sailing Charters** (Box 10697, Lahaina 96761, tel. 808/667–5667), **Maui–Molokai Sea Cruises** (831 Eha St., Suite 101, Wailuku 96793, tel. 808/242–8777), **Sail Hawaii** (Box 573, Kihei 96753, tel. 808/879–2201), **Scotch Mist Charters** (Box 831, Lahaina 96767, tel. 808/661–0386), and **Seabern Yachts** (Box 1022, Lahaina 96767, tel. 808/661–8110).

Scuba Diving Believe it or not, Maui is just as scenic underwater as it is above. In fact, some of the finest diving spots in Hawaii lie along the Valley Isle's western and southwestern shores. If you're a certified diver, you can rent gear at any Maui dive shop simply by showing your PADI or NAUI card. Unless you're familiar with the area, however, it's probably best to hook up with a dive shop for an underwater tour. Additionally, the only really decent shore dive is at Honolua Bay, a marine reserve above Kapalua Resort. The water is usually rough during the winter.

Popular Maui dive shops—stores that deal exclusively in the sale and rental of diving equipment, as well as lessons and certification—include **Capt. Nemo's Ocean Emporium** (150 Dickenson St., Lahaina, tel. 808/661–5555), **Central Pacific Divers** (780 Front St., Lahaina, tel. 808/661–8718), **Dive Maui** (Lahaina Market Place, Lahaina, tel. 808/667–2080), **Ed Robinson's Diving Adventures** (Box 616, 50 Koki, Kihei, tel. 808/879–3584); and **Lahaina Divers** (710 Front St., Lahaina, tel. 808/667–7496). All provide equipment with proof of certification, as well as introductory dives for those who aren't certified. Introductory boat dives generally run about $60.

Snorkeling The same dive companies that take scuba aficionados on tours will take snorkelers as well—for a lot less money. One of Maui's most popular snorkeling spots can be reached only by boat: Molokini Crater, that little bowl of land off the coast of the Makena Resort. For about $55, you can spend the day at Molokini, with meals provided. **Ocean Activities Center** (1325 S. Kihei Rd., Suite 212, Kihei 96753, tel. 808/879–4485) does the best job with a Molokini tour, although other companies also do this tour.

You can also find some good snorkeling spots on your own. Specifically, secluded **Windmill Beach** (take Hwy. 30 3½ miles north of Kapalua, then turn onto the dirt road to the left) has a superb reef for snorkeling. A little more than 2 miles south, another dirt road leads to **Honolua Bay;** the coral formations on the right side of the bay are particularly dramatic. One beach south of the Kapalua Resort, you'll find **Napili Bay,** which is also quite good for snorkeling.

Almost the entire coastline from Kaanapali south to Olowalu offers fine snorkeling. Favorite sites include the area just out from the cemetery north of Wahikuli State Park, near the lava cone called **Black Rock,** on which Kaanapali's Sheraton Maui Hotel is built (tame fish will take bread from your hand there); and the shallow coral reef at **Olowalu** (south of Olowalu General Store).

The coastline from Kihei to Makena is also generally good for snorkeling. The best is found near the rocks of **Kamaole Beach III** in Kihei and the rocky fringes of Wailea's **Mokapu, Ulua, Wailea,** and **Polo** beaches.

Between Polo Beach and Makena Beach (shortly before the turnoff to Ulupalakua) lies **Five Caves,** where you'll find a maze of underwater grottos below offshore rocks. This spot is recommended for experienced snorkelers only, since the tides can get rough. At Makena, the waters around the **Puu Olai** cinder cone provide great snorkeling.

If you need gear, **Snorkel Bob's** (5425 Lower Honoapiilani Rd., Napili, tel. 808/669–9603), in the Napili Village Hotel, will rent you a mask, fins, and snorkel and throw in a carrying bag, map, and snorkel tips for $15 a week.

Waterskiing Only one company tows water-skiers off the coast of Maui: **Lahaina Water Ski** (104 Wahikuli Rd., Lahaina, tel. 808/661–5988). For $25 per 15 minutes for one person, $45 per 30 minutes for one to three people, or $75 an hour for one to five people, Lahaina Water Ski provides the boat, driver, and equipment.

Windsurfing It's only been 11 years since Hookipa Bay was discovered by boardsailors, but in those years since 1980, the windy beach 10 miles east of Kahului has become the windsurfing capital of the world. The spot boasts optimal wave-sailing wind and sea conditions and, for experienced windsurfers, can offer the ultimate experience. Other locations around Maui are good for windsurfing as well—Honolua Bay, for example—but Hookipa is absolutely unrivaled.

Even if you're a windsurfing aficionado, chances are good you didn't bring your equipment. You can rent it—or get lessons—from these shops: **Kaanapali Windsurfing School** (104 Wahikuli Rd., Lahaina, tel. 808/667–1964), **Maui Magic Windsurfing School** (520 Keolani Pl., Kahului, tel. 808/877–4816), **Ocean Activities Center** (1325 S. Kihei Rd., Kihei, tel. 808/879–4485), and **Maui Windsurfari** (Box 330254, Kahului, tel. 808/871–7766). Lessons range from $30 to $60 and can last anywhere from one to three hours. Equipment rental also varies—from no charge with lessons to $20 an hour. For the latest prices and special deals, it's best to call around once you've arrived.

Spectator Sports

Golf Tournaments
Maui has a number of golf tournaments, many of which are televised on ESPN. Especially popular during the last two months of each year, Maui's golf tourneys are professional caliber and worth the watch. The **Isuzu Kapalua International Championship of Golf** held each November at the Kapalua Resort is the granddaddy of them all and now draws big names competing for a $600,000 purse. Also at Kapalua is the **Kirin Cup World Championship of Golf,** with teams representing the U.S. Professional Golf Association (PGA) tour, the European PGA tour, the Japan PGA Tour, and the Australia/New Zealand PGA tour. Golfing greats play on Kapalua's Bay Course for a $1.1-million purse each December. At Kaanapali, the **GTE Kaanapali Golf Classic** pits senior golfers in a battle for a $300,000 purse each December. Over in Wailea, the **Annual Asahi Beer Kyosan Golf Tournament** has a $100,000 purse, and the **LPGA Women's Kemper Open,** which moved from Kauai to Wailea starting with the February 1990 tourney. For more information on specific dates for all these tournaments, call Rolfing Productions, tel. 808/669–4844.

Windsurfing
Not many places can lay claim to as many windsurfing tournaments as Maui. The Valley Isle is generally thought to be the world's preeminent windsurfing location, drawing boardsailing experts from around the globe who want to compete on its waves. In April, the **Marui/O'Neil Invitational** lures top windsurfers from at least a dozen countries to vie for a $30,000 purse. The **Hawaiian Pro-Am Speed Slalom Windsurfing Competition** and **Wailea Speed Crossing** take place in September, and the **Maui Grand Prix** and the **Aloha Classic Wave Sailing World Championships** are held in October. The **Junior World Wave Sailing Championships,** for kids under 18 from around the world, is in May. All events are held at Hookipa Bay, right outside the town of Paia, near Kahului.

Dining

Maui cuisine consists of a lot more than the poi and pineapple you'll find at a local luau. It's also more than the burgers and fries doled out at the ubiquitous fast-food chains that in some towns seem to post a store on every other corner. Maui continues to attract fine chefs, some of whom have initiated the trend La Bretagne owner/chef Claude Gaty calls "nouvelle Hawaiian." This growing movement uses fruits and vegetables unique to Hawaii in classic European or Asian ways—spawning such dishes as breadfruit soufflé and papaya cheesecake. Sometimes a touch of California is added as well.

Of course, you can find plain old local-style cooking on the Valley Isle—particularly if you wander into the less touristy areas of Wailuku or Kahului, for example. Greasy spoons abound, and some of those places are where you can get the most authentic local food, or what residents call "plate lunch," for very little expense. A good plate lunch will fulfill your daily requirement for carbohydrates: macaroni salad, two scoops of rice, and an entrée of, say, curry stew, teriyaki beef, or *kalua* (roasted) pig and cabbage.

Some of the island's best restaurants are in hotels—not surprising, considering that tourism is the island's number-one industry. In the resorts, you'll find some of Maui's finest continental restaurants, and some good coffee shops as well. In addition, because many of the upscale hotels sit right on the beach, you'll often have the benefit of an oceanfront ambience.

Few restaurants on Maui require jackets. An aloha shirt and pants for men, and a simple dress or pants for women are acceptable in all but the fanciest establishments.

Restaurants are open daily unless otherwise noted.

Highly recommended restaurants in each price category are indicated by a star ★.

Category	Cost*
Very Expensive	over $60
Expensive	$40–$60
Moderate	$20–$40
Inexpensive	under $20

*per person, excluding drinks, service, and sales tax (4%)

West Maui

American **Sam's Upstairs.** This open-air bistro in a relatively uncrowded section of Lahaina gives good views of the ocean and Lanai beyond. Dinners feature tender steaks, fresh local fish, and Maine lobster. The more casual Sam's Pub downstairs serves lunch. *505 Front St., Lahaina, tel. 808/667–4341. Reservations advised. Dress: casual. AE, MC, V. Moderate–Expensive.*

★ **Longhi's.** Proprietor Bob Longhi has gotten a lot of notoriety for the way his young waiters and waitresses pull up a chair and recite the day's menu. But what makes this establishment worth a visit is the food. Homemade pasta and pastry—whipped up by the full-time pastry chef—as well as fresh-squeezed orange juice, fresh fish, and sandwiches you can't get your mouth around are only some of the choices here. Longhi's is an open-air establishment on its first floor; tile floors and casual wood tables invite celebrities, as well as more run-of-the-mill diners, to stop and watch the world go by while supping on an enormous burger, French onion soup made with Maui onions, or a lobster caught in waters right offshore. This is a good choice for breakfast and opens at 7:30. At night, the upper floor offers a fancier version of dinner, with dancing. *888 Front St., Lahaina, tel. 808/667–2288. No reservations. Dress: casual. AE, V. Moderate.*

Continental **The Bay Club.** Here's just the place to have a magical candle-
★ light dinner. This restaurant is situated on a lava-rock promontory overlooking the bay at the far end of Kapalua Beach, within the Kapalua Resort. Set in an open-air room, with richly paneled walls and rattan furniture, the Bay Club has an excellent wine list and nouvelle cuisine menu; the scaloppine of veal and fresh catch of the day from the Molokai Channel are both superior choices. *At the Kapalua Bay Resort, 1 Bay Dr., Kapalua, tel. 808/669–5656. Reservations required. Jacket required at dinner. AE, CB, DC, MC, V. Expensive.*

★ **Plantation Veranda.** Raffles fans stirring a gentle breeze above, hand-polished mahogany floors with hooked rugs, and Windsor chairs make this place reminiscent of an old Hawaiian plantation house. The menu is extensive: from saffron-poached fish of the day to escallops of spring lamb to chateaubriand for two. Try the homemade pâté, which is excellent, then move on to, perhaps, the galantine of young island duck or the paillard of veal with scampi and bay scallops. *Kapalua Bay Hotel, 1 Bay Dr., Kapalua, tel. 808/669–5656. Reservations required. Jacket required. AE, CB, DC, MC, V. Expensive.*

Swan Court. You enter by descending a grand staircase to the edge of a lagoon in which swans glide by. A waterfall splashes, and palm fronds sway slightly in the breeze—the Swan Court radiates grandeur and elegance. The international menu includes fresh island fish Eichenholz, which is baked on an oak plate with capers and mushroom garnish; roasted baby chicken in a sour-mash bourbon sauce; veal chop sauté Armagnac, in cream with sorrel mushrooms; and roast duck, chateaubriand, fresh fish, and more. The Swan Court's extensive wine list has won awards of excellence from *Wine Spectator* magazine. The restaurant is open for a breakfast buffet. *Hyatt Regency Maui, Kaanapali Beach Resort, 200 Nohea Kai Dr., tel. 808/661–1234. Reservations advised. Jacket required. AE, CB, DC, MC, V. Expensive.*

French **Chez Paul.** A mere wide spot in the road, 4 miles south of
★ Lahaina in Olowalu, provides the setting for this intimate French restaurant that's made a name for itself since 1975. Chez Paul has only 14 tables, each set with linen tablecloths, china, and fresh flowers. The menu changes daily, but specialties include scampi Olowalu, cooked with white wine, herbs, and capers; poisson beurre blanc, fresh island fish poached in white wine with shallots, cream, and capers; and veal à la Normande, sautéed with green apples in a Calvados sauce. If you're still hungry, try the Kahlua cheesecake. *On Hwy. 30, 4 mi south of Lahaina, tel. 808/661–3843. Reservations required. Dress: casual chic. AE, CB, MC, V. 2 dinner seatings nightly, at 6:30 and 8:30. Expensive.*

★ **La Bretagne.** Chef/owner Claude Gaty has only been in the kitchen for six years, but the native Frenchman turns out some of the tastiest cuisine this side of Paris. Such dishes as seafood à la Bretonne (in puff pastry), roast duckling with port wine and carmelized pearl onions, beef tournedos, and rack of lamb waltz out of Gaty's galley each night to satisfy the eager diners who pack the little restaurant. La Bretagne is set in a house the town sheriff built in 1920. It's now a little run-down but still reminiscent of a French country inn. Soft brocade wallpaper and flowered draperies decorate the inside, while a screened-in porch provides a more open-air ambience. Right inside the door, a gleaming brass espresso machine gives La Bretagne that nonchalant European touch. The lighting is low, the service is friendly, the food is fantastic. What else is there? *562-C Front St., facing Maluulu o lele Park, Lahaina, tel. 808/661–8966. Reservations advised. Dress: casual. AE, MC, V. Expensive.*

★ **Gerard's.** Set in the romantic, Victorian-style Plantation Inn, this restaurant is the creation of owner Gerard Reversade, who has a reputation as one of Hawaii's foremost chefs. Gerard's serves French cuisine, with a menu that changes daily. Two recommended dishes are rack of lamb and medallions of veal

Alex's Hole in the Wall, **8**
Avalon Restaurant and Bar, **9**
The Bay Club, **1**
Casanova Italian Restaurant & Deli, **25**
The Chart House, **20**
Chez Paul, **15**
Chopsticks, **4**
Dillon's, **23**
Erik's Seafood Grotto, **3**
Gerard's, **10**
Haliimaile General Store, **26**
Ichiban, **19**
La Bretagne, **11**
Lahaina Coolers, **12**
La Perouse, **31**
Longhi's, **7**
Mama's Fish House, **22**
Mark Edison's, **16**
Maui Onion, **28**
Ming Yuen, **21**
Moon Hoe Seafood Restaurant, **18**
Nikko, **5**
Palm Court, **29**
Plantation Veranda, **2**
Polli's on the Beach, **24,27**
Purple Parrot, **17**
Raffles, **30**
Sam's Upstairs, **14**
Swan Court, **6**
Tasca, **13**

Maui Dining

Hanokohau

Honolua

Napili

Kahakuloa

30

Kahana

Honoapiilani Hwy.

W E S T   M A U I   M T S.

Honokowai

Kaanapali

LAHAINA

Iao Valley State Park

Olowalu

Honoapiilani Hwy.

N

0 ——— 5 miles

0 ——— 5 km

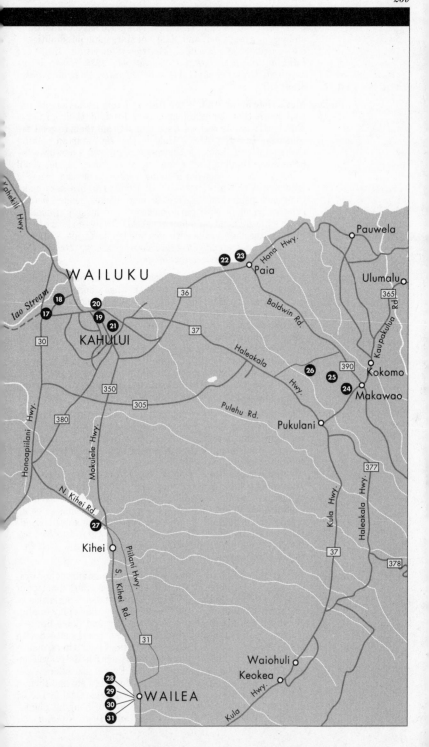

duxelles with ravioli. Other specialties include fresh fish, lamb, beef, veal, and 75 wine varieties. This place has a comfortable ambience, great food, and plenty of stargazing possibilities— it's a celebrity favorite. *At the Plantation Inn, 174 Lahainaluna Rd., Lahaina, tel. 808/661–8939. Reservations required. Dress: casual. AE, CB, DC, MC, V. Dinner only. Moderate.*

Italian

★ **Alex's Hole in the Wall.** When Alex and Tom Didio came to Hawaii more than 30 years ago, they brought their grandpa Marchetti's family recipes, determined to put them to good use someday. In 1971, Alex's Hole in the Wall started making Grandpa proud. Look for the restaurant down a narrow alley behind the Dolphin Gallery and up a staircase. Inside, you'll think you're in someone's living room, since the place is crammed with knickknacks of all kinds. The brothers make their own pasta and sausage; favorite dishes include *pollo e salsicce* (chicken with garlic sausage) and lasagne *imbottita* (with spinach, meat, and four cheeses). The desserts are to die for—try the cheesecake with rum and tropical fruit. *834 Front St., Lahaina, tel. 808/661–3197. No reservations. Dress: casual. AE, MC, V. Inexpensive–Moderate.*

Japanese

Nikko. This is Japanese food *teppan*-style. That means you'll be seated with other diners at a table that has a built-in grill. Together you'll watch the chef and his slicing, dicing, and chopping knives. He can perform amazing feats—and the best part is you get to eat the creations he prepares. Raw vegetables, such as green peppers, eggplant, and squash, as well as bite-size chicken, pork, and beef, are grilled to perfection. A lot of Japanese visitors find their way to Nikko—and you know what that says about a place. *Maui Marriott Hotel, Kaanapali Beach Resort, 100 Nohea Kai Dr., tel. 808/667–1200. Reservations required. Dress: casual. AE, CB, DC, MC, V. Moderate.*

Oriental

Chopsticks. When it opened, this was Maui's first restaurant featuring "grazing"—the sampling of several appetizer-sized portions in lieu of a single entrée. Here, you'll find yourself enjoying the cuisines of China, Japan, Thailand, and Polynesia. A typical meal might include the likes of Chinese dim sum (wonton-wrapped bits of meat and fish), Japanese sushi, and Thai spring rolls (like egg rolls only crisper and served with mint leaves, cucumber, and lettuce). The atmosphere is friendly, but keep an eye on your tab—watch what seems to be an inexpensive meal add up with each morsel you select. *Royal Lahaina Hotel, Kaanapali Beach Resort, 2780 Kekaa Dr., tel. 808/661–3611. No reservations. Dress: casual. AE, CB, DC, MC, V. Inexpensive–Moderate.*

Seafood

Erik's Seafood Grotto. This award-winning restaurant and oyster bar in the Kahana Villas Condominiums offers a netful of fresh island fish daily, plus such flavorful house specialties as cioppino and seafood curry. The fresh Hawaiian spiny or slipper lobster is filled with seafood stuffing and flame-broiled, while you can get your *opakapaka* (blue snapper) sautéed with butter. The mahimahi is especially delicious baked in vermouth with macadamia nuts. If you arrive between 5 and 6 PM you can sample the $10.95 early-bird special. Erik's also offers *keiki* dinners—a petite steak or medley of chicken, fish, and shrimp at $8.95 for children under 12. Erik's has a nautical feel to it, with a rustic open-beam ceiling and lots of hanging plants. *Kahana Villas, 4242 Lower Honoapiilani Hwy., Kahana, tel.*

808/669–4806. Reservations advised. Dress: casual. AE, MC, V. Dinner only. Moderate.

Spanish **Tasca.** This restaurant specializes in "tapas," the Spanish equivalent of "pupus" in Hawaii or "hors d'oeuvres" in America. The Mediterranean-style paella, ceviche, ratatouille, and other tasty nuggets hail from countries such as Greece, Portugal, Italy—and even Spain. *608 Front St., Lahaina, tel. 808/ 661–8001. Reservations advised. Dress: casual. AE, MC, V. Inexpensive–Moderate.*

Tropical/ Continental ★ **Avalon Restaurant and Bar.** This is one of Maui's trendiest restaurants, owned by Mark Ellman, a young Californian who came to Maui and opened his first commercial venture in January 1988. The decor at the Avalon is Hawaiian 1940s, with bright tropical prints on the chairs and tables, reminiscent of the days when you had to cruise to the Islands and, once there, would find a paradise of swaying palms and hula girls. Oversize dishware brings the food to the table—and what food it is! Called "Pacific Rim," features cuisine from California, Hawaii, Mexico, Indonesia, Thailand, Vietnam, and Japan. Ellman's signature items include roast duck with plum sauce and Chinese steamed dumplings; giant prawns in a garlic black-bean sauce; and fresh guacamole made right at your table. For dessert, try the pineapple upside-down cake served warm with whipped cream or the caramel Miranda—fresh exotic fruits in a homemade caramel sauce with sour cream and brown sugar. Celebrities love the Avalon: During one four-day visit, Yoko Ono was seen there three nights. *Mariner's Alley, 844 Front St., Lahaina, tel. 808/667–5559. Reservations advised. Dress: Casual. AE, DC, MC, V. Moderate.*

★ **Lahaina Coolers.** This surf bistro specializes in unusual food at reasonable prices. Try the pepper chicken linguini in a sauce of roasted bell peppers, or a spinach and feta quesadilla. *180 Dickenson St., Lahaina, tel. 808/661–7082. Reservations advised. Dress: casual. AE, MC, V. Inexpensive.*

Central Maui

American **Mark Edison's.** A romantic dining spot, Mark Edison's boasts one of Maui's most unusual locations. With views of the West Maui mountains and Iao Valley Park, this restaurant has a lush, tropical ambience unlike that of any other eating establishment. Specialties include chicken, steak, pasta, and fish, with a well-stocked salad bar. Each evening from 5:30 to 6:30, you can order prime rib and teriyaki chicken for $8.95. Mark Edison's has a large local following, especially at lunch. It also brings in good entertainment at least once a week. *Iao Valley Rd., just beyond Kepaniwai Park at the Iao Needle, tel. 808/242–5555. Reservations advised. Dress: casual. AE, MC, V. Moderate– Expensive.*

Chinese **★** **Ming Yuen.** This place is low-key, with unassuming decor, but locals love it and will line up to prove it. The menu is extensive and features mostly Cantonese cuisine, plus a few Szechuan dishes. The lemon chicken has made them famous, but also try the hot-and-sour soup to start and then go for the Kung Pau chicken: chicken stir-fried with chili peppers, garlic, peanuts, and chopped vegetables. The moo shu pork is also recommended. Ming Yuen's most unusual dish is a minced squab cooked in a Chinese mushroom sauce and served in lettuce pockets. *162 Alamaha St., Kahului, tel. 808/871–7787. Reservations advised. Dress: casual. AE, DC, MC, V. Inexpensive.*

Moon Hoe Seafood Restaurant. The second really good Chinese restaurant on Maui, Moon Hoe offers both Cantonese and Szechuan cuisines, with more than 100 different dishes to choose from, including a popular crispy roast chicken and a beef with snow peas. The fresh island-caught fish is superb. *752 Lower Main St., Wailuku, tel. 808/242–7778. Reservations advised. Dress: casual. MC, V. Inexpensive.*

Italian   Purple Parrot. This restaurant in downtown Wailuku caters largely to a local crowd, especially at lunch. The Purple Parrot has a friendly decor, with three shades of purple and tropical plants. It also serves good pasta. The fettuccine Alfredo primavera, for example, is a fine marriage of two popular pasta sauces, while the linguine in clam sauce with roasted red peppers is very tasty. The Purple Parrot also offers some delicious barbecue dishes and pizza. *2065 Main St., Wailuku, tel. 808/ 242–9650. Reservations advised. Dress: casual. AE, CB, DC, MC, V. Closed weekends. Inexpensive–Moderate.*

Japanese   Ichiban. If you've a hankering to try Japanese food in Maui, this is the place to do it. There's nothing fancy here, but you'll find authentic sashimi, teriyaki, and noodle dishes. The shrimp tempura and the combination dish are both popular and recommended. *Kahului Shopping Center, 2133 Kaohu St., tel. 808/ 871–6977. Dress: casual. MC, V. Inexpensive.*

Steakhouse   The Chart House. This dining spot is about as close to the ocean as you can get in a Kahului restaurant. Large aquariums that serve as partial walls contribute to the nautical decor. The menu includes steaks grilled to order; fresh fish sautéed, baked, broiled, or cooked in herbs and spices; and a well-stocked salad bar. One of the nicest dining establishments for both food and ambience in Kahului, the Chart House is very popular with the local after-work crowd. *500 Puunene Ave., Kahului, tel. 808/877–2476. Reservations advised. Dress: casual. AE, MC, V. Moderate.*

East Maui

American   Dillon's. Don't let the saloon-style exterior fool you. Dillon's is serious about its food. The bamboo-covered walls inside add to the rustic ambience, and there's also a tiny garden patio. The star of the lunch menu is a seafood salad heaped with Kula vegetables and fresh Kauai prawns. At dinner, look for such items as baked Kauai prawns stuffed with crab, and spinach pastas. *89 Hana Hwy., Paia, tel. 808/579–9113. Dress: casual. AE, MC, V. Inexpensive.*

Maui Onion. Set out by the pool at the Stouffer Wailea Hotel, this coffee shop has a small menu that includes salads and sandwiches. Maui Onion made it onto this list, however, because of its mouth-watering Maui onion rings. If you love onion rings, we recommend you make a special trip here. *Stouffer Wailea Hotel, Wailea Resort, 3550 Wailea Alanui Dr., tel. 808/879– 4900. Dress: casual. AE, CB, DC, MC, V. Inexpensive.*

Buffet   Palm Court. This is another Stouffer restaurant with a twist: At the Palm Court, you will find a huge buffet each night. What's more, the Palm Court rotates cuisines so that one night it will serve pasta, the next a paniolo steak fry, and two nights each week feature seafood or English cuisine. This isn't run-of-the-mill buffet food but rather top-of-the-line cuisine, as close to fine dining as you'll get, considering it's served from chafing dishes. Those who'd rather not partake of the buffet can order from the menu. *Stouffer Wailea Beach Resort, 3550 Wailea Alanui Dr., tel. 808/879–4900. Reservations advised. Dress: casual. AE, CB, DC, MC, V. Inexpensive–Moderate.*

Continental

★ **La Perouse.** This hushed, intimate room, richly paneled in koa and decorated with antiques and objets d'art, is named after the French explorer who discovered Maui in 1786. La Perouse serves as a worthy competitor to Raffles next door. Although the menu changes monthly, the accent here is on delicacies native to Hawaii—the Hawaiian shrimp on a bed of Hawaiian fiddlehead fern is excellent, as is the creamy callaloo of crab meat soup with Maui taro leaves, the deep water abalone with creamy dill sauce, and the island snapper in puff pastry. The seafood selections are extensive, but you can also get duck, lamb, chicken, or beef. Polish off your meal with the decadent chocolate mousse Brasilia. *Maui Inter-Continental Wailea Hotel, Wailea, tel. 808/879–1922. Reservations required. Dress: casual. AE, CB, DC, MC, V. Very Expensive.*

★ **Raffles.** The pride and joy of the Stouffer Wailea Beach Resort, Raffles is a luxurious, award-winning room that pays homage to British colonial elegance. In fact, the name was inspired by Sir Thomas Stamford Raffles (1781–1826), founder of the city of Singapore; the Raffles Hotel in that city is world-renowned. In this restaurant, Oriental rugs rest on shining teak floors, and bronze chandeliers illuminate the Chinese ceramics. The sophisticated Continental cuisine includes such treats as lobster ravioli with grilled shiitake mushrooms; warm quail salad with radicchio; and grilled ahi steak with eggplant, wasabe, ginger, cream, and green tea noodles. The Singapore-sling sorbet served between courses is a nice touch. Raffles also has an extravagant Sunday brunch that features, among other things, omelets and chocolate-dipped strawberries. *Stouffer Wailea Beach Resort, 3550 Wailea Alanui Dr., tel. 808/879–4900. Reservations required. Jacket required. AE, CB, DC, MC, V. Very Expensive.*

Italian

Casanova Italian Restaurant & Deli. Owned by three young native Italians—and a German brought up in Italy—this Upcountry establishment was once a modest deli. Now it's a real restaurant offering the best Italian food on Maui. A wood-fired pizza oven produces a variety of yummy pies; try the salsiccia with mozzarella, ham, and broccoli in a tomato sauce. You can also order pasta, chicken, or fresh fish. *1188 Makawao Ave., Makawao, tel. 808/572–0220. Reservations advised. Dress: casual. AE, MC, V. Moderate.*

Mexican

★ **Polli's on the Beach.** Who would've thought you could find two vegetarian Mexican restaurants on Maui? Native Arizonan Polli Smith and her husband opened a lively Mexican cantina called Polli's in Upcountry Makawao. It was so successful, they opened a Polli's on the beach in Kihei, which features an open-air atmosphere perfect for Maui sunsets. They've now added meat to the menu, but their meatless tacos, burritos, and enchiladas are just as good. Everything's offered à la carte, but you can get complete dinners, too. Polli's margaritas are the best in the state—take it from us. *1202 Makawao Ave., Makawao, tel. 808/572–7808, and 101 N. Kihei Rd., Kihei, tel.*

808/879–5275. Reservations advised. Dress: casual. AE, MC, V. Inexpensive.

Seafood **Mama's Fish House.** Looking for the best seafood on Maui? Put
★ your car on the Hana Highway and head toward Paia. About 1½
miles before Paia, you'll see an oceanfront building on your
left—Mama's, an Old Hawaiian-style restaurant serving hon-
est food. This is a lovely spot, well landscaped and well tended.
The fresh fish here has the reputation of being the best you can
find in the area, and you can get it sautéed in butter, poached in
white wine sauce with mushrooms, or broiled with lemon butter. One recommended dish is the stuffed fish Lani, a fresh fish
fillet baked with Mama's shrimp stuffing. Mama's also serves
meat and chicken. *799 Kaiholo Pl., Paia, tel. 808/579–9672.
Reservations required at dinner. Dress: casual. AE, MC, V.
Moderate.*

Tropical/ **Haliimaile General Store.** This delightful restaurant was a
Continental camp store in the 1920s, but you'd never know it now. From the
★ outside, its white, green, and peach tin exterior looks a little
out of place, sitting proudly in a pineapple field in Upcountry
Maui, literally in the middle of nowhere. Owner Beverly
Gannon has done wonders with this place, turning it into a
charming outpost that serves some of the best food in the state.
The contemporary menu uses Island products and changes
twice monthly. One of Haliimaile's staples is duck prepared in a
variety of ways, such as duck smoked with pineapple chutney.
Other specialties include the dynamite barbecued ribs, lobster
pasta with fresh tarragon, and spicy shrimp Diane. Since Mrs.
Gannon intended to open a deli with only 32 seats—although it
grew to 80 within one week—there's a stainless steel deli case
featuring all the different specials. A corner of this restaurant
looks like an old general store, with items for sale. Since its
opening in 1988, this has become one of Maui's most magnetic
restaurants, repeatedly attracting celebrities and a host of
other see-and-be-seen types. *Haliimaile Rd., 2 mi before
Pukalani, tel. 808/572–2666. Dress: casual. AE, MC, V.
Closed Mon. Inexpensive–Moderate.*

Lodging

Maui has the state's highest concentration of condominium units. More than half of the island's rental units, in fact, are
condos. Don't be put off by this; it's not what you're thinking.
For the most part, Maui's condos are not the tacky high rises
that boast thin walls and cheap appliances. These are top-of-
the-line units with all the amenities. Many are oceanfront and
offer the ambience of a hotel suite without the cost.

Maui also boasts the highest percentage of luxury hotel rooms
in the state. According to a national hotel-research firm, a full
50% of the Valley Isle's hotel rooms can be placed in the strato-
sphere when it comes to elegance. And although the figure for
luxury condominiums is lower, you can nonetheless find some
outrageously upscale condos on the Valley Isle.

Of course, the price you'll pay to stay on Maui reflects this attention to luxury. The island has the highest average
accommodation cost of any Hawaiian island, and hoteliers here
tend to raise rates with much greater abandon. In recent years,
this has created a greater willingness on the part of visitors to

try other islands, which is one reason Kauai and the Big Island have had higher visitor counts and occupancy rates. The average lodging rate on Maui can run as much as $70 more a night. Most lodgings come equipped with swimming pools, all of them outdoors to take full advantage of the gentle year-round climate.

What you'll pay depends in part on where you want to stay. West Maui is the center of tourism. More rooms are available on this part of the Valley Island than anywhere else, and most are high quality, and expensive. Two major resort areas anchor West Maui: the Kaanapali Beach Resort, with its six hotels and seven condominiums, and the Kapalua Bay Resort, with its one hotel and one condo.

Central Maui is a tough place to stay, mostly because the choices are so limited. It's a small area to begin with, and Central Maui is better known as home to the majority of the Valley Isle's residents. Wailuku is the county seat, and Kahului is the industrial/commercial center; neither place offers much in the way of accommodations.

East Maui is a mixed bag when it comes to accommodations. You can find just about any rate and just about any degree of comfort. That's partly because the area is so huge: it encompasses the Wailea and Makena resorts along the southwestern shore; Kihei, which runs in a strip above Wailea; Upcountry Maui, the area that rises into the clouds of Haleakala; and Hana, secluded in the easternmost end of the island.

Highly recommended hotels in each price category are indicated by a star ★.

Category	Cost*
Very Expensive	over $175
Expensive	$125–$175
Moderate	$75–$125
Inexpensive	under $75

*All prices are for a standard double room, excluding 9¼% tax and service charges.

West Maui

Very Expensive **Embassy Suites.** The Hawaiian Islands' first all-suite hotel opened north of Kaanapali in late 1988 with one- and two-bedroom apartments. The units are spacious, with a blue-and-beige decor that gently insists on being trendily tropical. Each suite has two phones (with separate phone lines), ceiling fans, air-conditioning, a refrigerator, a microwave oven, and a coffee maker, as well as a 36-inch color television with a VCR. Fine touches have been added, such as an inviting wicker chaise lounge perched next to an open window. The rates include a full breakfast each morning and a two-hour cocktail party with manager Gary Ettinger each evening. *104 Kaanapali Shores Pl., Lahaina 96761, tel. 808/661–2000 or 800/462–6284. 413 units. Beachfront. Facilities: sauna, health club, pool, tennis, golf, A/C, color TV. AE, CB, DC, MC, V.*
Hyatt Regency Maui. Want to stay in a fantasyland? This lavish property was built in 1980 by Chris Hemmeter, a developer

Maui Lodging

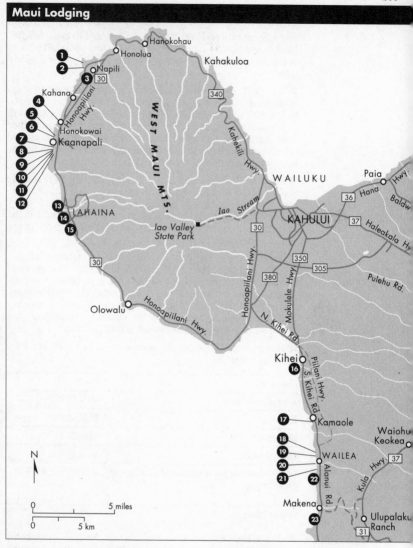

Aloha Cottages, **27**
Aston Kaanapali Shores, **5**
Aston Kamaole Sands, **17**
Coconut Inn, **3**
Embassy Suites, **6**

Four Seasons, **22**
Hana Kai-Maui, **26**
Heavenly Hana Inn, **25**
Hotel Hana-Maui, **28**
Hyatt Regency Maui, **12**
Kaanapali Alii, **10**
Kaanapali Beach Hotel, **8**
Kapalua Bay Hotel, **1**

Kula Lodge, **24**
Lahaina Hotel, **13**
Mana Kai-Maui, **18**
Maui Inter-Continental Wailea, **21**
Maui Lu Resort, **16**
Maui Marriott, **11**

Maui Prince, **23**
Napili Kai Beach Club, **2**
Papakea Beach Resort, **4**
Pioneer Inn, **15**
Plantation Inn, **14**
Royal Lahaina, **7**
Stouffer Wailea, **19**
Wailea Villas, **20**
Westin Maui, **9**

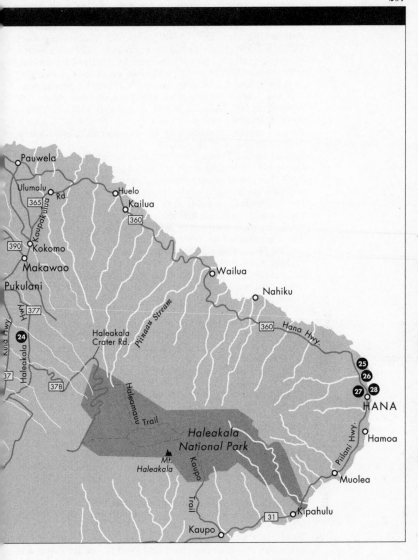

with a penchant for water fantasies and expensive art, and the hotel shows his biases. There are nine major waterfalls and several smaller ones. The 750,000-gallon pool is something every honeymooning couple should have access to—there's a secret, romantic grotto made more secluded by a waterfall cascading over the opening, as well as a 130-foot water slide, a swinging rope bridge, and a swim-up cocktail bar. Service here is good, and the room interiors have a tropical, upscale decor. *200 Nohea Kai Dr., Lahaina 96761, tel. 808/661–1234 or 800/233–9000. 815 rooms with bath. Beachfront. Facilities: 5 restaurants, 7 cocktail lounges, golf, tennis, color TV, A/C, library, health spa. AE, CB, DC, MC, V.*

Kaanapali Alii. This is a condominium, but you'd never know it; the four 11-story buildings are put together so well, you still have the feeling of seclusion. Instead of tiny rooms, you can choose from one- and two-bedroom apartments. Each features lovely amenities: a chaise in an alcove, a bidet, a sunken living room, a whirlpool, oak kitchen cabinets, and a separate dining room. Run by a company called Classic Resorts, the Kaanapali Alii is maintained like a hotel—with daily maid service, an Activities Desk, and a 24-hour front desk. If you can afford the nightly rate, it's well worth the price. *50 Nohea Kai Dr., Lahaina 96761, tel. 808/667–1400 or 800/642–MAUI. 264 1- and 2-bedroom units with bath. Beachfront. Facilities: sauna, pools, lighted tennis courts, golf, A/C, color TV. AE, CB, DC, MC, V.*

★ **Kapalua Bay Hotel.** Part of the Kapalua Bay Resort, this is one of the finest hotels in the state, winner of numerous awards and accolades. Built in 1978, the hotel has a California feel to it: the exterior is all understated white and natural wood. The open lobby, filled with flowering vanda and dendrobium orchids, has a fine view of the ocean beyond. The rooms are spacious and are undergoing renovation in furnishings and decor, which they needed because they'd begun to look dated. The impeccable staff is always ready to fill any need, and for the price, you certainly won't be disappointed. Although it's isolated from other resort areas, Kapalua has some of the island's finest restaurants and shops to make up for it. *1 Bay Dr., Kapalua 96761, tel. 808/669–5656 or 800/367–8000. 194 rooms with bath. (There are also 135 1- and 2-bedroom units in the Kapalua Villas on the Kapalua Resort. Condo rates are higher than hotel prices and often include a car.) Beachfront. Facilities: pool, 4 restaurants, shops, color TV, A/C, golf, and tennis. AE, CB, DC, MC, V.*

★ **Maui Marriott.** The Marriott sits on the same impressive Kaanapali beach as the Hyatt and Westin, but its rooms and service offer a lot less flash. The rooms are large—many with ocean views—and done in shades of mauve and mint, while the lobby is open and airy and filled with cascading orchids. The best thing about the Marriott, however, is the service. Most hotels talk about a guest-oriented staff; the Marriott lives the notion. These people are genuinely friendly and helpful. You almost think they'll invite you home for a visit. Maui's best Japanese restaurant, Nikko, is on the ground floor. *100 Nohea Kai Dr., Lahaina 96761, tel. 808/667–1200 or 800/228–9290. 720 rooms with bath. Beachfront. Facilities: 4 restaurants, 3 lounges, tennis, color TV, golf, pool. AE, CB, DC, MC, V.*

Westin Maui. The Westin is another property from the developer of the Hyatt Maui. Opened in the fall of 1987, the Westin is a make-over of a lower-end hotel called the Maui Surf. The design restrictions inherent in a renovation, unfortunately, have limited the room size, which is rather small for the price. This, however, is a hotel for people who aren't going to spend all their time in their rooms. *2365 Kaanapali Pkwy., Lahaina 96761, tel. 808/667–2525 or 800/228–3000. 761 rooms with bath. Beachfront. Facilities: 6 restaurants, lounges, shops, Jacuzzis, health club, beauty salon, 5 pools. AE, CB, DC, MC, V.*

Expensive   **Aston Kaanapali Shores.** Just north of Kaanapali beach in the area called Honokowai is a property run by Aston Hotels & Resorts, Hawaii's largest condominium manager. The locally owned company hasn't sacrificed quality in the name of size. The Kaanapali Shores is well run and was renovated at great expense; the tasteful, tropical decor combines new prints with rattan furnishings. Marble and modern art greet arrivals in the lobby, where the front desk is open 24 hours a day. The poolside restaurant—which happens to be beachside as well—is a great place to wind up the day. *3445 Honoapiilani Hwy., Lahaina 96761, tel. 808/667–2211 or 800/92–ASTON. 463 condo units with bath, including studios and 1- and 2-bedrooms. Beachfront. Facilities: pool, tennis, shops, restaurant, lounge, color TV. AE, CB, DC, MC, V.*

Kaanapali Beach Hotel. This property is right in the middle of all the Kaanapali action and offers much more reasonable rates than its neighbors. Instead of glitz and flash, you'll find a comfortable hotel with a friendly Hawaiian staff. The hotel conducts complimentary classes in hula, lei making, ukulele playing, and more. *2525 Kaanapali Pkwy., Lahaina 96761, tel. 808/661–0011 or 800/367–5170. 430 rooms with bath. Beachfront. Facilities: pool, golf, shops, color TV, A/C, restaurants, lounge. AE, CB, DC, MC, V.*

Lahaina Hotel. This once derelict hotel has reopened after more than $3 million in renovations by the Honolulu businessmen Rick Ralston and Alan Beall. Ralston, also responsible for the rebirth of the Manoa Valley Inn on Oahu, has stocked the 13-room Maui property with antique beds, wardrobes, and chests, as well as delightful country print curtains and spreads. The trendy David Paul's Lahaina Grill downstairs attracts diners. *127 Lahainaluna Rd., Lahaina 96761, tel. 808/661–0577. 13 rooms with bath. MC, V.*

★   **Napili Kai Beach Club.** Owner Dorothy Millar and her late husband created a homey little place on one of the finest beaches in Maui; it attracts a loyal following each year. The clean, Japanese-style rooms with shoji doors open onto your lanai, with the beach and ocean right outdoors. This place is particularly popular with honeymooners and Canadians. The weekly cocktail party Mrs. Millar continues to host encourages a friendly atmosphere. *5900 Honoapiilani Hwy., Lahaina 96761, tel. 808/669–6271 or 800/367–5030. 163 rooms with bath. Beachfront. Facilities: 4 pools, Jacuzzi, tennis courts, putting green. No credit cards. Advance payment or traveler's checks required.*

Royal Lahaina. California wholesaling giant Pleasant Hawaiian Holidays (PHH) recently purchased this 531-room property and depending on when you arrive, you may find the blue and green decor of old or PHH's new selections. The lanais will continue to have their stunning ocean or golf-course views, which are worth the price of the room. What distinguishes the Royal Lahaina is the two-story ocean cottages, each divided into four units. Lushly decorated, the bedrooms open to the tradewinds on two sides. The upstairs units have private lanais, while the downstairs share. Units also have small private pools. *2780 Kekaa Dr., Lahaina 96761, tel. 808/661–3611 or 800/621–2151. 531 rooms with bath. Beachfront. Facilities: 3 pools, shops, restaurants, tennis, golf, color TV, A/C. AC, CB, DC, MC, V.*

Moderate **Coconut Inn.** Although the management has changed, this hotel is still highly recommended. The Coconut Inn was a dumpy apartment building until California financial whiz George Gilman bought it and turned it into a small, personal country inn. Gilman has since sold out and opened a similar property called the Coconut Plaza in Waikiki, but the Coconut Inn retains much of its charm. The transformed hotel suites (once one-bedroom apartments) each come with a kitchen. A free-form pool and stream are located in the center courtyard, where guests congregate and become acquainted. The complimentary breakfast is served each morning in the lobby area. This is a comfortable place, and most people don't mind the trek to the beach. *181 Hui Rd. F, Napili 96761, tel. 808/669–5712 or 800/367–8006. 40 1-bedroom units with bath and kitchens. About ½ mi from beach. Facilities: pool, spa, color TV, continental breakfast, daily maid service. MC, V.*

★ **Papakea Beach Resort.** This resort is an active place to stay if you consider all the classes held here, such as swimming, snorkeling, and pineapple cutting. Located in Honokowai, Papakea has built-in privacy because its units are spread out among 11 low-rise buildings on some 13 acres of land. You aren't really aware that you're sharing the property with 363 other rooms. Bamboo-lined walkways between buildings and fish-stocked ponds create a serene mood. *3543 Honoapiilani Hwy., Lahaina 96761, tel. 808/669–4848 or 800/367–5637. 364 units with bath, including studios and 1- and 2-bedrooms. Beachfront. Facilities: 2 pools, whirlpool, spas, saunas, color TV, tennis, putting green. AE, MC, V.*

★ **Plantation Inn.** A nine-room property, the Plantation Inn is one of those places you just won't find everywhere. The inn resembles a renovated Victorian home on a quiet country street in the heart of Lahaina, within walking distance of the ocean and all the down-to-earth bars, restaurants, and shops in the old whaling port. Each room at the inn is decorated differently, with exquisite attention to detail. The owners have stocked the place with antiques, stained glass, brass beds, and ceiling fans and polished up the hardwood floors, wood trim, and wide verandas. Downstairs is one of Hawaii's best French restaurants, Gerard's, whose candlelit ambience definitely adds to the romantic European charm of the place. The Plantation Inn also offers meal, airfare, car, and dive packages. *174 Lahainaluna Rd., Lahaina 96761, tel. 808/667–9225 or 800/433–6815. 9 rooms with bath; suite available. Facilities: restaurant, refrigerators, pool, A/C, ceiling fans, color TV. AE, MC, V.*

Inexpensive **Pioneer Inn.** You want fancy? Don't check into the Pioneer Inn. If, however, you'd like to try a taste of old Lahaina, then this is the place for you. Downstairs is the boisterous saloon, where tourists and locals alike hang out—if you get a room over the bar, forget about sleeping until the bartender rousts the last revelers at about 1 AM. Rooms are on the second floor. In the older section up front, they're nothing fancy: smallish and rather dim, with ceiling fans and no air-conditioning. Ask about the Spencer Tracy–Katharine Hepburn suite in the newer section, which is brighter and quieter, with air-conditioning. In this newer wing, some rooms overlook the small hotel pool and courtyard, while others face Front Street. What you get at the Pioneer Inn is history—and plenty of it. *658 Wharf St., Lahaina 96761, tel. 808/661–3636. 48 rooms with bath. Near the ocean. Facilities: 2 restaurants, cocktail lounge, small pool. AE, CB, DC, MC, V.*

East Maui

Very Expensive

★ **Four Seasons.** Opened in mid 1990, the Four Seasons has quickly become a favorite Maui hotel. Part of the reason comes from its location: smack dab on one of the Valley Island's finest beaches with all the amenities of the well-groomed Wailea Resort. But the property's a stunner as well. Terraces, courtyards, gardens, waterfalls, and fountains combine to enhance the beachfront setting. Nearly all the rooms have an ocean view and, inside, are decorated in rattan and wicker with colors they call "sunset." Four Seasons couldn't decide whether to pamper guests with terry robes or Japanese yukatas, so they put both in each room. *3900 Wailea Alanui, Wailea 96753, tel. 808/874–8000 or 800/332–3442. 374 rooms with bath. Facilities: 3 restaurants, cocktail lounges, tennis, golf, nearby shopping, pool, health club. AE, CB, DC, MC, V.*

★ **Hotel Hana-Maui.** One of the best places to stay in Hawaii—if not the Western Hemisphere—is this small, secluded hotel in Hana. Rosewood Corporation of Dallas purchased the hotel and the 7,000-acre ranch that surrounds it, then proceeded to invest another $25 million or so in upgrading the hotel before selling it to a Japanese investor. The buildings now boast white plaster walls and trellised verandas, while inside, the rooms have bleached wood floors, overstuffed furniture in natural fabrics, and such decorator touches as art and orchids. A new addition is the Sea Cottages, 24 duplex units that have an old-time plantation look on the outside and that classy decorating touch inside. Prices at the Hotel Hana-Maui are outrageous, but they do include all meals. *Box 8, Hana 96713, tel. 808/536–7522, 808/248–8211, or 800/321–HANA. 96 large units with bath. Facilities: shuttle to secluded beach, pool, shops, restaurant, cocktail lounge, tennis, stables, library, jogging paths. All meals included in rate. AE, CB, DC, MC, V.*

★ **Maui Inter-Continental Wailea.** Many repeat guests swear that overall, the Inter-Continental is the finest hotel on Maui, and they may be right. Luxurious without being overwhelming, this is a genuine hotel—upscale, unpretentious, and expertly run, with its share of amenities, including a set of rooms right on the beach. All the quietly elegant rooms are decorated in subtle tones of white, peach, or lavender and have private lanais and spacious bathrooms. The grounds are beautiful, with walks along paths through jungles of palm, banana, and red-blossomed torch ginger. Activities abound here, and award-winning restaurants are located within the hotel. *Box 779, Wailea 96753, tel. 808/879–1922 or 800/33–AGAIN. 550 rooms with bath. Beachfront. Facilities: golf, tennis, restaurants, pools, Jacuzzi, shops. AE, CB, DC, MC, V.*

Maui Prince. The Prince is one of Maui's newer luxury hotels, opened in 1986. The attention to service, style, and presentation are apparent from the minute you walk into the delightful open-air lobby of the hotel, which is owned and managed by a Japanese company. Rooms on three levels surround the courtyard, which is home to a Japanese garden with carefully tended plants and a babbling stream. Each evening a three-piece string ensemble performs classical music in the courtyard. Rooms are not elaborately decorated—instead, they're rather understated, in tones of mauve and beige. Unfortunately, there's an earth berm between the hotel and the beach—part of the agreement the hotel had to make with the zoning commission and local residents—so an ocean view isn't possible from the first floor. *5400 Makena Alanui, Kihei 96753, tel. 808/874–1111 or 800/321–MAUI. 300 rooms with bath. Beachfront. Facilities: 4 restaurants, pool, golf, tennis, shops, color TV, A/C. AE, CB, DC, MC, V.*

★ **Stouffer Wailea.** This is the first hotel you'll come to once you enter the stylish Wailea Beach Resort. Nothing here is lean. Situated on fantastic Mokapu Beach, most of the hotel's luxury rooms are contained in a seven-story, T-shaped building, and the Mokapu Beach Club—26 cottagelike suites—is right on the water. Guest rooms, decorated in beige, burgundy, and blue, have refrigerators. The hotel emphasizes Hawaiian flavor, with gigantic contemporary tapestries and gorgeous carpets in the public areas; outside, you'll find gardens of exotic flowers, waterfalls, and reflecting ponds. Plenty of activities and award-winning restaurants are available right on the property. *3550 Wailea Alanui Dr., Wailea 96753, tel. 808/879–4900 or 800/9–WAILEA. 347 rooms with bath. Beachfront. Facilities: pool, Jacuzzi, restaurants, shops, cocktail lounges, color TV with HBO, A/C. AE, CB, DC, MC, V.*

Expensive **Wailea Villas.** The Wailea Resort has built three fine condominiums, calling them—appropriately—Wailea Ekahi, Wailea Elua, and Wailea Ekolu (Wailea One, Two, and Three). All three have beautifully landscaped grounds, large units with exceptional views, and access to one of the island's best beaches. Wailea Elua is usually considered the nicest of the three, with more expensive furnishings and rates to match. We recommend all three. It's an expansive property, with all the amenities of the fine Wailea Resort, including daily maid service and a concierge. *3750 Wailea Alanui, Wailea 96753, tel. 808/879–1595 or 800/367–5246. 598 units in 3 complexes, 2 of them beachfront. 1-, 2-, and 3-bedroom apartments with bath available. Facilities: pools, color TV, hotel restaurants and lounges nearby. MC, V.*

Moderate **Aston Kamaole Sands.** This is a huge property for Kihei—10 four-story buildings wrap around a grassy slope on which are clustered swimming and wading pools, a small waterfall, Jacuzzis, and barbecues. All units have laundry facilities but no air-conditioning. Managed by the well-run Aston Hotels & Resorts, this condominium property boasts a 24-hour front desk, an Activities Desk, and on-property food and beverage. *2695 S. Kihei Rd., Kihei 96753, tel. 808/879–0666 or 800/922–7866. 440 1-, 2-, and 3-bedroom condo units with bath. Across the road from Kihei Beach. Facilities: pool, Jacuzzis, wading pool, restaurant, tennis. AE, CB, DC, MC, V.*

★ **Hana Kai-Maui.** This small condominium is the only true beachfront property in the tiny town of Hana. The large and simply furnished units are set on lush, manicured grounds. One added benefit is the spring-fed swimming pool on one side of the property: It was built with lava rock and looks almost too unusual to swim in. *Box 38, Hana 96713, tel. 808/248–8426 or 808/248–7742. 17 units with bath. Beachfront. AE, MC, V.*

Kula Lodge. The Kula Lodge isn't your typical Hawaiian place, for two reasons: (1) it looks like a chalet property that should grace the Swiss Alps; and (2) three of its five units come with a fireplace. But the lodge is charming and cozy in spite of its non-tropical ambience. It's a perfect spot for a romantic interlude or reading a good book next to a roaring fire. The five units are in two wooden cabins; four of them have lofts in addition to the ample bed space downstairs. Set on three wooded acres, the lodge has a view of the valley and ocean, enhanced even more by the forest that surrounds it. Other amenities include a restaurant and lounge, as well as a gift shop and a protea co-op that will pack the unusual flowers for you to take home. The rates include breakfast. *RR1, Box 475, Kula 96790, tel. 808/878–1535. 5 units with bath. No phones or TVs. MC, V.*

★ **Mana Kai-Maui.** This lodging is a real find in Kihei, partly because of the property itself and partly because it sits on the end of one of the nicest beaches in the state, just down the strip from the Stouffer Wailea. Here you can get a studio without a kitchen, or a one- or two-bedroom unit with a kitchen. The decor is modest—what people in the Islands might call typical tropical—but the view of the ocean right outside the lanai overcomes any reservations you might have about the rooms' interiors. What's more, the rates usually include a car. The Mana Kai has a very good beachfront restaurant, open for all meals. *2960 S. Kihei Rd., Kihei 96753, tel. 808/879–1561 or 800/525–2025. 140 rooms. Beachfront. Facilities: pool, restaurant, lounge, shopping arcade, cable color TV, ceiling fans. AE, CB, DC, MC, V.*

Maui Lu Resort. The first hotel in Kihei, this place reminds one of a rustic lodge. The main lobby was the summer home of the original owner, and over the years, the Maui Lu has added numerous wooden buildings and cottages to its 28 acres. Of the 170 rooms, 50 are right on the beach, in their own secluded area. The rest are across Kihei Road, on the main property. In addition, 16 large, one-bedroom cottages have a garden setting and screened-in lanais. The decor isn't fancy, but it isn't motel-tacky either. *575 S. Kihei Rd., Kihei 96753, tel. 808/879–5881 or 800/92–ASTON. 170 rooms with bath. Facilities: restaurant, lounge, pool, shops, color TV, A/C, tennis. AE, DC, MC, V.*

Inexpensive **Aloha Cottages.** If you want to meet the people in little Hana town, check into one of these cottages, run by Fusae Nakamura. Tourism is Mrs. Nakamura's way of earning extra money for her family now that she's retired, and she takes it seriously. The three two-bedroom units and one studio all have kitchens. The rooms are sparsely furnished but clean and adequate. A special touch is the carefully tended fruit trees on the neighboring property—Mrs. Nakamura often supplies her guest with the harvest, which includes papaya, bananas, and avocados. *Hana 96713, tel. 808/248–8420. 4 cottages with bath. No credit cards.*

Heavenly Hana Inn. Whether you fly or drive to Hana, you'll pass the Heavenly Hana Inn and probably wonder what it is. An impressive Japanese gate flanked by two lions guards the property, making it look like a temple of sorts. Inside, the rustic and quiet inn goes for eccentric decor, with knickknacks everywhere. You can rent one of four two-bedroom units, each with a kitchenette and decorated with Japanese shoji screens, antique furniture, and Asian art. If the location, 2 miles from town, seems too remote (although, let's face it, all of Hana is remote), the inn also has a one-bedroom beach cottage and a family cottage near Hasegawa's General Store. *Box 146, Hana 96713, tel. 808/248–8442. 4 rooms, plus 1 cottage on Hana Bay and 1 in town. Kitchenettes, lanais, TVs. No credit cards.*

Bed-and-Breakfasts

Maui also has quite a few homes available for bed-and-breakfast rentals. Many have their units in separate guest houses, which allows privacy while still giving you a chance to get to know your hosts. Rates range from $30 a night to as much as $150. For more information about Maui B&Bs, write or phone:

Bed & Breakfast Hawaii (Box 449, Kapaa 96746, tel. 808/822–7771 or 800/567–7832). Headquartered on Kauai, this organization has listings throughout the state and handles about 35 B&Bs on Maui. A directory is available for $8.50.

Bed & Breakfast Honolulu (3242 Kaohinani Dr., Honolulu 96817, tel. 800/288–4666). This organization has statewide listings, with about 50 B&Bs, or nearly 100 units, on Maui.

Bed & Breakfast Maui-Style (Box 886, Kihei 96753, tel. 808/879–7865 or 800/848–5567). This organization has listings for about 25 B&Bs in Maui.

The Arts

Most of Maui's cultural activities are community efforts, with theater, film, and symphony productions held in the island's central towns of Kahului and Wailuku. For more specific information, check the daily newspaper, the *Maui News*.

Film

International Film Festival. This acclaimed salute to celluloid used to be restricted to Honolulu, but now festival films are also presented in Maui. Each year in late November and early December, the festival, sponsored by East-West Center, brings together filmmakers from Asia, the Pacific Rim, and the United States to view feature films, documentaries, and shorts. The films are shown at the Holiday Theaters at the Kaahumanu Center. To find out about specific films and dates, phone the East-West Center's International Film Festival Office (tel. 808/944–7200) in Honolulu.

Music

Kapalua Music Festival. Since 1982, the music festival has brought some of the world's finest musicians to Maui for several days each summer. Representatives from Juilliard and the Chicago and New York philharmonics, the Tokyo String Quartet, Israeli-born musical director Yishak Schotten, and violinist Joseph Swensen are only a few of those who've performed here in recent years. Kapalua usually has special room rates during the festival. *J. Walter Cameron Center, 95 Mahalani St., Wailuku 96793, tel. 808/244–3771. Tickets: $10 adults, $6 children 6–12.*

Maui Symphony Orchestra The symphony orchestra performs five season concerts and a few special musical sensations as well, including a July 4th concert on the Kaanapali Golf Course, complete with fireworks. The regular season includes a Christmas concert, an opera gala, a classical concert, and two pops concerts outdoors at Wailea. *Tel. 808/244–5439. Season tickets: $12 adults, $8 students; tickets for the July 4th concert: $3 adults, $1 children.*

Theater

Baldwin Theatre Guild. Dramas, comedies, and musicals for the entire island are presented by this group about eight times a year. The guild has staged such favorites as *The Glass Menagerie*, *Brigadoon*, and *The Miser*. Musicals are held in the Community Auditorium, which seats 1,200, while all other plays are presented in the Baldwin High School Mini Theatre. *1650 Kaahumanu Ave., Kahului, tel. 808/242–5821. Tickets: $6 adults, $4 seniors, $3 students.*

Maui Community Theatre. Now staging about six plays a year, this is the oldest dramatic group on the island, started in the early 1900s. Last season's productions included *Fiddler on the Roof*, *Amadeus*, and *Dracula: The Musical?*. Each July, the group also holds a fund-raising variety show, which can be a hoot. *Iao Theatre, 68 N. Market, Wailuku, tel. 808/242–6969. Tickets for musicals: $10 adults, $9 seniors, $5 children under 17. Nonmusicals are $1 less.*

Maui Youth Theatre. This theater program for children is one of the largest arts organizations in Hawaii; it takes plays into the schools around the county but also performs about 10 productions a year for the entire community. Plays have included name shows, such as *Mame*, and original plays and ethnic dramas. Performances are held in various locations. *Box 518, Puunene 96784, tel. 808/871–7484; box office 808/871–6516. Tickets: $3–$8.*

Nightlife

Nightlife on Maui can be of the make-your-own-fun variety. As on all the Neighbor Islands, the pace is a bit slower than what you'll find in Waikiki. Watching the sunset from a tropical perch, taking a moonlight stroll along one of the island's near-perfect crescent beaches, or dining in a meadow can be some of the best nightlife you'll find.

Dancing, luaus, dinner cruises, and so on are found mainly in the resort areas. Kaanapali and Wailea are the liveliest places to hear music and meet people. The old whaling port, Lahaina, also parties with the best of them.

Bars and Clubs

Contemporary Music

El Crab Catcher (Whalers Village, Kaanapali, tel. 808/661–4423). In addition to seafood, you'll find live music here nightly, 5:30–7:30. Often a contemporary Hawaiian duo or trio performs.

Molokini Lounge (Maui Prince Hotel, Makena Resort, tel. 808/874–1111). This is a pleasant bar with an ocean view, and you can even see Molokini Island before the sun goes down. Live music is presented, often Hawaiian in theme. There's a dance floor for late-night revelry.

Discos

Banana Moon (Maui Marriott, Kaanapali Beach Resort, tel. 808/667–1200). This is a lively spot in the Maui Marriott Hotel, open nightly from 9 to 2. It has high-tech decor and good music. Banana Moon is an enjoyable place to meet other young tourists and hotel employees out for a night on the town.

Inu Inu Lounge (Maui Inter-Continental Wailea, Wailea Resort, tel. 808/879–1922). There's dancing nightly here starting at 9, with live music—rock, big bands, or golden oldies. This is a very active spot for young crowds from Wailea, Kihei, and Makena. It also lures groups who are visiting the resort.

Spats II (Hyatt Regency Maui, Kaanapali Beach Resort, tel. 808/667–7474). This club is open for disco dancing Sunday through Thursday 10 PM –2 AM and Fridays and Saturdays until 4. (Spats is a Travel-Holiday Award–winning Italian restaurant from 6:30 to 9:30.) There's a cover charge on Friday and Saturday nights.

Jazz **Blackie's Bar** (Blackie's Boat Yard, on the mountain side of Honoapiilani Hwy. in an orange octagonal building, Lahaina, tel. 808/667–7979). Even without the finest jazz on Maui, Blackie's would be an interesting place to go. Take Blackie himself. The crusty proprietor often cruises the joint, making sure everyone's behaving and chastising those who put their feet on the chairs or spit or break some other rule he has set forth for his establishment. The jazz is terrific, featuring the Gene Argel Trio and other guest performers. The music stops at 8, however, because that's when Blackie goes to bed.

Dinner and Sunset Cruises

Genesis Sailing Charters. This dinner sail goes for 2½ hours and includes a gourmet catered meal on the 48-foot luxury sailing yacht *Genesis*. The cruise is limited to 20 passengers at a time. *Box 10697, Lahaina 96761, tel. 808/667–5667. Cost: $56 adults.*

Scotch Mist Charters. A two-hour champagne sunset sail is offered on the 19-passenger Santa Cruz 50 sloop *Scotch Mist II*. *Box 831, Lahaina 96767, tel. 808/661–0386. Cost: $30 adults.*

Stardancer. This 150-foot luxury yacht sails nightly, serving a gourmet buffet in its elegant dining room. The three-level ship also opens its disco after 10 PM. Shuttles run to the pier ever 20 minutes. *Lahaina Harbor, Lahaina 96761, tel. 808/871–1144. Cost: $50 for dinner; $5 for after-dinner dancing only.*

Windjammer Cruises. This cruise includes a sit-down meal and live entertainment on the 65-foot, 110-passenger *Spirit of Windjammer*, a three-masted schooner. *505 Front St., Suite 229, Lahaina 96761, tel. 808/667–6834. Cost: $49 adults.*

Luaus and Polynesian Revues

Drums of the Pacific. The Hyatt presents a fine Polynesian revue on the hotel's Sunset Terrace. The buffet dinner includes such fare as fresh fish, prime rib, chicken, and a native luau pupu platter. Afterward, the show features traditional dances and chants from such countries as Tahiti, Samoa, and New Zealand. *Hyatt Regency Maui, Kaanapali, tel. 808/661–1234 ext. 4420. Mon.–Wed., Fri., Sat. Dinner seating begins at 5:30. Tickets: $42 adults, $34 children 6–12.*

Maui's Merriest Luau. The Inter-Continental's oceanfront lawn is certainly a beautiful spot to hold a luau. The traditional feast begins with a rum punch welcome and *imu* (underground oven) ceremony, and the evening includes colorful Polynesian entertainment. *Maui Inter-Continental Wailea, Wailea, tel. 808/79–1922. Tues. and Thurs. 5:30.*

Old Lahaina Luau. This is the best luau you'll find on Maui—it's small, personal, and authentic. The Old Lahaina Luau is held on the beach at 505 Front Street in Lahaina, presumably the former Hawaiian entertainment grounds of the royals. You'll get all-you-can-eat traditional Hawaiian luau food: kalua (roasted) pork, long rice, lomi salmon, haupia cake, and other items, such as fresh fruit and salad. You'll also get all you can drink. Guests sit either on tatami mats or at tables. Then there's the entertainment, featuring a musical journey from Old Hawaii to the present with hula, chanting, and singing. Four young men started the Old Lahaina Luau in 1986, and their attention to detail is remarkable. *505 Front St., Lahaina, tel. 808/667–1998. Tickets: $42 adults, $21 children under 13, infants free.*

Shows

Maui Tropical Plantation's Hawaiian Country Barbecue & Buddy Fo Revue. This Hawaiian country evening with a *paniolo* (cowboy) theme starts with a narrated tram ride through about half of the 120-acre showcase of Hawaii's leading agricultural crops; then it moves to an all-you-can-eat barbecued steak dinner and open bar. After, Buddy Fo and his lively entertainers put on a Hawaiian country-and-western variety show; the audience can join in for some square dancing. *Maui Tropical Plantation, Wailuku, tel. 808/244–7643. Tickets: $42 adults, $21 children 5–12, $10 children under 5. Mon., Wed., Fri. 5:30–8:30.*

6 Molokai

by Marty Wentzel

Nicknames for Molokai have come and gone. In ancient times it was called Molokai of the Potent Prayers, for the island's powerful kahunas (priests) practiced their worship in solitude. During the late 1800s, it was dubbed the Forbidden Isle, because Hawaii's lepers were banished to a remote peninsula on its northern shore. Only in the last few decades has it worn a new nickname, the Friendly Isle.

Today Molokai is indeed friendly, and those who visit its shores quickly become aware of the down-to-earth charm of its 263 square miles. As other Neighbor Islands become increasingly crowded with high-rise hotel developments and visitor activities, Molokai quietly greets its guests with a handful of basic accommodations and unusual sightseeing alternatives.

Something else about Molokai makes it stand out from the other Neighbor Islands. You can smell it in the fresh mangos along the trail to Halawa Valley, where the earliest community on the island once lived (AD 650). You can see it in the way the sun hits the water in the ancient fish ponds of the south shore, which date back to the 13th century. You can hear it in the crashing of the waves as they rush up to 3-mile-long Papohaku Beach. All of these things evoke a mysterious sensuality that springs from the land and its past and that inspires its people in the present.

Most of the attractions of the Friendly Isle can be found in the great outdoors. The Molokai Mule Ride carries you on a switchback trail ride back in time, down a steep mountain to Kalaupapa. There you tour the historic colony once reserved for sufferers of Hansen's disease (leprosy), in a pristine town set at the base of dramatic sea cliffs. On a wildlife safari ride you can see rare African and Asian animals roaming the west end of the island. A horse-drawn-wagon tour takes you to Hawaii's largest *heiau* (outdoor shrine) and through enormous mango and coconut groves. And in the island's highest reaches you can explore the Kamakou Preserve, a 2,774-acre refuge for endangered birds, plants, and wildlife.

Molokai appeals to the visitor who enjoys adventuring at a personal pace. Plenty of opportunities are available for snorkeling, swimming, hiking, and sunbathing, but fewer possibilities exist for organized sports such as fishing, horseback riding, tennis, and golf. The more creative you are, the more you will enjoy Molokai, for it doesn't shout at you with things to do. Instead, it gently whispers, "Come play with me."

Big-city shoppers find little to rave about on the island. However, the one-road former plantation town of Maunaloa offers eclectic shops with unique creations such as homemade kites and hand-dyed shirts. The main town of Kaunakakai is equally unimpressive, but if you dig around you'll find such one-of-a-kind delights as Molokai bread from Kanemitsu's Bakery and local carvings at the Molokai Gallery.

The dining scene on Molokai is, once again, limited, which is why most visitors to the island stay in a condominium and cook their own food. There are, however, some great little local eateries where a slice of Molokai life is served up with every meal.

The best thing one can say about the Friendly Isle is that it is uncluttered. You can drive your rental car down any road and take your time looking around without fear of someone honking at you to maintain the speed limit. Sometimes yours is the only car on the road! There are no buildings higher than three stories, no elevators, no traffic jams, no stoplights, and no movie theaters. The fanciest hotels are bungalow-style low-rises. Molokai also has miles and miles of undeveloped countryside, like the rolling farmlands of the 60,000-acre Molokai Ranch (the island's largest local landholder) and the dozens of pineapple fields, which once did big business for Dole and Del Monte but have now been phased out of the island's economy.

Ten miles wide and 38 miles long, Molokai is the fifth largest island in the Hawaiian chain. As you drive along its roads you can see how its two main volcanic mountains are connected by a plain. To the west is Maunaloa, which is 1,381 feet high and the home of an ancient hula school. This dormant volcano overlooks dry, rolling countryside and hosts the island's only resort, Kaluakoi. To the east is Mt. Kamakou, which at 4,970 feet is the highest peak on the island. Kamakou's rain forests house a gentle system of plants and animals found nowhere else in the world.

At night, from the western shores of the island on the beach fronting Kaluakoi Resort, you can see the twinkling lights of Oahu, 25 miles across the channel. In spirit, however, Molokai is much, much farther away from its highly developed neighbor. With its slow pace of life and simple beauty, it is drowsing in another era; if its 6,000 proud people have their way, it's likely to remain so.

Essential Information

Arriving and Departing by Plane

Airports/Airlines The center of air traffic for Molokai is called **Hoolehua Airport** (tel. 808/567–6140), a tiny airstrip located just west of the island's center. It is 8 miles west of Kaunakakai and about 15 miles east of Kaluakoi Resort. With two gates and a baggage claim area without a carousel, the terminal is just big enough to get the job done.

If you want to fly from the mainland United States to Molokai, you must first make a stop in Honolulu; from there, it's a 25-minute trip to the Friendly Isle. **Hawaiian Airlines** (tel. 800/367–5320) offers the most flights daily between Oahu and Molokai aboard its Dash-7 aircraft, at a round-trip cost of $47 per person. **Panorama Air** (tel. 800/367–2671) runs its Piper Chieftains and charges $70 round-trip, while **Aloha IslandAir** (tel. 800/323–3345) flies 18-passenger deHaviland Dash-6 Twin Otters at a round-trip cost of $77. (Hawaiian Airlines, Panorama Air, and Aloha IslandAir serve Molokai from the other Hawaiian Islands as well as from Oahu.)

An even smaller airstrip serves the little community of **Kalaupapa** (tel. 808/567–6331), the former Hansen's-disease colony on the north shore. **Aloha IslandAir** flies directly into that town from Honolulu for about $60 round-trip. However, you must first have a land-tour confirmation for Kalaupapa, and your arrival should coincide with one of the authorized ground tours of the area (*see* Guided Tours, below). Otherwise you'll be asked to leave.

Between the Airport and Hotels By van, taxi, or rental car, a drive from Hoolehua Airport to Kaunakakai takes about 10 minutes. To the hotels and condominiums of Kaluakoi Resort, your driving time from the airport is 25 minutes. Since there's no rush hour on the Friendly Isle, you can count on an easy drive.

When arranging transportation from the airport to your accommodations, check to see if your hosts offer free airport shuttle service.

By Bus There is no public bus service on the island of Molokai.

By Van **Gray Line Molokai** (Box 253, Hoolehua 96729, tel. 808/567–9015) runs an airport shuttle service to lodgings in Kaunakakai and Kaluakoi Resort for $6, with a two-person minimum. Reservations should be made in advance of your arrival.

By Taxi Molokai has two taxi companies. **Molokai Taxi** (tel. 808/552–0041), which started in October 1988, currently operates with three air-conditioned 1987 Chevrolet Celebrities, plus one four-wheel-drive AMC Cherokee. Drivers are available 24 hours a day islandwide, and rates are $2.60 for the first mile and $1.60 for each additional mile. It costs about $14 from Hoolehua Airport to Kaunakakai, and about $25 to Kaluakoi Resort. You can also call **Teem Taxi** (tel. 808/553–3433 or 553–3786) for service around the island and around the clock.

By Car After renting a car at the Hoolehua Airport, it's easy to find your way around the island roads. Simply turn right on the main road (Hwy. 460) to reach Kaluakoi Resort and left if you're staying in Kaunakakai. **Avis, Budget, Dollar,** and **Tropical** are the four car-rental companies that serve Molokai. Their offices are located at the Hoolehua Airport (*see* Getting Around, below, for further car-rental information).

Getting Around

By Car You'll most likely want to get out and explore the island from one end to the other. However, options for guided tours are quite limited, so it's advisable to rent a car.

Driving Driving is a snap on Molokai, because there are just a few main roads to choose from. Highway 460, also known as Maunaloa Highway, is a wide, well-paved route running from Kaunakakai west to Maunaloa. Kaluakoi Road runs off it to the north and leads you to the accommodations of Kaluakoi Resort. Highway 450, or Kamehameha Highway, runs east to Halawa Valley, becoming narrower and extremely bumpy for the last 5 miles. Highway 470 runs north to Kalaupapa Lookout.

Gas stations are located in Kaunakakai and Maunaloa. Please note that most gas stations are closed on Sundays on Molokai. If you park your car somewhere, be sure to lock it. Even on the Friendly Isle, thefts have been known to occur. When driving, buckle your seat belt, because there's a $15 fine for noncompliance. Children up to age three must be seated in a federally approved car safety seat, which you can lease from your car rental agency. When you rent a car, you will receive the small but helpful *Molokai Drive Guide*.

Car Rentals Four car-rental agencies are available on Molokai, all of which have offices right at Hoolehua Airport. They are **Avis** (tel. 800/331–1212), **Budget** (tel. 800/527–0707), **Dollar** (tel. 800/367–7006), and **Tropical** (tel. 800/367–5140). Expect to pay around

$24.95 per day for a standard compact car, and $26.95 for one with air-conditioning. Rates are seasonal, however, and can run up to $45 per day during peak seasons, such as Christmas vacation and the winter months. Advance car reservations are usually necessary. If you're flying on Hawaiian Airlines, ask in advance if the airline has a fly/drive deal available. Sometimes it will offer you cheaper rates (around $15 per day) on a car from Avis.

By Taxi **Molokai Taxi Service** (tel. 808/552–0041) offers rates of $2.60 for the first mile and $1.60 for each additional mile. The company also offers exclusive tours to various points of interest and historic sites accessible only by dirt road. Or try **Teem Taxi** (tel. 808/553–3433 or 553–3786) for personalized service to any point on the island.

Important Addresses and Phone Numbers

Tourist Information **Destination Molokai Association** (Box 1067, Kaunakakai 96748, tel. 808/567–6255) offers advice on accommodations and tours and other visitor information.

Emergencies **General emergencies** (tel. 911).
Police (tel. 808/553–5355).
Ambulance (tel. 808/553–5911).
Fire (tel. 808/553–5401 in Kaunakakai, tel. 808/567–6555 at Hoolehua Airport).
Coast Guard (tel. 808/244–5626).

Doctors Round-the-clock medical attention is available at **Molokai General Hospital** (Box 408, Kaunakakai 96748, tel. 808/553–5331).

Pharmacy **Molokai Drugs** (tel. 808/553–5790) in Kaunakakai is the most reliable source for filling prescriptions. Open Monday–Saturday 8:45–5:45.

Opening and Closing Times

Banks are open Monday–Thursday 8:30–3, Friday 8:30–6.

Most stores are open Monday–Saturday 9–6; they are generally closed on Sundays.

Guided Tours

Ground Tours Two basic tours of Molokai are offered, both of them conducted in 14-passenger, air-conditioned vans. The three-hour, half-day tour includes stops at Kalaupapa Lookout, a macadamia nut farm, and a restored sugar mill in Kalae. The six-hour, full-day option begins at 8 AM and includes the half-day sights, plus tours of Kaluakoi Resort and the town of Maunaloa, lunch in Kaunakakai at the Hotel Molokai (not included in the price), and a drive east to the Halawa Valley Lookout. While the full-day trip requires a lot of travel time, it gives an excellent overview of the Friendly Isle. Two companies share the ground-tour business on Molokai: **Gray Line Molokai** (tel. 808/567–9015) and **Roberts Hawaii** (tel. 808/552–2751). *Cost varies according to pickup site. For airport pickup and drop-off, the rates are $12 half-day, $25 full-day. Airport pickup and hotel drop-off (or vice versa), $15.50 half-day, $28.50 full-day. Hotel pickup and drop-off, $18 half-day, $32 full-day.*

Helicopter Tours **Papillon Hawaii Pacific Helicopters.** This air tour of Molokai in a six-passenger Bell Long Ranger departs daily from behind the Hilton Hawaiian Village in Waikiki at 11:30 AM. After an aerial tour of the stunning north shore, it stops at the Kaluakoi Resort for a one-hour lunch. After more breathtaking flightseeing, you're returned to Waikiki by 3:30. *421 Aowena Pl., Honolulu 96819, tel. 808/836–1566 or 800/367–8047, ext. 142. Cost: $275.*

Kalaupapa Tours **Damien Molokai Tours.** Founded in the 1860s and now a National Historical Park, Kalaupapa was once a community of about 1,000 people who were banished from other parts of Hawaii due to their medical plight, Hansen's disease (leprosy). A caring priest named Father Damien committed himself to the care of the sufferers until he died there of the same disease in 1889. Today, the most sensitive tour guide through Kalaupapa is someone who actually lives there: Richard Marks, who happens to be the sheriff of the town. Marks and his staff will take guests on a fascinating four-hour van tour of the former settlement. The package includes air transportation from Hoolehua Airport to Kalaupapa and a look at historic sites such as Father Damien's memorial, St. Philomena Church, Mother Marianne's memorial, lonely graveyards, small wooden houses, and medical facilities. You also get a picnic lunch in a seaside park. *Box 1, Kalaupapa 96742, tel. 808/567–6171. Cost of total package: $65.*

Rare Adventures. This company offers you a most unusual method of reaching Kalaupapa: by mule. Tours depart the cliff-high stables on Molokai's north shore at about 10 AM and take about 1½ hours one-way. During the seven-hour mule-ride package, getting there is half the fun. You and about 20 other people are mounted on friendly, surefooted steeds who do the hard work for you. They wind their way along a 3-mile, 26-switchback trail that was built in 1886 as a supply route to the settlement below. While in Kalaupapa, you take a guided tour of the town and have a picnic in Kalawao Park, site of the first Hansen's-disease colony until 1888. It now offers views of the north coast, which is home to the world's highest sea cliffs. *Box 200, Kualapuu 96757, tel. 808/567–6088, 808/537–1845, or 800/843–5978. Cost of mule ride: $75 per person. Children under 16 not allowed. One tour daily.*

Exploring

Since Molokai is long and slipper-shaped, it takes at least two days to explore it: one day for the "heel" or western reaches, and one for the "toe" to the east. The imaginary dividing line is in the town of Kaunakakai, which is set right in the center of the island's southern shore. This guide divides the island into two car trips. On a third day, you might want to head on a short excursion north, which leads you to a spectacular overlook.

The eastern end of Molokai is flanked by Mt. Kamakou, the island's highest point at 4,970 feet. Kamakou presides over miles of rain forests burgeoning with fresh tropical fruit, misty valleys tickled with waterfalls, and ancient lava cliffs that rise above the sea as high as 3,000 feet. To the west is Maunaloa, a smaller dormant volcano that rises above rolling pastures, farmlands, and a town of the same name. The western portion of the island is much drier than the east, and boasts some magnificent long beaches by Kaluakoi Resort.

You'll have the most fun if you explore the island at your own pace in a rental car. Most of the highlights are natural landmarks—waterfalls, valleys, overlooks, and the like—and it's nice to get out of your car and wander around an area at your leisure without missing the tour bus. Those of you who want to make these trips on a guided tour should see Guided Tours in Essential Information, above. The half- and full-day ground tours cover most of the highlights.

Directions on the island are often referred to as *mauka* (toward the mountains) and *makai* (toward the ocean). You'll find these terms used in this chapter.

Highlights for First-time Visitors

Halawa Valley, Tour 2
Kalaupapa Lookout, Tour 3
Kalokoeli Fish Pond, Tour 2
Kaunakakai, Tour 1
Maunaloa, Tour 1
Molokai Mule Ride, Tour 3
Molokai Ranch Wildlife Safari, Tour 1

Tour 1: West Molokai

Numbers in the margin correspond with points of interest on the Molokai map.

The western portion of the island is warm, sunny, breezy, and basically untouched. Its two areas of "civilization" are Kaluakoi Resort and the sleepy town of Maunaloa. This driving trip includes a stop at a glorious sunbathing beach, so bring along your bathing suit and allow some time to linger there.

1 Begin the tour at **Kaluakoi Resort,** located on Kaluakoi Road. Molokai's only major development, it sprawls over approximately eight miles of beachfront property and looks tame and manicured next to the surrounding wilds of Molokai Ranch. Kaluakoi was developed in 1968 by Kaluakoi Corporation, a subsidiary of the Louisiana Land and Exploration Company. In 1987 the resort was sold to Tokyo Kosan Company, Ltd. The area is home to two bungalow-style condominiums and a hotel, plus residences, ranch properties, and the island's only public golf course.

2 Kaluakoi Resort is the starting point for the **Molokai Ranch Wildlife Safari,** hailed as one of the world's finest natural game preserves, with 1,000 acres of wildlife open to guided camera safaris. In comfortable 14-passenger vans that depart from the resort, passengers take the bumpy 1½-hour trek through a landscape that resembles African plains. Nearly 500 animals roam the area, including sika and axis deer, Barbary sheep, Indian black buck, oryx, greater kudu, eland, rheas, and wild turkeys. The driver stops along the way and calls to the animals, some of which come right up to the van in hopes of a snack. Bring your camera along on this trip, which takes you past some truly fascinating-looking creatures. Both adults and children enjoy this tour. *Wildlife Park Reservations Desk, Box 1977, Maunaloa 96770, tel. 808/552–2555, ext. 7553. Cost: $12 adults, $6 children under 12. 4 tours daily.*

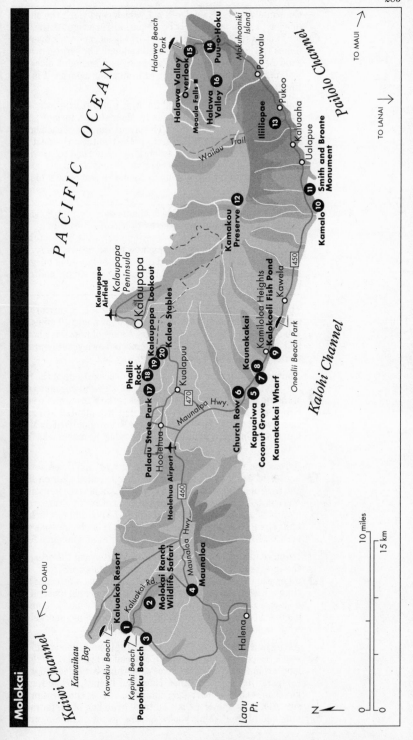

Molokai

Continue west on Kaluakoi Road, which runs along the shoreline past a number of lovely beach parks. Turn right at the sign
3 for **Papohaku Beach**, park in the parking lot, and walk over the dunes to the beach, which is 3 miles long. The largest white-sand beach in the islands, Papohaku is a splendid place for walking and sunbathing; in the calm summer months, it is also fine for swimming.

Return to Kaluakoi Road and follow it south to Highway 460.
4 Turn right and drive two miles to **Maunaloa**, a former sugar plantation town built in 1923. The layout and size of each house and garden indicate the hierarchy of the plantation when it was in full swing. Today this is essentially a one-road town whose pineapple fields are now overgrown. Maunaloa houses an attractive collection of shops run by a colorful assortment of local characters.

Time Out   **Jojo's Cafe** (makai [ocean] side of Maunaloa Hwy., tel. 808/552–2803). While in Maunaloa, stop by this local eatery run by Jojo Espaniola and her family. An antique bar adds to the funky, down-home atmosphere. The menu is the same every day, and the place is open for lunch and dinner. You get good burgers, hot dogs, salads, saimin (a Hawaiian noodle soup), and ribs, plus fresh tuna and butterfish.

The main road in Maunaloa is a dead-end street, so turn around at Jojo's and head east on Highway 460 for about 10 miles. As you drive along this section you get a view of how the island is laid out: two dormant volcanoes connected by a vast plain. Past the airport, follow the signs to Highway 450.

About a mile farther, look on the makai (ocean) side of the road for what seems, at first glance, to be a sea of coconut trees
5 standing tall and close together. This is the **Kapuaiwa Coconut Grove**, one of the last surviving royal groves planted by Prince Lot, whose nickname was Kapuaiwa. Prince Lot lived on Molokai and eventually became Hawaii's King Kamehameha V in 1863.

Across the street from the coconut grove, you'll see several
6 houses of worship along the road. This is called **Church Row**, and each one is attended primarily by Hawaiian congregations. You can see the unadorned, boxlike style of architecture, reminiscent of missionary homes, in each of the buildings, which are built along Hawaiian Homelands. On these lands, persons of at least half-Hawaiian blood can lease the sites at a nominal fee.

If you're interested in boats, turn makai (toward the ocean) at the intersection of Highway 450 and Ala Malama Street. This
7 takes you to **Kaunakakai Wharf**, the docks that were once bustling with pineapple exports and that now primarily send out honey, watermelons, cattle, and herbs. The wharf is home to deep-sea fishing boats, some of which offer sailing, snorkeling, whale watching, and diving excursions.

At the junction of Highway 450 and Ala Malama, head mauka to
8 reach the center of **Kaunakakai**, Molokai's "big" city. As the island's commercial hub, it leaves something to be desired when compared to cities on other Hawaiian islands. What Kaunakakai does have is character, similar to a 1930s Old West movie set. Along its one block is a cultural grab bag of restaurants, plus one of everything you're looking for: a gift shop, crafts

store, sporting goods shop, bakery, supermarket, liquor store, bank, and so on. Its people are generally friendly and willing to give you directions, and you'll never see anyone dressed in anything fancier than a muumuu or aloha shirt—more often, the preferred dress of Kaunakakai is shorts and a T-shirt.

Time Out **Kanemitsu Bakery** (mauka [mountain] side, Ala Malama St., tel. 808/533–5855). Anyone who has ever been to Molokai will tell you to stop by this bakery for a taste of its round Molokai bread, a pan-style white loaf that makes excellent French toast and cinnamon toast. In its glass display cases, Kanemitsu also shows off a calorie-laden assortment of rolls, buns, doughnuts, pies, and cakes. Try the *haupia* (coconut) jelly roll cake, the recipe for which is a guarded family secret. While there, you can sit right at the counter and have a diner-style breakfast or lunch.

Tour 2: East Molokai

This driving tour takes you through countryside that has been largely untouched. The road from Kaunakakai is 30 miles long, and much of it runs along the coast. It changes from a two-lane paved road to a narrow, bumpy track that dead-ends at Halawa Valley. You just might want to explore the valley on foot. In that case, bring shoes that you don't mind getting dirty, because the valley gets plenty of rain, which muddies up the trail.

Begin this tour heading east on Highway 450 out of Kaunakakai. After passing the **Pau Hana Inn, Molokai Shores,** and **Hotel Molokai,** you will see fewer houses and more natural countryside. About six miles out of Kaunakakai, look on the makai (ocean) side for the **Kalokoeli Fish Pond,** one of the many narrow ocean walls connecting two points of the shore. Kalokoeli is typical of the numerous fish ponds that line the southern shore, many of which were built around the 13th century. This early type of aquaculture is unique to Hawaii, and the fish ponds are well-preserved examples of man's early ingenuity.

⑩ Six miles farther on the makai side, look for a natural harbor called **Kamalo,** which was a stopping place for small ships carrying cargo along the coast in the 19th century. Here you'll also see one of the two churches built by Father Damien in the late 1800s.

⑪ In this vicinity, there is a monument on the makai side of the road. This is the **Smith and Bronte Monument,** dedicated to Ernest Smith and Emory Bronte, who crash-landed here in 1927. They were the first civilians to complete a transpacific flight from California, a noteworthy feat even if it did have a bumpy ending.

⑫ By now you are at the base of Mt. Kamakou, the island's highest peak. Hidden within the mountain is **Kamakou Preserve,** which harbors endangered birds and plants amid its lush 2,774 acres. Kamakou Preserve is a dazzling natureland full of wet ohia forests, rare bogs, native trees, and indigenous wildlife, which you can explore on a hike with the Nature Conservancy of Hawaii. *Contact Ed Misaki, Box 40, Kualapuu 96751, tel. 808/ 567–6680. Cost: $3. Hikers are picked up at Hoolehua Airport at 9 AM and returned by 4. Hikes are limited to 10 people. Ap-*

proximately 12 hikes are held each year, and reservations are required.

(13) Five miles east of Kamalo and 1/2-mile inland on the mauka (mountain) side of the road is **Iliiliopae**, a major heiau (outdoor shrine) that is listed in the National Registry of Historic Places. You can't miss it; it's as long as a football field. Treat this area with great respect, for it is the site of ancient human sacrifices and is said to hold great power to this day. *Park on the side of the road, look for the Wailau Trail sign, and walk about 10 minutes toward the mountains. A sign on the left will point you to the heiau. Tel. 808/558–8113. Admission free. Open all day.*

Time Out **Neighborhood Store and Snack Bar** (Kamehameha Hwy., Pukoo). Less than a mile past the Iliiliopae heiau is this family-run store, where there's a little something for everyone. It's your last chance to get food and drink before the end of Highway 450. A Filipino clan named the Quinones has run this slice of life for years, and their chicken papaya is worth sampling. Check out the pictures on the wall, which detail the rise of this modest business.

Now the coastline changes from rocks to white sandy beaches, and there are several bays where you may want to stop and take a breather. More and more potholes appear in the road, which hugs the shore as it twists and turns. Ten miles from Pukoo you
(14) make an ascent through **Puu-o-Hoku** (Hill of Stars), where you get panoramic views of West Maui. The small island off this coast is **Mokuhooniki,** where the United States military practiced its bombing techniques back in World War II.

(15) The road takes a hairpin turn left at **Halawa Valley Overlook**. By all means stop here and enjoy the vista of the mountains, the
(16) sea, and historic **Halawa Valley** (AD 650), the oldest recorded habitation site on Molokai. A busy community grew fruit and taro and fished here until it was struck by a fierce tidal wave in 1946. Now the valley is overrun with lush vegetation, although the remains of house platforms and garden walls are visible.

The road descends to a small church parking lot, where you can get out and hike the trail to **Moaula Falls**. It takes a muddy and mosquito-ridden hour one-way to reach the 250-foot cascade, but the effort pays off when you dive into the refreshing mountain pool at its base. Enjoy the hike back past taro patches, sweet-smelling forests of ginger and guava, and a freshwater stream that follows you back to your car.

Tour 3: A Short Excursion North

Here's an easy morning or afternoon trip, just the right diversion to break up your day. It takes you to the cooler highlands of the island, so you might want to bring along a light jacket.

(17) From Kaunakakai, follow Highway 460 and turn mauka on Highway 470. This leads you to **Palaau State Park**, one of the island's few formal recreation areas. At a 1,000-foot elevation, it sits in the center of the island on 233 acres. Forests of ironwood beckon to nature lovers. The park is well maintained, with camping facilities, washrooms, and picnic tables. *Admission free. Open daily 24 hours.*

Park in the lot at the end of the road, and follow the trail straight ahead to a distinctive formation jutting up from the ground. This is the **Phallic Rock**, also known as Kauleonanahoa by the ancient Hawaiians. Barren women would sit here to absorb its strength and gain fertility.

From the parking lot, follow the trail to the right that points to **Kalaupapa Lookout**. After walking for several minutes through a heady pine forest, you reach this magnificent overlook, which offers views of the tiny Hansen's-disease settlement, its airport, its main buildings, and the 2,000-foot-high sea cliffs protecting it. A series of informative plaques have been set up at the lookout with facts about Hansen's disease, Father Damien, and the colony itself.

Turn around in the parking lot and drive about ½ mile, until you reach a clearing on the right. This is the home of **Kalae Stables**, a hilltop corral 1,600 feet above Kalaupapa, and the start of the Molokai Mule Ride (*see* Guided Tours in Essential Information, above).

Two miles below Kalaupapa Overlook on the right is the **Meyer Sugar Mill**, built in 1878 and reconstructed to teach visitors about sugar's importance in Molokai's agricultural history. *Rt. 470, Kalae 96729, tel. 808/567–6436. Cost: $2.50. Open Mon.–Sat. 10–noon, Sun. 1–5.*

Molokai for Free

Purdy's All-Natural Macadamia Nut Farm. Molokai's only working macadamia nut farm is open to visitors for casual tours. This family business on Hawaiian homestead land takes up 1½ acres, and its flourishing grove of 45 trees is more than 60 years old. You learn how the trees are grown, how the nuts are harvested, and what makes them one of Hawaii's top products. The tour includes an opportunity to crack and sample the roasted nuts, plus a taste of yummy macadamia-blossom honey. Tropical flower stringing is demonstrated, leis are on sale, and fresh fruits are on hand for refreshment. *Box 84, Hoolehua Homestead 96729, tel. 808/567–6601; 808/567–6495 evenings. Open daily 9–1, or call for an appointment.*

Off the Beaten Track

Molokai Wagon Ride. This is a truly upbeat addition to the tourist attractions of Molokai. Island-born Larry Helm takes folks on a scenic and informative amble in a horse-drawn wagon. First you stop at the Iliiliopae heiau, the largest outdoor place of worship in Hawaii. It is elaborately constructed of stones, and only honored guests are taken there, for it is a very sacred place indeed. Next you tour the largest mango grove in the world. Afterward, you are regaled with a beach barbecue, coconut husking, fishing, traditional Hawaiian net throwing, and arts and crafts demonstrations on an exotic south-shore beach with views of Maui and Lanai. *Box 56, Hoolehua 96729, tel. 808/567–6773 or 808/558–8380. Cost: $25. Tours daily.*

Shopping

The shopping scene on the Friendly Isle can be divided into two districts: along Ala Malama Street in Kaunakakai and along Maunaloa Road in Maunaloa. Mind you, neither of these strips is a Rodeo Drive. Neither town has department stores or shopping malls, and the fanciest clothes you can find on the island are pretty muumuus and aloha shirts.

However, in each tiny hamlet you will find shops with flair and diversity. Some of the best bargains can be found in the stores that sell locally made goods, such as artwork and jewelry. For the most part, you can skip the small and insignificant emporia of Molokai's hotels, which sell high-priced clothing and gifts of little distinction.

Most stores are open Mondays through Saturdays between 9 and 6, but fewer stores open their doors on Sunday. You might want to call ahead to make sure of the particular store's hours. As is the case in any small town, the owner will simply close up shop if there's something else he'd like to do.

Kaunakakai

It takes about five minutes to walk from one end of the main street, Ala Malama, to the other. Here are some of the charming, family-run establishments you'll find along the way or right nearby:

Clothing The **Molokai Gift Shop** (tel. 808/553–5801), in the lobby of the Hotel Molokai, carries a little something for everyone: women's, men's, and children's aloha wear, hand-painted Molokai designer T-shirts, sportswear, and swimwear.

A small selection of casual wear, such as Levi's jeans and Nike shoes, is also for sale at the **Imports Gift Shop** (tel. 808/553–5734). **Molokai Island Creations** (tel. 808/553–5926) has unique designs in Hawaiian swimwear and tank tops that are made exclusively for the shop.

Grocery/Beverage Stores If you're staying in a condominium, you'll appreciate the services of the best-stocked supermarket on the island, the **Friendly Market Center** (tel. 808/553–5595). Its slogan is "Your family store on Molokai," and it lives up to the promise with hats, T-shirts, and other vacation needs as well as fresh produce, meat, groceries, liquor, and sundries. *Open weekdays 8:30–8:30, Sat. 8:30–6:30.*

Kaunakakai's other full-service grocery is **Misaki's Inc.** (tel. 808/553–5505). Misaki's traces its beginnings back to 1922, so it's a real island tradition. You can pick up liquor and dry goods here, as well as meat and produce. Its main advantage over the Friendly Market Center is that it's open on Sundays 9–noon.

Don't let the name **Molokai Wines 'n' Spirits** (tel. 808/553–5009) fool you. Along with a good selection of fine wines and liquors, it also carries gourmet foods and quality cuts of meat. *Open daily 8AM–10:30 PM.*

Jewelry James and Maria Watanabe own the **Imports Gift Shop** (tel. 808/553–5734), which features a decent collection of 14-karat-gold chains, rings, earrings, and bracelets, plus freshwater pearl jewelry. They also carry Hawaiian heirloom jewelry, which is unique to the islands. These stunning gold pieces are made to order with your Hawaiian name inscribed in Victorian-style black letters. A large percentage of the women who live in Hawaii have a piece of heirloom jewelry—or hope to receive one someday as a gift.

Leis   Cynthia and Donald Gutierres run **Kuualoha Flowers and Leis** (tel. 808/553–3455) and create leis from island flowers such as ginger and pikake. The couple specialize in the traditional circular *haku* lei, which is worn on the head.

Locally Produced Goods   **Molokai Island Creations** (tel. 808/553–5926) carries original Molokai glassware, exclusive Hawaiian notecards, jewelry made from coral right out of Hawaii's waters, and books on such Molokai subjects as history and fishing. It also sells authentic Molokai-design blouses and tank tops.

Outdoor Gear   **Molokai Fish and Dive** (tel. 808/553–5926) is Molokai's main source of sporting goods, from snorkeling rentals to free and friendly advice. Owner Jim Brocker knows the island inside out and can recommend the best spots for fishing and diving. Ask to see his Molokai T-shirts, an original design available nowhere else on the island. *Open weekdays 9–6, Sat. 8–6, Sun. 8–2.*

Maunaloa

The solitary shopping street in this old plantation town plays host to a handful of family-run businesses. Their owners are always happy to welcome a visitor through their doors.

Arts and Crafts   The **Plantation Gallery** (tel. 808/552–2364) is an arts and crafts emporium crammed with local works and goods from Bali, from sculptures and clothes to jewelry and musical instruments.

Grocery Store   The essentials are available at the **Friendly Market Center** (tel. 808/552–2443), run by the same owners as the FMC in Kaunakakai. This supermarket is convenient for guests who are staying at the condominiums of the Kaluakoi Resort. It carries meat, vegetables, fruit, dry goods, drugs, and liquor.

Kites   The **Big Wind Kite Factory** (tel. 808/552–2364) features custom-made kites to fly and display. Owner Jonathan Socher will give you a free kite-flying lesson if you call ahead. His stock includes kite kits, paper kites, minikites, and wind socks.

Shirts   Sol Kahalewai runs the popular **Molokai Red Dirt Shirt Shop** (tel. 808/552–2470), a small building where you can find one-of-a-kind Molokai T-shirts with Hawaiian graphics and other images unique to the Friendly Isle.

Beaches

On Molokai, don't be surprised if you're the only person sunbathing for miles. That's because the island has numerous beaches to choose from, many of them quite remote and undisturbed. You'll find the most spacious and beautiful beaches along the west coast, although you shouldn't venture into the high winter waves. Beaches fronting the Kaunakakai hotels and condominiums are narrow and less appealing, but the shallow waters are almost always calm for wading. At the extreme east of the island is the beach fronting Halawa Valley, a nice place for relaxing after the long drive getting there.

All of the beaches on Molokai are free and open to the public. None of them has a telephone number, so if you want to find out more about them, contact the **Department of Parks, Land and Natural Resources,** Box 153, Kaunakakai 96746, tel. 808/567–6083.

Halawa Beach Park. This long, curving beach at the head of Halawa Valley has safe swimming during the calm summer months, but watch out for the hazardous rip currents during the high surf of winter. Halawa's picnic facilities are some of the nicest on the island, making this an ideal beach for a family outing. Outdoor showers are available, and there are no life-guards. *Drive to the eastern end of Hwy. 450 until it dead-ends at the beach.*

Kawakiu Beach. One of the best swimming beaches on Molokai, this is part of the Kaluakoi Resort. It has also been set aside as a beach park in honor of its archaeological sites, including house platforms and structures from an ancient Hawaiian settlement. Outdoor showers are available at the resort. *At the northern end of the bay fronting Kaluakoi Resort, on Kaluakoi Rd.*

Kepuhi Beach. This white-sand beach stretches about ½ mile in front of Kaluakoi Resort on the west end of Molokai. It is fairly windy here all year long, which makes the swimming somewhat dangerous when the waves come up. This is a good beach for strolling and sunbathing. There are outdoor showers at the resort, but no lifeguards. From Kepuhi, the sunsets are a nightly extravaganza. *Kaluakoi Resort, Kaluakoi Rd.*

Onealii Beach Park. This is the only decent beach park along the island's south-central shore. The narrow and long beach has adequate swimming in calm waters year-round. From here you get smashing views of Lanai, 8 miles across the channel, and Maui. The beach park has rest rooms, outdoor showers, and picnic tables under the trees. There are no lifeguards. *On Hwy. 450, just east of Hotel Molokai.*

Papohaku Beach. Perhaps the most sensational beach on the is-land, Papohaku is a 3-mile-long strip of white-sand glory, the longest of its kind in the state. It's also quite wide, so you can relax in privacy. Some places are too rocky for swimming; look carefully before entering the water, and go in only when the waves are small (generally the summer months). Between the parking lot and the beach are outdoor showers, picnicking facil-ities, and a rest room. There are no lifeguards. *Kaluakoi Rd., 2 miles beyond the Kaluakoi Resort. Look for the big sign on the makai (ocean) side of the road.*

Pohakuloa Beach. The protective cove of this beach makes the waters calm and swimmable most of the year. As a result, many parents like to bring their children here, and it can get pretty busy during the weekends. An outdoor shower is available, but there are no lifeguards. *Drive about 1½ mi beyond Papohaku Beach to the end of the coastal road on the northwest end of the island. There is a sign on the makai side of the road pointing you to the parking lot.*

Sports

Molokai's untouched beauty and sunny skies make it a wise choice for the active-minded vacationer. Some sporting options can be arranged through the travel desk of your hotel, but in many cases you should call the companies directly for information and reservations.

Participant Sports

Fishing Based at the Kaunakakai docks, **Alele II Charters** (Box 121, Kaunakakai 96748, tel. 808/558–8266 or 808/558–8319) runs excursions on a 35-foot twin diesel cruiser. If you go in a group, the shared cost is about $120 a day, or $70 a half day for excellent sportfishing. On an exclusive basis, the full-day cost runs approximately $400, and $300 for a half day.

Golf Compared to the more commercialized Neighbor Islands, Molokai has a relatively mellow golf scene. The place to play is the **Kaluakoi Golf Course** (Kepuhi Beach 96770, tel. 808/552–2739) at the Kaluakoi Resort. At par 72, it features 18 holes on a 6,559-yard course designed by Ted Robinson, and its 160 manicured acres include five holes next to the beach. Facilities include a pro shop, rentals, a driving range, and a putting green. Greens fees and a cart cost $55 for nonguests, $40 if you're staying at the resort. There's also community duffing at the **Ironwoods Golf Course** (Hwy. 470, Kualapuu). Call Molokai Ranch (tel. 808/552–2767) for current rates.

Hiking Along with the mule ride (*see* Guided Tours in Essential Information, above), **Rare Adventures** (Box 200, Kualapuu 96757, tel. 808/567–6088, 808/567–6515, or 800/843–5978) offers a hiking excursion to Kalaupapa. The 7-hour hiking tour is only for the hale and hearty, because it's tricky maneuvering the 1,600-foot drop of the switchback mountain trail, whether you're hiking down it or back up. While in Kalaupapa, you get a guided tour of the town and have a picnic in Kalawao Park. The entire package costs $30 per person, including hiking permit, ground tour, and lunch.

For a free hike, try the trek into **Halawa Valley** on the east coast. It's a muddy but magnificent hike through groves of fruit trees and past taro patches and the remains of stone walls from centuries ago. The trail ends at Moaula Falls, a 25-foot cascade with refreshing swimming. The hike takes about 3 hours round-trip. (For detailed maps and information about this hike, consult Robert Smith's *Hawaii's Best Hiking Trails*, Wilderness Press.)

Horseback Riding Since many trails and dirt roads are impassable by car on Molokai, the island is perfect for exploring on horseback. Sarah Selnick operates **Hawaii Horsemanship Unlimited** (Box 94, Kualapuu 96757, tel. 808/552–0056), which presents a variety of supervised rides through the countryside. Cost for a full-day ride including lunch is $75. Her 5-hour guided tours of Kalaupapa's cliffs run $330 (for experienced riders only).

Hunting **Molokai Ranch** (Ala Malama St., Kaunakakai 96748, tel. 808/552–2767) provides guides and transportation for outings on private lands. Hunts for axis deer take place from February through October. During bird-hunting season, from November through January, you can look for ring-necked and green pheasant, quail, and wild turkeys. Occasionally, hunting for axis deer, Indian black buck, and audad sheep is also allowed at Molokai Ranch Wildlife Park. The cost is $400 a day for axis deer and $1,000 for black buck and audad. Nonguided hunts are allowed at $100 a day, plus $50 for any trophy animals taken.

Kayaking The remote windward shores of Molokai are flanked by chiseled cliffs, crashing waves, and serene beaches that rarely have seen footsteps during their centuries of existence. You can experience this landscape with **Island Adventures** (Box 90519, Honolulu 96835, tel. 808/737–4913, 808/735–1088, or 800/63–ISLES), which puts together adventure packages of camping and kayaking. The three-day experience includes equipment, an inflatable kayak, gourmet meals, ground transfers, and a guide. Cost: $375.

Sailing The 44-foot luxury sailing yacht *Whistling Swan* is your craft on **Whistling Swan Charters** (Box 1350, Kaunakakai 96748, tel. 808/553–5238). The company offers a three-day sailing expedition along the north shore, including a tour of Kalaupapa, for $450. If you don't mind sharing the yacht, the cost is $40 for a half day, $80 for a full day.

Snorkeling and Scuba Diving No Molokai-based companies take people on snorkeling and scuba excursions. However, equipment is available for rent at the main hotels of the island, including Kaluakoi Resort and Hotel Molokai. In addition, you can go through **Molokai Fish and Dive** (Ala Malama St., Kaunakakai, tel. 808/553–5926) for equipment rentals. The shop will be happy to give you information on good snorkeling and diving spots around the island.

Windsurfing Beginners as well as advanced windsurfers can take to the waves with **Windsurfing Molokai** (Star Route 329, Kaunakakai 96748, tel. 808/558–8253). It offers individual instruction in the calm waters of Ualapue Fish Pond and can also take you to the excellent windsurfing waters of Pailolo Channel, between Molokai and Maui. The cost of a two-hour beginners' lesson is $25 per person. Private lessons with equipment included are $25 an hour per person.

Spectator Sports

When it comes to cheering from the sidelines, there's really only one event for which Molokai is known: the **Molokai-to-Oahu Canoe Race** (call race coordinator Harry Anderson, tel. 808/525–5476). This is the world's major long-course event in the sport of outrigger canoeing, and the best in the field turn up on the Friendly Isle to participate. It begins on the southwest coast near the harbors of Halelono. After paddling across the rough Kaiwi Channel in traditional Hawaiian canoes, participants finish at Fort DeRussy Beach in Waikiki. The event takes place each September for the women and October for the men. Diehard fans watch the start on Molokai, hop on a plane, and fly to Oahu for the finish.

Dining

When it comes to going out for food and drink, the choices are limited on Molokai. In fact, during a week's vacation you can easily hit all the restaurants worth trying and return to your favorite places for a second round. Nevertheless, the dining scene is fun because it is a microcosm of Hawaii's diverse cultures. You'll find freshly baked Molokai bread, authentic Chinese dishes, spicy Filipino cuisine, and Hawaiian-style fish all in the same block of Ala Malama Street in Kaunakakai. What's more, the price is right at Kaunakakai's eateries; all of them fall into the Inexpensive category.

In addition, you can choose from one moderately priced establishment at the Kaluakoi Resort, one local-style gathering place in Maunaloa (*see* Tour 1 in Exploring, above), and a dining room at the Hotel Molokai. If these options don't sound appetizing, you had better rent a condominium and cook your own food.

Restaurants on Molokai do not require a jacket. They are open daily unless otherwise noted.

Highly recommended restaurants in each price category are indicated by a star ★.

Category	Cost*
Moderate	$20–$40
Inexpensive	under $20

*per person, excluding drinks, service, and 4% sales tax

Kaunakakai

Holo Holo Kai. Because of its diversified menu and pleasant surroundings, one might dare to say that this is Kaunakakai's fanciest restaurant. However, the atmosphere remains strictly casual. Set on the beach, Holo Holo Kai has a South Seas decor and views of the Pacific. Meals include such seafood as sautéed mahimahi and baked cod, generally prepared without fancy sauces. Other entrées include shrimp tempura, top sirloin, and teriyaki chicken or steak. Beef stew is a favorite here, served with rice or poi, and there's an all-you-can-eat soup-and-salad buffet with delicious Molokai bread. You'll see a lot of visitors eating at Holo Holo Kai, since it's part of the town's main hotel. *Hotel Molokai, tel. 808/553-5347. Reservations not necessary. Dress: casual. AE, DC, MC, V. Inexpensive.*

★ **Hop Inn.** From the outside it looks run down, but then, doesn't everything in Kaunakakai? Don't let appearances fool you, because inside you'll find a spotless restaurant specializing in the town's best Chinese food. Order a plate lunch and you always get more than enough food. The lemon chicken here is a local favorite, but don't overlook the chicken with cashew nuts, which is a deliciously chunky stew. Other good bets are the sweet and sour pork and shrimp chop suey, certainly nothing out of the ordinary but satisfying Chinese entrées just the same. *Ala Malama St., tel. 808/553-5465. Reservations not necessary. Dress: casual. No credit cards. Inexpensive.*

★ **Mid-Nite Inn.** Art Kikukawa runs this diner-style establishment, which is furnished with simple tables, booths, and counters. He says its name pays tribute to the departing travelers who would eat there in the old days while waiting to board the interisland steamer at midnight. His motto is "Best Fish Served Anywhere," which overstates things a bit, but the Mid-Nite Inn does provide the tastiest seafood in Kaunakakai. Try the fresh mahimahi fried in soy sauce with chopped green onions; it's served with a bowl of piping-hot rice and a side order of homemade kimchee (spicy Korean pickled cabbage). *Ala Malama St., tel. 808/553-5302. Reservations not necessary. Dress: casual. No credit cards. BYOB. Inexpensive.*

Oviedo's. As the main city of the island, Kaunakakai may seem lacking in many ways, but it does have good Filipino food at Oviedo's. The waitresses treat you like family, with a pat on the back, a wink, or a smile. The restaurant offers cheap prices on tasty lunch and dinner plates. Oviedo's specializes in adobos (stews) with a variety of traditional Filipino spices and sauces. Try the tripe, pork, or beef adobo for a real taste of tradition. A mixed plate comes with vegetables and rice. You can eat in or take out. *Ala Malama St., tel. 808/553-5014. Reservations not necessary. Dress: casual. No credit cards. Inexpensive.*

Pau Hana Inn Restaurant. This open-air restaurant is set by the sea, and its big doors open onto picturesque ocean views. A rustic setting is created by the big fireplace, although the room is usually too warm to light a fire. The cuisine is American, including honey-dipped chicken, New York strip steak, catch of the day, barbecued beef short ribs, and teriyaki steak. All entrées come with a starch and a beverage. In the evening, locals love to party here, and live bands provide loud music for dancing on weekends. *Pau Hana Inn, Kamehameha Hwy., tel. 808/553-5342. Reservations not necessary. Dress: casual. AE, DC, MC, V. Inexpensive.*

The West End

★ **Ohia Lodge.** The most sophisticated restaurant on Molokai, the Ohia Lodge offers continental dining by the sea. Its oversize doors add an informal touch to an otherwise elegant decor, and through its large picture windows you get lovely views of the sea and the lights of Oahu across Kaiwi Channel. Menus change nightly, with fresh fish spotlighted each evening. Cashew chicken, filet mignon béarnaise, and seafood tempura are regular features. The salad bar is especially good here, big enough to make a meal in itself, and you also have your choice of vegetarian platters, prime rib, prawns, and pasta dishes. *Kaluakoi Resort, Maunaloa, tel. 808/552-2555. Reservations advised. Dress: neat but casual. AE, CB, DC, MC, V. Moderate.*

Lodging

A visit to Molokai is an enriching experience, in part because the island is still highly undeveloped. While hotels and condos spring up like weeds on the more popular Neighbor Islands, Molokai has maintained an even keel with its accommodations. Its major resort area, Kaluakoi, will eventually expand to add the new multimillion-dollar luxury Kaiaka Rock Hotel, but it has been on the drawing board for so long that one wonders if even that will ever materialize.

Instead, Molokai appeals less to those who like impeccable furnishings and swanky amenities and more to those who appreciate genuine Hawaiian hospitality and relaxation in down-home surroundings. Hotel and condominium properties on Molokai range from the fine to the funky. Pools are outdoors. Kaluakoi Resort boasts the best hotel, while the condominiums of Kaunakakai are great for families, due to their proximity to the island's calmest, shallowest waters. None of the accommodations falls into the Very Expensive category, which is good news for the budget vacationer. Molokai hotel prices usually follow a European plan, meaning no meals are included.

Highly recommended lodgings in each price category are indicated by a star ★ .

Category	Cost*
Expensive	$90–$120
Moderate	$60–$90
Inexpensive	under $60

All prices are for a standard double room, excluding 9¼% tax and service charge.

Kaunakakai and Vicinity

Moderate
★
Hotel Molokai. Polynesian-style architecture graces a series of three-unit cottages at this laid-back hotel just a mile from the center of town. The furnishings are rustic, with basket swings on the lanais and wooden beams on the ceiling. Although the hotel is somewhat run-down, each room is kept clean, right down to the wall-to-wall carpet. Hotel Molokai is on the beach, but the swimming pool is a welcome addition since the waters in front of the property are shallow and not good for swimming. The hotel often offers overnight deals in conjunction with airlines and rental-car companies; ask about this when you make your reservation. *Box 546, Kaunakakai 96748, tel. 808/553–5347 or 800/922–7866. 56 rooms with bath. Facilities: pool, shops, restaurant, lounge. AE, DC, MC, V.*

Molokai Shores. Located between the Pau Hana Inn and the Hotel Molokai, this three-story condominium is also oceanfront, and each room offers a view of the water. Your condo also comes with a color TV and a fully equipped kitchen. The furnished lanais look out over four acres of tropical gardens. One-bedroom/one-bath units and two-bedroom/two-bath units are available. In addition, picnic tables and barbecue areas are available for outdoor family fun. *Box 1037, Kaunakakai 96748, tel. 808/553–5954 or 800/367–7042. 102 condominiums with kitchen. Facilities: pool, shops, putting green. MC, V.*

Wavecrest. Another condominium set right on the shore near Kaunakakai, the Wavecrest offers one- and two-bedroom apartments equipped with electric kitchens and color TV. The decor is your basic tropical design, with rattan furniture and a pastel color scheme. Each unit has a furnished lanai from which you have views of the islands of Maui and Lanai. The shallow water here is bad for swimming but great for fishing. *Star Route, Kaunakakai 96748, tel. 808/558–8101 or 800/367–2980. 216 condominium units with kitchen. Facilities: pool, shops, tennis. AE, CB, DC, MC, V.*

Inexpensive **Pau Hana Inn.** The somewhat funky accommodations of this
★ good-time hotel should be reserved for those who like to rough
it. It's composed of a ramshackle set of cottages with clean but
uninspired furnishings reminiscent of motels on the mainland.
It can get noisy here on weekend evenings, when there's live
entertainment. On the plus side, a nice swimming pool makes
up for the poor swimming beach fronting the property. If you
ask ahead of time, you can get one of the rooms with a kitchenette. *Box 860, Kaunakakai 96748, tel. 808/553–5342 or 800/
922–7866. 40 rooms with bath. Facilities: pool, restaurant,
lounge. AE, DC, MC, V.*

The Kaluakoi Resort

Expensive **Kaluakoi Hotel and Golf Club.** The only hotel at Kaluakoi, this
property does its best to provide a sense of laid-back elegance
for its guests. A series of two-level thatched-cottage complexes
are spread across ultragreen lawns, which are shaded by immense palm trees and brightened by bougainvillea bushes.
Rooms have high ceilings with exposed wooden beams, rattan
furnishings, and bright tropical colors. Each unit has a kitchenette and furnished lanai. If you want a room with an ocean view,
ask way in advance, because there aren't very many of them.
The beach fronting the property is one of Molokai's best for
sunbathing, and when the waves are small it's a popular
bodysurfing and swimming spot. *Box 1977, Maunaloa 96770,
tel. 808/552–2555 or 800/367–6046. 289 rooms with bath. Facilities: pool, shops, restaurant, lounge, snack bar, tennis, golf.
AE, CB, DC, MC, V.*

Ke Nani Kai. This is a decent condominium complex with two-
story buildings set back from the water. Your views are primarily of the gardens and golf courses, but the beach is a mere
five-minute walk away. Sliding screen doors open onto furnished lanais with flower-laden trellises, and the spacious
interiors are done in tropical rattans and pastels. Each unit has
a washer and dryer and a completely equipped kitchen. *Box
126, Maunaloa 96770, tel. 808/552–2761. 120 condominium
units with bath and kitchen. Facilities: pool, golf, spa, tennis,
whirlpool. AE, CB, DC, MC, V.*

★ **Paniolo Hale.** Considered by many to be Molokai's best condominium property, this one is perched high on a ledge
overlooking the beach, right next to the Kaluakoi Hotel.
Paniolo Hale has units with spectacular ocean-view and nice
garden views as well, with an option for one or two bedrooms.
The units have screened lanais, some of which even have hot
tubs for an additional charge. Kitchens are well stocked, and
the tidy decor is appropriately casual, to match the tropical
surroundings. Adjacent to the greens of the Kaluakoi Golf
Course, the property is sometimes a playground for wild turkeys and deer at night. *Box 146, Maunaloa 96770, tel. 808/552–
2731 or 800/367–2984. 77 condominium units with bath
and kitchen. Facilities: paddle tennis, pool, golf. AE, CB, DC,
MC, V.*

The Arts and Nightlife

Molokai has limited options for cultural activity. Most people who live on Molokai must fly to a neighboring island if they wish to hear a symphony performance or see a first-run movie or a community play. As for organized evening entertainment, most residents enjoy simply sitting around with friends and family, sipping a few cold ones, strumming ukuleles and guitars, singing old songs, and "talking story" (conversing).

Still, a handful of opportunities are offered for visitors to kick up their heels in the evening. Go into Kaunakakai, pick up a copy of the *Molokai Dispatch* or the *Molokai News* (the local papers, published every other week), and see if there's a church supper or square dance taking place. If you're looking for still more to do in the evening, why not take a walk on the beach and let the evening stars entertain you?

Films

The **Kaluakoi Resort** (tel. 808/552-2555) shows one movie nightly to its guests. The films are generally about three to five years old, or sometimes black-and-white classics; you sit on folding chairs in a recreation hall to watch them. It's free, so don't complain.

Bars and Clubs

Hotel Molokai. The bar is poolside and offers views of the ocean, Lanai, and Maui. What better place to relax with a drink or two? Once in a while the hotel also presents hula shows, but there's no set schedule. *Kamehameha Hwy., Kaunakakai, tel. 808/553-5347. Happy hour 11 AM–6 PM; live music Thurs.–Sat. evenings, 6:30–9.*

Ohia Room. Live bands take over the cozy lounge of this breezy seaside restaurant and play Top 40 and pop numbers for dancing. *Kaluakoi Resort, tel. 808/552-2555. Nightly 6:30–9:30.*

Pau Hana Inn. This is the island's liveliest forum for local music. The regulars can get pretty rowdy here on the weekends, but visitors are more than welcome to join in the fun. *Kamehameha Hwy., Kaunakakai, tel. 808/553-5342. Happy hour 4–6 PM; dinner music nightly 6:30–9; dance music Fri. and Sat. nights 9–1.*

7 Lanai

by Marty Wentzel

Look out the airplane window as you approach Lanai, and without any prompting you can guess its nickname: the Pineapple Island. As you gaze down upon Palawai Basin, a vast, fertile crater that has been flattened by centuries of erosion, you can see the 14,000 acres of pineapples for which the island is best known. Its historic nickname, Red Lanai, is equally apparent in the vermilion soil that covers almost all of its 140 square miles.

Lanai's one population center is called Lanai City, an old plantation town whose tiny houses have colorful facades, tin roofs, and tidy gardens. With its well-planned grid of paved roads and small businesses, Lanai City adds one of the few hints of civilization to an otherwise wild island.

Though the weather across much of the island is hot and dry, the Norfolk pines that line Lanai City's streets create a cool refuge. While there, you'll encounter some of the people who came from the Philippines to work in Lanai's pineapple fields. You'll also be exposed to the many other races of Hawaii, from Korean, Chinese, and Japanese to transplanted mainland *haoles* (Caucasians).

Lanai City is the only place to shop on the island, and its options are limited. It also offers a couple of diner-style eateries as well as the charming old Hotel Lanai, a 10-room hostelry that serves as a gathering place for locals and tourists alike.

But Lanai City is not the real reason for coming to Lanai. Visitors should be prepared to spend a lot of time outdoors, because Lanai has no commercial attractions, no movie theaters, and no bowling alleys. Instead you can visit sights such as the Garden of the Gods, where rocks and boulders are scattered across a crimson landscape as if some divine being had placed them there as his own sculpture garden. You can spend a leisurely day at Hulopoe Beach, where the waters are so clear that within a minute of snorkeling you can see fish the colors of turquoise and jade. And then there's the top of Lanaihale, a 3,370-foot-high, windswept perch from which you can see every inhabited Hawaiian island, except Kauai and Niihau.

While today it is an island that welcomes visitors with its friendly, rustic charm, Lanai has not always been so amiable. The earliest Polynesians believed it to be haunted by evil ghosts who gobbled up unsuspecting visitors. In 1836 a pair of missionaries named Dwight Baldwin and William Richards came and went after failing to convert the people of Lanai to their Christian beliefs. In 1854 a group of Mormons tried to create the City of Joseph on Lanai, but they, too, retreated in 1857 after drought forced them to abandon their endeavors.

One of Lanai's more successful visitors was a man named Jim Dole. In 1922, Dole bought the island for $1.1 million and began to grow pineapples on it. He built Lanai City on the flatlands where the crater meets the mountains. Then he planned the harbor at Kaumalapau, from which pineapples would be shipped. Four years later, as he watched the first harvest sail away to Honolulu, this enterprising businessman could safely say that Lanai's Dole Plantation was a success.

Not much has changed on the island since then; not much, that is, until recently. The third smallest of the islands, Lanai has always been the most intimate destination in the 50th state.

But, like so many good things in life, Lanai's simple charm may soon be faced with change. The island is already leaning more toward mainstream Hawaii as the finishing touches are put on two hotels created by Castle & Cooke, the parent company of Dole and 98% owner of the island. The 102-room Lodge at Koele and 248-room luxury Manele Bay Hotel are geared to the upscale-visitor market, and both should be completed by the time you read this. The effect of those accommodations upon the island remains to be seen.

For the residents of Lanai, life is simple. It begins at 5 AM, when workers take to the pineapple fields wearing floppy hats and colorful bandannas to guard against the sun and dirt. They follow behind huge cutting machines and pick up the pineapples by hand. At day's end, they return home, drink beer, eat dinner, and "talk story" (converse) as the stars fill the sky.

A visit to Lanai is equally straightforward. You can be all alone simply by leaving Lanai City. That is, unless you encounter the deer on the hillsides, or the spirits that linger amid the ancient fishing village of Kaunolu, or the dolphins that come into Manele Bay to swim with you. Bring casual clothes, because all your activities will be laid-back, whether you're riding the unpaved roads in a four-wheel-drive vehicle or having a drink on the front porch of the Hotel Lanai.

Everything on Lanai is leisurely and lovely. Come, take your time, and enjoy yourself before the island changes too much more.

Essential Information

Arriving and Departing by Plane

Airport As you land at the tiny Lanai airport (tel. 808/565–6757) you see a sign that welcomes you to "Lanai, the Pineapple Island, the world's premier pineapple plantation, grower of famous Dole Products." You might also see the glistening Falcon 50 jet owned by David Murdock, head of Castle & Cooke and the moving force behind the island's recent changes.

Airlines In order to reach Lanai from the mainland United States, you must first stop at Oahu's Honolulu International Airport; from there, it takes about a half hour to fly to Lanai. **Hawaiian Airlines** (tel. 800/367–5320) offers flights between Lanai and Oahu on an irregular basis, generally every day but Saturday. A round-trip on one of its 50-seat Dash 7s costs $50.95. **Aloha IslandAir** (tel. 800/323–3345) has two flights daily on its 18-passenger Twin Otters, at a round-trip cost of $77. (Hawaiian Airlines and Aloha IslandAir serve Lanai from the other Islands as well as from Oahu.)

Between the Airport and Hotels Lanai's airport is a 10-minute drive from Lanai City. If you're staying at the Hotel Lanai, the Lodge at Koele, or the Manele Bay Hotel, you will be met by a complimentary shuttle that will take you to your accommodations. Don't expect to see any public buses at the airport, because there are none on the island.

By Taxi **Oshiro U-Drive & Taxi** (tel. 808/565–6952) monopolizes the market for taxi transfers to and from the airport. The charge for the trip is $5.

By Car There is a distinct advantage to renting your own vehicle on Lanai, because public transportation is nonexistent and attractions are far apart. Make your car- or jeep-rental reservation way in advance of your trip, because Lanai is small and its fleet of vehicles is limited.

Three companies on Lanai rent vehicles to visitors. Contact **Lanai City Service** (Box N, Lanai City 96763, tel. 808/565–7227), **Oshiro U-Drive & Taxi** (Box 516, Lanai City 96763, tel. 808/565–6952), or **Dollar** (1600 Kapiolani Blvd., Honolulu 96814, tel. 800/342–7398). You'll pay from $35 a day for cars and $60–$90 a day for four-wheel-drive jeeps and vans. Each company offers airport pickup and drop-off for $5 round-trip.

Getting Around

Some sort of private transportation is advised on Lanai, unless you plan to stay in one place during your entire visit. Avoid that urge, because the island has natural splendors from one end to the other.

By Car Driving Driving around Lanai isn't as easy as on other islands, because most roads outside of Lanai City aren't marked. From town, the streets extend outward as paved roads with two-way traffic. Highway 44 runs north to Shipwreck Beach and south to Kaumalapau Harbor, while Highway 440 leads down to Manele Bay and Hulopoe Beach. The rest of your driving takes place on bumpy and muddy dirt roads, which are best navigated by a four-wheel-drive jeep or van.

The island has no traffic lights, and you'll never find yourself in a traffic jam. However, heed this word of caution: Before heading out on your explorations, ask one of the locals if you're going in the right direction. There are no signs by the major attractions, and it's easy to get lost.

Car Rentals *See* Between the Airport and Hotels, above, for information on renting a vehicle.

By Taxi It costs between $5 and $10 for a cab ride from Lanai City to almost any point on the paved roads of the island. **Oshiro U-Drive & Taxi** (tel. 808/565–6952) is Lanai's only taxicab service.

By Bicycle A mountain bike is a fun way to explore the pineapple fields and back roads of Lanai. Ask at the front desk of your hotel about renting one.

Important Addresses and Numbers

Tourist Information The two new hotels scheduled to open—the Lodge at Koele in 1990 and the Manele Bay Hotel in 1991—will most likely have information desks. In addition, you should write ahead of time to the **Maui Visitors Bureau** (380 Dairy Rd., Kahului 96732, tel. 808/871–8691), which offers information about Lanai as well as Maui.

Emergencies **Police, fire,** or **ambulance** (tel. 911).

Hospital The **Lanai Community Hospital** (628 7th Ave., Lanai City, tel. 808/565–6411) is the center of health care for the island. It offers 24-hour ambulance service and a pharmacy.

Opening and Closing Times

Lanai City basically shuts down on Sundays. **First Hawaiian Bank** (644 Lanai Ave., tel. 808/565-6969) is open Monday through Thursday 8:30 AM–3 PM, Friday until 6 PM. Shops open Monday through Saturday between 9 and 10 and close between 5 and 6.

Guided Tours

Off-Road Tours. Many of the highlights of Lanai are accessible only from the often-confusing unpaved back roads of the island. On a guided tour you can leave the navigation to a driver who knows what he's doing, while you simply hang on and enjoy the ride in a three-passenger Jeep Wrangler. Along the way you will see petroglyphs, the Garden of the Gods, and portions of the Munro Trail. Tours are at least two hours long and are limited to three people. Be sure to give advance notice. **Oshiro Tour & U-Drive** (Box 516, Lanai City 96763, tel. 808/565-6952) offers tours daily at $33 per hour per person.

Club Lanai. This is an option for touring Lanai without actually staying there. From Lahaina, on Maui, a 149-passenger tour boat departs at 8 AM and sails 35 minutes across the channel to an 8-acre beach estate on Lanai's eastern coast. The club is completely self-contained and offers a multitude of activities, including rides in a glass-bottom boat, snorkeling, wave skiing, whale watching, and historic guided bus tours to Lanai's oldest church, in the village of Keomuku. Continental breakfast is served on the cruise, and a buffet luncheon is available on Lanai. You leave the club at 4 PM for the cruise back to Maui. Club Lanai is a terrific introduction to the island, and one that may just entice you to return for more than a day. *355 Hukilike St., Suite 211, Kahului 96732, tel. 808/871-1144. Cost: $75 adults, $37 children under 13. (Half-day trips are also available.) Tours daily.*

Exploring

Lanai is small enough to explore in a couple of days of leisurely travel, depending on how you want to experience it. If you're a hiker, you'll want a day just to enjoy the splendors of Lanaihale, the mountain that rises above Lanai City. If you're a fan of water sports, you'll want to take time to jump into the water at Hulopoe Beach to the south or Shipwreck Beach to the north.

Most of the sights are out of the way; that is, you won't find them in Lanai City or along paved roads. You'll have to look to find them, but the search is worth it. Remember to ask directions at your hotel desk before setting out, because Lanai attractions aren't usually marked. Bring along a cooler with drinks and snacks for your explorations, because there are no places to stop for refreshments along the way—unless you return to your hotel or Lanai City.

All of the sights mentioned in this chapter are free.

Highlights for First-time Visitors

Garden of the Gods, Tour 3
Hulopoe Beach, Tour 1
Keomuku, Tour 2
Lanaihale, Tour 2
Manele Bay, Tour 1
Shipwreck Beach, Tour 2

Tour 1: Heading South

Numbers in the margin correspond with points of interest on the Lanai map.

Begin this tour in Lanai City. Head south on Highway 440 for about a mile, until you see an unmarked dirt road that heads left through some pineapple fields. At the end of that road, get out of the car and climb up another unmarked trail to the **①** **Luahiwa Petroglyphs,** ancient rock carvings. These simple stick figures represent man, nature, and life on Lanai as drawn by the Hawaiians of the early 19th century.

Return to Highway 440 and continue south by making a left; the highway is now called Manele Road. When this road makes a sharp left turn, continue straight on Kaupili Road, which leads you through pineapple fields. When you come to your fourth dirt road, take it toward the ocean until you reach **②** **Kaunolu,** an old fishing village once inhabited by King Kamehameha I. The Bishop Museum excavated these ruins, which include stone floors and platforms where 86 houses and 35 shelters once stood. You can also see house sites and terraces, all set atop the island's highest sea cliffs. In this area you can also find some petroglyphs, a series of intricate carvings that have been preserved in tribute to this once-thriving community. Just to the west of Kaunolu are the remnants of a sacred **③** gathering place called **Halulu Heiau.**

④ Return to Manele Road and follow it downhill to **Manele Bay.** Flanked by lava cliffs that are hundreds of feet high, the bay hosts a regular influx of little boats whose owners are generally from other Neighbor Islands. To the right of the harbor are the foundations of some old Hawaiian houses.

The road winds to the right and passes the new Manele Bay Hotel (scheduled to open in late 1990) on the right. To your left is a **⑤** sparkling crescent called **Hulopoe Beach,** whose broad expanse is one of the best beaches in all of Hawaii. It's an ideal spot for a picnic lunch, a dip in the water, and relaxing under the trees. The waves are gentle enough for beginning bodysurfers, and the waters are full of fish that are easily visible to snorkelers, since it is a marine life conservation area.

Retrace your route back up Manele Road to Highway 440, and take the highway until it meets up with Highway 440 west (Kaumalapau Highway). Turn left and drive about seven miles **⑥** to the ocean. This is **Kaumalapau Harbor,** a busy port used to ship millions of crates of—you guessed it—pineapples. The cliffs flanking the western shore are as high as 1,000 feet.

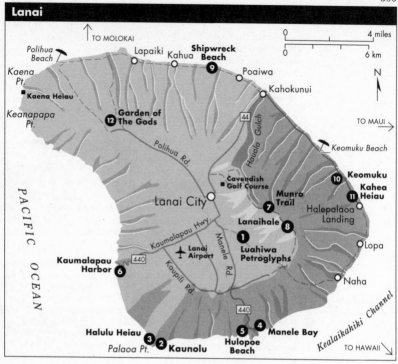

Lanai

TO MOLOKAI

Polihua Beach

Kaena Pt.

Kaena Heiau

Keanapapa Pt.

Lapaiki   Kahua   **Shipwreck Beach** ⑨   Poaiwa

Kahokunui

Garden of The Gods ⑫

Polihua Rd.

TO MAUI

Keomuku Beach

Hauola Gulch

44

Cavendish Golf Course

Lanai City

Munro Trail ⑦

⑩ **Keomuku**

⑪ **Kahea Heiau**

Halepalaoa Landing

Lanaihale ① ⑧

Luahiwa Petroglyphs

Lopa

Kaumalapau Hwy.

Lanai Airport

Manele Rd.

Naha

P A C I F I C   O C E A N

Kaumalapau Harbor ⑥

440

Kaupili Rd.

440

Halulu Heiau ③ ② **Kaunolu**

Palaoa Pt.

⑤ **Hulopoe Beach**   ④ **Manele Bay**

Kealaikahiki Channel

TO HAWAII

0   4 miles
0   6 km

N

Tour 2: Heading North

Once again, begin this tour in Lanai City. Head north on Highway 44 (Lanai Avenue), and two miles past the post office, turn right on a gravel road. A half mile past the cemetery on your right is the trailhead of the **Munro Trail,** an 8.8-mile route. From here only a jeep or your feet will take you up to **Lanaihale,** the high point of the island, at 3,370 feet. From its peak you'll get spectacular views of nearly all the Hawaiian islands. You can also see 2,000 feet down into Lanai's deepest canyon, Hauola Gulch. The trail, which winds through a lush tropical rain forest, was named after George Munro, a New Zealand naturalist who planted the pine trees in Lanai City in 1910.

Return to Highway 44 and continue north about eight miles, to the northern coast. Here you'll encounter **Shipwreck Beach,** so named because of the tricky winds that have caused many boats to crash on the reef. You can still see the remains of a World War II vessel here, not to mention sensational views of Molokai across the channel. If you want to see more petroglyphs, walk to the left along the beach and follow the white arrows painted on the rocks.

Highway 44 ends at Shipwreck Beach, but there's more excitement awaiting you if you feel adventurous. A word of caution: Do not continue along this road unless you have a four-wheel-drive vehicle. The going is rough and often muddy.

From Shipwreck Beach, go to the right (east) along the very bumpy dirt road. Five miles later you will come to an area where there are dozens of tall coconut trees. This is **Keomuku,** once a busy Lanai community, which was abandoned in 1901 after the collapse of the Maunalei Sugar Company. You can still go into the ramshackle old church, the oldest on the island. There's an eerie beauty about Keomuku, with its once-stately homes now reduced to weed-infested sites and crumbling stone walls.

A mile and a half farther down the road, you can see the ruins of a temple called **Kahea Heiau,** whose stone formations are visible amid overgrown shrubs and bushes. The dirt road ends three miles later, at the remnants of the old Hawaiian village of **Naha,** which you can skip unless you're a Hawaiian history buff. Here you must turn around and retrace your route—back to Highway 44.

Tour 3: Garden of the Gods

Once again, heed this advice: Ask for directions at your hotel before heading off on this excursion. It could very well be the most sought-after attraction on the island, yet it is also the most difficult to find.

From Lanai City, take Polihua Road north. This leads you to a dirt road, which cuts through pineapple fields for a couple of miles. Then you'll see a dirt road lined with ironwood trees, where you turn left. This road heads upward and eventually takes you to your destination: the **Garden of the Gods,** a heavily eroded canyon scattered with boulders of different sizes, shapes, and colors that seem to have been placed there with some purpose. Stop and enjoy this eerie scenery for a while, for its lunar appearance is unmatched in Hawaii. Anyone who's a geology buff will want to take photos of the area, and there are also magnificent views of the Pacific Ocean.

Shopping

Except for the specialty shops in the new Manele Bay Hotel, Lanai City is the only place on the island to buy what you need. Its main streets, 7th and 8th avenues, offer a small scattering of shops that look as if they're out of the 1920s. Each offers personal service and congenial charm.

Stores open their doors Monday through Saturday between 9 and 10 and close between 5 and 6. Shops are closed on Sundays and often between noon and 1:30 PM on weekdays.

General Stores

In the most literal sense, the four main businesses in town are what you would call general stores. That means they try to carry whatever customers need, and no business has a specialty.

You can get everything from cosmetics to canned vegetables at **Pine Isle Market** (356 8th Ave., tel. 808/565–6488).

In 1946, Richard Tamashiro founded **Richard's Shopping Center** (434 8th Ave., tel. 808/565–6047), which is run today by his sons Wallace, Robert, and Collin. Among other things, the store has a fun selection of Lanai T-shirts, which make great souvenirs.

You may not find everything the name implies at **International Food and Clothing Center** (833 Ilima Ave., tel. 808/565–6433). However, Andrew de la Cruz, whose parents started the store in 1952, does carry a good supply of everyday needs at this modest emporium.

If you're still looking for groceries and general necessities, go to **S.&T. Properties** (419 7th Ave., tel. 808/565–6537).

Beaches

Only a few beaches on Lanai are worth seeking out. All of them have good swimming in protected waters. None has a phone number, so if you need more information, try the Maui Visitors Bureau (380 Dairy Rd., Kahului 96732, tel. 808/871–8691), which is happy to hand out information on Lanai.

Hulopoe Beach is the island's only easily accessible white-sand beach. Residents enjoy spending the day there, cooking over the grills, swimming, and watching the sunset. The beach will certainly become more crowded with the opening of the new Manele Bay Hotel, but its broad, long stretch of sand ought to be able to accommodate everyone. The snorkeling here is ideal, and the scuba diving, swimming, and bodysurfing are fine. There are changing rooms, outdoor showers, picnic tables, grills, and lifeguards. *On the south shore of Hulopoe Bay, 10 mi south of Lanai City on Manele Rd.*

Polihua Beach. Due to its more obscure location and frequent high winds, this beach is often deserted. It is spectacular all the same, with a long white-sand beach and glorious views of Molokai. Swimming here is good when the wind dies down. *On the northwest shore, 11 mi from Lanai City, past the Garden of the Gods* (see *Tour 3* in Exploring, above). Ask in town for directions.

Shipwreck Beach. Don't let the name scare you away. This is a nice beach for exploring as well as swimming. More isolated and rustic than Hulopoe Beach, Shipwreck is a popular spot for snorkeling in shallow waters, thanks to the reef 200 yards offshore. Many people dive here for lobsters. The beach has no lifeguards, no changing rooms, and no outdoor showers. *On the north shore, 10 mi north of Lanai City at the end of Highway 44.*

Sports

Golf   For years, golfers have teed off from the pine-fringed greens of the **Cavendish Golf Course** (no phone number), which flanks the grounds of the Lodge at Koele, open as of April 1990. In 1990, greens fees for visitors were supposed to go up from the old rate of $5.

In addition, an 18-hole waterfront golf course has been designed by Arnold Palmer for the **Manele Bay Hotel** (tel. 808/548–3768), scheduled to open in early 1991.

Hiking   The most popular Lanai hike is the **Munro Trail**, a strenuous 8.8-mile trek that takes about eight hours. There is an elevation gain of 1,400 feet leading you to the lookout at Lanai's highest point, Lanaihale. You can also hike as far as 8 miles along **Shipwreck Beach,** all the way to Polihua Beach, if you're up for it. Along the way you'll see a whimsical assortment of seashells and ship debris. No permission is needed to venture along either of these routes.

Before taking off, fill a water bottle and arm yourself with provisions in case you get a little off the track. Also, look at Craig Chisholm's paperback, *Hawaiian Hiking Trails* (Touchstone Press, 1977), and Robert Smith's *Hawaii's Best Hiking Trails* (Wilderness Press, 1987).

Hunting Guided hunts on private lands are offered on Lanai courtesy of the **Koele Company** (Box L, Lanai City 96763, tel. 808/565–6661, 808/565–6955, or 808/565–7233), which provides guides, breakfast, lunch, skinning, and salting of the hide. The primary trophy animal here is the axis deer. Cost is $400 a day, $300 for each additional hunter in a party. Nonguided hunting is allowed at $200 a day, but only if you have hunted before on the island.

Snorkeling **Hulopoe Beach** is one of the most outstanding snorkeling destinations in all of Hawaii. It attracts brilliantly colored fish to its protected cove, in which you can also marvel at underwater coral and lava formations. Ask at your hotel's activities desk about renting equipment. If you visit the island as part of **Club Lanai,** you are invited to snorkel off a private beach on the north shore *(see* Guided Tours in Essential Information, above).

Tennis The new **Lodge at Koele** and **Manele Bay Hotel** (tel. 808/548–3768 for both properties) plan to include tennis courts for guest use. Call for rates.

Dining

Don't come to Lanai for gourmet cuisine. Your restaurant choices are limited enough that you'll have to be happy with what is available. In fact, you'll need to schedule your day's activities around the opening and closing times of each dining spot. Otherwise, you'll have to shop at a grocery store.

All of the restaurants listed here are located in Lanai City. Each is recommended for its home-style appeal and friendly service. Some new, upscale restaurants are opening in the Lodge at Koele and the Manele Bay Hotel, so you'll want to check with those properties regarding their offerings *(see* Lodging, below).

Each restaurant falls into the **Inexpensive** price category: under $20 per person, excluding drinks, service, and 4% sales tax.

Dahang's Pastry Shop. At breakfast, you won't be asked what you want, but how you want it. That's how things run at Dahang's, where the early morning fare is a pair of eggs, toast, hash browns, and your choice of meat. Lunchtime brings more selections, including the best hamburgers on the island. This is a real diner, with Formica-top tables, plastic chairs, and mismatched silverware. You order across the counter, then find a seat until the waitress brings your food. And yes, as the name implies, this is also a pastry shop, and a good one at that. Try the Filipino-style doughnuts coated with granulated sugar; freshly made, they're a real treat. *409 7th Ave., tel. 808/565–*

6363. *No reservations. Dress: casual. No credit cards. Breakfast and lunch only, as well as carryout food.*

Hotel Lanai. Over the years, this has been the only place where you could get three meals a day. Of course, that will change with the opening of the Lodge at Koele and Manele Bay Hotel. Still, don't overlook this charming spot with the island's most "gourmet" food. Banana pancakes and specialty omelets are offered at breakfast, soups and sandwiches at lunch, and American cuisine at dinner (steaks, chicken, and fish prepared simply). The pretty room is just off the hotel's lanai and features large wooden tables, a fireplace at one end, and stunning paintings and photographs by island artists. *828 Lanai Ave., tel. 808/565-7211. Reservations advised. Dress: casual. AE, MC, V.*

S.&T. Properties. Occupying part of a general store, this place has an old-fashioned soda fountain with a counter and swivel stools. The food is classic diner fare, such as burgers, fries, and sundaes. *419 7th Ave., tel. 808/565-6537. No reservations. Dress: casual. No credit cards.*

Lodging

Until recently, the only accommodation on the island was the comfy old Hotel Lanai in Lanai City. Now two swanky alternatives for the discriminating traveler plan to open by the end of this year. Let your tastes and your budget determine which place you choose.

Category	Cost*
Very Expensive	over $120
Inexpensive	under $60

*All prices are for a standard double room, excluding 9¼% tax and service charges.

Very Expensive

Lodge at Koele. One of the new additions to the hotel scene, the lodge was planned to resemble a luxurious private mountain retreat sprawled over 21 acres. Open as of April 1990, it sits on the edge of Lanai City, in the highlands, where the temperature is cool and the pine trees are plentiful. The two-story lodge features a reception building and a main hall with unusual art objects and rare Pacific artifacts. The porch is a generous space in which guests may enjoy the view and take refreshments, and the interiors have high beamed ceilings and natural stone fireplaces. In the Hawaiian fruit garden, visitors can pick and sample fruits from a variety of trees and shrubs, and there is more than a mile and a half of pathways through orchid gardens, macadamia forests, and Polynesian palm landscapes. *Box 2780, Honolulu 96803, tel. 808/548-3768. 102 rooms and suites with bath. Facilities: golf, tennis, croquet, lawn bowling, restaurant, 2 lounges, pool. AE, CB, DC, MC, V.*

Manele Bay Hotel. Scheduled to open in late 1990, this elaborate beachfront property will offer luxury villas and suites that command views of Hulopoe Bay, the coastline, and the island of Maui. Design will be reminiscent of traditional Hawaiian architecture, with lots of open-air lanais. Three two-story buildings will overlook a courtyard, and a reception building will house the lobby and specialty boutiques. Ground- and second-level guest rooms will feature private lanais and will be surrounded by courtyards, waterfalls, ponds, and lawns landscaped with bromeliads, canopy trees, and other exotica. *Box 2780, Honolulu 96803, tel. 808/548–3768. 250 rooms and suites with bath. Facilities: golf, tennis, croquet, 3 restaurants, lounge, pool. AE, CB, DC, MC, V.*

Inexpensive

Hotel Lanai. First built to house visiting plantation executives, this quaint 10-room inn was once the only accommodation on the island. Today, even though two new hotels are opening up, you shouldn't overlook this Lanai institution. The old front porch with the big wicker chairs has long been a meeting place for residents and locals alike, who gather to read the paper, order a drink, and "talk story" (converse). The rooms are simple, with single or twin beds, flowered wallpaper, and sometimes mismatched furniture, offering the feeling that you're in an eccentric great-aunt's country home. The grounds are well-maintained, with flower gardens and enormous Norfolk pines, and you can get three meals a day here (not included in the room fee). *Box A119, Lanai City 96763, tel. 808/565–7211 or 800/624 –8849. 10 rooms with bath. Facilities: restaurant. AE, MC, V.*

Nightlife

The locals entertain themselves by gathering on the front porch of the **Hotel Lanai** for drinks and "talk story" sessions.

The **Lodge at Koele** (tel. 808/548–3768) plans to feature music recitals and films in the octagonal corner rooms of its reception building. In addition, its Music Room will offer live entertainment, as yet unscheduled.

At the **Manele Bay Hotel** (tel. 808/548–3768), the Terrace will offer after-dinner dancing in a romantic garden setting next to a fountain and reflecting pool.

8 Kauai

by Marty Wentzel

Nicknamed "the Garden Isle," Kauai is Eden epitomized. In the mountains of Kokee, lush swamps ring with the songs of rare birds, while the heady aroma of ginger blossoms sweetens the cool rain forests of Haena. Time and nature have carved elegant spires along the remote northern shore, called the Pali coast, while seven powerful rivers give life to the valleys where ancient Hawaiians once dwelled. Visitors can become one with that Eden on land and sea or in the air, by hiking along the Kalalau Trail, or paddling a kayak along the Hanalei River, or taking an exhilarating helicopter ride above Mt. Waialeale, the wettest spot on earth.

Still, even Eden has its drawbacks. If you're looking for bright lights and big-city thrills, Kauai should not be your first destination in the Hawaiian Islands. Despite the addition of the ultraswank Westin Kauai Resort in Nawiliwili in the late '80s, the overall portrait that Kauaians like to paint of their home is laid-back, restful, and natural. Indeed, this is an island that appeals most to those with a love of the great outdoors.

During your days, you can take a boat ride up the Pali coast and go snorkeling. You can ride in a horse-drawn coach around a plantation-era sugar estate. You can play golf on the world-class greens of Princeville Resort, with views of the mountain ridge nicknamed Bali Hai. You can even take a ride in a glider above Waimea Canyon, called the "Grand Canyon of the Pacific." Tired yet? How about some tennis, horseback riding, and sportfishing?

One road runs almost all the way around the circumference of the island, although it dead-ends on either side of the 15-mile stretch of rugged Pali coast. Driving from one end to the other takes you past emerald blankets of sugarcane, an important economic force on the island since Hawaii's first sugar mill was built in Koloa in 1836. You pass the aquacultural tracts of Kilauea, where prawns and fish are raised in large rectangular pools reminiscent of the first Hawaiian fish ponds. You see such movie backdrops as Lumahai Beach, where *South Pacific* was filmed, and the Huleia River, where Indiana Jones made his daring escape at the beginning of *Raiders of the Lost Ark*.

Kauai is the fourth-largest island of the Hawaiian chain, and its capital is Lihue, a town whose governmental buildings look like something out of a little New England village. Lihue is the commercial center of the Garden Isle, yet its collection of businesses—a pair of banks, a library, a school, a museum, some family-run restaurants, and hotels—is small enough to keep the pace slow and relaxed. During rush hour, Lihue becomes citified, for its narrow roads have a hard time accommodating the traffic of residents as well as tourists. Some contemporary shopping complexes are also gently pushing Lihue into a more modern-day pace.

To the south of the island is the major resort of Poipu, whose sunny beaches and clear skies have spawned a crop of condos and hotels. Heading west beneath the slopes of the Hoary Head Mountains, you encounter such storybook plantation villages as Hanapepe, Kalaheo, and Waimea, where Captain James Cook made his first Hawaiian landing back in 1778. Beyond Waimea, you'll find the long, deserted sands of Polihale Beach, above which are the cool highlands of Kokee.

From the southwestern portion of the island you can see the island of Niihau, 17 miles off the southern coast. Until 1987, no uninvited guests were allowed to visit this family-owned island. Today most people who live in Hawaii still consider it off-limits, although this mysterious cay is now open to Kauai-based helicopter tours, which touch down on two Niihau beaches.

To the north of Lihue, the climate becomes cooler and wetter. Everything is green and growing, and the world feels rather untamed. The towns of Wailua and Kapaa offer several resort complexes along a picturesque shoreline, and as you head farther north to Anahola, Kilauea, and Hanalei, a kaleidoscope of vines and flowers takes over. At the end of the road in Haena, you'll encounter a misty otherworldliness conjuring up the legends of the ancients. Here, they say, is the birthplace of the hula; today's dancers drive to the end of the road to visit the area's huge *heiau* (a sacred stone platform for the worship of the gods) so they may pay tribute to Laka, the goddess of the hula.

More myths and legends are attached to the natural landscape of Kauai than to that of any other Hawaiian Island. A favorite among locals is the story of the legendary *menehune*, a community of tiny yet industrious workers who are said to have lived on Kauai before the Polynesians. Few people actually saw the menehune, because they worked in privacy at night. However, their stoneworks were impressive, and today you can see the bridges, walls, and structures that have been attributed to this mysterious race. It's still uncertain whether the menehune really existed, but no one has come up with an alternative regarding the source of the stoneworks.

Kauai may not be cosmopolitan, but as the sun sets on your day of play, the lights come up on a number of first-rate restaurants. Most of them are centered in the tourist resorts, including Poipu on the south shore and along the east coast from Wailua and Kapaa to Princeville and Hanalei. You can catch a couple of luaus in which performers take you back in time with the chants of Kauai's earliest inhabitants. Dinner shows touch on the contemporary as well and sometimes feature such island personalities as Charo, one of many entertainers who have chosen Kauai as their personal nirvana.

As it drifts in the Pacific just 95 miles northwest of Honolulu, Kauai makes no excuses for being less glamorous than Oahu. With unaffected natural beauty, it calmly welcomes all who step off the plane at the Lihue Airport and wraps them in a lei of ancient Hawaiian hospitality. With nearly 7,000 hotel rooms and condominiums on the island, it's no surprise that tourism is Kauai's number-one industry. The people involved in that business are working hard to keep its guests satisfied, and the aloha spirit is highly apparent. In fact, many think that Kauai's people are the friendliest in all of Hawaii.

The oldest of the Hawaiian Islands, Kauai has 350,000 acres that are ripe with natural history and reflections of cultures past. In the present, it boasts tourist attractions, commercial activities, and accommodations that have won awards for their services. With a sensitive eye toward the preservation of its rural charm, Kauai is always open to changes.

Essential Information

Arriving and Departing by Plane

Airports The **Lihue Airport** handles most of the air traffic in and out of Kauai. Located 3 miles east of the town of Lihue, the terminal is spacious, clean, contemporary, and friendly, and easily accommodates the growing number of visitors to the Garden Isle. Arriving passengers walk through automatic revolving doors to enter the baggage claim area, and gift and snack shops are available with essentials for the road. Once you arrive, if you have any immediate questions, stop by the **Lihue Airport Visitor Information Center** (tel. 808/246–1440), which is located right at the terminal. It's open all day.

To the north of Lihue is **Princeville Airport** (tel. 808/826–3040), a tiny strip in the middle of rolling ranch lands and sugarcane fields. The open-air design and single check-in counter of its terminal impart a distinctly easygoing atmosphere. Two car-rental counters are located right at the terminal.

Princeville Airport is just a five-minute drive from the Princeville development area, which is full of condos and has a hotel called the Sheraton Mirage Princeville. The airport is also about a 15-minute drive from the shops and accommodations of sleepy Hanalei.

Flights from the Mainland U.S. **United Airlines** (tel. 800/241–6522) is the only carrier that flies directly into Lihue Airport from the mainland (Los Angeles, Denver, Philadelphia, Chicago, and San Francisco). However, you must make one stop in Honolulu International Airport before reaching the Garden Isle. It takes about five hours to fly from the West Coast to Kauai, not including stopover time.

Flights from Honolulu Carriers flying from Oahu to Lihue Airport include **Aloha Airlines** (tel. 800/367–5250) and **Hawaiian Airlines** (tel. 800/367–5320). Each offers approximately 20 flights a day. The rates go up and down depending on which airline is trying to outdo the other, but the one-way, per-person fare generally is $44.95. When you call to make a reservation, ask if there are reduced rates for traveling on the first or last flight of the day. Sometimes that price drops to as low as $30 one-way. It's a 25-minute flight between Honolulu and Lihue. **Discovery Airways** (tel. 808/946–1500) started service to Kauai in early 1990.

Flights from Honolulu to Princeville Airport are offered by **Aloha IslandAir** (tel. 800/323–3345), formerly Princeville Airways. The cost per person from Honolulu is $47.95 one-way, and the flight takes about 45 minutes.

Lei Greetings Receiving a garland of fresh flowers as you step off the plane is a wonderful way to arrive at a new destination. You may decide to set up such a greeting for yourself or, better yet, for your traveling partner. Companies that cover the Lihue Airport include **Aloha Lei Greeters** (Box 29133, Honolulu 96820, tel. 808/836–0249), **Greeters of Hawaii** (Box 29638, Honolulu 96820, tel. 800/367–2669), **Hawaii 800** (Box 89696, Honolulu 96830-0810, tel. 800/367–5270), **Hawaii Resorts Transportation Company** (Box 183, Honokaa 96727, tel. 808/885–7484), and **Trans Hawaiian Services** (3111 Castle St., Honolulu 96815, tel. 800/533–8765). **Kauai Greeters** (Box 640, Poipu Beach 96756, tel. 800/443–

9180) will even meet you with music and hula dancers. Leis range from $6.95 for the simple orchid lei to $20 for the deluxe treatment. Some companies will also put together fruit baskets, bouquets, and other special orders.

Between the Airport and Hotels The driving distance from Lihue Airport to the town of Lihue is a mere five minutes. If you're staying in Wailua or Kapaa, your driving time from Lihue is 15 minutes, and to Princeville and Hanalei it takes 1¼ hours behind the wheel. If you're staying in Hanalei, try to fly into Princeville Airport to save on driving time.

To the south, it's a 20-minute drive from Lihue to Poipu, the major resort of that area. If you choose the rustic accommodations in the hills of Kokee, allow a good two hours of driving time from Lihue.

Before you look into one of the following methods of transportation to your lodgings, check with your hotel or condo to see if it offers free shuttle service from the airport.

By Bus Kauai has no public bus system. From Lihue Airport, **Gray Line Hawaii** (tel. 800/367–2420) offers an airport motor coach service, which costs $4 to Lihue, $8 to Poipu, $5 to Wailua, and $18 to Princeville. This is a shuttle service, so advance reservations are not necessary. You should call ahead, however, for exact departure times to your specific location.

From Princeville Airport, you can catch the free shuttle service (tel. 808/826–9644) offered by the Princeville Resort to its hotels and condos.

By Van **Shoppe Hoppers** (tel. 808/332–7272) is a shuttle service that takes you from the airport to various hotels around the island in 14-passenger air-conditioned vans. Charges differ according to distance; for instance, the per-person cost from the airport to Poipu is $6, to Kapaa $4. Shoppe Hoppers doesn't charge for your bags. There's no set schedule; just call the service as you would a taxicab.

By Taxi Fares around the island are $2.60 for the first mile and $1.60 for each additional mile. That means a taxicab from Lihue Airport to Lihue town runs about $5, and to Poipu costs $25. Two taxi companies that will take you to Lihue and Poipu are **Akiko's** (tel. 808/822–3613) and **Kauai Cab** (tel. 808/246–9544).

From the Princeville Airport to Hanalei, you'll pay about $10 when you ride with the **North Shore Cab Company** (tel. 808/826–6189), which serves only the northeast portion of the island.

By Limousine For luxurious transportation between the airport and your accommodations, contact **First Class Limousines** (Box 1027, Pearl City 96782, tel. 800/248–5101), whose hourly rates begin at $35. Another possibility for luxury travel is **Limo Limo Limousine Service of Kauai** (Box 636, Kapaa 96746, tel. 808/822–0393). Its rates are $38 to $68 per hour, with a two-hour minimum.

By Car Unless you plan to do all of your sightseeing as part of guided van tours, you will want a rental car on Kauai. The vast beauty of the island begs to be explored, and its attractions are sprinkled from one end to the other.

The main road north from Lihue Airport is Route 56 (also known as Kuhio Highway), which ends 38 miles later in Haena.

From Lihue south and west, the coastal highway is called Highway 50 (Kaumualii Highway), which ends about 40 miles later near Polihale Beach State Park. Highway 520 (Maluhia Road) runs south off Highway 50 to Poipu. On the west side, Highway 550 (Kokee Road) heads north from Kekaha up to the wilds of Kokee State Park.

Right across from the baggage claim area at Lihue Airport you'll find several rental-car firms, as well as vans that will shuttle you to offices nearby. These include **Alamo, Avis, Budget, Dollar, Hertz, National, Roberts, Thrifty, Tropical,** and **United.** There are also several lesser-known and local companies that offer slightly lower rates (*see* Getting Around, below, for specific car-rental information).

Arriving and Departing by Ship

From Honolulu A romantic way to visit Kauai for a short time is to book passage on an interisland cruise ship. These massive white "love boats" leave Honolulu each Saturday night and stop at Kauai, as well as Maui and the Big Island. At each port of call, you may get off the ship and sightsee for a day, sometimes two. **American Hawaii Cruises** (550 Kearny St., San Francisco, CA 94108, tel. 800/227–3666) has been presenting these successful excursions for several years on board the 800-passenger SS *Independence* and SS *Constitution*. Give one of the ships a whirl if you have the time and the money (weekly rates begin at $1,025, including meals).

Getting Around

Although Kauai is relatively small, its sights reach from one end of the island to the other. Often you can walk to the stores and restaurants in your resort area, but the important attractions of the island are generally not within walking distance of each other. As a result, you'll probably want to rent a car, unless you plan to do all your sightseeing with tour companies.

By Car It's easy to get around on Kauai, for it has one major road that
Driving almost encircles the island. Your rental-car company will supply you with a map with enlargements of each area of the island. The traffic on Kauai is pretty light most of the time, except in the Lihue area during rush hour (6:30–8:30 AM and 3:30–5:30 PM). The major attractions are indicated on the side of the road by a Hawaiian-warrior marker.

As is the case throughout Hawaii, a seat-belt law is enforced on Kauai for front-seat passengers. Children under the age of three must be in a car seat, which you can get from your car-rental company.

Although Kauai looks like paradise, it has its fair share of crime. Play it safe and lock up your car whenever you park it. Don't leave valuables in the car, and pay attention to parking signs, particularly in Lihue.

Car Rentals It is advisable to reserve your vehicle before you arrive, especially if you will be on Kauai during the peak seasons of summer, the Christmas holidays, and February.

Daily prices for a car from the major-name companies begin at $20. A fly/drive deal can sometimes reduce that cost to $14. If you sign up with a small or lesser-known local renter, prices range from $12 to $20.

Car-rental companies with offices at or near Lihue Airport are **Alamo** (tel. 800/327–9633), **Avis** (tel. 800/331–1212), **Budget** (tel. 800/527–0707), **Dollar** (tel. 800/367–7006), **Hertz** (tel. 800/654–8200), **National** (tel. 800/227–7368), **Roberts** (tel. 808/947–3939), **Thrifty** (tel. 800/367–2277), **Tropical** (tel. 800/367–5140), and **United** (tel. 800/657–7797).

Companies with Princeville Airport offices are **Avis** and **Hertz**. Several companies also operate reservation desks at the major hotels on the island. These include **Avis** (Stouffer Waiohai Beach Resort, tel. 800/426–4122), **Budget** (Kauai Hilton, tel. 800/445–8667), and **Hertz** (Kauai Hilton, tel. 800/445–8667, Sheraton Kauai and Sheraton Coconut Beach, tel. 800/325–3535, and Westin Kauai, tel. 800/228–3000).

You can get some good deals on a car if you book with one of Kauai's budget or used-rental-car companies. These include **Adventures Four-Wheel Drive Kauai** (tel. 800/356–1207), which offers four-wheel-drive vehicles for backcountry exploration. **Rent-A-Wreck of Kauai** (tel. 808/245–4755) provides used cars, minivans, and maxivans, which they keep in good shape. Or try the reliable **Westside U-Drive** (tel. 808/332–8644).

By Bus Kauai has no public bus system. There are, however, private buses that take visitors to specific commercial attractions (*see* Guided Tours, below).

By Taxi A taxicab will take you islandwide, but you'll pay dearly for that luxury. The cost for the first mile is $2.60, with $1.60 for each additional mile. So, from Lihue to Poipu the price is $25; from Lihue to Princeville, $40. Your best bet is to call a cab for short distances only (to a restaurant, for instance). A 5-mile cab ride will run you about $9. The drivers are often from Kauai, which means they'll give you information about the island. The major taxicab companies on the island are **Akiko's** (tel. 808/822–3613) and **Kauai Cab** (tel. 808/246–9544). Based in Princeville is the **North Shore Cab Company** (tel. 808/826–6189).

By Van An alternative to renting a car or calling a cab is to use **Shoppe Hoppers** (tel. 808/332–7272), whose 14-passenger air-conditioned vans shuttle you between shops, attractions, and activities. The service will also take you to the airport at the end of your stay. Shoppe Hoppers operates on a regular schedule daily from 9 to 3 between major hotels and specific locations; you can also call for special pickups and drop-offs. The price varies according to distance; for instance, a shopping trip from a Poipu hotel to old Koloa town costs $1.50 per person, one-way. Charter rates are available for groups.

By Limousine One doesn't see a lot of limousines cruising the country roads of Kauai, but if the idea intrigues you, contact **First Class Limousines** (Box 1027, Pearl City 96782, tel. 800/248–5101), whose hourly rates begin at $35. Another possibility for luxury travel is **Limo Limo Limousine Service of Kauai** (Box 636, Kapaa 96746, tel. 808/822–0393). Its rates are $38–$68 per hour, with a two-hour minimum.

By Moped/ Motorcycle A two-wheeler is an exciting way to cruise around the Garden Isle. Its country roads are generally uncrowded and safe, so you can ride along at your own pace and enjoy the views. This is also a safe island to explore by bicycle, as long as you exercise caution on the busier thoroughfares. **Pedal and Paddle** (tel. 808/826–9069) charges $30 a day (24 hours) for mopeds, $20 for bicycles. **South Shore Activities** (tel. 808/742–6873) rents mopeds for $22 a day and bikes for $15–$20, with hourly rates available.

Important Addresses and Numbers

Tourist Information
The **Hawaii Visitors Bureau** has its headquarters at 3016 Umi St., Lihue Plaza, Suite 207, Lihue 96766, tel. 808/245–3971. Umi Street runs off of Rice Street, Lihue's main thoroughfare, right near the Kauai Museum. The bureau has a good selection of brochures and other visitor literature, including two free weekly visitors magazines, *Spotlight Kauai* and *This Week on Kauai*.

The **Kauai Visitor Center** (Coconut Plantation Market Place, Waipouli, tel. 808/822–0987 or 822–5113) is another good source of information about the Garden Isle. It handles reservations for a variety of activities and has current brochures and schedules on hand.

Several activity centers will help visitors book tours, arrange sporting excursions, rent cars, reserve rooms in hotels and condos, and even plan weddings. These centers include **Aloha Destinations** (Box 1386, Poipu Beach 96756, tel. 800/443–9180), **Gilligan's Land of Bargains** (Box 1510, Kapaa 96746, tel. 808/822–0600), and **Paradise Club Activities** (Box 3477, Princeville 96722, tel. 808/826–7581 or 808/826–6880).

Emergencies
For police, ambulance, or fire department, dial 911.

Hospital Emergency Rooms
Wilcox Memorial Hospital (3420 Kuhio Hwy., Lihue 96766, tel. 808/245–1100).
Kauai Veterans Memorial Hospital (4643 Waimea Canyon Dr., Waimea 96796, tel. 808/338–9431).

Doctors
The **Kauai Medical Group** (KMG) offers 32 specialties to handle all medical problems. It features lab and X-ray facilities, physical therapy, optometry, and emergency rooms. The main clinic is located at 3420-B Kuhio Hwy., Lihue 96766, tel. 808/245–1500. Other KMG clinics can be found in Kilauea (tel. 808/828–1418), Princeville (tel. 808/826–6300), Kukui Grove (tel. 808/245–5651), Koloa (tel. 808/742–1621), and Kapaa (tel. 808/822–3431). *Open Mon., Thurs., Fri. 10:30–1:30; Sat. noon–6; Sun. 10–4. Physicians are on call 24 hours (tel. 808/245–1831 after hours).*

Shiatsu International Massage Clinic deals with stress, back pain, arthritis, injuries, headaches, fatigue, and the aches and pains of having too much fun on your vacation. Licensed staff members practice this ancient and respected system of pressure-point massage therapy. *1592 Kuhio Hwy., Kapaa 96746, tel. 808/822–9779. Open daily 9–9.*

Late-Night Pharmacies
The **Kauai Medical Group** (3420-B Kuhio Hwy., Lihue 96766, tel. 808/245–1500) offers an extensive pharmacy and features offices around the island. In Lihue, try **Long's Drugs** (Kukui Grove Center, Hwy. 50, tel. 808/245–8871), and in Kapaa, try **Shoreview Pharmacy** (4–1177 Kuhio Hwy., Suite 113, tel. 808/822–1447).

Opening and Closing Times

Most Kauai banks are open Monday through Thursday between 8:45 and 3 or 4:30, Friday until 6. Most financial institutions are closed on weekends and holidays.

Kauai attractions have their own specific hours, usually Monday through Saturday from 9 or 10 to 4:30 or 5. For instance, the Kauai Museum is open weekdays from 9 to 4:30, Saturday from 9 to 1. Most museums are closed on Christmas Day.

Kauai's major shopping centers are open daily from 10 to 5, although some close later. In Kapaa, Kinipopo Shopping Village is open daily from 9 to 9, while Princeville Center's hours are 9 to 5.

Guided Tours

There are three major methods for getting a good look at the Garden Isle: by land, by sea, and by air. You can book these tours through the travel desk of your hotel or call directly.

Tour Companies The companies that take you on guided ground tours of Kauai use big air-conditioned buses and stretch limousines as well as smaller vans. The latter seem to fit in more with the countrified atmosphere of Kauai. Whether you choose a bus or van tour, the equipment will be in excellent shape, because each of these companies wants your business. When you make your reservations, ask what kind of vehicle you'll be riding in and which tours let you get off and look around. The guides are friendly and generally know their island inside out. It's customary to tip them $1 or more per person for their efforts.

The helicopter and boat touring companies also use top-of-the-line equipment. The best-known and most reliable land, sea, and air tour companies on Kauai include the following:

Captain Zodiac Raft Expeditions (Box 456, Hanalei 96714, tel. 800/422–7824 or 808/826–9371) is known for its boat trips along the Pali coast.

Chandler's Kauai Tours (Box 3001, Lihue 96766, tel. 808/245–9134) has 14- and 17-passenger air-conditioned vans.

ERA Helicopters (tel. 808/245–9555 or 800/872–3642) offers around-the-island "flightseeing."

Gray Line Hawaii (tel. 800/367–2420) features tours by motor coach as well as by smaller vans.

Kauai Island Tours (tel. 800/733–4777) takes you around Kauai in an 11-passenger stretch limo and five-passenger Cadillac.

Menehune Helicopters (tel. 808/245–7705) has group rates and charters.

Na Pali–Coast Cruise Line (tel. 808/335–5078 or 246–1015) offers several options for touring the north-shore coastline by boat.

Polynesian Adventure Tours (tel. 800/622–3011) specializes in an all-day Kauai tour.

Roberts Hawaii Tours (tel. 808/245–9101) has top-of-the-line equipment, including stretch limos.

Trans Hawaiian Services (tel. 800/533–8765) offers multilingual tours.

Round-the-Island Ground Tour Sometimes called the Wailua River/Waimea Canyon Tour, this offers a good overview of the island, because you get to see all the sights, including the Russian Fort, Queen Victoria's Profile, Opaekaa Falls, and Menehune Fish Pond. Guests are transported in air-conditioned 17-passenger minivans. The trip includes a boat ride up the Wailua River to Fern Grotto, then a drive around the island to scenic views above Waimea Canyon. The tour stops at the Green Garden restaurant in Hanapepe for a no-host lunch. Companies offering round-the-island ground tours include Gray Line Hawaii, Polynesian Adventure Tours, and Roberts Hawaii Tours (*see* Tour Companies, above).

Helicopter Tours Kauai from the air is mind-boggling. In an hour you can see waterfalls, craters, and places which are inaccessible even by hiking trails. You depart from Lihue Airport or Burns Field in Hanapepe. *Papillon (Box 339, Hanalei 96714, tel. 808/826–6591) or Kenai (Box 3270, Lihue 96766, tel. 808/245–8591). Cost: $125.*

Great Outdoors Tours **Island Adventure's.** Hawaii's forests and marshes are the home of rare and exceptional flora and fauna, which often go unseen by visitor and resident alike. Island Adventure's takes inquisitive visitors on three-hour tours through Huleia National Wildlife Refuge to experience the joys of untamed nature. Your craft is a single-person fiberglass kayak, which you can easily paddle yourself. The number of people on the tour varies from 4 to 40, depending on demand. This is a beautiful one-way trip through the halcyon waters of Huleia Stream, with shuttle service back to your car at the end of the trip. *Box 90519, Honolulu 96835, tel. 800/634–7537. Tours daily at 8:45 and 12:45. Cost: $45.*

North Shore Bike, Cruise, and Snorkel. This is a great all-day tour for the ultimate outdoors person. Hotel pickups and drop-offs take place along the northeastern coast only. The company sponsors a bicycling tour plus a 6-mile cruise to two snorkel sites. Two guides and a support van accompany the group, which ranges from 6 to 13 people. Snorkeling instruction is included, as is a barbecue lunch. *Box 1192, Kapaa 96746, tel. 808/822–1582. Cost: $75.*

Historical Tours **History, Myth, and Legend Tour.** This 2½-hour tour, sponsored by **North Shore Cab Company,** focuses on the facts and fiction that spring from the lush north-shore landscape. The folks who put it together did plenty of research, and the guides are highly qualified to point out locations of historical value. You're driven around in 15-passenger air-conditioned vans, and along the way you learn about the myths associated with the north shore's natural formations. *Box 757, Hanalei 96714, tel. 808/826–6189. Cost: $40. Departs daily at 11:30 and 2. North Shore Cab Company will pick you up at your hotel if you are staying on the north or east side of the island. It will also pick you up at Lihue Airport.*

Niihau Tours Once the "Forbidden Isle," this area off Kauai's southern coast is now accessible to tourists, but only on a one- or two-hour tour with Niihau Helicopters (*see* Tour 4 in Exploring, below).

Exploring

The main road that runs along the edges of the island takes you past a variety of landscapes and attractions that can easily be explored in two or three full days. If you follow the road north from Lihue, you'll encounter green pasturelands, lush valleys, and untamed tropical wilderness. This area is rich in history and legend, for it was one of the primary communities of the first Polynesians, who settled here more than 1,000 years ago.

If you follow the road south from Lihue, the air feels warmer and dryer. This is Poipu, where the sun shines steadily on the populated beaches. A string of condos and hotels lines the sparkling sands, and an impressive variety of water sports is available for the asking.

Head west and you feel as if you're stepping back in time as you pass through one former plantation town after the next, each with its own story to tell: Waimea, home of the Menehune Ditch, which was supposedly built by a mysterious race of little people; Hanapepe, whose salt ponds were once farmed by the ancients; and in the middle of nowhere Fort Elizabeth, from which an enterprising Russian tried to take over the island in the early 1800s.

From Waimea you can drive upland to the crisp, cool climate of Kokee, 3,000 feet above sea level, where you'll see yet another side of this most ancient of the Hawaiian Islands. Here sequoia forests and swamplands provide a home for fascinating indigenous birds and plants, while a mountain lodge welcomes guests with old-style hospitality.

Each of the following driving tours can easily fill a day of sightseeing. If you need to cut your time short, allow one day for the north and east portion of the island and another day for sights to the south and west.

Mauka means on the mountain side of the road, while *makai* means on the ocean side. These terms will be used throughout this touring section.

Highlights for First-time Visitors

Fern Grotto, Tour 1
Fort Elizabeth, Tour 3
Kalalau Lookout, Tour 3
Kamokila, Tour 1
Kauai Museum, Tour 2
Kilauea Lighthouse, Tour 1
Kilohana, Tour 2
Opaekaa Falls, Tour 1
Spouting Horn, Tour 2
Waimea Canyon, Tour 3

Tour 1: The Heavenly Northeast

Numbers in the margin correspond with points of interest on the Kauai map.

Begin this tour by driving north on Highway 56 out of Lihue. If you're ready for an immediate scenic diversion, in about 10 minutes turn left on Highway 583, at the bottom of the hill in Kapaia. Drive 4 miles to reach **Wailua Falls,** an impressive cascade that you might recognize from the opening sequences of the old "Fantasy Island" television show.

Another 10-minute drive on Highway 56 takes you to **Wailua,** which means "sacred water" in Hawaiian. Kauai's first communities were built along the Wailua River, and tucked away along its banks are remnants of some *heiaus* (sacred stone platforms for the worship of the gods).

In Wailua, turn mauka (toward the mountains) onto Highway 580. This is nicknamed the King's Highway, for in ancient times monarchs were carried along this road because their feet were not supposed to touch the ground. On your immediate left is

❸ **Pohaku Ho'Ohanau**—a collection of rocks comprising a revered heiau. Oahu's Bishop Museum and the Kauai Historical Society joined forces to restore this sacred landmark, where sacrifices were once made to the gods.

Continue for 1 mile along Highway 580 to a lookout on the right.

❹ Here you see a dramatic vision called **Opaekaa Falls,** plunging hundreds of feet to the pools below. Opaekaa means "rolling shrimp," which refers to the little creatures that once tossed and turned at the base of the falls.

Across the street from the falls is a red sign with a Hawaiian

❺ warrior on it, pointing you to **Kamokila,** a restored Hawaiian village that sits on the banks of the peaceful Wailua River. Guests are invited to take guided tours of the houses and learn ancient crafts and games. Taro and banana patches surround the community. It's a great place to take the whole family. *Box 666, Kapaa 96746, tel. 808/822–1192. Admission: $5 adults, $1.50 children 6–12. Open Mon.–Sat. 9–4.*

Return to Highway 56 and continue heading north. On the

❻ mauka side awaits **Wailua Marina,** a pretty little set of docks from which cruise boats depart for **Fern Grotto.** This 3-mile trip up the Wailua River culminates at a yawning lava tube that is decorated with enormous fishtail ferns, an 80-foot waterfall, and other natural delights. On 150-passenger flat-bottom riverboats, the trip takes 1½ hours to reach the grotto, which is truly a tropical masterpiece. During the boat ride, good-natured musicians strum guitars and ukuleles and regale you with upbeat Hawaiian melodies. Fern Grotto is the setting for hundreds of weddings each year, and when you take a look at this romantic fairyland, you'll understand why. *Two companies offer several trips daily to Fern Grotto. One is Waialeale Boat Tours, Wailua Marina, Kapaa 96746, tel. 808/822–4908. Cost: $9.38 adults, $4.69 children 3–12. Also featured is a 2-hr. evening barbecue cruise. Cost: $45. The other company is Smith's Motor Boat Service, 174 Wailua Rd., Kapaa 96746, tel. 808/822 –4111. Cost: $9 adults, $4.50 children under 12. A 2½-hr. night trip includes a luau. Cost: $30 adults, $20 children under 12.*

Proceed north on Highway 56 and look makai (toward the oce-

❼ an) for **Lydgate State Park.** Here is a lovely coconut grove that was once a city of refuge for Hawaiian fugitives. If they made their way to this beachfront haven, their lives were saved (*see* Beaches, below).

❽ About 10 minutes farther north you reach **Waipouli,** the little town where the Coconut Marketplace holds forth. This overwhelming conglomeration of shops and restaurants offers just about anything a traveler might need, from tacky souvenirs to elegant strands of Niihau shells. If you're not in the mood for shopping, keep driving.

On the mauka (mountain) side you soon see a mountain ridge

❾ resembling a **Sleeping Giant.** This formation is said to be the giant Puni, who has dozed undisturbed since doing fierce battle

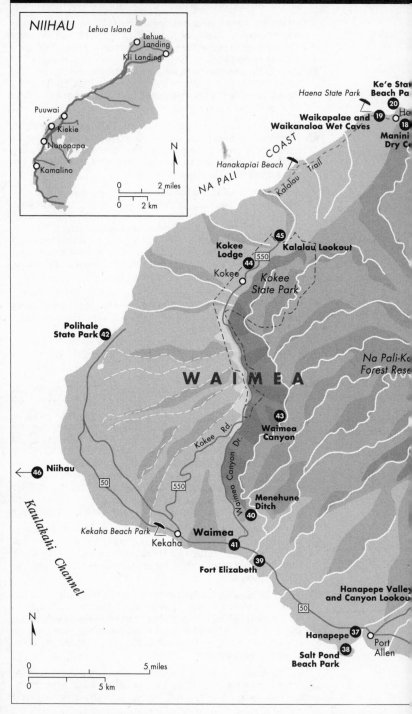

Kauai

NIIHAU

Lehua Island

Lehua Landing

Kii Landing

Puuwai

Kiekie

Nonopapa

Kamalino

N

0   2 miles
0   2 km

Haena State Park

Ke'e Stat
Beach Pa 20

Waikapalae and 19 Ha
Waikanaloa Wet Caves 18

Manini
Dry Ca

NA PALI COAST

Hanakapiai Beach

Kalalau Trail

45

Kokee
Lodge

44 550

Kalalau Lookout

Kokee

Kokee
State Park

Polihale
State Park 42

Na Pali-Ko
Forest Rese

WAIMEA

43

Waimea
Canyon

Kokee Rd.

Waimea Canyon Dr.

46 **Niihau**

50 550

Menehune
Ditch
40

Kekaha Beach Park

Kekaha

Waimea
41

39

Fort Elizabeth

Hanapepe Valley
and Canyon Lookou

Kaulakahi Channel

N

50

Hanapepe 37

Port
Allen

Salt Pond 38
Beach Park

0   5 miles
0   5 km

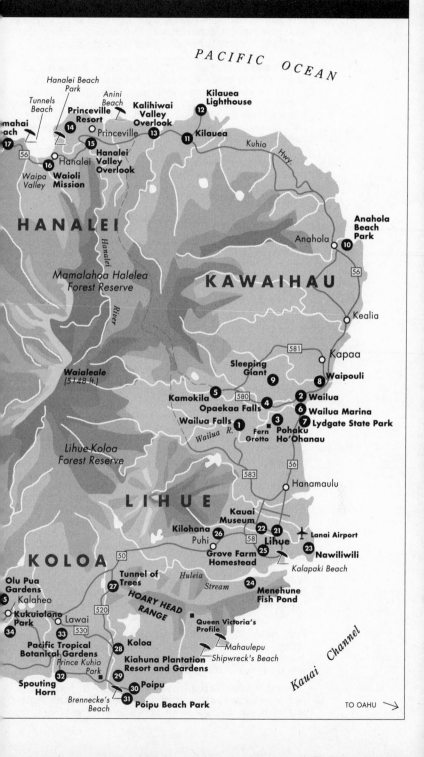

PACIFIC OCEAN

Tunnels Beach

Hanalei Beach Park

Anini Beach

Princeville Resort **14**

15 Princeville

Kalihiwai Valley Overlook **13**

Kilauea Lighthouse **12**

11 Kilauea

mahai ach **17**

56

16 Hanalei

Hanalei Valley Overlook

Waioli Mission

Waipa Valley

Kuhio Hwy.

HANALEI

Mamalahoa Halelea Forest Reserve

Hanalei River

Anahola

Anahola Beach Park

10

56

KAWAIHAU

Kealia

Waialeale (5148 ft.)

581

Kapaa

Sleeping Giant

9

8 Waipouli

Kamokila **5**

580

4

2 Wailua

6 Wailua Marina

7 Lydgate State Park

Opaekaa Falls

3

Wailua Falls **1**

Fern Grotto

Pohaku Ho'Ohanau

Wailua R.

Lihue-Koloa Forest Reserve

583

Hanamaulu

56

LIHUE

Kauai Museum

Kilohana **26**

22 **21**

Lanai Airport

Puhi

58 Lihue

25

23 Nawiliwili

Grove Farm Homestead

Kalapaki Beach

KOLOA

50

Tunnel of Trees

Huleia Stream

24 Menehune Fish Pond

Olu Pua Gardens

27

HOARY HEAD RANGE

5 Kalaheo

Kukuiolono Park

520

Lawai

Queen Victoria's Profile

34

33 530

33

Pacific Tropical Botanical Gardens

Prince Kuhio Park

Koloa

28

Mahaulepu

Shipwreck's Beach

Kauai Channel

Kiahuna Plantation Resort and Gardens

Spouting Horn

32

29 Poipu

30

Brennecke's Beach

31 Poipu Beach Park

TO OAHU →

with an island enemy. The next town you come to is **Kapaa,** a cozy hamlet that once bustled with plantation activity. Here you can see quaint storefronts and 19th-century buildings that have been restored to house souvenir shops and eateries.

Time Out **Ono Family Restaurant** (4-1292 Kuhio Hwy., Kapaa tel. 808/822–1710), is a family-style eatery that draws big crowds with its homemade Portuguese bean soup, gourmet hamburgers, and freshly baked pies. It's a great slice of local color, whether you stop here for breakfast or lunch. Get daring and order a buffalo burger, a specialty of the house, which is made with meat from the herds of Hanalei.

⑩ After the town of **Kealia,** you reach **Anahola,** best known as the home of **Anahola Beach Park.** This sleepy spot offers rest for the weary, shade for the overheated, and calm waters for the swimmers among you (*see* Beaches, below).

⑪ Continue north on Highway 56, and in a few miles you encounter **Kilauea,** another former plantation town. Today Kilauea is known for its aquacultural successes, especially with prawns. Turn right on Kolo Road when you see the post office, next to which is **Christ Memorial Episcopal Church** (2518 Kolo Rd., tel. 808/828–1791), which dates back to 1941. This church is constructed of native lava rock, and its stained-glass windows come from England.

⑫ Take the first left off Kolo Road, on Kilauea Road, and follow it to the end. This takes you to **Kilauea Lighthouse,** a beacon for passing air and water traffic since it was built in 1913. Once it boasted the largest lens of any lighthouse in the world. Now it is better known as the landmark of the **Kilauea Wildlife Refuge,** home to eight species of endangered seabirds. There are foot trails around the refuge, and guides inside the Visitor Center can fill you in on the various wildlife you may be lucky enough to spot. *Kilauea Rd., Kilauea, tel. 808/828–1413. Admission free. Open weekdays 10–4.*

Time Out On the mauka side of Highway 56 just past the center of Kilauea sits **Banana Joe's Tropical Fruit Farm** (5-2719 Kuhio Hwy., Kilauea, tel. 808/828–1092), a rustic shelter with a distinctly Polynesian look to it. This is the home of Banana Joe, whose fresh, ripe, Kauai-grown fruits are the perfect energy booster. He also sells fresh corn and other vegetables in season. If you're staying in a condo, pick up something for dinner. Joe also specializes in fruit smoothies, fruit salads, and delicious dehydrated tropical fruit, which you can eat here or take with you.

⑬ When you reach the 25-mile marker of Highway 56, you'll be at **Kalihiwai Valley Overlook.** There is room on the side of the road to pull over. This is a splendid vantage point for photographing the valley and its glimmering waterfall.

Turn right onto Kalihiwai Road on the northern side of the bridge, and take the left fork onto Anini Road. This will take you to **Anini Beach,** a good spot for beginning windsurfers and snorkelers (*see* Beaches, below).

⑭ The next highlight of Highway 56 is Princeville Airport, a small commuter airport on the mauka side of the road. **Princeville Resort** follows on the right, with its two Robert Trent Jones, Jr.

golf courses and tidy shopping center. Turn right on Princeville Road only if you're interested in seeing some fancy hotels and condominiums. Otherwise, skip it.

⓯ Directly across the street from the Princeville Shopping Center is the **Hanalei Valley Overlook,** identified by a Hawaiian-warrior marker. Here, in the 1850s, Robert Wyllie once attempted to establish a thriving coffee plantation. After that failed, the Chinese planted rice here until the early 1900s. Now the valley floor is filled with taro, the staple plant of the Hawaiian diet. From this panoramic overlook you can see more than a half mile of taro, plus the 900 acres that comprise a National Wildlife Refuge for endangered waterfowl.

⓰ Highway 56 now descends and crosses a rustic, arched one-lane bridge dating back to 1912, then swings into the town of **Hanalei.** This is the site of the 1837 **Waioli Mission,** once the home of missionary teachers Lucy and Abner Wilcox. Its prim and proper koa furniture and other furnishings are straight out of missionary Hawaii, and its tidy architecture feels like it belongs back in New England, from which the missionaries came. *Kuhio Hwy., Hanalei, tel. 808/245–3202. Admission free, although donations are accepted. Open Tues., Thurs., Sat. 9–3. Half-hour guided tours are available.*

Time Out **Tahiti Nui** (Kuhio Hwy. at Aku Rd., Hanalei, tel. 808/826–6277) is a favorite with locals; they love to gather on its funky front porch or inside the colorful bar to "talk story" (chat), have a few drinks, and eat pupus (hors d'oeuvres). Owned and operated by the Marston family from Tahiti, this restaurant is known in the area for its affordable meals, including fresh fish from the north shore and smoked ribs. It's a perfect place to watch the comings and goings of Hanalei.

⓱ Highway 56 north of Hanalei winds its way between the mountains and the sea and crosses a series of old one-lane bridges. The driving pace here is slow, so if you see a car coming the other way, just take your time and let him cross first. (It's the Kauai spirit!) As the road rises and curves left, look for the marker to **Lumahai Beach.** You can park on the makai side of the road and walk down the steep (and sometimes muddy) path to the beach, which was the setting for the film *South Pacific.* This ivory, mile-long strand is one of Kauai's best beaches, particularly for its spectacular setting of majestic cliffs, black lava rocks, and hala trees (*see* Beaches, below).

Back on the road going west, look for the 36-mile marker on Highway 56. A little farther, you'll see a right turn through a grove of trees. This takes you to **Tunnels Beach,** where the boats depart for Na Pali coastline trips. It's also a well-protected swimming beach (*see* Beaches, below).

⓲ A little farther on the mauka (mountain) side is **Maniniholo Dry Cave,** an eerie grotto said to have been dug by a menehune chief who was looking for an evil spirit. This cave was a site of ancient worship, and today you can walk back into it about 75 yards . . . if you dare. Across from the dry cave is **Haena State Park,** a fine beach for swimming when there's no current. A lunch wagon stands ready to feed hungry surf bums and sightseers (*see* Beaches, below).

Also on the mauka side, just north of the dry cave, are **②** **Waikapalae and Waikanaloa wet caves,** said to have been dug by the volcano goddess Pele. These watering holes used to be clear, clean, and great for swimming. Now stagnant, they're still photogenic and an example of the many haunting natural landmarks of Kauai's north shore.

When you reach the end of Highway 56 in Haena, you'll be at **②** **Ke'e Beach State Park,** an idyllic beach for viewing the spectacular Na Pali coastline. This is where you'll find the start of the 11-mile Kalalau Trail (*see* Beaches, below). From the beach, a path to the left leads to an open, grassy meadow with a stone altar called **Lohiau's Dance Pavilion.** They say that Laka, goddess of the hula, did most of her dancing on this very spot, and today's hula practitioners sometimes leave offerings here. Treat this beautiful site with reverence, for it is full of historical and spiritual *mana* (power).

Tour 2: Lihue and Southward

② Begin this tour on Rice Street, the main road of **Lihue.** This town is the commercial and political center of both Kauai and **②** Niihau. It is also the home of the **Kauai Museum,** whose exhibits present an informative overview of the Garden Isle. On permanent display at the museum is "The Story of Kauai," tracing the island's geological, natural, cultural, and mythological history and featuring a 20-minute aerial movie. Works by local artists are on display in the Plantation Gallery, and the gift shop offers a good selection of books and souvenirs. *4428 Rice St., Lihue 96766, tel. 808/245-6931. Admission $3. Open Mon.-Fri. 9:30-4:30.*

Time Out If you're looking for a decent breakfast to fuel you for the day, **The Eggbert's** (4483 Rice St., Lihue, tel. 808/245-6325), a rambling two-story restaurant, is your spot. Family fare at reasonable prices is the attraction here, with specialty omelets in two sizes (one huge), banana pancakes, fruits, juices, and such local taste treats as Portuguese sausage. Breakfast is served through midafternoon, and the place also offers lunch and dinner.

Follow Rice Street east until it dead-ends. Turn right on Waapa **②** Road, which takes you to **Nawiliwili,** Kauai's major port. Here you will see a host of little fishing and recreational boats, as well as tour boats that offer snorkeling and sightseeing adventures along the east and south coasts. In addition, Nawiliwili is where the luxury liners dock each week, as well as container ships and U.S. Navy vessels. **Kalapaki Beach** is nearby for protected swimming and sunbathing by the glitzy Westin Kauai Resort (*see* Beaches, below).

From Waapa Road, turn right on Mokihana Street, which becomes Halemalu Road. Here you follow the Huleia River, site of **②** the **Menehune Fish Pond.** Secretive little workers are said to have built these intricate walls 4 feet long and 5 feet high for a princess and prince. Today the structures rise above the water like a masterwork of engineering. Mullet are raised in the fish pond as they were in ancient times.

Return to Nawiliwili, take a left on Nawiliwili Road (Route 58), **②** and begin to look on your right for **Grove Farm Homestead.** One of Kauai's oldest plantation estates, it was founded in 1864 by George Wilcox; today it offers a look at 19th-century life on Kauai. On the 80 acres comprising this living museum are the original family mansion (filled with turn-of-the-century memorabilia), workers' quarters, and elaborate gardens of tropical flowers and tall palm trees. After your tour, you're invited to enjoy mint tea and sugar cookies made by the family cook. *Box 1631, Nawiliwili Rd., Lihue 96766, tel. 808/245–3202. Admission free. Guided narrated tours are available Mon., Wed., and Thurs. at 10 AM and 1:15 PM. Advance reservations required.*

At the intersection of Nawiliwili Road and Highway 50 stands **Kukui Grove Shopping Center,** a fairly new assemblage of department stores and smaller shops and restaurants. It feels like a mainland-style mall and holds little interest to the sightseer in search of the real Kauai.

26 Turn left and head west on Highway 50. Two miles farther, turn right at the entrance to **Kilohana.** Dating from 1835, this is the historic Wilcox sugar plantation house, which has been transformed into a 35-acre visitor attraction. There are agricultural exhibits, local arts and crafts, horse and carriage rides, specialty shops, and a pleasant restaurant called Gaylord's in the back courtyard. The estate is a beautiful showpiece from plantation days. *3–2087 Kaumualii Hwy., Lihue 96766, tel. 808/245–5608. Admission free. Open daily 9–5.*

Continue west on Highway 50, past the majestic slopes of the Hoary Head Mountains. On the top of the range is a formation called **Queen Victoria's Profile,** indicated by a Hawaiian-warrior marker. Some folks see a resemblance between the monarch and the mountain.

27 When you get to the intersection of Highways 50 and 520, you have reached **Koloa Gap,** which is the natural pass between Mt. Waialeale on your right and the Hoary Heads on your left. Turn left on Highway 520 (Maluhia Road), also called the **Tunnel of Trees** because of the long stretch of protective eucalyptus trees on either side of the road.

28 Highway 520 takes you to **Koloa,** site of Kauai's first sugar mill, dating back to 1835. You can see the remains of the mill on the right side of the road, where its old stone smokestack still stands. Adjacent to that is a sculpture depicting the various ethnic groups that made their mark on the sugar industry on Kauai. The main street of Koloa is lined with old buildings that have been beautifully restored to house expensive boutiques, an old general store, and a selection of restaurants.

Time Out Fourteen kinds of hot dogs, burgers made with such fresh fish as ono and mahimahi, and a big condiment bar make **Mustard's Last Stand** (corner of Hwy. 50 and Koloa Rd., Lawai, tel. 808/ 332–7245) an appropriate snack-time stop while you're touring the south of the island. The place also serves Lappert's Ice Cream, which is made in the Islands and features plenty of gourmet flavors. After you eat, why not play a round on the miniature golf course?

29 Head south on Highway 52, which is also called Poipu Road. At the fork, stay to the left. Look for a sign on the right to **Kiahuna Plantation Resort and Gardens,** the former home of Mr. and Mrs. Hector Moir. Their estate is now covered with Hawaiian

orchids, African aloes, lava-rock pools, and 4,000 varieties of
plants, which has earned it a listing in the book *Great Gardens
of America.* You can also visit a Hawaiian garden and learn how
herbs and plants were used by early settlers. *Poipu Rd., Poipu
96756, tel. 808/742–6411. Admission free. Open daily 9–6, with
a tour at 10.*

30 Poipu Road runs into Hoowili Road, which takes you through
the heart of sunny **Poipu,** the major resort of Kauai's south
shore. The boogey-boarding and swimming along these
beaches is spectacular, although you need to look out for occasional patches of coral, which can make a nasty cut on the foot
when stepped on.

31 On the makai (ocean) side of the road is **Poipu Beach Park,**
where you can park the car and look for the petroglyphs on
sandstone ledges at the far end of the beach. Here, too, is
Brennecke's Beach, well-known for its bodysurfing action. If
you follow Poipu Road to the end, it becomes a cane road. Turn
right on the first well-traveled byway and you'll find **Shipwreck's Beach.** Around the point is an even quieter stretch of
sand called **Mahaulepu** (*see* Beaches, below). On Poipu Road,
head back to the fork and turn left on Lawai Road. This takes
you past **Prince Kuhio Park,** honoring the birthplace of one of
Hawaii's most beloved congressmen.

32 At the end of this road is **Spouting Horn,** a waterspout that
shoots up out of an ancient lava tube like Old Faithful. Be sure
to follow the paved walkways around this area, because the
rocks are slippery and people have been known to fall in. You
may encounter a group of souvenir vendors along this walkway. Their wares are basically second-rate, so pass them by.

Time Out On your way back through Koloa, pull up to an open-air establishment called **Koloa Broiler** (Old Koloa Rd., Koloa, tel. 808/
742–9122), where you can help yourself to the best *mai tai* in
the Islands. The left side of the restaurant is the bar, a rustic
wood-paneled room. Sit by one of the huge open windows if you
can, and watch the world go by as you recap the day's events.
The dining room is on the right when you're ready for dinner.

Tour 3: The Western Route and Kokee

The west side of the island offers a look at the sleepiest, as well
as the most dramatic, sections of Kauai. Begin this tour by
heading west on Highway 50 out of Lihue. The first town you
come to is called **Lawai,** once the home of the Kauai Pineapple
Cannery. Although that operation has long since closed its
doors, Lawai has become a prolific producer of tropical fruits
and plants.

33 A good example of Lawai's green thumb can be found by
turning left on Hailima Road, which takes you to the **Pacific
Tropical Botanical Gardens,** a 400-acre scientific research center and estate property for botany and horticulture. The visitor
center presents a showcase of 6,000 different plant species.
There's a gift shop, too. *Box 340, Hailima Rd., Lawai 96765,
tel. 808/332–7361. Admission: $15. Open daily. An escorted
2½-hour narrated shuttle and walking tour is offered weekdays
9 and 1, Sat. 9, and Sun. 1. Advance reservations required.*

The next town along Highway 50 is **Kalaheo,** which means "proud day." Proud it should be, for it features one of Kauai's most scenic park areas. To see it, turn left on Papalina Road, which climbs to **Kukuiolono Park.** Translated "light of the god Lono," Kukuiolono offers serene Japanese gardens, an exhibit of old Hawaii, and spectacular panoramic views, which make this an ideal picnic spot. There is also a golf course spread across a nine-acre expanse (*see* Sports, below). *Admission to park free. Open 6–6.*

Just past Kalaheo, look on your right for macadamia nut groves and a Hawaiian-warrior marker indicating **Olu Pua Gardens.** If you just can't get enough of beautiful plants, turn right and drive a half mile up the private road to find yet another of Kauai's fine botanical showcases. Encompassing 12 acres, Olu Pua (which means "floral serenity" in Hawaiian) is a 1931 plantation estate. You can wander down shaded paths and enjoy the exotic flowers and plants, plus views of a pond shaped like a hibiscus blossom. *Hwy. 50, Kalaheo, tel. 808/332–8182. Admission: $10 adults, $5 children under 12. Open daily 8:30–5. Closed Christmas and New Year's Day. Tours at 9:30, 11:30, and 1:30.*

Continue along Highway 50 and soon, to your right, you will see a Hawaiian-warrior marker indicating the **Hanapepe Valley and Canyon Lookout.** This dramatic divide once housed a thriving Hawaiian community, and some of their taro patches are still in existence here. Hanapepe is a historic canyon, for it is the site of Kauai's last battle, led in 1824 by Humehume, the son of Kauai's King Kaumualii.

On your right you'll see an old-fashioned sign welcoming you to **Hanapepe,** dubbed by some "the Biggest Little Town on Kauai." As you come down the hill, take a right on Hanapepe Road to see the street that was used in the filming of the television miniseries *The Thorn Birds.* Hanapepe is a quiet farming town that supplies Kauai with much of its produce.

Time Out   **Lawai Restaurant** (2–3687 Kaumualii Hwy., Kalaheo, tel. 808/332–9550) is a slice of Kauai life if ever there was one. Lawai serves an eclectic variety of home-cooked Chinese, American, and Hawaiian food, and it's all quite good. You can go local by ordering some noodle soup and shave ice (a snow cone) or take the oriental route with sweet and sour pork topped off with a fortune cookie. Either way, the prices here are very reasonable, and it's open daily for breakfast, lunch, and dinner to suit your sightseeing schedule.

On the west end of Hanapepe, turn makai (toward the ocean) on Lele Road and follow it to the **Salt Pond Beach Park.** Here you can see how the Hawaiians have made salt for almost 200 years. They let the sun evaporate the sea water in mudlined drying beds, which leaves only the salt. This is also a safe area for swimming (*see* Beaches, below).

Near the ponds is **Burns Fields,** Kauai's first airfield and now the base of operation of several helicopter and glider-ride companies. Before you return to Highway 50, you might want to explore this coastal area just a bit more to see **Port Allen Harbor,** the shipping center for the west side of Kauai and the headquarters of the McBryde Sugar Company. You'll pass the humble Eleele Shopping Center, which was Kauai's first "modern" shopping center when it was built.

Return to Highway 50 and look on the makai side of the road for ❸❾ the Hawaiian-warrior marker to **Fort Elizabeth.** What's left of this stone fort, built in 1816 by an agent of the Imperial Russian government named Anton Scheffer, recalls the days when Scheffer tried to conquer the island for his homeland. King Kaumualii eventually chased the foreigner off the island.

Cross the Waimea River Bridge and take your first right on Menehune Road, which leads you 2½ miles up the Waimea ❹❶ Valley to **Menehune Ditch.** Archaeologists claim that this aqueduct was built before the first Hawaiians lived on Kauai, and it is therefore attributed to the industrious hands of the tiny menehune. The way the flanged and fitted cut-stone bricks are stacked and assembled indicates a knowledge of construction that is foreign to Hawaii, and the ditch is inscribed with mysterious markings. Until someone comes up with a better suggestion, the menehune once again take credit for this engineering feat.

❹❶ Next, enter **Waimea** and enjoy a look at the town that first welcomed Captain James Cook to the Sandwich Islands in 1778. An easy-to-miss monument on the mauka (mountain) side of the road commemorates his landmark arrival. Waimea was also the place where Kauai's King Kaumualii ceded his island to the unifying efforts of King Kamehameha.

Waimea played host to the first missionaries on the island, and if you take a right on Makeke Road you can see their old **Waimea Hawaiian and Foreign Church.** Built in 1846, the church is made of huge timbers, which were brought down from the mountains 8 miles away, as well as limestone blocks from a nearby quarry. The church took 12 years to construct, and services are still held there today.

Highway 50 next passes through the sugar town of **Kekaha,** beyond which lies Mana Drag Strip, an extremely straight shoreside road that runs through acres of cane fields. Eventually it passes the **Pacific Missile Range Facility,** an underwater test range for the Navy's antisubmarine-warfare training and weapons firing.

Turn left at the Hawaiian-warrior marker that points you to a dirt road through more sugarcane fields. It dead-ends at ❹❷ **Polihale State Park,** a long and beautiful stretch of unspoiled beach flanked by enormous sea cliffs. There are rest rooms, picnic pavilions, and showers here (*see* Beaches, below).

As you return to civilization, you have two choices for visiting ❹❸ **Waimea Canyon,** the "Grand Canyon of the Pacific." From Kekaha, Kokee Road makes a steep climb, with immediate views of the town and ocean below. The road up from Waimea, Waimea Canyon Drive, is narrower and in worse condition. A few miles up, the roads intersect, and you continue to climb past spectacular panoramas of the canyon, which is 3,600 feet deep, 2 miles wide, and 10 miles long. Created by an ancient fault in the Earth's crust, it has been eroding over the centuries due to weather, rivers, and streams. Its deep reds, greens, and browns are ever-changing in the light. Be sure to stop at the **Puu Ka Pele** and **Puu Hina Hina** lookouts for the most appealing views.

As the road rises to 3,000 feet, it passes through **Kokee State Park.** Here the air is cool and crisp, and the vegetation turns to evergreens and ferns. This 4,345-acre wilderness park is full of wild fruit, heady flowers, and the colorful rare birds that make their home in these forests. A 45-mile network of hiking trails takes you to some of Kauai's most remote places. *For information about the canyon and the park, contact: Division of State Parks, Box 1671, Lihve 96766, tel. 808/245–4444.*

Time Out 44 Treat yourself to a cup of coffee or a cocktail at **Kokee Lodge** (Waimea Canyon Dr., Kokee State Park, tel. 808/335–6061), a homespun mountaintop inn. Since the temperature can be nippy outside, the fireplace inside is almost always going. Afterward, peruse the gift shop, which carries T-shirts, postcards, and lots of Kokee memorabilia.

The road out of Kokee State Park leads you past the **NASA Tracking Station,** where a roomful of computers has kept track of the various goings-on in the wild blue yonder since 1960. This station recently shut down its operations for good due to the deployment of a $100-million satellite by the space shuttle *Discovery.*

45 Waimea Canyon Drive ends 4 miles above the park at the **Kalalau Lookout,** 4,120 feet above sea level. This is the beginning of a beautiful hiking trail. On a clear day at the lookout, you can gaze right down into the gaping valley, with its elegant ridges and waterfalls; if you look closely you can just barely see the shining sands of Kalalau Beach, like a tiny golden thread against the vast blue Pacific.

Tour 4: A Short Excursion to Niihau

46 Once it was called the Forbidden Isle. Now it takes only 12 minutes to fly from Kauai to **Niihau,** an island that few outsiders have set foot on since Elizabeth Sinclair bought it from King Kamehameha V in 1864. This 72-square-mile island just 17 miles from Kauai is now run by the Robinson family, which raises cattle and sheep on the barren, arid landscape. The Robinsons continue to preserve Niihau as a last refuge of primitive Hawaii. Residents of the island speak Hawaiian and do not use electricity, plumbing, or telephones; they ride bikes and horses to get around.

Bruce Robinson initiated Niihau Helicopters in 1987 in order to boost the struggling island economy. Tours avoid the western coastline, where Puuwai village—home to the island's 200 residents—is located. Flights depart from and return to Kauai's Burns Airfield near Hanapepe and are conducted in an Agusta 109 twin-engine, single-pilot helicopter. The first touchdown on the two-stop tour is near the sunken crater of Lehua. The second takes you to a cliff overlooking the beach coves of Keanahaki Bay. It's the perfect tour for those with a yen to explore untrammeled territory. *Niihau Helicopters, Box 370, Makaweli 96769, tel. 808/335–3500. Cost: 1-hour tour with 1 stop, $185; 2-hour tour with 2 stops, $250. Maximum of 4 flights per day, Mon.–Fri. No ground transportation available.*

Kauai for Free

Coconut Plantation Hula Show. In and around its 70 shops and restaurants, Coconut Plantation Market Place hosts a variety of free Hawaiiana demonstrations throughout the day, including songs and dances, lei making, and quilting. Its best-known freebie is the hula show on center stage. *4–484 Kuhio Hwy., Kapaa, tel. 808/822–3641. Thurs., Fri., Sat. at 4.*

Hilo Hattie Fashion Factory Tour. Hawaii's garment industry is booming, and Kauai is keeping in step with the other islands by presenting factory tours of this top fashion company. Here you can see how they make those colorful aloha shirts, muumuus, and other tropical togs. Aloha wear is on sale for the entire family, at factory-outlet values. Free alterations are available while you wait. *3252 Kuhio Hwy., Lihue, tel. 808/245–4724. Open daily 8:30–5. Free hotel pickup in Lihue and Coconut Plantation areas daily at 9, 11, 1, and 3. From Poipu, call for reservations on the 10 AM and 2 PM shuttle.*

Kilauea Lighthouse and Wildlife Refuge. *See* Tour 1, above.

Kilohana. *See* Tour 2, above.

Kokee Natural History Museum. Next door to the Kokee Lodge, this two-room museum presents intriguing displays about the natural wildlife of Waimea Canyon. Here you can learn about the rare birds and plants that are indigenous to the area. The museum also has maps, old photographs, petroglyph rubbings, artifacts, posters, souvenirs, and postcards. *Kokee Rd., Kokee, tel. 808/335–9975. Open daily 9–5.*

Montage Galleries. The beauties of the Garden Isle serve as inspiration for a large number of local painters, sculptors, weavers, and other handcrafters. This gallery displays a lovely variety of original pieces and spotlights a featured artist each month. Works are also available for sale. *Princeville Center, Kuhio Hwy., Hanalei, tel. 808/826–9151. Open daily 9–5.*

Waioli Mission. *See* Tour 1, above.

What to See and Do with Children

Kamokila. *See* Tour 1, above.

Smith's Tropical Paradise. Right next to Wailua Marina on the east side of the island, Smith's Tropical Paradise is 30 acres of family fun, with orchards, jungle paths, exotic foliage, tropical birds, ethnic village settings, tranquil lagoons, and a tram tour every hour. A luau banquet and live show are offered each evening from 5 to 9. *174 Wailua Rd., Kapaa 96746, tel. 808/822–4654. Admission: $4 adults, $2 children under 11. Tram tour: $7 adults, $3.50 children. Luau and show: $38 adults, $24 children. Open daily 8:30–4. A free shuttle runs from Wailua-area hotels and condominiums. Reservations required for the luau, shuttle, and show.*

Snorkeling with Blue Water Sailing. A fun excursion for all ages, this four-hour snorkeling sail off the southern shores of Kauai, includes gear, instruction, swimming, fishing, a gourmet picnic lunch, snacks, and beverages. During the winter season, you might catch glimpses of whales. Your craft is the 12-passenger, 42-foot luxury Pearson sailing yacht the *Lady*

Leanne II. Box 250, Eleele 96705, tel. 808/822–0525. Cost: $60 adults, $30 children 3–12.

Off the Beaten Track

Hawaiian Appreciation Classes. Kauai's people are extremely tuned in to their environment, and they are happy to help visitors learn more about the joys of Hawaiiana. Each week the beauty of Hawaiian dance, music, chanting, art, history, and folklore unfolds through the talents of local instructors. *Hawaiian Art Museum, 2488 Kolo Rd., Kilauea, tel. 808/828–1309. Cost: $5, which goes to a local preschool. Sat. 2–4.*

Hawaiian Farmers of Hanalei Ranch. The soil of lush Kauai produces vast amounts of delicacies, and the farmers who grow them for a living are an interesting and friendly bunch. They are working hard to renew the Waipa Valley and have plans to build a Hawaiian school there. They're happy to sell you their local produce and tell you about different ways to prepare Kauai's fruits and vegetables. *Waipa Valley, 1 mi west of Hanalei on the mauka (mountain) side of Kuhio Hwy. Tues. from 3 PM.*

Poetry and Prose Readings. Here's a wonderful way to get first-person insights into life on the Garden Isle. Amateur writers come together to read and discuss their original works and favorite materials. Visitors are welcome to come and listen and sip coffee or espresso. *West of the Moon Cafe, Kauhale Center, Kuhio Hwy., Hanalei, tel. 808/826–7460. Sat. 7 PM.*

Shopping

Kauai certainly doesn't have the myriad shopping alternatives of its cosmopolitan neighbor, Oahu. What the Garden Isle does have, however, is character. Along with a few major shopping malls, Kauai features some of the most delightful mom-and-pop shops and family-run boutiques imaginable.

Kauai also offers one-of-a-kind options for souvenir hunters, things you'd be better off buying here than on Oahu. For instance, the famous shell jewelry from Niihau is sometimes sold on Kauai for less than it is on other islands, due to the proximity of Kauai and Niihau.

Kauai is also known for its occasional outdoor markets, where you will find bargain prices on various souvenirs and produce; and get a chance to mingle with island residents.

Be sure to pay a visit to one of Kauai's many fashion stores and pick up some comfortable aloha shirts and muumuus. Almost every visitor buys at least one Hawaiian garment, no matter which island he or she visits.

Kauai's major shopping centers are open daily from 9 or 10 to 5, although some stay open until 9. Stores are basically clustered around the major resort areas and Lihue.

Shopping Centers

Kauai's largest assemblage of shops is **Kukui Grove Center** (3-2600 Kaumualii Hwy.; tel. 808/245-7784 for free shuttle service), on Highway 50, just west of Lihue. Besides the island's major department stores, it offers a **Long's Drugs** (tel. 808/245–7771) for personal needs and **Star Market** (tel. 808/245–7777) for groceries. You'll find fashions from the Orient at **See You in China** (tel. 808/245–8474), Hawaiian heirloom jewelry at **Capricorn Fine Gems** (tel. 808/245–6233), coral pieces at **Coral Grotto** (tel. 808/245–6619), and sundries at **Woolworth** (tel. 808/245–7702).

South of Lihue in Nawiliwili, **Kauai Lagoons Shopping Village** (Westin Kauai, Kalapaki Beach, tel. 808/245–5050) has such boutiques as Louis Vuitton, home of designer handbags and luggage.

West of Lihue in Puhi, **Kilohana Plantation** (3-2087 Kaumualii Hwy.) offers a unique collection of plantation-style shops. Its **Cane Field Clothing Co.** (tel. 808/245–5020) features cool island fashions, including hand-painted batik. **Plum Tuckered** (tel. 808/245–2208) is a fantasy gift shop, while **Stones at Kilohana** (tel. 808/245–6684) sells artwork collected from craftspeople around the South Pacific.

On the east coast of the island is **Waipouli Town Center** (4-901 Kuhio Hwy.) in Kapaa, a modest assemblage of 10 shops where you can buy a T-shirt at **Deja Vu** (tel. 808/822–7370), and then grab a sandwich at **Waipouli Delicatessen** (tel. 808/822-9311). Nearby in Waipouli you'll find the **Coconut Plantation Market Place** (4-484 Kuhio Hwy.), a shopping center that is part of a larger complex of resort hotels and restaurants.

On Kuhio Highway in Wailua is **Kinipopo Shopping Village** (4-356 Kuhio Hwy.), which has created a tropical garden setting for casual shopping. Here you'll find **The Goldsmith's Gallery** (tel. 808/822–4653), featuring handcrafted Hawaiian-style gold jewelry.

Princeville Center (5-4280 Kuhio Hwy., Princeville) is an upscale little gathering of trendy shops such as **Kauai Kite and Hobby Shop** (tel. 808/826–9144) and restaurants such as **Pizza Burger** (tel. 808/826–6070). Less fancy and more laid-back, **Ching Young Village** in Hanalei draws people to its **Village Variety Store** (tel. 808/826–6077), with cheap prices on beach towels, macadamia nuts, film and processing, wet suits, you name it.

Heading south, shoppers encounter old **Koloa**. It's not exactly a shopping center, but its main street, Old Koloa Road, is comprised of boutiques and eateries in one handy location. Favorites include **Koloa Ice House** (tel. 808/742–6005), which sells shave ice fantasies laced with tropical syrups, and **Progressive Expressions** (tel. 808/742–6041), which offers surfing and windsurfing accessories, swimwear, and beachwear. Farther south, in Poipu, is the **Kiahuna Shopping Village** (2360 Kiahuna Plantation Dr.), which features pricey stores worthy of a window-shopping excursion.

To the west of Kauai is a scattering of stores, including those at the no-frills **Eleele Shopping Center** on Highway 50 near Hanapepe. Waimea is proud of its new **Waimea Canyon Plaza** on Highway 50, which opened in 1988 and includes gift shops, fashion stores, and other family-run businesses.

Department Stores

As is true on the other major Hawaiian Islands, the primary department stores on Kauai are **Sears** (tel. 808/245–3325), **J. C. Penney** (tel. 808/245–5966), **F. W. Woolworth** (tel. 808/245–7702), and **Liberty House** (tel. 808/245–7751). You can find all of them at **Kukui Grove Center** in Lihue.

Flea Markets

Ready to shop and save in the great outdoors? A **Sunshine Market** takes place on the south shore each Monday at the Koloa Baseball Field. Stop by this Kauai-style swap meet from noon to 3 and chat with the local farmers, whose fruits and vegetables are worth trying.

Aloha Wear

Hilo Hattie Fashion Factory (tel. 808/245–3404) is the big name in aloha wear throughout the isles, and it creates more than 10,000 different types of garments. You can visit the factory at Waipouli's Coconut Plantation Market Place, then pick up floral duds at good savings. With three stores in Poipu, Lawai, and Waipouli, **Tropical Shirts** (Kiahuna Shopping Village, tel. 808/742–6691, Lawai Cannery, tel. 808/332–9497, and Coconut Plantation Market Place, tel. 808/822–0203) captures the beauty of Kauai with clothing that has been embroidered or hand-screened by local artists. For colorful aloha togs for tots, try **Traders** (tel. 808/742–7224), located at the Kiahuna Shopping Village. Kapaa's **Art to Wear** (1435 Kuhio Hwy., tel. 808/822–1125) offers hand-painted, hand-sewn originals decorated with flowers, seascapes, and animal motifs. At Coconut Plantation Market Place, **Tahiti Imports** (tel. 808/822–9342) carries the Polynesian *pareu*, a multicolored wraparound that can be tied in dozens of different ways to suit the occasion.

Books

Several fine books have been written about Kauai, and many more about Hawaii. **Waldenbooks** (tel. 808/245–7162) at Kukui Grove Center presents the island's broadest assortment of reading materials. Also try the **Hawaiian Art Museum and Book Store** (2488 Kolo Rd., Kilauea, tel. 808/828–1309).

Clothing

Liberty House (tel. 808/245–7751) in Kukui Grove Center carries high-quality designer labels as well as nice resort wear. Also at Kukui Grove, **Sears** (tel. 808/245–3325) features reliably handsome men's and women's clothing in mainland designs and some tropical stylings. In East Kauai, **Reyn's** (tel. 808/822–7800) at Coconut Plantation Market Place provides traditional sportswear and classic clothing for men, plus dresses, blouses, slacks, and shorts for women. **M. Miura Store** (4-1419 Kuhio Hwy., Kapaa, tel. 808/822–4401) has a great assortment of clothes for the outdoor fanatic, including tank tops, visors, swimwear, and Kauai-style T-shirts.

Exotica

Antique Chinese embroidery, Burmese tapestries, tribal woodcarvings, and many other arts and crafts from Indochina and the South Pacific are featured at the **Indo-Pacific Trading Company** in Lihue (4475 Rice St., tel. 808/245–9300). **Artlines** (tel. 808/246–0249), located in Kukui Grove Center, is the place for collectors, with its quartz crystals, antique silver, ethnic jewelry, pottery, and other handmade exotic gifts. **Half Moon Japanese Antiques** at Kilohana Plantation (tel. 808/245–4100) has a diverse collection of Japanese art, ceramics, and folk art, plus a selection of antique silk and cotton kimonos.

Food

Kauai has its own yummy specialties that you won't be able to resist while on the island. Kauai Kookies, taro chips, Kauai boiled peanuts, salad dressings, and jams and jellies from locally grown fruit make delicious gifts to take back home. For ideas, call the **Kauai Products Council** (tel. 808/246–0232).

In Kapaa, you can buy fresh pineapple, sugarcane, ginger, coconuts, local jams, jellies, and honey, plus Kauai-grown papayas, bananas, and mangos in season—all at the **Farm Fresh Fruit Stand** (4-1345 Kuhio Hwy., tel. 808/822–1154). Special gift packs are available, inspected and certified. At Coconut Plantation Marketplace, **Rocky Mountain Chocolate Factory** (tel. 808/822–1141) has hand-dipped chocolates including tropicals, macadamia clusters, and frozen chocolate bananas.

Macadamia nuts are a must-buy present for friends back home. Some of the best prices are available at **Star Market** (tel. 808/245–7777) in the Kukui Grove Center. Don't forget to try a big scoop of **Lappert's Ice Cream,** invented by Walter Lappert in Hanapepe in 1983 and now a favorite all over Hawaii. You'll find it just about anywhere you go on Kauai.

Flowers

Flowers Forever (Princeville Center, Princeville, tel. 808/826–7420) can help you ship leis, corsages, and flower arrangements back home, as well as take care of the agricultural inspection.

Flowers of the Rainbow (4–1300 Kuhio Hwy., Kapaa, tel. 808/822–4781) has a delightful selection of orchids.

Gifts

Eelskin is a popular item in the Islands, and you can buy it wholesale at **Lee Sands' Eelskin** at the intersection of Highway 50 and Koloa Road in Lawai (tel. 808/332–7404). This unusual store includes skin lines such as sea snake, chicken feet, and frog skin. A lizard card case is available for about $10.

How about a monkeypod bowl? That's just one of the gifts you can find in the warehouse-style setup of **Kauai's Hidden Treasures** in Kekaha (Hwy. 50, tel. 808/337–1680), located right next to the post office. The store offers free coffee or cold juice and gives each visitor a free shell lei and earrings.

Hawaiian Crafts

The Station (Hwy. 50, tel. 808/335–5731) used to be a run-down gas station on the west end of Hanapepe. Now it has been renovated into one of Kauai's most delightful craft and gift shops. Here you can pick up a variety of Hawaiian needlepoint and cross-stitch. **Kapaia Stitchery** (Kuhio Hwy., tel. 808/245–2281), a red general store just north of Lihue, features quilting and other fabric arts, plus kits for trying your own hand at various crafts. Kauai artist Peter Kinney specializes in scrimshaw pocket and army knives, available at **Ye Olde Ship Store & Port of Kauai** (tel. 808/822–1401) in Coconut Plantation Market Place.

Jewelry

At the Kauai Hilton (4331 Kauai Beach Dr.) in Hanamaulu, **Remember Kauai** (tel. 808/245–6650) offers mementos of your trip in the form of fashion jewelry. There's a branch in Kapaa as well (4–734 Kuhio Hwy., tel. 808/822–0161). **Kauai Gold** (tel. 808/822–9361) at the Coconut Plantation Market Place presents a wonderful selection of rare Niihau shell leis, strung by women from the Forbidden Isle and ranging from $20 to $200. The store also has a selection of 14K gold jewelry. In Kapaa, **Jim Saylor Jewelers** (1318 Kuhio Hwy., tel. 808/822–3591) showcases a good selection of gems from around the world, with black pearls, diamonds, and unique settings. Its pretty keepsakes are designed right on the premises. **Rainbow Rags** in Waimea (9905 Waimea Rd., tel. 808/338–0308) sells 100-year-old Chinese jewelry, plus a selection of marcasite, vintage, and contemporary jewelry. That, however, is just part of the inventory of this family-run store, housed in a building that is in the National Register of Historic Places. Among other things, the store sells antique cake molds, discounted resort fashions, and special finds.

Local Art

Kauai's natural beauty has served as the inspiration for many of Hawaii's best artists, and a painting or sculpture by a local creator can be a very special keepsake indeed. At the **James Hoyle Gallery** (3900 Hanapepe Rd., tel. 808/335–3582) in Hanapepe, a talented painter presents island landscapes in a personal, impressionistic style, focusing on two subjects: flowers and the distinctive architecture of the island. You can purchase the works of many other local artists—including seascapes by George Summer and Roy Tabora—at **Kahn Galleries** (tel. 808/822–4277 at the Coconut Plantation; tel. 808/826–6631 at the Sheraton Mirage Princeville). Then there's **The Art Shop** in Lihue, an intimate gallery that sells original oils, photos, and sculptures (3196 Akahi St., tel. 808/245–3810).

Kauai Images Gallery in Kapaa (937 Kuhi Hwy., tel. 808/822–1950) features original artwork by many of Hawaii's finest artists. Among the treats are hand-painted photographs by Diane Ferry, whose work has won numerous awards in Kauai art shows. Kauai Images also offers a large variety of quality frames, including koa, the rare and highly prized island wood.

Beaches

Of all the Hawaiian Islands, Kauai has had the most time to develop—and perfect—its beaches. The Garden Isle is embraced by stretches of magnificent ivory sands, many with breathtaking mountain backdrops. The waters that hug the island are clean, clear, and inviting, but be careful to go in only where it's safe.

The south shore is known for its enduring sunshine, which makes beaching in Poipu a popular activity. Here, too, is some of the island's best swimming, snorkeling, and bodysurfing in waters that are generally safe year-round, although the surf is a bit bigger in the summer.

The north shore is a different story altogether. While some of Kauai's most scenic beaches can be found here, they are treacherous during the winter months. In the summer, however, they are safe for swimming. No matter what time of year it is, be sure to exercise caution, because only a few of these beaches have lifeguards.

The beaches that front the hotels and condominiums along the eastern shore are conducive to seaside strolling but less favorable for swimming. The strong surf and rip currents of the winter months are unpredictable, and it's often quite windy.

If you want beaches with plenty of peace and quiet, drive to the west coast beyond Kekaha. This is where the locals often go to fish and swim, and you'll catch the best sunsets from this vantage point.

All of the beaches on Kauai are free, and none has a phone number. For information about beaches around the island, call the **County Department of Parks and Recreation** (tel. 808/245–8821) and the **State Department of Land and Natural Resources** (tel. 808/245–4444).

Anahola Beach Park. This is a quiet stretch of sand on the east shore whose calm waters are good for swimming and snorkeling. The Makalena Mountains are your backdrop here. There are rest rooms and showers. *Hwy. 56 heading north, between Anahola and Kilauea.*

Anini Beach. On the north shore, this is a good place for beginning windsurfers, snorkelers, and swimmers. There are public rest rooms, showers, and picnic tables. *Turn makai (toward the ocean) onto Kalihiwai Rd. on the Hanalei side of Kalihiwai Bridge.*

Brennecke's Beach. A steady stream of small- to medium-size waves makes this a bodysurfer's heaven. The waves are bigger here in the summer than in the winter months. Showers, rest rooms, and lifeguards are available, and there are several carryout-food stands across the street. *On Poipu Rd. on the south shore.*

Haena State Park. This is a good beach for swimming when the surf is down, which means summertime. There are rest rooms, showers, and snack vans. *On the north shore near the end of Hwy. 56.*

Hanakapiai Beach. This crescent of beach changes length and width throughout the year as fierce winter waves rob the shoreline of sand and summer's calm returns it. Be very careful swimming here in the summer, and don't even think of going in during the winter swells. There's a beautiful freshwater stream here, too. *At mile 2 of the Kalalau Trail, which begins at Ke'e State Park, at the northern end of Hwy. 56.*

Hanalei Beach Park. With views of the Pali coast and shady trees over picnic tables, this is a beach bum's heaven. However, swimming here can be treacherous. Stay near the old pier, where the water is a bit calmer. Rest rooms and showers are available. *In Hanalei, turn toward the ocean at Aku Rd. and right at the dead-end.*

Kalapaki Beach. This sheltered bay is ideal for swimming, sunning, surfing, and beginning windsurfing in the small waves. It fronts the Westin Kauai Resort, and there are rest rooms, lifeguards, and showers. *In Nawiliwili off Wapaa Rd., which runs east out of Lihue.*

Ke'e Beach. In the summer months, this is a fine swimming beach. In the winter, stay out of the water and enjoy the views of the Pali coast. This is where the Kalalau Trail begins. Extensive facilities are available, including showers and rest rooms. *At the northern end of Hwy. 56.*

Kekaha Beach Park. Stretching along the south shore for many miles is this strip of sand recalling the long beaches of California. The latest sport here is dune buggying. If you don't like the noise of those vehicles, stay away. There are no lifeguards, rest rooms, or showers. *Along Hwy. 50 west of Kekaha.*

Lumahai Beach. In the movie *South Pacific*, this is the place where Mitzi Gaynor sang, "I'm Gonna Wash That Man Right Outa My Hair." The beach is known for its striking natural beauty, flanked by high mountains and lava rocks. The swimming here is good only in the summer. There are no lifeguards, showers, or rest rooms. *On the winding section of Hwy. 56 north of Hanalei. Park on the ocean side of the road and walk down a steep path to the beach.*

Lydgate State Park. Depending on the wind, this beach can be a good place for family picnicking and swimming. Any time of year, it's a nice place for beachcombing and remembering the days when this was a Hawaiian city of refuge. Rest rooms and showers are available. *In Wailua, on Hwy. 56.*

Poipu Beach Park. Bodysurfers love the steady waves here, and sunbathers love the predictably clear skies. There are showers, rest rooms, and lifeguards. *On Poipu Rd. on the south shore.*

Polihale Beach Park. This is a magnificent stretch of sand, many miles long, flanked by impressive sea cliffs. Swim here only when the surf is small. Locals dune buggy here on the weekends. Polihale has no lifeguards, but there are showers, rest rooms, and picnic pavilions. *Drive to the end of Hwy. 50 and turn left at the Hawaiian-warrior marker. This takes you several bumpy miles on a dirt road through sugarcane fields.*

Salt Pond Beach Park. The waters here are particularly safe for swimming, so this is a real family spot. There are picnic tables, showers, and rest rooms. *Take Lele Rd. makai (toward the ocean) off Highway 50 in Hanapepe.*

Tunnels Beach. This is where boats depart for their trips up the Pali coast. Tunnels also offers one of Kauai's best-protected beaches for swimming and snorkeling. On the downside, there are no lifeguards, showers, or rest rooms. *Halfway between the 36- and 37-mi markers on Hwy. 56. Turn toward the ocean on a dirt road that runs through a grove of trees.*

Sports

Participant Sports

Golf   The Garden Isle has sprouted a healthy crop of golf courses, some with spectacular views. Best-known is the **Mirage Princeville Makai Course** (Box 3040, Princeville 96722, tel. 808/826–3580). Designed by Robert Trent Jones, Jr., it features a pro shop, a driving range, a practice area, lessons, club rental and storage, instruction, restaurants, a lounge, and a bar. Cost: $53 guests, $70 nonguests, including shared carts. The **Mirage Princeville "Prince" Course** has expanded to 18 holes, with new rates to be announced.

At the **Kukuiolono Golf Course** (Kalaheo 96741, tel. 808/332–9151) greens fees are $5 daily; carts are $5 for 9 holes and $10 for 18 holes. In the southern part of the island is the **Kiahuna Golf Club** (2545 Kiahuna Plantation Dr., Koloa 96756, tel. 808/742–9595). Robert Trent Jones, Jr., designed the 18-hole course, and there's a pro shop, rentals, a restaurant, and a bar. Greens fees with shared cart: $58. To the east, **Wailua Municipal Golf Course** (444 Rice St., Lihue 96766, tel. 808/245–8092) sits next to the Wailua River and beach. Its 18 holes have hosted national tournaments, and there's a pro shop, a driving range, and a restaurant. Cost: $10 weekdays, $11 weekends.

Horseback Riding   Kauai's scenic south shore can be explored on escorted rides along panoramic oceanside cliffs and beaches. **CJM Stables** (5598 Tapa St., Koloa 96756, tel. 808/245–6666) charges $25 an hour, $44 for two hours. Its three-hour *paniolo* (cowboy) beach breakfast ride is $55. Private rides are available on request at $45 an hour.

To the north, **Pooku Stables** (Box 888, Hanalei 96714, tel. 808/826–6777) offers guided horseback tours into the less-explored reaches of the island. A one-hour valley ride is $23 per person; a two-hour shoreline-vista ride is $44 per person; a three-hour waterfall picnic ride is $70, including lunch.

Hiking   Contact the **Department of Land and Natural Resources** (State Parks Division, Box 1671, Lihue 96766, tel. 808/254–4444) for information on the hiking trails throughout the island. The department has maps of state forest reserve and state park trails. For your safety, never hike alone, stay on the trail, and avoid hiking when it's wet and slippery. All hiking trails on Kauai are free.

Kokee State Park is a glorious 45-mile network of hiking trails of varying difficulty, all worth the walk. Its Kukui Trail takes hikers right down the side of Waimea Canyon. Awa'awapuhi Trail leads 4 miles down to a spectacular overlook into the canyons of the north shore. All hikers should register at Kokee

Park headquarters (tel. 808/335–5871), which offers trail maps and information. *To reach the park, follow Waimea Canyon Rd. 20 mi to reach Kokee.*

Kauai's prize hiking venue is the **Kalalau Trail,** which begins at the northern end of Highway 56 and proceeds 11 miles to Kalalau Beach. With hairpin turns and constant ups and downs, this hike is a true test of endurance and can't be tackled round-trip in one day. For a good taste of it, hike just the first 2 miles to Hanakapiai Beach (*see* Beaches, above).

Hunting If you want to hunt on Kauai, you need to visit during hunting season, which for game birds runs from November through mid-January. The schedule varies for other animals. You'll also need a license, so contact the **Division of Conservation Enforcement** (3060 Eiwa St., Lihue 96766, tel. 808/245–4444) for details.

Tennis Kauai offers 20 lighted public tennis courts and more than 70 private courts at the hotels. Six hard courts at **Coco Palms Resort** (Box 631, Lihue 96766, tel. 808/822–3831) are open to guests for $6, nonguests $8. The resort also has three clay courts at $8 for guests, $10 nonguests. **Hanalei Bay Resort** (Box 220, Hanalei 96714, tel. 808/826–6522) has 11 courts; cost: guests free, $5 per day nonguests. **Princeville Tennis Garden** (Box 3116, Princeville 96722, tel. 808/826–9823) has six courts; cost: $5 per hour per person. **Sheraton Coconut Beach Hotel** (Box 830, Kapaa 96746, tel. 808/822–3455) offers three courts; cost: $4 guests, $8 nonguests. **Stouffer Poipu Beach Resort** (2251 Poipu Rd., Koloa 96756, tel. 808/742–9655) has six courts; cost: $6 guests, $8 nonguests.

Water Sports No matter which company you choose, plan to spend $145–$150 *Fishing* for a full day of charter fishing on a shared basis, $85–$90 for a full day on a shared basis, $600–$900 for an exclusive full day, and $450–$500 for an exclusive half day. One reliable enterprise is **Alana Lynn Too Charters** (Box 137, Anahola 96703, tel. 808/245–7446), with a six-passenger, 33-foot Bertram boat. **Gent-Lee Fishing** (Box 1691, Lihue 96766, tel. 808/245–7504) has a 32-foot, six-passenger custom sportfisher, and **Gilligan's Coastal Charters Kauai Sportsfishing** (Box 3028, Lihue 96766, tel. 800/222–7756) runs a 30-foot, six-passenger custom sportsfisher. **Seascape Kauai** (Box 555, Hanalei 96714, tel. 808/826–1111) features a 50-foot luxury cabin cruiser that will carry up to 43 passengers.

For freshwater fishing, **Bass Guides of Kauai** (Box 3525, Lihue 96766, tel. 808/822–1405) goes inland freshwater-bass fishing for $95 a half day for one person, $135 for two, with a two-person maximum. A full day costs $180 for one person, $250 for two. All tackle, poles, and beverages are provided on this 17-foot Gragor bass boat.

Kayaking **Island Adventures** takes you on 2½-hour guided kayak tours through the Huleia National Wildlife Refuge (*see* Guided Tours in Essential Information, above).

Scuba Diving Contact **Dive Hawaii** (Box 90295, Honolulu 96835, tel. 808/922–0975). This nonprofit association of dive operations has a $3, 24-page guidebook of dive sites on all the islands. For Kauai dives in particular, **Aquatics Kauai** (733 Kuhio Hwy., Kapaa 96746, tel. 808/822–9213) offers an introductory half-day scuba excursion for $70. One-tank shore dives for certified divers cost $55, a refresher course is $60, and a five-day PADI (scuba-diving certification) course is $350. If you want to go out on a boat dive with two tanks, it costs $75, including lunch. Night dives are also available at $95, and underwater videotaping can be arranged.

Similar packages are offered by **Dive Kauai** (4-976 Kuhio Hwy., Kapaa 96746, tel. 808/822–0452), **Fathom Five Divers** (Box 907, Koloa 96756, tel. 808/742–6991), **Kauai Divers** (Box 56, Koloa 96756, tel. 808/742–1580), **Ocean Odyssey** (Box 807, Kapaa 96746, tel. 808/822–9680), and **Sea Sage** (4-1378 Kuhio Hwy., Kapaa 96746, tel. 808/822–3841).

Snorkeling Several companies offer snorkeling cruises. If you want to explore the waters off the south shore, **Captain Andy's Sailing Adventures** (Box 1291, Koloa 96756, tel. 808/822–7833) takes up to 20 passengers on its 37-foot trimaran, the *Dolphin II*. Rates for the four-hour morning "ultimate adventure" are $65 for adults, $50 for children under 12, including gear and lunch. Captain Andy's also features a two-hour sunset sail ($40 adults, $30 children) and presents whale watches during the winter months. Contact **Blue Water Sailing** (Box 250, Eleele 96705, tel. 808/822–0525), with comparable rates, for fun on a 12-passenger, 42-foot luxury Pearson sailing yacht.

For north-shore snorkeling, try **Blue Odyssey Adventures** (Box 10, Hanalei 96714, tel. 808/826–9033). The company offers 4½-hour morning and afternoon Na Pali coast snorkel sails at $65 for adults, $43 for children under 12, including lunch, drinks, equipment, and underwater camera. You get an exciting look into sea caves from on board a 28-foot motor raft, which holds 12 to 15 passengers. Other north-shore companies offering similar deals are the **Hawaiian Z-Boat Co.** (Box 3013, Princeville 96722, tel. 808/828–1124), **Na Pali Coast Cruise Line** (4402 Waialo Rd., Eleele 96705, tel. 808/335–5078), and **Raft Riders** (Box 1324, Hanalei 96714, tel. 808/828–1166).

Windsurfing This sport is growing in popularity around the islands, and two companies stand ready to help you get started. **Hanalei Sailboards Kauai** (Box 496, Hanalei 96714, tel. 808/826–9732) contributes to the north-shore windsurfing scene with a pro shop, rentals, and group and private lessons. A three-hour lesson costs $55 an hour for beginners; a private lesson for advanced windsurfers costs $35, and the six-hour certification course costs $110. Rentals run $38–$44 per day. Also try **Nawiliwili Marine** (3470 Paena Loop, Lihue 96766, tel. 808/245–5955), which offers private lessons for $55 an hour. Certification course: $100.

Spectator Sports

Golf In recent years, the **Mirage Princeville Makai Course** (Box 3040, Princeville 96722, tel. 808/826–3580) has been the setting for the LPGA Women's Kemper Open, including the Helene Curtis Pro-Am.

Rodeo In August, the **Po'oku Annual Hanalei Stampede** (Box 888, Hanalei 96714, tel. 808/826–6777) takes place. This statewide rodeo, held at Po'oku Stables in Hanalei, includes music and dancing, plus plenty of cowpunching.

Triathlons A triple challenge, the **Kauai Loves You Triathlon** is a world-championship event featuring a 1.5-mile swim, a 54-mile bike ride, and a 12.4-mile run; it begins and ends at Hanalei each October. In July, the **King Kong Ultra Triathlon** takes place, with a 2-mile swim, a 75-mile bike ride, and an 18-mile run in the Kauai wilderness. It doesn't cost a penny to cheer. Tel. 808/826–9343 for both events.

Dining

The sugar plantations of 19th-century Kauai brought together a universe of cultures as workers from other countries sought new jobs in Hawaii. With the workers came a delightful assortment of foods, which is reflected in the cuisine found today on Kauai. Depending on your mood, you can find restaurants preparing, among other cuisines, Chinese, Japanese, Thai, Mexican, Spanish, and French specialties, mixed with a heavy dose of traditional Hawaiian food, which is available in just about any town on the island.

Due to the growing numbers of visitors to Kauai, the finest restaurants are almost always found in the better hotels. Their menus are often continental by description, although Hawaii's island cuisine is gaining favor. Island cuisine takes advantage of the many fine products that come from native soil, and on Kauai, there is an especially heavy emphasis on the fruits of its extensive groves. Thanks to the abundance of fish in the waters surrounding Kauai, the catch of the day is always well worth trying.

The ambience of each Kauai restaurant is unique. Many capitalize on splendid views of the waterfront. Some are candlelit and serve meals on the finest china, while others present your food with plastic plates and silverware. The mood can be romantic, rollicking, or family-style.

When it's time for a snack, look for the carryout wagons that are often parked at the major beaches. They serve such local food as the plate lunch, in which two scoops of rice are served with every entrée, and shave ice, the ultimate snow cone, made with tropical-flavored syrups.

Few restaurants require jackets. An aloha shirt and pants for men, and a simple dress or pants for women are acceptable in all but the fanciest establishments.

Restaurants are open daily unless otherwise noted.

Highly recommended restaurants in each price category are indicated by a star ★.

Category	Cost*
Very Expensive	over $60
Expensive	$40–$60
Moderate	$20–$40
Inexpensive	under $20

*per person without sales tax (4%), service, or drinks

Lihue and Vicinity

American   **Oar House Saloon.** The theme here is nautical, with life preservers hanging from the beams and fish nets draped along the walls. Owners Bob Demond, Betty Garner, and Kimo Moncrief have created a relaxed setting in which to enjoy the views of Kauai's ever-green mountains. Step outside and you're right at the waterfront, next to the Westin Kauai Hotel. Broiler offerings include six-ounce burgers made with your choice of cheese, mushrooms, or bacon. The T-bone steak is a whopping 14 ounces, and the chef's salad comes with ham, turkey, Swiss, Cheddar, hard-boiled eggs, tomatoes, and more. During the afternoon and evening, the Oar House's dart board attracts a colorful local clientele. *Wapaa Rd., Nawiliwili, tel. 808/245–4941. No reservations. Dress: casual. AE, V. Inexpensive.*

Chinese   **Club Jetty.** This restaurant's simple Formica tables and chairs are arranged so as not to disrupt the picturesque views of the harbor from the large picture windows. As you dine, you can gaze at the comings and goings of cruise and pleasure boats sailing by. For more than 30 years, the club has been entertaining guests with such Chinese dishes as abalone with black mushrooms, shrimp Canton with fresh pineapple, and sweet and sour fish with fresh island vegetables. Dinner entrées also include steaks and seafood. *Nawiliwili Harbor, Nawiliwili, tel. 808/245–4970. Reservations advised. Dress: casual. AE, CB, DC, MC, V. Dinner only. Inexpensive.*

Continental   **Gaylord's.** A gracious plantation mansion from the 19th centu-
★   ry is the charming setting of this special restaurant. White tablecloths and pastel furnishings contribute to the cool ambience of the alfresco dining room, which opens to extensive gardens in back. Gaylord's prepares every dish to order, and each entrée is distinctive. Try the venison in blueberry-juniper sauce, or the pan-blackened and highly spiced fresh salmon. The roast duck breast features three sauces—peppercorn, port wine, and Madeira. For dessert, chef Chris Harris offers a truly decadent French Silk, which is whipped chocolate laced with raspberry-wine sauce. *Kilohana Plantation, 3–2087 Kaumualii Hwy., 1 mi south of Lihue, tel. 808/245–9593. Reservations required. Dress: casual. AE, CB, DC, MC, V. Moderate.*

Midori. East meets West at this mystical restaurant, which is decorated with Buddhas and other treasures from the Orient. The chef has created an inspired menu emphasizing ultrafresh ingredients. For instance, you can order grilled duck breast salad with shiitake mushrooms on exotic greens, or sliced Kauai tomatoes and sweet Maui onion topped with a raspberry vinaigrette. Seafood is particularly well prepared here. Try the fresh island fish of the day sautéed with papaya, ginger, and herb-lemon butter. You can order a prix fixe meal or à la carte. *Kauai Hilton, 4331 Kauai Beach Dr., Lihue, tel. 808/245–1955. Reservations advised. Collared shirt required. AE, CB, DC, MC, V. Dinner only. Moderate.*

Italian   **Casa Italiana.** This rambling, two-story restaurant has an old-world atmosphere, and its rooms feature murals of Italy. Northern and southern Italian cuisine is presented here, such as cannelloni and saltimbocca alla romano (veal in a sauce of marsala wine, mushrooms, and butter, layered with Swiss cheese and prosciutto). *2989 Haleko Rd., Lihue, tel. 808/245–*

9586. Reservations advised. Dress: casual. AE, CB, MC, V. Dinner only. Moderate.

Mexican **Rosita's.** Colorful piñatas, white stucco walls, and wrought-iron gates turn this Kukui Grove restaurant into a south-of-the-border party. Specialties of the house include an elegant version of arroz con pollo: a boneless chicken breast lightly sautéed with fresh tomatoes, onions, and bell peppers, flamed with sherry and served with rice. Rosita's homestyle lasagne is thickly layered with Italian meat sauce, ricotta cheese, Italian sweet sausage, mozzarella, and Parmesan cheese. The nachos supreme are spectacular, especially if you order them with turkey. Margaritas are a must here. Entrées come with soup or salad. *Kukui Grove Center, Hwy. 50 at Nawiliwili Rd., Lihue, tel. 808/245–8561. Dress: casual. AE, MC, V. Inexpensive.*

The East Shore

Asian **Hanamaulu Cafe.** Three miles north of Lihue is this tranquil
★ teahouse with interior gardens and carp-filled brooks. The immaculate setting creates a serene environment for the two spacious tearooms and authentic sushi bar with seating for 24. The *robatayaki*-style (cooked on an open grill) Japanese dishes include Tokyo steak, soft-shell crabs, and Kauai prawns. Chinese cuisine is also featured, including the chef's special nine-course dinner of pork and vegetable soup, crispy wonton, sweet and sour spareribs, fried shrimp, chop suey with noodles, crab claws with butter sauce, crisp fried chicken, beef with broccoli and tomatoes, and *char siu* (roast pork), plus rice, tea, and fortune cookies. *Hwy. 56, Hanamaulu, tel. 808/245–2511. Reservations required. Dress: casual. MC, V. Inexpensive.*

Mexican **Norberto's El Cafe.** This award-winning family restaurant has been a well-kept secret among locals for some time, but visitors are catching on to the joys of this little gem. Since 1977, Norberto's has prepared meals without lard or animal fat, using the freshest ingredients possible. One specialty is burritos rancheros: toasted flour tortillas rolled and stuffed with seasoned beef, Cheddar cheese, onions, and green chiles, smothered with Spanish sauce and cheeses. Norberto's fajitas are tender slices of prime Kauai steak or chicken sautéed with fresh mushrooms, bell peppers, and onions and served with Spanish rice and flour tortillas. Complete dinners come with soup, beans, and rice, plus chips and salsa. *4–1373 Kuhio Hwy., Kapaa, tel. 808/822–3362. Dress: casual. AE, MC, V. Dinner only. Inexpensive.*

Pizza **Wailua Pizza Stop.** For a fun meal eaten in or taken out, try this lively little spot in the Kinipopo Shopping Village. The dining room is casual and unpretentious, a good spot to relax after a long day of sightseeing. Pizzas have a medium-thick crust and are topped with fresh ingredients. The Hawaiian Delight features Canadian bacon and pineapple, while the Primo Pizza has sausage, pepperoni, mushrooms, olives, onions, and bell peppers. Grinders, pastas, soups, and salads are also available. Phone ahead for quicker service. *Kinipopo Shopping Village, Hwy. 56, Wailua, tel. 808/822–9222. Dress: casual. No reservations. No credit cards. Inexpensive.*

Steak and Seafood **Kapaa Fish & Chowder House.** The decor here combines thick hanging ferns and nautical memorabilia. Owners Jan and Glenn Lovejoy like Louisiana-style food and have included some

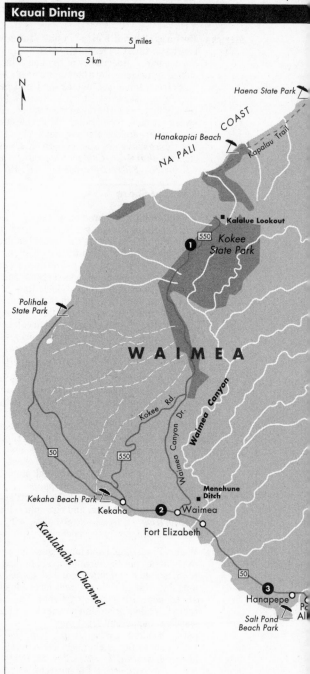

Kauai Dining

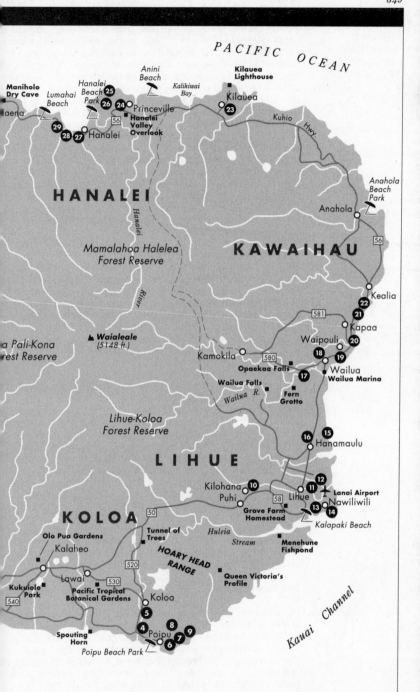

PACIFIC OCEAN

Maniholo
Dry Cave

Lumahai
Beach

Hanalei
Beach
Park **25**

Anini
Beach

Kilauea
Lighthouse

26 **24** Princeville
Kalihiwai
Bay

Kilauea

23

laena

29

28 **27** Hanalei

Hanalei
Valley
Overlook

56

Kuhio Hwy.

HANALEI

Hanalei River

Mamalahoa Halelea
Forest Reserve

Anahola
Beach
Park

Anahola

KAWAIHAU

56

a Pali-Kona
rest Reserve

▲ Waialeale
(5148 ft.)

Kealia

22

21 Kapaa

581

Waipouli

20

Kamokila

580

18

19

Opaekaa Falls

17

Wailua
Wailua Marina

Wailua Falls

Fern
Grotto

Wailua R.

Lihue-Koloa
Forest Reserve

16 **15**

Hanamaulu

LIHUE

Kilohana **10**

12

Puhi

11

Lanai Airport

Grove Farm
Homestead

Lihue

13

Nawiliwili

14

KOLOA

50

Kalapaki Beach

Olo Pua Gardens

Tunnel of
Trees

Huleia
Stream

Menehune
Fishpond

Kalaheo

520

HOARY HEAD
RANGE

Lawai

530

Queen Victoria's
Profile

Kukuiolo
Park

Pacific Tropical
Botanical Gardens

Koloa

540

5

4 **8**

7 **9**

Spouting
Horn

Poipu

6

Poipu Beach Park

Kauai Channel

dishes with a Cajun accent on the menu. For instance, the chef quickly sautées fresh shrimp, then coats it with some piquant Cajun spices that are sure to wake up the taste buds. Another unusual entrée served here is Alaskan snow crab legs and claws steamed in beer and served with drawn butter. The seafood fettuccine is recommended; stir-fried shrimp, scallops, clams, and fish are served on a combination of spinach and egg fettuccine blended with a white-wine sauce. Ask for a table in the Garden Room, a veritable Eden. *4-1639 Kuhio Hwy., Kapaa, tel. 808/822–7488. Reservations advised. Dress: casual. AE, MC, V. Dinner only. Moderate.*

Seashell. A tropical garden on a bluff overlooking the sea is the setting of the Seashell, next to Wailua Beach at the Coco Palms Resort. Seafood prepared Island-style is the fare here, including shrimp dim sum (bite-sized dumplings stuffed with the delectable Island shellfish). Opihi wontons use the highly prized, tiny shellfish, which is found on coastline rocks. Entrées include shrimp tempura, *onaga* (pink snapper) presented on a sizzling platter, and a fish stew called cioppino. A salad buffet and homemade desserts are featured, and tropical drinks are available during happy hour. *Coco Palms Resort, Hwy. 56, Wailua, tel. 808/822–3632. Reservations advised. Dress: casual. AE, CB, DC, MC, V. Dinner only. Moderate.*

★ **Bull Shed.** The A-frame design of this popular restaurant imparts a distinctly rustic feel, as do the exposed wood interior and big, family-style tables. Set on the shoreline and offering views of the ocean, the Bull Shed presents prime rib, teriyaki sirloin, chicken, and New Zealand rack of lamb; the fresh fish is particularly good. The salad bar is a real disappointment, however, so skip it and proceed directly to the entrées, which come with hot rolls and rice. *796 Kuhio Ave., Waipouli, tel. 808/822–3791. Reservations advised. Dress: casual. AE, MC, V. Dinner only. Inexpensive.*

Wailua Marina Restaurant. Technicolor bougainvillea and boats chugging along the charming Wailua River are your views from this dockside eatery, ideal for before or after the boat ride up to Fern Grotto. The open-air dining lanai is perched right on the water, next to shores where ancient Hawaiian communities once stood. For the large number of people it serves, the restaurant has a surprisingly thoughtful menu. For instance, the baked stuffed chicken is cooked in plum sauce and served with a lobster salad, and the baked salmon comes covered with a rich bacon sauce. A variety of steak and fresh seafood dishes are also on the menu. Complimentary transportation is available from Wailua-area hotels and condos in the evenings. *Wailua River State Park, Wailua Rd., Wailua, tel. 808/822–4311. Reservations advised. Dress: casual. AE, MC, V. Inexpensive.*

The North Shore

American **Pizza Burger.** With its tidy little wooden front porch and white railing, Pizza Burger is a fun indoor/outdoor emporium and a great place to watch the world go by. The pizzas here offer a variety of toppings in whatever combination you'd like: salami, Italian sausage, mushrooms, jalapeños, tomatoes, pineapple, and so on. The burgers are more interesting, including one made of a quarter-pound of 100% pure buffalo meat from Hanalei Garden Farms. The Fin Burger is four ounces of mahimahi fillet topped with Cheddar cheese, and another quarter-pounder combines pastrami and mozzarella. You pay a little more for your pizza if you carry it out. *Princeville Shopping Center, Hwy. 56, Princeville, tel. 808/826–6070. No reservations. Dress: casual. MC, V. Inexpensive.*

Chinese **Foong Wong's.** One story up in Ching Young Village, Foong Wong presents a striking first impression, with its predominantly red decor. The next thing you notice about the place is its wonderful views of the mountains of Hanalei, right outside the big picture windows. The interior is traditional, as is the presentation of the restaurant's Cantonese and Szechuan dishes. Owner Wing Yuen Leung and his wife, Mi Wah, have assembled a masterful menu of specialties, including three-flavored seafood sizzling plate, hot and sour soup, and chicken with cashew nuts. The abalone soup, enough for four or five persons, is an unexpected treat. *Ching Young Village, Hwy. 56, Hanalei, tel. 808/826–6996. No reservations. Dress: casual. AE, MC, V. Inexpensive.*

Continental **Nobles.** This is truly a beautiful restaurant. The centerpiece of
★ the newly renovated Sheraton Mirage Princeville, it features crystal chandeliers, hand-painted tile, and classical archways that lead you into a shimmering dining room. The cuisine is equally magical, including breast of duckling with black Bing cherries. Goose liver–brandy soufflé with brioche is the appetizer of choice, and venison with cognac cream and poached pears is one of the most popular entrées. Dinners are prix fixe, and the menu varies. You might want to call ahead and find out what the chef is currently featuring. *Sheraton Mirage Princeville Hotel, Princeville, tel. 808/826–9644. Reservations required. Jacket required. AE, CB, DC, MC, V. Dinner only. Very Expensive.*

The Lanai. Princeville has a lush, rolling countryside flanked by cliffs that have inspired generations of Hawaiians. That's the view that surrounds you at this alfresco restaurant. A pair of chefs—Androcles Handy and Mike Daigan—make the Lanai's victuals as memorable as the visuals. They share a keen interest in the preparation of fresh fish from Hawaii's waters and have come up with such crowd pleasers as fillets of ono in a sauce of tomato, garlic, shallots, and white wine. The 10-ounce steak is broiled and laced with a peppery sauce, while the medallions of veal are sautéed and presented with a sauce of mushrooms and marsala wine. Try the Lanai coffee, with hazelnut liqueur and coconut amaretto, topped with homemade whipped cream. *Makai Clubhouse, Princeville Resort, tel. 808/826–6226. Reservations advised. Dress: casual. AE, CB, DC, MC, V. Dinner only. Moderate.*

Deli **Cafe Zelo's.** This small deli and espresso bar is highly recommended for its gourmet sandwiches, which are perfect for a picnic at the beach. The curried almond chicken salad sandwich is particularly good, although you can select from a number of ingredients, including pastrami, turkey, avocado, and ham, plus a variety of fresh breads and rolls. Salads include a very nice fresh fruit compote with cinnamon-spiced yogurt. All items are available to take out, or you can eat there. Try a Zelo's breakfast of scrambled eggs with homemade salsa, topped with cheese and served with toast and cottage fries. *Princeville Shopping Center, Princeville, tel. 808/826–9700. No reservations. Dress: casual. MC, V. Breakfast and lunch only. Inexpensive.*

Italian **Casa di Amici.** A welcome addition to the north-shore dining
★ scene, Casa di Amici means "house of friends," and it feels that
way, too. The menu is broken down as it would be if you were
dining in Italy; that is, antipasti (starters), *zuppe* (soup), pasta,
insalate (salads), and *pietanza maggiore* (main courses). You
can mix your favorite pasta with your choice of sauce, including
pesto (fresh basil, pine nuts, garlic, and romano cheese) and
salsa di noci (walnut sauce with fresh romano cheese and mar-
joram in cream). The house scampi is prepared with garlic,
capers, fresh tomatoes, and olive oil on a bed of linguine. *2484
Keneke St. at Lighthouse Rd., Kilauea, tel. 808/828–1388. Reservations advised. Dress: casual. AE, CB, DC, MC, V.
Moderate.*

I'ulani Isle. Chef Jeff Farris runs this restaurant with his own
personal touches. A big-screen TV in the bar is available for
sports lovers, while conversationalists can sit in an open, relaxed dining room featuring arched doorways and arty posters
on the white walls. Farris combines Italian cuisine and seafood
quite well. The cheese lasagna layers pasta with provolone,
mozzarella, ricotta, and homemade marinara sauce. The captain's plate is loaded with shrimp, clams, calamari, and the
catch of the day, and the prime rib is blackened Cajun-style.
Seafood entrées come with french fries, rice, or spaghetti marinara, vegetable of the day, and homemade bread. The dinner
for two is a good deal at $30, and Farris also has a children's
menu. *Princeville Shopping Center, Princeville, tel. 808/826–
7680. Reservations advised. Dress: casual. AE, MC, V. Inexpensive.*

Mexican **Papagayo Azul.** The name of this restaurant means "blue parrot," which explains the aqua cockatoo perched above the sign.
Folding chairs and wooden tables are arranged on the covered
lanai, which is filled with hanging plants and cut tropical flowers. Although it's set right on the main drag, the front porch is
a comfy spot for lunch or dinner. The menu is highlighted by
the Papagayo burrito: green chiles covered with enchilada
sauce and cheese, then topped with sour cream, guacamole,
lettuce, and tomatoes. Barbecued specialties are also served,
such as beef and pork ribs, a whole or half chicken, and burgers. For dessert, go for a banana fritter rolled in a flour tortilla
with cheese, then deep-fried. *Ching Young Village, Hwy. 56,
Hanalei, tel. 808/826–9442. No reservations. Dress: casual.
No credit cards. Inexpensive.*

Mixed Menu **Charo's.** Famed for her "coochi coochi" act, Charo is a Kauai celebrity whose restaurant and nightclub draws in visitors by the
busload. The views of the ocean and magnificent north-shore
sunsets are heightened by floor-to-ceiling windows in this
high-ceilinged seaside restaurant. The entrance is designed
with lush plants and bamboo, while the Polynesian-style dining
room features aquariums used as room dividers. The food has
decidedly Island overtones. The teriyaki New York steak is
marinated in soy sauce, ginger, garlic, and wine, while the
large shrimp are lightly breaded with macadamia nuts and
deep-fried, then served with cocktail sauce and lemon. Try the
breast of chicken Bali Hai, topped with a sauce of Frangelica,
coconut milk, macadamia nuts, and shredded coconut. *Colony
Resort, Hwy. 56, Haena, tel. 808/826–6422. Reservations advised. Dress: casual. AE, CB, DC, MC, V. Moderate.*

Steak and Seafood **Chuck's Steak House.** A paniolo (cowboy) feeling permeates this place, right down to the saddles and blankets that hang from the open-beamed ceiling and the planters made out of wagon wheels. Choose from a very good salad bar with any entrée you order. From the land, try chunks of beef marinated in teriyaki sauce and showered with pineapple and bell peppers. From the sea, a good bet is the sea scallops sautéed in white wine with lime wheels and Canadian bacon. The barbecued beef ribs, lobster, chicken, and Alaskan king crab are also good. For dessert, Chuck's special mud pie is a winner, made with coffee ice cream and a chocolate and walnut crust, topped with cream. *Princeville Shopping Center, Princeville, tel. 808/826–6211. Reservations advised. Dress: casual. AE, CB, DC, MC, V. Moderate.*

Hanalei Dolphin. This is a favorite with many Hanalei residents because of its oceanside views and relaxed yet elegant ambience. True to its name, the Dolphin serves plenty of fresh seafood, such as charbroiled mahimahi served with tartar sauce, and calamari breaded, sautéed, and topped with a mild lemon-butter sauce. The Hawaiian chicken is lightly marinated in soy sauce and ginger. Light dinners are also featured, such as broccoli casserole made with mushroom sauce and Cheddar cheese. *Hwy. 56, Hanalei, tel. 808/826–6113. Reservations advised. Dress: casual. AE, CB, DC, MC, V. Dinner only. Moderate.*

The South and West

Continental **Tamarind.** The centerpiece of the Stouffer Waiohai Hotel, the ★ Tamarind lives up to the standards of the finest signature restaurants. It's decorated in soft earth tones, highlighted by elegant mirrors and chrome finishings, and the comfortable seats invite you to linger over your meal. A specialty of the house is the lamb, which is marinated in mustard and garlic. A different pâté is offered each night, and the duckling and lobster are good choices for entrées. As a sweet after-dinner touch, each diner receives a small chocolate cup filled with liqueur. *Stouffer Waiohai Hotel, 2249 Poipu Rd., Poipu, tel. 808/742–9511. Reservations advised. Jacket required. AE, CB, DC, MC, V. Dinner only. Expensive.*

Kiahuna Golf Club. Set practically on the green, this resort restaurant has a spacious alfresco ambience that's perfect for the consistently sunny clime of Poipu. The breakfasts are decadent in an Island fashion, especially the thick Hawaiian sweet-bread French toast, topped with macadamia nuts and strawberries. Lunch features sandwiches and salads with golf-oriented names; try the Birdie, half a strawberry papaya filled with chicken or tuna salad and topped with bay shrimp. If you're planning a private party, the staff is happy to help. They also do catering. *Kiahuna Shopping Village, 2360 Kiahuna Plantation Dr., Poipu, tel. 808/742–6055. Reservations advised. Dress: casual. AE, CB, DC, MC, V. Inexpensive.*

Mixed Menu **Mango's Tropical Restaurant.** Part of the Koloa dining scene, Mango's welcomes guests with a sleek decor combining nautical themes and garden designs. The place is decorated with lots of brass and wood, plus planters of tropical palms and crotons positioned around the dining room. The lunch menu of nearly 40 items touches on a variety of international influences. Oriental stir-fry chicken includes bean sprouts, broccoli, sugar pea pods, green and red peppers, sweet Maui onions, and mushrooms. The 50 dinner dishes include a fine Tennessee blackjack peppered steak laced with green peppercorns and a unique Jack Daniels bourbon sauce. *Koloa Rd., Old Koloa Town, tel. 808/742–7377. Reservations advised. Dress: casual. AE, CB, DC, MC, V. Moderate.*

Green Garden. With orchids on every table and an assortment of hanging and standing plants throughout the place, this family-run restaurant is aptly named. Formerly a five-bedroom home, it has been a favorite dining spot for Kauai residents and visitors since 1948. The Green Garden is very low-key, and the waitresses treat you like you're old friends. The food is no-frills local fare; you come here for the atmosphere first and the meals second. Dinner, which includes some 30 items, might consist of the Chinese plate, with pork chow mein, sweet and sour spareribs, and char siu (roast pork). The seafood special is breaded mahimahi fillet, scallops, oysters, and deep-fried shrimp. The homemade desserts are something special. Be sure to try the *lilikoi* (passion fruit) chiffon pie. *Hwy. 50, Hanapepe, tel. 808/335–5422. Reservations advised for dinner. Dress: casual. AE, CB, DC, MC, V. Closed Tues. nights. Inexpensive.*

Kokee Lodge. Set midway between Waimea Canyon and the Kalalau Lookout, this mountaintop lodge is protected on one side by a grove of pines. On the other side, picture windows open up to a rolling green lawn and clear blue Kokee skies (when the clouds haven't rolled in). This environment is a different slice of Kauai indeed. The food at the lodge consists of several types of cuisine, including Cornish game hen with mushroom and rice stuffing. The vegetarian fettuccine is quite good, or you can order steak, Island fish, or ribs. At breakfast, the pancakes sometimes come with tropical-flavored syrups. Try some mud pie for dessert; it's a chocolate lover's dream come true. *Kokee Rd., Kokee State Park, tel. 808/335–6061. No reservations. Dress: casual. AE, CB, DC, MC, V. Breakfast and lunch daily, dinner Fri. and Sat. only. Inexpensive.*

Wrangler's. This Waimea restaurant with paniolo (cowboy) overtones features Island beef raised in the hills of Kalaheo. Owners Colleen Faye and Kurt Vidinha have decorated the dining room with a fun assortment of furnishings, including antique hand lanterns and western saddles. The menu combines American, Mexican, Chinese, Japanese, and Korean influences. The shrimp and pork stir-fry is a spicy gathering of onions, bell peppers, garlic, and tomato salsa. For pork chops Kitano, the meat is sautéed in garlic butter with sliced onions, carrot sticks, and capers. You'll also get a good steak here. Try La Perouse, a rib steak panfried in its juices and garlic butter with fresh mushrooms, onions, and bell peppers, then topped with bordelaise sauce. *Ako Bldg., 9852 Kaumualii Hwy., Waimea, tel. 808/338–1218. Reservtions advised. Dress: casual. AE, CB, DC, MC, V. Closed for lunch Sun. Inexpensive.*

Steak and Seafood
★

House of Seafood. Owners Don Kubish and John Borales run this pretty restaurant, which overlooks the Poipu Resort tennis courts. Inside, the ceilings are so high that you feel you're dining outside, and tropical vines wrap themselves around the handsome exposed beams. The name says it all: This is a fine place to try island seafood, from ahi (tuna) to weke (goatfish). Preparations vary from night to night, and your server will tell you your options. A variety of shellfish dishes are available, including oriental shrimp and scallops, lobster and shrimp

Cantonese, and lobster tail. All entrées come with a cup of chowder or salad, fresh vegetables, almond rice pilaf, and freshly baked rolls. *1941 Poipu Rd., Poipu, tel. 808/742–6433. Reservations advised. Dress: casual. AE, CB, DC, MC, V. Dinner only. Expensive.*

★ **Brennecke's Beach Broiler.** Situated right across from Poipu Beach Park, this place has been around for years, and happily so. The names of Island fish are inscribed in big bold letters on the white walls, and pretty flower boxes brighten up the windows. You also have a view of the chef, who specializes in *kiawe*-broiled foods ("kiawe" is a mesquite-type wood). Along with the standard burgers, Brennecke's serves fresh clams, catch of the day, and exceptional homemade desserts, such as guava and mango sherbet. Ask to sit on the second floor so you can get better views of the ocean. *Ho'one Rd., Poipu, tel. 808/742–7588. Reservations advised. Dress: casual. MC, V. Moderate.*

Poipu Beach Club. Pastel pinks, freshly cut flowers, surrounding hibiscus gardens, and white tablecloths dress up this roomy restaurant, which overlooks the hotel's pool and the ocean beyond. Fresh fish is the specialty at dinner. You can begin with a sashimi appetizer, move on to Waimea seafood chowder, and top it off with pork ribs delicately seasoned with a ginger sauce. Breakfast is a good bargain here; be sure to order a macadamia nut roll with your eggs. *Stouffer Poipu Beach Resort, 2249 Poipu Rd., Poipu, tel. 808/742–1681. Reservations advised. Dress: casual. AE, CB, DC, MC, V. Breakfast and dinner only. Moderate.*

Lodging

Part of the appeal of the Garden Isle is its range of hotel properties, which cover the gamut from swanky and stuffy resorts to rustic mountaintop cabins to the bare-bones accommodations whose main appeal is the rock-bottom price. Here are some basic guidelines to help you make a choice.

Those seeking the sunshine often head south to the shores of Poipu, where high rises line the coast and the gentle surf offers ideal swimming. The hotels and condominiums of Poipu are in the Moderate to Very Expensive price range, although several shoreside cottages are in demand with the budget traveler.

Guests who are interested in the more historical and sacred sections of Kauai often stay on the east coast near the Wailua River, home of Kauai's first inhabitants. Many of the hotels here place an emphasis on the legends and lore of the area. Shops and restaurants are within walking distance of most accommodations, and the beaches are so-so for swimming but nice for sunbathing.

Farther north are the swanky hotels and condominiums of the Princeville Resort, generally reserved for the island's wealthiest patrons. You can't go wrong with a room here, because just about any hotel or condo offers views of Hanalei Bay, the Pali coast, and the chiseled mountain peaks of Hanalei. This is a duffer's paradise, for panoramic vistas are seen from every hole of the resort's golf course.

Bed-and-breakfasts are becoming a more attractive option for the many visitors to Kauai who wish to get a resident's point of view. These private homes are scattered around the island, and a good booking service can help you locate one.

You'll have no trouble finding a place to stay on Kauai if you make your reservations beforehand. Allow extra time during the peak months of February and August. When making your booking, ask about such extras as special tennis, golf, honeymoon, and room-and-car packages.

Highly recommended hotels in each price category are indicated by a star ★ .

Category	Cost*
Very Expensive	over $120
Expensive	$90–$120
Moderate	$60–$90
Inexpensive	under $60

All prices are for a standard double room excluding 9¼% taxes and service.

Lihue and Vicinity

Very Expensive **Kauai Hilton and Beach Villas.** The designers of this resort were sensitive to the history and scenery of the nearby Wailua River area. This explains why the low-rise, horseshoe-shaped structure surrounds a pool complex with rock-sculptured slopes, waterfalls, bright tropical flowers, and a cave resembling Fern Grotto. Each night at sunset, people in native dress light 100 tiki torches around the pools. Guest rooms and public areas are decorated in muted tones of peach, mauve, and teal against an off-white background, and each room has a lanai and views of mountains, gardens, or the sea. *4331 Kauai Beach Dr., Lihue 96766, tel. 808/245–1955 or 800/HILTONS. 350 hotel rooms and 135 condominiums with bath, on the beach. Facilities: 4 pools, 3 restaurants, 3 lounges, tennis, golf. AE, CB, DC, MC, V.*

★ **Westin Kauai.** While some residents feel that such opulence is out of place on a rural island, they do admit that this megaproperty can be very impressive. Guests are met at Lihue Airport in a limousine and driven on the resort's private road. The lobby boasts a $2.5 million art collection, and hotel amusements include horse-drawn-carriage rides and outrigger-canoe tours. Five towers of guest rooms have colonial furnishings and floor-to-ceiling sliding doors for ocean or mountain views. Rooms include robes, stocked minibars, big lanais, and a king or twin double beds. *Kalapaki Beach, Lihue 96766, tel. 808/245–5050 or 800/228–3000. 850 rooms with bath, on the beach. Facilities: Jacuzzis, health spa, golf, tennis, horse-drawn carriages, 12 restaurants and lounges, shops. AE, CB, DC, MC, V.*

Inexpensive **Hale Lihue Motel.** There are two advantages to staying at this hotel. First, it is located smack-dab in Lihue, making the sights of the north, south, and west portions of the island all within an easy hour's drive. Second, the price can't be beat. From the outside the low-rise building looks run-down, but the inside is clean. The rooms are very simple, with cinder-block walls and utilitarian furnishings. Kitchenettes are available. Ask in advance for one of the air-conditioned rooms. *2931 Kalena St., Lihue 96766, tel. 808/245–3151. 18 rooms with bath. No credit cards.*

The East and North Shores

Very Expensive **Sheraton Mirage Princeville Hotel.** After extensive remodel-
★ ing, this property is slated for an early 1991 opening. This hotel drapes down a cliff to maximize the views of the surrounding scenery. In one direction is Hanalei Valley's patchwork of rice and taro fields stretching back to the base of sheer, green mountains. Ocean-side views look to Hanalei Bay and the peaks known as Bali Hai. The interior design is dedicated to Kauai's ethnic heritage, and it blends modern amenities with furnishings whose origins date from the 1800s. The top-ranked 27-hole Princeville Golf Course is right outside the front door. *Box 3069, Princeville 96722, tel. 808/826–9644 or 800/325–3535. 300 rooms with bath. Facilities: pool, tennis, golf, shops, 3 restaurants, 2 lounges. AE, CB, DC, MC, V.*

Expensive **Aston Kauai Resort.** The constant care lavished on this property has resulted in a hotel that is clearly dedicated to its surroundings. Exotic flowers grace interiors and exteriors, and rooms feature pastel colors, rattan furnishings, and large windows. A Hawaiian story hour is available for children, who may also enter a daily flower-naming contest. For visitors with a yen to explore Kauai's past, each guest room has a booklet with legends of the Wailua River Valley and a self-guided tour of some of the historic Hawaiian temple ruins in the area. The hotel's Pacific Room features contemporary island entertainers each weekend. *3-5920 Kuhio Hwy., Kapaa 96746, tel. 808/ 245–3931 or 800/922–7866. 242 rooms with bath. Facilities: pool, shops, restaurant, lounge. AE, CB, DC, MC, V.*

★ **Coco Palms Resort Hotel.** The Coco Palms has a long history of hospitality. The queen of Kauai once owned these 45 acres, and the place is now done up like a Polynesian village, with lagoons, fish ponds, and thatched huts that keep alive the past. The lobby mirrors its cool, serene surroundings with soft sea colors and rattan furnishings. A white-on-pastel Pacific-colonial theme is the guest-room motif, and each bathroom has a giant clamshell washbasin. The resort also features the first clay tennis courts ever built in Hawaii, plus an eight-person Jacuzzi next to a lava-rock waterfall. *Box 631, Lihue 96766, tel. 808/ 822–4921 or 800/542–2626. 390 rooms with bath. Facilities: pools, tennis, shops, 3 restaurants, lounges. AE, CB, DC, MC, V.*

Moderate **Hanalei Bay Resort.** Part of the Princeville community, this re-
★ sort has a clifftop location and offers accommodations in 16 low-rise buildings overlooking Hanalei Bay and Kauai's north shore. Each unit is extremely spacious, some with as much as 2,000 square feet. What's more, the rooms have high, sloping ceilings and large private lanais with mountain or bay views. Rattan furniture and Island art add a casual feeling to each room, which comes with a fully equipped kitchen, a large dressing area, a color TV, and 24-hour switchboard service. Laundry facilities are on the property. The management hosts demonstrations and classes in hula, ukulele, lei making, and coconut-frond weaving, plus walking tours through the gardens. *Box 220, Hanalei 96714, tel. 808/826–6522 or 800/657–*

Kauai Lodging

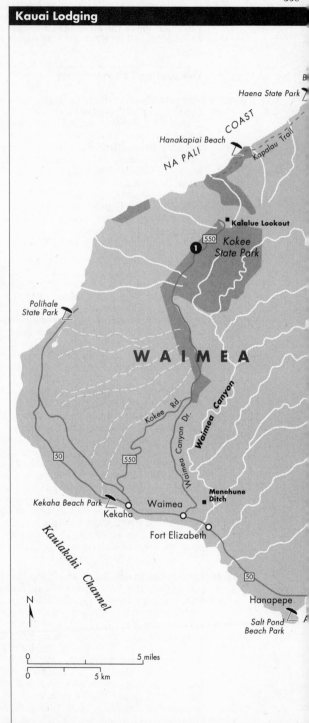

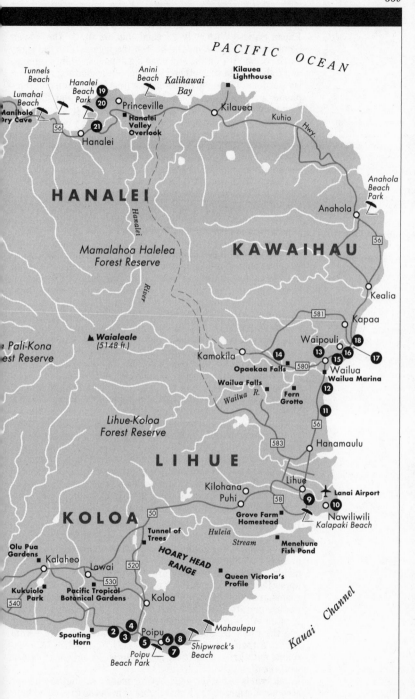

7922. *176 condominiums with bath. Facilities: 2 pools, tennis, golf, restaurant, lounge. AE, CB, DC, MC, V.*

Kapaa Sands. With only 23 condominium units, the Kapaa Sands is an intimate, off-the-beaten-track gem. Situated right by the ocean, it's on the site of an old Japanese Shinto temple, and today an old rock etched with Japanese characters graces the gardens. The small rooms come with a full kitchen plus telephone and TV, and some have dishwashers and garbage disposals. Furnishings are done in rustic wood with ceiling fans, appropriate for a beachside bungalow. Ask for an oceanfront room, because they offer great open-air lanais with gorgeous Pacific views. The landscaping around the eight two-story buildings is lush and lovely, with meandering pathways lined with palms, gingers, gardenias, and other tropicana. *380 Papaloa Rd., Kapaa 96746, tel. 808/822–4901 or 800/222–4901. 23 condominiums with bath and kitchen. Facilities: pool. AE, CB, DC, MC, V.*

Kauai Beachboy. Eight miles north of Lihue Airport, the Kauai Beachboy is well situated for east- and north-shore sightseeing. It's also a five-minute drive from the Wailua Golf Course and within walking distance of the Coconut Market Place shopping complex. The four-building, three-story hotel is set along an uncrowded, mile-wide stretch of Waipouli Beach. Rooms have large sliding screen doors, which open onto private lanais. The furnishings are heavy-handed in the Hawaiian motif department, with loud-colored bedspreads and gaudy prints on the white walls. On the plus side, guest rooms come with air-conditioning, color TV, daily maid service, and a refrigerator. *484 Kuhio Hwy., #100, Kapaa 96746, tel. 808/822–3441 or 800/ 367–8047 ext. 126. 243 rooms with bath. Facilities: pool, shops, restaurant, tennis, lounge. AE, CB, DC, MC, V.*

Sandpiper Village. If you want your own separate dwelling in the Princeville area, check out the Sandpiper Village, which rents two-bedroom/two-bath cottages. The garden setting is shaded and quiet, and picture windows in each unit offer views of the mountains of the Hanalei area. Inside each condo are high ceilings with ceiling fans, dark bamboo furnishings, and a kitchen with a dishwasher and washer/dryer. There's a central recreation and barbecue area for guest use only. *4770 Pepelani Loop, Princeville 96722, tel. 808/826–1176 or 800/526–1166. 74 condominiums with bath. Facilities: pool, sauna, golf, spa. AE, CB, DC, MC, V.*

Inexpensive   **Hotel Coral Reef.** An older hotel that has been well maintained, the Coral Reef is right on the sand's edge, although the swimming in front of the hotel is not as good as at the public beaches nearby. Colorful bedspreads liven up the somewhat stark furnishings of the rooms, which are clean and freshly painted. The upper floors have carpeting in each unit, while the ground-level rooms are done in terrazzo tile. Oceanfront accommodations feature private lanais and refrigerators. The property is ideally situated, near plenty of shopping, dining, and sightseeing, and the rates are attractive to budget travelers. *1516 Kuhio Hwy., Kapaa 96746, tel. 808/822–4481 or 800/843–4659. 26 rooms with bath. Facilities: pool, tennis, laundromat within walking distance. AE, MC, V.*

Kauai Sands. Another good bet for money-saving beachfront accommodations is the Kauai Sands, where the green and blue decor of the rooms is a reflection of the ocean right outside the windows. Each unit is carpeted and air-conditioned, and you can get one with a kitchenette for a few extra dollars. The restaurant and lounge offer up-close views of the sea. *420 Papaloa Rd., Kapaa 96746, tel. 808/822–4951 or 800/367–7000. 200 rooms with bath. Facilities: pool, shops, restaurant, lounge. AE, CB, DC, MC, V.*

The South and West

Very Expensive **Kiahuna Plantation.** With its reliably warm temperatures and ocean breezes, the southern coast is the perfect setting for a vacation in one of Kiahuna's one- or two-bedroom cottages, many of which are situated on the shoreline. Interiors are done in green and yellow and furnished with rattan-style chairs and couches. There's no television in the rooms, but you don't really need it, because the great outdoors beckons with the beaches, golf courses, swimming pools, shops, and restaurants of the bustling Poipu area. Each unit has a fully equipped electric kitchen and daily maid service. *2253 Poipu Rd., Koloa 96756, tel. 808/742–6411 or 800/367–7052. 333 rooms with bath. Facilities: pool, restaurant, tennis, golf. AE, CB, DC, MC, V.*

★ **Sheraton Kauai Hotel.** Stretching across 20 acres of prime Poipu Beach property, the Sheraton Kauai is comprised of low-rise Polynesian buildings that were designed to complement the surrounding beach, tropical gardens, and waterways. The Ocean Wing fronts the crescent of Poipu Beach and offers the best views, while the Garden Wing is set amid tropical foliage and lagoons filled with Japanese carp. Each room has a lanai, refrigerator, color TV, radio, telephone, and air-conditioning. Furnishings are appropriately Hawaiian, and rooms are very spacious. *2440 Hoonani Rd., Koloa 96756, tel. 808/742–1661 or 800/325–3535. 456 rooms with bath. Facilities: pools, shops, restaurants. AE, CB, DC, MC, V.*

★ **Stouffer Waiohai Beach Resort.** Fashionable travelers rave about this prize resort, touted by many as the south shore's classiest accommodation. The lobby boasts four-story, bronze-glazed atrium windows, an impressive welcome indeed. The building is designed like a *W* to allow the maximum number of ocean-view rooms, and two "super suites" sit right on the sand. Each room adjoins a private lanai decorated with outdoor furniture. All the carpeted and wood-shuttered units feature a large dressing area, a sit-down vanity, potted palms, and views of the ocean or gardens. Tiled bathrooms are designed with oval brass basins set in marble countertops. *2249 Poipu Rd., Koloa 96756, tel. 808/742–9511 or 800/426–4122. 426 rooms with bath. Facilities: tennis, shops, 3 lounges, 3 restaurants, 3 pools. AE, CB, DC, MC, V.*

Expensive **Kuhio Shores.** With an ideal waterfront location and an ingenious design, this condominium building makes a promise you won't hear from many other properties. Every unit in the complex offers a view of the water. Some of the large, clean windows and spacious lanais look out to the Pacific Ocean, while others offer harbor views. Accommodations are large here, with rattan furniture in the living rooms. The fully equipped kitchens come with microwaves, garbage disposals, and dishwashers. Each unit is individually owned and has its own personality. *R.R. 1, Box 70, Koloa 96756, tel. 808/742–6120 or 800/367–8022. 75 one- and two-bedroom condominiums with bath and kitchen. No pool. AE, MC, V.*

Stouffer Poipu Beach Resort. One of the smaller facilities on

Poipu Beach, this low-rise hotel is particularly appropriate for families, since the swimming nearby is usually safe for beginners. Each room has a kitchenette, a small refrigerator, and cooking utensils. The decor is no-frills, with dark tiled floors and simple Island-style furnishings. Rooms all have a lanai with patio tables and chairs, plus a color television, air-conditioning, maid service, and a telephone. *2251 Poipu Rd., Koloa 96756, tel. 808/742–1681 or 800/426–4122. 138 rooms with bath. Facilities: swimming pool, children's pool, shops, tennis, restaurant, lounge. AE, CB, DC, MC, V.*

Moderate
★ **Koloa Landing Cottages.** Just four accommodations are available in this garden complex near Poipu Beach, so advance reservations are a must. Once here, guests are treated like family by the owners, who invite their visitors to partake of fresh fruit picked from the trees right outside the door and who offer knowledgeable sightseeing advice. Koloa Landing has two two-bedroom cottages and two studios available for rent. Each has open-beamed ceilings, which keep the interiors cool, and batiks are used for decoration. Each cottage has a fully equipped kitchen with microwave, color cable television, and a telephone. Family swimming beaches and restaurants of all ilk are located within walking distance. *2740-B Hoonani Rd., Koloa 96756, tel. 808/742–1470. 4 cottages with private bath. Facilities: laundry, barbecue. MC, V.*

Inexpensive
★ **Garden Isle Cottages.** Here you'll find oceanside accommodations at budget prices. The theme of each interior is Hawaiian, and tropical flower gardens surround the cottages for an exotic yet homespun touch. Rooms have no telephones or televisions. Some do include kitchens, so ask in advance if you wish to reserve one. It's a five-minute walk to the restaurants of nearby Poipu. *2666 Puuhola Rd., Koloa 96756, tel. 808/742–6716. 13 cottages with bath. No pool. MC, V.*

★ **Kokee Lodge.** This may not fit the image of real Hawaiian lodgings held by first-time visitors: it's up in the mountains, where the air is considerably cooler than around the beachfront properties. Instead of palm trees there are pines, and accommodations are individual cottages rather than Poipu-style high rises. However, the Kokee Lodge offers the outdoors-oriented visitor a chance to experience the rare flora and fauna of Kauai's highlands. Housing is in 12 cabins that are rustic inside and out. Each has a fireplace (you pay a few dollars extra for wood) and comes with a fully equipped kitchen. The eight older wooden cabins are $10 cheaper than the four newer, log-cabin-type structures. Many Kauai residents head for Kokee for the weekend, so make your reservations in advance. *Box 819, Waimea 96796, tel. 808/335–6061. 12 cabins with bath. Facilities: shop, restaurant. AE, MC, V.*

Bed-and-Breakfasts

Bed & Breakfast Hawaii. This booker offers inexpensive single and double accommodations in family homes around the islands. The advantage here is that you get your morning meal as part of the deal, and you usually get an insider's view of Kauai from your congenial hosts. *Box 449, Kapaa 96746, tel. 808/822–7771 or 800/657–7832.*

Kay Barker's Bed & Breakfast. Kay Barker is a sprightly woman in her 80s who opens her home to guests and serves them a continental breakfast in the morning. Four inexpensive bedrooms are available, each with a private bath, and guests are invited to relax in the common rooms of the house as Kay shares her recollections of life on Kauai. *Box 740, Kapaa 96746, tel. 808/822-3073. 4 bedrooms with bath. Facilities: living room, TV room, library. No credit cards.*

The Arts

Very little classical arts activity happens on laid-back Kauai. The island doesn't have its own symphony, but the **Honolulu Symphony Orchestra** (tel. 808/537-6191) does perform on the Garden Isle from time to time. For a specific schedule, call the **Kauai Concert Association** (tel. 808/245-7464).

In Lihue, the **Kauai Regional Library** (4344 Hardy St., tel. 808/245-3617) often plays host to films, storytelling, musical presentations, and arts and crafts events.

The **Kauai Community Players** (tel. 808/822-7787) put on fun amateur productions throughout the year.

Nightlife

People on Kauai take great pride in their culture, and they like to share their unique traditions with those who come to call. As a result, on the Garden Isle you will find more traditional Hawaiiana and less Las Vegas–style glitz than on neighboring Oahu.

Because tourists are extremely important to Kauai's economy, most of the island's dinner shows and luaus take place within a hotel or resort. You will also find some pretty entertaining options on board the cruise boats. Hotel lounges and restaurant bars offer live music with no cover charge, and often they have discount drinks during happy hour.

Check the local newspaper, *The Garden Island Times*, for listings of weekly happenings. Two free magazines—*Spotlight Kauai* and *This Week on Kauai*—also offer listings of entertainment events. You can pick them up at the Hawaii Visitors Bureau and at Lihue Airport.

Bars and Clubs

For the most part, discos just don't fit into the serenity of Kauai, and the bar scene is extremely limited. If you want a nightcap or feel the urge to tap your feet, first check what's happening in your hotel lounge. The major resorts generally host their own live entertainment and happy hours.

The drinking age in Hawaii is 21, and if you look younger than that, you may be asked to show some identification. All bars and clubs that serve alcohol must close at 2 AM, except for those with a cabaret license, which close at 4 AM.

The following establishments present dance music on a regular basis.

Buzz's Steak & Lobster (Coconut Plantation Market Place, Kapaa, tel. 808/822-7491). The lounge area of this visitor-oriented restaurant features mellow Hawaiian music and Top

40 tunes. Happy hour daily 3–5, entertainment nightly 8:30–11:30.

Club Jetty (Nawiliwili Harbor, Nawiliwili, tel. 808/245–4970). This disco by the sea attracts crowds both young and old. Along with taped music, it hosts live bands from time to time. Wednesday–Saturday nights 10–3:30.

Paddling Club (Westin Kauai, Kalapaki Beach, Nawiliwili, tel. 808/246–5048). This high-energy, five-level, adult-entertainment discotheque features contemporary sounds from the past and present. It attracts the upscale resort crowd. Nightly 9–1.

Park Place Nightclub (Harbor Village Shopping Center, 3501 Rice St., Nawiliwili, tel. 808/245–5775). With the largest dance floor on the island, this fast-paced disco features Top 40 tunes in a garden setting. It caters to the under-30 age group. Happy hour on Wednesday lasts until midnight. Music nightly 9:30–4.

Dinner and Sunset Cruises

Choose a cruise along the north shore or the south. Either way, sunset is a magical time to watch Kauai from the water. Prices range from $45 to $75 per person for food and drink.

Na Pali Coast Cruise Line (4402 Waialo Rd., Eleele, tel. 808/335–5078). This two-and-a-half-hour cruise leaves Port Allen and serves drinks at twilight. The dinner headlines either prime rib or fresh fish. The views of the southern coastline make up for the lack of on-board musical entertainment. Wednesday, Friday, and Saturday 5:30–8:30.

Paradise Adventure Cruises (Kuhio Hwy., Hanalei, tel. 808/826–9999). This cruise line stands out from the others because it features Kauai's only singing captain. He'll take folks out on a personalized sunset excursion upon request. His boat is a 25-foot Boston Whaler, which holds six passengers.

Luaus

Each of the listings offers its own unique variation on the luau theme. The cost ranges from $30 to $40 for adults, $15 to $25 for children under 12.

Sheraton Coconut Beach Hotel Luau (Coconut Plantation, Kapaa, tel. 808/822–3455 ext. 651). The music, dance, and food of Polynesia come together at this hotel-based luau, regarded by many as the island's best. It takes place in a lovely setting of flaming tiki torches. Nightly at 6:45.

Smith's Tropical Paradise Luau (Wailua Marina, Wailua, tel. 808/822–4654). Set amid 30 acres of tropical flora and fauna, this luau begins with the traditional blowing of the conch shell and imu ceremony, followed by cocktails, an island feast, and an international show in the Lagoon Amphitheater. Week nights at 6.

Tahiti Nui Luau (Kuhio Hwy., Hanalei, tel. 808/826–6277). This is a welcome change from the standard commercial luau, because it's put on by a family that really knows how to party. A mood of fun and relaxation pervades this open-air restaurant. Emcee Auntie Louise keeps things rolling, with lots of good local entertainment. The menu is a luau with all the trimmings, from *kalua* (roasted) pig to *haupia* (gelatinlike dessert made from coconut). Monday, Wednesday, and Friday at 7.

Waiohai Luau (Stouffer Waiohai Beach Resort, Poipu, tel. 808/742–9511). The most elaborate of Kauai's luaus, this production takes place under the stars. It begins with live music by the Hawaiian Serenaders, who play while cocktails are served from the open bar. After the *imu* (underground oven) ceremony, there's the standard luau feast plus steak, chicken, and mahimahi for guests not interested in kalua pig. The Polynesian show is highlighted by fire dancers. Monday at 6.

Shows

The food is secondary to the entertainment at the following dinner shows. Prices range from $40 to $50 per person, including a cocktail and dinner.

Charo's (Colony Resort, Haena, tel. 808/826–6422). After years as an international dancer and guitarist, this Latin star has taken up residence on the north shore. Her show features Latin, flamenco, and island dancing by a well-choreographed ensemble, and Charo herself puts in an occasional appearance when she's not starring in her Waikiki-based act. The restaurant setting is lovely, right on the beach. A shuttle service is available from the Princeville area. Shows nightly at 8. Dinner 6–10.

Na Kaholokula (Sheraton Coconut Beach Hotel, Kapaa, tel. 808/822–3455). This is a nice way to get acquainted with authentic Hawaiian entertainment. These award-winning Kauai recording artists gather for an evening of casual Island-style music, while Puamohala performs the appropriate hula movements. Tuesday and Thursday at 6.

Polynesian Revue (Sheraton Kauai Hotel, Poipu Beach, tel. 808/742–1661). Perched next to the ocean with views from every table, the Outrigger Room is an appropriate setting for the pulsating rhythms and captivating dances of the South Pacific. This production features a good mix of the old and the new. Sunday and Wednesday at 6.

Hawaiian Vocabulary

The Hawaiian language is unlike anything heard by the average traveler. But given the chance, say at a traditional church service or a local ritual ceremony, visitors will find the soft, rolling language of the Islands both interesting and refreshing to the ear.

Although an understanding of Hawaiian is by no means required on a trip to the Aloha State, *malihinis*, or newcomers, will find plenty of opportunities to pick up a few of the local words and phrases. In fact, traditional names and expressions are still in such wide usage today, that visitors will be hard-pressed not to read or hear them each day of their visit. Such exposure enriches a stay in Hawaii. With a basic understanding and some uninhibited practice, anyone can have enough command of the local tongue to ask for directions and to order off the neighborhood restaurant menu.

Simplifying the learning process is the fact that the Hawaiian language contains only seven consonants—H, K, L, M, N, P, and W—and the five vowels. All syllables and all words end in a vowel. Each vowel, with the exception of the diphthong double vowels such as *au* (pronounced ow) or *ai* (pronounced eye), is pronounced separately. *A'a*, the word for "rough lava" for example, is pronounced ah-ah.

Although some Hawaiian words have only vowels, most also contain some combination consonants as well. Consonants are never doubled, and they always begin syllables, as in Ka-me-ha-me-ha.

The accent in most Hawaiian words falls on the next-to-the-last, or penultimate, syllable. Examples are KO-na, PA-li and KA-na. The exception occurs when the vowels in the second syllable become dipthongized, as in ha-PAI and ma-KAI, which are fundamentally ha-PA-i and ma-KA-i.

Pronounciation is simple. Use the following as a guide:

Pronounce *A* "uh" as in above; *E* "ay" as in weigh; *I* "ee" as in marine; *O* "oh" as in no; *U* "oo" as in true.

Consonants mirror their English equivalents, with the exception of W. When the letter begins the last syllable of a word, it is sometimes pronounced as a V. Awa, the Polynesian drink, is pronounced "ava"; Ewa is pronounced "Eva."

What follows is a glossary of some of the most commonly used Hawaiian words. Don't be afraid to give them a try. Hawaiian residents appreciate visitors who at least try to pick up the local language—no matter how fractured the pronunciation.

a'a—rough, crumbling lava, contrasting with *pahoehoe*, which is smooth.
ae—yes.
akamai—smart, clever, possessing savoir-faire.
ala—a road, path, or trail.
alii—a Hawaiian chief, a member of the chiefly class; also plural.

aloha—love, affection, kindness. Also a salutation meaning both greetings and farewell.

aole—no.

auwai—a ditch.

auwe—alas, woe is me!

ehu—a red-haired Hawaiian.

ewa—in the direction of Ewa plantation, west of Honolulu.

hala—the pandanus tree, whose leaves *(lauhala)* are used to make baskets and plaited mats.

hale—a house.

hana—to work.

haole—originally a stranger or foreigner. Since the first foreigners were Caucasian, *haole* now means a Caucasian person.

hapa—a part, sometimes a half.

hapa haole—part *haole*, a person of mixed racial background, part of which is Caucasian.

hauoli—to rejoice. *Hauoli Makahiki Hou* means Happy New Year.

heiau—an ancient Hawaiian place of worship.

holo—to run.

holoholo—to go for a walk, ride, or sail.

holoku—a long Hawaiian dress, somewhat fitted, with a scoop neck and a train. Influenced by European fashion, it was worn at court.

holomuu—a recent cross between a *holoku* and a *muumuu*, less fitted than the former but less voluminous than the latter, and having no train.

honi—to kiss, a kiss. A phrase that some tourists may find useful, quoted from a popular *hula*, is *Honi Kaua wikiwiki:* Kiss me quick!

hoomalimali—flattery, a deceptive "line," bunk, baloney, hooey.

huhu—angry.

hui—a group, club, or assembly. There are church *huis* and social *huis*.

hukilau—a seine; a communal fishing party in which everyone helps to drive the fish into a huge net, pull it in, and divide the catch.

hula—the dance of Hawaii.

ipo—sweetheart.

ka—the definite article.

kahuna—a priest, doctor, or other trained person of old Hawaii, endowed with special professional skills that often included the gift of prophecy or other supernatural powers.

kai—the sea, saltwater.

kalo—the taro plant from whose root *poi* is made.

kamaaina—literally, a child of the soil, it refers to people who were born in the Islands or have lived there for a long time.

kanaka—originally a man or humanity in general, it is now used to denote a male Hawaiian or part-Hawaiian.

kane—a man, a husband. If you see this word on a door, it's the men's room.

kapa—also called *tapa*, a cloth made of beaten bark and usually dyed and stamped with a geometric design.

kapakahi—crooked, cockeyed, uneven. You've got your hat on *kapakahi*.

kapu—keep out, prohibited. This is the Hawaiian version of the more widely known Tongan word *tabu* (taboo).

keiki—a child; *keikikane* is a boy child, *keikiwahine* a girl.

kokua—help.

kona—the south, also the south or leeward side of the islands from which the *kona* wind and *kona* rain come.

kuleana—a homestead or small plot of ground on which a family has been installed for some generations without necessarily owning it. By extension, *kuleana* is used to denote any area or department in which one has a special interest or prerogative. You'll hear it used this way: If you want to hire a surfboard, see Moki; that's his *kuleana*. And conversely, I can't help you with that; that's not my *kuleana*.

lamalama—to fish with a torch.

lanai—a porch, a balcony, an outdoor living room. Almost every house in Hawaii has one.

lani—heaven, the sky.

lauhala—the leaf of the *hala* or pandanus tree, widely used in Hawaiian handcrafts.

lei—a garland of flowers.

luna—a plantation overseer or foreman.

mahalo—thank you.

makai—toward the ocean.

malihini—a newcomer to the Islands.

mana—the spiritual power that the Hawaiians believed to inhabit all things and creatures.

manawahi—free, gratis.

mauka—toward the mountains.

mauna—mountain.

mele—a Hawaiian song or chant, often of epic proportions.

menehune—a Hawaiian pixie. The *menehunes* were a legendary race of little people who accomplished prodigious work, like building fish ponds and temples in the course of a single night.

moana—the ocean.

muumuu—the voluminous dress in which the missionaries enveloped Hawaiian women. Now made in bright printed cottons and silks, it is an indispensable garment in a Hawaiian woman's wardrobe.

nani—beautiful.

nui—big.

pake—a Chinese.

palapala—book, printing.

pali—a cliff, precipice.

panini—cactus.

paniolo—a Hawaiian cowboy.

pau—finished, done.

pilikia—trouble. The Hawaiian word is much more widely used here than its English equivalent.

puka—a hole.

pupule—crazy, like the celebrated Princess Pupule. This word has replaced its English equivalent in local usage.

wahine—a female, a woman, a wife, and a sign on the ladies' room door.

wai—fresh water, as opposed to saltwater, which is *kai*.

wikiwiki—to hurry, hurry up.

Pidgin English is the unofficial language of Hawaii. It is heard everywhere: on ranches, in warehouses, on beaches, and in the hallowed halls (though not in the classrooms) of the University of Hawaii. It's still English and not much tougher to follow than Brooklynese; it just takes a little getting used to.

Menu Guide

Much of the Hawaiian language encountered during a stay in the Islands will appear on restaurant menus and lists of luau fare. Often these menus will also include terms from Japanese, Chinese, and other cultures. Here's a quick primer.

ahi—locally caught tuna.

aku—skipjack, bonito tuna.

ama ama—mullet; it's hard to get, but tasty.

bento—a box lunch.

dim sum—Chinese dumplings.

chicken luau—a stew made from chicken, taro leaves, and coconut milk.

guava—This tasty fruit is most often used in juice and in jellies. As a juice, it's pink and quenches a thirst like nothing else.

haupia—a light, gelatinlike dessert made from coconut.

imu—the underground ovens in which pigs are roasted for luaus.

kalua—to bake underground. A *kalua* pig is the pièce de résistance of a Hawaiian feast.

kaukau—food. The word's derivation is Chinese, but it is widely used in the Islands.

kim chee—pickled Chinese cabbage made with garlic and hot peppers.

kona coffee—coffee grown in the Kona district of the Big Island; prized for its rich flavor.

laulau—literally, a bundle. In everyday usage, laulaus are morsels of pork, butterfish, or other ingredients wrapped along with young taro shoots in *ti* leaves for steaming.

lilikoi (passion fruit)—a tart, seedy yellow fruit that makes delicious desserts, jellies, and sherbet.

lomilomi—to rub or massage; also a massage. Lomilomi salmon is fish that has been rubbed with onions and herbs, commonly served with minced onions and tomatoes.

luau—a Hawaiian feast, also the leaf of the taro plant used in preparing such a feast.

luau leaves—cooked taro tops with a taste similar to spinach.

macadamia nuts—These little round, buttery-tasting nuts are mostly grown on the Big Island, but are available throughout the Islands.

mahimahi—mild-flavored dolphin, not to be confused with porpoise.

mai tai—Hawaiian fruit punch with rum.

malasada—a Portuguese deep-fried doughnut, dipped in sugar, with no hole.

manapua—dough wrapped around diced pork.

mango—a juicy sweet fruit, with a yellowish-red smooth skin and a yellow pulpy interior.

mano—shark.

niu—coconut.

okolehao—a liqueur distilled from the *ti* root.

onaga—pink snapper.

ono (adj.)—delicious.

ono (n.)—a long, slender mackerel-like fish; also called a wahoo.

opakapaka—blue snapper.

opihi—a tiny shellfish, or mollusk, found on rocks; also called limpets.

papaya—This little green or yellow melon-like fruit will grow on you; it's high in vitamin C and is most often eaten at breakfast with a squeeze of lemon or lime.

papio—a young ulua or jack fish.

poha—cape gooseberry. Tasting a bit like honey, the poha berry is often used in jams and desserts.

poi—a paste made from pounded taro root, a staple of the Hawaiian diet.

pupu—Hawaiian hors d'oeuvre.

saimin—long thin noodles and vegetables in a thin broth.

sashimi—raw fish sliced thin, usually eaten with soy sauce.

sushi—a variety of raw fish, served with vinegared rice and Japanese horseradish.

uku—deep-sea snapper.

ulua—crevelle, or jack fish; the giant trevally.

Index

Personal Itinerary

Departure   *Date*

Time

Transportation

Arrival   *Date*   *Time*

Departure   *Date*   *Time*

Transportation

Accommodations

Arrival   *Date*   *Time*

Departure   *Date*   *Time*

Transportation

Accommodations

Arrival   *Date*   *Time*

Departure   *Date*   *Time*

Transportation

Accommodations

Personal Itinerary

Arrival	*Date*	*Time*
Departure	*Date*	*Time*
Transportation		
Accommodations		

Arrival	*Date*	*Time*
Departure	*Date*	*Time*
Transportation		
Accommodations		

Arrival	*Date*	*Time*
Departure	*Date*	*Time*
Transportation		
Accommodations		

Arrival	*Date*	*Time*
Departure	*Date*	*Time*
Transportation		
Accommodations		

Personal Itinerary

Arrival Date   Time

Departure Date   Time

Transportation

Accommodations

Arrival Date   Time

Departure Date   Time

Transportation

Accommodations

Arrival Date   Time

Departure Date   Time

Transportation

Accommodations

Arrival Date   Time

Departure Date   Time

Transportation

Accommodations

Personal Itinerary

Arrival *Date*   *Time*

Departure *Date*   *Time*

Transportation

Accommodations

Arrival *Date*   *Time*

Departure *Date*   *Time*

Transportation

Accommodations

Arrival *Date*   *Time*

Departure *Date*   *Time*

Transportation

Accommodations

Arrival *Date*   *Time*

Departure *Date*   *Time*

Transportation

Accommodations

Personal Itinerary

Arrival *Date*   *Time*

Departure *Date*   *Time*

Transportation

Accommodations

Arrival *Date*   *Time*

Departure *Date*   *Time*

Transportation

Accommodations

Arrival *Date*   *Time*

Departure *Date*   *Time*

Transportation

Accommodations

Arrival *Date*   *Time*

Departure *Date*   *Time*

Transportation

Accommodations

Addresses

Name	*Name*
Address	*Address*
Telephone	*Telephone*
Name	*Name*
Address	*Address*
Telephone	*Telephone*
Name	*Name*
Address	*Address*
Telephone	*Telephone*
Name	*Name*
Address	*Address*
Telephone	*Telephone*
Name	*Name*
Address	*Address*
Telephone	*Telephone*
Name	*Name*
Address	*Address*
Telephone	*Telephone*
Name	*Name*
Address	*Address*
Telephone	*Telephone*
Name	*Name*
Address	*Address*
Telephone	*Telephone*

Addresses

Name	Name
Address	Address
Telephone	Telephone
Name	Name
Address	Address
Telephone	Telephone
Name	Name
Address	Address
Telephone	Telephone
Name	Name
Address	Address
Telephone	Telephone
Name	Name
Address	Address
Telephone	Telephone
Name	Name
Address	Address
Telephone	Telephone
Name	Name
Address	Address
Telephone	Telephone
Name	Name
Address	Address
Telephone	Telephone

Notes